ROUTLEDGE HANDBOOK OF SUSTAINABILITY INDICATORS

This handbook provides researchers and students with an overview of the field of sustainability indicators (SIs) as applied in the interdisciplinary field of sustainable development. The editors have sought to include views from the center ground of SI development but also divergent ideas which represent some of the diverse, challenging and even edgy observations which are prominent in the wider field of SI thinking.

The contributions in this handbook:

- clearly set out the theoretical background and history of SIs, their origins, roots and initial goals
- expand on the disciplines and modalities employed to develop SIs of various kinds
- assess the various ways in which SI data are gathered and the availability (over space and time) and quality issues that surround them
- explore the multiplex world of SIs as expressed in agencies around the world, via examples of SI practice and the lessons that have emerged from them
- critically review the progress that SIs have made over the last 30 years
- express the divergence of views which are held about the value of SIs, including differing theories on their efficacy, efficiency and ethics
- explore the frontier of contemporary SI thinking, reviewing ante/post and systemic alternatives.

This multidisciplinary and international handbook will be of great interest to researchers, students and practitioners working in sustainability research and practice.

Simon Bell is Professor of Innovation and Methodology at the Open University in the UK and CEO of the Bayswater Institute in London, UK. He has held a number of Visiting Professor roles. With over 100 published books and articles, Simon has written on subjects including information systems methodology, action research, participatory methods, coastal sustainability, systemic approaches to environmental problem structuring, sustainability indicators and fear management.

Stephen Morse is Chair in Systems Analysis for Sustainability in the Centre for Environment and Sustainability at the University of Surrey, UK. Steve has a background in applied ecology and the environment and his research and teaching interests are broad, spanning both the natural and social sciences. He is a Fellow of the Royal Geographical Society, the Royal Society of Biology and the Higher Education Academy and has published 18 books and over 140 academic papers, many of them on the assessment of sustainability (including indicators).

ROUTLEDGE HANDBOOK OF SUSTAINABILITY INDICATORS

Edited by Simon Bell and Stephen Morse

Routledge
Taylor & Francis Group

LONDON AND NEW YORK

First published 2018
by Routledge

2 Park Square, Milton Park, Abingdon, Oxfordshire OX14 4RN
52 Vanderbilt Avenue, New York, NY 10017

Routledge is an imprint of the Taylor & Francis Group, an informa business

First issued in paperback 2020

British Library Cataloguing-in-Publication Data
A catalogue record for this book is available from the British Library

Library of Congress Cataloging-in-Publication Data
A catalog record for this book has been requested

ISBN: 978-1-138-67476-9 (hbk)
ISBN: 978-0-367-49755-2 (pbk)

Typeset in Bembo
by Apex CoVantage, LLC

CONTENTS

List of figures ix
List of tables xii
List of boxes xiv
List of contributors xv
Foreword xxiii
Acknowledgements xxv
List of acronyms xxvi

1 Introduction: indicators and post truth 1
  Simon Bell and Stephen Morse

PART I

Theory and history 19

2 Bellagio STAMP: principles for sustainability assessment and measurement 21
  László Pintér, Peter Hardi, André Martinuzzi and Jon Hall

3 Contributions to the evolving theory and practice of indicators of
  sustainability 42
  Arthur Lyon Dahl

4 Substantiating the rough consensus on the concept of sustainable
  development as a point of departure for indicator development 59
  Walter J. V. Vermeulen

5 From crises and gurus to science and metrics: Yale's Environmental
  Performance Index and the rise of data-driven policymaking 93
  Daniel C. Esty and John W. Emerson

6 The limits of sustainability and resilience frameworks: lessons from
agri-food system research   103
Sarah Rotz and Evan Fraser

7 Lessons from the history of GDP in the effort to create better
indicators of prosperity, well-being, and happiness   117
Robert Costanza, Maureen Hart, Ida Kubiszewski, Steve Posner,
and John Talberth

8 A systems–theoretical perspective on sustainable development
and indicators   124
Paul-Marie Boulanger

PART II
Methods   **141**

9 World views, interests and indicator choices   143
Joachim H. Spangenberg

10 Sustainability indicators and certification schemes for the built environment   156
Catalina Turcu

11 Measuring water scarcity and water consumption   176
Jonathan Chenoweth

12 Participatory approaches for the development and evaluation of
sustainability indicators   188
Simon Bell and Stephen Morse

13 Environmental governance indicators and indices in support of
policy-making   204
Dóra Almássy and László Pintér

14 Environmentally sustainable national income, an indicator   224
Roefie Hueting and Bart de Boer

15 Green accounting: balancing environment and economy   235
Peter Bartelmus

16 Ecological Footprint accounts: principles   244
Mathis Wackernagel, Alessandro Galli, Laurel Hanscom, David Lin,
Laetitia Mailhes, and Tony Drummond

PART III
Agency experience   265

17 Governing by numbers: China, Viet Nam, and Malaysia's adaptation of
    the Environmental Performance Index   267
    Angel Hsu

18 The Human Sustainable Development Index   284
    Giangiacomo Bravo

19 The Environmental Performance Index: does this reflect reality?   294
    Elisabeth Conrad and Louis F. Cassar

20 Sustainability-related indicators developed for governments   308
    L. Reijnders

21 Sustainable development indicators, Finland: going from large
    descriptive sets to target-oriented actively used indicators   321
    Ulla Rosenström

22 The socio-ecological system (SES) approach to sustainable
    development indicators   329
    Gilberto C. Gallopin

23 UNEP and the CSD process for sustainable development indicators   347
    Arthur Lyon Dahl

24 Prospects for standardising sustainable urban development   364
    Simon Joss and Yvonne Rydin

25 Stakeholder-driven initiatives using sustainability indicators   379
    Ana Rita Domingues, Rodrigo Lozano, and Tomás B. Ramos

26 How evil is aggregation? Lessons from the dashboard of sustainability 392
    Jochen Jesinghaus

27 Criteria and indicators to audit the performance of complex, multi-
    functional forest landscapes   407
    *Dwi Amalia Sari, Chris Margules, Agni Klintuni Boedhihartono
       and Jeffrey Sayer*

28 The devil is in the detail! Sustainability assessment of African
    smallholder farming   427
    Wytze Marinus, Esther Ronner, Gerrie W. J. van de Ven, Fred Kanampiu,
    Samuel Adjei-Nsiah, and Ken E. Giller

PART IV
Critique of sustainability indicators and indices   **451**

29 Sustainable agricultural intensification and measuring the
    immeasurable: do we have a choice?   453
    Philip Grabowski, Mark Musumba, Cheryl Palm and Sieglinde Snapp

30 Relevance – a neglected feature of sustainability indicators   477
    Svatava Janoušková, Tomáš Hák, and Bedřich Moldan

31 Measurement matters: toward data-driven environmental policy-making   494
    Daniel C. Esty

32 Meta-evaluation of sustainability indicators: from organizational to
    national level   507
    Tomás B. Ramos and Sandra Caeiro

33 Ecological Footprint accounts: criticisms and applications   521
    Mathis Wackernagel, Alessandro Galli, Laurel Hanscom, David Lin,
    Laetitia Mailhes and Tony Drummond

In conclusion   **541**

34 What next?   543
    Simon Bell and Stephen Morse

Index   *557*

FIGURES

4.1	Three dimensions of the concept of sustainable development	60
4.2	Scientific articles published using the concept 'sustainable development' (1974–2016)	62
4.3	Scientific articles published: using the concept 'sustainable development' + definition (1984–2016)	63
4.4	Tensions in the practice of indicator construction and application	69
4.5	EC JRC Framework for best practices of impact characterization	77
4.6	Combining global initiatives for societal impact characterization in a societal category – activity midpoint–endpoint frameworks	80
4.7	17 SDGs characterized as steps in the logic model	82
4.8	Integrating the rough consensus in global scholarly practices of sustainability assessment and the 17 United Nations Sustainable Development Goals in a logic model representing the dual SD-agenda	83
5.1	Framework for the 2016 Environmental Performance Index	98
8.1	Form as the unity of distinction and indication	133
10.1	Siemens' Green City Index evaluates 16 quantitative and 14 qualitative indicators	161
10.2	Sustainable Seattle (S2): indicator trends in 1998	165
10.3	A hybrid set of sustainability indicators	166
10.4	CASBEE-UD information: BEEUD chart, radar chart, and six bar charts of credits	172
10.5	SPeAR visualisation	173
12.1	Some of the key questions in a participatory process	191
12.2	The dynamics of participatory research	195
12.3	A rich picture	200
13.1	Increase in the term "composite indicators" found by Google Scholar between 2005 and 2016	205
13.2	Themes covered by the composite indicators included in this review	210
13.3 and 13.4	Geographic scale and focus of the composite indicators included in this review	211
13.5	Map-based visualization of the Resource Governance Index for 2017	219

14.1A and B	Costs of elimination and revealed preferences for an environmental function; A: total curves, B: marginal curves	228
14.2	Translation of costs in physical units into costs in monetary units	230
15.1	Pricing the priceless	236
15.2	Outline of the SEEA	238
15.3	Environmentally adjusted net capital formation (ECF, percent of EDP)	239
15.4	Finding the balance. What are the trade-offs between economic production, consumption, and environmental quality?	240
16.1	Humanity's Ecological Footprint, 1961–2014	249
17.1	The 2016 Environmental Performance Index framework	270
17.2	The China EPI indicator framework with 39 indicators; the more recent report increased the number of indicators to a total of 47	272
17.3	The Viet Nam EPI framework	278
18.1	Geographical distribution of the 2015 HSDI	287
18.2	Binary correlations between the HSDI and HDI, and between all sub-indexes with corresponding scatterplots. The diagonal panels present the distribution of each index or sub-index	288
18.3	Binary correlations between the HSDI and all other indicators with corresponding scatterplots. The diagonal panels present the distribution of each variable	289
18.4	HSDI and Ecological Footprint by country	290
19.1	EPI – a proximity-to-target indicator	295
22.1	A representation of the socio-ecological system at the national scale as a framework for defining indicators of sustainable development	336
22.2	Trends of IDS for Honduras, years 1990–2000	341
26.1	Environmental pressures in the Netherlands	393
26.2	Avoidance vs. Damage Costs	395
26.3	The "Cake Share Model"	397
26.4	Agenda 21 and the UN CSD Dashboard of Sustainability	399
26.5	CSD Dashboard, disaggregated	400
26.6	A hierarchy of "welfare"	401
26.7	Environmental Sustainability Index for the USA	403
26.8	Essential steps to create a Policy Performance Index	404
27.1	The multi-layered audit mechanism	412
27.2	Audit design matrix (ISSAI) showing the process of designing an audit	413
27.3	Rich picture made by men and women group in SE Cameroon	414
28.1	Indicator score for the share of women's labour in agriculture, calculated for the most important grain crops	436
28.2	Nitrogen input and output at field (A, n=58) and farm level (B, weighted averages across fields per farm) for each of the 20 farms studied in Kenya	438
28.3	The percentage of field level and farm level (average across fields) nitrogen-use efficiency indicator outcomes that was either too high (NUE > 90%), good (NUE > 50%, < 90%), or too low (< 50%)	439
28.4	Average results across all households per research site in western Kenya (C, A) and northern Ghana (D, B)	440
28.5	Box and whisker plots of indicator results for Migori and Vihiga, Kenya	442

28.6	Example of individual household outcomes on the level of indicators for a household that scored poorly on most indicators (A) and a household that scored well on most indicators (B) when compared with the average for the case study area, Vihiga	443
28.7	Average indicators scores for households with a low legume intensity score and a high legume intensity score	445
29.1	Direct and indirect effects from a change in agriculture across all five domains	456
29.2	The pathways model for agriculture-nutrition linkages	462
29.3	Diagram of iterative co-learning cycle over time (a spiral) with several rounds of SAI assessment and the stages of development of an innovation labeled	465
29.4	Baseline diagram of tradeoffs and synergies for enset (false banana) in Ethiopia	469
29.5	Diagram of tradeoffs and synergies for enset for the scenario of successful productivity and marketing research	470
30.1	GDP per capita (constant 2010 US$); world, 1990–2015	486
30.2	GDP per capita (constant 2010 US$); world, 2015	486
30.3	Adjusted net savings (including particulate emission damage) (% of GNI); world, 1990–2014	488
30.4	Adjusted net savings (including particulate emission damage) (% of GNI); world, 2014	488
32.1	General meta-performance evaluation features of sustainability assessments	509
32.2	Conceptual framework for meta-performance evaluation of sustainability indicators	510
33.1	Mapping sustainable development outcome: HDI and the Footprint of nations, in 2013	524
34.1	Four indicators of measuring the size of the UK economy and the rank of the UK in the global 'league table' using those measures	550

TABLES

4.1 Descriptors of the sustainable development indicator formulation process, according to various authors   66

4.2 Popular sustainability pathways represented in terms of logic model concepts   71

6.1 Number of crops grown and farm size   109

6.2 Cover crops and forage integration by farm size   109

6.3 Mean farm size of farmers who did and did not choose the listed adaptation strategies   110

8.1 Synthetic representation of the main functional systems according to Luhmann   129

9.1 The world views of modificationists and transformationists and selected implications   145

10.1 Approaches to measuring sustainability in buildings/the built environment   159

10.2 European Common Indicators   160

10.3 The Reference Framework for Sustainable Cities (RFSC) has developed 30 indicators over five dimensions   162

10.4 Proposed indicators or targets for SDG Goal No 11 (Sustainable cities and communities: Make cities inclusive, safe, resilient and sustainable)   163

10.5 Examples of certification schemes for sustainable buildings and/or sustainable neighbourhoods   168

12.1 Sherry Arnstein's ladder of participation   193

13.1 Environmental governance capacity indices and their attributes (compilation of the authors) – in chronological order according to the year of introduction   207

13.2 Overview of the structure of the 8 indices studied in detail   214

19.1 EPI 2016 indicator scores for Malta (on a scale of 0–100) for ecosystem vitality, compared to average scores across 180 states, and ranking of Malta's performance relative to other states   297

19.2 EPI 2016 indicator scores for Malta (on a scale of 0–100) for environmental health, compared to average scores across 180 states, and ranking of Malta's performance relative to other states   301

19.3 Overview of survey exploring public perceptions of environmental quality in Malta   303

20.1	2030 Sustainable Development Goals in *Transforming Our World. The 2030 Agenda for Sustainable Development*	313
21.1	Comparison of the different phases	326
22.1	Indicators of Sustainable Development (IDS)	339
22.2	Comparison between the evolution in the available indicators for Honduras and the values for Latin America and the Caribbean	342
23.1	Brief chronology of the CSD work programme on indicators	351
24.1	Exemplars of urban sustainability frameworks categorised according to key governance functions	368
27.1a	Adoption of SDGs into Sustainability Auditing Standard Practice, numbers 1–9	417
27.1b	Adoption of SDGs into Sustainability Auditing Standard Practice, numbers 10–17	419
28.1	General characteristics of the selected N2Africa action sites	428
28.2	An example of criteria and indicators for the principle of productivity	432
28.3	Indicators collected in the household level survey and their units for the different principles	433
29.1	Examples of two indicators with metrics for each spatial scale	459
29.2	Examples of indicators and potential proxy indicators of system properties for specific objectives, many of which highlight temporal variability	461
30.1	Policy, science, and public perspectives of sustainability indicators with regard to thematic and indicator relevance	483
30.2	Indicator policy factsheet for "gross domestic product" indicator	486
30.3	Indicator policy factsheet for "adjusted net savings" indicator	488
32.1	Key good-practice factors and meta-performance evaluation indicators for sustainability assessment	512
32.2	Meta-evaluation indicators or good-practices factors used by the application examples	515
34.1	Summary of four indicators of economic 'size'	549

BOXES

16.1 The two principles underlying Ecological Footprint accounting   246
16.2 Calculating the Ecological Footprint of Gérard Depardieu in 6 easy steps   250
20.1 Examples of targets in *Transforming Our World. The 2030 Agenda for Sustainable Development*   312
20.2 Themes used by Eurostat for monitoring sustainable development   316
28.1 Important questions that must be addressed when developing a framework for indicators for sustainability   429
28.2 Selecting indicators through a hierarchical framework of principles, criteria, and indicators   430
28.3 An example of developing an indicator: nitrogen-use efficiency   434
33.1 Logical sequence for reviewing and criticizing research   533
33.2 'The Footprint is not perfect; therefore, we should not use it'   533

CONTRIBUTORS

Samuel Adjei-Nsiah is a trained Agronomist and holds a PhD in Production Ecology and Resource Conservation from Wageningen University, the Netherlands. He has several years of experience in integrated soil fertility management in smallholder farming systems in Ghana. His present research focuses on improving the productivity of grain legumes in smallholder farming systems.

Dóra Almássy is an Environmental Researcher, affiliated with the Central European University. Her main research interests concern various aspects of governance for sustainable development, including questions around monitoring and evaluation. She authored several studies and participated in international research projects focusing on environmental sustainability topics and the UN Sustainable Development Goals.

Peter Bartelmus holds a doctorate from the University of Heidelberg. He is an honorary professor of the Bergische Universität Wuppertal (Germany) and has been teaching economics of sustainable development at Wuppertal and Columbia universities. At the UN Environment Programme in Nairobi and the UN headquarters in New York, he developed international systems of environmental statistics and accounting. As director of the environment division of the Wuppertal Institute for Climate, Environment and Energy he sought to combine environmental and ecological economics in measurement and theory. His publications advanced new concepts and methods on green accounting and economics, including his latest book *Sustainability Economics* (Routledge).

Simon Bell is Professor of Innovation and Methodology at the Open University in the UK and CEO of the Bayswater Institute in London, UK. He has held a number of Visiting Professor roles. With over 100 published books and articles, Simon has written on subjects including information systems methodology, action research, participatory methods, coastal sustainability, systemic approaches to environmental problem structuring, sustainability indicators and fear management.

Agni Klintuni Boedhihartono has a background in Fine Arts and Anthropology. She has worked with conservation organizations in the tropics with multidisciplinary teams trying to find the balance between conservation and development. She is passionate about preserving traditional knowledge and the cultural diversity of forest peoples. She is based at University of British Columbia, Canada.

Paul-Marie Boulanger is a Belgian Sociologist and Computer Scientist born in 1950. After graduating in sociology at Strasbourg and Louvain, he spent two years lecturing at the University of Constantine (Algeria) then eight years as researcher with the Department of Population Studies at the University of Louvain (Belgium) where he focused on population aging, labour market and social security issues. Having left the university, he started a career as consultant and independent researcher specialized in the modelling and simulation of the interactions between human populations and their (natural and socio-economical) environments in a system dynamics perspective, as well as in the design and computer programming of information systems (indicators and interpretative models). From 1989 to 1997, he has been especially in charge of the methodological design and technical backstopping of the "Early Warning Systems" of famines in Chad, Mali and Madagascar, on behalf of the European Agency for Health and Development (AEDES), for which he developed original methods of prognosis and diagnosis using artificial intelligence techniques (fuzzy expert systems and Bayesian networks). In 1996 he launched the (French-speaking Belgian) Institute for Sustainable Development (IDD) which he chaired from 1999 to 2015. A senior researcher of the IDD, he coordinates, researches and studies on sustainable development indicators, impact assessment methods, sustainable consumption, energy and transition theory.

Giangiacomo Bravo is Professor at the Department of Social Studies and coordinates the computational social science group at the Centre for Data Intensive Sciences and Applications, Linnaeus University, Sweden. His main research interests cover collective action problems and environmental sustainability.

Sandra Caeiro, PhD, in Environmental Engineering, is Assistant Professor in the Department of Science and Technology at Universidade Aberta, Portugal and a Senior Researcher at the Centre for Environmental and Sustainability Research at New University of Lisbon. Her main research and teaching areas include environmental management and assessment and education for sustainable development.

Louis F. Cassar is Director of the Institute of Earth Systems of the University of Malta. He is a landscape ecologist and environmental planner by training, with experience from across the Mediterranean, West Africa, South America and South-East Asia in areas including biodiversity conservation and coastal management.

Jonathan Chenoweth is a senior lecturer in the Centre for Environment and Sustainability at the University of Surrey. His multi-disciplinary research focuses on water resources management and sustainable development in developed and developing countries. He has published over 55 refereed journal articles as well as book chapters, books and reports, with many of these publications on indicators of water resources development and sustainability.

Elisabeth Conrad is a Senior Lecturer in Environmental Management and Planning at the University of Malta, also holding adjunct status at James Madison University (Virginia, USA). Her experience spans work in environmental impact assessment and protected area management, as well as on research initiatives related to the use of sustainability indicators.

Professor Robert Costanza is a Vice Chancellor's Chair in Public Policy at the Crawford School of Public Policy at the Australian National University. He is also currently a Senior Fellow at the National Council on Science and the Environment in the US, a Senior Research

Fellow at the Stockholm Resilience Center, an Affiliate Fellow at the Gund Institute for Ecological Economics, a deTao Master of Ecological Economics at the deTao Masters Academy, China, and a Fellow of the Royal Society of Arts (UK).

Arthur Lyon Dahl is President, International Environment Forum; retired Deputy Assistant Executive Director, UNEP, coordinator UN System-wide Earthwatch; consultant on sustainability indicators to World Bank, World Economic Forum, UNEP; researcher on values-based indicators of education for sustainable development; biologist specialist on small islands and coral reefs; organizer of the Pacific Regional Environment Programme (SPREP).

Bart de Boer mastered in Automatic Control Engineering. He specialized in systems analysis of water quality management, with a project group researching regional water management. He continued this line of work with DHV Consulting Engineers. He joined Roefie Hueting in investigating and calculating the environmentally sustainable national income in 1991.

Ana Rita Domingues is currently a PhD candidate in Management at the University of Bologna (Italy) and is a researcher at the Center for Environmental and Sustainability Research (NOVA University of Lisbon, Portugal). She has previously worked as a research assistant and an environmental consultant. She has a MSc in Environmental Engineering (NOVA University of Lisbon). Her research activity is carried out within sustainability performance assessment and reporting, sustainability indicators and stakeholder engagement.

Tony Drummond, PhD, worked as Computational Scientist at Lawrence Berkeley National Lab and UC Berkeley on the development of high-performance numerical libraries and high-end computer simulation codes for earth sciences and high-energy physics applications. Currently, he serves as adjunct computational sciences faculty at San Diego State University and the Polytechnic University of Valencia in Spain.

John W. Emerson (Jay) is Director of Graduate Studies in the Department of Statistics and Data Science at Yale University. He teaches graduate and undergraduate courses as well as client workshops, tutorials and short courses. His interests are in computational statistics and graphics, Big Data, and environmental sustainability and performance metrics.

Daniel C. Esty is the Hillhouse Professor at Yale University. He is the author or editor of ten books and dozens of articles covering environmental law and policy, corporate sustainability, regulatory reform, and sustainability metrics – and for 20 years, he has led the team that produces the Environmental Performance Index (epi.yale.edu).

Evan Fraser is the Director of the Arrell Food Institute, a Tier I Canada Research Chair in Global Food Security and a Professor of Geography at the University of Guelph. His research focuses on threats and solutions to the challenge of sustainably and nutritiously feeding the world's growing population under climate change.

Alessandro Galli is Senior Scientist and Mediterranean Program Director at Global Footprint Network. His research focuses on historical changes in human dependence on natural resources and ecological services through the use of sustainability indicators and environmental accounting methods. He is co-author of several publications including 40 articles in peer-reviewed journals and various editions of WWF's *Living Planet Report*.

Dr. Gilberto C. Gallopin is an Independent Scholar and Associate Fellow, Tellus Institute. He is an ecological systems analyst, scenario builder and sustainable development expert. He worked in ecological systems analysis, global modelling, environmental impact assessment, environment and development nexus, scenario analysis, policy dialogues, sustainable development indicators and sustainability science.

Ken E. Giller is Professor of Plant Production Systems at Wageningen University. Ken's research focuses on smallholder farming systems in sub-Saharan Africa, in particular on soil fertility and the role of nitrogen fixation in tropical legumes. Ken earlier held professorships at Wye College, University of London and the University of Zimbabwe.

Dr. Philip Grabowski is an interdisciplinary social scientist focusing on sustainable development at Taylor University. His research focuses on documenting farmers' perspectives on sustainable technologies and analyzing how those technologies contribute to or detract from social, economic and environmental goals.

Tomáš Hák is Associate Professor and Researcher at Charles University Environment Center (Deputy Director 2003–2013). His field of research is indicators of resource use as well as on policy aspects of SIs. He is a member of the Environment Committee of the Czech Academy of Science and the Governmental Council for Sustainable Development, and he has cooperated with the Czech Statistical Office, Healthy Cities of the CR and international agencies such as UNEP and EEA.

Jon Hall has been working with indicators of well-being, progress and development since 2000. At the Australian Bureau of Statistics he designed Australia's first set of national progress measures. He led the Organisation for Economic Co-operation and Development's Global Project on Measuring the Progress of Societies (2005–2009) and now works on human development reporting for the United Nations.

Laurel Hanscom is Program Director at Global Footprint Network, spearheading their open data and sustainable development projects. She also contributes to the production of the National Footprint Accounts. Previously, Laurel worked at the Peace Corps, and in environmental analysis. She holds degrees in geography from San Diego State University, focusing on climate change and agriculture.

Peter Hardi is Professor Emeritus at Central European University, Budapest. His main field of research is sustainability, integrity and CSR. Prior to joining CEU he was Senior Fellow at the International Institute for Sustainable Development, Canada where he initiated the process that defined the first set of the Bellagio Principles.

Maureen Hart is President of Sustainable Measures and is an expert on sustainability indicators and the author of the *Guide to Sustainable Community Indicators*, used worldwide by organizations and communities working to measure progress toward long-term economic, social and environmental quality of life. She established Sustainable Measures in 1993. She is also the Acting Director of the Community Indicators Consortium, a network of organizations and individuals using information to foster informed discourse and decision-making about local, regional, national and global priorities.

Angel Hsu, PhD, is an Assistant Professor of Environmental Studies at Yale-NUS College and an Adjunct of the Yale School of Forestry and Environmental Studies, where she founded and directs the Yale Data-Driven Environmental Solutions Group.

Roefie Hueting is the first Ecological or Environmental Economist in the Netherlands and one of the first in the world. He designed the concept of the possible uses or functions of the environment defined as our non-human-made physical surroundings and the concept of the environmentally sustainable national income (eSNI).

Svatava Janoušková is Associate Professor at the Faculty of Science and researcher at Charles University Environment Center. Her main field of interest is the development and use of sustainability indicators at a local level. She cooperates on the development of sustainable development policies and programmes and conducts research into theoretical aspects of indicators. She is a member of the Governmental Council for Sustainable Development, cooperates closely with the Czech School Inspection and is a TIMSS board member.

Jochen Jesinghaus is an Economist and Engineer, and from 1992 to 2014 an Official of the European Commission. With Ernst Ulrich von Weizsäcker, he wrote *Ecological Tax Reform* (1992). He contributed to the 1993 *Delors White Paper on Growth, Competitiveness & Employment*, was a member of numerous indicator initiatives and created the 'Millennium Development Goals Dashboard of Sustainability'.

Simon Joss is Professor of Science & Technology Studies at the University of Westminster (London), where he directs the International Eco-Cities Initiative. His research focuses on governance innovation processes relating to contemporary environmental and urban issues. He works collaboratively with non-academic organizations on various applied research projects.

Fred Kanampiu is a Senior Scientist and N2Africa Project Coordinator at the International Institute of Tropical Agriculture. The focus of his research is on soil fertility and parasitic weed management in sub-Saharan Africa. Fred earlier worked as an agronomist with the International Maize and Wheat Improvement Center and the Kenya Agricultural Research Institute.

Professor Ida Kubiszewski is an Associate Professor at Crawford School of Public Policy at The Australian National University. She is the founding managing editor and current co-editor-in-chief of magazine/journal hybrid called *Solutions*.

David Lin is the Director of Research and leads the city sustainability programme at Global Footprint Network. He holds a BS in ecology from the University of California, Los Angeles and conducted his doctoral and postdoctoral research on greenhouse gas dynamics of Arctic ecosystems with the Systems Ecology Laboratory at the University of Texas, El Paso.

Rodrigo Lozano is Associate Professor at the University of Gävle, Sweden and former Editor-in-Chief for the *Journal of Cleaner Production*. He was previously Assistant Professor at Utrecht University, the Netherlands, and at Leeds, UK. For more than 15 years Rodrigo has been working towards Sustainability in NGOs, universities and corporations.

Laetitia Mailhes's writing career spans journalism and advocacy work. A former innovation correspondent of the *French Financial Times* and the co-author of two books about food systems, she has been writing extensively in English and French about sustainability issues. A Sciences-Po Paris graduate, she completed her education in the UK before moving to California where she currently lives.

Chris Margules led the Tropical Landscapes Program of CSIRO in Australia before becoming Senior Vice President, responsible for the Asia Pacific Division of Conservation International. He has worked in Africa, PNG and Australia and now spends much of his time working with Indonesian scientists and practitioners on conservation and development programmes in Indonesia. Chris is an Adjunct Professor at the University of Indonesia and James Cook University. He is a member in the general division of the order of Australia in recognition of his contributions to science.

Wytze Marinus is a PhD candidate at Plant Production Systems, Wageningen University. His research focuses on how model results can be used in co-learning cycles to develop options for sustainable intensification with smallholder farmers in the East African highlands. Wytze used several tools of farming systems analysis in research for development in earlier projects.

André Martinuzzi is founding director of the Institute for Managing Sustainability and professor at WU Vienna (www.sustainability.eu). He has coordinated projects funded by the EU Framework Programmes, on behalf of six EU DGs, Eurostat and UN organizations. His areas of research are corporate sustainability, evaluation and responsible innovation.

Bedřich Moldan is Professor at Charles University in Prague where he teaches. He also founded the Charles University Environment Center where he served as Director from 1991 to 2014. He started his public life as the first Minister of the Environment of the Czech Republic in 1990; between 2004–2010 he served as a Senator of the Parliament of the CR. He has held various international positions including Chairman of the UN Commission on Sustainable Development (2001) and Chairman of the EEA Scientific Committee (2000–2006).

Stephen Morse is Chair in Systems Analysis for Sustainability in the Centre for Environment and Sustainability at the University of Surrey, UK. Steve has a background in applied ecology and the environment and his research and teaching interests are broad, spanning both the natural and social sciences. He is a Fellow of the Royal Geographical Society, the Royal Society of Biology and the Higher Education Academy and has published 18 books and over 140 academic papers, many of them on the assessment of sustainability (including indicators).

Dr. Mark Musumba is an agricultural economist at the University of Florida. His research investigates the impacts of climate change on agricultural production, environment and health; the behavioural aspects of farmers' market participation; the factors that affect human capital movement and sustainability of agricultural intensification in sub-Saharan agricultural systems.

Dr. Cheryl Palm is a Tropical Ecologist and Biogeochemist at the University of Florida. Her research focuses on land degradation and rehabilitation, including soil nutrient dynamics in farming systems of Africa. Her most recent work investigates the trade-offs and synergies among agricultural intensification strategies, the environment and rural livelihoods.

László Pintér is Professor and Head of Department at the Department of Environmental Sciences and Policy at the Central European University and Senior Fellow at the International Institute for Sustainable Development. His work includes sustainability goals, strategies, indicators and outlooks, and he co-led the process that resulted in BellagioSTAMP.

Steve Posner is Policy Engagement Associate, who empowers scientists to transform, frame and catalyze the policy dialogue. He connects scientists and policymakers at the federal level, designs communications trainings for scientists and arranges briefings on natural resource issues. He creates the conditions for people to understand and use scientific knowledge about the environment. He has a PhD in natural resources and a certificate in ecological economics from the University of Vermont, and a bachelor's degree in astronomy and physics from Haverford College.

Tomás B. Ramos is Professor of Strategic Environmental Assessment and Planning at NOVA University Lisbon and researcher at CENSE, Center for Environmental and Sustainability Research. He has been working for the last 25 years with sustainability assessment, indicators and stakeholder engagement. He is Associate Editor of the *Journal of Cleaner Production* and member of the Board of the International Sustainable Development Research Society (ISDRS).

L. Reijnders is Emeritus Professor of Environmental Science at the University of Amsterdam. He published in the field of sustainability indicators with Hans Opschoor and Roefie Hueting. His main research interests are in the field of environmentally improved production, with a recent emphasis on biofuels, nanotechnology and resource conservation.

Esther Ronner is a PhD candidate at Plant Production Systems, Wageningen University. Her research focuses on the impacts of large-scale dissemination of improved grain legume technologies on smallholder farmers in Africa. With her background in International Development she has a keen interest in co-innovation and technology adoption and adaptation.

Dr. Ulla Rosenström is Chief Senior Specialist at the Finnish Prime Minister's Office. She is currently involved in leading the government strategy process and supporting the Prime Minister by reporting the impacts of the government programme. Ulla has led and participated in several national and international SDI working groups. She has conducted pioneering work on researching the use of SDIs resulting in over 50 articles and reports in the field.

Sarah Rotz is a Postdoctoral Fellow in the Department of Geography at the University of Guelph where she studies the political ecology of food systems. Sarah is a graduate of the University of Toronto and holds a Master's Degree in Environmental Studies from York University.

Professor Yvonne Rydin is Professor of Planning, Environment and Public Policy at University College London's Bartlett School of Planning. She specializes in urban planning, governance and sustainability. A collection on ANT and planning studies, *Actor Networks of Planning* (co-edited with Laura Tate), was published by Routledge in 2016.

Dwi Amalia Sari is an accountant and senior auditor for the Indonesia National Audit Office. She has audited government institutions in Indonesia since 2000. Her passion is to formulate mechanisms in auditing the sustainability of a governance in an interconnected multisectoral landscape in developing countries. Dwi is currently a PhD candidate at James Cook University, Australia.

Jeffrey Sayer is Professor in the Faculty of Forestry in the University of British Columbia in Vancouver. He has spent his career working to resolve trade-offs between conservation and development in low-income countries and has published widely on landscape approaches to achieve better environmental, social and economic outcomes. The development of integrated methods of assessing landscape performance is central to Jeff's current work. Jeff is currently focusing his attention on landscape scale initiatives in Indonesia.

Dr. Sieglinde Snapp is a Soils and Cropping Systems Ecologist at Michigan State University. Her research interests include international agricultural system design for a changing climate and understanding integrated nutrient management, ecological intensification and participatory action research. She has pioneered the development of multipurpose crops for food and environmental security.

Joachim H. Spangenberg is an Inter- and Transdisciplinary Researcher by education and dedication, with a PhD in economics, and an academic background in biology and ecology. His work focuses on sustainability of socio-ecological systems, ecosystem services, sufficiency and sustainable consumption. For more information please visit http://seri.academia.edu/ JoachimHSpangenberg

John Talberth is the Founder of Center for Sustainable Economy and currently serves as both President and Senior Economist. John coordinates consulting work with non-profits, businesses, universities and government agencies seeking environmental economics expertise and analysis to support their sustainability initiatives and programmes. He also leads work on CSE's Wild and Working Forests, Genuine Progress, and Green Infrastructure programmes. John holds a PhD in International and Environmental Economics from the University of New Mexico and an MA in Urban and Regional Planning from the University of Oregon.

Catalina Turcu is Senior Lecturer in Sustainable Development and Planning at the Bartlett, University College London. She is an expert on sustainability indicators, housing and urban energy. Catalina has also undertaken research in areas such as urban sustainability, urban regeneration, area deprivation, urban design and, more recently, pro-environmental behaviour.

Gerrie W. J. van de Ven is Assistant Professor at Plant Production Systems, Wageningen University. The focus of her work is on analysis of farming systems. Nutrient cycling, environmental impacts and indicators and the interaction between crops and livestock, both in the Western world and in Africa, have her special attention.

Walter J. V. Vermeulen has been Professor (Associate) in Environmental Social Science at Utrecht University since 1996. His work focuses on design, implementation and effectiveness of new strategies for improving the environmental and socio-ethical performance of production and consumption systems by means of co-production of sustainable development strategies. He is the President of the International Sustainable Development Research Society (www. isdrs.org). He is also connected as Associate Professor Extraordinary to Stellenbosch University, School of Public Leadership, and Sustainability Institute, Stellenbosch, South Africa. Web of Science Researcher-ID: B-4976–2008.

Mathis Wackernagel, PhD, is the Co-creator of the Ecological Footprint and CEO of Global Footprint Network. This international think tank focuses on bringing about a sustainable human economy in which all can thrive within the means of one planet. Mathis's awards include the IAIA Global Environment Award, the Blue Planet Prize, Kenneth E. Boulding Memorial Award, the Zayed International Prize for the Environment, and a Skoll Award for Social Entrepreneurship.

FOREWORD

There hasn't been a single point in my 45 years as a sustainability activist where indicators, of one sort or another, haven't been at the heart of what I was doing, haven't been fiercely contested and haven't both intrigued me and irritated the hell out of me!

Not many people cared about indicators in those very early days, although Fritz Schumacher's 'Small is Beautiful' in 1973 was one of the first books to suggest that a sustainable economy would remain forever a distant fantasy until we freed ourselves from the tyranny of using Gross Domestic Product as pretty much the sole proxy for progress. GDP is still the most controversial indicator we're wrestling with even now.

But today, as this wide-ranging and rather amazing book demonstrates so eloquently, the world of Sustainability Indicators is big, rapidly evolving, still as controversial as ever – and of critical importance to pretty much every citizen on Planet Earth.

That may sound like an overblown claim, but think about it. Back in 2016, governments the world over signed up to 17 big picture goals – the Sustainable Development Goals – underpinned by 169 targets, all of which are to be delivered by 2030. That's just 14 years in which the fate of humankind will be determined, one way or another: either we learn (finally!) to live within the Earth's Planetary Boundaries, and do so in far more equitable and compassionate economies than is the case today, or we don't.

Suffice it to say it's not going to be quite as binary as that – all target dates of that kind (2020, 2030, 2050, etc.) are more than a little arbitrary. But here's the thing: how will world leaders know, at any point between now and 2030, that we're moving in the right direction? At the right sort of speed? It's all in the data, in the metrics, and in the indicators through which that information is interpreted and mediated.

Sustainable development has proved notoriously difficult to pin down over the years – by way of *thematics* (what's in, what's not), by way of *levels* (global through to household, via countries, regions, cities, landscapes and communities), and by way of *agency* – exactly whose indicators are we talking about, designed, developed and delivered for what purpose? An impressive amount of light is shed on all these vexatious issues in this Handbook, revealing (somewhat reassuringly!) that the actual practice of sustainable development commands a much broader consensus than might be imagined.

Moreover, there's a deeper and hugely significant purpose at work here. Many of the core premises on which our current model of progress is based are currently under unprecedented assault. The pursuit of truth through the patient accumulation of empirical data is now seen by many as an obsolete irrelevance. Evidence-based policymaking is disparaged. And in what is chillingly described as our 'post-truth world', the very idea of objective expertise is ridiculed. This is a disaster for all of us.

Whether it's addressed explicitly by the Handbook's editors, or subtly implied by many of the authors, there's a story here about the critical importance of science, metrics and statistics deployed in defence of liberalism and rational Enlightenment values. The idea of the whole field of Sustainability Indicators being seen as part of a wider project 'to save human beings from their instinctive and irrational selves' sets the bar at an appropriately ambitious level.

Jonathon Porritt, CBE, is an eminent writer, broadcaster and
commentator on sustainable development

ACKNOWLEDGEMENTS

Primarily, we would like to express our thanks to our authors of chapters for this book. They have been good companions in our journey. Thanks to: László Pintér, Peter Hardi, André Martinuzzi, Jon Hall, Arthur Lyon Dahl, Walter J.V. Vermeulen, Daniel C. Esty, John W. Emerson, Sarah Rotz, Evan Fraser, Robert Costanza, Maureen Hart, Ida Kubiszewski, Steve Posner, John Talberth, Paul-Marie Boulanger, Joachim H. Spangenberg, Catalina Turcu, Jonathan Chenoweth, Dóra Almássy, Roefie Hueting, Bart de Boer, Peter Bartelmus, Mathis Wackernagel, Alessandro Galli, Laurel Hanscom, David Lin, Laetitia Mailhes, Tony Drummond, Angel Hsu, Giangiacomo Bravo, Elisabeth Conrad, Louis F. Cassar, Lucas Reijnders, Ulla Rosenström, Gilberto C. Gallopin, Simon Joss, Yvonne Rydin, Ana Rita Domingues, Rodrigo Lozano, Tomás B. Ramos, Jochen Jesinghaus, Dwi Amalia Sari, Chris Margules, Agni Klintuni Boedhihartono, Jeffrey Sayer, Wytze Marinus, Esther Ronner, Gerrie W. J. van de Ven, Fred Kanampiu, Samuel Adjei-Nsiah, Ken E. Giller, Philip Grabowski, Mark Musumba, Cheryl Palm, Sieglinde Snapp, Svatava Janoušková, Tomáš Hák, Bedřich Moldan and Sandra Caeiro.

ACRONYMS

AC	Avoidance Cost
ANS	adjusted net savings
ASI	Assessment of Sustainability Indicators
Asym	Asymmetrically booked cost(s) of environmental deterioration in the National Accounts
AWARE	Available Water Remaining index
BellagioSTAMP	SusTainability Assessment and Measurement Principles announced in a multistakeholder meeting in Bellagio, Italy
CGSDI	Consultative Group on Sustainable Development Indicators
CIAT	International Center for Tropical Agriculture
CIESIN	Center for International Earth Science Information Network
CLIMI	Climate Laws, Institutions and Measures Index
CNC/CRITINC	Critical natural capital
CSD	Commission on Sustainable Development
DC	Damage Cost
DPSIR	Driving forces – Pressures – State – Impact – Response
DSD	UN Division for Sustainable Development
DSR	driving-force/state-response
EBBF	Ethical Business Building the Future
ECF	Environmentally adjusted net Capital Formation
ECI	European Common Indicator
EC JRC	European Commission Joint Research Centre
ECLAC	UN Economic Commission for Latin America and the Caribbean
EDP	Environmentally adjusted net Domestic Product
EEA	European Environment Agency
EF	Ecological Footprint
EIA	Environmental Impact Assessment
EIS	Environmental Information System
eLCA	environmental Life Cycle Assessment
EPI	Environmental Performance Index

ES	Ecosystem Services
ESCAP	UN Economic and Social Commission for Asia and the Pacific
ESI	Environmental Sustainability Index
eSNI	environmentally Sustainable National Income
EVI	Environmental Vulnerability Index
FDES	Framework for the Development of Environment Statistics
FISD	Framework for Indicators of Sustainable Development
FSC	Forest Stewardship Council
GDP	Gross Domestic Product
GIS	Geographic Information Systems
GPI	Genuine Progress Index
GRI	Global Reporting Initiative
HANPP	Human Appropriation of Net Primary Product
HDI	Human Development Index
HSDI	Human Sustainable Development Index
IBRD	International Bank for Reconstruction and Development
ICSU	International Council of Scientific Unions/International Council of Science
ICT	information and communications technology
IDRC	International Development Research Centre
IHDP	International Human Dimensions of Global Environmental Change Programme
IISD	International Institute of Sustainable Development
ImPACT	Impact – Population size – Affluence – Consumption intensity – Technology
ISD	International Insititute for Sustainable Development
ISDRS	International Sustainable Development Research Society
ISO	International Organization for Standardization
ISSAI	International Standards for Supreme Audit Institution
ISSC	International Social Science Council
IUCN	International Union for Conservation of Nature
KPH	Forest Management Unit (in Indonesian)
LCA	Life Cycle Assessment
LCC	Life Cycle Costing
LCSA	Life Cycle Sustainability Assessment
LIME	Life-cycle Impact assessment Method based on Endpoint modelling
LPI	Living Planet Index
LUCAS	LCIA method Used for a CAnadian-Specific context
MDG	Millennium Development Goals
MIPS	Material intensity per unit of service
NCA	Natural Carbon Accounting
NEPA	National Environmental Policy Act
NGO	non-governmental organization
NI	national income
OECD	Organisation for Economic Co-operation and Development
PAR	Participatory Action Research
PEFC	Programme for the Endorsement of Forest Certification
PLA	Participatory Learning and Action

PPP or 3P	people, planet, prosperity (or people, planet, profit in other cases)
PRA	Participatory Rural Appraisal
PSR	pressure – state – response
ReCiPe	acronym represents the initials of the institutes developing the assessment method (RIVM, Radboud University, CML and PRé)
R&D	Research & Development
RFSC	Reference Framework for Sustainable Cities
RRA	Rapid Rural Appraisal
RSPO	Roundtable on Sustainable Palm Oil
S2	Sustainable Seattle
SAI	Sustainable agricultural intensification
SCOPE	Scientific Committee on Problems of the Environment
SD	sustainable development
SDGs	United Nations' Sustainable Development Goals
SDI	sustainable development indicator
SDSN	Sustainable Development Solutions Network
SEE	social, environmental (or ecological) and economic
SEEA	System of Integrated Environmental and Economic Accounts (now System of Environmental-Economic Accounting)
SES	Socio-Ecological System
SETAC	Society of Environmental Toxicology and Chemistry
SHDB	Social Hotspot Database
SI	sustainability indicator
SIDS	Small Island Developing States
SII	sustainability indicators and indices
sLCA	social Life Cycle Assessment
SNA	System of National Accounts
SOPAC	South Pacific Applied Geoscience Commission
SSA	sub-Saharan Africa
STIRPAT	STochastic Impacts by Regression on Population, Affluence and Technology
TBL	Triple Bottom Line
TLU	Tropical Livestock Unit
TRM	Total Material Requirement
UN	United Nations
UNCED	United Nations Conference on Environment and Development (Rio de Janeiro 1992)
UNCHE	United Nations Conference on the Human Environment (Stockholm 1972)
UNCSD	United Nations Conference on Sustainable Development (Rio de Janeiro 2012)
UNDP	United Nations Development Programme
UNEP	United Nations Environment Programme (now UN Environment)
UNSTAT	UN Statistical Office (now United Nations Statistics Division)
VMF	Variable Monthly Flow
WBCSD	World Business Council for Sustainable Development
WEF	World Economic Forum
WHO	World Health Organization

WRI	World Resources Institute
WSSD	World Summit on Sustainable Development (Johannesburg 2002)
WTA	willingness to accept
WTO-ITC	World Trade Organisation – International Trade Centre
WTP	willingness to pay
WWF	World Wildlife Fund/Worldwide Fund for Nature

1

INTRODUCTION

Indicators and post truth

Simon Bell and Stephen Morse

The moment we begin to fear the opinions of others and hesitate to tell the truth that is in us, and from motives of policy are silent when we should speak, the divine floods of light and life no longer flow into our souls.

– Elizabeth Cady Stanton

It would seem that this book is timely in a major and more important way than we thought at the outset when we began planning in 2015. When we began work, the major requirement for it had yet to emerge. Certainly, a book which brought together some of the most eminent and thoughtful authorities in the indicator universe had great merit. Definitely, a collection of essays on the topography of indicators and sustainable development is timely. Absolutely, to compare and contrast the thoughts of the authors of this landscape is priceless as we have never been so much in need of indicators to assess, in an impartial and confirmable manner, the outlines of our changing, developing, resilient and threatened world. But the main reason for this book was to emerge in the unravelling of the 20th century shared and liberal mindset which has been with us since the end of World War 2. This unravelling has been taking place since the second half of 2016. One would have to have a Panglossian mind to imagine that we are not now in a different place to the place we contemplated in 2015. We now know that a new and dangerous reality has emerged which not only threatens the stability of the complex world of indicators – from conception to verification – but the rational mindset which conceived of them as a good thing in the first place.

To the surprise of many and the bemusement of the majority of intellectuals, academics and just rational people, the world appears to be spinning towards what has been labelled a "post-truth" reality. What is post truth? The Oxford dictionary named it as the word of the year and has defined it as:

> Relating to or denoting circumstances in which objective facts are less influential in shaping public opinion than appeals to emotion and personal belief.

This is not a world with which we are unfamiliar. Those working in the indicator business (if we may so denote the field) are well aware of the 'emotion and personal belief' which helps to shape the selection, data gathering and assessment of many indicators. Indeed, in this book we have robust chapters which deal with this important aspect of indicator work. What has come as more of a surprise has been the destructive and senseless denial of the importance and value of objective expertise.

The first and most obvious precursor of the post-truth Weltanschauung in the UK appeared during the recent, divisive European Union referendum. In the comments by the then Justice Secretary, and at the time of writing the Secretary of State for Environment, Food and Rural Affairs, Michael Gove, objective data was called into question. The *Financial Times* reported the incident as follows:

> Michael Gove has refused to name any economists who back Britain's exit from the European Union, saying that "people in this country have had enough of experts"....
> He said that Vote Leave, the official Out campaign, would publish more details on its economic plans next week. So far it has said the UK could cut VAT on fuel and spend "additional millions" on the NHS.... Sky's political editor Faisal Islam said Mr Gove knew that figure was wrong, and accused him of importing the "post-truth" politics of Donald Trump to the UK. The UK Statistics Authority has said the figure "is misleading and undermines trust in official statistics", because it is a gross sum and does not account for Britain's rebate and funding received from the EU.
>
> (Mance 2016)

The source of post truth can be tracked back to the Trump campaign in the US presidential election, and the basis for the denial of facts and rational interpretation of collected data can be seen to have a ground zero in that troubled politics. In his brilliant article in the *Guardian* in January 2017, William Davies argued that we who look for accountability and empirical verification in our decision-making could be in trouble.

> Shortly before the November presidential election, a study in the US discovered that 68% of Trump supporters distrusted the economic data published by the federal government. In the UK, a research project by Cambridge University and YouGov looking at conspiracy theories discovered that 55% of the population believes that the government "is hiding the truth about the number of immigrants living here".
>
> (Davies 2017)

As Davies goes on to say:

> The declining authority of statistics – and the experts who analyse them – is at the heart of the crisis that has become known as "post-truth" politics. And in this uncertain new world, attitudes towards quantitative expertise have become increasingly divided. From one perspective, grounding politics in statistics is elitist, undemocratic and oblivious to people's emotional investments in their community and nation. It is just one more way that privileged people in London, Washington DC or Brussels seek to impose their worldview on everybody else. From the opposite perspective, statistics are quite the opposite of elitist. They enable journalists, citizens and politicians to discuss society as a whole, not on the basis of anecdote, sentiment or prejudice, but in ways that can be validated. The alternative to quantitative expertise is less likely to be democracy than an unleashing of tabloid editors and demagogues to provide their own "truth" of what is going on across society.
>
> (Davies 2017)

Let us lay one error to rest before it has a chance to emerge.

Those working in the area of indicator development have no issue with the importance of personal perspective and subjectivity in the area of indicators. We fully appreciate the value of the local and the personal in all stages of indicator formulation, selection, prioritization, assessment and outreach. Indeed, as long ago as 1999 the authors noted:

> Sustainability indicators were spawned from an understandable desire to 'do' sustainable development and not just talk about it, but no matter how much we try to convince ourselves otherwise they are still based upon what we each experience as a complex mix of cultural, social, ethical and professional aspirations and understandings. The dominant or emergent vision of sustainability, and the SIs that equate to it, will inevitably arise out of a negotiation between the visions of many individuals and groups. The emergent vision may well be that of scientists, planners, politicians, academics, environmentalists, interest groups, the public or a dynamic and changing coalition of all or some of these. They will invariably have views and ideas that are contested by other groups and which are not seen as being straightforward or absolute, 'true' or unchangeable. Sustainability indicators are, like all good statistics, measures of tendency interpreted to an agenda set by imperfect people.
>
> (Bell and Morse 1999 page XI)

The indicator community did not suggest that indicators should be expert impositions. Rather they are emergent from process. Many of the chapters in this book bear eloquent evidence of the time and trouble researchers have gone to make sure that they are inclusive and reflective of a range of emotional and empathetic issues and not merely the quantitative facts of empirical measurement. Within the pages of this book there is copious evidence.

What seems to be emerging in the early years of the 21st century appears to be a cynical and corrupting attempt to conflate prejudice with empathy, bias with inclusion and bullying with expertise. Of course, experts using numbers have a long tradition, Davies notes:

> The emergence in the late 17th century of government advisers claiming scientific authority, rather than political or military acumen, represents the origins of the "expert" culture now so reviled by populists. These path-breaking individuals were neither pure scholars nor government officials, but hovered somewhere between the two. They were enthusiastic amateurs who offered a new way of thinking about populations that privileged aggregates and objective facts. Thanks to their mathematical prowess, they believed they could calculate what would otherwise require a vast census to discover.
>
> (Davies 2017)

And Davies goes on to recognize that indicators are sharing issues which all figures, data collection and data interpretation now have:

> The crisis of statistics is not quite as sudden as it might seem. For roughly 450 years, the great achievement of statisticians has been to reduce the complexity and fluidity of national populations into manageable, comprehensible facts and figures. Yet in recent decades, the world has changed dramatically, thanks to the cultural politics that emerged in the 1960s and the reshaping of the global economy that began soon after. It is not clear that the statisticians have always kept pace with these changes. Traditional forms of statistical classification and definition are coming under strain from more

fluid identities, attitudes and economic pathways. Efforts to represent demographic, social and economic changes in terms of simple, well-recognised indicators are losing legitimacy.

(Davies 2017)

Davies is right but the indicator community has long been aware of the issue of legitimacy. What we have not been prepared for has been the brazen yet ignorant attack on the whole process of objective/subjective enlightenment rationalism. Davies chillingly concludes:

> A post-statistical society is a potentially frightening proposition, not because it would lack any forms of truth or expertise altogether, but because it would drastically privatise them. Statistics are one of many pillars of liberalism, indeed of Enlightenment. The experts who produce and use them have become painted as arrogant and oblivious to the emotional and local dimensions of politics. No doubt there are ways in which data collection could be adapted to reflect lived experiences better. But the battle that will need to be waged in the long term is not between an elite-led politics of facts versus a populist politics of feeling. It is between those still committed to public knowledge and public argument and those who profit from the ongoing disintegration of those things.

(Davies 2017)

It would seem that the post-truth phenomenon plays upon a natural tendency in human beings to go for an easy option in their decision-making. In his landmark book 'Thinking Fast and Slow', Daniel Kahneman fictionalizes the human mind to a System 1 and System 2 which he also calls the automatic and the effortful. He suggests:

> System 1 operates automatically and quickly, with little or no effort and no sense of voluntary control.
> System 2 allocates attention to the effortful mental activities that demand it, including complex computations. The operations of System 2 are often associated with the subjective experience of agency, choice, and concentration.

(Kahneman 2011 page 32)

System 1 is knee jerk and thoughtless to some extent. It takes time, effort and rationalism to engage with System 2. The post-truth world is a System 1 world where people of all political persuasions and none are buffeted from one idea to the next with scant or dubious information to support them, making decisions which may ultimately impact upon us all.

It is into *this* world that this book emerges.

In 2015 our aspiration for this book now appears startlingly naïve. In our pitch for the publication with Routledge we suggested that:

> Sustainable Development (SD) is a vast creator and consumer of indicators and indices (where an index comprises a number of indicators) of all kinds. The range of creators and potential users extends from government to non-governmental organizations, through professional practitioners in SD and Environmental Management (EM) to academics and researchers working in international research organizations and higher education institutions worldwide and of course the multitude of students who are studying in these various agencies.

4

Indeed, we did understand that indicators related to sustainable development were multiply produced and consumed. We recognized the conflicts surrounding sustainability indicators and indices (we used the abbreviation SII for them in the pitch).

> The numerous books and articles written on SIIs witness the popularity and topicality of the field and yet very few resources exist which tell the full story of the SII phenomena nor is the conflictual and contested story of SII development, assessment and use widely understood.

Please note, we understood the conflictual basis. What we were not to understand at that time was that a 'conflictual and contested story' might morph into a fundamental assault on the nature of data, fact and truth.

Our original objective was:

> to provide researchers and more general readers worldwide with an oversight of the field of SIIs as applied in the wide variety of fields embraced by SD. The handbook is intended to be provocative as well as being informative. In editing this book we have sought to include views from the centre ground of SII development but also divergent views which represent some of the diverse, challenging and even edgy observations which are prominent in the wider field of environmental indicator thinking.

And this remains true to this day but we need to now emphasize the 'edgy observations' and add that the book has a new and important mission.

We do support the need for empirical and verifiable and contestable indicators. We also urgently and defiantly register that this book provides a robust defence of the need for and the necessity to maintain the effort to produce resilient and honest measures and indicators.

So, what is this book about?

Sustainability indicators, environmental indicators and the indices which exist alongside them have been with us now for over 40 years. This duration has seen thinking change and adapt as the mission of the exercise moved and changed. If the intention was to provide a means to assess the durability of the earth system, then the path to make this assessment has been varied and precocious. For 40 years minds of all calibre have engaged in the means to measure the immeasurable – the concept of the sustainable world. If our work here is to bear witness to this huge, global and multidisciplinary work then it has to span many minds and many mindsets. This book is a map of the terrain so far traversed.

First, the book structure. The book is organized as a series of sections which build upon each other. There are four sections to the book:

Part I deals with the history and theory of indicators and indices in the field of sustainable development.

Part II looks at the main methods and approaches which have been used to gather and assess these indicators.

Part III contains a series of agency reports on the use of indicators.

Part IV provides some critiques of where we are, thoughts about where else we might be and how we might get there.

We do have to stress here that although we – as editors – were keen to have a structure and also to make sure that key places within the SI landscape were covered, we otherwise took a very 'hands-off' approach to the contributions of the authors. We did not wish to 'direct' authors in any particular way other than address any issues of clarity (of which, it has to be said, there were very few) and a desire to make sure that the authors were aware of what the others were doing and hence introduce a degree of cross-referencing where appropriate. After all, all the contributors to the book are experts in their field and while at times they may disagree with each other or perhaps arrive at the same point from quite different directions, we saw no reason to involve ourselves any further. The result, we hope the reader will agree, is a diverse, wide-ranging and thought-provoking series of essays on sustainability indicators and indices. Here follows a brief overview of the book chapters based on the abstracts provided by the authors.

Chapter 1 in which Simon and Steve set the scene for the book.

Part I: Theory and history

Chapter 2 Bellagio STAMP: principles for sustainability assessment and measurement
by László Pintér, Peter Hardi, André Martinuzzi, Jon Hall

Revisiting the way society defines and measures progress has been identified as one of the key levers in tackling the root causes of unsustainable development. The recent economic and food crises exposed a critical weakness in the ability of currently mainstream indicators of progress to provide early warning and take adequate preventive action.

Since the early 1990s a growing number of organizations have been involved in the development of indicator systems around the key socio-economic and environmental concerns of sustainable development within their own context. In order to provide guidance and promote best practice, in 1997 a global group of leading measurement and assessment experts developed the Bellagio Principles. The Bellagio Principles have become a widely quoted reference point for measuring sustainable development, but new developments in policy, science, civil society and technology have made their update necessary.

The Bellagio Sustainability Assessment and Measurement Principles (BellagioSTAMP) have in short been developed through a similar expert group process, using the original Principles as a starting point. Intended to be used as a complete set, the new BellagioSTAMP includes eight principles: (1) Guiding vision; (2) Essential considerations; (3) Adequate scope; (4) Framework and indicators; (5) Transparency; (6) Effective communications; (7) Broad participation and (8) Continuity and capacity. The chapter provides the rationale for the revision of the principles, their detailed description and guidance for their application.

Chapter 3 Contributions to the evolving theory and practice of indicators of sustainability
by Arthur Lyon Dahl

The first UN programme on indicators of sustainable development used a driving-force state-response framework by chapters of Agenda 21. A dialogue among scientists and policymakers produced a more policy-relevant grouping by key issues. The Environmental Vulnerability Index and Environmental Performance Index rated country status and performance against sustainability targets. Recent efforts have added a values or ethical dimension to indicators, and human well-being. The indicators for targets under the Sustainable Development Goals raise new challenges for more integrated indicator design and for the practicality of data collection and implementation. Systems approaches and modelling may generate more dynamic and integrated indicator frameworks to guide the transition towards sustainability.

Chapter 4 Substantiating the rough consensus on the concept of sustainable development as a
point of departure for indicator development by Walter J.V. Vermeulen

In this chapter Vermeulen maintains that, despite the endless condemnations of the vagueness of the concept and definition of sustainable development (SD), in practice we can see a rough consensus on what it includes. Claims about vagueness are the result of the ongoing, open and divergent discourses on what is needed for sustainable development. This divergence has its roots in the shared tendency to disagree within and between academic disciplines, in the political arena and in the competitive framings of the concept in the market arena. However, despite this noisy cacophony, we see, in a few globally oriented communities of practice (of voluntary standards, GRI [Global Reporting Initiative], LCA [Life Cycle Assessment], LCSA [Life Cycle Sustainability Assessment], some of the well-developed sustainable development indicators), a rough consensus on the core elements of the concept of sustainable development, which is also well in line with the UN Sustainable Development Goals (SDGs). Some sub-elements still need some refining, while some other key elements may still be further refined with additional sub-elements, but a core structure exists and is being widely worked with. In this chapter Vermeulen brings together widely shared views in diverse academic and practitioners' communities, which by smart combining can help to create an integrated view. Vermeulen reflects on the commonalities, some persistent confusion and shows routes for further refinement.

Chapter 5 From crises and gurus to science and metrics: Yale's Environmental Performance
Index and the rise of data-driven policymaking by Daniel C. Esty and John W. Emerson

First released as an Environmental Sustainability Index at the World Economic Forum in 2000, the Environmental Performance Index (EPI) emerged from an interdisciplinary team of researchers who believed that a data-driven approach to environmental policymaking would make it easier to spot problems, track trends, benchmark performance, highlight leaders and laggards, spotlight policy successes and failures, and identify best practices. Led by scholars at Yale and Columbia universities, the EPI ranks about 180 countries for which there are sufficient data on a series of performance indicators across a dozen environmental policy categories covering both environmental public health and ecosystem vitality – using a "proximity-to-target" methodology that tracks how close individual countries and the global community are to established environmental policy goals. Released on a biannual basis, the EPI has undergone continuous revision and refinement to reflect new learning and improved data, track trends over time, and provide a regularly updated performance scorecard. The policy impact of the EPI has been far-reaching. Dozens of nations have used the EPI to rethink their approach to policy and scholars across the world use the data in their analyses. More fundamentally, the EPI has helped to spark a trend toward more data-driven and empirical environmental policymaking including the world community's commitment to the 2015 Sustainable Development Goals.

Chapter 6 The limits of sustainability and resilience frameworks: lessons from
agri-food system research by Sarah Rotz and Evan Fraser

This chapter compares and contrasts resilience and sustainability indicators (SIs) and considers how each conceptual tool may build and enhance one another. The first section outlines the origins, utility and constraints for both SIs and resilience concepts. Rotz and Fraser begin by exploring how scholars have defined and applied each concept over time and reflect on the theoretical and methodological critiques of these definitions. They show that both concepts struggle with specific, and at times intractable, issues of comparability, scale and clarity. From here, the authors review scholarly attempts to address these critiques and assess the ways that SIs and resilience can be effectively integrated into contemporary research. They end this section of their chapter by emphasizing that concerns over political subjectivity still loom large for both concepts and thus consider the extent to which systems and programmes that claim to improve sustainability and resilience are actually doing so, and on whose terms this is being done. Key questions include: how do we examine characteristics of resilience or sustainability within systems that are fundamentally unsustainable or non-resilient? Further, is it useful to engage in such measurements when the system itself is dysfunctional? In the next section of their chapter they use a case study from agri-food research to reflect on these questions and explore whether such frameworks are able to measure resilience/sustainability in ways that meaningfully attend to larger social and political-economic issues. Here the authors focus on issues of conceptual framing, definition, appropriation and theoretical utility – as they often remain outside the scope of resilience-sustainability analysis. Specifically, the authors' data show the ways in which these aforementioned issues disincentivize livelihood sustainability and ecological resilience at the farm-scale. A key challenge that this case reveals is how fundamental systemic factors determine and limit the ways in which resilience and sustainability can be defined and legitimized. To close, Rotz and Fraser consider the utility of SIs and resilience for their study and illustrate various conceptual and programmatic tensions, as well as possible ways forward.

Chapter 7 Lessons from the history of GDP in the effort to create better indicators of prosperity, well-being, and happiness: for solutions
by Robert Costanza, Maureen Hart, Ida Kubiszewski, Steve Posner, and John Talberth

GDP was never designed as a measure of national progress, prosperity or well-being, and yet it has become the most widely accepted and influential goal for national economic policy. This chapter explores how this has come to be, why it is well past time for a change and what some of the alternatives to GDP might be. These alternatives focus on measuring sustainable human well-being, rather than marketed economic activity – what GDP measures. Because GDP measures only monetary transactions related to the production of goods and services, it is based on an incomplete picture of the system within which the human economy operates. As a result, GDP not only fails to measure key aspects of quality of life; in many ways, it encourages activities that are counter to long-term community well-being. As ecological, economic and social crises deepen, we desperately need new visions of a sustainable and desirable world and new ways to measure progress that have as broad a consensus and are therefore as influential as GDP has been in the past.

Chapter 8 A systems-theoretical perspective on sustainable development and indicators
by Paul-Marie Boulanger

Chapter 8 adopts a normatively distanced perspective on the issue of sustainability and its indicators. Taking a lead from the German sociologist and systems theorist Niklas Luhmann's writings, Boulanger argues that the disappointment manifested by many scholars and activists concerning the actual use of sustainability indicators in policymaking comes from an underestimation of the complexity of the modern society. The modern society's complexity lies in its (horizontal) differentiation into several autonomous, operationally closed subsystems (law, science, the economy, the mass media, etc.) structured around a binary code (legal/illegal, tradable/non-tradable, new/old). These different subsystems are open and structurally coupled to each other but not to their natural environment. The relation between society and nature is mediated by technology. Social systems observe each other with indicators, which are condensations of expectations with respect to the social environment. They make use of indicators if they change their structures and programmes according to their own observations and they are influenced by indicators if they react to the way they are themselves observed by their environment. The recent burgeoning of sustainability indicators, sustainability impact assessments methods and practices, etc., can be sociologically interpreted as the progressive emergence of a new functional system structured around the sustainable/unsustainable binary code. Whilst being a further diversification of the modern society, such a process would however overcome the current trade-off between complexity and sustainability, responsible for the coming ecological disasters.

Part II: Methods

Chapter 9 World views, interests and indicator choices by Joachim H. Spangenberg

Indicators may be derived from objective data, but the selection of data to be used and the methods to process them into indices are always subjective, based on what the author considers relevant information. This in turn is influenced by the world view he holds; the author here distinguishes archetypical modificationists and transformationists as two opposed camps. Their ontologies, epistemologies, anthropologies and axiologies differ, and so do their indicator choices. This chapter explains these different approaches and how they influence the indicator selection, based on examples from both camps.

Chapter 10 Sustainability indicators and certification schemes for the built environment by Dr Catalina Turcu

This chapter focuses on the role that SIs play in measuring sustainability in the built environment and is structured under three main sections. First, the chapter reflects on whether one can actually measure sustainability and briefly discusses various definitions of sustainability and why it is important to measure sustainability. The second part focuses entirely on sustainability indicators. It looks at their role and characteristics, and pauses on the main methodological models for their development: expert-led (or top-down) and citizen-led (or bottom-up). It also introduces a third and alternative methodological model, the hybrid model. The third section looks at certification schemes for sustainable built environments, such as BREEAM and LEED, which aggregate indicators into indices and are deployed to assess the sustainability performance of buildings and/or built areas. The chapter concludes by discussing some of the problems associated with the use of sustainability indicators and certification schemes in the built environment such as 'one size doesn't fit all', expert-biased processes and unequal consideration of sustainability pillars; but also their merits including raising awareness, dissemination of sustainability knowledge and evidence-based support in the decision-making process.

Chapter 11 Measuring water scarcity and water consumption by Jonathan Chenoweth

Water scarcity stems from the spatial and temporal mismatch between the supply and demand for freshwater. While water may be abundant globally, freshwater of suitable quality is frequently not available locally in the places where there is human demand. A range of indicators has been developed to assess water scarcity and the adequacy of access to water of appropriate quality faced by different human societies. Indicators have also been developed which focus not on the adequacy of water resources but on the measurement of water consumption itself, both direct and indirect consumption, on an individual, national or product basis. Such indicators raise questions about the adequacy of global water resources and whether water resources on a planetary basis are sufficient for all of humanity to achieve a decent quality of life while maintaining the natural environment in an adequate state. Indicators attempting to measure the sustainability of global human water consumption compared to the environment's ability to cope with that consumption have been proposed but require further development if we are to realistically assess how close humanity is to reaching a global water scarcity threshold that limits future growth.

Chapter 12 Participatory approaches for the development and evaluation of sustainability indicators by Simon Bell and Stephen Morse

The idea of employing an element of stakeholder participation in the identification of sustainability indicators (SIs) as well as how they can best be assessed and indeed used is well established and many examples exist in the literature since the 1990s, when the concept of Local Agenda 21 was first proposed at the Rio Earth Summit. The logic is very clear; the inclusion of those who have a 'stake' (interest) in achieving what the SIs are meant to help achieve (i.e.

sustainable development) would greatly enhance the chances of success. However, while the logic is clear, the definition of what is meant by stakeholder has been somewhat fraught. Indeed, the very term 'stakeholder participation' has two contestable elements; just what is a stakeholder and what is participation? In this chapter, adapted from a chapter in *Resilient Participation: Saving the Human Project?* published by Earthscan, London, Simon and Steve try to bring some clarity to the understanding of these two elements.

Chapter 13 Environmental governance indicators and indices in support of policy-making
by Dóra Almássy and László Pintér

The proliferation of environmental sustainability-related policy initiatives over the last decades brought about increasing interest in their functioning as instruments of governance and their role in influencing environmental outcomes. While there is no lack of interest in setting environmental goals, the gap between aspirations and actual results is often increasing. As capacity is an important aspect of the implementation of environment-related policy mechanisms, the assessment of environmental capacities to implement environmental goals can support the understanding of why implementation is lagging behind. One way to provide such assessment is via composite indicators (indices) that can summarize multidimensional problems and evaluations in a simplified manner for policymakers and the general public. Over the last years several indices have been developed that focus on the capacity dimension of environmental governance. Given the proliferation of measurement tools it is important to understand their methodological soundness and applicability. Presenting the state-of-the-art in existing environmental governance indices and their methodological approaches, this chapter provides an overview of some of the most widely known indices. The methodological soundness is presented based on the ten-step OECD EC JRC composite indicator development methodology, leading to some insight related to the applicability of the indices in policymaking.

Chapter 14 Environmentally sustainable national income, an indicator
by Roefie Hueting and Bart de Boer

All economic action is directed to the satisfaction of wants, or in other words: to welfare. Welfare is defined as the satisfaction of wants derived from our dealings with scarce goods. It is a category of personal experience and not measurable in cardinal units. Nevertheless, information can be given with the aid of indicators that are measurable in cardinal units and that are arguably influencing welfare. Economic growth is generally defined as increase of the production as measured in national income (NI or GDP). However, it can mean nothing other than increase in welfare, which is dependent on more factors such as employment, income distribution, labour conditions, leisure time and the scarce possible uses of the non-human-made physical surroundings: the environmental functions. The latter are the most fundamental scarce and consequently economic goods at the disposal of humanity. These fall outside the market and outside the measurement of NI. Environmentally sustainability national income (eSNI) is the production level that does not threaten future generations. The difference with the standard NI indicates the part of the production that is not sustainable. This equals the minimal costs of the measures to arrive at environmental sustainability, calculated with a static general economic equilibrium model, resulting in the level of eSNI.

Chapter 15 Green accounting: balancing environment and economy by Peter Bartelmus

GDP is blamed for distorting the assessment of socio-economic progress. GDP bashing ignores, though, that the national accounts provide the only well-defined objective measures of economic performance, an essential ingredient of national progress. This is not to deny that a number of environmental and social obstacles might lie in the way of progress. The greening of the national accounts, as suggested by the System of Environmental-Economic Accounting, corrects the accounting indicators for hitherto ignored environmental costs. Internalizing these costs into the budgets of households and enterprises and into environmental-economic policies would ground the integration of environmental and economic policies on facts rather than rhetoric.

Chapter 16 Ecological Footprint accounts: principles by Mathis Wackernagel,
Alessandro Galli, Laurel Hanscom, David Lin, Laetitia Mailhes and Tony Drummond

The Ecological Footprint emerged as a response to the challenge of sustainable development, which aims at securing human well-being within planetary constraints. It aims to support needed sustainable development efforts by offering a metric for this challenge's core condition: keeping the human metabolism within the means of what the planet can renew. Therefore, Ecological Footprint accounting seeks to answer one particular question: How much of the biosphere's (or any region's) regenerative capacity does any human activity demand? The condition of keeping humanity's material demands within the amount the planet can renew is a minimum requirement for sustainability. While human demands can exceed what the planet can renew for some time, exceeding it leads inevitably to (unsustainable) depletion of nature's stocks. Such depletion can only be maintained temporarily. In this chapter the authors outline the underlying principles that are the foundation of Ecological Footprint accounting.

Part III: Agency experience

Chapter 17 Governing by numbers: China, Viet Nam, and Malaysia's adaptation of the
Environmental Performance Index by Angel Hsu

The Environmental Performance Index (EPI) is a biennial global ranking of countries' efforts to protect human environmental health and manage natural resources and ecosystems. Since researchers at Yale and Columbia universities created it more than a decade ago, the EPI has inspired several sub-national adaptations of composite environmental indices in Asia. This article examines and compares the sub-national EPIs in China, Malaysia and Viet Nam. Focusing on the motivations, policy rationale and practical challenges involved in each case, Hsu discusses underlying trends and themes that explain why these countries adopted the global EPI framework to measure and track sub-national environmental implementation. These case studies exemplify a growing trend that sees rapidly developing countries that employ top-down environmental policymaking and execution adopting quantitative tools to assess results at the local levels. These countries face common challenges that many other nations would likely encounter when adopting indicators or composite indices for environmental management, including issues of poor data availability and quality, institutional fragmentation and organizational constraints. Describing the pathways each of these Asian countries took to adapt their sub-national EPIs, this chapter distils lessons for other countries that seek to develop indicator systems for environmental management.

Chapter 18 The Human Sustainable Development Index by Giangiacomo Bravo

The Human Sustainable Development Index (HSDI) has been proposed as a way to amend the United Nations' Human Development Index (HDI) by adding an environmental dimension. After a slow start, the use of HSDI has slowly gained traction within and outside the scientific community. This chapter aims to critically review the HSDI, including a complete description of the procedure leading to its calculation and a critical assessment of its relation with some established environmental indicators.

Chapter 19 The Environmental Performance Index: does this reflect reality?
by Elisabeth Conrad and Louis F. Cassar

The 2016 Environmental Performance Index (EPI) ranked the Mediterranean island state of Malta 9th out of 180 countries. This result was met with surprise in at least some quarters because of a common perception that Malta's environmental performance is weak, especially given the country's high population density, placing great pressure on environmental resources. In this chapter, the authors take a closer look at the EPI metric, using the case of Malta to evaluate whether and to what extent it accurately represents the country's environmental performance in different priority areas. Conrad and Cassar also consider how the EPI evaluation compares to public opinion on environmental quality. Results show several mismatches between the EPI ranking and actual performance, with the EPI generally providing a more positive assessment than that suggested by other data. On the basis of this review, the authors conclude that the EPI has a poor ability to serve as a gauge of environmental performance in Malta, with reasons including limitations of the index itself as well as mismatches of scale. However, Conrad and Cassar argue that the EPI's utility could potentially be enhanced via modifications tailoring the index to reflect regional and/or local priorities.

Chapter 20 Sustainability-related indicators developed for governments by L. Reijnders
Indicator sets for sustainability or sustainable development constructed for governments vary very much. Variations are linked to divergent interpretations of sustainability or sustainable development, to the range of objectives to be met and to differences in available data. The sustainability and sustainable development indicator sets surveyed in this chapter often regard a variety of economic, social and environmental aspects. Available objective statistics (e.g. turnout at elections) are often used but subjective data (e.g. trust in institutions) have also been included in such indicator sets. The indicator set proposed in 2016 for the 2030 Sustainable Development Goals is to be based on objective statistics. National implementation of the 2030 Sustainable Development Goals is likely to lead to indicator sets diverging from the latter indicator set. Justice between the generations (operationalized as decision-making as if one does not know to which generation one belongs) and the conservation of natural capital as a prerequisite to sustainable development appear not to be central to the development of the sustainability-related indicator sets constructed for governments surveyed in the chapter. Many sustainability-related indicator sets do not allow for a single or definite answer to the question whether or not there is progress towards sustainability. It would seem that sustainability-related indicator construction for national governments currently mainly aims at monitoring developments in view of what might be considered a more or less responsible good life of the present generation. There is a case for refocusing on intergenerational justice and on the conservation of natural capital as a prerequisite to sustainable development in the construction of indicator sets.

Chapter 21 Sustainable development indicators Finland: going from large descriptive sets
to target-oriented actively used indicators by Ulla Rosenström
The history of efforts to promote utilization of sustainable development indicators (SDIs) is long and the challenges hindering their utilization have remained largely the same: the sets are often too large and vague to give clear policy guidance, while poor data availability and time lags further contribute to weak interest by the intended users. Finland has been among the forerunners in developing SDIs since the late 1990s and has made special efforts to enhance their use. The unique location of the leadership of indicator work, first at the Ministry of the Environment and later at the Prime Minister's Office, has enabled experimentation and innovation, which have increased the use and influence of the indicators.

This article describes the efforts made in improving the indicator sets and enhancing their use. The efforts and outcomes can be divided and presented in four phases, although they may overlap. Phase I (1996–2000): large sets that measured what experts thought relevant for sustainable development. Phase II (2001–2008): tailoring of smaller indicator sets to be used for specific purposes (the leaflets). Phase III (2009–2016): www.findicator.fi online service that included more than just national SDIs. In the Findicator service the indicators were updated automatically and a Google search was optimized, which emphasized timeliness and accessibility. Phase IV (2017–today): the Findicator service needs to be renewed and the national SDIs moved to a new location with stronger emphasis on use.

The agency experience described in this chapter is written from the point of view of a civil servant and is not a scientific analysis of the indicators or their use. Use is largely considered as direct use.

Chapter 22 *The socio-ecological system (SES) approach to sustainable development indicators*
by Gilberto C. Gallopin

An attempt is made to clarify the concepts of sustainable development, sustainability and indicators using a systemic approach. It is argued that such an approach is required to do justice to the different functionally interconnected aspects involved in the quest for sustainable development at the global, national and local levels. The concept of the socio-ecological system (SES) is proposed as a useful neutral and universal systemic framework for identifying and ordering indicators of sustainable development. It is argued that, with very few exceptions, among the indicators generally available at the country level no single indicator can provide information on the dual nature of sustainable development, but a set of carefully selected indicators can, collectively, do the task. An example of application at the national level (Honduras) and the aggregate regional level (Latin America and the Caribbean) is presented. The framework has also been officially employed by Argentina and the Catalonian Region of Spain. The chapter ends with a discussion of the importance of including the critical causal interlinkages among subsystems of the considered SES and its implications for the feasibility of advancing towards the Sustainable Development Goals (SDG) adopted by the United Nations.

Chapter 23 *UNEP and the CSD process for sustainable development indicators*
by Arthur Lyon Dahl

Agenda 21 called for indicators of sustainable development, and UNEP, through the UN System-wide Earthwatch, helped to take this forward. Experts and diplomats met to lay a framework for an indicators process at the Commission on Sustainable Development, producing three sets of indicators and country testing for initial implementation. Two SCOPE projects and a Consultative Group on Sustainable Development Indicators addressed the conceptual development of indicators. After 15 years, 66 countries were using indicators in national environmental reporting. The UN-led process combined research and development sensitive to political context, policymakers convinced of the usefulness of indicators, and capacity building sharing innovative approaches.

Chapter 24 *Prospects for standardising sustainable urban development*
by Simon Joss and Yvonne Rydin

This chapter goes beyond the well-established debate over how urban sustainability indicator sets should be constructed, and what purposes such indicators might serve, to examine what has actually happened as theory has turned into widespread practice. This involves two levels of analysis. First, there is consideration of how impacts on the ground involve negotiation between shifting networks of heterogeneous actors in particular local settings. Specific examples are given of how the outcomes of adopting sustainable indicator sets are indeterminate until these detailed local circumstances are considered. Second, there is a survey of the available urban sustainability frameworks at the global level, emphasizing their sheer variety. Such frameworks are shaped by the proposer's particular agendas and by expectations of their adopter's needs. The field of frameworks is therefore constituted by emergent co-production both at the level of concrete results and of the frameworks themselves. At both levels, real-world innovation is enabled and constrained by divergent systems of motivations; it does not flow in a linear fashion from abstract principles of urban sustainability, however these may be defined. This emphasizes the need for ongoing critical evaluation of the practices surrounding the adoption and mobilization of these frameworks.

Chapter 25 Stakeholder-driven initiatives using sustainability indicators
by Ana Rita Domingues, Rodrigo Lozano and Tomás B. Ramos

Sustainability indicators have been extensively used to measure and communicate the state and progress of sustainability issues by covering robust and meaningful information for a variety of stakeholders. Sustainability indicators allow informal and, many times, sporadic actions of sustainability data collection and evaluation that can be conducted by stakeholders, covering different phases of the sustainability assessments. Stakeholder involvement in sustainability-related initiatives can increase the quality of environmental and sustainability decisions, since the information in these initiatives is then taken into consideration in more comprehensive ways. There have been new approaches to enhance the interaction and empowerment of stakeholders in environmental and sustainability indicator initiatives. Stakeholders can have an active role as part of the team that selects, develops and evaluates sustainability indicators, as well as participating actively in data collection in the monitoring phase. This chapter aims to explore and describe voluntary and collaborative stakeholder initiatives that use sustainability indicators as evaluation and communication tools. The chapter analyzes worldwide initiatives, including technology-based examples. The findings show that in a majority of cases, the examples focus on empowering stakeholders in the selection of sustainability indicators and monitoring data collection of sustainability-related initiatives. These examples appear to have been governmental entities and non-governmental organizations. The integration of stakeholders, as active actors, could: enhance social ties; improve the communication grid, including the vision on what was being implemented; and increase co-responsibility of the shared resources. Stakeholders, thus, can, and should, become part of the environmental and sustainability indicator initiatives, especially when they feel that their opinions are part of decision-making processes that have impacts in their daily lives or are important for their community. An increase of interaction between experts and non-experts of sustainability indicators could enhance transparency of sustainability-related initiatives and help the transition to more sustainable societies.

Chapter 26 How evil is aggregation? lessons from the dashboard of sustainability
by Jochen Jesinghaus

In democratic societies, voters have the right to be informed about the current government's performance in advancing progress. But only a handful of objective figures reach the public, namely GDP growth, unemployment and inflation rates, and stock indices. After decades of watching the news, the brainwashed voter will believe that a good government is one that cares for GDP growth and the Dow Jones. This absurd situation has triggered numerous initiatives to either 'green' GDP, or to replace it with an index composed of the most relevant indicators, e.g. in areas like health, equity, environment, justice, etc. While 20 years ago data availability was the bottleneck, official statistics produce nowadays hundreds of 'key' indicators. Obviously, voters and journalists alike cannot digest huge batteries of indicators with cryptic names, therefore aggregation is a must. The author shows the pitfalls of aggregation but concludes that a transparent methodology based on surveys among experts and voters could provide a convincing alternative index of societal progress. Unfortunately, this would require a commitment from governments, in financial and political terms. Since governments are clearly unwilling to do that, the author suggests that journalists take a clear stance on GDP growth, and in particular denounce its abuse as a misleading labour market predictor.

Chapter 27 Criteria and indicators to audit the performance of complex, multi-functional forest landscapes by Dwi Amalia Sari, Chris Margules, Agni Klintuni Boedhihartono and Jeffrey Sayer

The landscape is a widely preferred scale for initiatives that seek to balance development and conservation. Governments, aid donors, NGOs and the corporate sector are all attempting to reconcile economic development and environmental conservation actions at this scale. New forms of polycentric and multilevel governance are emerging to operate at the landscape scale. By definition these initiatives are seeking to deal with the conflicting goals of diverse stakeholders – they are often a way of addressing wicked problems. Most assessment systems to date have aimed to verify compliance with social and environmental safeguards. However since these integrated approaches now command significant government, corporate and aid agency investments, it will be necessary to go beyond compliance and audit the full range of benefit flows that they generate for society. Landscape approaches are effectively being asked to deliver on the Sustainable Development Goals in a defined area. The authors discuss the challenges of developing performance metrics for these complex and uncertain endeavours. They propose that outcome metrics will differ for all situations and that generalizable indicators will rarely be available. However process indicators will be valuable in confirming best practice and the deployment of appropriate process indicators should ensure that measurable outcome indicators will be identified. Adaptive management will be required. Process indicators will have to be used to inform reflection and learning so that outcome indicators can be continuously updated to deal with changing conditions.

Chapter 28 The devil is in the detail! sustainability assessment of African smallholder farming
by Wytze Marinus, Esther Ronner, Gerrie W. J. van de Ven, Fred Kanampiu,
Samuel Adjei-Nsiah and Ken E. Giller

Indicators for sustainability are a hot and debated topic. Sustainable intensification of agriculture is also widely debated due to the divergent views on the future of agriculture and the wide variety of indicators used. Legumes are seen as a key option for sustainable intensification of smallholder farming systems in sub-Saharan Africa (SSA). The authors developed a framework for assessing the sustainability of contrasting farming systems to illustrate the complex balancing act involved, using a case study of the N2Africa project. N2Africa offers legume options to farmers in SSA (www.N2Africa.org). The authors worked at farm household level and used a hierarchical framework of principles and criteria to select the indicators for sustainability.

One of the main outcomes is a list of questions and hurdles the authors ran into when developing the framework. This can be used by others as guidance both when choosing indicators and to critically evaluate existing sustainability assessments. The authors illustrate that many of the decisions made in developing an indicator framework are subjective and that they include important but easily overlooked details. The chapter concludes that, only by being explicit about the steps taken and the assumptions and decisions made, one can develop a sustainability framework that results in meaningful outcomes.

Part IV: Critique of sustainability indicators and indices

Chapter 29 Sustainable agricultural intensification and measuring the immeasurable:
do we have a choice? by Philip Grabowski, Mark Musumba,
Cheryl Palm and Sieglinde Snapp

Sustainable agricultural intensification (SAI) aims to balance the demand for increased yields with a range of social, economic and environmental goals for agriculture. The authors outline a framework for selecting and assessing indicators across five domains of SAI (productivity, economic, environmental, human condition and social). The authors summarize several important challenges that make it difficult to implement a system of indicators for sustainable agricultural intensification.

The chapter focuses on three main challenges:

- challenges associated with mismatches in spatial and temporal scales of sustainable biogeo-chemical and socio-economic processes
- challenges associated with dealing with indirect links among indicators, complexity and 'disciplinary' biases
- challenges related to the diversity of values and different priorities among agricultural stakeholders.

The authors then highlight how their efforts have met the challenges and what further work is needed. They also provide examples of their initial efforts for implementing a participatory, iterative co-learning approach, and how indicators can help guide the process of developing innovations for SAI.

Chapter 30 Relevance – a neglected feature of sustainability indicators
by Svatava Janoušková, Tomáš Hák and Bedřich Moldan

This chapter critically reviews the state-of-the-art in assessing the quality of sustainability indicators and focuses attention on an important feature – relevance. The indicator quality has several dimensions, including relevance of the content, credibility of the source and process, originality, timeliness, legitimacy, etc. Although mostly well-defined theoretically, the validation criteria are far from being ready to use. Relevance, in particular, is a characteristic employed by all indicator developers and promoters; however, it is often totally unclear what they mean by that term. To make the relevance concept operational and usable for practical purposes, the authors distinguish two types of relevance – thematic relevance and indicator relevance. Since indicators serve a multitude of purposes, the authors categorize relevance first and foremost by the user to which they refer: i.e. from policy, science and public perspectives. Finally, they introduce an "indicator user factsheet" model allowing the indicator user to take advantage of the knowledge on different relevance types when using indicators in decision-making.

Chapter 31 Measurement matters: toward data-driven environmental policy-making
by Daniel C. Esty

Environmental decision-making has long been plagued by uncertainties and incomplete information. Historically, governments, companies, communities and individuals have lacked the data necessary for thoughtful and systematic action to minimize pollution harms and to optimize the use of natural resources. As a result, choices were made on the basis of generalized observations, average exposures and best guesses – or worse yet, rhetoric and emotion. But breakthroughs in information technologies now permit a much more careful, quantitative, granular, empirically grounded and systematic approach to pollution control and natural resource management. This chapter explores why and how better and cheaper data and greater emphasis on statistical analysis promise to strengthen environmental policymaking.

Chapter 32 Meta-evaluation of sustainability indicators: from organizational to national level
by Tomás B. Ramos and Sandra Caeiro

Despite the diversity of methods and tools to evaluate sustainable development at any level from organizational to national level, indicators are one of the approaches most used. However, these tools do not usually include evaluation of the performance measurement instrument itself. The main objective of this chapter is to present a conceptual framework to design and assess the effectiveness of the sustainability indicators themselves. To put the proposed tool into practice, a set of key good-practice factors and meta-performance evaluation indicators is proposed. This framework allows one to evaluate how appropriate a set of sustainability indicators is and allows an evaluation of overall performance of indicator monitoring, assessment, reporting and implementation activities and their results/impacts. Stakeholder involvement is an essential component of the proposed framework, exploring the role that could be played by stakeholders (non-experts and experts) as informal meta-evaluators. The stakeholders' assessment of sustainability indicators can also be used as an indirect way for formal results evaluation, allowing for cross-validation. The proposed framework should be implemented through gradual and prioritized steps to mitigate practical difficulties, due to the complexity of institutional assessment and reporting processes. Successful application cases worldwide demonstrate the usefulness of this approach and how this tool could support continuous improvement in the performance of ongoing sustainability indicator initiatives, allowing greater guidance, objectivity and transparency in sustainability assessment processes.

Chapter 33 Ecological Footprint accounts: criticisms and applications by Mathis Wackernagel, Alessandro Galli, Laurel Hanscom, David Lin, Laetitia Mailhes and Tony Drummond

Ecological Footprint accounting can be applied to any scale, from the planet down to an individual or a product. By mapping the size of an economy's physical metabolism, compared to what nature can renew, it provides an important input for decision-makers concerned with making economic success last. Through the many applications of the tool, the method has also met with criticism. Both the range of applications as well as the raised criticisms are discussed in this chapter.

In conclusion

Chapter 34 What next?

In this final chapter Simon and Steve set out their top takes on the chapter themes and ideas and look to the future. The future is not clear. There have been many missteps with indicators and indices and we now know that there is a future which finds indicators in confusion, which confounds the integrity of factual measurement with Fake News and Un-truth. We tend to a more optimistic scenario, one which sees the opportunity for indicators and indices to act with greater and greater degrees of particularity to specific human issues while retaining the unambiguous capacity to promote important news and messages at a global scale. But at this time (late 2017) the future is far from clear and a new generation of practitioners will need to be active in promoting a positive outcome.

Finally, indicators have a place in history and a coherent but complex set of fundamental theories which support them. Indicators did not merely leap out of cultural history as a tyranny to coerce. They are a part of enlightenment thinking related to concepts of empiricism and democratic civic transparency.

Whoever is careless with the truth in small matters cannot be trusted with important matters.
– Albert Einstein

References

Bell, S. and S. Morse. 1999. *Sustainability Indicators: Measuring the Immeasurable*. London: Earthscan.

Davies, W. 2017. "How Statistics Lost Their Power – and Why We Should Fear What Comes Next". *The Guardian Online*.

Kahneman, D. 2011. *Thinking Fast and Slow*. London: Penguin.

Mance, H. 2016. "Britain Has Had Enough of Experts, Says Gove – Brexit Campaigner Offers to Have Disputed EU Contribution Figure Audited". *Financial Times*.

PART I

Theory and history

2

BELLAGIO STAMP

Principles for sustainability assessment and measurement

László Pintér, Peter Hardi, André Martinuzzi and Jon Hall

Introduction

Changing the way society measures progress represents a key leverage point in tackling the root causes of unsustainable development (Hjorth & Bagheri, 2006; Meadows, 1998). The recognition is not new, but the gap between the mainstream practice of measuring progress and what the public (and, increasingly, policy-makers) believes should be measured has grown.

The severity and interlinkages of the global crises in financial markets, food and climate that broke into the open in 2008 after many years in the making presented societies with unprecedented challenges. The fact that the overall crisis caught major institutions by surprise indicates underlying problems with measurement, assessment and early warning. Societies and major institutions were caught off guard to a significant extent because key indicators they were (and still are) using were blind to problems that turned out to be critically important in triggering the crisis. Managing the complex web of problems now facing corporations, local communities, national economies and multilateral institutions requires much improved planning and accountability tools and practices. We know we must be much better at tracking and assessing financial risk and performance, both at the macro- and microeconomic level. But we also need to develop and mainstream better metrics for tracking poverty, food security, carbon, water availability and a host of other issues that are not well captured by traditional economic accounts (see, e.g., Costanza et al., 2009; Dasgupta, 2010).

Questions have been raised concerning the role of indicators used in setting targets, tracking impacts, evaluating performance and designing policies with real accountability in mind. This has been confirmed recently by the Commission on the Measurement of Economic Performance and Social Progress and iterated in the Istanbul Declaration adopted at the Second Organisation for Economic Co-operation and Development (OECD) World Forum on Statistics, Knowledge and Policy, both representing high-level calls for action (OECD, 2007; Stiglitz, Sen & Fitoussi, 2008). Perhaps most importantly, a link is increasingly being made between the meaning, purpose and measurement of economic growth in a finite world and the primacy of mainstreaming structural changes in macroeconomic policy – policy that includes, as a central element, a redefinition of the goal of development from growth to sustainability.

For at least the three past decades, there has been a recognition that this requires a systematic revision of our monitoring, statistical data collection and reporting system. Hundreds, if not thousands, of initiatives have been started and more are born every day (International Institute for Sustainable Development [IISD], 2009; OECD, 2009a). Many of the initiatives involve science–policy dialogues and engage civil society in a discourse on the key constituents and targets of sustainability, well-being and quality of life and the actions needed to get us closer to these targets.

While this represents an encouraging trend, it also represents considerable challenges. Although on some levels progress has been made, such as the development of satellite accounts or the United Nations' System of Integrated Environmental and Economic Accounts (SEEA), attempts to agree on common indicator sets or indices at levels that would allow them to be mainstreamed into policy-making have had limited success. Various high-level aggregate indices such as the Human Development Index (HDI), the Genuine Progress Index (GPI), the Environmental Performance Index (EPI) and the "Ecological Footprint" that capture some of the dimensions left out of mainstream economic metrics have become better known. Although not as regularly published and certainly not as systematically used, they are increasingly available alongside economic measures. We continue moving toward an indicator zoo, characterized by a multitude of approaches but still limited impact on policy and outcomes that are priorities for sustainable development (Pintér, Hardi & Bartelmus, 2005).

In recognition of the risk and opportunities associated with the growing measurement movement, in 1996 an international group of leading measurement practitioners developed the Bellagio Principles ("the Principles") to provide high-level guidance for measuring and assessing progress toward sustainable development (Hardi & Zdan, 1997; IISD, 1997). They recognized that measurement reform is about more than selecting new indicators and technical revisions to our statistical data collection and reporting mechanisms. The idea behind the Bellagio Principles was that harmonization is not simply a matter of selecting common frameworks and indicators, but of following a common approach of developing and using measurement systems as an integral part of how institutions and society function. The Principles were not expected to lead directly to common indicator sets, but to help guide overall indicator system design and analysis that – over time – will result in better and more accountable convergence.

The original Principles became widely known and referenced by the measurement community. In order to keep them up to date and reflect the current context for measurement, a review and update was organized, following a similar approach used for developing the original Principles. The review meeting, involving internationally recognized measurement practitioners, was held in April 2009 at the Rockefeller Foundation's Bellagio Center in Bellagio, Italy, where the original group had gathered. The meeting was co-organized by the International Institute for Sustainable Development (IISD) and the OECD. The policy context for the meeting was provided by the OECD's Measuring the Progress of Societies initiative, a key global policy coordination forum on the use of measurement in driving strategic policy change compatible with sustainable development (OECD, 2009b).

In preparation for the meeting, a draft discussion paper was prepared to point out changes in context that justify reviewing the Principles and identify some of the key issues with individual Principles that would need to be considered. Building on the discussion paper, the Principles were discussed in plenary and in breakout groups. In order to finalize their text drafting, groups were set up to focus on specific Principles.

Renamed the Sustainability Assessment and Measurement Principles, or STAMP, the Principles are more succinctly phrased and eliminate some of the ambiguities and duplications that were present in the original set. The number of Principles has been reduced from ten to eight. While still aiming for brevity, this paper provides the rationale for the revision of the Principles and additional guidance to aid in their interpretation and use.

Foundations

Problems with the food and energy supply, climate change and turmoil in financial markets that arose in 2008 are some of the symptoms of systemic problems associated, among others, with how we make decisions, what we value and what we measure. Governance for sustainable development requires policy coherence and policy integration (Ruddy & Hilty, 2008). Managing the complex web of problems now facing corporations, local communities, national economies and multilateral institutions requires much improved navigation and accountability tools. There is an emerging need for optimizing the development of policy measures (Dilly & Hüttl, 2009), based on the recognition that we must be much better at tracking and assessing financial risk and performance at the macro- and microeconomic levels. We also need to develop and mainstream much-improved metrics for tracking poverty, carbon Footprint, water availability and a host of other issues that are not well captured by traditional economic accounts.

Sustainable development is an integrative concept. Consequently, any assessment of progress toward sustainability must also be an integrative process with a corresponding framework for decision-making (Ginson, 2006). For 60 years, Gross Domestic Product (GDP) has been the dominant way in which the world has measured and understood progress. This approach has failed to explain several of the factors that impact most on people's lives (European Commission, 2007; European Commission, 2009; Stiglitz, 2009; Thornhill, 2009). Over the last decade, a large amount of work has been carried out to understand and measure what true progress is made in the world. A plethora of approaches available to measure welfare and sustainable development exist, without a consensus on which one is correct (Kulig, Kolfoort & Hoekstra, 2010). Now the development of measurement paradigms focused on the well-being of all citizens is vital to the design of more effective policies with increased accountability (Stiglitz, Sen & Fitoussi, 2008). Initiatives to do just this are being run in many countries, rich and poor, by governments, by civil society, by academics and by the private sector. Some of the most successful have been run in novel partnerships that span the different sectors and that are integrated into decision-making, implementation and management (e.g., *Sierra Business Council*, 2009; *Resort Municipality of Whistler*, 2007).

Conceptual frameworks for new performance measures in a global context, as well as integrative sustainability assessment methods also capable of analyzing the normative, systemic and procedural dimensions of sustainability-focused policy-making, have been developed lately – as shown, for example, in the cases of global and multistakeholder agricultural programmes (Iskandarani & Reifschneider, 2008) and indicator-based sustainability assessments in agriculture (Binder, Feola & Steinberger, 2010).

The attention to the evolution of the economic, social and environmental phenomena, especially their long-term trends, as well as to evidence-based policy-making, has started to affect political decision-making. Evidence-based policy-making represents a contemporary effort to reform or re-structure policy processes in order to prioritize data-based decision-making. At the same time, empirical research suggests that the level of policy analytical capacity available to implement evidence-based policy-making is low in many governments and non-governmental organizations; thus the failure of evidence-based policy-making is highly probable (Howlett, 2009). We may observe more emphasis on efforts aimed at developing a sound evidence base for policies, including long-term impact evaluations of programmes. These evaluations need to be theory-based and use "multi-method" approaches (Sanderson, 2002). While the call for "evidence-based policy" accompanied by "green" policy instruments is strengthening, as is shown in an analysis of the practice in the United Kingdom (Boaz et al., 2008), experience from the European Union and OECD countries shows that decisions that are based on the principles of sustainable development and balance environmental, social and economic targets are scarce and mainly ineffective. According to a recent synthesis paper that brings together literature from the fields of political science, geography, sociology and science and technology studies, many policies directly contradict available "evidences" (Juntti, Russel & Turnpenny, 2009).

Democracy can be seen as an ally of long-term policy design, to the extent that it can generate public legitimacy and accountability, and potentially foster more equitable and just outcomes. Recent debates on how to "manage" policy transitions to sustainability have been curiously silent on governance matters, despite their potential implications for democracy (Hendriks, 2009). Evidence-informed practice and policy at the macro level is capable of dealing also with ethical issues and providing answers to such central questions as how to reflect ethically on problems of scarce resources, social and economic justice, and empowerment of clients (Gambrill, 2008).

From the perspective of measurement, two general aspects of the science agenda that emerged over the last decade and a half need to be highlighted: the emergence of post-normal science and the increasing demand for policy-relevant science. With regard to the first, *post-normal science*, a term coined by Funtowicz and Ravetz (1993), underlines the importance of uncertainty and the need to recognize multiple perspectives in trying to understand the nature of an increasingly complex and interlinked world. This is particularly relevant for areas of research that study the interaction of "linked socioecological" systems, often studied in the context of a place, whether it is a community, a country or a particular ecosystem, or in the context of a particular problem.

Science that is defined more by the nature of the problem rather than by the tools and framework of a particular discipline also has contributed to the emergence of sustainability science (Kates et al., 2001). Essentially a new field of science sitting on the boundary of pure and applied research, it also emphasizes the growing role and responsibility of science in tackling real-world, practical problems that require integrative approaches that connect not only across disciplinary fields, but also in terms of temporal and spatial scales.

The new perspectives offered by new paradigms such as post-normal and sustainability sciences call for adaptive, flexible approaches where both scientific inquiry and subsequent management and policy are designed with flexibility and adaptive capacity in mind. Broad holistic questions posed in policy formation cannot be answered by narrow reductionist questions that are susceptible to scientific method. Approaches to building policy to help establish a framework in applied ecology and environmental management, by which reductionist science can underpin decision-making at the policy level, are already offered in the health services as a model (Pullin, Knight & Watkinson, 2009). Measurement under these conditions plays an increasingly important role, as the need for diagnosing and adapting to constant changes and potential systemic surprises requires regular monitoring of a wide range of parameters, interpretation of trends from multiple possible perspectives, exploration of alternative future trajectories and interlinkages between various science and policy domains (Gunderson & Holling, 2001; Swanson & Bhadwal, 2009).

Another element with a strong connection to policy is related to the development of monitoring and data collection methods and mechanisms. While data quantity and quality continue to be serious problems due partly to the erosion of capacity in public institutions to maintain monitoring systems, in other areas progress is being made. The *Group on Earth Observation* (2009) represents a major international initiative aimed at significantly and systematically improving the availability and quality of geospatial data. The availability of cheaper monitoring tools combined with pervasive wireless technology and growing access to the Internet enables a type of *civic science* where data collected through traditional methods and institutions of science can be organically combined ("mashed up") with both quantitative and qualitative information gathered by citizens for use in public policy and even individual decision-making (Backstrand, 2003).

Over the last ten years, statistical data providers and research centres have heavily invested resources to improve their communication tools, especially the use of the Internet. But new ICT (information and communications technology) tools and the success of the Internet are also profoundly changing the way in which people, especially new generations, look for and find data. For example, according to Internet experts, 95 per cent of those persons using Google do not go beyond the first page of occurrences; the way in which "discovery metadata" are structured is fundamental to their placement in the first page of Google's results, but these metadata have nothing to do with the intrinsic quality of the information provided. Therefore, sources able to structure well their "discovery metadata" can appear higher than those having better quality information but not investing in this kind of metadata. These developments, as well as the use of advanced technologies and of very interesting visualization tools (charts, maps and so on), mean several research centres have been able to produce indicators (including composite indicators) and make them visible and popular.

More recently, the development of Web 2.0 (social networking sites, wikis and so on) has opened new opportunities to producers and users of information. The main difference between the first and the second generation of Internet platforms is that the former are mainly "repositories of information", while the latter are "marketplaces" where people exchange and share information, meet people and discuss ideas, among other things. Of course, reliable statistics cannot be generated using "collective intelligence", but this approach does have a huge impact on the way in which statistics are used and discussed by interested communities. New formats for web-based databases are already proposed to provide required information in accessible form, for example, in current conservation practice (Sutherland et al., 2004).

The planetary challenge of climate change and its consequences offers an excellent example for illustrating why understanding risk and uncertainty is important. It also illustrates the vital importance of a strong monitoring and accounting system, including but not limited to the measurement of carbon, which is a cornerstone of not only macro-level policy mechanisms but also underpins market-based transactions (Jonas et al., 1999).

These developments have strongly influenced business attitudes and practices with regards to sustainable development and, more specifically, to assessment of and reporting on sustainable development performance. In this perspective, we should recognize that the Bellagio Principles have not been applied in the business world to assess the progress of individual companies toward (or away from) sustainability, and, in our opinion, they have had very limited influence on the assessment of the performance of whole business sectors with regard to sustainable development. One of the reasons for this failure is that business entities have a special interpretation of sustainable development or sustainability. In the business context, their primary objective is to focus on the management of issues that are dominated by the market system. Managing non-market issues, such as social and environmental performance, is important only as long as business can demonstrate how voluntary social and environmental management contributes to the competitiveness and economic success of the company. According to the most common business views of sustainable development, it helps achieve a "triple win potential" that is the basis of any kind of sustainability management of profit-oriented organizations in a market system (Schaltegger & Wagner, 2006). It also influences local authorities in their efforts to report on local sustainability issues (McKeand, 2007). There is a potential in the concept of "triple bottom line", or TBL, for capturing a more systematic approach to sustainable development so far as it "demands that a company's responsibility be to stakeholders rather than shareholders" (Wikipedia, 2009a).

The standard business interpretation of sustainable development, helped by the TBL concept, has made the application of a specific reporting framework not only easy but almost inevitable. This framework is the Global Reporting Initiative (GRI, 2006), now in its third iteration. The widespread use of the GRI indicators in business is another major impediment to the application of the Bellagio Principles for business, but it has led to the expansion of sustainability reporting and already thousands of companies (some of the world's largest included) report social and environmental information (The Global Reporters, 2004). Obviously, the GRI has important merits, including the availability of metrics and indicators in traditionally non-business-related issues such as environmental and social performance (Paul, 2008), but offering a menu of loosely linked indicators from which to choose does not reflect the basic values and systemic, let alone holistic, approach to sustainable development.

An integrative assessment and reporting process, including the GRI, needs a reference frame in order to be credible. The assessment process itself needs to comply with accountability standards that are based on an analysis of the content of their underlying norms, the implementation processes they suggest, and their context of application. Models that allow such applications are already being developed; Rasche (2009) discusses see a recent application of such a model to the United Nations Global Compact.

The coordination of different stakeholder interests may lead to a more comprehensive and holistic interpretation of sustainable development, and that interpretation, projected to business entities, may help define a strategy of sustainable development, but in all practical cases, this remains just that: an unused potential.

Since the beginning of the 1990s, the strength of civil society has significantly increased in setting and advancing public policy objectives. This is very clear in the case of articulating and pushing forward a broader measurement agenda. Civil society's interest in measurement cuts across many scales, from local neighbourhoods and communities to larger political jurisdictions and ecosystems, up to the global/international level. Whether measurement is the main focus or part of a broader civil society strategy to raise awareness or strengthen accountability related to public policy issues, civil society has clearly taken a strategic interest in measurement.

The Internet has added greatly to civil society's ability to organize and form the sort of ad hoc coalitions of partners and stakeholders typically necessary to make an indicator system work. Initiatives such as Community Accounts in Canada's East, the GEOCities initiatives in some of the largest metropolises in Latin America and many others are combining grassroots and multistakeholder activism and participation with technological innovation. The trade-off in civil society activism is the proliferation of many different approaches that reflect local concerns, but lack harmonization.

Another characteristic of civil society initiatives – although not only theirs – is the active and increasing interest in networking with others involved in similar work. Some of the networks that sprung up over the last few years, such as the mostly U.S.-based International Sustainability Indicator Network (ISIN, 2009), initially withered but later became successfully reincarnated and also developed an educational form – in the case of ISIN, the Community Indicators Consortium (CIC, 2009). Others, such as the Canadian Sustainability Indicators Network, have grown rapidly and even integrated a wide range of government and business members. A multistakeholder global umbrella network has been formed around the Measuring the Progress of Societies initiative (OECD, 2009a). Beyond the networks, extensive online participatory policy-making foresight exercises are conducted to ensure governments' acknowledgements of the value of collective intelligence from civil society, academic and private-sector participants in participative policy-making (Hilbert, Miles & Othmer, 2009).

These developments represent a great challenge, but also a key opportunity, for developing an effective framework to assess progress toward sustainable development.

Overview of the principles

Principle 1: guiding vision

Assessment of progress toward sustainable development will be guided by the goal of delivering well-being within the capacity of the biosphere to sustain it for future generations. Before one can assess progress, one needs to know what "sustainable development" looks like. Sustainable development is – by definition – about looking to the future. It requires a vision of what "development" means for a society, as well as an understanding of whether that development can be sustained by future generations.

The Stiglitz-Sen-Fitoussi commission note that "at a minimum, in order to measure sustainability, what we need are indicators that inform us about the change in the quantities of the different factors that matter for future well-being" (Stiglitz, Sen & Fitoussi, 2009, p. 11).

And so it follows that one needs first to define what "well-being" is, as well as to understand the factors that matter for it in the future.

Discussions about "well-being" and "development" are essentially political: there is no one way to characterize what well-being means for a society and a variety of approaches have been taken (see, for example, the Canadian Index of Wellbeing, 2009, and the Australian Treasury, n.d.). Discussions about what pattern of activity is, or is not, sustainable are more scientific. Both are necessary to prepare the guiding vision. Citizens may have different views about what "well-being" means, and experts may disagree over whether different development paths are sustainable (Hall, 2005). But first reaching agreement on an overall guiding vision is an important step toward these more detailed conversations: a vision helps us to assess progress by defining, in general terms, the direction for desirable change without making more detailed pronouncements about the progress or sustainability that could be contentious. The vision can also provide a foundation for more detailed alternative scenarios.

The process of developing the vision may be just as – or even more – important than the vision itself. Participation and social engagement during the development of the vision are an important attribute of the process and can better ensure that the final assessment is owned by, and resonates with, the peoples whose progress one seeks to assess (Hall et al., 2005).

Principle 2: essential considerations

Assessment of progress toward sustainable development will consider:

* the underlying social, economic and environmental system as a whole and the interactions among its components, including issues related to governance
* dynamics and interactions between current trends and drivers of change
* risks, uncertainties and activities that can have an impact across boundaries
* implications for decision-making, including trade-offs and synergies.

Achieving sustainable development depends on a myriad of interconnected factors and the entire system needs to be considered holistically. It is simply not enough to try to consider each part in isolation. Many of the most significant problems that jeopardize sustainable development are "wicked": that is, they are problems that are "difficult or impossible to solve because of incomplete, contradictory, and changing requirements that are often difficult to recognize. Moreover, because of complex interdependencies, the effort to solve one aspect of a wicked problem may reveal or create other problems" (Wikipedia, 2009b). Tackling these problems requires understanding and analysis of the dynamics and interactions within the system and of the risks and uncertainties.

Many different approaches have been used to label the component parts of the system, but, however the parts are labelled, it is important to look at a broad range of social, economic and environmental concerns. The OECD recommends considering the following domains: Human Well-being (comprising Individual and Social Well-being, Culture, Economy and Governance) and Ecosystem Condition (OECD, 2009b).

It is also important to understand the links between current trends and drivers of change. This need not attempt to be exact, but it needs to be included;

> [n]o limited set of figures can pretend to forecast the sustainable or unsustainable character of a highly complex system with certainty. The purpose is, rather, to have a set of indicators that give an "alert" to situations that pose a high risk of non-sustainability.
>
> (Stiglitz, Sen & Fitoussi, 2009; p. 269)

Sustainable development is, as we have already noted, about looking to the future. And any forecasts about the future will be plagued by risk and uncertainties. But these need to be recognized and included in an assessment, as do the effects of activities that cross boundaries:

> Sustainability involves the future and its assessment involves many assumptions and normative choices. This is further complicated by the fact that at least some aspects of environmental sustainability (notably climate change) is affected by interactions between the socio-economic and environmental models followed by different countries. The issue is indeed complex, more complex than the already complicated issue of measuring current well-being or performance.
>
> (Stiglitz, Sen & Fitoussi, 2009, pp. 16–17)

Finally, it is important not to lose sight of the purpose of the assessment. It needs to be a useful tool to aid decision-making, either through direct influence on policy-making or through a more diffuse influence on citizens. Assessments of progress toward sustainable development can be helpful in the political economy of reform. By explaining the directions in which a society is heading, and by highlighting the likely impacts of competing decisions elsewhere in the system (for example, by explaining the trade-offs and synergies likely to flow into other areas from a policy decision in one area), an assessment can help societies make tough choices in a more informed way. David Walker, past U.S. Comptroller General, put this well when he said,

> Comprehensive, objective, and reliable information that's readily available to the public can also put pressure on politicians to make difficult but necessary policy choices. With greater public awareness, elected officials are more likely to consider the greater good,

the bigger picture, and the longer term. With greater public awareness, elected officials are less likely to shirk their stewardship responsibilities to future generations.... Indicators can help average individuals better understand complex issues and may encourage greater citizen engagement in the public policy process.

(Walker, 2007, p. 25)

Principle 3: adequate scope

Assessment of progress toward sustainable development will adopt:

- an appropriate time horizon to capture both short- and long-term effects of current policy decisions and human activities
- an appropriate geographical scope.

One of the most significant challenges of any policy framework for sustainable development is the temporal scale, i.e., the unavoidable long-term vision incorporated into the very concept of sustainable development. Sustainability makes sense only over time – which frequently extends over the horizons of policy-makers – and in reference to the future, while it also demands immediate actions. Hence, an appropriate time horizon means that, in the assessment, we need to capture both short- and long-term effects of current policy decisions and human activities, including those on future generations. At the same time, it is important to adopt a time horizon long enough to capture ecosystem time scales that may far transcend the span of a generation's time horizon. A long enough time scale is a precondition to build on historic and current conditions to anticipate future trends and determine where we want to go or where we could go.

Despite the importance of intergenerational equity and thus a long-term perspective for sustainable development policy, most indicator initiatives actually limit their attention to short-term perspectives or do not explicitly specify their time horizons (Kates, Parris & Leiserowitz, 2005). While this may be acceptable in cases when the issue being tracked is stable or in positive territory, the importance of time scale becomes immediately clear once one deals with problems that are close to or beyond critical thresholds, as is the case with regard to a series of global ecological problems (Rockström et al., 2009). Thus what matters, particularly in the case of critical problems, is not just where critical thresholds are and how far we are from breaching them, but also the time it might take before thresholds are crossed, with and without various policy measures (Sicherl, 2002).

A similar problem emerges in the assessment of sustainable development concerning the spatial scale. In an integrative approach, sustainability must extend to the global scale, even if actions are also needed on the local scales. Hence, the appropriate geographical scope of an assessment must range from local to global scales in order to capture the impacts of actions; the space of the assessment must be large enough to include not only local, but long distance, impacts on people.

Principle 4: framework and indicators

Assessment of progress toward sustainable development will be based on:

- a conceptual framework that identifies the domains within which core indicators to assess progress are to be identified
- standardized measurement methods wherever possible, in the interest of comparability
- comparison of indicator values with targets, as possible.

An important starting point of the assessment process is to develop a conceptual framework that defines the issues to be measured, the priorities for the reference community whose actions are to be assessed, and the specific domains that core indicators have to cover.

The assessment is an ongoing process that starts with the measurement of a baseline and includes follow-up measures to determine progress. This is possible only if the measures are comparable and are standardized, which helps comparability. Another desired feature of the assessment is the ability to make projections and models based on the most recent data and infer trends and build scenarios on their basis.

With good indicator systems, policy-makers are not flying blind. They have factual information to guide them to where they can most effectively deploy their efforts. Furthermore, such systems help all those involved in the decision-making to work off the same information base. Moreover, it seems the very process of constructing an indicator set – when it involves a cross-section of society and is developed from the bottom up – can build a shared sense of vision, broker consensus and mobilize communities to action.

The assessment is also a policy tool to indicate progress toward set goals of sustainability; hence the definition of targets corresponding to the goals and a comparison of indicator values with targets and benchmarks (when possible) is desirable.

Principle 5: transparency

Assessment of progress toward sustainable development will:

- ensure the data, indicators and results of the assessment are accessible to the public
- explain the choices, assumptions and uncertainties determining the results of the assessment
- disclose data sources and methods
- disclose all sources of funding and potential conflicts of interest.

The transparency principle addresses two crucial issues:

- the importance of the public understanding of the employed methods, data and assumptions on which the assessment process is built
- public assurance that results of the assessments are reliable and subject to control.

The selected methods can seriously influence the results of the assessments and may limit the range and scope of data collected for an assessment. The methods also may have an impact on the relative weight of certain issues and can attach increased weight to specific data. If these choices are not revealed or are not transparent, the interpretation(s) of the assessment results may be misleading or, in extreme cases, simply false.

Similarly, if the limitations in data selection, the lack of relevant data sources and the use of substitute or proxy data in case of the unavailability of the originally proposed or selected data are not revealed, the uncertainties in the final assessments can be easily overlooked, leading to inadequate or wrong policy decisions.

Both the purpose and the outcome of measurement may be influenced by the clients who order and finance the measurement/assessment activities. If the identity of the funding agents remained hidden, the eventual biases might distort the outcome of the assessment and the professional independence of the evaluators could be questioned. Both cases would lead to public mistrust and a decreased efficiency of the recommended processes.

Principle 6: effective communications

In the interest of effective communication, to attract the broadest possible audience and minimize the risk of misuse, assessment of progress toward sustainable development will:

- use clear and plain language
- present information in a fair and objective way that helps to build trust
- use innovative visual tools and graphics to aid interpretation and tell a story
- make data available in as much detail as is reliable and practicable.

In contrast with common perception, the knowledge utilization literature is quite clear that decision-makers do not necessarily seek out the best information they need to make a decision. In order to increase the probability that information relevant for a particular decision-making context is considered, it would need to be actively brought to the attention of the relevant audiences (Webber, 1991–1992).

The value of proactive communication has been pointed out by many authors with regard to sustainability and the environment, where issues are often characterized not only by high degrees of complexity and uncertainty, but also by relevance for policy and the everyday life of the public (see, e.g., Denisov & Christoffersen, 2001; Denisov et al., 2005; Pintér, 2002). Effective communication requires sophistication, a strategic approach that goes beyond packaging and transmission of information and recognizes the value of dynamic engagement between the producers and consumers in a process of joint information and knowledge construction (Chandler, 1994; Thorngate, 1996). While engagement is covered by Principle 7, Principle 6 addresses the "packaging" and presentation of information.

Considering that the audience for many sustainability issues is broad, presenting indicator analyses and assessment in non-technical language is essential. Although very important, this can be a challenge for those more accustomed to technical and scientific writing, but it is all the more important particularly when the interpretation of the data is subject to debate but has major policy consequences, as in the case of climate change. Although not always feasible, peer review and making use of the expertise of a language editor can help weed out difficult-to-understand language.

In order to make proper use of indicators and their assessments, people need to trust them. There are several factors that contribute to building trust, but one of the most critical is presenting information objectively, without any apparent bias. This can be challenging, because many sustainability issues involve conflict either in the present or between the present and future generations. This may put the analyst working on the boundary of a technical or scientific field and policy in a challenging position, as expectations and perceptions of what is "objective" may vary by the audience. On balance, assessments that recognize and learn to manage multiple audiences and expectations are believed to be perceived as more objective and effective (Cash et al., 2002).

Although people may understand indicator trends by reading analyses, the impact of the information can be greatly increased by presenting data visually and attractively. This is no longer difficult: one of the areas where the last ten years produced significant change is with regard to data visualization. Once good quality, reliable data are available, the number of options for presenting it in a way most relevant for the problem at hand *and* attractively is possible at a reasonable cost.

When presenting indicators, it is increasingly important to think about presenting not only statistical data, but broader contextual information in different formats. This may not only include text, but map-based data or stories in multimedia format accompanying the indicators. Increasingly, tools are being developed that attempt to combine the dynamic presentation of different types of information – quantitative and qualitative – into integrated platforms (e.g., International Institute for Information Design (IIID), 2008; Pintér, 2008).

In order to make data contextually as relevant as possible, often it needs to be presented at different scales. Drilling down from the global level to continental, national, community or neighbourhood is technically feasible and, if allowed by data, presenting aggregates on multiple scales can be helpful. It not only helps reveal more granular detail that may be hidden in higher-level averages, but also engages audiences in a process of inquiry.

Principle 7: broad participation

To strengthen its legitimacy and relevance, assessment of progress toward sustainable development should:

- find appropriate ways to reflect the views of the public, while providing active leadership
- engage early on with users of the assessment so that it best fits their needs.

Measurement and assessment initiatives need strong leadership, coordination and governance mechanisms, balanced with meaningful public involvement. Finding the right balance is a delicate matter and navigating the process requires cultural, social and political sensitivity. No – or only token – participation may simplify the measurement process, but also may result in reduced legitimacy and use of the results. Weak leadership, however, may bog the process down in the multitude of perspectives among stakeholders regarding what needs to be measured, how to agree on priorities and how to move from the general importance of measurement to concrete action.

Active leadership is needed to maintain momentum and direction in a multi-stage process and to ensure continuity over multiple reporting cycles. Leadership is also needed to formally represent the initiative to general society and the media and decision-makers, to organize and manage working groups and to commission background research related to substantive aspects.

Strong leadership must be complemented by broad participation for several reasons. As Stiglitz, Sen and Fitoussi (2008) observed, one of the main concerns with regard to a mainstream measurement system is that the indicators used provide an inadequate representation of the real values and priorities of society. In order to bridge the gap, measurement and assessment systems should reflect not only the best scientific understanding of sustainability, but also key values that are missing from measurement tools such as the GDP (Meadows, 1998). This requires representatives of the public to be involved in the indicator development process.

Public participation is also important for making measurement systems more relevant and increasing the legitimacy of results in the eyes of those involved. Based on the analysis of the effectiveness of global and subglobal assessment processes, legitimacy and relevance have been identified as key factors of effectiveness and influence (Mitchell et al., 2006). Involvement in indicator selection, particularly when the process feeds into decision-making, has been shown to empower communities in cases when conventional development approaches failed (Fraser et al., 2005). There are many options for involving the public through focus groups, Internet fora, interviews and others. Besides choosing the appropriate modality, participation should also be timed to ensure its results can inform the design of the measurement system rather than be considered an opportunity to legitimize decisions already made.

Principle 8: continuity and capacity

Assessment of progress toward sustainable development will require:

- repeated measurement
- responsiveness to change
- investment to develop and maintain adequate capacity
- continuous learning and improvement.

Sustainable development requires an ongoing process of planning, management, evaluation, adaptation and accountability, based on a regular flow of information (Dalal-Clayton & Bass, 2002). One-off or short-term measurements may be useful, but in order to recognize long-term trends, consistent time series data are needed.

Although monitoring, data collection and indicator systems need stability and consistency, they also need periodic review and adjustment to make sure they cover important emerging issues and do not allocate resources to collecting irrelevant data. This is particularly important related to sustainability issues such as climate change, where new science and quickly evolving policy agendas frequently produce new data requirements.

The costs of systematic data collection, monitoring and reporting are often grossly underestimated, and budgets for statistical data collection are easy targets for cost-cutting in times of crisis. This has been well documented for environmental statistics, but even socio-economic data collection capacities in developed countries can be inadequate (Reamer, 2009; United Nations Environment Programme [UNEP], 2004). Repeated measurement requires that organizations in charge of data collection and monitoring have stable mandates, capacity and resources to carry out these activities on an ongoing basis. In reality, capacity and independence are not givens. Agencies responsible for data collection, monitoring and reporting can be subject to budget cuts and political pressures, particularly when the story told by data is politically or economically inconvenient. Recognizing the risks in these, calls have been made to grant statistics agencies autonomy similar to that provided to central banks (Totaro, 2009).

Ultimately, measurement and indicator systems are not only elements of the mechanisms of social organizations, but they need to be subject to continuous review and revision (see, e.g., Déri, Swanson & Bhandari, 2007). This can take the shape of formal reviews by external experts but also involve public participation, where stakeholders are engaged to assess the relevance of the design and elements of measurement and indicator systems.

Options and guidance for the application of the STAMP

Over the last two decades, sustainable development has evolved from a vague vision to an integral aspect of decision-making in the public and private sectors. At the same time, several elements of good governance and evidence-based decision-making – such as long-term objectives, policy coherence, openness and participation, effectiveness and accountability – became more frequently considered. In order to base decisions on reliable information, different types of feedback mechanisms were established, focusing on different elements of the policy or management cycle:[1]

Baseline studies explore states, trends and pressures and are conducted mostly at the initiation stage of the policy or management cycle. They serve to set the agenda and as the starting basis for measuring progress toward sustainable development. Sustainability science is characterized by an interdisciplinary and problem-centred approach, strong links between the production of knowledge and its influence on society, a higher degree of responsibility of researchers (for more than merely scientific outputs) and, as a result, a high level of reflexivity (Nowotny, Scott & Gibbons, 2001). The benefits of promoting and applying the STAMP in this area are numerous:

- The STAMP supports the dissemination of the principles of sustainability science in the broader field of "conventional" research.
- The STAMP offers a normative orientation and encourages researchers to make normative implications explicit.
- The STAMP strengthens interdisciplinary research and multidimensional frameworks, as well as transformation-oriented and systemic knowledge.
- The STAMP highlights the importance of participation of societal and field experts and advocates the consideration of context-factors in the research process.

While the *Quality Criteria of Transdisciplinary Research* guide (Bergmann et al., 2005) focuses on the genuine characteristics of transdisciplinary research (focusing on problems from everyday life, involving actors from civil society, co-production of knowledge), the STAMP distinguishes between researchers and decision-makers.

Impact Assessments or Appraisals (ex ante) serve to assess the effects of decisions in advance and support choice between various options. Typical examples on the E.U. level are the Impact Assessment procedure (European Union, 2002) and the Strategic Environmental Assessment (European Union, 2001), and, on the national level, various forms of Regulatory Impact Assessment, Sustainability Assessment and other types of appraisal and integrated assessments (e.g., in the United Kingdom, Switzerland and forthcoming in Germany). A common characteristic is that these instruments are concerned with decisions with high potential for societal conflict and therefore the assessment serves not only to assess the potential effects of a decision in a scientific and neutral way, but also to support a (more or less democratically legitimized) valuation and decision. The origins of this kind of feedback mechanism lie in the Environmental Impact Assessment (EIA), established in 1969 by the U.S. National Environmental Policy Act (NEPA). Since then, we can observe three tendencies: (1) broadening of the impact area to an integrated assessment of environmental, economic and societal effects; (2) broadening of the object of assessment from projects only to include programmes and policies; and (3) conducting the assessment at an earlier stage of project (policy, programme) preparation to include more fundamental upstream decisions (e.g., in land use planning). Considering these tendencies, as well as the assessment stages identified in the new Impact Assessment Guidelines (European Union, 2009) and the results of an evaluation of the E.U. Impact Assessment System (Watson et al., 2007), the following benefits of promoting and applying the STAMP in this field can be expected:

The STAMP highlights key elements of sustainable development (e.g., holistic approach, geographical scope, dynamics, risks and uncertainties) when applying the principle of "proportionate level of analysis" to determine the likely impacts of a proposed action.

By finding appropriate ways to reflect the views of the public, the STAMP encourages a participative approach going beyond "consultation of interested parties".

The STAMP improves the standardization of Impact Assessments: although the current Impact Assessment System provides great flexibility, it lacks basic uniform standards.

The STAMP could easily be integrated into more specific checklists and guidelines for Impact Assessments and Appraisals. Therefore, it will be necessary to expand the aspects of "trade-offs and synergies" mentioned in Chapter 2 of the STAMP. Especially with respect to Impact Assessments, it is desirable to assess and integrate effects across multiple dimensions, and on this basis to formulate recommendations and make decisions. A wide selection of applicable evaluation methods is available, such as cost-benefit analysis, cost-effectiveness analysis or multi-criteria analysis. Although widespread in practice (see, e.g., www.sustainabilitya-test.net), these are not detailed in the STAMP. The methods of participatory multi-criteria analysis especially possess significant potential; see, for example, Multi-Scale Integrated Assessment (Giampetro, 2004) and Social Multi-Criteria Evaluation (Munda, 2003), which explicitly address the structure of the evaluated problem and focus on whose perspectives are represented and how. In addition, the STAMP could be taken into account when organizing future monitoring and evaluation systems and defining core indicators of key policy objectives, important steps when conducting an Impact Assessment.

Monitoring systems are key components of permanent feedback mechanisms accompanying the whole policy or management cycle. They serve to systematically and periodically collect and analyze data, many of them based on or leading to indicator systems. In order to increase the relevance of monitoring systems for decision-makers, an approach called "from studies to streams of information" is necessary (Rist & Stame, 2005). This is reflected in the STAMP from a number of angles. It emphasizes the importance of regular assessment and the requisite institutional capacity, but it also brings attention to systematic and effective communication that should no longer follow a linear model but instead engage citizens in a process of jointly creating assessment content, in effect practising "citizen science" (Harvey, 2006).

While many of the assessments in this category still produce their flagship main report, they rely on continuously updated databases and indicator systems and a wide range of thematic or subglobal reports that are issued between major reports. One example where several elements of STAMP have particular relevance is the United Nations Environment Programme's (UNEP's) Global Environment Outlook (GEO). GEO is a multi-scale, science-based but policy-oriented assessment that is produced in a global participatory process (UNEP, 2007). The assessment makes use of the most recent monitoring data to provide definitive information on the state and directions of the global environment with subglobal detail, to evaluate the effectiveness and impacts of policies affecting the environment (and, through that, human well-being) and to explore policy options for the future. Based on GEO, UNEP and IISD developed an extensive capacity-building programme targeting subglobal audiences interested in preparing Integrated Environmental Assessments (IEAs). Assessment and reporting systems such as GEO, its subglobal IEAs and the related capacity-building programme represent opportunities for applying the STAMP in a practical context.

Evaluations (ex post) serve to identify, analyze and evaluate short-, medium- and long-term effects triggered by the intervention and are usually employed at the end of a policy or management cycle.[2] In contrast to baseline and monitoring studies, the intervention is placed in the centre of interest in order to fully capture substantial, territorial and temporal dimensions of effects and their causality. Evaluation mirrors the tension between legitimization and learning, with a variety of evaluation approaches and models.[3] Inspired by the U.S. Joint Committee on Standards for Educational Evaluation and on the basis of their Program Evaluation Standards, new Standards for Evaluation have been developed. These serve the purposes of training, orientation and meta-evaluation, but offer no certification of evaluators or evaluation reports. They are intentionally left thematically unspecific and focus not on programme evaluation only, in order to remain applicable for all kinds of evaluations in various policy areas. Combining Evaluation Standards and the STAMP could lead to an integrated guideline for sustainability evaluations:

- *Utility Standards* are intended to ensure that an evaluation will serve the information needs of intended users. The STAMP broadens the U1 standard (stakeholder identification) to a broader kind of participation and adds to the U4 standard (value identification) the normative perspective of sustainable development ("delivering well-being within the capacity of the biosphere").

- *Propriety Standards* are intended to ensure that an evaluation will be conducted legally, ethically and with due regard for the welfare of those involved in the evaluation, as well as those affected by its results. The STAMP would expand the P6 standard ("evaluation findings are made accessible to the persons affected by the evaluation and any others with expressed legal rights to receive the results") to "ensure the date, indicators and results are accessible to the public".
- *Accuracy Standards* are intended to ensure that an evaluation will reveal and convey technically adequate information about the features that determine worth or merit of the evaluand. The STAMP broadens the A2 standard (context analysis) by highlighting the "appropriate time horizon to capture both short- and long-term effects" and an appropriate geographical scope. *(Feasibility Standards are not affected by the STAMP.)*

All of these types of feedback mechanisms are closely related and mutually supportive.[4] Applying the STAMP in all cases highlights a broad variety of questions that should be answered and therefore it has a strong influence on the scope of assessment. At the same time, the STAMP pays attention to the assessment process by applying participatory approaches on the one hand, and by focusing on decision-makers in the public and private sectors on the other.

Conclusions

As the convergence of financial, environmental and food crises of 2008 demonstrated, *Anthropocene* (a term coined by Crutzen and Stoermer [2000], the new planetary phase of development characterized by a distinct human influence on Earth System scale processes) is a phase with potential for increased risk and vulnerability. In order to tackle, and in the long run prevent, such risks, society must develop qualitatively better governance mechanisms across all stages of the policy cycle. Having better measurement approaches, capacity and practices in place is seen as part of this governance challenge, and the STAMP attempts a principled transition from current practices to practices more tailored to the challenges at hand.

Focused on sustainable development, the STAMP builds on a rich and growing science, policy and management tradition that grew after the Brundtland Commission's report in 1987. The need for strengthening the evidence base is a common element of this tradition, but although the recognition of this need is widespread, there is no consensus on how this can be achieved and how different interested actors, both in the public and private sectors, should harmonize their approaches. Although these actors and their interests are diverse, the STAMP tries to go to a level of generality where it is applicable to most.

Perhaps the three distinct audiences that would benefit most include the communities involved in developing alternative metrics systems, the communities focused on integrated assessment and reporting, and those practising project- or policy-focused evaluation. As Part 4 of this paper pointed out, these interests and the communities may overlap, but they also have their specific methods and interests and applicability for the STAMP. The STAMP may provide soft guidance or be more formally adopted or incorporated into formally established codes of conduct, standard or best practice. Whether this is indeed possible at this point is not known and it would be up to the relevant practitioner groups or professional organizations to debate the merits of such a move.

In order to facilitate the use and adoption of the original Bellagio Principles, IISD developed a series of case studies to illustrate how the Principles may work in practice. The case studies demonstrated not only the broad applicability of the Principles to various sectors and stages of the governance cycle, but also their practical use (Hardi & Zdan, 1997). Given the early stage of the sustainability measurement movement, however, the history and selection of such cases was limited and the case studies were selected to fit the Principles retroactively, without actual project application. Building the Principles proactively into actual case studies, along with a richer selection of case studies, may see a similar effort for the STAMP result in practical and more useful guidance.

Returning, in a sense, to its roots, one area where the STAMP may have particular relevance is in the context of the 20th anniversary conference of the first Earth Summit, which took place in 2012.[5] While most attention may be focused on forward-looking issues such as the green economy or global environmental governance, the conference also would be an opportunity for organizations, from the global level to the local level, to carry out an assessment of their successes and failures and reasons over the last 20 years. *How* this can be done will be an important question that may even determine the objectivity and usefulness of the assessments. The Bellagio STAMP may well be an important guide that raises the standard of these assessments to the necessary level.

Notes

1 Until now, no unified terminology or systematization of the various feedback mechanisms has been established. Therefore, in different languages terms such as assessment, appraisal, evaluation and monitoring have slightly different meanings and different levels of differentiation. In international comparison we can see various cultures of evidence-based policy-making and varying foci of discussion in various communities.

2 For the sake of clarity, the authors chose to identify assessment with "ex ante" and evaluation with "ex post" approaches, even though such a differentiation is fuzzy. Formative ex ante evaluations also exist (e.g., in the framework of the E.U. Structural Funds), but due to limited space these have not been addressed in the text.

3 Stufflebeam and Shinkfield (2007) describe 26 different evaluation models.

4 Several additional and relevant areas with developed guidelines for feedback mechanisms have not been addressed in detail in this text (e.g., the Guide to the Evaluation of Socio-Economic Development in E.U. Structural Funds programmes, the United Nations Development Programme's Handbook on Monitoring and Evaluation for Results, the G3 Guidelines of the Global Reporting Initiative, several tools and guidelines for Life Cycle Assessment, and OECD/DAC Evaluation Criteria on evaluating development assistance).

5 For more information, see United Nations (2012) Report of the United Nations Conference on Sustainable Development. Rio de Janeiro, Brazil, 20–22 June 2012. Available at <http://www.un.org/ga/search/view_doc.asp?symbol=A/CONF.216/16&Lang=E>

References

Australian Treasury. (n.d.). Available at <www.treasury.gov.au/documents/876/HTML/docshell.asp?URL=Policy_advice_Treasury_wellbeing_framework.htm>

Backstrand, K. 2003. Civic science for sustainability: Reframing the role of experts, policy-makers and citizens in environmental governance. *Global Environmental Politics*, Vol. 3, Issue 4, pp. 24–41.

Bergmann, M., B. Brohmann, E. Hoffmann, M.C. Loibl, R. Rehaag, E. Schramm and J.-P. Voß. 2005. *Quality criteria of transdisciplinary research – A guide for the formative evaluation of research*. ISOE Studientexte No. 13. Frankfurt am Main: Institute for Socio-Ecological Research (ISOE).

Binder, C.R., G. Feola and J.K. Steinberger. 2010. Considering the normative, systemic and procedural dimensions in indicator-based sustainability assessments in agriculture. *Environmental Impact Assessment Review*, Vol. 30, Issue 2, February, pp. 71–81.

Boaz, A., L. Grayson, R. Levitt and W. Solesbury. 2008. Does evidence-based policy work? Learning from the UK experience. *Evidence and Policy*, Vol. 4, Issue 2, pp. 233–253.

Canadian Index of Wellbeing. 2009. Available at <www.ciw.ca/en/TheCanadianIndexOfWellbeing/DomainsOfWellbeing.aspx>

Cash, D., W.C. Clark, F. Alcock, N. Dickson, N. Eckley and J. Jäger. 2002. *Salience, credibility, legitimacy and boundaries: Linking research, assessment and decision making.* Faculty Research Working Papers Series RWP02–046. Kennedy School of Government. Cambridge, MA: Harvard University. November 2002. Available at <http://papers.ssrn.com/sol3/Delivery.cfm/SSRN_ID372280_code030203530.pdf?abstractid=372280&mirid=2>

Chandler, D. 1994. *The transmission model of communication.* Aberystwyth, UK: University of Wales. February 10, 2001. Available at <www.aber.ac.uk/media/Documents/short/trans.html>

CIC. 2009. *Community indicators consortium.* Available at

Costanza, R., M. Hart, S. Posner and J. Talberth. 2009. *Beyond GDP: The need for new measures of progress.* The Pardee Papers No. 4. The Frederick S. Pardee Center for the Study of the Longer Range Future. Boston, MA: Boston University. January. Available at <http://vip2.uvm.edu/~gundiee/publications/Pardee_Paper_4_Beyond_GDP.pdf>

Crutzen, P.J. and E.F. Stoermer. 2000. *The anthropocene.* IGBP Newsletter 41, August 30. Available at <www.mpch-mainz.mpg.de/~air/anthropocene/>

Dalal-Clayton, B. and S. Bass. 2002. *Sustainable development strategies: A resource book.* London: Earthscan.

Dasgupta, P. 2010. Nature's role in sustaining economic development. *Philosophical Transactions of the Royal Society B – Biological Sciences*, Vol. 365, Issue 1537, January, pp. 5–11. Available at <http://rstb.royalsocietypublishing.org/content/365/1537/5.full.html#ref-list>

Denisov, N. and L. Christoffersen. 2001. *Impact of environmental information on decision-making processes and the environment.* UNEP/GRID-Arendal Occasional Paper 01–2001. Arendal, Norway: UNEP/GRID-Arendal. Available at <www.grida.no/impact/papers/fullimpact.pdf>

Denisov, N., K. Folgen, I. Rucevska and O. Simonett. 2005. *Impact II – Telling good stories: We have the message but how to communicate it using the right messengers.* A collection of practices and lessons. Arendal, Norway: UNEP/GRID-Arendal Occasional Paper 01 2005. Available at <www.grida.no/_res/site/file/publications/impact2-occasional-paper1-2005.pdf>

Déri, A., D. Swanson and P. Bhandari. 2007. "Training module 8: Monitoring, evaluation and learning – for improvement and increased impact of the IEA process". In L. Pintér, D. Swanson and J. Chenje, Eds., *IEA Training Manual.* Nairobi: UNEP. Available at <http://hqweb.unep.org/ieacp/_res/site/File/iea-training-manual/module-8.pdf>

Dilly, O. and R.F. Hüttl. 2009. Top-down and Europe-wide versus bottom-up and intra-regional identification of key issues for sustainability impact assessment. *Environmental Science & Policy*, Vol. 12, Issue 8, pp. 1168–1176.

European Commission. 2007. *Beyond GDP: Measuring progress, true wealth, and the well-being of nations.* Conference Proceedings. Brussels: European Communities. Available at <www.beyond-gdp.eu/news.html>

European Commission. 2009. *GDP and beyond: Measuring progress in a changing world.* Communication from the Commission to the Council and the European Parliament #52009DC0433. Brussels: Commission of the European Community. Available at <www.beyond-gdp.eu>

European Union. 2001. *Directive on Strategic Environmental Assessment, 2001/42/EC.* Directive 2001/42/EC of the European Parliament and of the Council of 27 June 2001 on the assessment of the effects of certain plans and programmes on the environment). Official Journal of the European Communities, July 21. Available at <http://eur-lex.europa.eu>

European Union. 2002. *Directive on impact assessment, COM(2002)276 final (Communication from the Commission on Impact Assessment).* Brussels, June 5. Available at <http://eur-lex.europa.eu>

European Union. 2009. *Impact assessment guidelines, SEC(2009) 92.* January 15. Available at <http://ec.europa.eu/governance/impact/commission_guidelines/commission_guidelines_en.htm>

Fraser, E.D.G., A.J. Dougill, W.E. Mabee, M. Reed and P. MacAlpine. 2005. Bottom up and top down: Analysis of participatory processes for sustainability indicator identification as a pathway to community empowerment and sustainable environmental management. *Journal of Environmental Management*, Vol. 78, Issue 2, pp. 114–127.

Funtowicz, S.O. and J.R. Ravetz. 1993. Science for the post-normal age. *Futures*, Vol. 25, Issue 7, pp. 735–755.

Gambrill, E. 2008. Evidence-based (Informed) macro practice: Process and philosophy. *Journal of Evidence-Based Social Work*, Vol. 5, Issues 3–4, pp. 423–452.

Giampetro, M. 2004. *Multi-scale analysis of agroecosystems.* Boca Raton: CRC Press.

Ginson, R.B. 2006. Beyond the pillars: Sustainability assessment as a framework for effective integration of social, economic and ecological considerations in significant decision-making. *Journal of Environmental Assessment Policy and Management*, Vol. 8, Issue 3, pp. 259–280.

The Global Reporters. 2004. *Risk and opportunity: Best practice in non-financial reporting.* The Global Reporters 2004 survey of corporate sustainability reporting. London: UNEP.

GRI. 2006. *Global reporting initiative: G3 core indicators.* Version 3.0. Available at <www.globalreporting.org/ReportingFramework/G3Online/>

Group on Earth Observation. 2009. Available at

Gunderson, H. and C.S. Holling. 2001. *Panarchy: Understanding transformations in systems of humans and nature.* Washington, DC: Island Press.

Hall, J. 2005. Measuring progress – An Australian travelogue. *Journal of Official Statistics*, Vol. 21, Issue 4, pp. 727–746.

Hall, J., C. Carswell, R. Jones and D. Yencken. 2005. Collaborating with civil society: Reflections from Australia. Canberra: Australian Bureau of Statistics. Available at <http://www.ausstats.abs.gov.au/ausstats/subscriber.nsf/0/171BBD3184985F9ECA25709F00759B87/$File/1351055008_oct%202005.pdf>

Hardi, P. and T. Zdan, Eds. 1997. *Assessing sustainable development: Principles in practice.* Winnipeg: IISD. Available at <www.iisd.org/pdf/bellagio.pdf>

Harvey, K. 2006. Monitoring change: Citizen science and international environmental treaty-making. *Papers on International Environmental Negotiation: Ensuring a Sustainable Future*, Vol. 15, pp. 77–90.

Hendriks, C.M. 2009. Policy design without democracy? Making democratic sense of transition management. *Policy Sciences*, Vol. 42, Issue 4, pp. 341–368.

Hilbert, M., I. Miles and J. Othmer. 2009. Foresight tools for participative policy-making in inter-governmental processes in developing countries: Lessons learned from the eLAC Policy Priorities Delphi. *Technological Forecasting and Social Change*, Vol. 76, Issue 7, pp. 880–896.

Hjorth, P. and A. Bagheri. 2006. Navigating towards sustainable development: A system dynamics approach. *Futures*, Vol. 38, Issue 1, February, pp. 74–92.

Howlett, M. 2009. Policy analytical capacity and evidence-based policy-making: Lessons from Canada. *Canadian Public Administration*, Vol. 52, Issue 2, pp. 153–175.

IIID (International Institute for Information Design). 2008. *Data designed for decisions: Enhancing social, economic and environmental progress.* A joint IIID and OECD Conference, Paris, June 18–20, 2009. Available at <www.dd4d.net>

IISD (International Institute for Sustainable Development). 1997. *Complete Bellagio Principles.* Winnipeg: IISD. Available at <www.iisd.org/measure/principles/progress/bellagio_full.asp>

IISD (International Institute for Sustainable Development). 2009. *Compendium of sustainable development indicator initiatives.* Available at <www.iisd.org/measure/compendium/searchinitiatives.aspx>

ISIN. 2009. *International sustainability indicators network.* Available at

Iskandarani, M. and F.J.B. Reifschneider. 2008. Performance measurement in a global program: Motivation, new concepts and early lessons from a new system. *Science and Public Policy*, Vol. 35, Issue 10, pp. 745–755.

Jonas, M., S. Nilsson, A. Shvidenko, V. Stolbovoi, M. Gluck, M. Obersteiner and A. Öskog. 1999. *Full carbon accounting and the Kyoto Protocol: A systems-analytical view.* Laxenburg, Austria: IIASA.

Juntti, M., D. Russel and J. Turnpenny. 2009. Evidence, politics and power in public policy for the environment. *Environmental Science and Policy*, Vol. 12, pp. 207–215.

Kates, R., W. Clark, R. Corell, J. Hall, C. Jaeger, I. Lowe, . . . H. Mooney. 2001. Sustainability science. *Science*, Vol. 292, Issue 5517, pp. 641–642.

Kates, R., T. Parris and A. Leiserowitz. 2005. What is sustainable development? Goals, indicators, values, and practice. *Environment: Science and Policy for Sustainable Development*, Vol. 47, Issue 3, pp. 8–21.

Kulig, A., H. Kolfoort and R. Hoekstra. 2010. The case for the hybrid capital approach for the measurement of the welfare and sustainability. *Ecological Indicators*, Vol. 10, Issue 2, pp. 118–128.

McKeand, K. 2007. *Embedding sustainability in local government through triple bottom line.* Melbourne: ICLEI-A/NZ Sustainability Services.

Meadows, D.H. 1998. *Indicators and information systems for sustainable development.* A Report to the Balaton Group. Hartland Four Corners, VT: Sustainability Institute.

Mitchell, R.B., C.C. William, W.C. David and M.D. Nancy, Eds. 2006. *Global environmental assessments: Information and influence.* Cambridge: Massachusetts Institute of Technology Press.

Munda, G. 2003. Social multi-criteria evaluation: Methodological foundations and operational consequences. *European Journal of Operational Research*, Vol. 3, Issue 158, pp. 662–677.

Nowotny, H., P. Scott and M. Gibbons. 2001. *Rethinking science: Knowledge and the public in an age of uncertainty.* Cambridge: Polity Press.

OECD. 2007. *The Istanbul declaration*. Paris: OECD. Available at <www.oecd.org/newsroom/38883774.pdf>

OECD. 2009a. *Measuring the progress of societies knowledge base – Inventory of initiatives*. Available at <www.measuringprogress.org/knowledgeBase/>

OECD. 2009b. *A framework to measure the progress of societies*. Available at <www.oecd.org/progress/taxonomy>

Paul, K. 2008. Corporate sustainability, citizenship and social responsibility reporting. *Journal of Corporate Citizenship*, Vol. 32, Winter, pp. 63–78.

Pintér, L. 2002. *Making global integrated environmental assessment and reporting matter*. PhD Thesis. Minneapolis/St. Paul: University of Minnesota. Available at <www.iisd.org/pdf/pinter_thesis.pdf>

Pintér, L. 2008. *Balaton trend: An experiment in building next generation stakeholder information systems for indicator and multimedia commentary visualization*. Presented at the OECD and Statistics Sweden Seminar on turning statistics into knowledge. Stockholm, May 26. Available at <www.oecd.org/dataoecd/47/22/40010783.pdf?contentId=40010787>

Pintér, L., P. Hardi and P. Bartelmus. 2005. *Sustainable development indicators: Proposals for a way forward*. New York, NY: UN Division on Sustainable Development.

Pullin, A.S., T.M. Knight and A.R. Watkinson. 2009. Linking reductionist science and holistic policy using systematic reviews: Unpacking environmental policy questions to construct an evidence-based framework. *Journal of Applied Ecology*, Vol. 46, Issue 5, pp. 970–975.

Rasche, A. 2009. Toward a model to compare and analyze accountability standards – The case of the UN global compact. *Corporate Social Responsibility and Environmental Management*, Vol. 16, Issue 4, pp. 192–205.

Reamer, A. 2009. *In dire straits: The urgent need to improve economic statistics*. Washington, DC: Brookings Institution. Available at <www.brookings.edu/opinions/2009/0304_census_reamer.aspx>

Resort Municipality of Whistler 2020. 2007. Available at <https://www.whistler.ca/sites/default/files/related/2007-06-whistler_2020_plan-second_edition.pdf>

Rist, R. and N. Stame, Eds. 2005. *From studies to streams: Managing evaluative systems*. New Brunswick: Transaction Publisher.

Rockström, J., W. Steffen, K. Noone, Å. Persson, F.S. Chapin, III, E.F. Lambin, . . . J.A. Foley. 2009. A safe operating space for humanity. *Nature*, Vol. 461, 24 September, pp. 472–475. Available at <www.nature.com/nature/journal/v461/n7263/full/461472a.html>

Ruddy, T.F. and M.H. Hilty. 2008. Impact assessment and policy learning in the European Commission. *Environmental Impact Assessment Review*, Vol. 28, Issues 2–3, pp. 90–105.

Sanderson, I. 2002. Evaluation, policy learning and evidence-based policy making. *Public Administration*, Vol. 80, Issue 1, pp. 1–22.

Schaltegger, S. and M. Wagner. 2006. *Managing and measuring the business case for sustainability*. Oxford: Greenleaf Publishing, pp. 2–3.

Sicherl, P. 2002. *Time distance: A missing link in comparative analysis*. Presented at the RC33 Research Committee on Logic and Methodology in Sociology, Session 13, XVth World Congress of Sociology, Brisbane, Australia, July 7–13. Available at <www.sicenter.si/pub/Brisbane14.pdf>

Sierra Business Council. 2009. Available at <www.sbcouncil.org/Home>

Stiglitz, J. 2009. Towards a better measure of well-being. *Financial Times*, September 13.

Stiglitz, J.E., A. Sen and J.-P. Fitoussi. 2008. *Issues paper*. Paris: Commission on the Measurement of Economic Performance and Social Progress. Available at <www.stiglitz-sen-fitoussi.fr/documents/Issues_paper.pdf>

Stiglitz, J.E., A. Sen and J.-P. Fitoussi. 2009. *Report by the commission on the measurement of economic performance and social progress*. Available at <www.stiglitz-sen-fitoussi.fr>

Stufflebeam, D. and A. Shinkfield. 2007. *Evaluation theory, models, and applications*. San Francisco, CA: Jossey-Bass.

Sutherland, W.J., A.S. Pullin, P.M. Dolman and T.M. Knight. 2004. The need for evidence-based conservation. *Trends in Ecology and Evolution*, Vol. 19, Issue 6, pp. 305–308.

Swanson, D. and S. Bhadwal. 2009. *Creating adaptive policies: A guide for policymaking in an uncertain world*. Los Angeles: Sage Publications. Available at <www.iisd.org/publications/pub.aspx?id=1180>

Thorngate, W. 1996. *Measuring the effects of information on development*. Available at <www.idrc.ca/books/focus/783/thorn2.html>

Thornhill, J. 2009. A measure remodeled. *Financial Times*, January 27. Available at <https://www.ft.com/content/638d2ba8-ecab-11dd-a534-0000779fd2ac>

Totaro, L. 2009. Statistics agencies need ECB-like independence, ISTAT head says. *Business Week Internet Edition*, December 31. Available at <www.businessweek.com/news/2009-12-31/statistics-agencies-need-ecb-like-independence-istat-head-says.html>

UNEP (United Nations Environment Programme). 2004. *Strengthening the scientific base of the United Nations Environment Programme: Environmental statistics: Status and challenges: An assessment of joint United Nations Statistics Division/United Nations Environment Programme data collection.* Prepared for the 23rd session of the Governing Council/Global Ministerial Environment Forum Nairobi, February 21–25, 2005. UNEP/GC.23/INF/15. Nairobi: UNEP. Available at <www.unep.org/GC/GC23/documents/GC23-INF15.doc>

UNEP. 2007. *Global Environment Outlook 4.* Nairobi: UNEP. Available at <www.unep.org/geo/geo4/report/GEO-4_Report_Full_en.pdf >

Walker, D. 2007. "Key national indicators can improve policy making and strengthen democracy in statistics, knowledge and policy". In *Measuring and Fostering the Progress of Societies.* Paris: OECD Publishing, pp. 23–26. Available at: <https://www.oecd-ilibrary.org/docserver/9789264043244-en.pdf?expires=1524861283&id=id&accname=guest&checksum=0875549C15AFA6C5DD1EC968492AC238>

Watson, J., J. Wolff, M. Kuehnemund, B. Ward, S. Burke and M. Mitchener. 2007. *Evaluation of the Commission's Impact Assessment System.* The Evaluation Partnership, Contract Number SG-02/2006, April 2007. Available at <http://ec.europa.eu/governance/impact/key_docs/docs/tep_eias_final_report_executive_summary_en.pdf>

Webber, D.J. 1991–1992. The distribution and use of policy knowledge in the policy process. *Knowledge and Policy, the International Journal of Knowledge Transfer and Utilization,* Vol. 4, Issue 4.

Wikipedia. 2009a. Triple bottom line. Available at <http://en.wikipedia.org/wiki/Triple_bottom_line>

Wikipedia. 2009b. *Wicked problems.* Available at <http://en.wikipedia.org/wiki/Wicked_problem>

3

CONTRIBUTIONS TO THE EVOLVING THEORY AND PRACTICE OF INDICATORS OF SUSTAINABILITY

Arthur Lyon Dahl

Introduction

The concept of sustainability has been difficult to define, both in diplomacy and in academia. This is an advantage in diplomacy, as it is always easier to agree on a text when each country can read into it what it wants to. Since sustainability really refers to a dynamic process rather than an end point (Dahl 1996a), the challenge of defining it is understandable. It is much easier to identify what is unsustainable that needs to be reduced or eliminated in order to maintain a sustainable balance over time.

In the absence of a precise definition of "sustainable development", indicators of sustainable development or sustainability have become a primary tool for defining the parameters that need to be included in measuring sustainability. This paper focuses on the United Nations (UN) process, and follows the evolution of the theory and practice of sustainability indicators since Agenda 21, adopted at the Rio Earth Summit in 1992, which called for indicators of sustainable development to support decision-making and "to contribute to a self-regulating sustainability of integrated environment and development systems" (UN 1992, §40.4). It shares some insights into the intellectual history of the concept of indicators of sustainability within the UN framework, and in particular the struggle to address integration. It complements the separate paper in this volume on the events and processes through which this evolution proceeded (Dahl, Chapter 23, this volume).

My own interest in indicators had deep roots, starting with my research on complex biological systems like coral reefs (Dahl 1973), and continuing with indicators to define the conservation importance of islands (Dahl 1986, 1991). After helping to draft Agenda 21 in the UN Conference on Environment and Development (UNCED) secretariat, the United Nations Environment Programme (UNEP) assigned me the challenge to implement its Chapter 40 calling for information for decision-making, and I had to reflect deeply on the meaning of sustainable development (Dahl 1996b). My function was to try to provide some overall strategic vision to the challenge of measuring and guiding the world towards sustainability using indicators.

The starting point

The inclusion of a call for indicators of sustainable development in Chapter 40 of Agenda 21 launched a process within the United Nations system to develop such indicators, but without any clear concept of what was involved. When governments at the early meetings of the Commission on Sustainable Development (CSD) were divided between those that saw the importance of measuring progress and those that expressed the fear that such indicators would be used to determine conditionality in development financing, it seemed important to launch a dialogue between scientists and policymakers about what such indicators might consist of and how they might be used, and within the scientific community about the design and content of such indicators (Bell and Morse, Chapter 12, this volume).

To start the process of implementation, UNEP commissioned an overview of environmental indicators: state of the art and perspectives led by Jan Bakkes of Rijksinstituut voor Volksgezondheid en Milieu (RIVM) (Netherlands) with Cambridge University which suggested a pressure/state/response (PSR) approach to interactions between the socio-economic system, the human population and the environment (UNEP/RIVM 1994).

The World Resources Institute (WRI) organised a Workshop on Environmental Indicators in Washington, DC, in December 1992, bringing together leading researchers from around the world to explore the state of the art in environmental indicators. One of the issues discussed was how to go beyond environmental indicators to indicators of sustainability, but it was felt that an index of sustainable development was not yet practical or advisable. The workshop and subsequent work contributed to a WRI report on environmental indicators (Hammond et al. 1995).

UNEP and the UN Statistical Office (UNSTAT) then convened a Consultative Expert Group Meeting on Environmental and Sustainable Development Indicators in Geneva on 6–8 December 1993. UNEP, UNSTAT and the International Development Research Centre (IDRC) all proposed conceptual models at the meeting. My opening working paper discussed some policy-oriented indices like Net Resource Product, Environmental Capital Index, Global, National and Individual Environmental Impact Indices, Net International Product, Industrial Efficiency Index, Social Equity Index, Intergenerational Equity Index, Human Welfare Index and a Capacity Building Index. It reviewed the challenges of developing policy-relevant indicators of sustainable development, and suggested vector indicators giving both speed and direction of progress towards (or away from) various sustainability targets (Dahl 1993). Peter Bartelmus of UNSTAT presented a draft Framework for Indicators of Sustainable Development (FISD) as a cross-reference between the internationally endorsed Framework for the Development of Environment Statistics (FDES) and the System of Environmental-Economic Accounting (SEEA) which represent the producer side of indicators, and the clusters of Agenda 21 of UNCED which reflected a key international use aspect (Bartelmus 1994).

Over time, a core group of indicator specialists formed a Consultative Group on Sustainable Development Indicators (CGSDI) that contributed creative thinking, participated in multiple processes and helped to maintain continuity and coherence between them. Some of the key members were:

Robert B. Wallace, Chairman of the CGSDI
Albert Adriaanse, a pioneer of environmental indicators and senior adviser at the Dutch Ministry of Environment (in the early years);
Jan Bakkes of RIVM in the Netherlands drawing on an important pool of expertise in his institute;
Peter Bartelmus and Reena Shah, of the UN Statistics Division;
Arthur Dahl, Coordinator of the UN System-wide Earthwatch, UNEP;
Gilberto Gallopin, Stockholm Environment Institute;
Allen Hammond, director of World Resources Institute's Resource and Environmental Information programme;

Peter Hardi, and later László Pintér, of the International Institute for Sustainable Development (IISD);

Jochen Jesinghaus of EUROSTAT and later the EU Joint Research Centre;

Donella Meadows, lead author of the 1972 report to the Club of Rome *The Limits to Growth* and updates, and adjunct professor at Dartmouth College;

Bedřich Moldan, first Minister of Environment in the Czech Republic, a vice president (and later president) of the Commission on Sustainable Development, on the Scientific Committee on Problems of the Environment (SCOPE), and Director of the Environment Center at Charles University in Prague;

John O'Connor, senior advisor at the World Bank;

Ismail Serageldin, World Bank vice president; and

Manuel Winograd, first at Ecological Systems Analysis Group, Bariloche, Argentina, and then at International Center for Tropical Agriculture (CIAT) Colombia.

CSD work programme on indicators

As the UN Division for Sustainable Development (DSD) worked with UN agencies to prepare an indicators programme for the Commission on Sustainable Development (CSD), it adopted a driving-force/state/response (DSR) framework, a modification of the pressure/state/response framework. A matrix of this framework across the chapters of Agenda 21 grouped in economic, social, environmental and institutional categories (often called the "four pillar model"), was used to organise indicators. There was no attempt at integration, simply trying to achieve the best coverage of indicators for issues across the framework. Ultimately a "blue book" of 134 indicators with methodologies was produced for trialling by governments (UN 1996; EUROSTAT 1997). The DSR framework was later expanded into a DPSIR framework, including both drivers and pressures, and adding impacts along with states and responses.

To support the evolution of the indicator programme, DSD organised a series of expert meetings to discuss progress at a technical level and to propose improvements, as well as a programme of country testing in a number of pilot countries (Dahl, Chapter 23, this volume). A number of complementary initiatives concerned approaches to aggregation and linkages, including by the World Resources Institute (WRI)/Wuppertal Institute Total Material Requirements, IISD highly aggregated indices, the World Bank on wealth measures and Genuine Savings, the International Union for Conservation of Nature (IUCN) Barometer of Sustainability, World Health Organization (WHO) aggregated health indicators, and UNSTAT integrated environmental and economic accounting (Bartelmus, Chapter 15, this volume). These still faced challenges of selection, scaling, weighting, aggregation and visualisation (UN 1997). In addition, many research projects on sustainable development indicators were funded by the European Union and other donors.

Drawing on the experience of 22 countries that tried out the DSR indicator framework during the testing phase, the Fifth Expert Group Meeting on Indicators of Sustainable Development, United Nations, New York, 1999, which I chaired in part, proposed the adoption of a theme/sub-theme framework and a smaller set of core indicators as being more relevant to policymakers (UN 1999a). These proposals were then elaborated for the workshop of testing countries in Barbados in December 1999 (UN 1999b). Social themes like equity, health, education, housing, security and population; environmental themes including atmosphere, land, oceans/seas/coasts, freshwater and biodiversity; economic themes for economic structure and consumption and production patterns; and institutional themes of framework and capacity, were broken down into 38 sub-themes, each with one or more indicators, for a total of 58 core indicators to which countries could add those relevant to their specific situation. For institutional indicators, which had been the weakest dimension of the previous list, the Wuppertal Institute introduced a project to develop institutional indicators in the CSD framework. Agenda 21 was analysed regarding its institutional contents focusing on organisations, mechanisms and orientations, leading to suggestions for cardinal performance indicators. A number of existing CSD indicators were shown to be institutionally meaningful although specific for one or two of the sustainability dimensions (UN 1999b).

The second edition of the indicators handbook (UN 2001a) emphasised that "a successful framework should reflect the connections between dimensions, themes and sub-themes" and "the goals of sustainable development to advance social and institutional development, to maintain ecological integrity, and to ensure economic prosperity" (UN 2001a, p. 27). However, in practice, the result was still just a list of individual indicators integrated by the framework, rather than indicators of integration. DSD did explore the issues of linkages and aggregation during this process. It first commissioned an extensive review of existing examples of indicators with linkages and of indices based on aggregation, as well as geographic integration (Guinomet 1999). A commentary on this review noted the importance of distinguishing interlinkages of indicators and indicators of interlinkages (Spangenberg 1999). The latter are more difficult to develop, since they raise issues of dynamic interactions and decoupling. DSD summarised the key issues in a background paper for the Ninth CSD in 2001 (UN 2001b). The basic problem in most cases was the subjectivity of methods of aggregation.

Reena Shah of UNSTAT prepared a review of recent developments and activities (Shah 2004). DSD commissioned a paper on proposals for a way forward (Pintér et al. 2005). It reviewed recent trends in the development and implementation of SD indicators, discussed continuing interest in the development of aggregate indices, and in core sets of "headline indicators", and looked at the emergence of goal-oriented indicators. Another theme was making better use of indicators in performance measurement (Almássy and Pintér, Chapter 13, this volume).

A third edition of the "blue book" was prepared in 2007, including 50 core indicators in a larger set of 96 indicators for sustainable development. It retained a themes and sub-themes approach with slightly modified 14 themes: Poverty, Governance, Health, Education, Demographics; Natural hazards, Atmosphere, Land, Oceans, seas and coasts, Freshwater, Biodiversity, Economic development, Global economic partnership, Consumption and production patterns; without categorisation into the four pillars of sustainable development. It reviewed a variety of indicator frameworks, including: Driving-force state-response frameworks, Issue- or theme-based frameworks, Capital frameworks, Accounting frameworks, Aggregated indicators, and other indicator approaches (UN 2007).

The research dimension

Alongside the intergovernmental process, the Scientific Committee on Problems of the Environment (SCOPE) of the International Council of Scientific Unions (ICSU, now the International Science Council) organised two SCOPE/UNEP projects on indicators of sustainable development (1994–1997) and (2004–2007). These projects brought together leading researchers in the field with those like Peter Bartelmus of the UN Statistical Division and myself for UNEP at the science-policy interface, to collect and assess the state of the art in indicators and stimulate further research. The projects became the research dimension of the CSD programme of work on indicators.

After its first meeting in Ghent between scientists and diplomats to address the political issues, the first SCOPE/UNEP project organised a Scientific Workshop on Indicators of Sustainable Development at the Wuppertal Institute in Germany on 15–17 November 1995 (Billharz and Moldan 1996; Dahl 1995). After an introduction to comprehensive approaches (Dahl 1997), over 50 leading researchers addressed topics such as environmental indicators of materials flows, spatial indicators from Geographic Information Systems (GIS), socio-economic indicators for sustainable development, frameworks and linkages, and the meaning of sustainable development for indicators, and made proposals for coherent indicator development and use. It was clear from the results that much progress had been made since the WRI workshop three years before, with many prominent new approaches. The SCOPE project concluded with the production of a book on *Sustainability Indicators* (Moldan et al. 1997).

When a UN Expert Meeting on Methodologies for Indicators of Sustainable Development was held in February 1996 to finalise the first "blue book", it requested the SCOPE/UNEP project to explore linkages and to develop highly aggregated indicators based on different themes of sustainability.

One of the issues reviewed at the Fourth Expert Group Meeting on Indicators of Sustainable Development in 1997 was approaches to aggregation. It noted that

> Several approaches to aggregation have been developed and are in different stages of application. Some examples include inter alia: (1) The World Bank work on Wealth Measures and Genuine Savings, (2) The IUCN Barometer of Sustainability, (3) UNDP's Human Development Index, (4) UN work on integrated environmental and economic accounting, (5) The joint effort of the Wuppertal Institute and the WRI to develop among many flows an index of total material requirements (TMR). The WRI is also developing a strategic approach that would lead to a limited number of indices in the environmental field, (6) Work by EUROSTAT on pressure indices, (7) Global Environmental Change and Human Security Project (GECHS), and (8) Asian Development Bank's Regional Technical Assistance Project on Environmental Indices.
>
> (UN 1997, §59)

The International Institute for Sustainable Development (IISD) organised "Beyond Delusion: Science and Policy Dialogue on Designing Effective Indicators of Sustainable Development" on 6–9 May 1999 in San Jose, Costa Rica, with 40 participants (www.iisd.ca/crs/scipol/ [accessed 12 December 2016] and summary at IISD 1999). It supported the dashboard approach, and debated the advantages of a single Sustainable Development Index or a set of sub-indices. It agreed on the need to present indicators in clusters and to embed them in decision-making processes. The greatest challenges were:

> the difficulty of grappling with a difficult concept; the use of the same indicators for a variety of levels; the importance of accounting for everyone's interests; the need for indicators that reflect specific contextual situations without losing comparability; the difficulty of determining how much time is left before irreversible damage occurs; the inequality of nations on the global level; the need to convince decision-makers to think long term; the need to ensure indicators make an impact on decisions; and the use of indicators to address changing needs and consumption patterns.
>
> (IISD 1999, p. 5)

The science of indicators advanced so rapidly that SCOPE initiated a second project, the SCOPE/UNEP/IHDP/EEA Assessment of Sustainability Indicators (ASI) project (2003–2007) with the International Human Dimensions of Global Environmental Change Programme (IHDP) and the European Environment Agency (EEA), to make a scientific assessment of progress and to define outstanding challenges, paralleling the preparation by the UN of the third edition of its guidelines and methodologies. The central activity was the ASI Workshop on 10–14 May 2004 in Prague, Czech Republic. Based on over 60 working papers presenting many indicator approaches, and three cross-cutting working groups on meeting conceptual challenges, identifying methodological challenges and ensuring policy relevance, the results were written up in a comprehensive volume *Sustainability Indicators: A Scientific Assessment* with 23 chapters by groups of leading experts (Hak et al. 2007). The introductory chapter provided an overview of the issues still faced, starting with the definition of sustainability itself. It identified the multiple ways in which indicators could be made policy relevant, and the need for many approaches to respond to the diversity of situations around the world, and to meet the needs of different users. It highlighted the need to consider the ethical component of sustainability in designing indicator programmes. It also commented and compared selected indicators, indices and indicator programmes (Moldan and Dahl 2007). The conceptual challenges included going from pillars to linkages to systems; expanding temporal and spacial scales; finding planetary limits; exploring vulnerability, resilience and irreversibility; and adding meaning with reference values, trends and targets. They also concerned issues of process and universality, such as cultural diversity, comparing countries and closing in on equity (Karlsson et al. 2007; Reijnders, Chapter 20, this volume). One important issue flagged in the book is the need for better approaches to the integration of many indicators into more comprehensive assessments of sustainability (Dahl 2007). This issue has emerged again in the design of the UN 2030 Agenda and its Sustainable Development Goals, targets and indicators (UN 2015). The ASI project provided a definitive review of the science of sustainability indicators as the CSD programme of work was coming to completion.

Efforts at integration

While governments refused to consider indicators that might be used for comparisons between countries, the scientific, academic and civil society communities have had no such qualms, leading to efforts to develop composite indices that could combine many indicators into an integrated measure to rank countries and motivate improvements. The review by SCOPE is reasonably comprehensive (Hak et al. 2007, especially Moldan and Dahl 2007). Some of the most popular indices, such as the Ecological Footprint (Wackernagel et al., Chapters 16 and 33, this volume) or the Worldwide Fund for Nature (WWF) Living Planet Index, are designed to be communications tools rather than assessments of sustainability in all its complexity, and are successful in their intended purpose. The examples that follow have been selected to illustrate some of the challenges with composite indices that include many dimensions of sustainability.

Environmental Vulnerability Index (EVI)

The Barbados Conference of Small Island Developing States (1994) called for the development of a vulnerability index or indices for Small Island Developing States (SIDS). The UN followed up by organising an ad hoc expert group on vulnerability indices in New York on 15–16 December 1997. While Lino Briguglio (1995) had pioneered work on the economic vulnerability of islands, I noted at the meeting that little had been done to address the environmental vulnerability of islands apart from the economic impact of natural disasters. The South Pacific Applied Geoscience Commission (SOPAC) in Fiji decided to take up the challenge of developing indicators of environmental vulnerability, and in 1999 invited me to contribute to their conceptualisation. For the first time, each indicator was related to a scientifically designed end point of sustainability or resilience, rather than just relative measures comparing countries, none of which might have been sustainable. The result was a set of 50 indicators for various dimensions of environmental vulnerability particularly relevant to islands but appropriate for all countries. To extend this work to the world level, I co-organised and participated in the SOPAC/ UNEP Global Environmental Vulnerability Indicators Meeting in Geneva in 2001 (Kaly et al. 2001) which made this work available to a wider audience. The resulting Environmental Vulnerability Index (EVI) was launched at the SIDS preparatory session of the UN Commission on Sustainable Development (CSD) in New York in 2004. The work was finalised at an EVI Think Tank II at SOPAC, Suva, Fiji, in 2004 (Alder et al. 2004), and a graphic presentation showing a country profile for environmental vulnerability with the 50 indicators was developed. I was then part of the SOPAC delegation to present the EVI calculated for a hundred countries in a side event at the Mauritius International Meeting on further implementation of the Programme of Action for Small Island Developing States in January 2005. The effectiveness of the EVI was demonstrated when I was given 3 minutes to explain it to the Irish Minister of Development Cooperation, who was to speak for the European Union at the side event, using Ireland's own country profile. He understood immediately, seized its significance and spoke enthusiastically about its importance at the side event. Unfortunately, SOPAC had no mandate to take the work further at the global level, so it has not been updated since 2005.

Environmental Sustainability Index (ESI) and Environmental Performance Index (EPI)

The Environmental Sustainability Index was an academic initiative of the Yale Center for Environmental Law and Policy and the Center for International Earth Science Information Network (CIESIN) at Columbia University, in collaboration with the World Economic Forum (WEF) and the Joint Research Centre of the European Commission. It was produced in a pilot version in 2000 and revised in 2001, 2002 and 2005. The 2002 version, produced for the Global Leaders of Tomorrow Environment Task Force, World Economic Forum Annual Meeting in 2002, aimed to measure overall progress of 142 countries towards environmental sustainability using 20 indicators each combining two to eight variables, for a total of 68 underlying data sets. It tracked relative success in five core components: Environmental Systems, Reducing Stresses, Reducing Human Vulnerability, Social and Institutional Capacity, and Global Stewardship (Esty et al. 2002). As with all such aggregated indicators, it faced challenges of the selection of themes to be measured and the aggregation methodology, in this case equal weighting of the themes with relative rankings from worst to best in the combined index. In the initial versions, there were strong criticisms of the rankings, which seemed to have a bias towards developed countries. I attended a Workshop on the Environmental Sustainability Index at the World Economic Forum in Geneva in 2001, and the World Economic Forum asked me to advise them whether they should continue to collaborate in the ESI. I was then brought in as advisor to the World Economic Forum and Yale University in the redesign of the ESI for 2005 where we made major improvements and also qualified the interpretation of the rankings (Esty et al. 2005). However, the ESI still ranked countries by their performance relative to other countries, so even if everyone was doing badly, some would still rank highly.

At the same time, we developed the concept for a new Environmental Performance Index (EPI) first issued as a pilot in 2006 (Esty et al. 2006) and updated every two years (Esty and Emerson, Chapter 5, this volume). Drawing on the experience with the Environmental Vulnerability Index (EVI), the indicators making up the EPI were all related to scientifically determined targets of sustainable environmental performance, so that a high score would really show that a country was approaching environmental sustainability. The 2016 EPI ranks 180 countries on how well they perform in two broad policy areas: protection of human health from environmental harm, and protection of ecosystems, scoring country performance in nine issue areas comprised of 20 indicators (Hsu et al. 2016). There are still issues of the selection of measures and their weighting. While the comparisons of country performance in a particular year can be very policy relevant, adding or revising a few indicators can produce wide variations in the rankings, as illustrated by the significant shifts between the 2014 and 2016 EPIs, which can raise issues of credibility (Hsu et al. 2014, 2016; Conrad and Cassar, Chapter 19, this volume). One point with respect to these indices that rank countries is that their greatest value is in peer comparisons between countries in similar situations and stages of development, where the indicators can signal best practices.

CGSDI

Another initiative to address the intellectual challenges in measuring sustainability was the creation of the Consultative Group on Sustainable Development Indicators in 1996 as a kind of think tank about the process. We were a small group, initially of eight, supported by the Wallace Global Fund and with a secretariat at IISD, whose mission was to promote cooperation, better coordination and strategising among key individuals and institutions working on developing and using sustainable development indicators. The path we followed suggests some of the continuing conceptual difficulties with integrating sustainability indicators.

Our first focus was on developing highly aggregated measures of sustainable development. We started working on a sustainability index, which proved conceptually too challenging, before shifting the emphasis from one index to a set of highly aggregated indices and exploring an appropriate framework for defining clusters to integrate indicators. We discussed new aggregate indices and ways to normalise indicators to show sustainability levels. We identified a need for welfare-related indicators. Our tasks included defining a set of new indices, finding a powerful index to mobilise decision-makers, finding a methodology to overcome gaps in existing evaluations and making comparisons to desirable or targeted levels (UN 1997).

After its first year of work, the CGSDI suggested that highly aggregated indices could be arranged in nested arrays with ever higher levels of aggregation within internally consistent units: nature/environment in physical units, economy in monetary units, social and institutional dimensions in social science units, and individual welfare in demographic, percent population or per capita units. Each parameter should include state/stock, flow/trend, driving forces and responses, and a direction, target or trajectory towards sustainability. To make this complex framework accessible to decision-makers, we discussed if the four components could be arranged as compass directions, but also could be related along another axis to the ultimate goals of human satisfaction and biosphere sustainability. Simple colour-coded graphic presentations could provide warning signals of unsustainable trends for decision-makers and the public. Models could be developed to show underlying linkages in human and natural systems (summarised in UN 1998, §21–23).

With some further work, a main product of the group shifted to the Dashboard of Sustainability, created by Jochen Jesinghaus to present complex indicator data sets in an easy-to-understand graphic form, while making it possible to burrow down for the details for those who were interested. It could be used for a variety of data sets (Jesinghaus collected over 400), and could allow users to try different weightings of indicators and to see their effect on the final indices. This showed how composite indices are sensitive to underlying assumptions and choices of indicators, and can even produce results that are counter-intuitive depending on how measures are selected and interpreted.

Beyond the tool to make the indicators understandable, much of the CGSDI discussion was about the content, selecting the most appropriate indicators for all the significant dimensions of sustainability, such as whether GDP should be included or replaced by a better indicator, and avoiding hidden underlying assumptions. We also debated whether statistical analyses would add anything. One continuing problem was the adequacy of available data sets to cover all the essential components of sustainability assessment, as well as the bias introduced by data being most available in industrialised countries and emphasising their definition of desirable development.

The CGSDI also faced the challenge of deciding who should be the target audience: policymakers to influence short-term decisions with marginal effects, system planners to demonstrate the need for a fundamental transformation of the system or even the general public. What would be required for a sustainable development index to be quoted in the media and widely used like GDP? How do you go beyond a purely intellectual exercise to make a difference? Despite various attempts, we never really found the answers to these questions.

An ultimate dream of some of us in the CGSDI was to achieve dynamic systems modelling of the whole sustainability challenge, beyond what the World 3 model was able to for the research on *The Limits to Growth* (Meadows et al. 1972, 1992, 2004). By placing all the indicators into a coherent dynamic framework, since they are all interdependent, it should be possible to derive secondary indicators of processes and rates of change, interactions, and positive and negative feedbacks, that would say much more about the sustainability of the whole system.

Exploring new directions

The focus of most indicators of sustainable development has been at the technical level of planetary systems and resources, components of the economic system, and collective social impacts and behaviours. Yet, apart from the institutional aspects, it is individual human beings who decide to be more or less sustainable in their lifestyles, consumption patterns and political choices at least in democratic systems. Even at the highest levels of policy, decisions are usually based on the values and ideological perspectives of political leaders. Education for sustainable development is recognised as an important dimension of any programme for sustainability, but indicators of the impact of such education on individuals are largely lacking, especially with respect to values and behaviour (Dahl 2012b). Exploring the role of values and ethics in achieving sustainability, and developing indicators of the state and trends in values in individuals and populations, and of the impact of efforts in education and public information on these values, would have considerable potential for leveraging change.

With colleagues, I helped to design and lead a research programme in 2008–2011 on values-based education for sustainable development, with a focus on finding indicators of the ethical dimension that could be used to assess the success of educational efforts. With financial support from the European Union Seventh Framework Programme, research teams at the University of Brighton (UK) and Charles University in Prague collaborated with several civil society organisations, including the Earth Charter Initiative, the Alliance of Religions and Conservation, EBBF (Ethical Business Building the Future) and The Peoples' Theatre (Germany) to crystallise their own values and to identify how they were expressed in their own context in ways that could be objectively measured to generate indicators. Pilot projects looked at indigenous school children in Mexico, a university programme in sustainability, a Red Cross project with former child soldiers in Sierra Leone, a cosmetics company in Italy, a youth theatre project in Germany, inner city Moslem women in London, and as a control a financial services company in Luxembourg. The results were launched at an international conference at the University of Brighton in December 2010 (https://iefworld.org/conf14). The resulting indicator methodologies have now been applied to the youth programmes of the International Federation of the Red Cross and Red Crescent Societies, with the Earth Charter Initiative educational programmes and in toolkits for use in secondary education (Dahl et al. 2014a, b, c), among others. Descriptions of various dimensions of the research have been published (Podger et al. 2010; Dahl 2011; Dahl 2013; Burford et al. 2013; Burford et al. 2015; Podger et al. 2015; Ribeiro et al. 2016).

In addition to the research coming directly out of the programme, various dimensions of values in education have been explored with reference to individual motivation (Dahl 2012a, 2012d, 2014a; Howell 2013), individual accountability (Dahl 2015b), sustainable consumption and production (Dahl 2012c), ethics (Dahl 2015a) and higher education (Dahl 2014c), as well as a more general framework for values-based indicators (Dahl 2013) and a recent update (Dahl 2016a).

A related approach concerns indicators of happiness and well-being, which could be seen as an outcome of greater sustainability. The concept was pioneered by the Government of Bhutan, which has developed and refined its Gross National Happiness index as a more culturally appropriate replacement for GDP including a values dimension (Ura et al. 2012). The concept has gradually been taken up by other countries and was presented by Bhutan at the United Nations in 2012, inspiring among other things the *World Happiness Report* (Helliwell et al. 2012, 2013, 2016; Sachs et al. 2016). In one of the papers in the 2013 report, co-author Jeffrey Sachs particularly highlights the happiness that comes from leading a virtuous life (Sachs 2013). This has led to a proposal for a whole set of indicators for individual well-being to support the transition to sustainability (Dahl 2014b).

There is another significance to this new research into the ethical or values dimension of sustainability. Effective large-scale social transformation depends on social cohesion, and failures in social cohesion can lead to chaos (Turchin 2010) which will regress rather than advance sustainability. A recent analysis by Peter Turchin of the factors that enabled more complex and large-scale levels of social organisation and civilisation to emerge suggests that an ethical transformation mediated by religion tipped the balance towards altruism and enabled multi-cultural and multi-ethnic societies to flourish over large areas (Turchin 2016). The transition to sustainability requires a strongly altruistic focus on the protection of the environment and the well-being of future generations. All of the efforts to put in place the technical requirements for sustainable development will fail if the political, social and economic actors all give priority to their selfish personal, national or corporate interests. Developing indicators of the ethical content or orientation of the different social actors will be an important guide to the success or failure of programmes for sustainability.

The UN 2030 Agenda

The latest framework for indicators of sustainability is the United Nations 2030 Agenda and its 17 Sustainable Development Goals (SDGs), with 169 targets and over 240 indicators (UN 2015; IAEG-SDGs 2016). Space does not permit more than a short mention of the new challenges and opportunities in the development of the SDG indicators.

While the early discussion of sustainable development indicators recognised the need for indicators of planetary sustainability with reference to global resources and life-support systems, it was only when researchers began to identify and quantify planetary boundaries (Rockström et al. 2009; Wijkman and Rockström 2012; Steffen et al. 2015) that such indicators became possible. The 2030 Agenda responds to this recognition that we are at or beyond sustainable planetary limits and must make a fundamental and rapid transition to sustainability. The SDGs are the first updated and globally accepted definition of the content and meaning of sustainable development since Agenda 21. The targets are global, and need to be translated into corresponding efforts at the national level, much as the CSD indicators were developed two decades ago.

There was already a wide debate as the SDG indicators were being developed. The Inter-Agency and Expert Group on Sustainable Development Goal indicators, advising the UN Statistical Commission, revised and updated its proposals several times before agreeing on a first workable set of indicators (IAEG-SDGs 2016). Meanwhile, the Sustainable Development Solutions Network (SDSN), taking a more scientific perspective as opposed to that of the statisticians, made its own series of proposals for indicators for each of the SDG targets (SDSN 2015). A critique by the International Council for Science (ICSU) and the International Social Science Council (ISSC) raised questions about the drafting of the targets that often made it difficult to measure and assess progress properly (ICSU and ISSC 2015). Groups of researchers are also contributing to the debate (Pintér et al. 2015, Sachs et al. 2016), and this will certainly continue as the indicators are developed and refined between now and 2030.

To illustrate the complexity of the challenge, my comparison of the indicators proposed for SDG 14 on oceans, between those proposed by the Statistical Commission, those of the SDSN from a science perspective, and those of the Global Oceans Commission as seen from the Law of the Sea perspective, showed little overlap between the different sets of indicators (Dahl 2015c). Another study has compared the UN approach and a values-based approach for one educational target (4.7) to show that there are important gaps in the traditional approach and to demonstrate the complementarity of values-based locally relevant indicators, requiring a conceptual shift from education for transmission to education for transformation (Burford et al. 2016).

While the 2030 Agenda and its SDGs are explicitly an integrated whole, there is still much to be done to make that integration a practical reality, a challenge that has been with indicators programmes since the beginning. Some targets would seem to be conflicting, if not incompatible, such as those for continuing economic growth and environmental protection. The SDGs themselves call for new indicators, for example alternative indicators to GDP for the economy. One integrated approach is material flow analysis, and the International Resource Panel has recently prepared a first global data set of material flow indicators (UNEP 2016). The International Council for Science has launched a project to explore SDG integration in more detail (Nilsson et al. 2016a, Nilsson et al. 2016b; ICSU 2017).

While the 2030 Agenda is supposed to be an agenda of, by and for the people, it has inevitably been largely a top-down UN process, even with widespread stakeholder participation. The SDGs are global goals, and it is governments that are expected to develop national implementation and to report on progress. Yet governments by themselves cannot achieve sustainability without the cooperation of business, civil society and the public in general. There is thus enormous scope for other actors to take on the SDGs as their own and to work for their implementation, producing their own indicators of progress. It is even possible to explore the implementation of the SDGs as communities and individuals (IEF 2016) and to create SDGs that individuals can take on as their own goals (Dahl 2016b). This would obviously lead to indicators for individual behaviour and achievement.

The SDGs provide a new mapping of the key characteristics of a sustainable world system with a detail never achieved before. Perhaps it will now be possible to place all the indicators into an integrated systems framework (Capra and Luisi 2014), and to determine its emergent properties with a new set of indicators of integration, finally realising our dream in the CGSDI 20 years ago.

References

Alder, Jackie, Arthur Dahl, Ursula Kaly, Jonathan Mitchell, Ned Norton, Craig Pratt, and Michael Witter. 2004. *Report on the Environmental Vulnerability Index (EVI) Think Tank II.* Suva, Fiji, 4–6 October 2004. SOPAC Preliminary Report 149; Technical Report 377. South Pacific Applied Geoscience Commission, Suva, Fiji, October 2004. Available online: www.vulnerabilityindex.net/wp-content/uploads/2015/05/EVI%20Think%20Tank%20II%20FINAL.pdf

Bartelmus, Peter. 1994. *Towards a Framework for Indicators of Sustainable Development.* Department for Economic and Social Information and Policy Analysis, Working Paper Series No. 7. New York: United Nations.

Billharz, Suzanne and Bedřich Moldan. (Eds.). 1996. *Scientific Workshop on Indicators of Sustainable Development,* Wuppertal, Germany, 15–17 November 1995. Report. Scientific Committee on Problems of the Environment (SCOPE). Prague: Charles University Environmental Center.

Briguglio, Lino. 1995. Small Island Developing States and Their Economic Vulnerabilities. *World Development* 23(9): 1615–1632.

Burford, Gemma, Elona Hoover, Arthur L. Dahl, and Marie K. Harder. 2015. "Making the Invisible Visible: Designing Values-Based Indicators and Tools for Identifying and Closing 'Value-Action Gaps'", pp. 113–133. In Victoria W. Thoresen, Robert J. Didham, Jorgen Klein, and Declan Doyle (eds.), *Responsible Living: Concepts, Education and Future Perspectives.* Heidelberg and Switzerland: Springer. doi:10.1007/978-3-319-15305-6_9

Burford, Gemma, Elona Hoover, Ismael Velasco, Svatava Janoušková, Alicia Jimenez, Georgia Piggot, Dimity Podger, and Marie K. Harder. 2013. Bringing the "Missing Pillar" into Sustainable Development Goals: Towards Intersubjective Values-Based Indicators. *Sustainability* 5: 3035–3059. doi:10.3390/su5073035 www.mdpi.com/2071-1050/5/7/3035

Burford, Gemma, Peter Tamás, and Marie K. Harder. 2016. Can We Improve Indicator Design for Complex Sustainable Development Goals? A Comparison of a Values-Based and Conventional Approach. *Sustainability* 8: 861. doi:10.3390/su8090861

Capra, Fritjof and Pier Luigi Luisi. 2014. *The Systems View of Life: A Unifying Vision.* Cambridge: Cambridge University Press.

Dahl, Arthur Lyon. 1973. Surface Area in Ecological Analysis: Quantification of Benthic Coral Reef Algae. *Marine Biology* 23: 239–249.

Dahl, Arthur Lyon. 1986. *Review of the Protected Areas System in Oceania* (including Oceania island list). Gland and Cambridge: International Union for Conservation of Nature and Natural Resources. 73 + 239 p.

Dahl, Arthur Lyon. 1991. *IUCN/UNEP Island Directory.* UNEP Regional Seas Directories and Bibliographies, No. 35. Nairobi: United Nations Environment Programme. 573 p. Available online: http://islands.unep.ch/isldir.htm and http://yabaha.net/dahl/isldb/isldir.htm

Dahl, Arthur Lyon. 1993. *Environmental and Sustainable Development Indicators: Some Points for Discussion.* Paper presented at UNEP/UNSTAT Consultative Expert Group Meeting on Environmental and Sustainable Development Indicators, Geneva, 6–8 December 1993. Available online: http://yabaha.net/dahl/papers/1993g/Dahl1993g.html

Dahl, Arthur Lyon. 1995. *Towards Indicators of Sustainability.* Paper presented at the SCOPE Scientific Workshop on Indicators of Sustainable Development, Wuppertal, 15–17 November 1995. Available online: www.un.org/earthwatch/about/docs/inddahl.htm

Dahl, Arthur Lyon. 1996a. Measuring the Unmeasurable. *Our Planet* 8(1): 29–33.

Dahl, Arthur Lyon. 1996b. *The Eco Principle: Ecology and Economics in Symbiosis.* London: Zed Books Ltd, and Oxford: George Ronald.

Dahl, Arthur Lyon. 1997. "The Big Picture: Comprehensive Approaches – Introduction", Chapter 2, pp. 69–83. In Bedřich Moldan, Suzanne Billharz, and Robyn Matravers (eds.), *Sustainability Indicators: A Report on the Project on Indicators of Sustainable Development.* Scientific Committee on Problems of the Environment, SCOPE 58. Chichester: John Wiley and Sons.

Dahl, Arthur Lyon. 2007. "Integrated Assessment and Indicators", Chapter 10, pp. 163–176. In Tomas Hak, Bedřich Moldan, and Arthur Lyon Dahl (eds.), *Sustainability Indicators: A Scientific Assessment, SCOPE Vol. 67.* Washington, DC: Island Press.

Dahl, Arthur Lyon. 2011. *Values-based Indicators for Responsible Living.* Paper presented at the PERL International Conference, Istanbul, Turkey, 14–15 March 2011. Available online: https://iefworld.org/ddahl11b

Dahl, Arthur Lyon. 2012a. *Ethical Sustainability Footprint for Individual Motivation.* Presented at Planet Under Pressure 2012 Conference, London, United Kingdom, 26–29 March 2012. Available online: https://iefworld.org/ddahl12d

Dahl, Arthur Lyon. 2012b. Achievements and Gaps in Indicators for Sustainability. *Ecological Indicators* 17: 14–19. June 2012. Available online: http://dx.doi.org/10.1016/j.ecolind.2011.04.032

Dahl, Arthur Lyon. 2012c. *Values Education for Sustainable Consumption and Production: From Knowledge to Action.* Paper presented at the Global Research Forum on Sustainable Consumption and Production, Rio de Janeiro, Brazil, 13–15 June 2012. Available online: https://iefworld.org/ddahl12i

Dahl, Arthur Lyon. 2012d. *Changing Mentalities and Motivations: Values for the Sustainability Transition.* Paper presented at the 16th IEF Conference event at the Peoples' Summit, Rio de Janeiro, Brazil, 21 June 2012. Available online: https://iefworld.org/ddahl12j

Dahl, Arthur Lyon. 2013. "A Multi-Level Framework and Values-Based Indicators to Enable Responsible Living", pp. 63–77. In Ulf Schrader, Vera Fricke, Declan Doyle, and Victoria W. Thoresen (eds.), *Enabling Responsible Living.* Berlin and Heidelberg: Springer Verlag. doi:10.1007/978-3-642-22048-7_6 and available online: www.springer.com/environment/sustainable+development/book/978-3-642-22047-0

Dahl, Arthur Lyon. 2014a. *The Ethics of Hope: Values as Positive Drivers for a Sustainable Future.* Presented at the Global Research Forum on Sustainable Production and Consumption, Fudan University, Shanghai, China, 8–11 June 2014. Available online: https://iefworld.org/ddahl14b

Dahl, Arthur Lyon. 2014b. "Putting the Individual at the Centre of Development: Indicators of Well-being for a New Social Contract", Chapter 8, pp. 83–103. In François Mancebo and Ignacy Sachs (eds.), *Transitions to Sustainability.* Dordrecht: Springer. doi:10.1007/978-94-017-9532-6_8 and available online: http://yabaha.net/dahl/papers/2014i_chpt8.pdf and https://iefworld.org/ddahl13a

Dahl, Arthur Lyon. 2014c. "Sustainability and Values Assessment in Higher Education", Chapter 9, pp. 185–195. In Zinaida Fadeeva, Laima Galkute, Clemens Mader, and Geoff Scott (eds.), *Sustainable Development and Quality Assurance in Higher Education: Transformation of Learning and Society.* Houndsmill, UK: Palgrave Macmillan. doi:10.1057/9781137459145. Available online: http://yabaha.net/dahl/papers/2014j.pdf

Dahl, Arthur Lyon. 2015a. "Ethics in Sustainability Education", pp. 27–40. In Victoria W. Thoresen, Robert J. Didham, Jorgen Klein, and Declan Doyle (eds.), *Responsible Living: Concepts, Education and Future Perspectives.* Heidelberg and Switzerland: Springer. doi:10.1007/978-3-319-15305-6_3

Dahl, Arthur Lyon. 2015b. *Personal and Professional Accountability: An Ethical Challenge.* Presented in the IEF side event on "Principles of Accountability for Climate Change Agreements" at the UN Climate Change Conference (COP21), Paris, France, 10 December 2015. Available online: https://iefworld.org/ddahl15h

Dahl, Arthur Lyon. 2015c. *Resource Efficiency Improvements and Marine Resources Management in the Sustainable Development Goals (SDGs).* Paper presented at the International Resource Panel Scoping Workshop on Marine Resources, UNEP, Paris, 14–15 April 2015. Available online: http://yabaha.net/dahl/papers/2015i.html

Dahl, Arthur Lyon. 2016a. *Values-based Education for Environment and Sustainable Development.* Based on a paper prepared for the United Nations Environment Programme, January 2016. Available online: https://iefworld.org/ddahl16a

Dahl, Arthur Lyon. 2016b. *Looking at the Sustainable Development Goals from the Bottom Up.* Paper presented at the International Environment Forum 20th International Conference, Nur University, Santa Cruz de la Sierra, Bolivia, 7 October 2016. Available online: https://iefworld.org/ddahl16j

Dahl, Arthur Lyon, Marie K. Harder, Marilyn Mehlmann, Kirsi Niinimaki, Victoria Thoresen, Onno Vinkhuyzen, Dana Vokounova, Gemma Burford, and Ismael Velasco. 2014a. *Measuring What Matters: Values-Based Indicators.* A Methods Sourcebook. PERL Values-Based Learning Toolkit 1. Partnership for Education and Research about Responsible Living (PERL). Available online: https://iefworld.org/fl/PERL_toolkit1.pdf

Dahl, Arthur Lyon, Marie K. Harder, Marilyn Mehlmann, Kirsi Niinimaki, Victoria Thoresen, Onno Vinkhuyzen, Dana Vokounova, Gemma Burford, and Ismael Velasco. 2014b. *Discovering What Matters: A Journey of Thinking and Feeling.* Activities Developed with Students, for Students. PERL Values-Based Learning Toolkit 2. Partnership for Education and Research about Responsible Living (PERL). Available online: https://iefworld.org/fl/PERL_toolkit2.pdf

Dahl, Arthur Lyon, Marie K. Harder, Marilyn Mehlmann, Kirsi Niinimaki, Victoria Thoresen, Onno Vinkhuyzen, Dana Vokounova, Gemma Burford, and Ismael Velasco. 2014c. *Growing a Shared Vision:*

A Toolkit for Schools. Activities for Organisational and Staff Development. PERL Values-Based Learning Toolkit 3. Partnership for Education and Research about Responsible Living (PERL). Available online: https://iefworld.org/fl/PERL_toolkit3.pdf

Esty, Daniel C., Marc Levy, Ilmi M.E. Granoff, Kim Samuel-Johnson, Manny Amadi, Francisco Gutierrez-Campos, John Manzoni, Alicia Barcena Ibara, Guy Hands, Liavan Mallin, Ugar Bayar, Molly Harriss-Olson, Jonathan Mills, Matthew Cadbury, George M. Kailis, Rodrigo Navarro Banzer, Carlos E. Cisneros, Shiv Vikram Khemka, Patrick Odier, Craig A. Cohon, Loren Legarda, Paul L. Saffo, Colin Coleman, Maria Leichner, Simon Tay, Christopher B. Leptos, Thomas Ganswindt, Philippa Malmgren, Kiyomi Tsujimoto, Barbara Ruth, Marguerite Camera, Bob Chen, Kobi Ako Abayomi, Maarten Tromp, Alex de Sherbinin, Francesca Pozzi, and Antoinette Wannebo. 2002. *2002 Environmental Sustainability Index.* An Initiative of the Global Leaders of Tomorrow Environment Task Force, World Economic Forum, Annual Meeting 2002, in collaboration with the Yale Center for Environmental Law and Policy, Yale University, and the Center for International Earth Science Information Network (CIESIN), Columbia University. Available online: http://archive.epi.yale.edu/files/2002_esi_report.pdf

Esty, Daniel C., Marc Levy, Tanja Srebotnjak, and Alexander de Sherbinin. 2005. *2005 Environmental Sustainability Index: Benchmarking National Environmental Stewardship.* New Haven: Yale Center for Environmental Law & Policy. Available online: http://archive.epi.yale.edu/files/2005_esi_report.pdf

Esty, Daniel C., Marc A. Levy, Tanja Srebotnjak, Alexander de Sherbinin, Christine H. Kim, and Bridget Anderson. 2006. *Pilot 2006 Environmental Performance Index.* New Haven: Yale Center for Environmental Law & Policy. Available online: http://archive.epi.yale.edu/files/2006_pilot_epi_report.pdf

EUROSTAT. 1997. *Indicators of Sustainable Development: A Pilot Study Following the Methodology of the United Nations Commission on Sustainable Development.* Statistical Office of the European Communities (EUROSTAT). Luxembourg: Office for Official Publications of the European Commission.

Guinomet, Isabelle. 1999. *The Relationship Between Indicators of Sustainable Development: An Overview of Selected Studies.* Background paper for the Fifth Expert Group Meeting on Indicators of Sustainable Development, New York, 7–8 April 1999. 183 p.

Hak, Tomas, Bedřich Moldan, and Arthur Lyon Dahl. (Eds.). 2007. *Sustainability Indicators: A Scientific Assessment, SCOPE Vol. 67.* Washington, DC: Island Press, 413 p.

Hammond, Allen, Albert Adriaanse, Eric Rodenburg, Dirk Bryant, and Richard Woodward. 1995. *Environmental Indicators: A Systematic Approach to Measuring and Reporting on Environmental Policy Performance in the Context of Sustainable Development.* Washington, DC: World Resources Institute. May 1995. Available online: http://pdf.wri.org/environmentalindicators_bw.pdf

Helliwell, John, Richard Layard, and Jeffrey Sachs. 2012. *World Happiness Report.* New York: Earth Institute, Columbia University. Available online: www.earth.columbia.edu/articles/view/2960

Helliwell, John, Richard Layard, and Jeffrey Sachs. (Eds.). 2013. *World Happiness Report 2013.* New York: Sustainable Development Solutions Network and Earth Institute, Columbia University. 154 p. Available online: http://unsdsn.org/files/2013/09/WorldHappinessReport2013_online.pdf

Helliwell, John, Richard Layard, and Jeffrey Sachs. (Eds.). 2016. *World Happiness Report 2016, Update (Vol. I).* New York: Sustainable Development Solutions Network. Available online: http://worldhappiness.report/#happiness2016

Howell, Rachel A. 2013. It's Not (Just) "The Environment, Stupid!" Values, Motivations, and Routes to Engagement of People Adopting Lower-Carbon Lifestyles. *Global Environmental Change* 23: 281–290.

Hsu, A., J. Emerson, M. Levy, A. de Sherbinin, L. Johnson, O. Malik, J. Schwartz, and M. Jaiteh. 2014. *The 2014 Environmental Performance Index.* New Haven, CT: Yale Center for Environmental Law and Policy. Available online: http://archive.epi.yale.edu/files/2014_epi_report.pdf

Hsu, A. et al. 2016. *2016 Environmental Performance Index.* New Haven, CT: Yale University. Available online: http://epi.yale.edu/sites/default/files/2016EPI_Full_Report_opt.pdf

IAEG-SDGs. 2016. *Report of the Inter-Agency and Expert Group on Sustainable Development Goal Indicators,* 19 February 2016 – United Nations E/CN.3/2016/2/Rev.1. Available online: http://unstats.un.org/unsd/statcom/47th-session/documents/2016-2-SDGs-Rev1-E.pdf

ICSU and ISSC. 2015. *Review of Targets for the Sustainable Development Goals: The Science Perspective.* Paris: International Council for Science and International Social Science Council. Available online: www.icsu.org/publications/reports-and-reviews/review-of-targets-for-the-sustainable-development-goals-the-science-perspective-2015/SDG-Report.pdf for the full report accompanying supplement "Sustainable Development Goals and Targets". Available online: www.icsu.org/publications/reports-and-reviews/review-of-targets-for-the-sustainable-development-goals-the-science-perspective-2015/sdgs-report-supplement-goals-and-targets

International Council for Science (ICSU). 2017. *A Guide to SDG Interactions: From Science to Implementation* [David J. Griggs, Måns Nilsson, Anne-Sophie Stevance, David McCollum (Eds.)]. Paris: International Council for Science. Available online: www.icsu.org/cms/2017/05/SDGs-Guide-to-Interactions.pdf

International Environment Forum (IEF). 2016. *Implementing the Sustainable Development Goals as Communities and Individuals*. Report of the International Environment Forum 20th Annual Conference, Nur University, Santa Cruz, Bolivia, 7–9 October 2016. Available online: https://iefworld.org/conf20

International Institute for Sustainable Development (IISD). 1999. Beyond Delusion: Science and Policy Dialogue on Designing Effective Indicators for Sustainable Development. *Sustainable Developments* 25(1): 1–5. 12 May 1999. Costa Rica, 7–9 May 1999. Available online: www.iisd.ca/download/pdf/sd/sdvol25no1e.pdf

Kaly, Ursula, Craig Pratt, Elizabeth Khaka, Arthur Dahl, Lino Briguglio, and Emma Sale-Mario. 2001. *Globalising the Environmental Vulnerability Index (EVI)*. Proceedings of the EVI Globalisation Meeting, 27–29 August 2001, Geneva, Switzerland. SOPAC Technical Report 345, 54 p., 3 appendices, 14 tables. Available online: http://ict.sopac.org/VirLib/TR0345.pdf

Karlsson, Sylvia, Arthur Lyon Dahl, Reinette (Oonsie) Biggs, Ben J. E. ten Brink, Edgar Gutiérrez-Espeleta, Mohd Nordin Hj. Hasan, Gregor Laumann, Bedřich Moldan, Ashbindu Singh, Joachim Spangenberg, and David Stanners. 2007. "Meeting Conceptual Challenges", Chapter 2, pp. 27–48. In Tomas Hak, Bedřich Moldan and Arthur Lyon Dahl (eds.), *Sustainability Indicators: A Scientific Assessment, SCOPE Vol. 67*. Washington, DC: Island Press.

Meadows, Donella H., Dennis L. Meadows, and Jorgen Randers. 1992. *Beyond the Limits: Confronting Global Collapse, Envisioning a Sustainable Future*. White River Junction, VT: Chelsea Green Publishing Company.

Meadows, Donella H., Dennis L. Meadows, Jorgen Randers, and William W. Behrens III. 1972. *The Limits to Growth*. A Report for the Club of Rome's Project on the Predicament of Mankind. New York: Universe Books. 205 p.

Meadows, Donella, Jorgen Randers, and Dennis Meadows. 2004. *Limits to Growth: The 30-Year Update*. White River Junction, VT: Chelsea Green Publishing Company. 338 p.

Moldan, Bedřich, Suzanne Billharz, and Robyn Matravers. (Eds.). 1997. *Sustainability Indicators: A Report on the Project on Indicators of Sustainable Development*. Scientific Committee on Problems of the Environment, SCOPE 58. Chichester: John Wiley and Sons.

Moldan, Bedřich and Arthur Lyon Dahl. 2007. "Challenges to Sustainability Indicators", Chapter 1, pp. 1–24. In Tomas Hak, Bedřich Moldan, and Arthur Lyon Dahl (eds.), *Sustainability Indicators: A Scientific Assessment, SCOPE Vol. 67*. Washington, DC: Island Press.

Nilsson, Måns, Dave Griggs, and Martin Visbeck. 2016a. Policy: Map the Interactions Between Sustainable Development Goals. *Nature* 534: 320–322. 16 June 2016. doi:10.1038/534320a

Nilsson, Måns, Dave Griggs, Martin Visbeck, and Claudia Ringler. 2016b. *A Draft Framework for Understanding SDG Interactions*. ICSU Working Paper. Paris: International Council for Science, June 2016. Available online: www.icsu.org/publications/reports-and-reviews/working-paper-framework-for-understanding-sdg-interactions-2016/SDG-interactions-working-paper.pdf

Pintér, László, Dóra Almássy, Kate Offerdahl, and Sarah Czunyi. 2015. *Global Goals and the Environment: Progress and Prospects*. Winnipeg: International Institute for Sustainable Development, May 2015. Available online: www.iisd.org/library/global-goals-and-environment-progress-and-prospects

Pintér, László, Peter Hardi, and Peter Bartelmus. 2005. *Sustainable Development Indicators: Proposals for a Way Forward*. Prepared for the United Nations Division for Sustainable Development (UN-DSD). Winnipeg: International Institute for Sustainable Development. Available online: www.iisd.org/pdf/2005/measure_indicators_sd_way_forward.pdf

Podger, Dimity, Elona Hoover, Gemma Burford, Tomas Hak, and Marie K. Harder. 2015. Revealing Values in a Complex Environmental Program: A Scaling up of Values-Based Indicators. *Journal of Cleaner Production* August 2015. doi:10.1016/j.jclepro.2015.08.034

Podger, Dimity, Georgia Piggot, Martin Zahradnik, Svatava Janouskova, Ismael Velasco, Tomas Hak, Arthur Dahl, Alicia Jimenez, and Marie K. Harder. 2010. The Earth Charter and the ESDinds Initiative: Developing Indicators and Assessment Tools for Civil Society Organizations to Examine the Values Dimensions of Sustainability Projects. *Journal of Education for Sustainable Development* 4(2): 297–305.

Ribeiro, Maria Miguel, Elona Hoover, Gemma Burford, Julia Buchebner, and Thomas Lindenthal. 2016. Values as a Bridge Between Sustainability and Institutional Assessment. *International Journal of Sustainability in Higher Education* 17(1): 40–53. January 2016. doi:10.1108/IJSHE-12-2014–0170

Rockström, Johan, Will Steffen, Kevin Noone, Åsa Persson, F. Stuart Chapin, III, Eric F. Lambin, Timothy M. Lenton, Marten Scheffer, Carl Folke, Hans Joachim Schellnhuber, Björn Nykvist, Cynthia

A. de Wit, Terry Hughes, Sander van der Leeuw, Henning Rodhe, Sverker Sörlin, Peter K. Snyder, Robert Costanza, Uno Svedin, Malin Falkenmark, Louise Karlberg, Robert W. Corell, Victoria J. Fabry, James Hansen, Brian Walker, Diana Liverman, Katherine Richardson, Paul Crutzen, and Jonathan A. Foley. 2009. A safe operating space for humanity. *Nature* 461: 472–475. 24 September 2009. doi:10.1038/461472a. Published online on 23 September 2009. Available online: www.nature.com/news/specials/planetaryboundaries/index.html and Planetary Boundaries: Exploring the Safe Operating Space for Humanity. *Ecology and Society* 14(2): 32. Available online: www.ecologyandsociety.org/vol14/iss2/art32/

Sachs, Jeffrey D. 2013. "Restoring Virtue Ethics in the Quest for Happiness", Chapter 5, pp. 80–97. In John Helliwell, Richard Layard, and Jeffrey Sachs (eds.), *World Happiness Report 2013*. New York: Sustainable Development Solutions Network and Earth Institute, Columbia University. Available online: http://unsdsn.org/files/2013/09/WorldHappinessReport2013_online.pdf

Sachs, Jeffrey, Leonardo Becchetti, and Anthony Annett. 2016. *World Happiness Report 2016, Special Rome Edition (Vol. II)*. New York: Sustainable Development Solutions Network. Available online: http://worldhappiness.report/#happiness2016

Sachs, J., G. Schmidt-Traub, C. Kroll, D. Durand-Delacre, and K. Teksoz. 2016. *SDG Index and Dashboards – Global Report*. New York: Bertelsmann Stiftung and Sustainable Development Solutions Network (SDSN). Available online: http://sdgindex.org/download/ http://sdgindex.org/assets/files/sdg_index_and_dashboards_compact.pdf and http://sdgindex.org/assets/files/sdg_index_and_dashboards_indicator_profiles.pdf

Shah, Reena. 2004. *CSD Indicators of Sustainable Development – Recent Developments and Activities*. SCOPE/UNEP/IHDP/EEA Assessment of Sustainability Indicators (ASI) project, ASI Workshop 10–14 May 2004, Prague, Czech Republic. New York: United Nations. Available online: https://sustainabledevelopment.un.org/content/documents/scopepaper_2004.pdf

Spangenberg, Joachim H. 1999. *Comments on the Input Paper by Isabelle Guinomet "The Relationship Between Indicators of Sustainable Development"*. Produced for the Fifth Expert Group Meeting on Indicators of Sustainable Development, New York, 7–8 April 1999.

Steffen, Will, Katherine Richardson, Johan Rockström, Sarah E. Cornell, Ingo Fetzer, Elena M. Bennett, Reinette Biggs, Stephen R. Carpenter, Wim de Vries, Cynthia A. de Wit, Carl Folke, Dieter Gerten, Jens Heinke, Georgina M. Mace, Linn M. Persson, Veerabhadran Ramanathan, B. Reyers, Sverker Sörlin. 2015. Planetary Boundaries: Guiding Human Development on a Changing Planet. *Science* Vol. 347, Issue 6223. 13 February 2015. *Science*, Published online on 15 January 2015. doi:10.1126/science.1259855

Sustainable Development Solutions Network (SDSN). 2015. *Indicators and a Monitoring Framework for Sustainable Development Goals: Launching a Data Revolution for the SDGs*. 12 June 2015. A report to the Secretary-General of the United Nations by the Leadership Council of the Sustainable Development Solutions Network. Available online: http://unsdsn.org/wp-content/uploads/2015/05/150612-FINAL-SDSN-Indicator-Report1.pdf

Turchin, Peter. 2010. Political Instability May Be a Contributor in the Coming Decade. *Nature*, Vol. 463, Issue 7281: 608. 4 February 2010. doi:10.1038/463608a

Turchin, Peter. 2016. *Ultrasociety: How 10,000 Years of War Made Humans the Greatest Cooperators on Earth*. Chaplin, CT: Beresta Books.

UN. 1992. *Agenda 21*. Adopted at the United Nations Conference on Environment & Development, Rio de Janeiro, Brazil, 3–14 June 1992. New York: United Nations. Available online: https://sustainabledevelopment.un.org/content/documents/Agenda21.pdf

UN. 1996. *Indicators of Sustainable Development Framework and Methodologies*. New York: United Nations. 428 p.

UN. 1997. *Fourth Expert Group Meeting on Indicators of Sustainable Development*, United States, 23–24 October 1997. Available online: https://sustainabledevelopment.un.org/content/dsd/dsd_aofw_ind/ind_egm1097.shtml

UN. 1998. *Report of the Fourth International Workshop on Indicators of Sustainable Development*, Prague, Czech Republic, 19–21 January 1998. E/CN.17/1998/15. New York: United Nations. Available online: www.un.org/ga/search/view_doc.asp?symbol=E/CN.17/1998/15%20&Lang=E

UN. 1999a. *Fifth Expert Group Meeting on Indicators of Sustainable Development*, United States, 7–8 April 1999. Available online: https://sustainabledevelopment.un.org/content/dsd/dsd_aofw_ind/ind_egm0499.shtml

UN. 1999b. *International Workshop on CSD Indicators of Sustainable Development*, Bridgetown, Barbados, 7–9 December 1999. Available online: https://sustainabledevelopment.un.org/content/dsd/dsd_aofw_ind/ind_ws1299.shtml

UN. 2001a. *Indicators of Sustainable Development: Guidelines and Methodologies.* Second Edition. New York: United Nations. 320 p. Available online: https://sustainabledevelopment.un.org/content/documents/indisd-mg2001.pdf

UN. 2001b. *Report on the Aggregation of Indicators for Sustainable Development.* Commission on Sustainable Development, Ninth Session, 16–27 April 2001, Background Paper No. 2. E/CN.17/2001/BP/2.

UN. 2007. *Indicators of Sustainable Development: Guidelines and Methodologies.* Third Edition. New York: United Nations. 93 p. and methodology sheets 398 p. Available online: https://sustainabledevelopment. un.org/content/documents/guidelines.pdf and https://sustainabledevelopment.un.org/content/documents/methodology_sheets.pdf

UN. 2015. *Transforming Our World: The 2030 Agenda for Sustainable Development.* Outcome document of the Summit for the adoption of the Post-2015 Development Agenda, New York, 25–27 September 2015. A/70/L.1. New York: United Nations. Available online: www.un.org/ga/search/view_doc. asp?symbol=A/70/L.1&Lang=E

UNEP. 2016. *Global Material Flows and Resource Productivity.* An Assessment Study of the UNEP International Resource Panel: H. Schandl, M. Fischer-Kowalski, J. West, S. Giljum, M. Dittrich, N. Eisenmenger, A. Geschke, M. Lieber, H. P. Wieland, A. Schaffartzik, F. Krausmann, S. Gierlinger, K. Hosking, M. Lenzen, H. Tanikawa, A. Miatto, and T. Fishman. Paris: United Nations Environment Programme.

UNEP/RIVM. 1994. *An Overview of Environmental Indicators: State of the Art and Perspectives.* UNEP Environment Assessment Technical Reports UNEP/EATR. 94–01; RIVM/402001001. Nairobi: United Nations Environment Programme, Environmental Assessment Sub-Programme; Bilthoven: Rijksinstituut voor Volksgezondheid en Milieu RIVM, 30 June 1994. Available online: http://hdl.handle. net/10029/10006

Ura, Karma, Sabina Alkire, Tshoki Zangmo, and Karma Wangdi. 2012. *A Short Guide to Gross National Happiness Index.* Thimphu, Bhutan: Centre for Bhutan Studies. 96 p. Available from Bhutan Gross National Happiness Commission. Available online: www.gnhc.gov.bt/

Wijkman, Anders and Johan Rockström. 2012. *Bankrupting Nature: Denying Our Planetary Boundaries.* A Report to the Club of Rome. London: Earthscan from Routledge. 206 p.

4

SUBSTANTIATING THE ROUGH CONSENSUS ON THE CONCEPT OF SUSTAINABLE DEVELOPMENT AS A POINT OF DEPARTURE FOR INDICATOR DEVELOPMENT

Walter J. V. Vermeulen

4.1 Introduction

Indicators and indexes are useful metrics to assess progress in achieving goals. This is also true for the field of sustainable development, where the goals are complex and may be difficult to explain. With a history of academic discourses of more than three decades, the concept of 'sustainable development' is often referred to as being vague, unspecified or intuitive (Christen and Schmidt, 2012; Cobbinah et al., 2015; Daly, 1990; Lele, 1991; Mebratu, 1998; Pope et al., 2004; Redclift, 2005; Robinson, 2004; White, 2013). Some scholars even argue that the concept should be set aside and replaced (Dernbach and Cheever, 2015; Viñuales, 2013, p. 3). However, the number of scientists applying the concept continues to grow rapidly, with 9000–12000 articles published annually during the last decade in Scopus registered journals.

Simultaneously, industries are developing sustainability solutions at a vast rate, and voluntary initiatives, in collaborations between producers and civil society, are rapidly expanding in number, scope and global uptake. Meanwhile, in the multilateral policy arena, growing concerns about the still on-going degradation of ecosystems and persistent poverty and inequality have leveraged the political process of formulation and acceptance of the UN Sustainable Development Goals (SDGs) in September 2015 (General Assembly UN, 2015).

The continuous criticisms on the concept versus the dynamic practices are in sharp contrast. While scientists are endlessly discussing the details, practitioners seem to be finding their way in the forest of opinions, at least the most advanced initiatives amongst them.

As I argued elsewhere, making sense of the concept is especially essential for well-motivated executives in the economy, who may previously have been fairly inactive on the scene of sustainability, but are willing to jump on the bandwagon (Vermeulen and Witjes, 2016). For them the first challenge is to find their way through the cacophony of opinions. These range from – on one side – aspiring to a reticent position of just complying with regulatory requirements (which, in itself, is confusing due to contradictions and diversity in and between regulatory regimes in our >200 nations), with – in the centre – a wide variety of opinions available in the scientific, political and market arenas (Du Pisani, 2006; Robinson, 2004) to – on the other side – eco-fundamentalists in civil society and academics taking extreme positions, which might even almost exclude the mere existence of businesses and modern mankind from the picture of Gaia (Callicott, 2005; Lovelock, 2003).

The so-called problem of vagueness of the concept is not so much the problem of that concept itself, but rather a symptom of the dominant tendency in contemporary open societies to disagree. This results in on-going, open and divergent discourses on what is needed for sustainable development. This divergence partly has its roots in endless debates about the 'correct' meaning of the concept of sustainable development in and between *academic disciplines*. It also is partly rooted in the same tendency to disagree in the *political arena*. And we also see this common practice of competing by means of different framings of the concept in the *market arena*. These *three processes of divergence* are mutually reinforcing, and do not help companies in making substantial steps in the right direction, especially the smaller ones.

How can one still help companies and others find their way? There is a way out of this; despite this noisy cacophony, discourses on the supranational level have resulted in a fairly well-supported *rough consensus* on the core elements of the concept of sustainable development. Some sub-elements may still need some refining, some other key elements may still be further complemented by additional sub-elements, but a core structure exists and is widely being worked with.

Pragmatic choices are needed. What is the contribution to be made; continue endlessly impeaching the concept, or work with the well-supported rough consensus and have it further fine-tuned by exposing it to communities of practice?

For the last purpose, I have had good experiences in presenting the concept of sustainable development in the context of discourses on vision and strategy development as a Rubik's Cube (see Figure 4.1), combining the issues dimension (people, planet, prosperity; or PPP), with the time dimension (past, now and then) and the place dimension (I, here and there) (Vermeulen

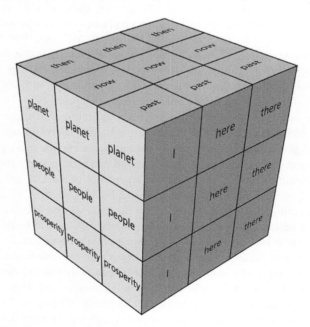

Figure 4.1 Three dimensions of the concept of sustainable development: issues (people, planet, prosperity; or PPP), time and place, containing 3x3x3 boxes

and Witjes, 2016; Witjes, 2017). The time dimension includes the most clear point of consensus on the concept: that of intergenerational justice. The place dimension reflects the connectedness of mankind and ecosystems through global networks of value chains. In this chapter, we focus mostly on the issue dimension.

The challenge is to further detail this by reviewing the *crucial choices* to be made and being made in practice in parcelling out the playing field of sustainable development. This requires a few steps:

- We should apply sustainable development as a *goal-oriented* concept and not as a fixed end-state concept. It is oriented towards solving issues of unsustainability; in other words, minimizing the negative ecological and societal impacts that are covered by the concept, or even reversing them into positive impacts.
- We need a clear *demarcation* between *causes and impacts*, with causal pathways from societal root causes, via interventions (what and how) to effects of interventions in terms of termination of the negative impacts.
- We need to *separate* the *means* from the *ends*.
- We also need to *distinguish* the *impacts* from the *fields of application*.
- We need to apply scientifically well-founded *rules for categorization* of impacts, both at the level of the main elements (in practice mostly a three-pillar approach is suggested, whereas others suggest four or more main categories) and for the sub-elements.

During the last decade, the field of sustainability science and the practices of sustainability initiatives have delivered a wide range of approaches and elaborated instruments to assess sustainability more or less holistically.[1] This in itself is an encouraging progress. However, in many cases these initiatives have elaborated their approach without acknowledging work on the same topic in other forums, often for understandable reasons (limited resources and time). But recent efforts have been more helpful in creating overviews in the various fields. For our purpose of identifying the *rough consensus*, these aggregation activities are useful sources.

At least three fields of practice[2] related to economic activities by companies in the market are relevant:

- voluntary sustainability initiatives in the international trade of products (supply chain perspective)
- voluntary reporting on corporate sustainability (firm level perspective)
- efforts to synthesize life cycle assessment on environmental and social aspects (eLCA, sLCA, LCSA) (product perspective).

In each of these fields either scientific scholars or collaborative knowledge institutes have recently produced reviews and developed aggregated reviews, often closely related to policy developments at the global level (UN, OECD, World Bank) or global stakeholder representation organizations (ISEAL Alliance, WBCSD, GRI). Simultaneously, in the scientific arena clear ideas have been presented about proper and valid ways of developing indicators and formulating (policy) goals.

In this chapter I will link these various fields, identify commonly occurring confusions and suggest a way out. I will first discuss what sustainable development is about; then reflect on key principles for goal definition and indicator development, stressing the need to link *problems* with *practices*, and via *interventions* to *goals*. After that I will compare key demarcations in the concept of sustainable development as three issue fields and give a criticism of some of the commonly applied confusions and the way to go beyond them. I will then map the environmental issues (*planet*) and the societal issues (*people and prosperity*). By doing so I will be able to integrate the various separated discourses and link them to the SDGs.

4.2 What is sustainable development about?

After its first usage in the 1980s the concept of sustainable development has become common-place, especially after the first global conference on sustainable development in 1992, but even more so after the second in 2002 and the third in 2012. More recently some fatigue seems to be occurring. In Figure 4.2 we see a sharp rise in scientific publications on sustainable development in the 1990s, up to some 127000 in total in 2016, with some 11000–12000 additional contributions per year the last decade.

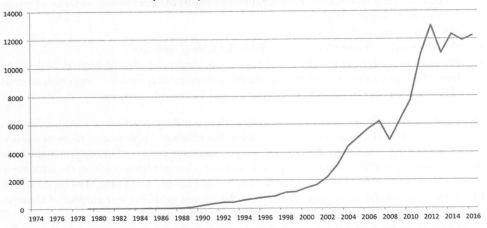

Scientific articles published using the concept *'sustainable development'* (1974–2016) (appr. 127000 in Scopus)

Figure 4.2   Scientific articles published using the concept 'sustainable development' (1974–2016)
Source: Scopus

The same trend can be seen with a more specified search for conceptual debates (Figure 4.3).

Various authors have been mapping and aggregating the diverse perspectives in this debate. Some of the best recognized historical reviews are by Lele, Robinson, Pezzoli and Hopwood et al., who clearly show the diversity of conceptions with diverging views on the balance between two key elements: fair equitable development of the poor versus protection of our ecology against human impacts (Bolis et al., 2014; Hopwood et al., 2005; Lele, 1991; Pezzoli, 1997; Robinson, 2004; Sartori et al., 2011). Going back to the earliest publications, most authors clearly stress the equal importance of this dual challenge (Clausen, 1982; Daly, 1990; Goodland and Ledec, 1987), which is generally seen as the original core message of the Brundtland Commission (World Commission on Environment and Development, 1987).

In this sense, sustainable development clearly combines two major ambitions: the ambition of ecological precaution and the ambition of fair and equitable societal development. The common elements in both are the *extractive practices of human societies*, both with respect to the ecological and the societal system. Many contributions have been made on the dual and mutually

Scientific articles published using the concept *sustainable development* + definition (1984–2016) (appr. 355 in Scopus)

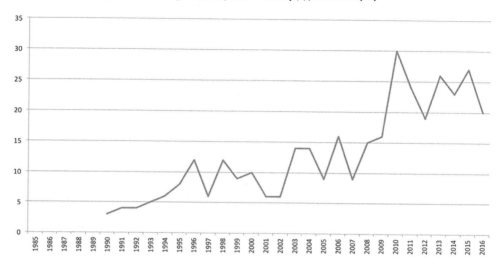

Figure 4.3 Scientific articles published: using the concept 'sustainable development' + definition (1984–2016)

Source: Scopus

reinforcing relationship between these two elements. In the past scholars have stressed the threats of the rapid increase in poor populations to long-term sustainability, often as a threat to nature or to the rest of mankind (Hardin, 1974, 1968, Meadows et al., 1972, 2004), while others were focussed more on ecology as a prerequisite for economic development (Pearce, 1988).

We can see a shift away from the original meaning of sustainable development as addressing fair and equitable development (intra- and intergenerational justice), while simultaneously respecting planetary boundaries. Various authors observe this shift away from the fairness and equity component, towards stronger emphasis of the ecological agenda, partly because it allows business to create win-wins on the ecological element, rather than on the fair distribution element. Hadden and Seybert have clearly shown this original intention of the concept with their content analysis of speeches by heads of states in UN meetings. In the 1992 discourse the original focus was on the 'development gap', 'poverty', 'equity' and 'solidarity', which recently has shifted to the 'development gap' and 'green economy' in 2012 (Hadden and Seybert, 2016, p. 246). We observed a comparable trend in the academic teaching on sustainable development (Vermeulen et al., 2014). Others show the same trend in global business initiatives (Barkemeyer et al., 2014), while White illustrated this same point by analyzing popular definitions of sustainable development by creating a word cloud, based on the count of words used in definitions. Remarkably, a clear reference to the poverty, equity and solidarity element only shows up in 24th place with the word 'equity' (White, 2013, p. 216).

However, despite these analyses, there is one convincing argument to state that we need to continue seeing the concept of sustainable development as an integral ecological and societal fairness agenda. They are equally important, and mutually dependent and reinforcing: it is about 'planet' and about 'people and prosperity'. This has been well acknowledged in the supranational policy processes preparing for the 2012 summit on sustainable development,[3] as well as finally in the accepted SDGs: having six goals addressing the societal fairness agenda at individual human level (goals 1, 2, 3, 4, 5, 11) and four goals at societal level (goals 8, 9, 10, 16), while five goals are linked to the ecological agenda (goals 6, 7, 13, 14, 15). I will later discuss this in more detail.

4.3 Key principles for goal definition and indicator development

Before we proceed to detail the key elements, we need to look at what the scientific community sets as key principles for (sustainable development) indicator construction. Sustainability indicators are also developed at various levels: nations, regional/urban, projects, companies and products. Examples of nations' indicators are discussed in Hueting and de Boer, Chapter 14; Hsu, Chapter 17; Conrad and Cassar, Chapter 19; Rosenström, Chapter 21; Gallopin, Chapter 22; while Joss and Rydin, Chapter 24 discuss examples of urban indicators. In this chapter, we focus on the discourse related to production and products, but our discussion on the core vision also applies to the other levels. Another complication is that many indicator approaches also limit themselves to specific issues under the wider flag of sustainability, such as only environmental issues or even one environmental issue, for example, climate change or biodiversity (see for example Wackernagel et al., Chapter 16; Sari et al., Chapter 27). Therefore, anyone embarking on gauging sustainable development faces the challenge of measuring something that is not precisely defined. The possibility of finding an objective measure for a concept that is loaded with values and constrained by uncertainties and data availability is still, scientifically, an open challenge (Bell and Morse, 2008; Bradley Guy and Kibert, 1998, p. 40). Goal development and indicator construction are the contact points between policymaking and evaluating policy implementation. They are reflected upon both by practitioners in policy agencies and researchers in academic circles. Engaging in the multifaceted discourses in these circles will inevitably confuse scholars, due to the wide variety of languages used by the various 'communities of experts'.

In common sense usage, the word '*goal*' would be understood as the intended result of any effort aiming at achieving a specific point, just as in sports. In this sense, it could be anything. In the context of policies or governance a 'policy goal' would be the outcome of a political process accommodating diverse societal stakeholders' individual goals. Various theories of the policy process describe this process differently, but remarkably, most authors hardly try to define the concept of 'policy goals' (see for example Cairney and Heikkila, 2014; Mukherjee and Howlett, 2015; Sabatier and Weible, 2014). However, various authors, also in the field of sustainable development, explicitly call for more specific goal formulation and distinguish a pathway of *policy outputs* (regulation, instruments, projects, plans, etc.), *intermediate outcomes* (behavioural response of target groups) and the ultimate intended '*end-outcome*' (as improved environmental or societal conditions). In their view policies will be more effective if the goals are specified as such '*end-outcomes*' (Biddle and Koontz, 2014). This is in line with the common approach in policy and program evaluation studies, to distinguish input, throughput, output and outcomes (also known as '*logic models*') (see for more detail Cooksy et al., 2001; Kaplan and Garrett, 2005; McCawley, 2002; McLaughlin and Jordan, 1999; Millar et al., 2001; Morra Imas and Rist, 2009, p. 223). It stresses the need to distinguish between direct policy outputs affecting target group behaviours, and long-term outcomes in terms of the desired 'end state'. This is the type of reasoning that we will need to clarify the concept of sustainable development.

In the scholarly discourse about sustainable development we see two distinct approaches towards 'end states': sustainability seen as a fixed end state or endpoint versus a development or learning process towards a less fixed destination (Bell and Morse, 2007, 2001). In the first approach one would develop goals as very clear quantitative targets, whereas in the second approach one would rather describe problem areas, in terms of a desired 'end state', but in both cases one should avoid fixing the required solutions (these are inputs or outputs, but not the outcomes). Here the *means* and the *ends* do need to be clearly separated.

Goals need to be translated into indicators to measure progress. The concept of '*indicator*' is generally described as well-justified measurements, representing a wider complexity in reality, but based on a convincing reasoning assumed to be valid for describing that complex reality. As a specific subset 'indexes' are deliberate simplifications of a wider set of measurements, mainly to guide decisions and behaviour (Mayer, 2008, p. 278).

Both defining goals and related indicators and indexes are in themselves societal activities, either in the policymaking arena (serving policy formulation and planning, as well as evaluation), or in the policy implementation arena serving collaborative policymaking (Bell and Morse, 2005), or in academic circles (serving curiosity-driven or contract-driven research), or finally, in civil society circles (as a tool to push policymakers) (see also Dahl, Chapter 3; Rotz and Fraser, Chapter 6; Spangenberg, Chapter 9). Remarkably, here we see very different approaches, which can be understood from the specific positions these actors hold in the societal governance processes (either close to governments at national level or in supranational agencies; or as consultants or facilitators to open policy processes; or merely within the academic circles; or as civil society actors in public discourses) (Parris and Kates, 2003, pp. 572–577). No wonder we get a cacophony.

However, looking at these diverging debates we can distinguish some consensual lines of reasoning. Goals and indicators are to be logically linked and to be used to guide action (at any level of governance). Regardless of whether the process of construction is intended as a 'top-down expert' or a 'bottom-up practitioner' activity (see also Bell and Morse, Chapter 12; Turcu, Chapter 10; Domingues et al., Chapter 25), there is a common pathway. In working with indicator systems, it will be very fruitful to combine the lines of thought in the policy evaluation community (logic models, focus on outcomes) with guidelines for creating indicators in the academic (mostly environmental) indicator community.

Various scholars have either critically reviewed the practices of sustainable development indicators or proposed systematic approaches for it. Table 4.1 combines the core massages of five well-recognized examples of such contributions (see also Pintér et al., Chapter 2). Each of them, starting from different intentions and foci, propose steps, factors, requirements, criteria and more for creating and applying indicators systems. Table 4.1 suggests a synthesis, which includes partly methodological aspects and partly considerations for useful application.

Combining the articles, we can observe that they mostly entail comparable steps and related considerations: first, with creation of a core structure of the indicator system (A and B). This needs to feed and justify choices made in the operationalization (C). Methodological rigour needs to be established in the steps of data manipulation (D) and in the process of final aggregation into a final composite result (E). In all these scholarly contributions, the link between each of these steps or elements is crucial: all choices need to be well founded in systemic core reasoning. In that sense steps A and B are to be seen as guidance.

In practice, cohesion between the five steps or elements is often challenged. Reviews such as the articles used here often observe that indicators systems either have a narrow focus on available data, an over-simple guiding vision, or inadequately apply steps C, D and/or E. This can be

Table 4.1 Descriptors of the sustainable development indicator formulation process, according to various authors

Authors	Pintér et al., 2005/Hardi and Zhan 1997	Bohringer and Jochem, 2007	Boulanger, 2008	Mayer, 2008	Bradley Guy and Kibert, 1998
Relevance (as # citations; field weighed citation impact and percentile)[1]	45 3.38 96th percentile	241 40.77 percentile n.a.	12 0.43 65th percentile	138 2.74 88th percentile	59 6.69 90th percentile
Description of considerations or purpose	Bellagio STAMP: "8 **principles** to promote common approach of developing/using measurement systems as integral part of how institutions and society function" *(based on expert meeting)*	"6 **Key requirements** for selecting appropriate SD indicators" *(referring to various other authors)*	"Successive **phases** of the construction of indicators" *(cf. work of the empirical sociologist Lazarsfeld)*	"Prevent bias due to 4 **factors** influencing inappropriate index behaviour" *(scientific work)*	"12 **criteria** for indicators" *(position: selection of sustainability indicators as an inevitably human value-driven process)*
Focus	Content and procedures for giving guidelines	Procedures for Comparing existing indicator sets	Procedures for Giving guidelines	Procedures for Comparing existing indicator sets	Process of Developing sector indicators
A. Scope and core concept	1. **Guiding vision** *Includes well-being, within biosphere capacity, also for future generations*	1. Rigorous **connection to definitions** of sustainability	1. **Concept** *As: aggregate, multi-dimensional umbrella concept*	–	–
B. Key elements	2. **Essential considerations** *Includes holistic systems approach*	2. Selection of **meaningful** indicators representing **holistic** fields	2. **Dimensions** *As: logical main elements of concept, but still multifaceted, to be broken down in separate variables*	–	• Linkage environment, economic, and social issues; • Representative: cover important dimensions of focus area

Article

Methodological elements

Methodological elements					
C. Data specification	3. **Adequate scope** *Time and geographical*	3. Reliability and availability (measurability) of **data** for quantification over **longer time horizons**	3. **Measure** *Measure theoretically relevant variables with appropriate indicators*	1. **Scale** of the available data	• Valid measurement of state of the system • Include focus on long term • Act locally, think globally: prevent acting at the expense of others
D. Data manipulation	4. **Framework and indicators** *Define issues, priorities with targets, and proper baseline and benchmarks to compare*	4. Process- orientated **indicator selection** 6. **Adequate normalization, aggregation and weighting** of the underlying variables ensuring **scientific quality**	— 4. **Aggregate** *Combine results in synthetic indicators: in a common unit, or by standardization, well justified*	2. Choice of **system boundaries** 3. **Aggregation** method	—
E. Compilation of final result	—	—	5. **Weighing** *Major challenges in weighing the relative importance of the 3 dimensions (PPP)*	4. **Inclusion, transformation and weighting** of indicator data	—

(Continued)

Table 4.1 (Continued)

Authors	Pintér et al., 2005/Hardi and Zhan 1997	Böhringer and Jochem, 2007	Boulanger, 2008	Mayer, 2008	Bradley Guy and Kibert, 1998
I. Accountability	5. **Transparency** *Publicly accessible, choices justified and sources disclosed*	–	–	–	• Stable and reliable: a systematic and fair method
II. Outreach	6. **Effective communications** *Broad public, avoid misuse*	5. Possibility of **deriving political** (sub)**objectives**	–	–	• Understandable for lay persons
	7. **Broad participation** *Reflect public interests, engage users*		–	–	• Community involvement Relevant to public or corporate policy
III. Long-term impact	8. **Continuity and capacity** *Ensure long-term capacity and adaptability*		–	–	• Available and timely data on annual basis • Responsive to changes • Flexible: include possible future available important data

Application aspects

[1]: Using the metrics on the document details page in Scopus (22–2–2017)

seen as the result of practices of indicator construction and application struggling with the conflicting expectations and needs on two conflicting lines: theoretical soundness versus applicability for engagement; and methodological rigour versus data availability (see also the discussion in Dahl, Chapter 3; Esty and Emerson, Chapter 5; Boulanger, Chapter 8). The elements A to D and I to III identified in the review in Table 4.1 all relate to specific sides of these tensions (as shown on Figure 4.4). Limited resources and the position of the developers in society often determine the choices they can make in this field of tensions.

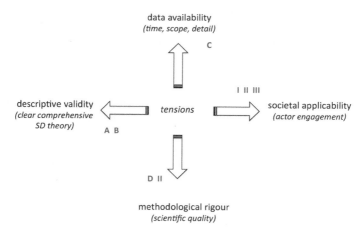

Figure 4.4   Tensions in the practice of indicator construction and application (and relation to elements A to D and aspects I to III described in Table 4.1)

4.4 Linking problems with practices, and via interventions to goals

Apart from balancing these tensions, as indicated before and also stressed in Janoušková et al., Chapter 30, it is crucial to work with a guiding core reasoning (elements A and B). For this, our discussion in Part 4.2 is essential, framing sustainable development as a twin integral ecological and societal fairness agenda. End states need to be described as the final targets in both these domains. From those endpoints, logic models are required to specify the *pathways* from policy outputs (as regulations, projects, policy instruments, plans, etc.) via intermediate outcomes (responses of target groups) to the end-outcomes. Such pathways then serve to improve the quality of choices made in elements C and D. The composition of the final outcome parameter should again be based on the SD vision (elements A and B).

Various models for describing such pathways or causal routes are popular, in both academic literature and policy practice, originally rooted in the field of environmental sciences. In most cases they do not (explicitly) link to the thinking in terms of logic models common in the field of policy evaluation. Popular pathway models are the *pressure-state-response* model (Kee and de Haan, 2007; Orians and Policansky, 2009; Pintér et al., 2005; Singh et al., 2009; Tanguay et al., 2010), or (more extended) the *driver-pressure-state-impact-response* model (Ness et al., 2010; Smeets and Weterings, 1999); various *capital* approaches (like CRITINC) (Bebbington, 1999; Ekins et al., 2003; Joint UNECE et al., 2013; Worldbank, 1997), and causal models like *IPAT* or *ImPACT* or *STIRPAT* (Chertow, 2000; Fischer-Kowalski and Amann, 2001; Waggoner and Ausubel, 2002; York et al., 2003). Contributions about indicators from policy agencies and accounting or statistical bureaux tend to be strongly data driven; presenting and discussing large numbers of indicators, stressing the technical issues which are shown in Table 4.1 under elements C and D. These reviews often have weak conceptual foundations, more or less bypassing methodological aspects A and B and presenting the work with categorizations of policy fields (Joint UNECE et al., 2013; Leadership Council of the Sustainable Development Solutions Network (SDSN), 2015; United Nations, 2007). In Table 4.2, I compare some of these logic pathway models. In the left column, in the lowest five rows, it shows the elements in logic models. With their roots in evaluation studies, logic models tend to focus on the logic *after* policy formulation. So I have added four rows before it, describing the origins of SD issues in human activity, current problem states, its recognition and the take-up in any governance activity (as varied forms of multi-actor activity, see for a discussion Driessen et al., 2012), thus also describing the policy formulation phase. We need this combination to contextualize the sustainability pathways in this perspective.

In the nine columns to the right I show various popular pathway models and their academic context. It shows that these models mostly focus on the causation and to some extent make an (implicit) jump to end-outcomes.

In most cases the models do not clarify how societal (governance) responses to the issues result in achieving the goals, e.g. end-outcomes. The PSR and DPSIR approach implicitly aggregates inputs, throughputs, output and outcomes under an unspecified 'Response'. The IPAT model and related variations merely a causal model, not reflecting societal response, while the capital approaches assume that a balanced presence of the five or six capitals ensures achievement of sustainability more or less as a black box. As a result of these lines of reasoning the end-outcomes are not very explicitly identified.

The first six approaches, all focussing on a 'impact' category, are rooted in environmental sciences and describe impacts as environmental impacts, either using a 'receiver' categorization (the nature component that receives the impacts: air, water, soil, human) or more sophisticated categorization describing the problem-causation mechanism of the impacts (climate change, eutrophication, depletion, etc.) which has become accepted as the proper way of working in the sub-discipline of environmental life cycle analysis (which I will discuss in Parts 4.6 and 4.7).

The various capital approaches tend to present the capitals as valid indicators for the concept of sustainable development, with many authors suggesting that these also represent the three elements of sustainable development: the environmental (natural capital), the social (human and social, or also intellectual capital) and the economic aspect (built, or physical and financial capital).

The fundamental shortcomings of such approaches are twofold: (1) they fail to display the causal pathway from problem, via governance response and its outputs, to the defined end-outcomes (goals) of sustainable development; and (2) the end-outcomes are not clear and instructive for actors in society.

These various pathway approaches have a long history and are well known and widely applied in the indicator communities. Earlier I argued that the inclusive scope and core concept and its key elements (Part 4.2; elements A and B in Table 4.1) should be guiding. This implies that we need to frame both the problem identification (row -2-) and the goals (row -9-) as the twin SD-agenda of integral ecological and societal fairness. Assessing the popular pathway models in this way, we cannot but observe that most do not explicitly and clearly do so. In many cases the complexity of the issue is reduced by working towards one of the corners of

Table 4.2 Popular sustainability pathways represented in terms of logic model concepts

Environmental sciences Representations (disciplines)	PSR (OECD, 2003, p. 21) (environmental sciences)	DPSIR (Bell, 2012; Kim, Ness et al., 2010; OECD, 2003; Smeets and Weterings, 1999) (environmental sciences)	CNC/CRITINC (Critical natural capital) (Ekins et al., 2003; Joint UNECE et al., 2013) (environmental sciences)	IPAT (Chertou, 2000; Daily and Ehrlich, 1992; Diesendorf, 2002; Roca, 2002; Schulze, 2002) (environmental sciences)	ImPACT (Waggoner and Ausubel, 2002) (environmental sciences)	STIRPAT (stochastic impacts by regression on population, affluence and technology) (York et al., 2003) (ecological economics)	5 Capitals (as prerequisites for development at national level) (Lehtonen, 2004; Pretty, 2008; Worldbank, 1997) (ecological economics)	6 Capitals (Deloitte and Deloitte Netherlands, 2016) (business studies; accounting)	5 Capitals (for rural livelihood development at local level) (Bebbington, 1999; DFID, 1999; Garnett et al., 2007) (development studies, ecology; agro-economics)
Logic model elements[1]									
1 (human activities causing SD issues [PPP]) →	**Pressure**	**Driving forces Pressures**	Influences	**Population size Affluence Technology**	**Population size Consumption intensity Affluence Technology**	**Population size Affluence Technology**	n.a.	n.a.	n.a.
2 (current problematic states of environment and/or society) →	**State**	**State Impact**	Natural Capital (elements and functions); Functions for people	(environmental) Impact (of a population)	(environmental) Impact (of a population)	(environmental) Impact (of a population)	Natural capital	Natural capital	Natural capital
3 (knowledge and societal pressure) →	n.a.	n.a.	n.a.	n.a.	n.a.	n.a.	n.a.	(Intellectual capital)	

(Continued)

Table 4.2 (Continued)

Representations (disciplines)	PSR (OECD, 2003, p. 21) (environmental sciences)	DPSIR (Bell, 2012; Kim, 2010; Ness et al., 2010; OECD, 2003; Smeets and Weterings 1999) (environmental sciences)	CNC/CRITINC (Critical natural capital) (Ekins et al., 2003; Joint UNECE et al., 2013) (environmental sciences)	IPAT (Chertow, 2000; Daily and Ehrlich, 1992; Diesendorf, 2002; Roca, 2002; Schulze, 2002) (environmental sciences)	ImPACT (Waggoner and Ausubel, 2002) (environmental sciences)	STIRPAT (stochastic impacts by regression on population, affluence and technology) (York et al., 2003) (ecological economics)	5 Capitals (as prerequisites for development at national level) (Lehtonen, 2004; Pretty, 2008; Worldbank, 1997) (ecological economics)	6 Capitals (Deloitte and Deloitte Netherlands, 2016) (business studies; accounting)	5 Capitals (for rural livelihood development at local level) (Bebbington, 1999; DFID, 1999; Garrett et al., 2007) (development studies, ecology, agro-economics)
Logic model elements[1]									
4 *(governance responses: formulation and decision-making)*	**Response**	**Response**	n.a.	n.a.	n.a.	n.a.	Social capital	Social capital	Social capital
5 **INPUTS** *(resources: time, funds, people, etc.)*			n.a.	n.a.	n.a.	n.a.	Physical capital Financial Capital	Physical capital Financial Capital	Built capital Financial Capital
6 **THROUGHPUTS** *(processes, activities, implementation, . . .)*			n.a.	n.a.	n.a.	n.a.	Human capital	Human capital	Human capital
7 **OUTPUTS** *(plans, projects, enforcement)*			n.a.	n.a.	n.a.	n.a.	n.a.	n.a.	n.a.
8 *(intermediate)* **OUTCOMES** *(behaviours, . . .)*			n.a.	n.a.	n.a.	n.a.	n.a.	n.a.	n.a.
9 **END-OUTCOMES**	*(reduced)* **Pressure**/ *(adjusted)* **State**	*(adjusted)* **Driving** forces, **Pressures** and **States**	Human **Welfare**/ Ecological **Well-being**	*(goals not specified)*	*(goals not specified)*	*(goals not specified)*	SD measured as maintenance of 5 capital 'stocks'	Sustainable business	Sustainable livelihood

[1]: Using (Cooksy et al., 2001; Kaplan and Garrett, 2005; McCawley, 2002; McLaughlin and Jordan, 1999; Millar et al., 2001), being based in the discipline of policy evaluation it starts after the initial policymaking, expressing these prior steps here *(between brackets and in italics)*; n.a. = not addressed

the tension fields shown in Figure 4.4. Either using available data or generating a simple and attractive message towards user publics seems to motivate such simplification steps. The way the sustainability pathways approaches describe the end state does not link substantially to the twin SD-agenda. PSR and DPISR implicitly limit the intended end-outcome to environmental conditions; CNC and CRINTINC refer to combined ecological and human well-being, but do not detail it; the IPAT, ImPACT and STIRPAT approaches do not specify end-outcomes, while finally, the various capitals approaches propose the balanced and sustained availability of the various capitals as the end-outcome, but detail them in very different ways. The need for stronger focus on implementation and effectiveness is also stressed in Almássy and Pintér, Chapter 13.

For the sake of maintaining a clear meaning for the concept of sustainable development I therefore argue that we need stronger focus on the first elements in the indicator formulation process approaches: the inclusive scope of the concept, well-linked to a holistic systems theory approach. This implies a stronger reasoning for subdividing sustainable development into a small number of key elements.

In literature, such subdivisions are framed with various different wordings ('aspects', 'domains', 'pillars', 'spheres', 'dimensions', 'circles', etc.). The number of elements also differs, often three, but we also find versions of two, four or five more key elements. Mostly used are subdivisions into *social*, *environmental* (or *ecological*) and *economic* elements (SEE) and in *people*, *planet*, *profit* (PPP, or 3P), also referred to in business contexts as *triple bottom line* (TBL). They may be seen as nearly identical, but once we look into the ways these three elements are further detailed, we get a chaotic picture, both in scientific literature and in policy- and practices-related literature. It may be useful to analyze the roots and history of such diverse operationalizations, but with the limited space here I only briefly reflect on this.

4.5 Commonly found confusions and the way to go beyond them

Many of the existing approaches are created in the context of production and consumption systems and business, to assess and decide upon productive activities, projects, plans and product redesigns etc., in the context of corporate sustainability and the impacts of production throughout value chains. In these contexts the assessment of *environmental* impacts has relatively the longest history. In this subfield, a fairly clear consensus on showing the pathways of impacts has developed (which I will discuss in Part 4.6). It uses a clear midpoint-endpoint pathway reasoning,[4] as I described in Part 4.4.

But working towards an integrated sustainability assessment in relation to production activities also has a long history. The *people*, *planet*, *profit* (PPP, or 3P) framing has become very popular after Elkington's critical book on firms' behaviour, called *Cannibals with Forks* (Elkington, 1998), stressing that with unsustainable practices the business community is cutting up its own flesh. The key point here was the argument to extend economic decision-making beyond the single bottom line of profit and include environmental and social impact considerations. In this way 'profit' as a concept sneaked into the framing of sustainability. It makes perfect sense to assess improvement options in the context of the relative efficiency of various alternative solutions, and thus allow for identifying alternatives that can create win–win situations for both producers and customers. But with the concept becoming more and more attractive and enabling previously closed boardroom doors to open, practitioners and academics started to distort the clear framing of sustainable development (as the twin SD-agenda of integral environmental and societal fairness) by putting individual firms' *profit*-making at the same outcome level as *people*- and *planet*-related issues. Individual firms' profits can never serve as intended *end-outcomes* of the process towards sustainable development. For scholars who are not convinced by the argument, I suggest that they check the text of the UN decision on the SDGs. They will look for the word 'profit' in this document in vain (General Assembly UN, 2015).

A comparable development is seen where sustainable development is summarized as social, environmental and economic (SEE). Here the element 'economic' is often without clear theoretical reasoning filled at random with concepts or metrics related to economic growth. Examples are: summing up profit margins, total labour costs (Kruse et al., 2009); revenues (Ocampo, 2015); investments made (Joung et al., 2013); R&D expenditures (Krajnc and Glavič, 2005), just to name a few of the overwhelming number of examples. The crucial issue here is that in the development of indicators and indexes, steps A and B are ignored. *Any costs made in production, profits resulting from it and even the resulting economic growth in itself, are not elements of the concept of sustainable development.* Sustainable development is about abating the *negative environmental and societal externalities* created in our production and consumption systems (Benoît and Mazijn, 2009, pp. 15–16; Sala et al., 2015, pp. 18–19). To include any element of the internalities (being: all costs and benefits that are intrinsically connected to goods and service brought on the market) is a major fallacy in using the concept of sustainability: it relates neither to creating societal fairness, nor to ecological protection. Here the problem is that the decision-making context (throughput in Table 4.2) is confused with the intended end-outcomes. In decision-making one needs to know the financial implications and the strategic business opportunities. It makes sense to identify and specify them. But they need to be used in clear separation from the sustainability end goals.

A comparable confusion is found in the literature about developing integrated sustainability life cycle assessment methodologies. In many proposals the solution suggested is to see this as the sum of eLCA + sLCA + LCC (Finkbeiner et al., 2010; Halog and Manik, 2011; Heijungs et al., 2013; Kloepffer, 2008; Swarr et al., 2011b; Zamagni, 2012). In the next part I will discuss the first two in more detail. But first we need to address the applicability of Life Cycle Costing as representation of one of the three key elements of sustainable development. At the current stage in most cases LCC does not address the fair economic development framing we identified as a core element of sustainable development. Historically LCC is about the production costs in the full supply chain, translated to the full costs for the user per unit of product or service (Cole and Sterner, 2000). Again, this is a very useful concept, but it analyzes the *internalities*,[5] not the externalities (Meester et al., 2013; Swarr et al., 2011a, 2011b) or it addresses the environmental and/or social externalities in monetary units, thus risking double counting. The micro-economic parameters can be used to assess the efficiency and feasibility of improvement options, which in simple terms can be presented as:

$$\frac{\text{'total sustainability improvement' (as planet, people, prosperity) per unit}}{\text{'total life cycle costs' per unit}}$$

But micro-economic parameters should be used properly. In the above-mentioned cases the numerator and the divisor in this equation are mixed up, using the 'total life cycle costs' in the place of 'prosperity'. The numerator needs to express only the twin SD-agenda of integral ecological and societal fairness.

In more recent approaches some scholars propose forms of LCC, which include models following a midpoint and endpoint reasoning, and offer a pathway reasoning including the macro-economic 'areas of protection' as 'economic stability' and 'wealth generation' (Neugebauer et al., 2016). This is a step in the right direction, but these are not yet explicitly linked to the sustainable development discourse as described in Part 4.2. The related midpoints are still profitability, productivity and consumer satisfaction, which are neither connected to the twin SD-agenda, nor to be seen as externalities. Although in these new approaches the concept of prosperity is also embraced, the theoretical reasoning is still fairly weak, close to the neo-liberal economic agenda of economic growth, capital investment and export-stability. Some links are made to the issue of inequality, but it is not yet explicitly addressed in the framework they propose (Neugebauer et al., 2016, p. 6).

At this point the LCA, LCSA and LCC community are weakly connected to wider discourses on sustainable development and the SDGs. Looking beyond their epistemological homeland could enrich the methodological development. Looking to the academic field of economic history and development economics could strengthen the theoretical thinking on the societal fairness side of the twin SD-agenda. In these disciplines, the crucial question is to what extent core institutional features of societies matter for achieving prosperity, and which specific institutions are most relevant. This question has been extensively addressed with long-term historic cross-country comparative research in the last decade, backed up by empirical analysis of assumed causal mechanisms. Extensive empirical data is used to prove key assumptions, even going back to colonial periods (Acemoglu et al., 2000). With this approach the group around Acemoglu, Johnson and Robinson developed their *theory of political transitions* (Acemoglu and Robinson, 2001), which was illustrated in their extensive book *Why Nations Fail – The Origins of Power, Prosperity and Poverty* and many other publications (Acemoglu et al., 2014; Acemoglu and Robinson, 2013). Their main point is that continuous development toward prosperity can only be achieved by states organized around *inclusive political institutions* combined with *inclusive economic institutions*. History shows a long development of historical and contemporary elites building *extractive political and economic institutions*; where during crucial historical junctures (decolonization, post–First World War and post–Second World War and after collapse in Eastern Europe) new (more) extractive regimes were often created, recycling earlier institutions in new forms. With their approach they built on the earlier work of the Nobel Prize-winning economic historian North, who argued that we should derive the key elements of what a state is from the 'exploitation or predatory theory of the state', where the agency is a group, class or elite, which uses the state to extract income from the rest of the constituents in the interest of that group (North, 1989, 1979). The most fundamental institutions in the political and economic domain are closely linked. It includes *property* and *contract law, tax systems* and a *control system* for this: *jurisdiction*. Yet, as North argues, this builds in fundamentally inherent tensions which cause the continuous historical turmoil within and between states: rent maximizing for the rulers and safeguarding tax revenues via juridification of transaction costs creates tensions between groups close to the elite, as it builds in some diffusion of power and creates its own future failure. It is essential that societies are able to make the transition away from extractive political and economic institutions towards *pluralist and inclusive institutions*. Only with pluralist regimes can entrepreneurs engage in innovation, and new knowledge be used without the countervailing activities of incumbent interests and creative destruction, which are crucial elements for progress to take place. Based on this school of research the critical *political institutions* are identified, enabling an open political system; fair taxation; distributional systems; and rules for free association. Key *economic institutions* are related to property rights and land and resources ownership; price formation and open markets; and rights of workers and consumers.

Remarkably, these well-proven theories are hardly used in the SD indicator arenas, while they offer a good theoretical justification of the methodological choices to be made in our field of study. It allows us to better elaborate the prosperity element at the macro level of society as a social system and thus link it also to the SGs that address this level (SDG 8, 9, 10, 16).

In this way, we can translate the twin SD-agenda of integral ecological and societal fairness into that of *planet* and of *people and prosperity*, where the 'people' element addresses (in the context of productive activities) the individuals and their communities directly related to value-chain activities, and the 'prosperity' element relates to the macro-economic institutions that are essential for creating fair and equitable development.

With this in mind, we can now review the common approaches for mapping these elements by: (1) voluntary sustainability initiatives in the international trade of products (supply chain perspective); (2) voluntary reporting about corporate sustainability (firm level perspective); and (3) efforts to synthesize life cycle assessment on environmental and social aspects (eLCA, sLCA, LCSA).

4.6 Mapping environmental issues: *planet*

The first pillar of 'planet'-related impacts has the longest history of scientific discourses on the most valid method for characterization of the damage impacts. This discourse also includes a focus on integrating causal pathways from human activity to final impacts. This is the core activity of the field of environmental life cycle (impact) assessment (LCA, LCIA, eLCA). First approaches were developed in the 1980s (Klöpffer, 1997), with methodologies elaborated in various parts of the world and a longer history of collaborative approaches to harmonizing the key principles (guided by UNEP/SETAC, EC-JRP, and others). Being one of the core applied methodologies in environmental sciences, from its first days it combined impacts both on eco-systems and on mankind, but related to the production of products and services, thus already focussing on planet and people, but with a limited perspective. Many publications are available describing the principles of environmental life cycle (impact) assessment (Guinée, 2002; Pennington et al., 2004; Rebitzer et al., 2004), and the methods are also standardized with various ISO standards (most recent ISO 14044:2006).

For our debate in this chapter, the question on the core categories of environmental damages is the most crucial. In LCA terminology, this relates to the 'characterization' step of mapping the pathway of human impact on ecosystems and mankind in terms of midpoints, endpoints and areas of protection. Various slightly different approaches for this have been developed and are widely used. Some of the most important examples from various continents are the CML-method (Guinée et al., 1993; Udo De Haes et al., 2000; Udo de Haes, 1993), ImPACT 2002+ (Jolliet et al., 2003), LUCAS (Toffotetto et al., 2006), the EcoIndicator-method (Goedkoop and Spriensma, 2000), the LIME approach (Itsubo and Inaba, 2003), and ReCiPe (Goedkoop et al., 2009). Understandably this diversity of approaches has led to confusion and some loss of confidence in the field of science. The good thing is that this academic community has joined forces and worked towards a consensus on the best practices for characterization, created by all lead researchers in the field (see Hauschild et al., 2013). In this key publication 156 characterization models were reviewed belonging to 12 different LCIA methods, and a best practice framework was proposed, as shown in Figure 4.5, synthesizing the discourse into 15 midpoints and three endpoints.[6]

Remarkably, not all relevant environmental impacts have found their way into this apparent LCA consensus, such as various forms of nuisance (noise, odour, light), which are also seen as essential (Marchand et al., 2013; Müller-Wenk, 2004; Ongel, 2016).

The field of life cycle (impact) assessment is strongly matured, but is not the only subfield of sustainable development research. In this context, I want to briefly refer to the growing field of resilience research, which takes a planetary system's approach and defines the crucial thresholds to be guarded, described as nine boundaries. These are also depicted in Figure 4.5. We see a strong overlap of the two approaches, but the planetary boundaries approach mixes midpoint and endpoint reasoning and ignores some issues, such as depletion of mineral resources.

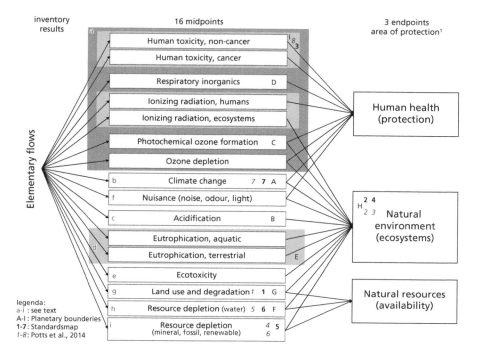

Figure 4.5 EC JRC Framework for best practices of impact characterization

Source: Based on Hauschild et al., (2013) compared with planetary boundaries concept elements (Rockström et al., 2009; Standardsmap and Potts et al 2014).

Legend: Planetary boundaries **A – I**: A: Climate change; B: Ocean acidification; C: Stratospheric ozone depletion; D: Atmospheric aerosol loading; E: Biogeo-chemical flows: interference with P and N cycles; F: Global freshwater use; G: Land-system change; H: Rate of biodiversity loss; I: Chemical pollution;

[1]: Endpoint descriptions also based on (Huijbregts et al., 2017*)*;

a–b: simplifications explained in text;

1–7: categories in Standardsmap (WTO-ITC, 2017): 1: soil; 2: forests; 3: chemicals, organic inputs; 4: biodiversity; 5: waste; 6: water; **7**: energy / *1–8*: categories in review of voluntary standards (Potts et al., 2014, p. 70) *1*: soil; *2*: biodiversity; *3*: GMO prohibition; *4*: waste; *5*: water; *6*: energy; *7*: greenhouse gas; *8*: synthetic inputs.

Combining these approaches is fertile, as the resilience community adds knowledge about specific threshold values to be respected, which is weak in the LCA community.

With a stronger collaboration between these various research communities, a clearer consensus would be possible. However, scientists would not be scientists if some of them would not, after this consensus, jump like frogs out of the wheelbarrow again. After this joint publication some new adjustments to the framework have been published, such as the ReCiPe2016 approach (Huijbregts et al., 2017). In this new version, some of the 15 midpoints are again detailed into separate midpoints, adding up to a total of 17 midpoints, and, more importantly, more details have been added on pathway categories.

However, for our purpose I would rather move in the other direction, that of aggregation, which I also illustrate in Figure 4.5, with the blue 'a' to 'h'. Indeed, looking through one's lashes, a rough consensus on the short list of midpoints and the reasoning in midpoints and three endpoints is strongly vested.[7] We could even further summarize this synthesis into a shorter list of nine general midpoint categories: (1) human health-related pollution, (2) climate change,

(3) acidification, (4) eutrophication, (5) eco-toxicity, (6) nuisance (of noise, smell, light), (7) land use and (8) water depletion and (9) resource depletion (mineral, fossil, renewable).

4.7 Mapping social issues and societal issues: *people and prosperity*

The development of a comparable methodology for the social and societal issues is far more recent; it has mostly taken off in the 21st century. I will briefly compare the approaches in the fields of social-LCA, product standards and corporate reporting.

As approaches for social-LCA grew in the womb of the eLCA community, right from the start scholars have tried to continue applying the logic of causal pathways, midpoints and end-points (Parent et al., 2010; Russo Garrido et al., 2016) and have tried to link to other relevant research communities and communities of practice. Now, in the middle of the second decade of the 21st century, various efforts of reviewing and integration have already been accomplished (Benoît-Norris et al., 2011; Benoît et al., 2010; Benoît and Mazijn, 2009; Benoît and Vickery-Niederman, 2011; Fontes, 2016; Russo Garrido et al., 2016; Sala et al., 2015). However, various scholars argue that the theoretical foundations are weak and a stronger justification of social goals is needed (Parent et al., 2013; Sala et al., 2015). Some sustainability pathway approaches have been suggested, including a stakeholder approach (Benoît and Vickery-Niederman, 2011, p. 14), an impact categories approach (such as human rights, working conditions, health and safety, cultural heritage, etc. see Benoît-Norris et al., 2011, p. 683) and also the capabilities or capitals approach (Reitinger et al., 2011; Sala et al., 2015, p. 82). However, looking at the commonly used approaches, the stakeholder categorization appears to be the dominant one (Benoît and Mazijn, 2009; Eisfeldt, 2016; Fontes, 2016), sometimes applied in combination with the other two. It focusses on five general stakeholder groups: *workers*, (local) *communities*, *consumers* and *suppliers* (or 'value-chain actors') and as last '*society*'. In this way life cycle thinking is applied for the first four stakeholder groups, combining it with a societal network approach, implicitly referring to what is also called the netchain approach (Omta et al., 2001).

However, it is not yet fully mature. The last category is especially problematic. Using '*society*' as a main stakeholder group is a regularly repeated conceptual blunder. In social sciences 'society' stands for the total collection of actors and their encounters, embedded within meso-structures of organizational units and macro-structures of institutions, stratifications and cultures (Turner, 2014, 2012a, 2012b, 2010). In that way 'society' cannot be a stakeholder. The roots of this confusion are the common practices in the field of business studies, where 'society' is more or less used as everything outside the firm. However, also in stakeholder theory a stakeholder is commonly defined as "any *group* or *individual* who can affect or is affected by the achievement of the organization's objectives" (Freeman, 1984, p. 46; Mitchell et al., 1997, p. 856). As a result of this conceptual inaccuracy we see a problematic diversity in the application of this category in practice. We see very diverse notions under the heading of 'society', as in the UNEP/SETC Guidelines 'public commitment'; 'economic development'; 'prevention of armed conflicts'; 'technology development' and 'corruption' (Benoît and Mazijn, 2009, p. 49; also applied in PSILCA, see Ciroth and Franze, 2011, p. 80), but in the same report it also refers to: government, banks, media and more financial institutions (p. 26). Other approaches replaced 'society' by 'governance', like the SHDB, using it to contain 'legal system' and 'corruption' (Sala et al., 2015, p. 40) combining it with an impacts categories approach (using labour rights, human rights, etc.). In these ways 'society' functions as a trash bin category.

This choice of five key categories has also been endorsed by the initiative of a large group of industry stakeholders in their Roundtable for Product Social Metrics, which published their *Handbook for Product Social Impact Assessment 3.0* (Fontes, 2016). This report makes a valuable contribution with the review of 19 comparable global initiatives in its Appendix 9 (including GRI,

ISO 26000, OECD Guidelines), mapping the social impacts and illustrating the level of consensus on most of the topics categorized under the same five stakeholder groups (see Fontes, 2016, pp. 127–133). However, it also implicitly makes an interest-biased choice in shortlisting, thus reducing the methods they propose to only three of the five stakeholder categories (workers, consumers and communities), not elaborating the categories of value-chain 'actors' and 'society', only justified as allowing more focus and presenting it as an initial shortlist (Fontes, 2016, pp. 28, 127).

Further evidence for a rough consensus in the field of 'people'-related impacts can be found in two comprehensive reviews of the state-of-the-art in the field of voluntary sustainability standards, by the International Institute of Sustainable Development (IISD) and by WTO-ITC. The vastly growing number of product-oriented standards (see for a discussion Vermeulen, 2015) have specified requirements for many categories of internationally traded products. These requirements have been determined in open stakeholder processes. The IISD and WTO-ITC review reports provide a good overview of which issues are seen as being relevant for sustainable products. In these reports a bottom-up process of aggregation resulted in a categorization which is described above as the *impact categories* approach – using eight categories: human rights; labour rights; gender; health and safety; employment conditions; employment benefits; community involvement; and humane treatment of animals (Potts et al., 2014, p. 69).

The second knowledge hub in this field, the WTO-International Trade Centre, in describing voluntary sustainability standards in the social dimension, distinguishes three main categories: social aspects, management aspects and ethical aspects (ITC, 2016, 2015; ITC and EUI, 2016), which however again cover the same issues as the approaches discussed above, while the category 'management aspects' describes the means rather than the intended end-outcome (in terms of applying management system practices: plan-do-check-act activities, such as having proper chemicals storage facilities and warnings, and anti-erosion plans, etc.).

A third community of practice addressing (in addition to environmental issues also) the social and societal issues are the organizations that provide the current global guidelines for corporate sustainability and reporting about it: ISO 26000 and GRI:G4. In these cases, the focal point is not the product but the organization, which results in a mixture of end-outcome-oriented metrics and throughput and output metrics. It also includes an explicit life cycle perspective. Both guidelines do use different categorizations, but also provide guidance in how these relate to each other (ISO and GRI, 2014). If we focus on the end-outcomes, we see the same categories as applied in the sLCA and voluntary standards community. This like-mindedness is the strongest on the issues concerning *workers*. For the *community* stakeholder group, the ISO 26000 and GRI:G4 include more detail than the LCA and the product standard communities, also looking at rights of communities not directly working for companies, and issues like protecting cultural heritage and informal property rights. For the consumer, it also includes protection against misleading marketing.

These guidelines also more extensively address issues related to the macro-economic institutions that are essential for creating fair and equitable development. They include anti-corruption, fair competition, fair value-chain contracting, and responsible political involvement.

There are still a few key elements of the *theory of political transitions* (Part 4.5) that these three communities have hardly adopted, but that have been increasingly addressed in the last few years: the crucial quest for fair taxation systems and reduction of inequality. This translates to tax evasion and tax avoidance as corporate behaviours, which deprives developing countries from substantial incomes, which are needed for their development (Hollingshead, 2010; Makunike, 2015; Verstappen et al., 2016). The issue of inequality is also only sometimes addressed in measurements of corporate or product sustainability, but practical methods have recently been proposed (Croes and Vermeulen, 2016).

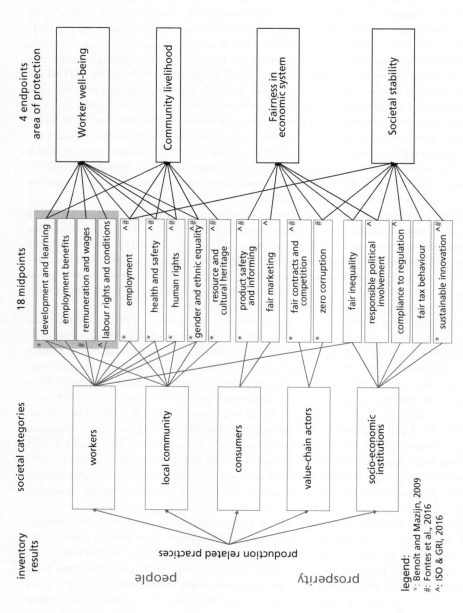

Figure 4.6 Combining global initiatives for societal impact characterization in a societal category – activity midpoint–endpoint frameworks

Sources: Benoît and Mazijn (2009, pp. 45, 49); Fontes (2016, pp. 29, 127–133); ISO and GRI (2014)

If we now combine the approaches discussed in this section, taking the strong elements of the various approaches, we can map the societal pathways in a way that enables them to be integrated with the commonly accepted approach for the 'planet' element. Figure 4.6 combines the 'people' element, addressing the individuals and their communities directly related to value-chain activities (stakeholder groups workers, communities and consumers), and the 'prosperity' element relates to the macro-economic institutions that are essential for creating fair development, such as the transactional institutions in value-chain exchanges and corporate activity related to political and economic institutions at the macro-societal level.

4.8 Synthesizing and reconnecting to the SDGs

Every time we review specific subfields in the academic study and communities of practice of sustainable development, we may be tempted to dive deeper and deeper with further detailing. Working in this very complex field (from any of the many possible positions in relation to the full (value-chain) production and consumption system), when we choose to narrow down to what may seem a feasible way forward, we tend to reduce our scope and build in biases (like the example of the Roundtable for Product Social Metrics discussed above). This understandable tendency partly accounts for the alleged vagueness of the concept of sustainable development, which I addressed in the introduction. For the purpose of this chapter I focus on the common ground and attempt to strengthen the argument that in general we know what we are looking for and that this is actually validated by high-level UN decision-making.

Following the argument in this chapter,

- We need to build indicators and index systems based on a clear guiding vision and key elements.
- There is a clear systemic vision of sustainable development as the twin SD-agenda of integral ecological and societal fairness.
- This can be described as PPP with prosperity as the third P, explicitly separating profits of firms as internalities from the externalities addressed in this twin SD-agenda.
- The goal setting should apply the reasoning of logic models, clarifying the logic causal pathways from inputs, policy outputs via intermediate outcomes to the end-outcomes.
- This is applied in the field of environmental impacts and can also very well be applied in the field of societal impacts.
- And thus, this allows us to present the twin SD-agenda as addressing the planet, people and prosperity issues in terms of end-outcomes, or as it is called in the (s)LC(S)A community: as the intended 'areas of protection'.
- But in the area of 'prosperity' a stronger theoretical foundation is still required.

This line of reasoning can strengthen both the governance agenda and the (academic) impact assessment practices. For this we need to have a closer look at the 17 SDGs, politically validated in the UN General Assembly on September 25, 2015 (General Assembly UN, 2015). These 17 goals[8] are formulated in very different forms and further detailed in 169 sub-goals, with between five and 19 sub-goals per SDG (a detailed explanation is available in Osborn et al., 2015). Figure 4.7 shows our analysis of these sub-goals in terms of the logic model discussed in Part 4.3 and Table 4.2. We see that only 25% of these goals have the nature of a 'end-outcome' goal, formulated in terms of a reduced impact, or in other words: as an achieved level of either planetary or societal well-being. Most of the sub-goals (39%) are formulated as policy outputs (plans, projects, regulations), and as policymaking (inputs or throughputs) (15%). A small part (12%) is formulated as intermediate outcome (behaviour response of target groups). Others

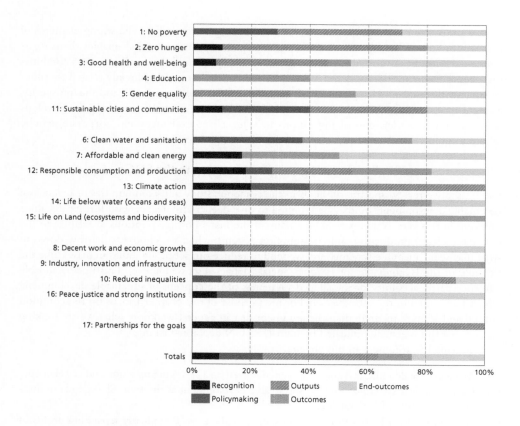

Figure 4.7 17 SDGs characterized as steps in the logic model (for more details see Appendix 4.1)

stress in a comparable analysis that the SDGs focus mostly on government roles, ignoring the role of businesses and other actors (Spangenberg, 2016).

But regardless of the weakness in this political result of 17 SDGs in clarifying pathways of creating the necessary end-outcomes, they turn out to be very valuable, as they are far more inclusive in describing the twin SD-agenda of integral ecological and societal fairness. The SDGs are very explicit, especially in the area of socio-economic institutions and the endpoint of fairness in the economic system and societal stability: such as SDG 8.5 (achieve full and decent employment by 2030); SDG 10.1 (income growth of the bottom 40% of the population at a rate higher than the national average); SDG 16.4 (significantly reduce illicit financial and arms flows, strengthen recovery and return of stolen assets) and SDG 16.5 (substantially reduce corruption and bribery). These 'prosperity' goals have not yet properly found their way into the sustainability assessment practices of products and companies, which I discussed in Parts 4.5 to 4.7.

As a result of the extensive literature review in this chapter, aiming at finding common ground, which is also validated by the various synthesizing activities in global communities of practice, I suggest an integrated representation of the rough consensus on the key components of the concept of sustainable development as the intended end-outcomes.

Figure 4.8 combines the results of Parts 4.5 to 4.7 and uses the logic model approach to display the main pathways, while avoiding the abundance of detailing that most communities of practice tend to present, especially when they make the steps from goal formulation (which should be in terms of end-outcomes) towards indicators for measurement of progress. The goals are to be the two final areas of protection, which are well agreed upon: planetary and human well-being. The six endpoints also each have their own strong foundations in various academic fields, even though they are often not yet sufficiently connected.

Further detailing the 9+18 midpoints is the actual minefield. We have seen that both the academic community and the communities of practices have made strong efforts to come to a widely shared view on various parts of this. The presentation in Figure 4.8 intends to balance the elements of PPP in a way that respects the twin SD-agenda of integral ecological and societal fairness.

With this argumentation, I stress the need to describe sustainable development as the intended end-outcome and not to mix up SD indicators with parameters describing means or policy inputs, throughputs and outputs. This is one of the sources of confusion about the concept.

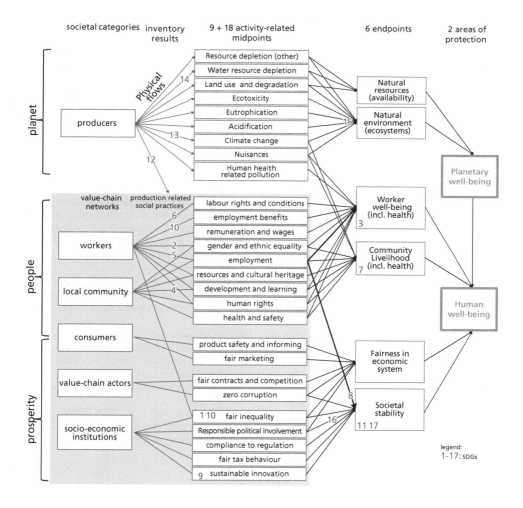

Figure 4.8 Integrating the rough consensus in global scholarly practices of sustainability assessment and the 17 United Nations Sustainable Development Goals in a logic model representing the dual SD-agenda. Legend: 1–17 = SDGs.

A second source of confusion is the incorrect and obscuring use of all kinds of economic parameters, and using profit, production costs and investment costs as data in assessing the level of sustainability. Instead I stressed and elaborated the use of 'prosperity' as the third element of the triple P, referring to macro-economic system elements as key pathways. This is also better in line with the UN SDGs. The micro-economic parameters can be used to assess the efficiency and feasibility of improvement options, but in Part 4.5 we saw that in many cases the numerator and the divisor in this equation is being mixed up, using the 'total life cycle costs' in the place of 'prosperity'.

With this extensive review, the concept of sustainable development has been recalibrated as aiming for the *'planet, people, prosperity'* triple-P, as shown in the Rubik's cube (Figure 4.1) instead of the obscuring triple bottom line (TBL). The 'time' and 'place' dimension were not discussed in detail, but 'place' refers to applying the full value-chain system approach, while the 'time' dimension refers to translating the long-term challenges for each of the triple-P issues as input for defining the planetary boundaries, which serve as reference points for outcome evaluations. In this way the 'time' dimension addresses to most clear point of consensus on the concept: that of intergenerational justice.

Our joint challenge as assessment and indicator communities is to link our diverse practices in further detailing the parameters and maintaining the suggested focus on the common ground presented here. This needs to enable application in the many decision-making contexts on any human activity in such a way that it acknowledges the full spectrum of potential impacts on the three issues domains, and avoids successes for some issues at the expense of increased impacts for other issues and at other places, while simultaneously respecting the needs of future generations.

Notes

1 See for an overview www.iisd.org/measure/compendium/
2 It would be interesting to also include a review of efforts framed as 'performance measurement' or 'key performance indicators', but due to limitations of space in this chapter I will do so elsewhere.
3 As a clear example, in the report presented to the UN General Assembly about the preparation for the SDGs it was stated: "moving towards a green economy in the context of sustainable development and poverty eradication is as much about structural change in the institutions governing economies at different levels as about technological change" (Preparatory Committee for the United Nations Conference on Sustainable Development, 2010, p. 2).
4 Remarkably this is not recognized at the level of *national* or *regional projects* or *country* comparisons. In those fields of study the environmental aspects are often still subdivided as the receiving components of the earth's system: air, water, soil, etc., as indicated in Part 4.1. In this chapter I focus on production-related approaches.
5 Kloepffer gives a remarkable justification for this, clarifying my point here: "to sum up, LCC is a useful complement to LCA (and SLCA), since sustainable products should be profitable and not unreasonably expensive, otherwise they will not be accepted in the market" (Kloepffer, 2008, p. 91). Thus it is not about the SD end-outcomes, but about the direct customer/consumer interest.
6 I have also added the categories for the planet issues used in the community of voluntary sustainability standards, which will be discussed in Part 4.7.
7 A recent example of such a simplified aggregation is to be found in (Sala et al., 2015, p. 56).
8 When clarifying the concept of sustainable development as intended end-outcomes, we could better talk in terms of only 16 SDGs, as SDG 17 only refers to collaborative policy activities.

References

Acemoglu, D., Gallego, F.A., and Robinson, J.A., 2014. Institutions, Human Capital, and Development. *Annual Review of Economics* 6, 875–912. doi:10.1146/annurev-economics-080213–041119
Acemoglu, D., Johnson, S., and Robinson, J.A., 2000. The Colonial Origins of Comparative Development: An Empirical Investigation. *American Economic Review* 91, 1369–1401.

Acemoglu, D. and Robinson, J.A., 2001. A Theory of Political Transitions. *American Economic Review* 91, 938–963. doi:10.1257/aer.91.4.938

Acemoglu, D. and Robinson, J.A., 2013. *Why Nations Fail – The Origins of Power, Prosperity and Poverty*, 1st paperback ed. Profile Books Ltd, London.

Barkemeyer, R., Holt, D., Preuss, L., and Tsang, S., 2014. What Happened to the "Development" in Sustainable Development? Business Guidelines Two Decades after Brundtland. *Sustainable Development* 22, 15–32. doi:10.1002/sd.521

Bebbington, A., 1999. Capitals and Capabilities: A Framework for Analyzing Peasant Viability, Rural Livelihoods and Poverty. *World Development* 27, 2021–2044. doi:10.1016/S0305–0750X(99)00104–00107

Bell, S., 2012. DPSIR = A Problem Structuring Method? An Exploration from the "imagine" Approach. *European Journal of Operational Research*. Elsevier B.V., 222(2), 350–360. doi: 10.1016/j.ejor.2012.04.029

Bell, S. and Morse, S., 2001. Breaking through the Glass Ceiling: Who Really Cares about Sustainability Indicators? *Local Environment* 6, 291–309. doi:10.1080/1354983012007328

Bell, S. and Morse, S., 2005. Holism and Understanding Sustainability. *Systemic Practice and Action Research* 18, 409–426. doi:10.1007/s11213-005-7171-9

Bell, S. and Morse, S., 2007. Problem Structuring Methods: Theorizing the Benefits of Deconstructing Sustainable Development Projects. *Journal of Operational Research Society* 58, 576–587. doi:10.1057/palgrave.jors.2602311

Bell, S. and Morse, S., 2008. *Sustainability Indicators: Measuring the Immeasurable?* Earthscan, London.

Benoît, C. and Mazijn, B., 2009. *Guidelines for Social Life Cycle Assessment of Products*. UNEP/SETAC, Paris.

Benoît, C., Norris, G.A., Valdivia, S., Ciroth, A., Moberg, A., Bos, U., Prakash, S., Ugaya, C., and Beck, T., 2010. The Guidelines for Social Life Cycle Assessment of Products: Just in Time! *International Journal of Life Cycle Assessment* 15, 156–163. doi:10.1007/s11367-009-0147-8

Benoît, C. and Vickery-Niederman, G., 2011. Social Sustainability Assessment Literature Review. *Sustainablility Consortium White Paper* 1–34.

Benoît-Norris, C., Vickery-Niederman, G., Valdivia, S., Franze, J., Traverso, M., Ciroth, A., and Mazijn, B., 2011. Introducing the UNEP/SETAC Methodological Sheets for Subcategories of Social LCA. *International Journal of Life Cycle Assessment* 16, 682–690. doi:10.1007/s11367–11011–10301-y

Biddle, J.C. and Koontz, T.M., 2014. Goal Specificity: A Proxy Measure for Improvements in Environmental Outcomes in Collaborative Governance. *Journal of Environmental Management* 145, 268–276. doi:10.1016/j.jenvman.2014.06.029

Böhringer, C. and Jochem, P.E.P., 2007. Measuring the Immeasurable – A Survey of Sustainability Indices. *Ecological Economics*, 63(1), 1–8. doi: 10.1016/j.ecolecon.2007.03.008

Bolis, I., Morioka, S.N., and Sznelwar, L.I., 2014. When Sustainable Development Risks Losing Its Meaning: Delimiting the Concept with a Comprehensive Literature Review and a Conceptual Model. *Journal of Cleaner Production* 83, 7–20. doi:10.1016/j.jclepro.2014.06.041

Boulanger, P.-M., 2008. Sustainable development indicators: a scientific challenge, a democratic issue. *Sapiens*, 1(September), 44–59. doi: 10.5194/sapiens-1-59-2008

Bradley Guy, G. and Kibert, C.J., 1998. Developing Indicators of Sustainability: US Experience. *Building Research and Information Journal* 26, 39–45. doi:10.1080/096132198370092

Cairney, P. and Heikkila, T., 2014. A Comparison of Theories of the Policy Process, in: *Theories of the Policy Process*. pp. 363–389.

Callicott, J.B., 2005. Animal Liberation and Environmental Ethics: Back Together Again, in: *Environmental Philosophy: From Animal Rights to Radical Ecology*. pp. 130–138.

Chertow, M.R., 2000. The IPAT Equation and Its Variants. *Journal of Industrial Ecology* 4, 13–29. doi:10.1162/10881980052541927

Christen, M. and Schmidt, S., 2012. A Formal Framework for Conceptions of Sustainability – a Theoretical Contribution to the Discourse in Sustainable Development. *Sustainablility Development* 20, 400–410. doi:10.1002/sd.518

Ciroth, A. and Franze, J., 2011. *LCA of an Ecolabeled Notebook: Consideration of Social and Environmental Impacts along the Entire Life Cycle*. GreenDelta TC GmbH, Berlin.

Clausen, A.W., 1982. Sustainable Development : The Global Imperative. *Environmentalist* 2, 23–28.

Cobbinah, P.B., Erdiaw-Kwasie, M.O., and Amoateng, P., 2015. Rethinking Sustainable Development within the Framework of Poverty and Urbanisation in Developing Countries. *Environmental Development* 13, 18–32. doi:10.1016/j.envdev.2014.11.001

Cole, R.J. and Sterner, E., 2000. Reconciling Theory and Practice of Life-Cycle Costing. *Building Research and Information Journal* 28, 368–375. doi:10.1080/096132100418519

Cooksy, L.J., Gill, P., and Kelly, P.A., 2001. The Program Logic Model as an Integrative Framework for a Multimethod Evaluation. *Evaluation and Program Planning* 24, 119–128. doi:10.1016/S0149-7189(01)00003-00009

Croes, P.R. and Vermeulen, W.J.V., 2016. In Search of Income Reference Points for SLCA Using a Country Level Sustainability Benchmark (part 1): Fair Inequality: A Contribution to the Oiconomy Project. *International Journal of Life Cycle Assessment* doi:10.1007/s11367-015-1018-0

Daily, G. and Ehrlich, P., 1992. Population, Sustainability, and Earth's Carrying Capacity, *Bioscience*, 42(10), 761–771. doi: 10.2307/1311995

Daly, H.E., 1990. Toward Some Operational Principles of Sustainable Development. *Ecological Economics* 2, 1–6. doi:10.1016/0921-8009(90)90010-R

Deloitte Netherlands, 2016. *Integrated Reporting Moving towards Maturity: Are We Truly Maximizing the Benefits of Integrated Reporting?* Amsterdam.

Dernbach, J.C. and Cheever, F., 2015. Sustainable Development and Its Discontents. *Transnational Environmental Law* 4, 247–287. doi:10.1017/S2047102515000163

DFID, 1999. *Sustainable Livelihoods Guidance Sheets*. UK Department for International Development, London.

Diesendorf, M., 2002. I=PAT or I=PBAT?, *Ecological Economics*, 42(1–2), p. 3. Available at: http://www.ncbi.nlm.nih.gov/pubmed/22067794.

Driessen, P.P.J., Dieperink, C., Laerhoven, F., Runhaar, H.A.C., and Vermeulen, W.J.V., 2012. Towards a Conceptual Framework for the Study of Shifts in Modes of Environmental Governance – Experiences from the Netherlands. *Environmental Policy of Government* 22, 143–160. doi:10.1002/eet.1580

Du Pisani, J.A., 2006. Sustainable Development – Historical Roots of the Concept. *Environmental Science* 3, 83–96. doi:10.1080/15693430600688831

Eisfeldt, F., 2016. *Introducing PSILCA 1.0 – A Comprehensive and Transparent Database for Social LCA*. GreenDelta TC GmbH, Berlin.

Ekins, P., Simon, S., Deutsch, L., Folke, C., and De Groot, R., 2003. A Framework for the Practical Application of the Concepts of Critical Natural Capital and Strong Sustainability. *Ecological Economy* 44, 165–185. doi:10.1016/S0921-8009(02)00272-00270

Elkington, J., 1998. Cannibals with Forks: The Triple Bottom Line of Sustainability. *New Society Publishers* 37–51. doi:10.1002/tqem.3310080106

Finkbeiner, M., Schau, E.M., Lehmann, A., and Traverso, M., 2010. Towards Life Cycle Sustainability Assessment. *Sustainability* 2, 3309–3322. doi:10.3390/su2103309

Fischer-Kowalski, M. and Amann, C., 2001. Beyond IPAT and Kuznet Curves: Globalization as a Vital Factor in Analyzing the Environmental Impact of Socio-Economic Metabolism. *Population Environment* 23, 7–47.

Fontes, J., 2016. *Handbook for Product Social Impact Assessment 3.0*. Roundtable for Product Social Metrics & PRé Consultants, Amersfoort.

Freeman, R.E., 1984. *Strategic Management: A Stakeholder Approach*. Pitman ser. ed. Cambridge University Press, Cambridge. doi:10.1017/CBO9781139192675

Garnett, S., Sayer, J. and Toit, J.T. Du, 2007. Improving the Effectiveness of Interventions to Balance Conservation and Development: A Conceptual Framework'. *Ecology and Society*, 12(1). Available at: https://works.bepress.com/johan%7B_%7Ddutoit/18/.

General Assembly UN, 2015. *Transforming Our World: The 2030 Agenda for Sustainable Development*. United Nations, New York.

Goedkoop, M., Heijungs, R., Huijbregts, M., Schryver, A. De, Struijs, J., Zelm, and R. van, 2009. *ReCiPe 2008. A Life Cycle Impact Assessment Method Which Comprises Harmonised Category Indicators at the Midpoint and the Endpoint Level*, Report 1: Characterization. Ministerie van VROM, Den Haag.

Goedkoop, M. and Spriensma, R., 2000. *The Eco-Indicator 99 – A Damage Oriented Method for Life Cycle Impact Assessment – Methodology Annex*. doi:10.1007/BF02979347

Goodland, R. and Ledec, G., 1987. Neoclassical Economics and Principles of Sustainable Development. *Ecology Modelling* 38, 19–46. doi:10.1016/0304-3800(87)90043-90043

Guinée, J.B., 2002. *Handbook for Life Cycle Assessment: Operational Guide to the ISO Standards, Dordrecht*. Kluwer, Dordrecht.

Guinée, J.B., Heijungs, R., Udo de Haes, H.A., and Huppes, G., 1993. Quantitative Life Cycle Assessment of Products. *Journal of Cleaner Products* 1, 81–91. doi:10.1016/0959-6526(93)90046-E

Hadden, J. and Seybert, L.A., 2016. What's in a Norm? Mapping the Norm Definition Process in the Debate on Sustainable Development. *Global Governance* 22, 249–268. doi:10.1007/s13398-014-0173-7.2

Halog, A. and Manik, Y., 2011. Advancing Integrated Systems Modelling Framework for Life Cycle Sustainability Assessment. *Sustainability*. doi:10.3390/su3020469

Hardi, P. and Zdan, T., 1997. Assessing Sustainable Development: Principles in Practice, Winnipeg, Manitoba: The International Institute for Sustainable Development. doi: 10.1002/msj.20251

Hardin, G., 1968. The Tragedy of the Commons. *Science* 162, 1243–1248. doi:10.1126/science.162.3859.1243

Hardin, G., 1974. Lifeboat Ethics: The Case Against Helping the Poor. *Psychology Today* 1–8, September.

Hauschild, M.Z., Goedkoop, M., Guinée, J., Heijungs, R., Huijbregts, M., Jolliet, O., Margni, M., De Schryver, A., Humbert, S., Laurent, A., Sala, S., and Pant, R., 2013. Identifying Best Existing Practice for Characterization Modeling in Life Cycle Impact Assessment. *International Journal of Life Cycle Assessment* 18, 683–697. doi:10.1007/s11367-012-0489-5

Heijungs, R., Settanni, E., and Guinée, J., 2013. Toward a Computational Structure for Life Cycle Sustainability Analysis: Unifying LCA and LCC. *International Journal of Life Cycle Assessment* 18, 1722–1733. doi:10.1007/s11367-012-0461-4

Hollingshead, A., 2010. *The Implied Tax Revnue Loss from Trade Mispricing.* Washington, DC.

Hopwood, B., Mellor, M., and O'Brien, G., 2005. Sustainable Development: Mapping Different Approaches. *Sustainability Development* 13, 38–52. doi:10.1002/sd.244

Huijbregts, M.A.J., Steinmann, Z.J.N., Elshout, P.M.F., Stam, G., Verones, F., Vieira, M., Zijp, M., Hollander, A., and van Zelm, R., 2017. ReCiPe2016: A Harmonised Life Cycle Impact Assessment Method at Midpoint and Endpoint Level. *International Journal of Life Cycle Assessment* 22, 138–147. doi:10.1007/s11367-11016-11246-y

ISO and GRI, 2014. *GRI G4 Guidelines and ISO 26000 : 2010 How to Use the GRI G4 Guidelines and ISO 26000 in Conjunction.* ISO, Geneva.

ITC, 2015. *The State of Sustainable Markets: Statistics and Emerging Trends 2015.* Internation Trade Centre, Geneva.

ITC, 2016. *Building Sustainable Supply Value Chains.* Geneva, International Trade Centre, Switzerland.

ITC, EUI, 2016. *Social and Environmental Standards: Contributing to more Sustainable Value Chains.* Geneva, International Trade Centre, Switzerland.

Itsubo, N. and Inaba, A., 2003. A New LCIA Method: LIME Has Been Completed. *International Journal of Life Cycle Assessment* 8, 305–305. doi:10.1007/BF02978923

Joint UNECE, Eurostat, Development, O.T.F. on M.S., 2013. *Framework and Suggested Indicators to Measure Sustainable Development.* United Nations Economic Commission for Europe (UNECE).

Jolliet, O., Margni, M., Charles, R., Humbert, S., Payet, J., Rebitzer, G., and Robenbaum, R.K., 2003. IMPACT 2002+: A New Life Cycle Impact Assessment Methodology. *International Journal of Life Cycle Assessment* 8, 324–330. doi:10.1007/BF02978505

Joung, C.B., Carrell, J., Sarkar, P., and Feng, S.C., 2013. Categorization of Indicators for Sustainable Manufacturing. *Ecological Indicators* 24, 148–157. doi:10.1016/j.ecolind.2012.05.030

Kaplan, S.A. and Garrett, K.E., 2005. The Use of Logic Models by Community-Based Initiatives. *Evaluation and Program Planning* 28, 167–172. doi:10.1016/j.evalprogplan.2004.09.002

Kee, P. and de Haan, M., 2007. Accounting for Sustainable Development Performance. Statistics Netherlands (CBS), Den Haag.

Kim, C., 2010. Environmental Performance Index Preliminary Results. *Law & Policy* (January), 1–73.

Klöpffer, W., 1997. Life Cycle Assessment: From the Beginning to the Current State. *Environmental Science and Pollution Research International* 4, 223–228. doi:10.1007/BF02986351

Kloepffer, W., 2008. Life Cycle Sustainability Assessment of Products (with Comments by Helias A. Udo de Haes, p. 95). *International Journal of Life Cycle Assessment* 13, 89–95. doi:http://dx.doi.org/10.1065/lca2008.02.376

Krajnc, D. and Glavič, P., 2005. A Model for Integrated Assessment of Sustainable Development. *Resources, Conservation and Recycling* 43, 189–208. doi:10.1016/j.resconrec.2004.06.002

Kruse, S.A., Flysjö, A., Kasperczyk, N., and Scholz, A.J., 2009. Socioeconomic Indicators as a Complement to Life Cycle Assessment – An Application to Salmon Production Systems. *International Journal of Life Cycle Assessment* 14, 8–18. doi:10.1007/s11367-11008-10040-x

Leadership Council of the Sustainable Development Solutions Network (SDSN), 2015. *Indicators and a Monitoring Framework for Sustainable Development Goals – Launching a Data Revolution for the SDGs.* New York.

Lehtonen, M., 2004. The Environmental-Social Interface of Sustainable Development: Capabilities, Social Capital, Institutions. *Ecological Economics* 49, 199–214. doi: 10.1016/j.ecolecon.2004.03.019

Lele, S., 1991. Sustainable Development: A Critical Review. *World Development* 19, 607–621.

Lovelock, J., 2003. Gaia: The Living Earth. *Nature* 426, 769–770. doi:10.1038/426769a

Makunike, C., 2015. *Towards Measuring Fairness of Tax Systems in Developing Countries.* Tax Justice Network Africa, The Hague.

Marchand, M., Aissani, L., Mallard, P., Béline, F., and Réveret, J.-P., 2013. Odour and Life Cycle Assessment (LCA) in Waste Management: A Local Assessment Proposal. *Waste and Biomass Valorization* 4, 607–617. doi:10.1007/s12649–12012–19173–z

Mayer, A.L., 2008. Strengths and Weaknesses of Common Sustainability Indices for Multidimensional Systems. *Environmental International* 34, 277–291. doi:10.1016/j.envint.2007.09.004

McCawley, P.F., 2002. *The Logic Model for Program Planning and Evaluation*. University of Idaho.

McLaughlin, J.A. and Jordan, G.B., 1999. Logic Models: A Tool for Telling Your Programs Performance Story. *Evaluation and Program Planning* 22, 65–72. doi:10.1016/S0149–7189(98)00042–00041

Meadows, D. et al. 1972. The Limits to Growth. New York: Universe Books.

Meadows, D.H., Randers, J., and Meadows, D.L., 2004. *Limits to Growth: The 30-Year Update*. Chelsea Green Publishing Company, White River Junction, VT.

Mebratu, D., 1998. Sustainability and Sustainable Development: Historical and Conceptual Review. *Environmental Impact Assessment Review* 18, 493–520. doi:10.1016/S0195–9255(98)00019–00015

Meester, S. De, Vorst, G. van der, Langenhoive, H. van, and Dewulf, J., 2013. Sustainability Assessment Methods and Tools, in: . . . and Processes from. . . . pp. 55–88.

Millar, A., Simeone, R.S., and Carnevale, J.T., 2001. Logic Models: A Systems Tool for Performance Management. *Evaluation and Program Planning* 24, 73–81. doi:10.1016/S0149–7189(00)00048–00043

Mitchell, R.K., Agle, B.R., and Wood, D.J., 1997. Toward a Theory of Stakeholder Identification and Salience: Defining the Principle of Who and What Really Counts. *Academy of Management Review* 22, 853–886. doi:10.5465/AMR.1997.9711022105

Morra Imas, L.G., and Rist, R.C., 2009. *The Road to Results: Designing and Conducting Effective Development Evaluations*. doi:10.1596/978-0-8213-7891-5

Mukherjee, I. and Howlett, M., 2015. Who Is a Stream? Epistemic Communities, Instrument Constituencies and Advocacy Coalitions in Public Policy-Making. *Politics and Government* 3, 65–75. doi:10.17645/pag.v3i2.290

Müller-Wenk, R., 2004. A Method to Include in LCA Road Traffic Noise and Its Health Effects. *International Journal of Life Cycle Assessment* 9, 76–85. doi:10.1007/BF02978566

Ness, B., Anderberg, S., and Olsson, L., 2010. Structuring Problems in Sustainability Science: The Multilevel DPSIR Framework. *Geoforum* 41, 479–488. doi:10.1016/j.geoforum.2009.12.005

Neugebauer, S., Forin, S., and Finkbeiner, M., 2016. From Life Cycle Costing to Economic Life Cycle Assessment – Introducing an Economic Impact Pathway. *Sustainability* 8, 23. doi:10.3390/su8050428

North, D.C., 1979. A Framework for Analyzing the State in Economic History. *Explorations in Economics History* 16, 249–259. doi:10.1016/0014–4983(79)90020–90022

North, D.C., 1989. Institutions and Economic Growth: An Historical Introduction. *World Development* 17, 1319–1332. doi:10.1016/0305–0750X(89)90075–90072

Ocampo, L.A., 2015. A Hierarchical Framework for Index Computation in Sustainable Manufacturing. *Advances in Production Engineering and Management* 10, 40–50. doi:10.14743/apem2015.1.191

OECD, 2003. *OECD Environmental Indicators: Development, Measurement and Use*. Paris. doi: 10.1016/j.infsof.2008.09.005

Omta, O., Trienekens, J., and Beer, G., 2001. Chain and Network Science. *Journal on Chain Network Sciences* 1, 77–85.

Ongel, A., 2016. Inclusion of Noise in Environmental Assessment of Road Transportation. *Environmental Modeling and Assessment* 21, 181–192. doi:10.1007/s10666–10015–19477–z

Orians, G.H. and Policansky, D., 2009. Scientific Bases of Macroenvironmental Indicators. *Annual Review of Environment and Resources* 34, 375–404. doi:10.1146/annurev.environ.020608.151439

Osborn, D., Cutter, A., and Ullah, F., 2015. Universal Sustainable Development Goals: Understanding the Transformational Challenge for Developed Countries. London: Stakeholder Forum

Parent, J., Cucuzzella, C., and Revéret, J.-P., 2010. Impact Assessment in SLCA: Sorting the sLCIA Methods According to Their Outcomes. *International Journal of Life Cycle Assessment* 15, 164–171. doi:10.1007/s11367-009-0146-9

Parent, J., Cucuzzella, C., and Revéret, J.-P., 2013. Revisiting the Role of LCA and SLCA in the Transition towards Sustainable Production and Consumption. *International Journal of Life Cycle Assessment* 18, 1642–1652. doi:10.1007/s11367-012-0485-9

Parris, T.M. and Kates, R.W., 2003. Characterizing and Measuring Sustainable Development. *Annual Review of Environment and Resources* 28, 559–586. doi:10.1146/annurev.energy.28.050302.105551

Pearce, D., 1988. Economics, Equity and Sustainable Development. *Futures* 1, 598–605.

Pennington, D.W., Potting, J., Finnveden, G., Lindeijer, E., Jolliet, O., Rydberg, T., and Rebitzer, G., 2004. Life Cycle Assessment Part 2: Current Impact Assessment Practice. *Environment International* 30, 721–739. doi:10.1016/j.envint.2003.12.009

Pezzoli, K., 1997. Sustainable Development: A Transdisciplinary Overview of the Literature. *Journal of Environmental Planning and Management* 40, 549–574. doi:10.1080/09640569711949

Pintér, L., Hardi, P., and Bartelmus, P., 2005. *Sustainable Development Indicators: Proposals for the Way forward, International Institute for Sustainable Development.* New York, USA.

Pope, J., Annandale, D., and Morrison-Saunders, A., 2004. Conceptualising Sustainability Assessment. *Environmental Impact Assessment Review* 24, 595–616. doi:10.1016/j.eiar.2004.03.001

Potts, J., Lynch, M., Wilkings, A., Huppe, G., Cunningham, M., Voora, V., Huppé, G., Cunningham, M., and Voora, V., 2014. *State of Sustainability Initiatives Review 2014 Standards and the Green Economy.* International Institute for Sustainable Development (IISD) and International Institute for Environment and Development (IIED), Winnipeg.

Preparatory Committee for the United Nations Conference on Sustainable Development, 2010. *Objective and Themes of the United Nations Conference on Sustainable Development Report of the Secretary-General.* United Nations, New York.

Pretty, J., 2008. Agricultural sustainability: concepts, principles and evidence. *Philosophical transactions of the Royal Society of London. Series B, Biological sciences* 363(July 2007), 447–465. doi: 10.1098/rstb.2007.2163

Rebitzer, G., Ekvall, T., Frischknecht, R., Hunkeler, D., Norris, G., Rydberg, T., Schmidt, W.P., Suh, S., Weidema, B.P., and Pennington, D.W., 2004. Life Cycle Assessment Part 1: Framework, Goal and Scope Definition, Inventory Analysis, and Applications. *Environmental International.* doi:10.1016/j.envint.2003.11.005

Redclift, M., 2005. Sustainable Development (1987–2005): An Oxymoron Comes of Age. *Sustainability Development* 13, 212–227. doi:10.1002/sd.281

Reitinger, C., Dumke, M., Barosevcic, M., and Hillerbrand, R., 2011. A Conceptual Framework for Impact Assessment within SLCA. *International Journal of Life Cycle Assessment* 16, 380–388. doi:10.1007/s11367-11011-10265-y

Robinson, J., 2004. Squaring the Circle? Some Thoughts on the Idea of Sustainable Development. *Ecological Economics* 48, 369–384. doi:10.1016/j.ecolecon.2003.10.017

Roca, J., 2002. The IPAT Formula and Its Limitations. *Ecological Economics* 42(1–2), 1–2. doi: 10.1016/S0921-8009(02)00110-6

Rockström, J., Steffen, W., Noone, K., Persson, Å., Chapin, F.S., Lambin, E., Lenton, T.M., Scheffer, M., Folke, C., Schellnhuber, H.J., Nykvist, B., de Wit, C.A., Hughes, T., van der Leeuw, S., Rodhe, H., Sörlin, S., Snyder, P.K., Costanza, R., Svedin, U., Falkenmark, M., Karlberg, L., Corell, R.W., Fabry, V.J., Hansen, J., Walker, B., Liverman, D., Richardson, K., Crutzen, P., Foley, J., Wit, C.A. De, Hughes, T., Leeuw, S. Van Der, Rodhe, H., Snyder, P.K., Costanza, R., Svedin, U., Falkenmark, M., Karlberg, L., Corell, R.W., Fabry, V.J., Hansen, J., Walker, B., Liverman, D., Richardson, K., Crutzen, P., Foley, J., 2009. Planetary Boundaries: Exploring the Safe Operating Space for Humanity. *Ecology and Society* 14, 472–475. doi:10.1038/461472a

Russo Garrido, S., Parent, J., Beaulieu, L., and Revéret, J.-P., 2016. A Literature Review of Type I SLCA – Making the Logic Underlying Methodological Choices Explicit. *International Journal of Life Cycle Assessment.* doi:10.1007/s11367-11016-11067-z

Sabatier, P.A. and Weible, C., 2014. *Theories of the Policy Process.*

Sala, S., Vasta, A., Mancini, L., Dewulf, J., and Rosenbaum, E., 2015. *Social Life Cycle Assessment – State of the Art and Challenges for Supporting Product Policies.* Luxemburg. doi:10.2788/253715

Sartori, S., Latrônico, F., and Campos, L.M.S., 2011. Sustainability and Sustainable Development: A Taxonomy in the Field of Literature. *Ambient Society* 17, 1–22. doi:10.1590/1809-44220003491

Schulze, P.C., 2002. I=PBAT. *Ecological Economics*, 40(2), 149–150. doi: 10.1016/S0921-8009(01)00249-X

Singh, R.K., Murty, H.R., Gupta, S.K., and Dikshit, A.K., 2009. An Overview of Sustainability Assessment Methodologies. *Ecological Indicators* 9, 189–212. doi:10.1016/j.ecolind.2008.05.011

Smeets, E. and Weterings, R., 1999. *Environmental Indicators : Typology and Overview, Technical Report.* Copenhagen.

Spangenberg, J.H., 2016. Hot Air or Comprehensive Progress? A Critical Assessment of the SDGs. *Sustainable Development.* doi:10.1002/sd.1657

Swarr, T.E., Hunkeler, D., Klopffer, W., Pesonen, H.-L., Ciroth, A., Brent, A.C., and Pagan, R., 2011a. Environmental Life Cycle Costing : A Code of Practice. *Society of Environmental Toxicology and Chemistry.*

Swarr, T.E., Hunkeler, D., Klöpffer, W., Pesonen, H.-L., Ciroth, A., Brent, A.C., and Pagan, R., 2011b. Environmental Life-cycle Costing: A Code of Practice. *International Journal of Life Cycle Assessment* 16, 389–391. doi:10.1007/s11367-011-0287-5

Tanguay, G.A., Rajaonson, J., Lefebvre, J.F., and Lanoie, P., 2010. Measuring the Sustainability of Cities: An Analysis of the Use of Local Indicators. *Ecological Indicators* 10, 407–418. doi:10.1016/j.ecolind.2009.07.013

Toffotetto, L., Bulle, C., Godin, J., Reid, C., and Deschênes, L., 2006. LUCAS – A New LCIA Method Used for a Canadian-Specific Context. *International Journal of Life Cycle Assessment* 12, 93–102. doi:10.1065/lca2005.12.242

Turner, J.H., 2010. *Theoretical Principles of Sociology, Volume 2 Microdynamics, Theoretical Principles of Sociology.* Springer, New York, Dordrecht, Heidelberg and London. doi:10.1007/978-1-4419-6221-8

Turner, J.H., 2012a. *Theoretical Principles of Sociology, Volume 1 Macrodynamics, Theoretical Principles of Sociology.* Springer, New York, Dordrecht, Heidelberg and London. doi:10.1007/978-1-4419-6221-8

Turner, J.H., 2012b. *Theoretical Principles of Sociology, Volume 3 Mesodynamics, Theoretical Principles of Sociology.* Springer, New York, Heidelberg, Dordrecht and London. doi:10.1007/978-1-4419-6221-8

Turner, J.H., 2014. *Theoretical Sociology: A Concise Introduction to Twelve Sociological Theories.* Sage Publications, Thousand Oaks, London and New Dehli.

Udo De Haes, H., Heijungs, R., Huppes, G., Van Der Voet, E., and Hettelingh, J.P., 2000. Full Mode and Attribution Mode in Environmental Analysis. *Journal of Industrial Ecology* 4, 45–56.

Udo de Haes, H.A., 1993. Applications of Life Cycle Assessment: Expectations, Drawbacks and Perspectives. *Journal of Cleaner Products* 1, 131–137. doi:10.1016/0959–6526(93)90002-S

United Nations, 2007. *Indicators of Sustainable Development: Guidelines and Methodologies.* New York.

Vermeulen, W.J.V., 2015. Self-Governance for Sustainable Global Supply Chains: Can It Deliver the Impacts Needed? *Business Strategy and Environment* 24, 73–85. doi:10.1002/bse.1804

Vermeulen, W.J.V., Bootsma, M.C., and Tijm, M., 2014. Higher Education Level Teaching of (Master's) Programmes in Sustainable Development: Analysis of Views on Prerequisites and Practices Based on a Worldwide Survey. *International Journal of Sustainable Development and World Ecology* 21, 430–448. doi:10.1080/13504509.2014.944956

Vermeulen, W.J.V. and Witjes, S., 2016. On Addressing the Dual and Embedded Nature of Business and the Route Towards Corporate Sustainability. *Journal of Cleaner Products* 112, 2822–2832. doi:10.1016/j.jclepro.2015.09.132

Verstappen, R., Akker, M. van den, and Kamp, L., 2016. *Tax Transparency Benchmark 2016.* Utrecht.

Viñuales, J.E., 2013. The Rise and Fall of Sustainable Development. *Review of European, Comparative and International Environmental Law* 22, 3–13. doi:10.1111/reel.12021

Waggoner, P.E. and Ausubel, J.H., 2002. A Framework for Sustainability Science: A Renovated IPAT Identity. *Proceedings of National Academy of Sciences of U.S.A.* 99, 7860–7865. doi:10.1073/pnas.122235999

White, M.A., 2013. Sustainability: I Know It When I See It. *Ecological Economics* 86, 213–217. doi:10.1016/j.ecolecon.2012.12.020

Witjes, S., 2017. *Leapfrogging through Retrospection: Ferreting out Sustainability Integration within Organisations.* Utrecht University, Utrecht.

World Commission on Environment and Development, 1987. *Our Common Future (The Brundtland Report).* doi:10.1080/07488008808408783

Worldbank, 1997. *Expanding the Measure of Wealth: Indicators of Environmentally Sustainable Development.* The World Bank, Washington, DC.

WTO-ITC, 2017. *Standardsmap.* URL: www.standardsmap.org (accessed 4.5.17).

York, R., Rosa, E.A., and Dietz, T., 2003. STIRPAT, IPAT and ImPACT: Analytic Tools for Unpacking the Driving Forces of Environmental Impacts. *Ecological Economics* 46, 351–365. doi:10.1016/S0921–8009(03)00188–00185

Zamagni, A., 2012. Life Cycle Sustainability Assessment. *International Journal of Life Cycle Assessment* 17, 373–376. doi:10.1007/s11367-012-0389-8

Appendix 4.1

CONTENT ANALYSIS OF UN SDGS ON ELEMENTS IN LOGIC MODEL ADDRESSED PER SUB-GOAL

SDG	Logic model element cf. Table 4.2 (# 1...x + a...d)	Recognition and activation				Stages in logic model				
		causes	states	knowledge	Governance response	INPUT	THROUGHPUT	OUTPUT	OUTCOME	END-OUTCOME
1 End poverty	5 + 2						1a–1b	1.3–1.4–1.5		1.1–1.2
2 End hunger and provide good food	5 + 3			2a				2.1–2.2–2.3–2.5–2b–2c	2.4	2.1–2.2
3 Health and well-being	9 + 4			3b				3.5–3.7–3.8–3a–3d	3c	3.1–3.2–3.3–3.4–3.6–3.9
4 Education	7 + 3								4.7–4a – 4b – 4c	4.1–4.2–4.3–4.4–4.5–4.6
5 Gender equality	6 + 3							5a–5b–5c	5.4–5.6	5.1–5.2–5.3–5.7
6 Water and sanitation	6 + 2					6b	6.5–6a		6.3–6.4–6.6	6.1–6.2
7 Affordable and clean energy	3 + 2			7a					7a – 7b	7.1–7.2–7.3
8 Growth and employment	10 + 2			8a		8.1		8.3–8.8–8.9–8b		8.1–8.2–8.4–8.5–8.6–8.7
9 Infrastructure and innovation	5 + 3			9.5–9b				9.3–9.6–9c	9.1–9.2–9.4	
10 Reduce inequality	7 + 3					10.6		10.2–10.3–10.4–10.5–10.7–10a–10b–10c		10.1
11 Cities and settlements	7 + 3			11c			11.3–11.4–11a	11.1–11.2–11.7–11b		11.5–11.6

(Continued)

Appendix 4.1 (Continued)

SDG	Logic model element cf. Table 4.2 (# 1…x + a…d)	Recognition and activation				Stages in logic model				
		causes	states	knowledge	Governance response	INPUT	THROUGHPUT	OUTPUT	OUTCOME	END-OUTCOME
12 Consumption and production	8 + 3			12.8–12b		12a		12.1–12.7–12c	12.2–12.4–12.6	12.3–12.5
13 Climate change	3 + 2			13.3		13b		13.1–13.2–13a		
14 Oceans and seas	7 + 3			14a				14.2–14.3–14.4 14.5–14.6–14b–14c	14.7	14.1–14.4
15 Ecosystems and biodiversity	9 + 3					15a –15b	15.9–15c	15.1–15.2– 15.3–15.4– 15.5–15.6–15. 7–15.8		
16 Peaceful and inclusive societies	10 + 2			16.1		16a	16.7–16.8	16.3–16.6–16b		16.1–16.2– 16.4–16.5– 16.9
17 Global partnership	19			17.6– 17.8– 17.18– 17.19		17.1– 17.9– 17.16– 17.17	17.13–17.14– 17.15	17.2–17.2– 17.3–17.4– 17.7–17.10– 17.11–17.12		
Totals	126 + 43 = 169	-	-	8 + 8 = 16	-	6 + 6 = 12	9 + 5 = 14	50 + 17 = 67	14 + 6 = 20	43
%[1]				9,3%		6,9%	8,1%	38,9%	11,6%	25%

[1] = Column total divided by 172 as some goals are mentioned in 2 columns

5

FROM CRISES AND GURUS TO SCIENCE AND METRICS

Yale's Environmental Performance Index and the rise of data-driven policymaking

Daniel C. Esty and John W. Emerson

Minimata and severe neurological disorders from mercury poisoning. *Silent Spring* and the loss of songbirds due to DDT exposure. Fire on Cleveland's Cuyahoga River providing indisputable evidence of severe water pollution. Love Canal and cancer clusters tied to abandoned toxic waste sites. The *Exxon Valdez* oil spill and a vast swath of contamination that killed thousands of fish and birds and wreaked havoc on the ocean habitat in Alaska's Prince William Sound. These and other crises around the world drew attention to environmental problems and motivated new efforts on pollution control and land conservation in the 20th century.

The waves of emotion triggered by vivid disasters helped launch a powerful environmental movement, led to the creation of hundreds of new non-governmental organizations (NGOs), built the careers of a phalanx of environmental advocates, and generated political momentum for action (Farber, 1992; Lazarus, 2013). But the laws and policies that emerged were not always grounded in thoughtful analysis and systematic attention to science and data (Esty, 2017). These high-profile events drove spending on pollution control, but the money did not always deliver improved environmental results. As the 20th century drew to a close, the pace of pollution control and conservation progress actually slowed in many places as a result of a backlash against legal frameworks and programs that overpromised and under-delivered, proved to be disconnected from the facts on the ground, or failed to balance economic costs and environmental benefits (Glicksman, 2010).

In the wake of this backlash and propelled by the data analytics revolution that had begun to transform many dimensions of modern life, a push emerged for greater analytic rigor and empirical foundations for decision-making in the environmental arena (Breggin & Amsalem, 2014; Charnley & Elliot, 2002; Esty, 2004). But the existing data sources on pollution and natural resource were limited. Oftentimes, the metrics available were neither methodologically rigorous nor consistent across jurisdictions or problems (Emerson et al., 2010). Furthermore, the perception of the environmental realm as a "soft" field, dominated by emotion rather than facts, slowed progress toward more data-driven policymaking (Esty & Porter, 2000).

At the same time, a new generation of environmental leaders began to emerge. They were not steeped in the crisis-fueled advocacy of the 1960s and '70s, but rather motivated to deliver better environmental outcomes based on firmer analytic foundations. This group fundamentally appreciated the inescapable reality of tradeoffs and believed that the use of solid data and performance metrics could help to ensure that policy choices and programs delivered the maximum return in a world of tight budget constraints (see the Boulanger's Chapter 8 in this volume; Revesz & Livermore, 2008). Chapter 2 by Pintér et al. in this volume chronicles the rise of sustainability-oriented indicators in the 1990s, highlighting a number of the individuals and institutions pushing for better measures of societal progress and an invigorated set of socio-economic and environmental metrics. Likewise, Chapter 23 reviews how the United Nations embraced the challenge of developing indicators to track performance on sustainability targets.

In this spirit, at the World Economic Forum in 1999, a dozen "global leaders for tomorrow" from ten different countries convened as an Environment Task Force to find concrete ways to push the presidents, prime ministers, and corporate leaders in Davos to pay more attention to the "sustainability" of the planet. The group, led by Canadian businesswoman Kim Samuel, set out to produce an Environmental Sustainability Index (ESI) that would rank countries on their performance in meeting the spectrum of challenges pertaining to environmental public health and ecosystem vitality (Esty, 2001). Just as the World Economic Forum's (WEF) competitiveness rankings had helped to sharpen the focus of political and corporate leaders on the underpinnings of sustained economic growth and business success in the marketplace, the Global Leaders for Tomorrow Environment Task Force reasoned that a similar scorecard, which would highlight various elements of national performance related to environmental progress, might spur attention to sustainability issues. Dan Esty was thus commissioned to organize a research team to develop a pilot Environmental Sustainability Index with intellectual and financial support from the WEF's Global Leaders for Tomorrow community across the world.

The team Esty initially assembled included several colleagues at Yale University (including Jay Emerson) and others from the Center for International Earth Science Information Network (CIESIN) at Columbia University. With a goal of developing a sustainability-oriented counterpart to the WEF competitiveness ranking using the same basic data strategy, the researchers focused on assembling quantitative gauges of performance – called *metrics* or *indicators* – for an array of critical environmental policy issues that could then be aggregated into a composite index.

This approach required addressing a number of methodological issues. First, given the commitment to a *multidimensional* scorecard, relevant performance indicators needed to be identified. With the aim of providing an overarching signal about national outcomes on the range of sustainability challenges facing countries, the ESI research team started with a review of the scientific literature, developing a list of the critical issues that national governments were being asked to address. The Yale and Columbia scholars scoured journals across the spectrum of ecological sciences and environmental policy. After developing a draft list of concerns, they convened a workshop at Yale with environmental policy experts from across the world to review the issues that were candidates for inclusion in the index. The initial list was quite broad, and it expanded further as the experts added new topics that they judged to be critical policy elements of any government's sustainability agenda.

Second, the research team began assembling all available data sets to track performance on the specified issues of importance. Given that the proposed index centered on nation-state performance, data were required at the national level with coverage across a large number of countries. With this mandate, the ESI team pursued data from a wide variety of sources: international organizations, including the World Bank, the World Health Organization, and the Food and Agriculture Organization; university-based research centers; and environment-oriented think tanks, such as the World Resources Institute (WRI). The environmental metrics "dashboard" assembled during the late 1980s by a team at the Organization for Economic Cooperation and Development proved to be especially useful as a guide to the indicators available across the world (OECD, 1987; see also Jesinghaus's Chapter 26 in this volume).

The third step of the process involved review of the data sets that the expert group had suggested might serve as potential performance indicators for each issue identified in the literature review. The team assessed each potential metric for *suitability* – how closely the data tracked the issue – as well as *reliability* and methodological rigor (Levy, 2002). Where no data set was available for a particular issue, the group sought to find a proxy metric that would provide some indication of national performance on the concern in question. Potential proxy metrics were subject to special scrutiny for their suitability and reliability. For some issues, metrics were unavailable, judged to be insufficiently reliable, or lacked adequate country coverage. Because the goal was worldwide benchmarking, the research team required data for at least 80–100 nations in any data set. Unfortunately, many metrics fell short of this standard. In those instances, the issue dropped out of the proposed index and moved onto a list of topics to be highlighted for their lack of data and metrics (Esty et al., 2000).

After looking worldwide for suitable metrics, there remained a surprisingly large number of critical issues that had no broad-based quantitative data available on a methodologically consistent basis across a sufficient number of countries. Even very fundamental environmental policy challenges – such as solid waste disposal, toxic waste management, surface water quality and quantity, and wetlands protection – lacked data that were both standardized and covered a reasonably large number of nations. Highlighting these data gaps has been a regular theme of the project ever since its first iteration in 2000 (Esty et al., 2000; Esty et al., 2002; Esty et al., 2005; Esty et al., 2006; Esty et al., 2008; Emerson et al., 2010; Emerson et al., 2012; Hsu et al., 2014; Hsu et al., 2016; Wendling et al., 2018). While the ESI and now the Environmental Performance Index (EPI) have continued to highlight data deficiencies, many gaps persist to the present day. The lack of progress in developing appropriate metrics for so many critical issues represents a source of ongoing distress to the research team, especially as the world has placed new emphasis on quantitative metrics as a guide to progress on the global policy commitments reflected in the 2015 Sustainable Development Goals (UN General Assembly, 2015).

Creating the index

Moving from a wide-ranging set of indicators to a single score for each country required further methodological work. The team built the aggregation model around a "basket of baskets" approach, which entailed creating an Environmental Sustainability Index score from 64 "variables" (data sets or performance measures) combined into 21 "factors" (each representing a core issue of concern), which were then consolidated into five "components": Environmental Systems, Stresses and Risks, Human Vulnerability, Social and Institutional Capacity, and Global Stewardship. These five components were then averaged to produce the overall ESI score.

In January 2000, a Pilot Environmental Sustainability Index was introduced at the World Economic Forum annual meeting in Davos. The report accompanying the Pilot ESI offered three primary conclusions (Esty et al., 2000):

1. It would be "possible to construct a single index measuring Environmental Sustainability, generating results that appear to be both plausible and useful".

2. By comparing the ESI score with economic competitiveness rankings, light might be shed on the "degree to which economic and environmental objectives are in conflict".

3. There was "considerable work to be done" to move the Pilot Index forward and that "serious limitations in the available data relevant to environmental sustainability drastically limit the ability of the world community to monitor the most basic pollution and natural resource trends".

Nearly two decades later, these conclusions remain valid. Much work has been done to refine the framework first introduced in 2000. Indeed, one of the hallmarks of this effort has been its openness about the limitations of the data and the need for improved methodologies and analytic tools. With a firm commitment to complete data transparency, the ESI team has published all of its underlying data online and has benefitted from critique and commentary from many sources. Indeed, the 2002 and 2005 ESI Reports highlight a number of refinements to the analysis that emerged from the ensuing academic and policy discussions (Esty et al., 2002; Esty et al., 2005).

Emerging policy conclusions

The ESI modeling revealed several important empirical results (Esty et al., 2000; Esty et al., 2002; Levy, 2002; Esty et al., 2005). Most notably, it became clear that the sustainability challenge had two quite distinct dimensions – one associated with the environmental infrastructure obstacles facing developing nations and the other driven by the natural resource consumption and pollution impacts that plague industrialized nations. As the data team unpacked the overarching ESI score and looked at the component metrics, the statistical evidence confirmed that developed nations outperformed the developing world in terms of access to sanitation and safe drinking water. Indeed, on issues that relate to the capacity of societies to make investments in environmental systems (waste management, drinking water, etc.), the correlation with per capita income proved to be very high (Esty et al., 2000; Levy, 2002; Esty et al., 2002; Esty et al., 2005; Esty et al., 2006; Esty et al., 2008; Emerson et al., 2010; Emerson et al., 2012; Hsu et al., 2014; Hsu et al., 2016; Wendling et al., 2018). On the other hand, industrialized nations suffer more when it comes to pollution impacts, although the most developed nations (and those with greater access to clean energy) often will be able to bring down their levels of emissions (Esty et al., 2002; Esty et al., 2005; Esty et al., 2006; Esty et al., 2008; Emerson et al., 2010; Emerson et al., 2012; Wendling et al., 2018).

2002 reconceptualization

The question of the appropriate scope of "sustainability" remained a topic under discussion over the first several iterations of the ESI. In 2002, after considerable feedback from a range of sources, including a number of environment ministries, the team decided to explore reframing the analysis as an Environmental Performance Index. This alternative structure promised to tighten the conceptual frame in several ways. First, in shifting from a broad sustainability structure to *environmental performance*, the new EPI focused more sharply on the issues that an environment ministry would be expected to manage – tracking pollution control and natural resource management challenges rather than wider-ranging social or governance concerns. Second, the EPI dropped metrics that simply gauged underlying societal endowments, such as water availability, to hone in on environmental outcomes over which governments had some control. This emphasis made the EPI more useful as a benchmarking tool for environment ministries but less of a *sustainability* index.

Likewise, this tighter frame – and the elimination of indicators that tracked broader social dimensions of sustainability – made the index more useful to environmental policymakers and the broader community of NGOs, business and industry leaders, legislators, and media who participate in the conversation about environmental results and policy successes. The research team recognized, of course, that the more extensive set of sustainability issues – including education, healthcare, and labor rights – would be relevant in other contexts. But the project leaders concluded that, with a core focus on tracking performance on environmental sustainability, "less is more". Finally, by sharpening the focus on "outcome" measures of performance, the recast

EPI more cleanly separates the dependent from independent variables, thus providing a better framework for analyzing the "drivers" of good environmental results, such as good governance.

With the support of several dozen members of the World Economic Forum's Global Leaders for Tomorrow Environmental Task Force, the Yale and Columbia researchers continued to refine the EPI and its underlying methodologies. In 2006, after several cycles in which both the original ESI and the new EPI were produced and feedback from across the world reviewed, the Yale and Columbia teams concluded that the tighter focus of the EPI methodology provided a more analytically rigorous framework for analysis and a more useful benchmarking tool for policymakers. Thus, as demonstrated in Figure 5.1, the EPI became the framework of choice with its focus on two broad objectives – environmental health and ecosystem vitality – broken out into ten policy categories: air quality, water & sanitation, heavy metals, biodiversity & habitat, forests, fisheries, climate & energy, air pollution, water resources, and agriculture. Each of the categories has one or more underlying indicators, meaning a total of two dozen metrics undergird the EPI score (Wendling et al., 2018).

With some minor refinements, including a ramped-up focus on climate change alongside sustainable energy, this framework has now been used for a decade. The most recent 2018 iteration of the EPI scores 180 nations from Switzerland at the top to Burundi at the bottom (Wendling et al., 2018). It provides not only a snapshot that gauges current performance on the issues being tracked, but also a backcasted score from approximately a decade ago that signals which nations are delivering improved results and which are deteriorating. In this regard, China has moved out of the bottom tier while India's performance has deteriorated.

Over the course of nine iterations and nearly two decades of work, the EPI team has refined the methodology for benchmarking environmental performance in several important ways. Most importantly, metrics need to be carefully normalized so that scores provide an accurate comparative picture – without regard to a nation's size, population, density, or other factors that might skew the picture if raw numbers were used. In addition, the scores developed for each issue category reflect a "distance from target" methodology. Thus, for each indicator, the EPI team has identified a relevant target drawn from international agreements, a consensus of national standards, or the policy literature. Where no such target proved to be available, the team studied the distribution of actual performance metrics, setting the target at or near the high end of the outcomes being achieved. This "distance from target" approach allows the distribution of scores to highlight issues on which many countries are doing well (e.g., preventing deforestation) from ones where nearly the whole world is falling short (such as greenhouse gas emissions control) of critical policy targets (Rockstrom et al., 2009).

After the initial measurements and resulting scores for each sub-indicator and indicator of each country are assembled, a careful analysis is needed to identify possible outliers or suspicious values. Experience has taught the EPI team that anomalous results are often a function of faulty data reporting or entry errors – not truly off-the-charts performance. To further ensure that outlier metrics do not torque the aggregate results, the data team uses a combination of statistical transformations and trimming the tails of the distributions ("winsorizing"), which has the effect of reducing the possibility of distortion from anomalies. Each raw metric is then scaled to establish a negative polarity, meaning that low scores signal bad performance and high scores translate into good results. All these steps together transform the raw metrics into scores from 0–100 that can be easily understood, compared, and communicated. These metrics, or indicators, are then aggregated via the "basket of baskets" approach first to the level of the issue categories, then to broad policy objectives, and finally to the single EPI.

Metrics that have less than complete country coverage (with recently about 180 nations in the scorecard) are reviewed carefully to determine whether the gaps can be systematically filled

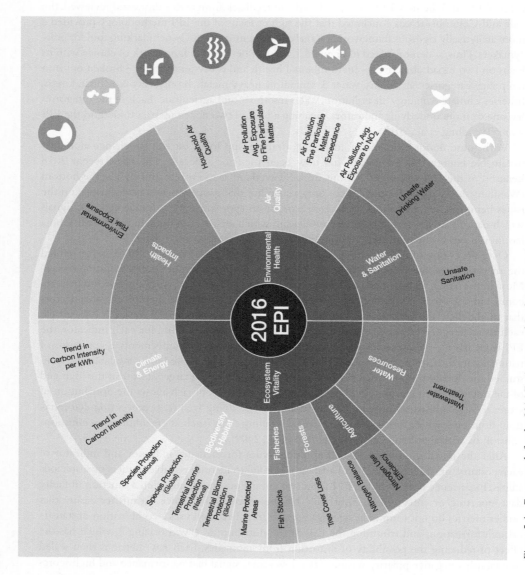

Figure 5.1 Framework for the 2016 Environmental Performance Index

through extrapolation, interpolation, or averaging around the data hole using available time series data. Proposed metrics with data coverage that is too sparse are dropped.

As noted earlier, the EPI team has always been committed to complete transparency. In this spirit, each biennial report presented data appendices with the sources of the metrics, calculation methodologies, and assumptions embedded in the analyses. Sensitivity analyses examined the effects of various assumptions and methodological choices, and were conducted both internally and, in some years, externally by the Joint Research Centre of the European Commission in Ispra, Italy (Athanasoglou et al., 2014). These analyses provided an independent cross-check on the data analytics.

Making sense of the results

The EPI team specifically emphasizes the limitations of the results presented, including the fact that important policy issues remain missing from the index. While the overarching EPI scores are indicative of which nations are doing well and which are not, the data team has always stressed that the limitations of the aggregation methodology make it difficult to draw conclusions about small differences in the topline scores. The indicators at the component or issue category level offer much greater insight on who is doing well on which issues. Moreover, the EPI team has always invited critique and commentary on its methodology and data sources. The EPI framework continues to evolve in response to this feedback and to new or improved data sets – and the team is careful to emphasize what can and cannot be concluded from the data and analysis. The Conrad and Cassar chapter in this volume continues that ongoing conversation.

In recent EPI reports, the analysis presented has gone beyond a simple performance "snapshot" to try to capture trends (Emerson et al., 2012; Hsu et al., 2016; Wendling et al., 2018). In particular, for countries with similar scores, it is useful to know whose performance is improving and whose is deteriorating over time. In addition, by looking at both top-tier performance and trend leaders, it becomes easier to find "best practices" and to extract policy guidance from the results. In this regard, as the data foundations for future environmental policy evaluation become stronger, even more emphasis should be put on analysis of the "drivers" of good results. Being able to tell policymakers not only *which* countries are doing well, but *why*, has thus emerged as a valuable dimension of the EPI project.

Even with all of its recognized limitations, the EPI has helped shift environmental policy debates toward being more fact-based and empirical. Media coverage of each new EPI release has generated hundreds of articles across the world and hundreds of thousands of hits on the EPI website. This intensity of interest in the EPI has demonstrated the value of a more data-driven approach to policymaking in general and to environmental decision-making in particular (Esty & Rushing, 2007; Gerken, 2009). And it has sharpened the focus on environmental best practices at many scales of governance: global, national, state/provincial, and municipal. The EPI project has also provided a data framework for hundreds of academic studies that have helped to illuminate which policy interventions deliver good results and which do not (Niemeijer, 2002).

One of the core conclusions from the nearly 20 years of producing the ESI and EPI is that the arraying of countries – issue by issue and at various levels of aggregation – provides valuable feedback to policymakers. By benchmarking results and demonstrating what others have achieved, the EPI spurs improved performance. Indeed, in terms of driving policy ambitions, there is nothing more convincing to a skeptical government official than to show what others whom he or she considers to be peers have achieved. Thus, the EPI's cross-country comparisons have sparked competition to deliver better environmental public health and ecosystem vitality on many issues and in many circumstances.

Environment ministries that find themselves with outcomes lower than they had anticipated often follow up with the EPI team. It turns out, in fact, that every country has something to learn from the comparative analysis of the EPI. Even top-performing nations lag on some policy categories. Dozens of nations – including Belgium, China, Mexico, Norway, South Korea, Turkey, and the United Arab Emirates – have therefore used the ESI or EPI to recast their own policy approaches. Furthermore, Angel Hsu's chapter in this volume (Chapter 17) shows how the EPI methodology is currently being deployed at the sub-national scale. This broad degree of government interest and follow-up leads to perhaps the most dramatic conclusion of the EPI project: that the simple exercise of transparently arraying data in an easy-to-understand format and highlighting subpar results can be a powerful policy tool.

Another important conclusion from the two decades of work on the EPI is that countries benefit most from comparisons to *relevant* peers. Top-to-bottom scores across 180 nations are not what motivate attention. What does attract the interest of policymakers is the underperformance of their nation compared to others that are similarly situated. Haiti, for example, never thought that it could compete with Finland or Switzerland. But when Haitian officials are made aware that they trail the Dominican Republic (with whom they share the island of Hispaniola), they pay attention. The EPI team has therefore tried to provide a range of peer groups for comparison – including regional groupings, trade partners, countries at similar levels of economic development, clusters by geographic or demographic circumstances (high population density or arid nations), and statistically derived "clusters" of nations with similar profiles (Esty et al., 2006; Esty et al., 2008; Emerson et al., 2010; Emerson et al., 2012). In this way, government officials can choose for themselves which peer comparisons are most meaningful.

Conclusion

Policymakers the world over now recognize the opportunity to improve outcomes and ensure that limited environmental investment funds are well spent by bringing better data, carefully defined metrics, and rigorous analysis to a wide range of decision processes (Gerken, 2009; Sunstein & Thaler, 2009; Ibrahim, 2012). Enormous effort is thus being put into "smarter governance" – with data-driven policymaking as one of the pillars of this movement (Esty, 2017; Novek, 2015). While policy choices will always entail a degree of political judgment, the promise of undergirding these decisions with better performance measurement metrics, trend indicators, and systematic data analytics looms large as information and communications technologies advance.

The EPI has helped to promote this commitment to more data-driven and empirical policymaking – and to demonstrate the value of metrics and systematic data analysis. But even after multiple iterations over nearly two decades, the EPI remains a work in progress. The data limitations that have plagued the project from its earliest days have begun to be addressed but only modestly so. There remain significant data gaps in both issue coverage and country scope. The methodologies for gauging performance have improved to some degree but, in many cases, require further work.

On a positive note, the range of parties now committed to metrics development and data-driven environmental policymaking has expanded dramatically. The world community's commitment to the 2015 Sustainable Development Goals provides a particular impetus for ramped-up efforts to produce carefully defined quantitative metrics to guide policymakers. As the data advance and the statistical tools of the Information Age flow more fully into the environmental arena, the potential for even more rigorous environmental decision-making by governments, businesses, and the academic community looks significant.

References

Athanasoglou, S., Weziak-Bialowolska, D., & Saisana, M. 2014. *Environmental Performance Index 2014: JRC analysis and recommendations.* (Report EUR 26623 EN). Luxembourg: Publications Office of the European Union. doi: 10.2788/64170.

Breggin, L. & Amsalem, J. 2014. Big Data and the Environment: A Survey of Initiatives and Observations Moving Forward. *Environmental Law Reporter News & Analysis,* 44, 10984–10995.

Charnley, G. & Elliot, E. D. 2002. Risk Versus Precaution: Environmental Law and Public Health Protection. *Environmental Law Reporter News & Analysis,* 32(3), 10363–10366.

Emerson, J., Esty, D. C., Levy, M. A., Kim, C. H., Mara, V., de Sherbinin, A., & Srebotnjak, T. 2010. *2010 Environmental Performance Index.* New Haven: Yale Center for Environmental Law and Policy.

Emerson, J., Hsu, A., Levy, M. A., de Sherbinin, A., Mara, V., Esty, D. C., & Jaiteh, M. 2012. *2012 Environmental Performance Index and Pilot Trend Environmental Performance Index.* New Haven: Yale Center for Environmental Law and Policy.

Esty, D. C. 2001. Toward Data-Driven Environmentalism: The Environmental Sustainability Index. *Environmental Law Reporter,* 31(10603).

Esty, D. C. 2004. Environmental Protection in the Information Age. *New York University Law Review,* 79(1), 115–211.

Esty, D. C. 2017. Red Lights to Green Lights: From 20th Century Environmental Protection to 21st Century Sustainability. *Environmental Law,* 47(1), 101–175.

Esty, D. C., Levy, M. A, Granoff, I., & de Sherbinin, A. 2000. *Pilot Environmental Sustainability Index.* New Haven: Yale Center for Environmental Law & Policy.

Esty, D. C., Levy, M. A, Granoff, I., & de Sherbinin, A. 2002. *2002 Environmental Sustainability Index.* New Haven: Yale Center for Environmental Law & Policy.

Esty, D. C., Levy, M. A., Kim, C. H., de Sherbinin, A., Srebotnjak, T., & Mara, V. 2008. *2008 Environmental Performance Index.* New Haven: Yale Center for Environmental Law & Policy.

Esty, D. C., Levy, M. A., Srebotnjak, T., & de Sherbinin, A. 2005. *2005 Environmental Sustainability Index: Benchmarking National Environmental Stewardship.* New Haven: Yale Center for Environmental Law & Policy.

Esty, D. C., Levy, M. A., Srebotnjak, T., Sherbinin, A., Kim, C. H., & Anderson, B. 2006. *Pilot 2006 Environmental Performance Index.* New Haven: Yale Center for Environmental Law & Policy.

Esty, D.C. & Porter, M.E. 2000. 'Measuring national environmental performance and its determinants', in M.E. Porter and J. Sachs (eds), The Global Competitiveness Report 2000, New York: Oxford University Press.

Esty, D. C. & Rushing, R. 2007. *Governing by the Numbers: The Promise of Data-Driven Policymaking in the Information Age.* Washington, DC: Center for American Progress.

Farber, D.A. 1992. Politics and Procedure in Environmental Law. *Journal of Law, Economics, and Organization,* 8(1), 59–81.

Gerken, H. 2009. *The Democracy Index: Why Our Election System Is Failing and How to Fix It.* Princeton, NJ: Princeton University Press.

Glicksman, R. L. 2010. Anatomy of Industry Resistance to Climate Change: A Familiar Litany. In David Driesen, *Economic Thought and US Climate Change Policy.* Cambridge: MIT University Press.

Hsu, A., Emerson, J., Levy, M. A., de Sherbinin, A., Johnson, L., Malik, O., Schwartz, J., & Jaiteh, M. 2014. *2014 Environmental Performance Index.* New Haven, CT: Yale Center for Environmental Law & Policy.

Hsu, A., Levy, M.A., de Sherbinin, A., & Esty, D. C. 2016. *2016 Environmental Performance Index.* New Haven, CT: Yale University.

Ibrahim, M. 2012. *Better Data, Better Policy Making.* New York: McKinsey & Company.

Lazarus, R. J. 2013. Environmental Law at the Crossroads: Looking Back 25, Looking Forward 25. *Michigan Journal of Environmental & Administrative Law,* 2(2), 267–284.

Levy, M. A. 2002. *Measuring Nations' Environmental Sustainability: Environmental Performance Measurement: The Global Report 2001–2002.* New York: Oxford University Press.

Niemeijer, D. 2002. Developing Indicators for Environmental Policy: Data-Driven and Theory-Driven Approaches Examined by Example. *Environmental Science & Policy,* 5(2), 91–103.

Noveck, B. S. 2015. *Smart Citizens, Smarter State: The Technologies of Expertise and the Future of Governing.* Cambridge: Harvard University Press.

Organization for Economic Cooperation and Development. 1987. *Environmental Data Compendium, 1987.* Paris: OECD Publishing.

Revesz, R. L. & Livermore, M. A. 2008. *Retaking Rationality: How Cost-Benefit Analysis Can Better Protect the Environment and Our Health.* Oxford: Oxford University Press.

Rockström, J., Steffen, W., Noone, K., Persson, A., Chapin, F. S. III, & Lambin, E. 2009. A Safe Operating Space for Humanity. *Nature*, 461, 472–475.

Sunstein, C. & Thaler, R. 2009. *Nudge: Improving Decisions about Health, Wealth, and Happiness.* New York: Penguin.

UN General Assembly. 2015. *Transforming Our World: The 2030 Agenda for Sustainable Development.* Report A/RES/70/1. New York: United Nations.

Wendling, Z., Emerson, J., Esty, D. C., Levy, M. A., de Sherbinin, A., et al. 2018. *2018 Environmental Performance Index.* New Haven, CT: Yale Center for Environmental Law & Policy. epi.yale.edu.

6

THE LIMITS OF SUSTAINABILITY AND RESILIENCE FRAMEWORKS

Lessons from agri-food system research

Sarah Rotz and Evan Fraser

Introduction

In response to the complex environmental challenges facing the world, there has been rapid growth in the development and application of sustainability indicators (SIs). Broadly speaking, sustainability indicators are collections of data-gathering frameworks or tools aimed at holistically evaluating the social, environmental and economic impact of humanity's behaviour on the planet. One of the first and most notable attempts to institutionalize SIs was the United Nations Programme on Sustainable Development Indicators established at the 1992 Rio Earth Summit (Bell and Morse 2008). Since then, countless sustainability commissions, working groups, projects and reports have been developed. Just recently, over 20 years after Rio, the UN unveiled its Sustainable Development Goals.

A consistent challenge for these efforts has been determining the scope and breadth of indicators that can be included before the framework becomes un-interpretable (Barnett *et al.* 2008, Bell and Morse 2008, Dahl 2012). Another problem has to do with the general lack of theory and causal analysis in SI development (Bossel 1999, Milman and Short 2008). Generally, SIs are rather descriptive, and while they may reveal correlations, they provide little insight into the sort of causal relations that are amendable to political and policy intervention. For instance, Turner *et al.*'s sustainability framework (2003) demonstrates how nested and spatially contextual sustainability operates, but does not offer any theoretical analysis of the social, political and economic dynamics at work – dynamics that often determine the nature and structure of 'sustainability' within the given context.

In light of this challenge, some have turned to resilience, which is defined in a number of ways including the capacity of a system to absorb stress before fundamentally changing states (Gunderson and Holling 2002, Folke *et al.* 2010). Unfortunately, and as will be illustrated below, problems have arisen as resilience has been proposed, developed and applied across various social and ecological systems. For instance, many resilient systems are not desirable (e.g. economic systems that create poverty are built on maximizing exploitation and/or imperial wealth production). In light of these tensions and complexities, the purpose of this paper is to use an agri-food system case study to contrast the conceptual and methodological challenges associated with both sustainability and resilience indicator frameworks. In doing so, we explore the strengths and weaknesses of these tools and consider specific limits to their utility. Before detailing the study, however, we outline the main debates in SI and resilience research.

Sustainability indicators and resilience

Sustainability indicators

SIs are founded on a positivist approach to theory and methodology that argues singular, objective 'truths' can be derived through empirical quantitative data analysis (King 2016). SIs have evolved as a means of codifying the complex and messy facets of environmental health and sustainability – a wicked problem to be sure (Frame 2008). The purpose of SIs, therefore, is typically to determine whether systems, or components therein, are becoming more or less sustainable. Hence, measurement, standardization and calculation are central to the design and implementation of SIs (United Nations 2007, Bell and Morse 2008, Hsu *et al.* 2016).

The mechanisms of quantification inherent to SIs have generated critique from post-structural and critical scholarship specifically (Rutherford 2007, Rydin 2007, Darian-Smith 2016). More broadly, environmental and sustainability measures have received criticism on a range of epistemological, political, socio-cultural, economic and programmatic issues (Morse and Fraser 2005, Fiala 2008, Ilcan and Phillips 2010, Lautensach and Lautensach 2013). A common thread across critiques is that while it is crucial to monitor and assess environmental change, we cannot assume that all means of tracking and analyzing such change are accurate or beneficial (Dahl 2012, Bulkeley *et al.* 2013, Linner and Selin 2013).

A major challenge then becomes how to design, monitor and interpret SIs in a way that is robust, holistic and fair. As a number of cases show, "indicators are only as good as the data behind them" (Dahl 2012, p. 16; Esty Chapter 31). The scarcity, or inappropriate use, of data has led to interpretations that are irrelevant, inaccurate, exclusionary and clumsy (Morse and Fraser 2005, Fraser *et al.* 2006, Dahl 2012). Accordingly, another major challenge facing those who would like to use SIs is how to select, gather and interpret a vast array of – varyingly accurate – descriptive statistics (Dahl Chapter 3). Decisions about which indictors to include and how to organize them, how to gather, manipulate and analyze data, as well as how data is scaled and weighted are all central in determining for whom the indicator set serves (Morse and Fraser 2005). Such decisions are indeed power-laden. Hence, arguments for SIs on the grounds that they are 'apolitical', 'objective' and 'value neutral' must be considered very critically (e.g. see Morse and Fraser 2005 for an exploration of this issue as it pertains to one key SI initiative).

Another challenge for SIs is how to account for the subjective and political-economic forces that constrain action to improve sustainability. For instance, how do SIs effectively account for the offsetting of industrial activity from so-called Global North nations onto the Global South? We know that wealth accumulation (derived through capitalism, imperialism and colonialism) has created the conditions for such spatial and ecological fixes (Harvey 2001, Ekers and Prudham 2015), but should this political complexity be integrated into a model that was built for standardization? If so, how? Although still fraught with such concerns, the clear aim of SIs is to *measure* sustainability. What is less clear, however, is its ability to assess how we should act on these measures (the 'software' of SIs) (Dahl 2012, Bell and Morse Chapter 12). This raises the question of for whom does this data serve, and what does it mean for policy and practice?

This final point brings us to another key theme in the SI literature, which is focused on the 'rolling-out' of SIs, and is thus more process-based. A goal of SI discussions is to provide guidance on *how* to engage with different groups to define their own SIs, in turn allowing them to uncover the causes of unsustainability within their own context. We might call this the 'bottom-up' approach to SIs, as opposed to the 'top-down' approach, which typically misses the qualitative nuance, and has too often failed communities in the past (Fraser *et al.* 2006, Bell and Morse 2008). A key argument being that active and ongoing community ownership remains constrained by the quantifiable and comparative nature of SIs as well as inattention to various political dynamics of 'inclusion' (Fraser *et al.* 2006). SIs too often circulate within rather closed loops of 'expert' knowledge and information, which, in turn, produces simplistic conclusions about sustainability and fails 'to align with community values' and objectives (Morse and Fraser 2005, Fraser *et al.* 2006, Miller 2007, p. 6). At the same time, focusing on the stressors and state of sustainability, as many traditional models do, is insufficient for explaining the dynamics of the system and the relations between components (Turner *et al.* 2003, Bell and Morse 2008).

For us, this debate also highlights the relative intractability concerning issues of comparability and scale. If SIs can effectively be scaled down in a way that empowers communities to uncover contextually relevant, nuanced and comprehensive indicators, how do we use them to engage in a broader (e.g. national or global) discussion?

Resilience

In some ways, more recent scholarship on resilience emerged out of critiques of SIs, particularly concerning analytical nuance and integration of system dynamics (Turner *et al.* 2003, Adger *et al.* 2005, Adger 2006, Turner 2010). Initially, resilience was defined by ecologists as the ability of an ecosystem to experience disturbance and maintain its basic structure and functions (Holling 1973, Gunderson and Holling 2002). Over time, the concept of social-ecological resilience took shape, which integrates ecology with society, and highlights the need for social change by identifying indicators of persistence, adaptability and transformation (Folke *et al.* 2010).

More recently, resilience has been taken up across the social sciences, such as economics, environmental policy and security, organizational strategy, development, social psychology and international relations. As a result, numerous scholars argue that resilience has become methodologically and conceptually ambiguous, leading to a co-optation of sorts (Frerks, Warner and Weijs 2011, Reid 2012, Walker and Cooper 2011). Specifically, the conceptual expansion of resilience facilitated a redirection into neoliberal discourses of economic flexibility and adaptation, which claim to increase wealth and freedom while concurrently increasing "the prosperity and security of life itself" (Reid 2012, p. 77).

Additionally, inherent to resilience is the assumption that self or social preservation within a system is intrinsically positive. In other words, it is assumed that resilience is necessarily a good thing. Yet, resilience does not seem prudent under all cases such as systems of authoritarianism, systemic poverty, racism, colonialism or unfettered free-market capitalism (Cote and Nightingale 2011, Anderies *et al.* 2013). This has led scholars to problematize resilience by illustrating how feedback cycles can encourage and entrench prevailing states, thus increasing systemic connectivity and dependence on prevailing conditions, which reduces the system's ability to adapt to change (e.g. see Cote and Nightingale 2011, Walker and Cooper 2011). That said, resistance to change *can* be effective and beneficial under other kinds of systems and conditions, such as the ability for an ecosystem to withstand flood disturbance and remain functional. The question then becomes, for which kinds of systems is a resilience analysis relevant and useful, and for which is it not?

Finally, resilience has been critiqued for taking for granted – or completely ignoring – the systemic forces that produced the perturbation in the first place. In this way, some resilience scholarship seems focused on maintaining current systems of accumulation, and has thus become a "test of one's right to survive in the global order of things" (Walker and Cooper 2011,

Watts 2011, p. 90). Critics argue that social dynamics cannot be naturalized through ecological principles like resilience, as it treats them as "inevitable rather than as objects of struggle" (Walsh-dilley *et al*. 2016, p. 5). Without such nuance, resilience's focus on 'chaos' divorces cause and effect, individualizes adaptive capacity building, and brushes systemic forces into the realm of the unknown (Aradau 2014).

Many of these critiques have been addressed by a range of scholars including Neil Adger, Katrina Brown (Adger 2000, Adger and Brown 2009) and members of the 'Resilience Alliance' who describe resilience as a framework for understanding processes of change by examining the ability of social and ecological systems to adapt, learn and evolve in ways that support better core functions. While this approach shows considerable promise, this broad definition puts us back into a similar position that has plagued SIs. Namely, and as will be discussed in the following section, that the definition may become so broad and holistic as to render it amenable to problematic political and social interventions.

Aligning SIs and resilience?

To address the conceptual and methodological ambiguousness of both SIs and resilience, scholars have established indicators, which include, for instance: (1) capacity to absorb change, (2) self-organization and (3) adaptive capacity (Adger 2006, Anderies *et al*. 2013, Engle *et al*. 2014, Milestad and Darnhofer 2003). Similar to sustainability, therefore, resilience scholars argue that such a framework must be established in order to apply resilience effectively (Frerks *et al*. 2011). However, attempts to instrumentalize resilience bring us back, again, to concerns expressed with SIs. Specifically, how do we build indicators that are fair and comprehensive, how do we 'roll them out', and how do we assess who these indicators serve and what they mean for policy and practice? (Bell and Morse Chapter 12). Moreover, such a framework does little to address the critique that resilience ignores structural causes, risks and dynamics.

This concern has been addressed by some recent resilience scholarship. Anderies *et al*. (2013), for instance, call for a careful alignment between the concepts of resilience, robustness and sustainability, wherein sustainability is the distinguished goal, while the process is developed around the concepts of resilience and robustness. Anderies *et al*. (2013) recognize that resilience is not normative, and thus ought to be used within a context of sustainability. Thus, system-level processes such as building skills, knowledge and/or capacity can be considered from a resilience lens (i.e., to increase adaptive capacity), but these processes should be developed within the broader goal of improving sustainability. Resilience then gives us information about what might need to happen at the system level for sustainability to improve. Meanwhile, having sustainability as the goal means that resilience does not always imply persistence or resistance to transformation, which, they argue, is where robustness becomes useful (Anderies *et al*. 2013).

Still, issues of both systemic risk and social justice do not seem inherent to such a sustainability-resilience framework either. For instance, while the introduction of a new hydroelectric dam may allow regional energy needs to be met without the use of fossil fuels (a common indicator of improved sustainability), it may also produce new risks and issues around artificial stabilization, disaster management, water and food contamination (e.g. heavy metals accumulation) and community dislocation and land dispossession. Indeed, both sustainability and resilience continue to be flexibly adopted in ways that permit inequitable and exclusionary development projects (Reid 2013). This highlights the aforementioned centrality of *sustainability and resilience for and by whom?* In other words, we must resist the de-politicization of sustainability and resilience that is working in the interests of institutional capital, timelines and strategies.

So, while sustainability and resilience *may* respectively help us understand where we want to go and how to get there, the issue of political subjectivity still looms large (Joss and Rydin Chapter 24). The question then becomes whether systems and programs that claim to improve sustainability and resilience are actually doing so, and on whose terms this is being done. In the following case study, we consider the extent to which such frameworks are able to measure resilience in a way that attends to socio-political issues within a fundamentally unsustainable system. Primarily, we examine issues of conceptual framing, definition, appropriation and theoretical utility – as they often remain outside the scope of resilience-sustainability analysis (Cote and Nightingale 2011, Anderies *et al.* 2013, Reid 2013). A key challenge this case should reveal is how fundamental systemic factors determine and limit the ways in which resilience and sustainability can be defined and legitimized. From here, we reflect on the utility of SIs and resilience for this study and illustrate various conceptual and programmatic tensions.

Wrestling with resilience in unsustainable systems: the case of industrial agriculture in Ontario

The Ontario agri-food context

Ontario's agri-food system is a product of nearly a century of agricultural industrialization, itself built on European settler colonization. Mechanization and capitalization took hold in the 1940s, which initially increased productivity and income, but subsequently created a crisis of overproduction that has led to declining commodity prices – a pattern that has repeated itself sequentially. In turn, Ontario agriculture has experienced a structural 'cost-price squeeze' for the past several decades, which occurs when agricultural production costs continue to rise while farm-gate prices and incomes remain stagnant (Smithers *et al.* 2008, Troughton 1989, van der Ploeg 2006). For instance, in Canada's central and populace province of Ontario, input costs have risen faster (between 1995–2008 the cost of seeds doubled) than the rise in prices farmers receive (National Farmers Union 2013). As crop prices have remained fairly constant from the mid 1970s until about 2007, the viability of producing crops could only be captured through increasing economies of scale, which has drastically reorganized the size and structure of Ontario farms (Winson 1993). This has fuelled a wave of industrialization that has driven farmers to consolidate land, capitalize and intensify cropping in order to stay in production. Meanwhile, this trajectory has heightened corporate power, while eroding the power of small- and medium-scale farmers to set their prices and act alternatively (Hendrickson and James 2005, Rotz and Fraser 2015).

As a result, many farmers have been forced out of production, exacerbating farmland consolidation further. For instance, since 1921, Ontario agricultural land has fallen by 42%, while the average farm size nearly doubled from 114 to 233 acres (National Farmers Union 2013). This trend continues today, with a loss of 23,643 farms (10.3%) in Canada between 2006 and 2011, along with a 10% reduction in the number of farm operators over this same period (Statistics Canada 2011).

Additionally, the political-economic imperatives of capitalization and mechanization have led to crop and livestock specialization at the farm-scale. While grains have long been a staple of Ontario food production, traditional crops such as oats, barley, rye, buckwheat, mixed grain and pulses have been outflanked by a simpler corn-soy-wheat rotation (Statistics Canada 2011). The commercial viability of these three crops is no accident, instead it was generated through extensive university, government and corporate research and support programs for crop breeding and modification, especially for the purposes of pesticide compatibility (Reaman 1970). Further, the growing market flexibility for corn and soy as low-cost, high-quantity industrial inputs continues to re-structure the industry and the character of Ontario farms. For their industrial utility to be realized, crops must be sold below their true cost of production, further exacerbating farm consolidation and price subsidization. Indeed, the 'big three' crops have been promoted to farmers for decades by agri-business, whose profits have risen steadily as a result. Yet, the economic benefits remain unrealized for most farmers, as their debt loads grow alongside corporate profits. For instance, the average amount of farmer debt in Canada is now 23 dollars for every dollar of net income (National Farmers Union 2010).

These trends have only intensified as neoliberalization has taken hold. The unloading of public sector programming to private actors together with laissez-faire governance has emboldened the corporatization of production and inputs specifically. During this time, Ontario agriculture has become increasingly export-oriented. For instance, Canadian export values of agriculture and agri-food products increased from $10.9 billion in 1988 to $35.5 billion in 2010 (AAFC 2012). Concurrently, Ontario consumers increasingly rely on imported fruit and vegetables (Desjardins *et al.* 2009, National Farmers Union 2013).

Defining SIs and resilience in the Ontario agri-food context

At the outset of the research, sustainability indicators were deployed to analyze the context of Ontario grain farming. The first step in assessing social-ecological resilience within a sustainability lens (Ostrom 2009, Folke *et al.* 2010) was to conduct 107 surveys with grain farmers across Ontario, which consisted of six main sections.[1]

Initially, we found SIs and resilience to be a useful heuristic guide for identifying problems within this social-ecological system (Ostrom 2009). For instance, SI frameworks inevitably focus on landscape changes that affect ecosystem services, such as biodiversity and habitat. Resilience frameworks similarly focus on biodiversity, as they assume that landscapes rich in biodiversity are better able to adapt to environmental perturbations. In turn, the evaluation of sustainability and resilience in Ontario's agricultural sector revealed that crop pattern homogenization had negative consequences for both ecological resilience and sustainability. Similarly, our evaluation of social resilience and sustainability revealed that the race to accumulate land, rising farmer debt, price volatility and declines in farm numbers and farmer power were deeply problematic for the system (see Rotz, Fraser and Martin 2017 for further details on the methods and data collected).

However, very quickly, this research project ran into conceptual and methodological challenges. Principally, in assessing resilience and sustainability, we found there were few significant differences in farm characteristics and practices across the survey population. For instance, we did not find that smaller farmers who were assumed to be less embedded in capitalist systems had more complex rotations, used fewer inputs per acre or adopted more agro-ecological practices generally (Tables 6.1 and 6.2). In fact, we found that, because large farmers were more financially secure, they tended to integrate cover crops more regularly and were better able to introduce new crops into their rotation. And while we did find that smaller farmers were more interested in diversifying their farm and setting land aside for ecological preservation, they were not significantly more likely to do so in practice due to financial and structural constraints. In other words, the indicators revealed nothing about the important underlying forces that led towards (or away from) greater resilience and sustainability.

Moreover, for the few farmers who did choose to adopt the more deeply agro-ecological practices (on-farm diversification and organic production alongside livestock integration), few financial benefits were observed. In fact, organic farmers – who were also comparatively small

Table 6.1 Number of crops grown and farm size

Number of crop species typically grown per year	Farm size (acres)
< 3	333 (n = 12)
> = 3	769 (n = 89)
< 4	556 (n = 40)
> = 4	823 (n = 61)
< 10	685 (n = 94)
> = 10	1160 (n = 7)

Table 6.2 Cover crops and forage integration by farm size

Do you grow cover crops or forages?	Yes	No
Farm Size (acres)	791	469

in acreage – had a significantly lower income change (a proxy for economic resilience) over the past ten years than conventional respondents. Generally, there was no correlation between rotation, yield and income or income change at all. Rather, the most significant financial differences were correlated with farm size. Larger farmers had significantly higher (gross and net) incomes than small- and medium-sized farmers. And since many farmers defined sustainability and resilience through yield and cost/debt/income measures, they tended to focus on growth and land accumulation.

Other indicators that should have signified resilience or sustainability displayed a similar trend. For instance, in collecting data on 'adaptation strategies', we aimed to specify whether farms of different sizes or organizational structures used adaptation strategies that were more or less resilient/sustainable. Again, we found no differences. Indeed, all types of farmers expressed similar adoption levels of drought resistant seeds, change in crop rotation, the purchase of irrigation, introduction of cover crops, and the construction of water catchment reservoirs (Table 6.3). Meanwhile, the disparities that were observed are likely a result of resource and economic factors. For instance, larger farmers were more likely to adopt technology and equipment, increase crop insurance and add organic material to their soil as adaptation strategies. These strategies each have significant financial implications, which is possibly why we see large farmers more likely to adopt them. Yet larger farmers (912 and 900 acres respectively) were also more likely to change their pesticide application and increase crop residue and mulching than smaller farmers (671 and 568 acres respectively), which is less easily explained by economic factors. At the same time, very few farmers overall adopted more agro-ecological practices, such as on-farm diversification (5 out of 104 respondents), transitioning to organic (3), and introducing shrubs and trees onto their farm (0), and the farm size of adoptees was not significantly smaller. In fact, the only adaptation strategy that was adopted by small farmers specifically (253 acre average between 2 respondents) was to reduce livestock on their farm, which again is likely due to financial constraints.

Overall, there were few meaningful differences in on-farm practices across farm size. Hence, in this context, small acreage did not imply superior agro-ecological practices, as observed elsewhere (Woodhouse 2010, Rudel *et al.* 2016). Instead, small acreage predicted greater financial insecurity, which seemed to hinder their capacity for environmental stewardship. At the same time, while small farmers did show greater interest in setting aside land for ecological

Table 6.3 Mean farm size of farmers who did and did not choose the listed adaptation strategies

Adaptation strategy	Mean farm size (acres)	
	Adopted	Not adopted
Bought drought resistant seeds	704	712
Changed crop rotation	639	735
Purchased irrigation	797	705
Introduced cover crops	757	682
Built water reservoirs	662	715

conservation and less interest in selling their land to corporate developers, non-economic attachments and anti-corporate political views were not clearly divided along farm size (Flinn and Buttel 1980). And again, there was no indication that such sociological and political perspectives resulted in better environmental stewardship in practice.

So, how do we make sense of these findings? Taken at face value, the results of this SI/resilience analysis may suggest that there are no real differences in the sustainability of larger or smaller farms (in fact, some may take our data to suggest that larger farmers are more resilient and sustainable). Nevertheless, much of the literature on sustainable farming systems would disagree and point to the significant issues that large-scale production produces, including excessive input use, the loss of the rural infrastructure and rising farmer debt. Is our data, then, showing that large-scale farms, driven by economies of scale, are indeed more sustainable than small-scale operations? When we examine the broader context of the system, our data does not support any such conclusion. Rather, our findings should make clear that ecological issues are merely symptoms of much deeper phenomena that must be examined before a substantive transition to sustainable agriculture can occur. Hence, in this case, downloading notions of resilience, adaptive capacity and sustainability onto the farm-scale served to individualize systemic issues and naturalize what is in fact an unprecedented environmental and climate crisis. In turn, we want to focus on the factors creating and perpetuating these conditions. After all, the dynamics of this system are deeply complicated, with variegated social, political, economic and cultural aspects operating at multiple scales. As such, reflecting on our own research reveals that using sustainability and resilience as frameworks to guide indicators and data collection could only take us so far into our analysis. We will now briefly outline these reflections.

Reflecting on the framework

One of the most significant issues uncovered by our research was that respondents did not share our understanding of resilience or sustainability. Hence, the very rights-based resilience framework grounded in goals of sustainability were not "relevant to local struggles and policies in the same way (Blesh and Wittman 2015, p. 532). Respondents viewed resilience from a lens of economic rather than socio-ecological sustainability, which was strongly linked to farm size under this system. For farmers, the logical result – to accumulate land – was their path toward farm-scale sustainability. Of course, this was creating deeply unsustainable conditions at the system-scale. From our observation, it was largely the case that farmers saw well-being, health and resilience through a lens of economic improvement. To become more resilient and adaptive under this paradigm, many farmers are now focusing their efforts on new ways to understand and manage the 'unknowns'[2] (Chandler 2014). This is specifically linked to the growing adoption of 'big data' methods for 'managing' and adapting to weather fluctuations and climate change. Resilience is working here to move farmers "fairly swiftly from thinking about the dynamics of systems to emphasising individual responsibility, adaptability and preparedness" (Joseph 2013, p. 40). Moreover, it is working directly for agri-business capital accumulation. The disparity in definitions together with the trends observed in on-farm practices made it challenging to move ahead with the development of indicators, and, in particular, to adopt participatory development methods (Bélanger *et al.* 2012). Hence, we were not confident that an ecologically rigorous indicator set could be developed under these conditions, as indicators that were – for us – fundamental would likely be rejected during the process (As occurred with 'energy use' for Bélanger *et al.* [2012]). While we do not entirely disagree with Bélanger *et al.* that "farm sustainability must start with farmers" (2012, p. 428), we must also be clear about how different *kinds* of alternatives become made available to farmers. For us, what needed more attention was, instead, why farmers are being directed to 'manage the unknowns' via big data by articulated forces of neoliberal agri-food in the name of sustainability and resilience, and how this shapes the way farmers see and make sense of their conditions.

It seems clear that 'neoliberal doctrines of economy' can easily appropriate any model or framework of sustainability or resilience (Reid 2013). As, in this case, farmer representatives, organizations and agri-business are focused on constructing a kind of sustainability and resilience that works for their pocketbooks. In practice, activities are not judged by the degree to which they improve sustainability. Rather, potential activities are limited to those that improve economic outcomes for system actors, as long as they can be claimed to have any sort of ecological benefit, however marginal or controversial. In this context, conversations intended to centre on sustainability resulted in debates over the economic and yield benefits of practices like no-till and genetically modified soy or corn seed. It seems that 'sustainability' and 'resilience' as concepts or indicators have done little to widen or challenge that conversation. At this point, holding onto a sustainability-resilience framework seemed to distract attention from the critical work of naming the systemic causes and forces in ways that are theoretically specific and robust. Attention thus moved toward investigating why and how resilience and sustainability were being so profoundly coopted for particular socio-cultural and political-economic interests.

To clarify, the issue became whether a sustainability-resilience framework could provide the theoretical and conceptual depth needed to adequately investigate how these conditions are shaped, maintained and reproduced within the system. In effect, the Ontario grain production system does not fit with many of the successful applications of resilience in other agri-food systems, such as Blesh and Wittman's (2015) study. We wanted to understand trade-offs and synergies in the system, but socio-cultural, political, and economic stabilizations (Howarth 2010, Berardi *et al.* 2011) created systemic distortions in power and social domination. This in turn limited the effectiveness and relevance of such assessment tools. Indeed, without performing a broader analysis of systemic drivers and the entrenched and long-standing functions of systemic bias, one cannot measure the system effectively.

Additionally, as we turned toward the deeper factors contributing to unsustainability, we found that each needed a distinct conceptual framework, none of which could be attended to through a broad resilience or SI lens. Specifically, there were far more analytically relevant methods for examining farmland capitalization and tenure (Rotz *et al.* 2017), the socio-materialities of settler colonialism and racial hierarchy (Rotz 2017b), and discursive and social power (Rotz 2017a) within the agri-food system than resilience and sustainability.

Considering the limits of resilience and sustainability frameworks

The purpose of the discussion is to build on the case study and provide some practical reflections for academics and practitioners interested in SIs or resilience. First, one ought to be quite clear about the sources and dynamics of 'unsustainability' before applying assessment tools. In other words, prior to identifying indicators of sustainability or resilience, it is essential to study the "most significant driving forces and impacts and their causal relationships" (Dahl 2012, p. 17). In effect, we wanted to understand the *behaviour* of the system, which took us conceptually well outside the realm of sustainability and resilience. We see this as a good thing, especially if one aims for critical analysis. In this sense, we find that while indicators can be a useful measure of the state of things, they are descriptive in nature, which places significant limits on their utility for critical analysis.

Second, practitioners need to ask: 'what exactly is the system to which we are ascribing some notion of quality?' The main issue in our study was that the system had divested itself from any attention to sustainability. Larger factors created the conditions wherein ecological sustainability was not – and frankly could not – factor into decision-making, never mind become prioritized. As a result, many practices that may have met standards of sustainability were arbitrary, and told us little about how sustainability could be improved at the farm-scale or systemically. There were little to no clear determining factors for high social and ecological sustainability, as the two rarely coincided, if at all. If we were to simply apply a framework similar to Turner *et al.* (2003), many of the more complex issues of social and racial domination may have been undetected or ignored. However, these turned out to be the key drivers of unsustainability in the system, even though they seemed disconnected at the outset. Moreover, adequate time and space needs to be made to theorize these drivers, as they are deeply complex and historically constituted. Hence, we find that in many cases, resilience and SIs may only be useful at the outset – to identify the state of things – or after a certain degree of systemic transformation has occurred. Understanding when it is applicable, and when it is not, seems most useful then.

Finally, one's ability to locate sustainability is deeply context specific. This point has been made repeatedly, and does not need to be detailed again (Fraser *et al.* 2006, Barnett *et al.* 2008, Ericksen 2008, Beroya-Eitner 2016, Pupphachai and Zuidema 2017). It is important to add, however, that context specific does not only imply how and at what scale indicators are to be designed, developed, implemented and monitored, but whether they ought to be adopted at all. In this case, addressing some of the key systemic drivers of unsustainability are necessary before attempting to apply assessment tools. Foundational shifts must be made before we can see this system as moving toward any state of ecological sustainability. At that point, an SI-resilience assessment may be useful for measuring the conditions of the transition. Of course, the reasons for abandoning SIs are also context specific. For instance, we argue that SIs are fairly useless for measuring a system such as the Alberta tar sands for many of the same reasons observed in our example. But, they may also need to be abandoned in communities that, for instance, may choose a more culturally appropriate methodology, which ought to be respected on those grounds alone.

Conclusion

The work being done to identify and carve a path toward a more sustainable future is laudable, necessary and crucial. Given the profound environmental crises we are facing, tracking our progress is essential. Yet, our case study should illustrate that building tools and frameworks to measure, quantify and monitor things only take us so far. As we have shown, measuring progress is fraught with challenges, which often re-creates (although in different ways) already explored critiques of SIs and resilience. Moreover, assuming that these tools are 'solutions' in themselves risks distracting us from the deeper forces at work within systems. Indeed, we must remain focused on understanding the conditions within which sustainability and resilience get manipulated in the interests of political-economic and social empowerment and capital accumulation. How are these concepts deployed by different groups, and for what possible ends? For our study, certain systemic conditions prevented us from applying these concepts instrumentally, and with confidence. Instead of trying to 'make things fit', we refocused our analysis onto the structural forces at work. Of course, this will often take researchers and practitioners well outside of the sustainability and resilience scholarship, but we see this as a strength.

Therefore, from a methodological and operational perspective, two key problems need to be highlighted. First, we must acknowledge the limits of sustainability and resilience both as concepts and tools. Knowing when and how they should and should not be applied was a key takeaway from our research. Our case study showed that the conceptual and instrumental challenges that arose were in fact deeply linked. Conceptual confusion, appropriation and legitimization made it impossible (and rather pointless) to instrumentalize these tools.

Second, if they can be appropriately applied, indicators need to be nested in a broader analysis that helps to make sense of context-specific dynamics. This is a real challenge since it forces us to be attentive to multiple spatial and institutional scales. Meanwhile, the effectiveness of both SIs and resilience depends not only on the dynamics of each scale, but the relations between scales (Rydin 2007). For us, institutional (corporate and provincial/federal government and agency) and cultural scales were impacting the landscape and farm-scale in ways that categorically limited political, economic and social definitions, behaviours and imaginaries. Alternatives were restricted to ideas and activities that facilitated persistence in the system. The evidence of this was clear, but could not be sufficiently understood through these concepts and tools alone. Indeed, there was little sense in trying to understand what farm-scale resilience meant when farmers were operating within a system that is structurally disinterested in sustainability. This hurdle was even clearer at the landscape scale, wherein even when farmers were interested in environmental practices, they were deeply sceptical that others would participate or support such efforts.

For others, these concepts may be of more sustained utility. We only hope that they are perceived as one of many tools, as opposed to 'the' solution. A great deal of well-intentioned environmental and climate research and work has had deeply negative impacts due to assumptions about 'the solution', often already framed within what is deemed 'do-able' and 'appropriate' for global conditions and actors (Evans and Reid 2015, p. 155). While 'bottom-up' community-led research has worked to address many of these issues, the problem is by no means solved – after all, much of the problem continues to be found in our own assumptions as researchers. In turn, it seems to us that knowing when to listen and be open to change, even in cases that require you to set aside your long-studied tools and frameworks, is essential for moving research from a state of good intention to constructive impact. That is, by directing it to where the power lies.

Notes

1 (1) Demographics; (2) farm socio-economics; (3) resource use including feed, fertilizer, pesticides, fuel and manure; (4) crop and agriculture analysis which detailed crop rotation, soil texture, livestock integration, organic practices, cover crops and forages, and pest and weed control; (5) climate and environmental conditions including ecological buffering, protection and enhancement, soil health (fertility, mineral balance, organic matter, erosion, leaching, etc.), indicators of farm health, and responses to extreme weather and climate change; (6) organizational and community relationships such as

knowledge and information gathering, local involvement and participation, interest in localizing production and participating in environmental enhancement programming, farm transition and sale, and community dynamics and openness.

2 E.g. focusing efforts on carbon sequestration is not an effective means to nurture system resilience. First, because we don't know how it will interact within the larger system, and we likely can't know this. But also, it is not working to address the host of other practices that are producing the erosion of health and well-being in the climate system: biotic and abiotic health, which includes but is not limited to ocean and air currents, and vegetative health, soil and water health, etc., which contribute to the functioning of the global carbon cycle.

References

AAFC, 2012. *An Overview of the Canadian Agriculture and Agri-Food System.* Ottawa, Canada: Agriculture and Agri-Food.

Adger, W.N., 2000. Social and Ecological Resilience: Are They Related? *Progress in Human Geography*, 24 (3), 347–364.

Adger, W.N., 2006. Vulnerability. *Global Environmental Change*, 16 (3), 268–281.

Adger, W.N., Arnell, N.W., and Tompkins, E.L., 2005. Successful Adaptation to Climate Change Across Scales. *Global Environmental Change*, 15 (2), 77–86.

Adger, W.N. and Brown, K., 2009. Vulnerability and Resilience to Environmental Change: Ecological and Social Perspectives. *In*: N. Castree, D. Demeritt, D. Liverman, and B. Rhoads, eds. *A Companion to Environmental Geography*. Blackwell Publishing Ltd., 109–122.

Anderies, J. M., C. Folke, B. Walker, and E. Ostrom. 2013. Aligning key concepts for global change policy: robustness, resilience, and sustainability. *Ecology and Society*, 18 (2), 8.

Aradau, C., 2014. The Promise of Security: Resilience, Surprise and Epistemic Politics. *Resilience*, 2 (2), 73–87.

Barnett, J., Lambert, S., and Fry, I., 2008. The Hazards of Indicators: Insights from the Environmental Vulnerability Index. *Annals of the Association of American Geographers*, 98 (1), 102–119.

Bélanger, V., Vanasse, A., Parent, D., Allard, G., and Pellerin, D., 2012. Development of Agri-environmental Indicators to Assess Dairy Farm Sustainability in Quebec, Eastern Canada. *Ecological Indicators*, 23, 421–430.

Bell, S. and Morse, S., 2008. *Sustainability Indicators: Measuring the Immeasurable?* London, Sterling, VA: Earthscan.

Berardi, G., Green, R., and Hammond, B., 2011. Stability, Sustainability, and Catastrophe: Applying Resilience Thinking to U.S. Agriculture. *Research in Human Ecology*, 18 (2), 115–125.

Beroya-Eitner, M.A., 2016. Ecological Vulnerability Indicators. *Ecological Indicators*, 60, 329–334.

Blesh, J. and Wittman, H., 2015. Brasilience: Assessing Resilience in Land Reform Settlements in the Brazilian Cerrado. *Human Ecology*, 43, 531–546.

Bossel, H., 1999. *Indicators for Sustainable Development: Theory, Method, Applications.* Winnipeg: International Institute for Sustainable Development.

Bulkeley, H., Jordan, A., Perkins, R., and Selin, H., 2013. Governing Sustainability: Rio+20 and the Road Beyond. *Environment and Planning C: Government and Policy*, 31 (6), 958–970.

Chandler, D., 2014. Beyond Neoliberalism: Resilience, the New Art of Governing Complexity. *Resilience*, 2 (1), 47–63.

Cote, M. and Nightingale, A.J., 2011. Resilience Thinking Meets Social Theory: Situating Social Change in Socio-Ecological Systems (SES) Research. *Progress in Human Geography*, 36 (4), 475–489.

Dahl, A.L., 2012. Achievements and Gaps in Indicators for Sustainability. *Ecological Indicators*, 17, 14–19.

Darian-Smith, E., 2016. Mismeasuring Humanity: Examining Indicators through a Critical Global Studies Perspective. *New Global Studies*, 10 (1), 73–99.

Desjardins, E., MacRae, R., and Schumilas, T., 2009. Linking Future Population Food Requirements for Health with Local Production in Waterloo Region, Canada. *Agriculture and Human Values*, 27 (2), 129–140.

Ekers, M. and Prudham, S., 2015. Towards the Socio-ecological Fix. *Environment and Planning A*, 47, 2438–2445.

Engle, N. L., Bremond, A., Malone, E. L., & Moss, R. H. (2014). Towards a resilience indicator framework for making climate-change adaptation decisions. *Mitigation and Adaptation Strategies for Global Change*, 19(8), 1295–1312.

Ericksen, P.J., 2008. Conceptualizing Food Systems for Global Environmental Change Research. *Global Environmental Change*, 18 (1), 234–245.

Evans, B. and Reid, J., 2015. Exhausted by Resilience: Response to the Commentaries. *Resilience*, 3 (2), 1–6.

Fiala, N., 2008. Measuring Sustainability: Why the Ecological Footprint Is Bad Economics and Bad Environmental Science. *Ecological Economics*, 67 (4), 519–525.

Flinn, W.L. and Buttel, F.H., 1980. Sociological Aspects of Farm Size: Ideological and Social Consequences of Scale in Agriculture. *American Journal of Agricultural Economics*, 62 (5), 946–953.

Folke, C., Carpenter, S.R., Walker, B., Scheffer, M., Chapin, T., and Rockström, J., 2010. Resilience Thinking: Integrating Resilience, Adaptability and Transformability. *Ecology and Society*, 15 (4).

Frame, B., 2008. 'Wicked', 'Messy', and 'Clumsy': Long-term Frameworks for Sustainability. *Environment and Planning C: Government and Policy*, 26 (6), 1113–1128.

Fraser, E.D.G., Dougill, A.J., Mabee, W.E., Reed, M., and McAlpine, P., 2006. Bottom up and Top down: Analysis of Participatory Processes for Sustainability Indicator Identification as a Pathway to Community Empowerment and Sustainable Environmental Management. *Journal of Environmental Management*, 78 (2), 114–127.

Frerks, G., Warner, J., and Weijs, B., 2011. The Politics of Vulnerability and Resilience. *Ambiente & Sociedade*, XIV (2), 105–122.

Gunderson, L.H. and Holling, C.S., 2002. *Panarchy: Understanding Transformations in Human and Natural Systems.* Washington, DC: Island Press.

Harvey, D., 2001. Globalization and the "Spatial Fix". *Geographische Revue*, 23–30.

Hendrickson, M.K. and James, H.S., 2005. The Ethics of Constrained Choice: How the Industrialization of Agriculture Impacts Farming and Farmer Behavior. *Journal of Agricultural and Environmental Ethics*, 18 (3), 269–291.

Holling, C.S., 1973. Resilience and Stability of Ecological Systems. *Annual Review of Ecology and Systematics*, 4, 1–23.

Howarth, D., 2010. Power, Discourse, and Policy: Articulating a Hegemony Approach to Critical Policy Studies. *Critical Policy Studies*, 3 (3–4), 309–335.

Hsu, A., Alexandre, N., Cohen, S., Jao, P., Khusainova, E., Mosteller, D., Peng, Y., Rosengarten, C., Schwartz, J.D., Spawn, A., Weinfurter, A., Xu, K., Yin, D., and Zomer, A., 2016. *2016 Environmental Performance Index.* New Haven, CT: Yale University.

Ilcan, S. and Phillips, L., 2010. Developmentalities and Calculative Practices: The Millennium Development Goals. *Antipode*, 42 (4), 844–874.

Joseph, J., 2013. Resilience as Embedded Neoliberalism: A Governmentality Approach. *Resilience*, 1 (1), 38–52.

King, L.O., 2016. Functional Sustainability Indicators. *Ecological Indicators*, 66, 121–131.

Lautensach, A. and Lautensach, S., 2013. Assessing the top performers : Mindful conservatism and 'sustainable development'. *In: The 3rd World Sustainability Forum.* doi: 10.3390/wsf3-f004

Linner, B.-O. and Selin, H., 2013. The United Nations Conference on Sustainable Development: Forty Years in the Making. *Environment and Planning C-Government and Policy*, 31 (6), 971–987.

Miller, C.A., 2007. *Creating Indicators of Sustainability: A Social Approach.* Winnipeg: International Institute for Sustainable Development.

Milestad, R., & Darnhofer, I. (2003). Building Farm Resilience: The Prospects and Challenges of Organic Farming. *Journal of Sustainable Agriculture*, 22(3), 81–97. https://doi.org/10.1300/J064v22n03_09

Milman, A. and Short, A., 2008. Incorporating Resilience into Sustainability Indicators: An Example for the Urban Water Sector. *Global Environmental Change*, 18 (4), 758–767.

Morse, S. and Fraser, E.D.G., 2005. Making 'Dirty' Nations Look Clean? The Nation State and the Problem of Selecting and Weighting Indices as Tools for Measuring Progress Towards Sustainability. *Geoforum*, 36, 625–640.

National Farmers Union, 2010. *Losing Our Grip: How a Corporate Farmland Buy-up, Rising Farm Debt, and Agribusiness Financing of Inputs Threaten Family Farms and Food Sovereignty.* Saskatoon.

National Farmers Union, 2013. *Farms, Farmers and Agriculture in Ontario.* Saskatoon.

Ostrom, E., 2009. A General Framework for Analyzing Sustainability of Social-Ecological Systems. *Science*, 325, 419–422.

Pupphachai, U. and Zuidema, C., 2017. Sustainability Indicators: A Tool to Generate Learning and Adaptation in Sustainable Urban Development. *Ecological Indicators*, 72, 784–793.

Reaman, G.E., 1970. *A History of Agriculture in Ontario.* Volume Two. Toronto: Saunders of Toronto.

Reid, J., 2012. The Disastrous and Politically Debased Subject of Resilience. *Development Dialogue*, April, 67–79.

Reid, J., 2013. Interrogating the Neoliberal Biopolitics of the Sustainable Development-Resilience Nexus. *International Political Sociology*, 7 (4), 353–367.

Rotz, S. (2017a). Drawing lines in the cornfield: an analysis of discourse and identity relations across agri-food networks. *Agriculture and Human Values*. https://doi.org/10.1007/s10460-017-9838-0

Rotz, S. (2017b). "They took our beads, it was a fair trade, get over it": Settler colonial logics, racial hierarchies and material dominance in Canadian agriculture. *Geoforum*, 82, 158–169. https://doi.org/10.1016/j.geoforum.2017.04.010

Rotz, S. and Fraser, E.D.G., 2015. Resilience and the Industrial Food System: Analyzing the Impacts of Agricultural Industrialization on Food System Vulnerability. *Journal of Environmental Studies and Sciences*, 5, 459–473.

Rotz, S., Fraser, E. D. G., & Martin, R. C. (2017). Situating tenure, capital and finance in farmland relations: implications for stewardship and agroecological health in Ontario, Canada. *The Journal of Peasant Studies*, 1–23. https://doi.org/10.1080/03066150.2017.1351953

Rudel, T., Kwon, O.-J., Paul, B., Boval, M., Rao, I., Burbano, D., McGroddy, M., Lerner, A., White, D., Cuchillo, M., Luna, M., and Peters, M., 2016. Do Smallholder, Mixed Crop-Livestock Livelihoods Encourage Sustainable Agricultural Practices? A Meta-Analysis. *Land*, 5 (1), 6.

Rutherford, S., 2007. Green Governmentality: Insights and Opportunities in the Study of Nature's Rule. *Progress in Human Geography*, 31 (3), 291–307.

Rydin, Y., 2007. Indicators as a Governmental Technology? The Lessons of Community-based Sustainability Indicator Projects. *Environment and Planning D: Society and Space*, 25 (4), 610–624.

Smithers, J., Lamarche, J., and Joseph, A.E., 2008. Unpacking the Terms of Engagement with Local Food at the Farmers' Market: Insights from Ontario. *Journal of Rural Studies*, 24 (3), 337–350.

Statistics Canada, 2011. *2011 Census of Agriculture*. Ottawa.

Troughton, M.J., 1989. The Role of Marketing Boards in the Industrialization of the Canadian Agricultural System. *Journal of Rural Studies*, 5 (4), 367–383.

Turner, B.L., 2010. Vulnerability and Resilience: Coalescing or Paralleling Approaches for Sustainability Science? *Global Environmental Change*, 20 (4), 570–576.

Turner, B.L., Kasperson, R.E., Matson, P.A., McCarthy, J.J., Corell, R.W., Christensen, L., Eckley, N., Kasperson, J.X., Luers, A., Martello, M.L., Polsky, C., Pulsipher, A., and Schiller, A., 2003. A Framework for Vulnerability Analysis in Sustainability Science. *Proceedings of the National Academy of Sciences of the United States of America*, 100 (14), 8074–8079.

United Nations, 2007. *Indicators of Sustainable Development: Guidelines and Methodologies*. Third Edition. New York: United Nations.

van der Ploeg, J.D., 2006. Agricultural production in crisis. *In*: P. Cloke, T. Marsden, and P. Mooney, eds. *Handbook of Rural Studies*. Thousand Oaks, CA: Sage Publications, 258–271.

Walker, J. and Cooper, M., 2011. Genealogies of Resilience: From Systems Ecology to the Political Economy of Crisis Adaptation. *Security Dialogue*, 42 (2), 143–160.

Walsh-Dilley, M., Wolford, W., and Mccarthy, J., 2016. Rights for Resilience: Food Sovereignty, Power, and Resilience in Development Practice. *Ecology and Society*, 21 (1).

Watts, M.J., 2011. Ecologies of rule: African environments and the climate of neoliberalism. *In*: C. Calhoun and G. Derluguian, eds. *The Deepening Crisis: Governance Challenges after Neoliberalism*. New York, USA: New York University, 67–91.

Winson, A., 1993. *The Intimate Commodity: Food and the Development of the Agro-Industrial Complex in Canada*. Aurora, ON: Garamond Press.

Woodhouse, P., 2010. Beyond Industrial Agriculture? Some Questions about Farm Size, Productivity and Sustainability. *Journal of Agrarian Change*, 10 (3), 437–453.

7

LESSONS FROM THE HISTORY OF GDP IN THE EFFORT TO CREATE BETTER INDICATORS OF PROSPERITY, WELL-BEING, AND HAPPINESS

Robert Costanza, Maureen Hart, Ida Kubiszewski,
Steve Posner, and John Talberth

There has been a long overdue flurry of recent activity in developing better indicators of national progress, prosperity, well-being, and happiness. This activity has arisen from the growing recognition of the inappropriate misuse of Gross Domestic Product (GDP) as a proxy for these goals. This article reviews the history of GDP and what we can learn from that history in creating new and better indicators of societal well-being.

For over a half century, the most widely accepted measure of a country's economic progress has been changes in GDP.[1] GDP is an estimate of market throughput, adding together the value of all 'final' goods and services that are produced and traded for money within a given period of time. It is typically measured by adding together a nation's personal consumption expenditures (payments by households for goods and services), government expenditures (public spending on the provision of goods and services, infrastructure, debt payments, etc.), net exports (the value of a country's exports minus the value of imports), and net capital formation (the increase in value of a nation's total stock of monetized capital goods).

Since its creation, economists who are familiar with GDP have emphasized that GDP is a measure of economic activity, not economic or social well-being. In 1934, Simon Kuznets, the chief architect of the United States national accounting system and GDP, cautioned against equating GDP growth with economic or social well-being. The US Bureau of Economic Analysis's description of GDP (McCulla and Smith 2007) states that the purpose of measuring GDP is to answer questions such as how fast is the economy growing? what is the pattern of spending on goods and services? what percent of the increase in production is due to inflation? and how much of the income produced is being used for consumption as opposed to investment or savings? To understand how GDP continues to be misused as a scorecard for national well-being, it is important to consider history and how the current national accounting system has evolved.

When GDP was initially developed in the US[2] in the 1930s and 1940s, the world was in the midst of major social and economic upheaval from two global wars and the Great Depression. President Roosevelt's government used the statistics to justify policies and budgets aimed at bringing the US out of the depression. As it became more likely that the US would become involved in World War II (WWII), there was a concern about whether this would jeopardize the standard of living of US citizens who were just beginning to recover from the depression. GDP estimates were used to show that the economy could provide sufficient supplies for fighting WWII while maintaining adequate production of consumer goods and services (Marcuss and Kane 2007).

The use of GDP as a measure of economic progress was further strengthened as a result of the Bretton Woods Conference. A key factor in the outbreak of WWII was economic instability in a number of countries caused by unstable currency exchange rates and discriminatory trade practices that discouraged international trade. In 1944, in order to avoid a recurrence, leaders of the 44 allied nations gathered in Bretton Woods, New Hampshire, to create a process for international cooperation on trade and currency exchange. The intent of the meeting was to "speed economic progress everywhere, aid political stability and foster peace" (UN Monetary and Financial Conference at Bretton Woods 1944). International trade would create jobs in all countries. Those jobs would provide income, allowing people everywhere to obtain adequate food, housing, medical care, and other amenities. Improving economic well-being was thus key to creating lasting world peace. Growing the economy was seen as the path to economic well-being.

The key outcomes of the meeting were the establishment of the International Monetary Fund (IMF) and the International Bank for Reconstruction and Development (IBRD – now part of the World Bank). The IMF was created as a forum for collaborative management of international monetary exchange and for stabilization of the exchange rates of countries' currencies. The World Bank was established to provide investment funds for infrastructure reconstruction and development in war-torn areas and less developed nations. In theory, the governing structures of these institutions were supposed to provide an equal voice to all member countries. In practice, because of its political and economic strength following WWII, the US dominated both institutions for the first quarter century. As a result, the US dollar, economy, and economic policies became the de facto standards against which other countries were compared. In addition, the work done by the US and UK Treasuries developing GDP methodologies for analyzing economic activity informed much of the discussion at the Bretton Woods meeting. As a result, GDP came to be used by the IMF and the World Bank as the primary measure of economic progress in the ensuing 60 years. With the restructuring of these institutions in the 1970s, the US has a less dominant position within the World Bank and the IMF; however, GDP remains the most widely cited measure of economic progress.

Economists have warned since its introduction that GDP is a *specialized* tool, and treating it as an indicator of general well-being is inaccurate and dangerous. However, over the last 70 years economic growth – measured by GDP – has become the *sine qua non* for economic progress. Per capita GDP is frequently used to compare quality of life in different countries. Governments often use changes in GDP as an indicator of the success of economic and fiscal policies. In the US, GDP is

> one of the most comprehensive and closely watched economic statistics: It is used by the White House and Congress to prepare the Federal budget, by the Federal Reserve to formulate monetary policy, by Wall Street as an indicator of economic activity, and by the business community to prepare forecasts of economic performance that provide the basis for production, investment, and employment planning.
>
> (McCulla and Smith 2007, p. 1)

Internationally, the IMF and the World Bank both use the changes in a country's GDP to guide policies and determine how and which projects are funded around the world.

Today, GDP in particular, and economic growth in general, is regularly referred to by leading economists, politicians, top-level decision-makers, and the media *as though* it represents overall progress. In fact, a report released by the World Bank states that long-term high rates of GDP growth (specifically a doubling of GDP each decade) is necessary to solve the world's poverty problem (Commission on Growth and Development 2008, p. 1). Essentially, this is like measuring a building's energy use and saying that the more electricity used, the better the quality of life of the building's inhabitants. Although electricity powers some of life's amenities, a higher electric bill, as many people are beginning to find out, does not equate to a better life.

In presenting GDP to Congress in 1934, Simon Kuznets discussed its uses and limits. After presenting an itemized list of the things measured by the GDP, Kuznets noted, "The boundaries of a 'nation' in 'national' income are still to be defined; and a number of other services, in addition to those listed above, might also be considered a proper part of the national economy's end-product". He went on to list "services of housewives and other members of the family", "relief and charity", "services of owned durable goods", "earnings from odd jobs", and "earnings from illegal pursuits" among others (Kuznets 1934, pp. 3–5). His stated reasons for excluding these things from the GDP largely boil down to his intent that GDP be a precise and above all a *specialized* tool, designed to measure only a narrow segment of society's activity. This is reflected in his fear that the simplicity of the GDP makes it prone to misuse:

> The valuable capacity of the human mind to simplify a complex situation in a compact characterization becomes dangerous when not controlled in terms of definitely stated criteria. With quantitative measurements especially, the definiteness of the result suggests, often misleadingly, a precision and simplicity in the outlines of the object measured. Measurements of national income are subject to this type of illusion and resulting abuse, especially since they deal with matters that are the center of conflict of opposing social groups where the effectiveness of an argument is often contingent upon oversimplification.
>
> (Kuznets 1934, pp. 5–6)

Because GDP measures only monetary transactions related to the production of goods and services, it is based on an incomplete picture of the system within which the human economy operates. As a result, GDP not only fails to measure key aspects of quality of life; in many ways, it encourages activities that are counter to long-term community well-being.

Of particular concern is that GDP measurement encourages the depletion of natural resources faster than they can renew themselves. Another concern is that current economic activity is degrading ecosystems thereby reducing the services that, until now, have been provided to humans virtually for free. In 1997, research by Costanza and colleagues estimated that the world's ecosystem provides benefits valued at an average of US$33 trillion per year. This is nearly double the total *global* economic GDP at the time as measured by NIPA (Costanza et al. 1997). However, in GDP terms, clear-cutting a forest for lumber is valued more than the ecosystem services that forest provides if left uncut. These services – including biodiversity habitat, reducing flooding from severe storms, filtration to improve water quality in rivers and lakes, and the sequestration of carbon dioxide and manufacture of oxygen – are not part of the market economy and as a result are not counted in GDP. As Herman Daly, formerly the senior economist at the World Bank, once commented, "the current national accounting system treats the earth as a business in liquidation" (cited in Cobb et al. 1995, digital edition).

Text Box

"Our Gross National Product . . . counts air pollution and cigarette advertising, and ambulances to clear our highways of carnage. It counts special locks for our doors and the jails for the people who break them. It counts the destruction of the redwood and the loss of our natural wonder in chaotic sprawl. It counts napalm and counts nuclear warheads and armored cars for the police to fight the riots in our cities . . . and the television programs which glorify violence in order to sell toys to our children. Yet the gross national product does not allow for the health of our children, the quality of their education or the joy of their play. It does not include the beauty of our poetry or the strength of our marriages, the intelligence of our public debate or the integrity of our public officials. It measures neither our wit nor our courage, neither our wisdom nor our learning, neither our compassion nor our devotion to our country, it measures everything, in short, except that which makes life worthwhile. And it can tell us everything about America except why we are proud that we are Americans". Robert F. Kennedy, speech at the University of Kansas, March 18, 1968 (Kennedy 1968)

Another concern about GDP as a measure of progress is what is known as the 'threshold effect.' As GDP increases, overall quality of life increases, but only up to a threshold point. Beyond this point, increases in GDP often result in no further increases or even decreases in well-being. This is due to the fact that the benefits provided by the increase in expenditures are offset by the costs associated with income inequality, loss of leisure time, and natural capital depletion (Max-Neef 1995, Talberth et al. 2007, Kubiszewski et al. 2013). In fact, an increasingly large and robust body of research confirms that beyond a certain threshold, further increases in material well-being are poor substitutes for community cohesion, healthy relationships, knowledge, wisdom, a sense of purpose, connection with nature, and other dimensions of human happiness (Kubiszewski et al. 2013). A strikingly consistent global trend suggests that as material affluence increases, these critical components of psychic income often decline amidst rising rates of alcoholism, suicide, depression, poor health, crime, divorce, and other social pathologies (McKibben 2007).

In addition, GDP also conceals a growing disparity between the haves and have-nots. Income disparity has been linked to poorer overall health in a country, decreased worker productivity, and increased social unrest (Bernasek 2006, Wilkinson and Pickett 2009).

> A highly unequal distribution of income can be detrimental to economic welfare by increasing crime, reducing worker productivity, and reducing investment. Moreover, when growth is concentrated in the wealthiest income brackets it counts less towards improving overall economic welfare because the social benefits of increases in conspicuous consumption by the wealthy are less beneficial than increases in spending by those least well off.
>
> (Talberth et al. 2007, p. 2)

The way forward

At the time it was conceived, GDP was a useful signpost on the path to a better world: a path where increased economic activity provided jobs, income, and basic amenities to reduce worldwide social conflict and prevent a third world war. That economic activity has created a world very different from the one faced by the world leaders who convened at Bretton Woods in 1944. We are now living in a world overflowing with people and man-made capital, where the emphasis on growing GDP and economic activity is leading the world back towards increasing conflict and environmental degradation. As Herman Daly said:

> Economists have focused too much on the economy's circulatory system and have neglected to study its digestive tract. Throughput growth means pushing more of the same food through an ever larger digestive tract; development means eating better food and digesting it more thoroughly.

> (Daly 2008, p. 2)

Now, the world is in need of new goals, goals with a broader view of interconnectedness of long-term, sustainable economic, social, and ecological well-being. We also need new ways to measure progress towards those goals. There is a need for a global dialogue on these issues.

In any new context, we first have to remember that the goal of an economy is to sustainably improve human well-being and quality of life. Material consumption and GDP are merely means to that end, not ends in themselves. We have to recognize, as both ancient wisdom and new psychological research tell us, that material consumption beyond real need can actually reduce overall well-being. Such a reorientation leads to specific tasks. We have to identify what really does contribute to human well-being, and recognize and gauge the substantial contributions of natural and social capital, both of which are coming under increasing stress. We have to be able to distinguish between real poverty in terms of low quality of life versus merely low monetary income. Ultimately we have to create a new vision of what the economy is and what it is for, and a new model of development that acknowledges the new full-world context (Costanza 2008).

To solve this problem, the time is right to embark on a new round of consensus-building that will re-envision what was institutionalized over the last 65 years. The consensus is already clear about the need for (1) new goals with a broader view of interconnectedness among long-term, sustainable economic, social, and ecological well-being; (2) better ways to measure progress towards international goals; (3) and an invigorated campaign for the realization of this evolved economic system. What is missing is a "New Bretton Woods". This series of meetings would function somewhat like the original Bretton Woods meetings in that they would set the goals, institutions, and measures for progress at multiple scales, from communities to states, countries, and the whole world. There would be major differences with the original Bretton Woods meetings, however. The new meetings would have additional clarity of purpose: to create solutions to today's global challenges, with care to bring onboard all the new thinking about what progress is and how to measure it. The goal of such a series of meetings would be broad consensus, with broad participation, high-level input, and transparent discussion and incorporation of the various complex measurement issues.

One method of building consensus is to create a global shared vision that is both desirable to the vast majority of humanity and ecologically sustainable (Prugh et al. 2000, Costanza and Kubiszewski 2013). Envisioning can also be seen as a key, but often missing, element in a true democracy. Democracy is about much more than simply voting for representatives. It is about building consensus around the kind of world we really want. The New England town meeting is a good example of real democracy. It is a gathering where an entire town sits down, once a year, to discuss where they are, where they want to go, and how to get there. Can we scale up this process? In order to do that, we need an ongoing discussion about how that world might look. Global communications made possible by the Internet might make sharing visions and scaling up real democracy possible.

As ecological, economic, and social crises deepen, we desperately need new visions of a sustainable and desirable world and ways to measure progress toward those visions. Isolated initiatives will not form an adequate response to our interconnected plights. Envisioning must also be seen as an ongoing process in which community members collectively identify shared values, describe the future they seek, and develop a plan to achieve common goals. Meeting these goals will require ways to measure progress that have as broad a consensus and are therefore as influential as GDP has been in the past.

Only after such a broad consensus is achieved about alternative indicators will it be possible to move beyond GDP to measures of what we really want and to achieve these goals.

Acknowledgements

This article is adapted from a paper by Costanza, Hart, Posner, and Talberth titled: "Beyond GDP: The Need for New Measures of Progress" originally published by the Frederick S. Pardee Center for the Study of the Longer-Range Future at Boston University.

Notes

1 The Gross National Product (GNP) is another frequently mentioned measure of economic progress. The difference between GDP and GNP is the production boundaries used. GDP measures all goods and services produced in the country whether by domestic or foreign companies. It excludes goods and services produced in other countries. GNP measures all production by domestic companies regardless of where in the world that production takes place. Because its boundaries coincide with the boundaries used to measure a country's population and employment, GDP is more useful for setting domestic policies and evaluating programs. To simplify the discussion in this document, the term GDP will be used throughout this paper to refer to the measure of economic activity although at times in the past, the actual measure used was GNP.
2 Work by the US and UK Treasuries in the 1930s and 1940s was the foundation of National Income and Product Accounts (NIPA) and GDP methodologies. Since then the work has been expanded on by many nations and has been formalized in the System of National Accounts (SNA) 1993 documentation available at http://unstats.un.org/unsd/nationalaccount/

References

Bernasek, A. 2006. Income Inequality, and Its Cost. *New York Times*, New York. June 25.
Cobb, C., T. Halstead, and J. Rowe. 1995. If the GDP Is up, Why Is America Down? *The Atlantic Monthly*, pp. 59–78.
Commission on Growth and Development. 2008. *The Growth Report: Strategies for Sustained Growth and Inclusive Development*. World Bank, Washington, DC.
Costanza, R. 2008. Stewardship for a "Full" World. *Current History*, 107: pp. 30–35.
Costanza, R., R. d'Arge, R. de Groot, S. Farber, M. Grasso, B. Hannon, S. Naeem, K. Limburg, J. Paruelo, R. V. O'Neill, R. Raskin, P. Sutton, and M. van den Belt. 1997. The Value of the World's Ecosystem Services and Natural Capital. *Nature*, 387: pp. 253–260.
Costanza, R. and I. Kubiszewski. 2013. Envisioning a Sustainable and Desirable Future. *World Scientific*. Singapore.
Daly, H. 2008. *A Steady-State Economy*. Sustainable Development Commission: London, UK.
Kennedy, R. F. 1968. *Speech at Lawrence Kansas. [cited 2008 July 12, 2008]*. Available from: www.jfklibrary.org/Historical+Resources/Archives/Reference+Desk/Speeches/RFK/RFKSpeech68Mar18UKansas.htm
Kubiszewski, I., R. Costanza, C. Franco, P. Lawn, J. Talberth, T. Jackson, and C. Aylmer. 2013. Beyond GDP: Measuring and Achieving Global Genuine Progress. *Ecological Economics*, 93: pp. 57–68.

Kuznets, S. 1934. *National Income 1929–1932, Senate Report, B.o.E.a.D.C. Division of Economic Research and B.o.E.a.D.C.* National Income Senate Report Division of Economic Research, Editors. US Government Printing Office, Washington, DC.

Marcuss, R. D. and R. E. Kane. 2007. U.S. National Income and Product Statistics: Born of the Great Depression and World War II. In *Bureau of Economic Analysis: Survey of Current Business*, pp. 32–46.

Max-Neef, M. 1995. Economic Growth and Quality of Life: A Threshold Hypothesis. *Ecological Economics*, 15 (2): pp. 115–118.

McCulla, S. H. and S. Smith. 2007. *Measuring the Economy: A Primer on GDP and the National Income and Product Accounts.* Bureau of Economic Analysis, US Department of Commerce, Washington, DC.

McKibben, B. 2007. *Deep Economy: The Wealth of Communities and the Durable Future.* Time Books, New York.

Prugh, T., R. Costanza, and H. Daly. 2000. *The Local Politics of Global Sustainability.* Island Press, Washington, DC. 173 pp.

Talberth, D. J., C. Cobb, and N. Slattery. 2007. *The Genuine Progress Indicator 2006: A Tool for Sustainable Development.* Redefining Progress, Oakland, CA.

United Nations Monetary and Financial Conference at Bretton Woods. July 22, 1944. Summary of Agreements. *World War II Resources 1946* [cited July 27, 2008]. Available from: www.ibiblio.org/pha/policy/1944/440722a.html

Wilkinson, R. G. and K. Pickett. 2009. *The Spirit Level: Why Greater Equality Makes Societies Stronger.* Bloomsbury, New York.

8

A SYSTEMS-THEORETICAL PERSPECTIVE ON SUSTAINABLE DEVELOPMENT AND INDICATORS[1]

Paul-Marie Boulanger[2]

1. Introduction

With the publication of the Brundtland report in 1987 (WCED 1987) and, more solemnly, at the United Nations Conference in Rio in 1992, the (world) society (Luhmann 1997) formalized a new way of observing itself and, in so doing, institutionalized a new self-description. From then on, society was to regard itself as "unsustainable". During the three decades following World War Two, the possibility of a nuclear war between the two opposing blocks had already given rise to a worldwide anxiety about the prospect of humanity destroying itself through the obliteration of its living environment. Likewise, a new way of observing the relations between society and the natural environment had become apparent in the early seventies, with several now almost legendary publications such as *The Limits to Growth* (Meadows, Meadows, Randers and Behrens III 1972), *Blueprint for Survival* (Goldsmith, Allen, Allaby, Davull and Lawrence 1972), *The Population Bomb* (Ehrlich 1968), *The Closing Circle* (Commoner 1971) and other less famous manifestos. At the end of the eighties, following the collapse of the communist block, the world society was confronted to a new challenge: becoming at once fully global and fully developed. The challenge was that development, as it was understood, could not become global without putting in peril its ecological basis but, at the same time, development that could not be extended to the whole humanity was not considered real development. A new model of development was to be imagined that could be shared by all people immediately without jeopardizing the future. This was called "sustainable development". As a result, at the 1992 UN Conference on Environment and Development, in Rio-de-Janeiro, 178 countries adopted the Agenda 21 action program by which they committed themselves to a host of resolutions and actions deemed able to put the world society on the path of sustainable development. Among these measures was the identification and use of indicators (see Dahl, Chapter 23). The use of indicators for assessing sustainable development is called for at several places in Agenda 21. It is mentioned in particular in Chapter 8 ("Integrating Environment and Development in Decision-Making"), with Article 8.5 stating that: "Countries could develop systems for monitoring and evaluation of progress towards achieving sustainable development by adopting indicators that measure changes across economic, social and environmental dimensions". (This, incidentally, is one of the earliest mentions of the so-called "three pillars of sustainable development".) Indicators were also called for in almost every chapter of Part 1 ("Social and Economic Dimensions"), in Chapter 35 ("Science for Sustainable Development") and in Article 40.4 where one reads that:

> Commonly used indicators such as the gross national product (GNP) and measurements of individual resource or pollution flows do not provide adequate indications of sustainability. Methods for assessing interactions between different sectoral environmental, demographic, social and developmental parameters are not sufficiently developed or applied. Indicators of sustainable development need to be developed to provide solid bases for decision-making at all levels and to contribute to a self-regulating sustainability of integrated environment and development systems.

As a consequence, from 1992 onwards, we have witnessed an important intellectual and financial investment in the production and discussion of indices of sustainability and sustainable development and the development of conceptual frameworks for the cognitive and normative integration of those indicators in the assessment of progress towards SD. Despite undeniable achievements in both domains (as this book testifies), there is a widely shared sentiment amongst researchers and activists in sustainable development that this increase in "ecological communication" has not delivered the expected (officially, at least, by the countries that endorsed the Agenda 21 program) changes in political and economical practices (Gudmundsson, Lehtonen, Bauler, Sebastien and Morse 2009; Lyytimäki, Gudmundsson and Sørensen 2014; Lyytimäki, Tapio, Varho and Söderman 2013; Lehtonen, Sébastien and Bauler 2016). It is nowadays common knowledge that the relation between information and decision is not the simple, linear, straightforward one assumed by the rationalist theory of decision. In this context, indicators, even if not explicitly mobilized in the policy-making process, can and do influence it in several ways (Boulanger 2007; Gudmunsson 2003). The success of the somewhat naïve calls for "evidence-based policies" – admittedly, in less obfuscate domains than sustainable development – has not come without criticisms (Saltelli and Giampietro 2017; Strassheim and Kettunen 2014). We have recently come to a more realistic, less utopian understanding of the relations between knowledge in general, indicators in particular and policy-making. We now know that the path from evidence-based policy to policy-based evidence is short, and at times the two are difficult to disentangle. Yet we still lack a theoretically based interpretation of the adequacy or otherwise of indicators generally and this is even more the case in sustainable development. Various classifications of the types of indicators (descriptive, normative, etc.), of their use or misuses, of their influences, consequences, etc., are mostly derived from inductive reflections and, on the whole, they lack the consistency and explanatory power of observations which one would have if a general theory were to be available. On the other hand, one may think that the way in which these issues have been dealt with so far has been overly influenced by what some have called "unreflected normativity"[3] (Irwin 2006). If there is no shortage of reflections that are anchored in Habermas's or other philosophers' perspectives on communicational rationality, the ethics of discussion, on deliberative democracy and on democratic participation, we will probably never have too much of that kind of "reflected normativity". Yet, what is probably lacking the most at this moment is an uncompromising "reflected positivity". What do we mean by that? We invite our reader to follow us in an analysis which takes its lead from a thinker who can be considered the anti-Habermas par excellence: the German sociologist Niklas Luhmann. Luhmann's absence of claim to normativity – a position that could be described as ambitious modesty (King and Schütz 1994) – should enable us to adopt an "analytically sceptical but not dismissive perspective" (Irwin 2006, p. 300) on the whole SI industry. The excessively (?) abstract nature of Luhmann's theories allows us to escape the traps of an overly "politically correct" view point as well as, hopefully, put aside for a moment our own axiological commitments. Hans-Georg Moeller maintains that "Luhmann's social theory is the best description and analysis of contemporary society presently available" (Moeller 2012, p. 3). Without going as far as Moeller, we note that a growing number of sociologists find in Luhmann's writings one of the deepest, far-reaching and sophisticated sociological theories of society.

The present chapter is organized as follows: as introduction, we briefly present Luhmann's vision of modern society as functionally differentiated, his theory of systems as the unity of a distinction system/environment, and the concepts of autopoiesis and operational closure. We conclude this section with a characterization of sustainability as a problem specific to modern society that has to accept a trade-off between the necessary reduction of the complexity of its environment and its environmental sustainability, an avenue already explored by Vladimir Valentinov. The next section deals in more detail with the way functional subsystems are structured around a binary code that regulates all their communications. It introduces the concept of "structural coupling" which describes the relations they maintain with each other and gives an interpretation of indicators as structures (i.e. condensation of expectations) used by systems in observing each other and observing how others observe them. This enables us to formalize in a system-theoretical way the difference between use and influence of indicators. We then turn to the problem of the structural couplings (if any) of society with its non-social environment. We argue that the reduction of its complexity is taken care of by technology, in fact by a whole machinery of reduction of the complexity of natural non-living and living systems or aggregates. This leads to the question of the reference class of sustainability indicators: is it nature as such or technologies and therefore decisions on technological choices and their risks? Going back to indicators, we show that they are also technological beings and therefore complexity-reduction devices, as "forms" in Spencer-Brown sense and as punctuations (discretizations) of continuous processes. After having summarized some of the ideas and arguments presented in the whole chapter in a section devoted to the Ecological Footprint, we conclude with some prospective considerations on the possible emergence of a new fully autonomous autopoietic functional system in charge of the survival of the world society (as a functionally differentiated one) thanks to the handling of the binary code "sustainable/unsustainable" and its programs (sustainability assessments methods and models) and structures (indicators).

2. Why (or how) is modern society unsustainable?

While the world society that began observing itself through the sustainable/unsustainable distinction was not wholly developed, it was nevertheless roughly "modern". At least, there was a universal consensus on the fact that it was impossible not to be modern because there was literally no alternative unless one decided to exclude oneself from world society. But what did "to be modern" exactly mean? Few words have been as thoroughly discussed and commented than "modernity". In some ways, it has been the main – if not the only – concern of sociology since its inception. This has been true for its founding fathers (Emile Durkheim, Karl Marx, Vilfredo Pareto, Max Weber, Ferdinand Tönnies) and it remains so for most pro-eminent contemporary scholars such as Talcott Parsons, Anthony Giddens, Zygmunt Bauman, Alain Touraine, Jürgen Habermas and Niklas Luhmann. They have all emphasized and analyzed different facets of modernity but its most often acknowledged and highlighted singularity, compared to any other society, is its mode of internal differentiation. In particular, with the exception perhaps of Durkheim and Parsons, no other sociologist has given more attention and importance to the internal mode of differentiation of modern society than Luhmann. According to him, societies can be differentiated from one another by the existence or non-existence of a principle of internal differentiation and, if any, by the nature of the principle of differentiation at work. He distinguishes four principles of differentiation: segmentation, centre-periphery, social stratification and functional differentiation. It is the latter which characterizes the society which gradually formed within Europe during the sixteenth to eighteenth centuries. Modern society is differentiated in functional subsystems: law, economics, politics, science, religion, education, mass media, art, etc. This does not mean that other forms of internal differentiation have completely disappeared – for instance, being a plurality of national states, the world political system is still structured in a segmentary way – but the dominant and structuring principle of modern society is the differentiation into subsystems organized around the fulfilment of a societal function: economy deals with scarcity; politics provides collectively binding decisions, science is in charge of the production of knowledge, education ensures the preparation of psychic systems for communication, etc. These different functions, formerly closely intertwined, gradually broke apart from each other and are nowadays performed by different, specialized systems. It is therefore a fully functionally differentiated society that began to observe itself through the distinction "sustainable/unsustainable" and to combine this with two other already established distinctions: global/local and developed/underdeveloped. It is then very natural to assume that there is some relation between functional differentiation and unsustainability. In order to understand why, or more exactly, in what way a society composed (mainly) of functionally differentiated systems compromises its ecological basis, it is necessary to clearly appreciate both the systemic and the social character of the functional subsystems. The systemic character is summarized by two (somewhat pedantic) concepts: operational closure and autopoiesis.

Contrary to almost the entire tradition in systems theory, the founding principle of modern system theory and Luhmann's in particular, is not the whole-parts relationship but the system-environment distinction. Luhmann used to say that a system is not a unity, nor a totality but a difference, or, more exactly, the unity of a difference system-environment. Systems are flow of operations that connect and interlink with one another over time, with the result of perpetuating a system-environment distinction of its own. In other words, the system continuously reproduces itself as distinguished from its environment with its own elements as building blocks. This is the phenomenon of autopoiesis (Maturana and Varela 1980). For instance, consciousness (which Luhmann calls "the psychic system") is the uninterrupted flow and mutual linking of thoughts in one's mind, and what constitutes the identity of a "psychic system" (as consciousness) is the singularity of its thoughts compared to anyone else's. The same is true for what constitutes a human organism as a biological system, which enables its immune system to preserve it as a unique living entity, different from any other (except a perfect twin) and explains the rejections that occur after an organ transplant.

Systems are operationally closed. A system can "act" only inside its own boundaries. It is incapable of intervening directly on the operations of other systems and in return, they are unable to interfere with it. In other words, no system can intervene in the autopoiesis of another system. According to Luhmann, this is true even for the political system of modern society. It cannot – unless it renounces to be modern – decide in place of science on what is true or not about the world and the communist experience has shown that it cannot without much trouble abolish the difference between political and economic operations. Operational closure does not mean closeness to their environment. On the contrary, operational closure is a correlate to causal opening to the environment. The relationship between a system and its environment will be discussed in more detail hereafter with the concept of structural coupling.

The operations of autopoietic systems are recursive, that is to say, they are based on the results of previous operations. The operations of the system at any time depend on its present state, which is the outcome of its past operations, and on the present state of its environment. In other words, the system is always a mixture of self-reference and other-reference. The self-reference functions as a binary code which decides, during the interval between t and t + 1, on the acceptance or rejection of the operation to come. It presupposes the ability to observe itself, which amounts to recapitulating the sequence of its past operations and characterizing them.

What makes systems social is the nature of their operations. Social systems consist of communications, and only communications.[4] Communication events are essentially, but not exclusively, linguistics. A monetary transaction, a vote, a decision (inasmuch as it is not confined to the consciousness of the person who takes it) are communications. Functional systems constitute environments for each other, of which they are distinct but with which they maintain relationships. The economy is an environment for politics, the legal system, science, arts, education, the mass media, etc., and they in turn are environments for politics, economy, the legal system, and so on. More generally, functional systems, as belonging to society, constitute for each other a societal environment, an environment made only of communications, differently coded than their own. In addition to its societal environment, each subsystem (and society in general) is facing an extra-societal environment consisting of non-social systems or objects, in which Luhmann puts human beings both as living organisms and as psychic systems and, the bio-physical environment (which is not a system to Luhmann).[5]

We can now be somewhat more specific about sustainability and sustainable development: it has to do with the relation between social systems (systems made of communications) and their non-social environment, which is not made of communications but of bodies, minds and thoughts for the human environment, and a lot of inert matter, energy and living systems for the bio-physical one. The *raison d'être* of the differentiation of society in functional subsystems is the reduction of the complexity of this environment. Modern system theory (as opposed to classical system theory) maintains that for any system, its environment is more complex than itself and that any system has to reduce this complexity in order to survive. No system can handle the full complexity of its environment. It would be quickly overwhelmed if it tried to do so. Since modern society reduces the complexity of its non-social environment by differentiating itself in subsystems, it does so at the expense of an increase in its own complexity. It follows that, as Vladimir Valentinov (2014) elegantly puts it, there is a "trade-off between sustainability and complexity". The complexity of human beings is reduced by "slicing" them in as many parts as the functional systems to which they participate, a slicing responsible for the feeling of alienation and meaninglessness that accompanies modernity. As for the complexity of nature, it is reduced through technology. This trade-off obtains at the level of the causal relations between systems and their environment, which is the domain of what (modern) system theorists call "structural couplings".

3. Binary coding, structural couplings and indicators

Functional systems have all their communications shaped by a binary code: true/untrue for the scientific system; payment/non-payment for the economy; government/opposition for policy; information (i.e. new)/non-information (i.e. old) for mass media; legal/illegal for law, etc.

> A code must fulfil the following requirements: (1) it must correspond to the system's function, which is to say, it must be able to translate the viewpoint of the function into a guiding difference; and (2) it must be complete. . . . The code must completely cover the functional domain for which the system is responsible. It must therefore (3) be selective with regard to the external world and (4) provide information within the system. (5) The code must be open to supplements (programs) that offer (and modify)

criteria to determine which of the two code values is to be considered in any given case. (6) All of this is cast into the form of a preferential code, that is, into an asymmetrical form that requires a distinction between a positive and a negative value. The positive value can be used within the system; at the least, it promises a condensed probability of acceptance. The negative value serves as a value of reflection; it determines what kinds of program are most likely to fulfil the promise of meaning implied in the positive code value.

(Luhmann 2000a, p. 186)

If the binary coding determines the ultimate meaning of communications for the functional subsystems, it is at the level of programs that they open themselves causally to their environment. Programs are guidelines, methods, criteria that allow the code to be applied. Theories and methods are science's programs; for the legal systems these are norms, constitutions, etc.; political parties' programs are parts of the program of the political system in democracy, and so on. The nature of the relations between functions, codes and programs for the different functions system is synthesized in Table 8.1.

The execution of functional programs necessitates resources supplied by the social environment. Therefore, every functional system is dependent on the others. The political system needs (growing) financial resources for satisfying (ever growing) demands from the other systems. The economy needs laws to ensure that contracts are being honoured or that sanctions are applied; all systems need competent individuals able to execute their programs and they expect the education system to provide them. And all need the mass media because "Whatever we know about

Table 8.1 Synthetic representation of the main functional systems according to Luhmann

System	Function	Efficacy	Code	Program	Organizations
Law	Elimination of the contingency of normative expectations	Regulation of conflicts	Legal/illegal	Laws, constitutions, etc.	Courts
Politics	Making collectively binding decisions	Practical application of collectively binding decisions	Government/ opposition Power/ no-power	Political parties' programs, government's programs	Parties
Science	Production of knowledge	Supply of knowledge	True/false	Theories, methods	Laboratories, universities
Religion	Elimination of contingency	Spiritual and social services	Transcendence/ immanence	Holy scriptures, dogmas	Churches, sanctuaries in general
Economy	Prevention of shortages	Satisfaction of needs	Payment/non- payment	Budgets, investments	Firms
Etc. (Mass media, education, health...)	...	...	...	...	...

Source: Adapted from Moeller (2006, p. 29)

our society, or indeed about the world we live in, we know through the mass media" (Luhmann 2007, p. 1), etc. These kinds of linkages between systems are called "structural couplings".

> [C]oupling mechanisms are called structural couplings if a system presupposes certain features of its environment on an ongoing basis and relies on them structurally . . . structural coupling is a form, too, and a two-sided [*sic*] at that, and that means it is a distinction. What it includes (couples with) is as important as what it excludes. Accordingly, the forms of a structural coupling *reduce* and so *facilitate* influences of the environment on the system.
>
> (Luhmann 2004, p. 382)

Indicators are structures[6] that systems use in order to observe their environment. They condense expectations with respect to it. More precisely, the systems expect that things do not change too quickly or too radically in their environment (otherwise the indicators would have to be permanently changed), but also that these expectations could be invalidated (otherwise they would not monitor it in this way). Changes (positive or negative) can occur and it is important for the systems to be informed sufficiently early to react, possibly by adapting their programs and structures (including, if necessary, their indicators). Functional systems observe each other in conformity with their own (binary) codes and structures, according to their structural couplings with their environment. For the economic system, something has meaning if it relates to actual or possible payments (markets, prices); for science, if it consists of statements open to verification so that they can be classified *in fine* as true or untrue; for politics, what matters is how it connects to the government/opposition or majority/minority distinction and what are the consequences in the perspective of future elections, which depends on public opinion (through which it is structurally coupled with the system of the mass media) and so on. Viewed in terms of structural couplings, the GDP, even if made of economic data, is a political indicator, not an economic one. Through the GDP, and the distinction growth/stagnation, the political system (and perhaps other systems as well) monitor its structural coupling with the economy. The same is true for other seemingly economic indicators such as the unemployment rate. The distinction growth/stagnation is particularly important for the political system because its budgetary resources are closely dependent on (are structurally coupled with) the level of economic activity. The political system's legitimacy and the credibility of its programs are indexed on economic growth which makes possible both the reduction of unemployment and the response to the growing demands made on it as a welfare state. As for the economic system, it observes itself through markets (notably the stock markets of which the Dow Jones is the leading indicator) that provide a representation of the economy as a whole to its various subsystems and it concentrates its external observations on its political and legal environment with indicators of safety of investments in the countries of the world, of competitiveness, of taxations levels, of trade-unions influence and so on.[7] The political system observes itself in the mirror of public opinion[8] (through which it is coupled to the mass media); the scientific system has its H–index and G–index; and so on.

Functional systems observe each other but they also know that they are being observed. They observe how others observe them and may be "irritated" (that is, stimulated) by it. An interesting example of the process of mirroring observations with resulting consequences for the observed system is given by the performance indices of the education system, such as, for example, the PISA indicator of the Program for International Student Assessment OECD, the Shanghai Academic Ranking of World Universities or the QS World University Ranking (QSWUR). The success of these rankings is understandable when one considers the coupling of almost any other system with the education system as their functioning needs people with the required skills.

The education system must also meet the expectations that families, who want the best possible career prospects for their children, maintain towards the school. About the role of rankings on America's law schools, Espeland and Sauder (2012) remark:

> Law school rankings have influenced almost every aspect of legal education, despite the fact that they were initially denounced by most administrators and by virtually all of the professional organizations associated with legal education. They have changed which schools students apply to and attend. They have changed how resources are distributed within the schools; for example, schools have shifted money from need-based to merit-based scholarships in order to raise their median LSAT scores and improve their rank. Rankings have also changed the work routines and career paths of many administrators; career service personnel, for instance, now spend much more time tracking down students to find out if they are employed – a key component of the ranking formula – often at the expense of additional individual career counseling or networking with employers.
>
> (Espeland and Sauder 2012, p. 89)

In the language of system theory, the distinction between use and influence of indicators can be stated as follows: A system *uses* an indicator if it changes its structures and programs according to its own observations. Conversely, it is influenced by an indicator if it adapts its programs in reaction to the way it is observed by the systems in its environment.

4. What structural couplings: with nature or technology?

Functional systems observe their societal environment with a particular focus on their structural couplings. In the SD domain, we are concerned with non-social environments, which are, according to Luhmann, human beings, nature and technology. We will leave aside here the important question of the structural couplings between society and the human beings[9] and focus on the society-nature-technology relations. Whilst the topic has not been investigated in these terms by Luhmann, there are some indications that he considered that modern society's coupling with nature was nowadays mediated by technology.[10] In his last opus, he wrote:

> The structural coupling of the physical world and society can no longer be captured by the concept of nature. . . . The nature concept is replaced in this context by the paired concepts energy/work and energy/economy. Technology consumes energy and performs work and in this manner links physical givens with society.
>
> (Luhmann 2012, p. 322)

We have mentioned Valentinov's (2014, 2017) analysis of the sustainability problem as a trade-off between societal internal complexity and full awareness of the complexity of its environment. We think it necessary to add to Valentinov's analysis[11] a consideration of the role technology is playing as a medium between society and nature, but also in some way between human beings and nature. As an organism, the human individual is coupled with its ecological environment through its perception and motion organs but nowadays it rarely has access to a genuine, pristine natural environment. The air humans breathe, the water they drink, the food they eat, the scenery they contemplate are so modified by technologies that it is almost impossible to disentangle what is nature and what is culture. What is important about technologies is that they are the most powerful and pervasive complexity reduction machinery the social systems make use of in their relation with nature. At the more abstract level, technology is driven by the distinction "work/doesn't work". This distinction supposes selecting some causal forces operating in the environment and transforming or diverting them in order to make them work as (or in) an artefact:

> What is called technology is a functioning simplification in the medium of causality. We could also say that within the simplified area strict (functioning under normal circumstances, recurrent) couplings are established. This is, however, possible only if interference by external factors is to a large extent excluded. Technology can therefore also be understood as the extensive causal closure of an operational area.
>
> (Luhmann 2008, p. 87)

Abstracting or insulating some mechanisms or processes from their original context of functioning constitutes a reduction of the complexity of nature that has already been dramatic in its consequences with rather simple substances like DDT and can be still more so with "high technologies" such as nuclear plants, GMOs, nanotechnologies, etc. It is tantamount to cutting, as with a scalpel, in the complex network of interacting factors and feedbacks of which natural (and especially living and ecological) systems are made of. The distinction "works or not" boils down to "successful or unsuccessful reduction of complexity", or to "controllable or uncontrollable states of affairs". Yet, "we also know . . . that complexity itself can be captured in no reduction, can be represented in no model. Even if it works, we must also expect something to be left over. 'Successful' reduction thus amounts to harmless ignoring" (Luhmann 2013, p. 317). The problem is that, sometimes, what looked first as "harmless ignoring" reveals itself to be quite risky if not definitively catastrophic. The burning of fossils fuels, the spreading of DDT, the handling of asbestos, the habit of smoking, etc., are but dramatic examples of such mistakes. If all important relations between society and its bio-physical environment are mediated by technology, it follows that the issue of environmental sustainability can be stated in terms of technological risks,[12] which means in terms of decisions regarding which technology to adopt (and, beforehand, to develop), and this for any organization, whatever the functional system it belongs to. As Bartelmus (Chapter 15, this volume) remarks, there has been much GDP bashing in the SI (and SD) community and sometimes for good reasons, but if we agree that the couplings of functional systems with the bio-physical environment are mediated by technology, there is no particular reason for blaming the economy more than any other system for society's unsustainability. Of course, not all functional systems are coupled at the same degree to technologies. The scientific system, the health system or the mass media – not to mention the army – certainly make a more intensive use of energy and materials than the legal system, religion or arts but all contribute to the environmental crisis. Yet, it is the economy and economic growth in particular that is most generally blamed for it. This was already apparent in the Agenda 21 program, which focused mainly on indicators complementary or alternative to GDP and was more than neutral with respect to technologies. In fact, most references to technologies in the document concerned transfer of technologies from developed to developing countries, as if the technologies of developed countries were more benign than the ones of less developed countries. Because the economy, like any social system, consists of – and only of – communications and observations, it cannot directly intervene in the functioning of ecosystems. Payments as such have no impact on the bio-physical environment of society. The financial system, which is a subsystem of the economy, gives a clear demonstration that economical communications can be totally disconnected from any linkage with the material world (precisely what many activists blame it for!), except through the information technologies they make use of. On the other hand, the simple idea of giving more importance to one or another functional system at the expense of others in the fate of the whole society is totally foreign to Luhmann's perspective (Luhmann 1987). There is no overarching system and no "determination in last instance". The economy is what it is because all other systems are what they are and they are all structurally coupled to energy and material through their use of housing, transportation, information processing . . . technologies. Technology is indeed one of the three factors taken in consideration in the IPAT identity but the SD community is divided as to which factor to highlight: T, A or P[13]? Actually, several of the founding fathers (or grandfathers) and mothers of our contemporary ecological consciousness such as Oswald Spengler, Lewis Mumford, Rachel Carson, Jacques Ellul, Gunther Anders, Fritz Schumacher, Ivan Illich, Bertrand de Jouvenel and others thought that the role of technology and of the technological mindset in the coming environmental crises was deeper than the responsibility of the economy or the politics.

5. Indicators as reduction of complexity

What is true of technology in general is also true of indicators, because they are (information) technologies. Like all technologies they reduce complexity, and they do so in two important respects:

1   Indicators are observation devices, but what is observing? According to George Spencer-Brown (1969) observing is the unity of a distinction and an indication. You cannot observe something until you distinguish it from something else (at least, everything else) and focus on one side of the distinction, which is then called indicated or "marked", and leaving the other "unmarked". The unity of a distinction and an indication is called a "form" (Figure 8.1).

It is important to be aware that both sides of the distinction are important, even if only one is focused on. The marked side makes sense only in reference to the unmarked one. For instance, the "risk" in a risk/safety distinction is different from the same word in a risk/danger distinction. As Luhmann (2008) shows, the two lead to very different observations. Indicators are "forms" also; they focus only on the marked space and leave as much if not more of the "world" unobserved, including the operation of distinction itself. For instance, in the SD community, GDP is blamed (once again) for leaving "unmarked" a lot of (supposedly) important non-monetary phenomena. Of course, this is true as it is true of any observation.

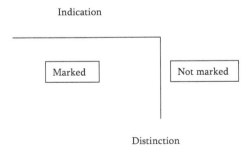

Figure 8.1   Form as the unity of distinction and indication

Source: Spencer-Brown (1969)

133

GDP divides the world in monetized and non-monetized things and it is important to understand that both sides of the distinction are important. It is the unity of the distinction that matters. There must be some non-monetized things in the world in order to make sense of the monetized ones. Therefore, by attempting to bring back on the monetized side (the indicated one) as many elements from the non-monetized one (unmarked) as possible, we run the risk of abolishing the distinction itself and therefore of condemning oneself to being unable to observe anything. It is only at a second level of observation that the system (or another one), making use of another distinction, is able to observe the first observation, and discover its contingent character. The distinction sustainable/unsustainable can thus be considered the leading distinction of a second-order observation of the first-order observation using the developed/underdeveloped form.

2   Indicators digitalize (make discrete) analogous (continuous) processes. To be useful for binary coded systems and for decision-making in organizations, indicators must reduce the complexity of a continuous phenomenon to a very limited number of significant (for the user) categories (an operation sometimes called punctuation), if not simply to the binary code itself. It is particularly true in SD where the set of values of observations should be separated in two subsets: sustainable and unsustainable. This is in many cases (if not all of them) an obvious reduction of the complexity of the nexus of mechanisms and processes of positive and negative feedback.[14] Yet it is indispensable: without threshold values for ppm of GHG in the atmosphere (445) or for the increase in average temperature at a given horizon (+ 2 degrees Celsius), the mission of the parties at the United Nations Convention on Climate Change would be impossible. The "punctuation" of continuous processes for usability in policy-making can only very rarely be based only on scientific evidence. It involves taking account of uncertain social consequences whose assessment mixes necessarily scientific and normative considerations and there is necessarily some arbitrariness in this. It is at this stage that participation of the public can be the more legitimate and effective (Bell and Morse, Chapter 12, this volume). As Bell and Morse write in their introduction:

> The indicator community did not suggest that SIs should be expert impositions, and neither should we pretend that there can only be one set of "true" SIs that apply. Rather they are emergent from process, and hence can be contestable. This goes against the grain of science and for some it is an uncomfortable and maybe even unacceptable position. To suggest that we do not have the "truth" and the best or only way to represent that "truth" is to play into the hands of those who wish to dominate with their own agendas.

If reducing complexity is unavoidable, the challenge is to determine the level and scope of reduction necessary and sufficient for "irritating" society's functional systems. In that respect, one can wonder if we are not going too far in an excessive reduction of complexity with some "mashup" indices (Ravaillon 2010) of SD. Throughout the Agenda 21 and almost all of the literature that followed, GDP is criticized not only because of its blindness to environmental damages but also because it gives an inaccurate and partial vision of the psychological comfort of people ("well-being"). Hence, the development of indices attempting to capture in one figure as many sectors of the bio-physical environment as possible together with the human state of well-being. We refer here to various attempts to enrich the GDP with environmental and welfare dimensions such as with the Index of Sustainable Economic Welfare, the Genuine Progress Indicator, the Genuine Savings Index, the Happy Planet Index, etc. Pretending to condense in one single index the complexity of two of the non-social environments of society, that is, the human being as an arrangement of organic and psychic systems, and the bio-physical environment in all its diversity, constitutes a formidable challenge in terms of reduction of complexity. It is also being oblivious to the complexity of the social world to believe that there exists something like a central agency inside society able to steer on such a basis the whole system's relations with its environments, or otherwise, that each functional subsystem can extract from them the required and relevant information it needs to adapt itself. Both assumptions are false, Luhmann argues. Indeed, by pointing only to the economic system or to the political one (but giving it the mission to steer the economy), "Beyond GDP" indices assume either that it is possible to reduce the complexity of society to only one of its subsystems: the economy or the political system or, still worse, that society exists outside or above its subsystems and the organizations that belongs to them. There is no overarching principle or centre in contemporary society that could play the role God, the King, the nobility or empires' capitals played in past societies.

The case of the Ecological Footprint

An indicator is intended to transform data into information, for instance data about rising temperatures and about GHG emissions are transformed into information on the relation between human production and consumption patterns and global change. However there is no such thing as information, period. "Information is a purely system-internal quality. There is no transference of information from the environment into the system. The environment remains what it is. At best, it contains data" (Luhmann 1989, p. 18). It follows that each system considers the data about temperatures and GHG emissions differently: some ignore them altogether; others can be irritated by them but only on the basis of their own codes and programs. Take for instance the Ecological Footprint indicator (Wackernagel et al., Chapter 16, this volume). It is interpreted in a totally different way by the scientific research system and by the system of the mass media. The science system cannot but look at it with the lenses of its binary code: true/untrue. Yet, whilst born of the scientific system, the EF doesn't convince everyone in the scientific community (van den Bergh and Verbruggen 1999; Kitzes et al. 2009; Giampietro and Saltelli 2014; Galli et al. 2016). Still, and despite its uncertain scientific status, the EF can be considered a success story: a Google search done at the 02/02/2015 date delivers about 1.760.000 references, compared to 461.000 for the Index of Sustainable Economic Welfare, 448.000 for the Genuine Savings Index and 272.000 for the Genuine Progress Indicator. This can be attributed to its endorsement by several NGOs (WWF, the New Economic Foundation, Redefining Progress) but also to some idiosyncratic features of the index which make it well suited to the need of the system of the mass media. The (general) mass media system whose internal code is information/no-information (which boils down to new/old) has been interested in the EF and could easily include it in its autopoiesis for several reasons that are worth exploring a bit. First of all, like the GDP's growth rate or the unemployment rate, it is a quantity and Luhmann (2000c, pp. 28–29) observes:

> Quantities are a particularly effective attention-grabber. Quantities are always informative, because any particular number is none other than the one mentioned – neither larger nor smaller. And this holds true regardless of whether one understands the material context (that is, whether or not one knows what a gross national product is. . .). The information value can be increased in the medium of quantity if one adds comparative figures, whether they be temporal (the previous year's rate of inflation), or factual, for example, territorial.

So quantification can generate sudden moments of insight without any substance and simultaneously more information for those who already have some knowledge.

But, of course, this is not enough. Almost all indicators are quantities (more or less) but not all of them receive the same attention from the general mass media. The second characteristic of the EF, which makes it well suited to the mass-media requirements, is its multi-level relevance. Because it can be computed at the levels of the household, the city, the region, the country and the world, information is given a local if not a personal reference and this feature has greatly contributed to the surfacing and diffusion of the ecological topic in society's communications. Referring to the diffusion of the ecological concerns, as Luhmann explains,

> The speed with which this complex of topics has been introduced and spread is certainly due partly to protest movements operating in close collaboration with the media, but above all to the mass media themselves. Many selection criteria come together in this context: high figures, a steady supply of disasters, events triggered by technology and therefore contingent, ideological and political conflicts about the appropriate attitude to adopt. Then there are the local and at the same time supralocal relevance and the largely invisible form of threat.
>
> (Luhmann 2013, p. 317)

6. Conclusion: an emerging sustainability functional system?

In a functionally differentiated society whose systems are articulated around a binary coding, which system is able to take care of the ecological question? This is the question posed by Luhmann in 1989 by publishing *Ecological Communication*. Three years after the publication of this book, at the United Nations Conference on Environment and Development, world society formalized its self-observation with the categories sustainable/unsustainable and described itself as unsustainable. There is no trace of the sustainability concept and therefore of the sustainable/unsustainable distinction in Luhmann's 1989 opus, nor even in the two articles published around or just after the Rio Conference addressing the ecological issue (Luhmann 1993, Luhmann 1998). We had no clue that Luhmann's foresight would be the birth of a new functional subsystem. Yet, the burgeoning of indicators, (and the controversies about them), conceptual frameworks and assessments methods that followed the 1992 Rio Conference can be interpreted as the possible emergence of a new functional social system, striving to find its place next to the extant incumbent ones. This means that an additional row would have to be inserted in Table 8.1 with, in the "code" column, the distinction "sustainable/unsustainable", and in the "Program" one: indicators and Sustainability Impact Assessment frameworks and methods. This new system's function would be to take care of the survival of humanity and of its living environment and its efficacy would be assessed in terms of sustainable human well-being. Therefore, whilst being a further diversification of the modern society, the coming of this new system would however overcome the current trade-off between complexity and sustainability, responsible for the coming ecological disasters. In the "Organizations" column we would probably see institutions like the IPPC. perhaps with a more participatory component. Being distinct from science, politics or law, etc., its basic binary code "sustainable/unsustainable" would not be reducible to true/false, power/no-power or legal/illegal, or any other distinction used by the social systems in its environment. As for sustainability indicators, for instance, they would still have to be underpinned by scientific theories, methods and observations but their logic would nevertheless remain distinct from the scientific one, if only because they involve a risk evaluation component foreign to pure scientific communication. Of course, structural couplings would have to be established with the other systems and the "ecological communication" would have to be understood and translated in their own semantics. In order to be effective, the sustainability function system should be able to trigger new applications of the "true/false", "government/opposition", "tradable/non-tradable", "legal/illegal", etc., distinctions, but in no ways try to substitute its own code to theirs. In short, it would have to accept a functionally differentiated society and respect the autonomy of the other systems. As a social system, it would also be a meaning-constituted one, made of communications only. It would not (and could not) communicate with the bio-physical environment but only with other social systems. It would focus on the decisions taken in the organizations of the other functioning systems: the state, administration and parties for the political system; firms and corporations for the economic system; universities and research centres for the science system; hospitals for the health system and so on, and screen them with its sustainable/unsustainable sieve. All this is already on the way, more or less, and only the future will tell if it will continue but there exist temptations to return to a less differentiated society, with science, politics or even religion taking an hegemonic position and, in the very name of sustainability, pretending to decide alone what is collectively binding or not, legal or illegal (for science or religion); true or false, legal or illegal, transcendent or immanent (for politics), etc. The risk exists that a sustainability functional system, once fully developed, becomes able to claim the superiority of the sustainable/unsustainable distinction over all other binary codes and in the name of human survival as preeminent value, erodes the autonomy of the others social systems and gives rise to a differently structured society, possibly far away from what we understand today by "sustainable development". This means that even if we are impatient with the slowness with which the incumbent systems (mainly the political, the economical and the educational ones) react and adapt to the messages of our indicators, we maybe have to refrain the temptation to deprive them of their autonomy and to put them under (our?) control.

Notes

1 I want to thank Simon Bell and Stephen Morse for their support and patience; Andrea Saltelli and Vladislav Valentinov for their responsiveness and suggestions and Pascale Boulanger for her invaluable help. Errors and clumsiness are mine.

2 E-mail: pm.boulanger@skynet.be

3 And we don't clear one's name from the grievance.

4 One would be tempted to add observations except that observations are communications too.

5 To which Luhmann sometime adds technology. More on technology shortly.

6 Luhmann uses the term "structure" in a different way than most sociologists. A "structure" consists of expectations a structure holds with respect to its environment. Learning, for instance, means changing one's expectations, changing one's structures.

7 For a comprehensive list of the various indices used by functional systems to observe each other, see Bandura (2008).

8 See "Die öffentliche Meinung" in Luhmann (2000b). For a French translation, *cfr.* Luhmann (2001).

9 It is a topic explored in details by Luhmann, for the most part with the concept of "interpenetration".

10 The status of technology in Luhmann's writings is unclear. Luhmann (1990, 2013: 312–324) didn't consider technology as a system or at least, not as a social or autopoietic one (Chaskiel 2008), but see Reichel (2011).

11 In a recent article written with Spencer Thompson, Valentinov does in fact consider technology, albeit only at the micro level of the firm (Thompson and Valentinov 2017).

12 Technology is of course one of the three factors taken in consideration in the IPAT identity. However, it is more often than not the A factor more than the T one or the P one which is emphasized in the SD community.

13 In Chapter 9, this volume, Spangenberg distinguishes between "modificationists" and "transformationists". It is tempting to assimilate the former to T-champions and the latter to A-ones. But things are not that simple: there can be modificationists and transformationists in both camps.

14 Analog communication is of a higher level of intrinsic complexity than digital communication. However the latter is of a higher logical level. See Wilden (1980). Especially Chapter VII "Analog and Digital Communication: On Negation, Signification and Meaning".

References

Bandura, R. 2008. *A Survey of Composite Indices Measuring Country Performances, 2008 Update*. Office of Development Studies, United Nations Development Programme (UNDP), New York.

Boulanger, P.-M. 2007. Political uses of social indicators: Overview and application to sustainable development indicators. *International Journal of Sustainable Development*. 10(1–2): 14–32.

Chaskiel, P. 2008. Luhmann et le mystère du risque technologique: Un retour de l'opinion publique? *Réseaux*. 151: 63–90.

Commoner, B. 1971. *The Closing Circle: Nature, Man and Technology*. Random House, New York.

Ehrlich, P.R. 1968. *The Population Bomb*. A Sierra Club-Ballantine Book, New York.

Espeland, W.E. and Sauder, M. 2012. The dynamism of indicators. In Davis, K.E, Fischer, A., Kingsbury, B., and Merry, S.E. (Eds.). *Governance by Indicators: Global Power through Quantification and Rankings*. Oxford University Press, Oxford, pp. 86–110.

Galli, A., Giampietro, M., Goldfinger, S., Lazarus, E., Lin, D., Saltelli, A., Wackernagel, M. and Müller, F. 2016. Questioning the Ecological Footprint. *Ecological Indicators*. 69: 224–232.

Giampietro, M. and Saltelli, A. 2014. Footprints to nowhere. *Ecological Indicators*. 46: 610–621.

Goldsmith, E., Allen, R., Allaby, M., Davull, J., and Lawrence, S. 1972. *Blueprint for Survival*. Houghton Mifflin, Boston.

Gudmundsson, H. 2003. The policy use of environmental indicators – learning from evaluation research. *The Journal of Transdisciplinary Environmental Studies*. 2: 1–12.

Gudmundsson, H., Lehtonen, M., Bauler, T., Sebastien, L., and Morse, S. 2009. Process and results of analytical framework and typology development for POINT. In *Point: Policy Influence of Indicators*. Technical University of Denmark, Lyngby.

Irwin, A. 2006. The politics of talk coming to terms with the 'new' scientific governance. *Social Studies of Science*. 36(2): 299–320.

King, M. and Schütz, A. 1994. The ambitious modesty of Niklas Luhmann. *Journal of Law and Society*. 21(3): 261–287.

Kitzes, J., Galli, A., Bagliani, M., Barrett, J., Dige, G., Ede, S., Erb, K.-H., Giljum, S., Haberl, H., Hails, C., Jungwirth, S., Lenzen, M., Lewis, K., Loh, J., Marchettini, N., Messinger, H., Milne, K., Moles, R., Monfreda, C., Moran, D., Nakano, K., Pyhälä, A., Rees, W., Simmons, C., Wackernagel, M., Wada, Y., Walsh, C. and Wiedmann, T. 2009. A research agenda for improving national Ecological Footprint accounts. *Ecological Economics*. 68: 1991–2007.

Lehtonen, M., Sébastien, L., and Bauler, T. 2016. The multiple roles of sustainability indicators in informational governance: Between intended use and unanticipated influence. *Current Opinion in Environmental Sustainability*. 18: 1–9.

Luhmann, N. 1987. The representation of society within society. *Current Sociology*. 35(101): 101–108.

Luhmann, N. 1989. *Ecological Communication*. Chicago University Press, Chicago.

Luhmann, N. 1990. Technology, environment and social risks: A system perspective. *Industrial Crisis Quarterly*. 4: 223–231.

Luhmann, N. 1993. Ecological communication: Coping with the unknown. *System Practice*. 6: 527–539.

Luhmann, N. 1997. Globalization or world society? How to conceive of modern society. *International Review of Sociology*. 7(1): 67–79.

Luhmann, N. 1998 The ecology of ignorance. In Luhmann, N. *Observations on Modernity*. Stanford University Press, Stanford, pp. 75–115.

Luhmann, N. 2000a. *Art as a Social System*. Stanford University Press, Stanford.

Luhmann, N. 2000b. *Die Politik der Gesellschaft*. Suhrkamp, Frankfurt.

Luhmann, N. 2000c. *The Reality of the Mass Media*. Polity Press, Cambridge.

Luhmann, N. 2001. L'opinion publique. *Politix*. 14(55): 25–59.

Luhmann, N. 2004. *Law as a Social System*. Oxford University Press, Oxford.

Luhmann, N. 2007. *The Reality of the Mass Media*. Polity Press, Cambridge.

Luhmann, N. 2008. *Risk: A Sociological Theory*. Aldine, New Brunswick, London.

Luhmann, N. 2012. *Theory of Society*. Vol 1. Stanford University Press, Stanford.

Luhmann, N. 2013. *Theory of Society*. Vol 2. Stanford University Press, Stanford.

Lyytimäki, J., Gudmundsson, H., and Sørensen, C.H. 2014. Russian dolls and Chinese whispers: Two perspectives on the unintended effects of sustainability indicator communication. *Sustainable Development*. 22(2): 84–94.

Lyytimäki, J., Tapio, P., Varho, V., and Söderman, T. 2013. The use, non-use and misuse of indicators in sustainability assessment and communication. *International Journal of Sustainable Development & World Ecology*. 20(5): 385–393.

Maturana, H.R. and Varela, F. 1980. *Autopoiesis and Cognition*. Reidel, Dordrecht.

Meadows, D.H., Meadows, D.L., Randers, J., and Behrens III, W.W. 1972. *The Limits to Growth: A Report for The Club of Rome's Project on The Predicament of Mankind*. Universe Book, New York.

Moeller, H.-G. 2006. *Luhmann Explained: From Souls to Systems*. Open Court, Chicago and La Salle.

Moeller, H.-G. 2012. *The Radical Luhmann*. Columbia University Press, New York.

Ravaillon, M. 2010. Mashup indices of development. *The World Bank: Policy Research Working Paper 5432*.

Reichel, A. 2011. Technology as system: Towards an autopoietic theory of technology. *International Journal of Innovation and Sustainable Development*. 5(2/3): 105–118.

Saltelli, A. and Giampietro, M. 2017. What is wrong with evidence based policy, and how can it be improved? *Futures*. 91: 62–71.

Spencer-Brown, G. 1969. *Laws of Form*. Allen & Unwin, London.

Strassheim, H. and Kettunen, P. 2014. When does evidence-based policy turn into policy-based evidence? Configurations, contexts and mechanisms. *Evidence & Policy: A Journal of Research, Debate and Practice*. 10(2): 259–277.

Thompson, S. and Valentinov, V. 2017. The neglect of society in the theory of the firm: A systems-theory perspective. *Cambridge Journal of Economics*. 41(4): 1061–1085.

Valentinov, V. 2014. The complexity-sustainability trade-off in Niklas Luhmann's Social Systems Theory. *Systems Research and Behavioral Sciences Syst. Res.* 31: 14–22.

Valentinov, V. 2017. Wiener and Luhmann on feedback: From complexity to sustainability. *Kybernetes*. 46(3): 386–399.

van den Bergh, J.C.J.M. and Verbruggen, H. 1999. Spatial sustainability, trade and indicators: An evaluation of the ecological footprint. *Ecological Economics*. 29: 63–74.

WCED (The World Commission on Environment and Development). 1987. *Our Common Future*. Oxford University Press, Oxford, New York.

Wilden, A. 1980. *System and Structure*. Tavistock, Abingdon, Oxon.

PART II

Methods

9

WORLD VIEWS, INTERESTS AND INDICATOR CHOICES

Joachim H. Spangenberg

World views

Which challenges are perceived, issues are emphasised, policies suggested and changes endorsed in order to approach sustainable development depends on the world views (also described as pre-analytic visons, e.g. by Herman Daly et al. [1990] and similar to metaphysics) held by the respective agents.

The elements constituting a world view are its ontology including an anthropology, its epistemology and its axiology including a societal vision (Hedlund-de Witt 2012; Spangenberg 2016). Ontology deals with questions concerning what entities exist or may be said to exist and how such entities may be grouped, related within a hierarchy and subdivided according to similarities and differences. Epistemology is a branch of philosophy dealing with the theory of knowledge; it studies the nature of knowledge, justification and the rationality of belief. Axiology is one branch of ancient philosophy, encompassing a range of approaches to understanding how, why, and to what degree humans should or do value objects, whether the object is physical (a person, a thing) or abstract (an idea, an action), or anything else. In philosophy, value is a property of such objects, representing their degree of importance. An object with philosophic value may be termed an ethic or philosophic good. Different kinds of value can be distinguished, based on different philosophical traditions and approaches (for a more detailed overview see Spangenberg and Settele 2016).

World views are comprehensive systems of perceiving reality; they cannot be proven right or wrong but can be assessed and compared regarding their plausibility, their 'fit' with logical conclusions and with observations. Different value systems shape the perception of what is important in reality: from an objective value perspective, there are no instrumental values, only means to things which may be valuable; the means may be valuable in themselves but not by their mean function. From an instrumental perspective, all values can be described in instrumental terms, bequest and existence value included (instrumental for enhancing one's own life satisfaction – a 'feel good' or 'warm glow' effect, and moral nihilism).

Modificationists versus transformationists

In the sustainable development discourse, as in other discourses, two basic camps can be distinguished; deriving a name from their attitudes and avoiding established classifications they can be called modificationists and transformationists (Spangenberg 2015). Both groups are as old as the sustainability discourse itself, represent different societal groups and generate assessments of past events and future trends which often are in clear contradiction to each other. Both camps can be found in almost all disciplines and political organisations (except for those denying the need for change, or even advocating a transition towards more unsustainability).

Both camps are aware that sustainable development requires decisions, and that their advice can influence them. However, both groups undertake analyses and derive recommendations in the context of and shaped by their own world view. As a result, they tend to take their respective body of knowledge as the relevant set of information on which decisions should be based, often unable to recognise their respective limits and the 'safe operating space' for their tools.

Of course in each of the camps discussed here various schools of thought exist and individual variations occur, so this brief description and the presentation in Table 9.1 can only capture some archetypical traits of each camp.

Modificationists

Modificationists consider sustainability to be something that can be brought about by minor and incremental modifications of the current system, believing that technology always offers solutions, free markets are providing optimal welfare and efficiency is the key to a sustainable society. Thus the current socio-economical model (market economy, neoliberal society, privatised or limited welfare systems and non-disruptive environmental policy) is perceived as basically the right approach, and only modifying a limited number of elements is required to overcome malfunctioning traits. Consequently, what is missing for more sustainable policy and management decisions is better information, data and indicators; better informed decision makers will set the course towards sustainability (less so to sustainable development, see Gallopin, Chapter 22). As the system as such is more or less adequate, descriptive indicators and indices are sufficient, causal analyses and theories of change are not important (Rotz and Fraser, Chapter 6; and Janoušková et al., Chapter 30), and as the system is legitimate, stakeholders are considered data sources rather than agents shaping targets and indicators (Domingues et al., Chapter 25).

The conflict of camps is particularly prominent in the discipline of economics, which currently dominates much of the sustainability discourse. The disciplinary basis for the modificationists is environmental economics (an extension of neoclassical economics integrating the environment). For both neoclassical and environmental economics and thus for most of the modificationists camp, the axiology is one of instrumental values, anthropocentric, with a utilitarian or hedonist ethics with all values (except intrinsic and spiritual values) reducible to exchange values. They are usually expressed as suggested or realised prices in real or hypothetical markets (for an exemption in this aspect see Hueting and de Boer, Chapter 14, or Bartelmus, Chapter 15). The anthropology is one of self-centred individuals with rational decision-making maximising their utility (or with bounded rationality at best), progressing by technical means. The epistemology is one of science-cum-technology confident positivism, and the societal vision one of a free-market society. The ontology is different between neoclassical and environmental economics as for neoclassical economics there are no such things as society or the environment, while environmental economics acknowledges the existence of the environment and conceptually integrates it into an extended economic system.

In the case of environmental economics dominating in the modificationist camp, this results in substituting prices for all other characteristics of objects (as this is the only metric available to standard economists), and it is justified by assuming full substitutability between natural, social and human-made assets: "The world can, in effect, get along without natural resources,

Table 9.1 The world views of modificationists and transformationists and selected implications

	Modificationists	Transformationists
Ontology	Nature as natural capital, nature and society are subsystems of the economy	Elements of Platonism and naturalism. Economy as a subsystem of society, which is a subsystem of nature
Epistemology	Positivism, methodological naturalism	Diverse, with elements of critical rationalism and empiricism
Anthropology	*Homo economicus, homo faber*	*Homo sapiens, homo socialis*
Axiology	Instrumental values, anthropocentric (valuable if useful), consequentialist ethics, utilitarist or hedonist	Value pluralism, including ideal, absolute and subjective values, the latter including inherent and instrumental values, deontological or rule consequentialism ethics
Social vision	Free-market society, globalisation, economic growth to overcome poverty	Solidary society/welfare state to overcome poverty, strengthening local cohesion and social resilience, limits to growth/post-growth/degrowth

Some selected implications

	Modificationists	Transformationists
Sustainability	Sustaining sum of capital stocks, substituting human-made capital for natural and human capital possible. Sustainability through 'green growth' or 'sustained and sustainable growth'	Limiting human impact, long-term resilient and healthy ecosystems providing ecosystem services. Earth closed system with limited resources, complexity enhancing energy use efficiency, no permanent growth possible
Future value	Exponential discounting, positive discount rates	Object dependent: no, hyperbolic or exponential discounting
Dynamics	Equilibrium, series of equilibria, largely predictable, reversible	Nature as a process of continuous irreversible change, path dependent but unpredictable
Target group of policy recommendations	Economic and fiscal policymakers, business	Policymakers, civil society

Source: Neugebauer 2012, modified; Daly 1996, modified; Rink and Wächter 2002; Spangenberg 2005; Renn 2012, modified

so exhaustion is just an event, not a catastrophe" (Solow 1974, p. 11). Thus one of the most prominent modificationists' proposals is to correct market failures by internalising external cost, assuming that a functioning market would provide optimal results also regarding environmental concerns, achieving a "sustained and sustainable growth" (United Nations General Assembly 2012; 2015) or "green growth" (OECD 2011b).

Monetising achievements in all dimensions of sustainable development generates commensurability and the possibility to aggregate, at the price of losing view of the dimension-specific characteristics – which may lead to severe mistakes when providing advice if these characteristics are of importance in the case to be decided (Gerber, Scheidel 2018). Value theory, which could have been considered an indispensable centrepiece of economics, is in neoclassical economics and its derivates generally considered to be "nothing more than metaphysical speculation and therefore completely irrelevant to 'real' economics" (Söllner 1997, p. 178).

Transformationists

Transformationists consider modifications as necessary but insufficient, and call for a structural transformation of society and economy of Polanyian depth as the only viable way towards sustainable development; change is considered inevitable and urgent (Polanyi 1944). They think that technology is indispensable but suspect that it is not the solution, and that sufficiency needs to complement efficiency. They hold that not a lack of information, but dominant interests are the cause of unsustainable decisions, that an analytical, theory-backed approach is necessary (Rotz and Fraser, Chapter 6), that information (indicators, indices) must be relevant to transformative decision-making (Janoušková et al., Chapter 30), and that both such strategies and the information underpinning them requires a high level of legitimacy unachievable without stakeholder participation and empowerment (Domingues et al., Chapter 25). These perspectives resonate well with its main supporters and users, a strong group of development and environment NGOs, some trade unions, selected scientific representatives and organisations. However, as an approach incorporating contributions from civil society (Martinez-Alier et al. 2014), it remains a minority position in the policy domain, and hardly receives support from international organisations, business and governments. Its historical roots reach as far back as those of the mainstream camp.

The transformationist camp and ecological economics in particular hold a fundamentally different ontology of nested systems (Gunderson and Holling 2001): nature is considered the metasystem into which society is embedded, and the economy is seen as a subsystem of society. The anthropology perceives humans as multi-facetted social beings, complex individuals with interacting egoistic and social inclinations, part of social communities and processes and driven by both intrinsic and extrinsic motivations. Their behaviour is not only shaped by selfish rationalism, but also by habitual learning and various forms of norm-driven behaviour. For most of the transformationist camp, the axiology emphasises non-instrumental (objective and ideal) values as complementary perspectives with incommensurable results (they cannot be added up). Such value pluralism approaches do not impose a universal vocabulary on the discourse about environmental values instead of many vernaculars, and do not strive for one final result, one right answer or one optimal solution. The approach is either enlightened anthropocentric (recognising the personal benefits from safeguarding the public good – an overlap with parts of the modificationists camp), or more biocentric, emphasising the inherent right of nature and (some of) its elements to exist in a healthy state. The ethics combines deontological (moral principle based) and consequentialist elements (expected outcome based); their blend is known as rule consequentialism. Both views are not compatible with unlimited substitutability, thus transformationists are opposed to the commodification of nature and see economic valuation, in particular if it is assumed to cover consumer and citizens, individual and social values as misguided.[1]

Technological change is considered urgently necessary, but the epistemology is characterised by sceptism regarding the unlimited possibilities of science and technology; uncertainty is considered omnipresent and a real-world empirical foundation is considered crucial (empiricism). The societal vision combines the call for environmental limitations to economic activities (limits for resource consumption or their degrowth) with a vision of intra- and intergenerational justice including poverty eradication, both derived directly from the Brundtland Commission's definition of sustainable development more than 30 years ago (WCED 1987). The means of measurement and the languages describing observations emphasise the necessity to analyse physical and social data, and are sceptical against methods to aggregate incommensurable parameters (Martinez-Alier et al. 1998).

Both views are coherent in themselves, and the figures and indicators they use are usually based on the best available data and rigorous methodologies. Nonetheless, and although over-lapping in some points and both geared towards sustainable development, the world views of modificationists and transformationists are essentially distinct and incommensurable (Spangenberg 2016). Both don't recognise other kinds of values than those they deal with themselves, practising monistic approaches by trying to express all environmental value within their own framework of analysis. This has severe policy implications and helps explain a variety of environmental policy conflicts, as throughout the world it is the incrementalists who dominate public policy (Cassandra has a reputation not to win elections).

It is quite obvious and will be shown in the next section in some more detail that the fundamental differences affect and shape the choice of sustainability indicators and their application: the suitability and relevance attributed to an indicator (an often neglected key criterion, Janoušková et al., Chapter 30) depends on the world view. The ontology decides which system hierarchy between economy, society and nature is assumed to exist, the epistemology determines which data we have, need and trust in (climate change denial is an epistemological mistake) and the axiology gives weight to different arguments in calculating trade-offs and seeking balanced decisions.

Sustainable development indicators

Sustainable development indicators are tools to reduce the complexity of a process of sustained change (Gallopin, Chapter 22), designed for specific purposes, to provide a relevant, credible and legitimate but easily understandable information base for public and private decision-making (Janoušková et al., Chapter 30). However, what is considered relevant or credible is a matter of the epistemology. Interests motivate action; they can be self-regarding (egoistic or hedonistic) or other-regarding (altruistic or socially utilitarian, 'the greatest good for the greatest number', a matter of ethics) (Hansjürgens et al. 2017). In the former case, the ontology shapes which means are considered effective to realise it, while in the latter case the axiology shapes what priorities are to be set. In both cases the societal vision legitimates the objectives, and the ethics (be it deontological or consequentialist) legitimises the measures to be taken.

In all cases sustainability indicators can be used to describe a state or to monitor change – in the latter case at best indicating the progress achieved towards a target described as a future state using the same parameters; then they would be classified as performance indicators. For this behalf they have to be measurable, be it on a nominal, ordinal or cardinal scale – see e.g. the Environmental Performance Index (EPI; Esty and Emerson, Chapter 5). Sustainable development indicators deal with a different challenge: with development understood as a dynamic, path dependent, evolutionary trajectory, not a strategy towards a well-defined goal that has to be monitored, but a process and its sustainability quality (which en passant modifies the targets) and the efforts to create and use bifurcation points to change course: sustainability is then no well-defined target but a *leitbild*, the joint vanishing point of the desirable and the possible (Gallopin, Chapter 22). For indicator quality (on criteria see Spangenberg 2015) this implies that

- To be relevant, they have to address crucial aspects of sustainability/sustainable development as identified by the ontology and axiology/societal vision, they have to have a clear message and be indicative, i.e. a true representation of the state or trend of the phenomenon the indicator is intended to report about. To be effective, they have to resonate with the target audience – different audiences may require different sets or subsets of sustainable development indicators, the choice being influenced by the anthropology.

• To be credible, they have to be based on a sound scientific basis including a well-defined method and reliable data to guarantee the reproducibility of results. They should be simultaneously robust (immune against small variations in data and method not indicating a change of state or trend) and sensitive, i.e. react early and clearly to relevant changes in what they are designed to monitor, an obvious case of trade-offs between criteria.

• To be legitimate, they have to be transparent regarding data sources and data processing methods to support credibility – again an issue of epistemology. Discursive processes and stakeholders participating as partners, with influence on process and outcome, can enhance credibility – but only if conflicting groups and interests are involved in a balanced manner (Domingues et al., Chapter 25).

Thus, although indicators are data based and have to comply with quality standards such as those mentioned, they are no 'objective' base for decision-making: both the definition and selection of indicators are inevitably influenced by the ontology, epistemology and societal vision of their authors and promoters. Their subjective choices determine who should be the target audience, if data should be aggregated for the sake of reducing complexity, or not so to enhance transparency, and the like. The most important decision to make is which are the crucial trends and states to be monitored for sustainable development, and the answer is again heavily dependent on the world views the authors hold and the interests they are motivated by. In particular the fact that indicators support decision-making processes by indicating priority issues and the direction of measures to be taken makes their definition and acceptance a political and frequently controversial process: world views shape the policy arena.[2]

Different world views lead to different assessments of the same facts, trends and events (for an example see Conrad and Cassar, Chapter 19). This was very obvious in the aftermath of the Paris climate conference, and after the adoption of the Sustainable Development Goals (SDGs) by the United Nations. Most comments praised both as historical break-throughs (the modificationists' view), while transformationists criticised them as a major failures. A bonmot about the Paris results said that compared to what could be reasonably expected, they were a miracle, but compared to what was needed, they were a disaster: modificationists focus on relative improvements and celebrate the miracle, while transformationists emphasise absolute thresholds and targets and mourn the disaster.[3] So the same facts can lead to diverging assessments, with implications for the meaningfulness of the indicators used. Indicators have a purpose, they convey a message, and they are chosen by the messenger to illustrate their respective point of view. World views influence the judgements, and the judgements determine the choice of indicators.

Modificationists' indices and indicator systems

Modificationists also modify indicators: as development is understood as GDP growth, and sustainability as greening that growth (distributional issues play a secondary role), indicators are modified from GDP to Green GDP, ISEW (Index of Sustainable Economic Welfare) and GPI (Genuine Progress Index; www.ecodynamics.unisi.it/?p=1233&lang=en). Modificationists measure resource intensity and improvements as compared to status quo scenarios, often relative to GDP growth (see for instance OECD 2011a). Indicators and indices promoted are derived from market prices or, for non-market goods, explored by contingent valuation including willingness to pay (WTP) analyses. Only recently, in the context of the discussion about monitoring the Sustainable Development Goals, social issues have gained prominence (again).

Another rather recent development is the attempt to measure not only the aggregate welfare in monetary terms, but also the subjective well-being by measuring happiness or life satisfaction, based on the same methodological individualism approach (Layard 2005; Veenhoven 2010). However, the validity of happiness measurement is disputed (Johns and Ormerod 2008) and their policy relevance appears questionable – nobody wants a national happiness provision system.

Unsustainable development is considered a misallocation of capital caused by a market failure, in line with the modificationists' ontology; the latter is seen in the fact that environmental (rarely mentioned: social) damages are externalised, having no cost in the market system. Consequently, monetisation of such damages and their internalisation into the market system is considered as problem-solving strategy. This is the main reason why monetary measurements and indicators play such a major role in the sustainable development indicators developed by this camp. Prominent examples include

- the World Bank Capital Stock Approach, distinguishing human-made, natural, human and social capital stocks (Serageldin 1997)
- Adjusted Net Savings or Genuine Savings, derived from standard System of National Accounts (SNA) accounting measures by making several adjustments (Pearce 2000),
- the ISEW and GPI which as well take the GDP as their starting points, and distract the monetary value of 'bads' while adding the money value of 'goods' (Lawn 2003),
- the System of Environmental-Economic Accounting (SEEA; better known as 'Green Accounting') complementing the SNA by introducing satellite accounts which can be monetary or not (Bartelmus, Chapter 15). The latest version was introduced in 2013, and a second part dealing with the integration of biodiversity and ecosystem services, partly in monetary terms (Natural Capital Accounting), into the accounting system is still being tested.

Multidisciplinary indicator sets have been developed in particular by international bodies like the UN, the OECD and the EU, stimulated by the development of national sustainable development indicator programs in some countries and stimulating the development of such programs in others (however, the EU initiative "Beyond GDP" which was started with high optimism but did not produce any tangible results and while it lingers on, it has lost its focus).

These indicator sets blend economic indicators with biophysical and social (rarely institutional) indicators partly originating from earlier traditions, partly from competing schools of thought including the transformationists. The systems are data hungry; collecting and processing the data requires significant human and financial resources. Well-known indicator systems include (see also Dahl, Chapter 23; and Boulanger, Chapter 8):

- the OECD PSR indicator system (OECD 1991, 1993),
- the UNCSD Indicators for Measuring Sustainability (UNDPCSD 1996; UNDESA 2007; Dahl, Chapter 23),
- the SDG indicators recently developed (Inter-Agency and Expert Group 2016; Reijnders, Chapter 20) to monitor the implementation of Agenda 2030 (United Nations 2015).

The SDG set comprises 230 indicators on which agreement had been reached after intense debates involving both camps. As a result, in particular the social targets and indicators reflect a transformationist position, while economic targets, instruments and agency are shaped by modificationists; environmental targets and indicators fall in between (Spangenberg 2017).

Mixed indicator sets include monetary indicators combined with non-monetary ones (otherwise the results could have been added up into one index). One reason why this combination is predominant in national SDI systems is the public information demand: people do not want to know about the economic loss due to unemployment or air pollution, they want to know how many people are unemployed and what they breathe. The Stiglitz-Sen-Fitoussi Commission on the Measurement of Economic Performance and Social Progress initiated by the French government suggested to replace the GDP by a mixed set of indicators for the short term and to develop new indicators for the longer-term sustainability measurement (Stiglitz et al. 2010; http://library. bsl.org.au/jspui/bitstream/1/1267/1/Measurement_of_economic_performance_and_social_progress.pdf). However, it was thwarted by the French and the German Statistical Offices.

Transformationists' indicators and indicator systems

Transformationists consider development not as growth but as improving the quality of life. As far as livelihood improvements are dependent on income growth, they support it while emphasising the need for equitable distribution. While a strong correlation of life satisfaction and income has been found below a certain threshold (about 15,000 US\$/cap*yr in the 1990s), above it the correlation vanished (Max-Neef 1995). In this camp, average income figures are thus considered to provide little information about how many people are living below the life satisfaction threshold. The environmental condition of sustainability is considered to be a physical steady-state system, with the smallest-feasible flows of resources at the (functionally, not geographically defined) input and output boundaries between the technosphere and the ecosphere leaving intact – for an infinite length of time – the stability of the internal evolutionary processes of the biophysical ecosphere. Thus transformationists exchange the indicators used, substituting for instance social or horizontal Multi Criteria Analyses (MCA) for Cost Benefit Analyses (CBA),[4] or physical accounting combined with social data like income distribution, working hours, poverty rate, literacy and institutional indicators for GDP and its derivates (on the concept of environmentally sustainable national income, an intermediary, see Hueting, de Boer, Chapter 14, this volume). They measure absolute levels and changes in resource consumption, work and social status, soil fertility and environmental quality, and refrain from monetising as this is considered to imply substitutability of incommensurable objects.

Biophysical measurement indicators include for instance

* In the field of energy, embodied energy (also known as emergy) is the sum of all energy consumed in the process of producing, distributing and maintaining a product (Odum 1989; Ulgiati and Brown 1998) and exergy is an indicator describing the available energy inherent to a product, and thus the potential to actively interact with its environment (Jørgensen 2010). In bio-economic descriptions based on thermodynamics (Georgescu-Roegen 1971), scholars distinguish and assess depletable stocks, reproducing funds and physical flows (Daly 1996), with a few scholars linking them to human labour and value production (Giampietro et al. 2006).
* In the field of resource consumption, Material Flow Analysis (MFA) is a tool to measure the total materials activated (Total Material Requirement [TMR]) or actually used (Total Material Consumption [TMC]), or the material used for domestic consumption (Domestic Material Consumption [DMC]) (Schmidt-Bleek et al. 1998). Due to data problems, the European Commission uses a simplified indicator called Raw Material Consumption (RMC) in monitoring its Resource Efficiency Strategy (http://ec.europa.eu/archives/commission_2010-2014/potocnik/expert_group/pdf/DGENVResEffIndicsonlyFin.pdf).

The Vienna school of Marina Fischer-Kowalski links these material flows to the human appropriation of net primary production (Weisz et al. 2006). Substance Flow Analysis throughout the industrial metabolism monitors individual substances of special interest.

- In the field of land use the probably best known indicator is the Ecological Footprint (Rees and Wackernagel 1996; Wackernagel et al, Chapter 16; Chapter 33). It calculates the area of land needed for food, fuel and fibres, plus the land hypothetically needed to absorb carbon emissions from fuel consumption, but is considered misguided by other authors (Giampietro and Saltelli 2014). The land use intensity is assessed by measuring the human appropriation of net primary production (HANPP; www.uni-klu.ac.at/socec/inhalt/1191.htm), an indicator reflecting the disturbance effects of human interventions in natural landscapes (Haberl et al. 2007).
- In the field of biodiversity, ecosystems and their services the indicator system adopted by the Convention on Biological Diversity (CBD) (CBD 2003, endorsed 2006, www.cbd. int/2010-target/framework/indicators.shtml) consists of a rather unsystematic mix, does not conform to the quality standards mentioned earlier and is rarely used; the EU SEBI biodiversity indicators (SEBI, Streamlining European Biodiversity Indicators, is a pan-European initiative led by the European Environment Agency EEA; European Commission 2008, www.eea.europa.eu/themes/biodiversity/indicators#c7=all&c5=all&c10=SEB I&c13=20&b_start=0) follow closely the UN CBD approach, with minor adaptations. Biodiversity indices like the Shannon Index (www.tiem.utk.edu/~gross/bioed/bealsmodules/shannonDI.html) measure diversity and are frequently used in science, but do not communicate well to the public. Species richness and abundance (www.britannica.com/science/biodiversity#ref922447) address specific aspects of biodiversity, but are often used in public and policy circles (but also by institutions such as the OECD) to characterise total biodiversity, overstretching the meaning of an otherwise good indicator.

Monodisciplinary indices for measuring sustainable development do not exist in the transformationist camp as emergy, TMC, HANPP and species abundance have no common denominator and therefore cannot be aggregated. The same holds true in the social domain: unemployment, life expectancy at birth, participation rights and discrimination may be correlated but have no common denominator, cannot be aggregated and have to be reported and weighed separately.

However, indices have been developed to aggregate the information about specific sub-issues, such as the consumption of food, feed and fibre (the Ecological Footprint), or the total use or consumption of raw materials (TMC, TMR, etc.). In the social field, 'healthy life years' is a simple index, and the Human Development Index (HDI; http://hdr.undp.org/en/content/human-development-index-hdi) a complex index, with the Human Sustainable Development Index (HSDI) adding an environmental dimension to the HDI (see Bravo, Chapter 18). They are helpful as long as not considered to be describing the totality of the state and/or changes of the environment, but as tools to measure important aspects of it.

A subjective index from this camp is the Happy Planet Index (http://happyplanetindex.org/) developed by the UK New Economics Foundation (NEF; Marks et al. 2006).

Political reality: unhappy coexistence in mixed systems

International conventions do not follow a scientific logic but are political compromises, and so are their accompanying indicator systems. This was already obvious in the first sustainable development indicator set developed to support the implementation of Agenda 21 (UNDPCSD 1996), and it did not change with the second (UNDSD 2001) and third version (UNDESA

2007) (Janoušková et al., Chapter 30, describes the lost battle for scientific rigour; Dahl, Chapter 3, the development process). Such political compromises are also a key reason behind the deficits of the initial versions of the biodiversity indicators adopted by the CBD and the EU, as described above.

The latest victim to this unhappy coexistence are the Sustainable Development Goals (SDGs; for the process, see Reijnders, Chapter 20). They are not only characterised by an inherent weaknesses of target formulation – the International Council for Science (ICSU) and the International Social Science Council (ISSC) found only 29% of the 169 targets to be well-defined and based on latest scientific evidence, while 54% were classified as needing more work and 17% as weak or non-essential (ICSU, ISSC 2015).

The European Commission decided that 100 indicators would be enough and delegated the task of choosing them to the EU Statistical Agency – which despite consultations within the Commission and with the public implied that the choice of monitoring priorities was not made as a policy issue, but based on data availability (in which case old problems with time series of data tend to be monitored, while emerging problems are not suitably covered). Fortunately, the international dynamics forced the EU to take the full international indicator set into account as well, although the reporting will highlight the 100 long-established indicators.

However, indicator sets can only be as good as the targets or processes they are designed to monitor, and as coherent. In the case of the SDGs, while necessary changes of state and impacts are rather well covered (excellently in the social domain, less so for the environment – the influence of transformationist thinking is evident), the pressures causing the impacts are not named in the SDGs and thus go unmonitored. Even worse, the driving forces behind them, including the aspiration for high economic growth even in the most affluent countries, plus deregulation, globalisation and free trade are not scrutinised for their sustainability impacts and framed accordingly, but are unambiguously endorsed (which is 'more of the same', even less than a modificationists' approach). As a result, it is foreseeable that that the economic and trade targets as they stand, and the social and environmental targets cannot be reached in harmony – either the drivers will have to be domesticated, or the pressures and impacts will continue increasing (Spangenberg 2017).

In this situation, an indicator system measuring progress towards each target will be of little help as long as it does not show how reaching one target undermines others. Consequently, the indicator development process has been a dispute if such contradictions should be masked or highlighted by the monitoring system. The next years will show how the inherent contradictions of targets will be recorded, and if the future revisions of the indicator system will provide a level of coherence their underlying targets are lacking. Indicators can serve to highlight the need for action, but they can also be used as camouflage: in the end it is the political will which is decisive.

Conclusion

Established ruling elites, and thus the beneficiaries of the status quo, apparently tend to be inclined to behave as modificationists, while transformationists can be geared towards different societal visions, one of them being sustainable development. As modificationists rely on science and technology, they try to avoid type one errors, accepting false truth. However, the more they do so they are prone to fall victim to type two errors, falsely rejecting findings not fully proven yet. That attitude may help managing challenges of unsustainable development, but often falls short of preventing upcoming threats.

Take for instance the frequent call to base new indicator systems on existing data with sufficient time series: such data have been collected for, say, a decade, and the collection was initiated another decade earlier, setting up the necessary institutions, developing and refining the methods of data gathering and processing. Consequently, existing good data series answer questions and respond to concerns at least 20 years old, while for emerging problems neither the methods nor the data are available. Fortunately, at the international level (EU and UN), the awareness regarding this problem has grown and stand-in indicators are used while final indicators are being developed.

Indicator users should be aware of the limitations each indicator, index or indicator system has, partly from the method of calculation, but also from the often-hidden assumptions inherent to the world views from which they have been derived. Practitioners should chose and combine the indicators they use carefully, being fully aware of these biases and their impacts on both the measurement and the messages derived from it, implicitly or explicitly.

Notes

1 Resistance against commodification is not new: Martin Luther (obviously an effective transformationalist) revolted against the commodification of sins, spirituality and god's forgiveness by means of indulgence letters by publishing in 1517 his theses initiating the reformation, more than 500 years ago. Another early reformer, Thomas Müntzer said in 1524, as reported by Karl Marx in 1843: "It is intolerable that every creature should be transformed into property – the fishes in the water, the birds in the air, the plants on the earth: the creature too should be free" (Kovel 2011, p. 5).

2 As political priorities cannot be decided by statistical offices, and as these are not free of the same world view influences, delegating indicator development or selection to them (as the European Commission decided to do for the SDG indicators) does not provide 'objectivity' but could undermine the legitimacy of results.

3 Praise versus condemnation of free trade agreements in the 2016 US elections may be another example of world views shaping the assessment of trends and events, with both sides using selected indicators to illustrate their points, and a different kind of transformationist (not towards sustainability) winning against promises of gradual improvements and minor modifications.

4 Multi Criteria Analyses (MCA) use stakeholders to develop an extended list of decision criteria and assessment of their fulfilment (de Marchi et al. 2000). The majority of studies and tools weighs the criteria according to the preferences of a decision maker (who can also be the analyst), while a minority accepts diverse preferences and thus has no overall weighing scheme to offer. As the former (supported by most MCA software) ends up with a clear hierarchy it can be called a 'vertical MCA'. Accepting the legitimacy of partly mutually exclusive value systems rules out the definition of hierarchies as result of an MCA, instead providing equally legitimate alternatives as input to the policy process; since creating a level playing field it has been called 'horizontal' (Spangenberg 2001) or 'social MCA' (Munda 2004).

References

CBD Convention on Biological Diversity. 2003. *Proposed Indicators Relevant to the 2010 Target.* Document UNEP/CBD/SBSTTA/9/inf/26. CBD, Montreal, Canada.

Daly, H.E. 1996. *Beyond Growth: The Economics of Sustainable Development.* Beacon Press, Boston, USA.

Daly, H.E., Cobb, John B. Jr., with contributions by Cobb, C.W. 1990. *For the Common Good: Redirecting the Economy towards Community, the Environment and a Sustainable Future.* Green Print, London, UK.

de Marchi, B., Funtowicz, S., Lo Cascio, S., and Munda, G. 2000. Combining Participative and Institutional Approaches with Multicriteria Evaluation: An Empirical Study for Water Issues in Troina, Sicily. *Ecological Economics* 34: 267–284.

European Commission. 2008. Commission Staff Working Document. Accompanying document to the Communication from the Commission to the Council, the European Parliament, the European Economic and Social Committee and the Committee of the Regions: *A Mid-Term Assessment of Implementing* the EC Biodiversity Action plan, COM(2008) 864 final: *SEBI 2010 Biodiversity Indicators*. European Commission, Brussels, Belgium.

Georgescu-Roegen, N. 1971. *The Entropy Law and the Economic Process*. Harvard University Press, Cambridge, MA, USA.

Gerber, J.-F., and Scheidel, A. 2018. In Search of Substantive Economics: Comparing Today's Two Major Socio-Metabolic Approaches to the Economy – MEFA and MuSIASEM. *Ecological Economics* 144: 186–194.

Giampietro, M., Mayumi, K., and Munda, G. 2006. Integrated assessment and energy analysis: Quality assurance in multi-criteria analysis of sustainability. *Energy* 31: 59–68.

Giampietro, M. and Saltelli, A. 2014. Footprints to Nowhere. *Ecological Indicators* 46: 610–621.

Gunderson, L.H., and Holling, C.S. 2001. *Panarchy: Understanding Transformations in Systems of Humans and Nature*. Island Press, Washington, DC, USA.

Haberl, H., Erb, K.H., Krausmann, F., Gaube, V., Bondeau, A., Plutzar, C., Gingrich, S., Lucht, W., and Fischer-Kowalski, M. 2007. Quantifying and Mapping the Human Appropriation of Net Primary Production in Earth's Terrestrial Ecosystems. *Proceedings of National Academy of Sciences USA* 104(31): 12942–12947.

Hansjürgens, B., Schröter-Schlaack, C., Berghöfer, A., and Lienhoop, N. 2017. Justifying Social Values of Nature: Economic Reasoning Beyond Self-Interested Preferences. *Ecosystem Services* 23: 9–17.

Hedlund-de Witt, A. 2012. Exploring Worldviews and Their Relationships to Sustainable Life-Styles: Towards a New Conceptual and Methodological Approach. *Ecological Economics* 84: 74–83.

Inter-Agency and Expert Group on Sustainable Development Goal Indicators. 2016. *Final List of Proposed Sustainable Development Goal Indicators*, UN Document E/CN.3/2016/2Rev.1. United Nations, New York, USA.

International Council for Science ICSU, International Social Science Council ISSC. 2015. *Review of Targets for the Sustainable Development Goals: The Science Perspective*. ICSU, Paris, France.

Johns, H., and Ormerod, P. 2008. The Unhappy Thing about Happiness Economics. *Real-world Economics Review* 46: 139–146.

Jørgensen, S.E. 2010. Ecosystem Services, Sustainability and Thermodynamic Indicators. *Ecological Complexity* 7(3): 311–313.

Kovel, J. 2011. On Marx and Ecology. *Capitalism Nature Socialism* 22: 4–17.

Lawn, P.A. 2003. A Theoretical Foundation to Support the Index of Sustainable Economic Welfare (ISEW), Genuine Progress Indicator (GPI) and Other Related Indexes. *Ecological Economics* 44: 105–118.

Layard, R. 2005. *Happiness: Lessons from a New Science*. Penguin Press, New York, USA.

Marks, N., Abdallah, S., Simms, A., and Thompson, S. 2006. *The Happy Planet Index 1.0*. New Economics Foundation, London, UK.

Martinez-Alier, J., Anguelovski, I., Bond, P., Del Bene, D., Demaria, F., Gerber, J.-F., Greyl, L., Haas, W., Healy, H., Marín-Burgos, V., Ojo, G., Porto, M., Rijnhout, L., Rodríguez-Labajos, B., Spangenberg, J.H., Temper, L., Warlenius, R., and Yánez, I. 2014. Between Activism and Science: Grassroots Concepts for Sustainability Coined by Environmental Justice Organizations. *Journal of Political Ecology* 21: 19–60.

Martinez-Alier, J., Munda, G., and O'Neill, J. 1998. Weak Comparability of Values as a Foundation for Ecological Economics. *Ecological Economics* 26: 277–286.

Max-Neef, M. 1995. Economic Growth and Quality of Life: A Threshold Hypothesis. *Ecological Economics* 15(2): 115–118.

Munda, G. 2004. Social Multi-Criteria Evaluation: Methodological Foundations and Operational Consequences. *European Journal of Operational Research* 158: 662–677.

Neugebauer, F. 2012. *A Multidisciplinary Sustainability Understanding for Corporate Strategic Management*. Paper presented at the 18th ISDRC Conference, Hull, UK, June 24th-26th.

Odum, H.T. 1989. Self-Organization, Transformity, and Information. *Science* 242: 1132–1139.

OECD. 1991. *Environmental Indicators. A Preliminary Set*. OECD, Paris, France.

OECD. 1993. OECD core set of indicators for environmental performance reviews. OECD Environmental Directorate Monographs N° 83. OECD, Paris, France.

OECD. 2011a. *Monitoring Progress Towards Green Growth – OECD Indicators*. OECD Council Paper C(2011)30. OECD, Paris, France.

OECD. 2011b. *Towards Green Growth*. OECD, Paris, France.

Pearce, D.W. 2000. The Policy Relevance and Uses of Aggregate Indicators: Genuine Savings. *OECD Proceedings: Frameworks to Measure Sustainable Development*. OECD, Paris, France: 79–82.

Polanyi, K. 1944. *The great transformation: Economic and political origins of our time*. Rinehart Publ., New York, USA.

Rees, W.E., and Wackernagel, M. 1996. *Our Ecological Footprint – Reducing Human Impact on Earth*. New Society Publishers, Gabriola Islands, British Columbia, Canada.

Renn, O. 2012. Sustainability: The Need for Societal Discourse. O. Renn, A. Reichel and J. Bauer (Eds.), *Civil Society for Sustainability: A Guidebook for Connecting Science and Society*. Europäischer Hochschulverlag, Bremen, Germany: 18–37.

Rink, D., and Wächter, M. 2002. Naturverständnisse in der Nachhaltigkeitsforschung. I. Balzer and M. Wächter (Eds.), *Sozial-ökologische Forschung: Ergebnisse der Sondierungsprojekte aus dem BMBF-Förderschwerpunkt*. Ökom Verlag, München, Germany: 339–360.

Schmidt-Bleek, F., Bringezu, S., Hinterberger, F., Liedtke, C., Spangenberg, J.H., Stiller, H., and Welfens, M.J. 1998. *MAIA Einführung in die Material-Intensitäts-Analyse nach dem MIPS-Konzept*. Birkhäuser Verlag, Basel, Berlin, Boston, Switzerland, Germany and USA.

Serageldin, I. 1997. *Expanding the Measure of Wealth; Indicators of Environmentally Sustainable Development*. The World Bank, Washington, DC, USA.

Söllner, F. 1997. A Reexamination of the Role of Thermodynamics for Environmental Economics. *Ecological Economics* 22: 175–201.

Solow, R.M. 1974. The Economics of Resources or the Resources of Economics. *The American Economic Review* 64(2): 1–14.

Spangenberg, J.H. 2001. Investing in Sustainable Development. *International Journal of Sustainable Development* 4(2): 184–201.

Spangenberg, J.H. 2005. Economic Sustainability of the Economy: Concepts and Indicators. *International Journal of Sustainable Development* 8(1–2): 47–64.

Spangenberg, J.H. 2015. Indicators for Sustainable Development. M. Redclift and D. Springett (Eds.), *Routledge International Handbook of Sustainable Development*. Routledge, Taylor & Francis Group, Abingdon, Oxford, UK: 308–322.

Spangenberg, J.H. 2016. The World We See Shapes the World We Create: How the Underlying Worldviews Lead to Different Recommendations from Environmental and Ecological Economics – the Green Economy Example. *International Journal of Sustainable Development* 19(2): 127–146.

Spangenberg, J.H. 2017. Hot Air or Comprehensive Progress? A Critical Assessment of the SDGs. *Sustainable Development* 25(4): 311–321.

Spangenberg, J.H., and Settele, J. 2016. Value Pluralism and Economic Valuation – Defendable if Well Done. *Ecosystem Services* 18: 100–109.

Stiglitz, J., Sen, A., and Fitoussi, J.P. 2010. *Mismeasuring Our Lives*. The New Press, New York, USA.

Ulgiati, S., and Brown, M.T. 1998. Monitoring patterns of sustainability in natural and man-made ecosystems. *Ecological Modelling* 108(1): 23–36.

UNDESA UN Department of Economic and Social Affairs (2007). *Indicators of Sustainable Development: Guidelines and Methodologies*, 3rd ed. United Nations, New York, USA.

UNDPCSD UN Division for Sustainable Development: Department of Policy Co-ordination and Sustainable Development. 1996. *Indicators of Sustainable Development, Framework and Methodologies*, 1st ed. United Nations, New York, USA.

UNDSD Division for Sustainable Development: UN Department of Economic and Social Affairs. 2001. *Indicators of Sustainable Development: Guidelines and Methodologies*, 2nd ed. United Nations, New York, USA.

United Nations General Assembly. 2012. *The Future We Want*. UNGA 66th Session, Agenda Item 19, Document A/66/L.56, July 24th, 2012, New York.

United Nations General Assembly. 2015. *Transforming Our World: The 2030 Agenda for Sustainable Development*. Resolution 70/1 adopted by the General Assembly on 25 September 2015. Document A/RES/70/1. United Nations, New York, USA.

Veenhoven, R. 2010. Greater Happiness for a Greater Number: Is That Possible and Desirable? *Journal of Happiness Studies* 11: 605–629.

WCED World Commission on Environment and Development. 1987. *Our Common Future (The Brundtland Report)*. Oxford University Press, Oxford, UK.

Weisz, H., Krausmann, F., Amman, C., Eisenmenger, N., Erb, K.-H., Hubacek, K., and Fischer-Kowalski, M. 2006. The Physical Economy of the European Union: Cross-Country Comparison and Determinats of Material Consumption. *Ecological Economics* 58(4): 676–698.

10

SUSTAINABILITY INDICATORS AND CERTIFICATION SCHEMES FOR THE BUILT ENVIRONMENT

Catalina Turcu

Introduction

This chapter focuses on the role that SIs play in measuring sustainability in the built environment and is structured under three main sections. First, the chapter reflects on whether one can actually measure sustainability and briefly discusses various definitions of sustainability and why it is important to measure sustainability. The second part focuses entirely on sustainability indicators. It looks at their role and characteristics, and pauses on the main methodological models for their development: expert-led (or top-down) and citizen-led (or bottom-up). It also introduces a third and alternative methodological model, the hybrid model. The third section looks at certification schemes for sustainable built environments, such as BREEAM and LEED, which aggregate indicators into indices and are deployed to assess the sustainability performance of buildings and/or built areas. The chapter concludes by discussing some of the problems associated with the use of sustainability indicators and certification schemes in the built environment such as 'one size doesn't fit all', expert-biased processes and unequal consideration of sustainability pillars; but also their merits including raising awareness, dissemination of sustainability knowledge and evidence-based support in the decision-making process.

Part I: measuring sustainability

Any measurement should start with a definition of what is being measured. Sustainability is a contested term, with a long history which can be traced back to the work of the German forester, Hans Carl von Carlovitz, who coined the term in an environmental context while looking at how forests can be managed on a long-term basis. The term was relatively forgotten until the 1960s and 1970s when it re-emerged with the birth of the contemporary environmental movement. The 1987 Brundtland Report, however, brought it back into a wider currency and defined it as:

> development that meets the needs of the present without compromising the ability of future generations to meet their own needs.
>
> (WCED, 1987, p. 43)

'This definition is, however, imprecise: it is holistic and attractive, but too elastic' (Turcu, 2013, p. 697). It does not give an indication of what sustainability is precisely and what one may contemplate to measure. For example, what needs; what type of ability; which generations; and over what period of time?

A consistent definition of sustainable development or sustainability has proved to be elusive. Both concepts can be used to cover very divergent ideas and encompass a complex range of meanings (Adams, 2001; Adams, 2006; Lele, 1991). For example, Parkin (2000) found more than 200 formal definitions of sustainable development. The lack of agreement and uncertainty over the definition, however, has not reduced the popularity of the concept. 'Sustainability' and 'sustainable development' have generally been defined as an aggregate of characteristics, including economic security and growth (economic pillar); environmental quality and integrity (environmental pillar); social cohesion and quality of life (social pillar); and, more recently, empowerment and governance, and/or historic and cultural circumstances (institutional/cultural pillar).

The complex interdependencies between economic, social and environmental phenomena, and the need to balance or harmonise these over time, have also been the focus of particular attention in defining sustainability. However, over what period of time should one view sustainable development and sustainability? Five, ten or 100 years? This is an open question which highlights the fact that sustainability could look very different in a short-, medium- or long-term perspective. In fact, Brandon and Lombardi (2005) note the evolving nature of sustainability and that sustainability should be seen as a *process of change* and not as an end goal or destination. This is important for sustainability discourses within built environment studies and suggests that both the spatial and temporary dimensions of built environments are equally important when discussing sustainability, as they constantly adapt, change and are re-interpreted because of changes in circumstances and advances in knowledge. This is not an easy consideration as the built environment remains firmly grounded into and concerned with spatiality, physicality and locality, and time escapes that.

Bearing in mind the difficulty that scholars encounter to define the concept, it does not come as a surprise that there is no agreed way of defining the extent to which sustainability is being achieved. On the one hand, it is argued that sustainability is a moving target and so, developing measures at any one point in time is not worth the effort (Hempel, 1999). On the other hand, it is important to monitor progress, as people need a 'reality check' to ensure that things are moving into the right direction (Brandon and Lombardi, 2005, Hemphill et al., 2004, Hemphill et al., 2002, Innes and Booher, 2000). There is no textbook which gives a methodology that is generally accepted and applicable across regions and sectors (Hardi et al., 1997) and, as such, many authors employ rather ad hoc checklists of sustainability without a clear methodological framework.

The area of built environment studies echoes most of the ideas above and uses sustainability to coin and unpick concepts such as compact cities, sustainable urbanism, green urbanism, smart growth, low-carbon development and ecological/eco-urbanism, among others. Thinking underlying some of these concepts offers some communalities and/or refers to discussions of reduced consumption and impacts; increased density, proximity, diversity and access; enhanced equity, and so on. As a result, there is a sheer variety of frameworks at the global level that seek to 'standardise' sustainable development within the built environment and Chapter 24 by Joss and Rydin offers a fuller discussion of this.

This infiltration of sustainability ideas in planning and urbanism studies, however, has attracted much criticism. It is argued the built environment relies on too many resources crossing its boundaries to be sustainable and only by, for example, 'rehabilitating' natural capital resources (such as local fisheries, forests and agricultural land) it can become more self-reliant and so, sustainable (Rees, 1997; Rees and Wackernagel, 1996; Renn et al., 1998). Moreover, Owens (1992) points out that the notion of urban sustainability is a contradiction. Urban areas will always be net consumers of resources, drawing them from the world around them. They are also likely to be major degraders of the environment, simply because of the relative intensity of economic and social activity taking place in such places (Owens, 1992).

There is a range of approaches looking at gauging sustainability performance in the built environment. Among these, however, two have recently received more extensive attention in both academia and practice. They are the *Ecological Footprint*, which has been applied at a range of scales (from building, through city, to regional and national level); and *Ecosystem Services*, mainly applied at the city and national scales (Karadimitriou et al., 2016). Both approaches use a natural resources – flows – systems framing and use Natural Carbon Accounting (NCA). NCA calculates the total stocks and flows of natural resources and services in a given ecosystem or area and translates that into a carbon equivalent. The concept of accounting for natural capital has been around for more than 30 years but was re-launched by the UN Statistical Commission of the System for Environmental and Economic Accounts (SEEA) in 2012. It provides an internationally agreed method to account for material natural resources like minerals, timber and fisheries and can use one of the following methods: *dashboards of indicators*, i.e. Eurostat Sustainable Development Indicators; *indices*, i.e. Environmental Sustainability Index; *adjusted GDP*, i.e. Green GDP; and *overconsumption indices*, i.e. adjusted net savings (ANS) and Ecological Footprint accounts.

For example, the Ecological Footprint – for a fuller account of this see Chapter 16 by Wackernagel and colleagues – and Ecosystem Services, two relatively popular approaches to measuring sustainability, use NCA and advance a strong 'carbon and natural resources first' framing. They are firmly grounded in natural and environmental sciences (i.e. environmental science/biology/Earth science) and engineering, therefore being weaker in accounting for socio-economic flows and processes. Sustainability measures can be monetary or quantifiable (i.e. length of cycle lanes), non-monetary (i.e. the overall cost/benefit of improved environmental conditions) and non-quantifiable (they cannot be translated easily in money and/or do not take a physical form, i.e. happiness). For example, while some ecosystems services, like fish or wood, are bought and sold in markets, many ecosystem services, like a day of wildlife viewing or a view of the ocean, are intrinsically hard to measure let alone trade in markets.

Alongside NCA-based approaches, other measures are also proposed to measure the sustainability of the built environment including those derived from costs and benefits analysis and balancing environment and development needs (MIPS, Emergy, Life Cycle Analysis). A brief overview of these is given by Table 10.1. To sum up, it is clear that measuring sustainability is complex (Bell and Morse, 2003) and this is also challenging in the area of planning and built environment. However, perhaps the most popular approach with both policy makers and scholars has been sustainability indicators (SIs) which are discussed at length in the following section.

Part II: sustainability indicators (SIs) for the built environment

Sustainability indicators (SIs) are individual credit-scoring variables that provide specific measurements, but also are seen as defining and operationalising sustainability. They play an important role in formulating local and national sustainability policy (Brugmann, 1997a; Brugmann, 1997b; Pinfield, 1996; Pinfield, 1997) and have been widely employed by urban policy makers to ensure the continued success of their cities (Habitat, 2009; Ravetz, 2000; Mega and Pedersen, 1998; Maclaren, 1996). However a gap still exists between policy aspirations and actual results (see Chapter 13 by Almássy and Pintér for a fuller discussion).

Table 10.1 Approaches to measuring sustainability in buildings/the built environment

Approach	Description	Limitations/Criticism
Cost Benefit Analysis (CBA)	Comparison of financial values of the costs of achieving sustainability in a building/built area with the benefits.	CBA does not provide unbiased information and efforts to use monetary values for environmental and safety regulations erode the self-evident values upon which our society is based. CBA has been shown to mask theoretical and technical difficulties of measuring sustainability and has been discredited as a valid approach for decision-making for sustainability (Lave and Gruenspecht, 1991).
Balancing environment and development **Life Cycle Analysis (LCA)**	Assessment of environmental impacts associated with (all) stages of a building/built area; also associated to cradle-to-cradle and eco-balance analysis.	It tends to be limited to the cost of service life of building in engineering or accounting. It does not consider the full life cycle of assessment, i.e. planning, design, costing, budgeting, financing, operations, maintenance, repair, recycling, reuse and evaluation (Neuman and Whittington, 2000).
Material intensity per unit of service (MIPS)	Mass of material input per total units of service delivered by building/built area over its entire lifespan.	Does not take into account eco-toxicity of materials (i.e. non-toxic materials). The current climate change and CO_2-emissions debates show vast amounts of non-toxic materials may contribute to environmental problems.
(Solar) Emergy	Converts inputs/flows in a building/built area into an energy equivalent (usually solar energy).	Criticised by economists, physicists and engineers. Some critics have focused on detailed practical aspects of the approach, while others have taken issue with specific parts of the theory and claims.
Natural Capital Accounting (NCA) **Ecological Footprint (EF)**	A spatial unit (e.g. country or urban area) can be described in terms of its carrying capacity or impact in terms of the land area required to support it.	Does not account for all aspects of sustainability, i.e. social. A static model – whilst all domains of sustainable development are dynamic – cannot directly take into account things such as the adaptability of social systems or technological change.
Ecosystem Services (ES)	Benefits to humans resulting from use of ecosystems (supporting, provisioning, regulating, cultural services) in built areas	Still at an early stage of application. Cultural services (i.e. non-material benefits people draw from ecosystems through spiritual enrichment, cognition, reflection, aesthetic experiences, etc.) are particularly difficult to quantify. Criticised for commodifying nature and promoting an exploitative human-nature relation (Schröter et al., 2014).

Source: Adapted from Turcu (2010)

What are their characteristics? On the one hand, SIs should be objective. That is to say they have to be objective or measurable, easy to understand, eye-catching, reflect local circumstances and address a range of issues across the four pillars of sustainability (environmental, economic, social and institutional/cultural). On the other hand, SIs are subjective. They are socially constructed. 'Beloved indicators' tend to exist at the back of our minds and this may bias their selection and our interpretation; because of this, SIs can measure what is measurable, rather than what is important and needs to be measured (see Chapter 9 by Spangenberg for a fuller discussion). Generally, there are three types of indicators: counts (i.e. census indicators); ratios (i.e. GDP per capita); and composites (i.e. HDI, MDG, SDG indicators). Counts are the simplest types, ratios are the most established and composites the most powerful (used in ranking performance), but also the most contested.

SIs have different functions. They can be used to produce scientific knowledge about sustainability, facilitate organisational management, i.e. monitor sustainability performance and help to reform/improve sustainability agendas. Two methodological approaches dominate the development of SIs (Reed et al., 2005; Eckerberg and Mineur, 2003; Turcu, 2012). They are expert-led or top-down and citizen-led or bottom-up models of development. There is a third and emerging approach, called the hybrid or integrated development of SIs, which aims to address the limitations of the two previous approaches, by bringing together their strengths (Turcu, 2010; Turcu, 2012; Turcu, 2013).

The expert-led or top-down, also called government SIs, are based on traditional and formal hierarchies that define complex system dynamics. They tend to be 'scientific' or quantitative and measure, for example, economic activity, average annual consumption of electricity, election turnout, etc. They draw on large datasets collected via statistically randomised surveys and rely primarily on 'expert' knowledge. That is to say, they are developed with input from academics and/or other sustainability 'experts' such as government bodies, policy makers and other professionals (planners, architects, engineers, urban economists, etc.) working with sustainability in the built environment.

One such example is illustrated by the ten European Common Indicators (ECIs) in Table 10.2, which aim to measure the environmental sustainability of cities and towns across the European context (EC, 2000). Another example is the 30 indicators from the European Green City Index (Figure 10.1) developed by Siemens and the Economist's Intelligence Unit which measures the

Table 10.2 European Common Indicators

	Indicator
1.	*Satisfaction with the local community*
2.	*Local contribution to global climate change (carbon Footprint of town/city)*
3.	*Mobility and passenger transportation*
4.	*Availability of public space and services*
5.	*Local air quality*
6.	*Children's journeys to and from school*
7.	*Sustainable management of the local authority and local businesses*
8.	*Noise pollution*
9.	*Sustainable land use*
10.	*Products promoting sustainability*

Source: EC (2000)

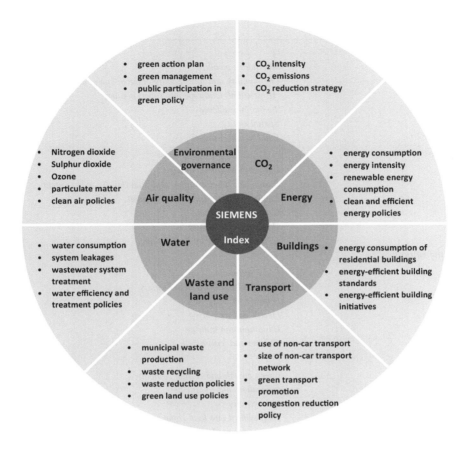

Figure 10.1 Siemens' Green City Index evaluates 16 quantitative and 14 qualitative indicators

Source: Adapted from Siemens AG (2009, p. 9)

current environmental performance of major European cities, as well as their commitment to reducing their future environmental impact (Siemens AG, 2009).

Widely employed examples of top-down-developed SIs include the 30 indicators from the Reference Framework for Sustainable Cities (RFSC) which support and measure the delivery of 2007 Leipzig Charter and European Union's vision for sustainable cities (EU, 2008) – see Table 10.3; and the recently 13 indicators proposed to measure the Sustainable Development Goal (SDG) No 11 (Sustainable cities and communities: Make cities inclusive, safe, resilient and sustainable) (UN, 2016). See Table 10.4, and for a fuller discussion of SDGs see Chapter 6 by Rotz and Fraser.

Other sets of indicators, often assessing sustainability, include the European Green Capital Award (by European Commission); Urban Ecosystem Europe (by ICLEI and Ambiente Italia); European Metabolism Framework (by European Environmental Agency); Urban Sustainability Indicators (by European Foundation for the Improvement of Living and Working Conditions); Urban Audit indicators (by Eurostat); Global City Indicators Programme (by World Bank); City

Table 10.3 The Reference Framework for Sustainable Cities (RFSC) has developed 30 indicators over five dimensions

Spatial	
1.	*Alternative mobility*
2.	*High quality and functionality of public spaces and living environment*
3.	*Architectural, landscape and urban heritage*
4.	*Territorial resilience*
5.	*Spatial equity*
6.	*Land resources saving*
Governance	
7.	*Integrated territorial strategy*
8.	*Sustainable administration and financial city management*
9.	*Monitoring of continual improvement*
10.	*Citizen participation*
11.	*Widening governance*
12.	*Capacity building and networking*
Social and cultural	
13.	*Social inclusion*
14.	*Social and intergenerational equity*
15.	*Housing for everyone*
16.	*Health and well-being*
17.	*Education and training*
18.	*Culture and leisure*
Economic	
19.	*Green growth and circular economy*
20.	*Innovation and smart cities*
21.	*Connectivity*
22.	*Employment and local economy*
23.	*Sustainable production and consumption*
24.	*Cooperation and innovative partnerships*
Environment	
25.	*Water resources*
26.	*Climate change and energy*
27.	*Biodiversity and ecosystems*
28.	*Pollution reduction*
29.	*Natural and technological risks*
30.	*Natural resource management and waste reduction*

Source: EU (2008)

Blueprints (by Waternet Amsterdam and KWR Water Cycle Research Institute); China Urban Sustainability Index (by Urban China Initiative), etc.

The criticism of SIs developed from the top down is threefold. First, they are 'conditioned' by the existence of available and, usually, centralised collection of statistical data. That means that where data is not available, an indicator cannot be measured and so, it might be discounted from a shortlist of potential indicators. For example, both ECIs and RFSC indicators have been developed with data availability and comparability across national contexts in mind. In addition, a wider range of data and statistics is readily available for cities and urban areas in developed

Table 10.4 Proposed indicators or targets for SDG Goal No 11 (Sustainable cities and communities: Make cities inclusive, safe, resilient and sustainable)

Indicators SDG Goal 11
1. *Proportion of urban population living in slums, informal settlements or inadequate housing*
2. *Proportion of the population that has convenient access to public transport, disaggregated by age group, sex and persons with disabilities*
3. *Ratio of land consumption rate to population growth rate*
4. *Percentage of cities with a direct participation structure of civil society in urban planning and management which operate regularly and democratically*
5. *Share of national (or municipal) budget which is dedicated to the preservation, protection and conservation of national cultural natural heritage, including World Heritage sites*
6. *Number of deaths, missing people, injured, relocated or evacuated due to disasters per 100,000 people*
7. *Percentage of urban solid waste regularly collected and with adequate final discharge with regard to the total waste generated by the city*
8. *Annual mean levels of fine particulate matter (e.g. PM2.5 and PM10) in cities (population weighted)*
9. *The average share of the built-up area of cities that is open space for public use for all, disaggregated by age group, sex and persons with disabilities*
10. *Proportion of women subjected to physical or sexual harassment, by perpetrator and place of occurrence (last 12 months)*
11. *Cities with more than 100,000 inhabitants that implement urban and regional development plans integrating population projections and resource needs*
12. *Percentage of cities that are implementing risk reduction and resilience strategies aligned with accepted international frameworks (such as the successor to the Hyogo Framework for Action 2005–2015 on disaster risk reduction) that include vulnerable and marginalized groups in their design, implementation and monitoring*
13. *Percentage of financial support that is allocated to the construction and retrofitting of sustainable, resilient and resource-efficient buildings*

Source: UN (2016)

countries, than in transition and developing countries, which make implementation and comparison of SIs difficult.

Second, this type of indicators can miss what is important at the local level as they take a view from the top (Morse and Fraser, 2005) and only sparingly include consultation and involvement of groups at the bottom. It has been argued, for example, that European level indicators fail to reflect regional perspectives of sustainability (Zeijl-Rozema and Martens, 2010).

Third, top-down indicators are little sensitive to change in built environment circumstances and processes. As they involve considerable financial and human resources in their development, once developed, they do not change to include, for example, new indicators arising from new urban conditions. To sum up, top-down SIs are data driven and tend to be a reflexion of Western expertise and models, more often than not and imposed on the developing context. The most successful ones tend to be supported by strong institutions and financial resources hence, they represent certain groups and ideologies in society (Turcu, 2017).

The citizen-led or bottom-up, also called governance, SIs build on community or grassroots participation and a thorough understanding of the local context. They rely on 'popularity' and prioritisation of indicators within a certain locality and learning by doing. Bottom-up indicators tend to favour soft or qualitative indicators such as 'level of community activity', 'satisfaction with local area' and 'perceptions of community spirit'. It is argued that, in addition, they have the ability to measure changes in process and policy, besides outcomes (Kline, 2001); and promote truly participatory and democratic qualities, which in time can bring about changes in the policy status quo (Eckerberg and Mineur, 2003).

One such well-known example is represented by the set of Sustainable Seattle (S2) indicators, first of this kind and acknowledged worldwide as a leader in the development of indicators based on citizens' values and goals for their community (Atkisson, 1999; Holden, 2006). A model that has been noted in the Bellagio Principles for Assessment of sustainability indicator projects (Zdan, 1997) and from which many bottom-up indicator sets have grown. S2 have been at the centre of the Brugmann–Pinfield debate in the late 1990s, when the former criticised S2's failure to formally change policy at the city level thus casting doubt on the importance of such process which could only be 'catalytic' at best, while the latter responded by defending the importance the citizen-based process spearheaded by S2 (Brugmann, 1997a; Brugmann, 1997b; Pinfield, 1997).

The first set of S2 indicators was launched in 1993 and reviewed thereafter in 1995 and 1998. It consists of some 40 indicators across four themes (environment, population and resources, economy, and culture and society) including some very specific-to-Seattle indicators such as 'wild salmon runs through local steams' (Figure 10.2). Outcomes are measured as 'sustainability trends' i.e. indicators moving toward or away from sustainability; and staying stable/neutral. Figure 10.2 illustrates S2 trends in 1998 (Sustainable Seattle, 1998).

Citizen-led or bottom-up developed indicators, however, come with their caveats and Chapter 12 by Bell and Morse discusses this in greater detail. They are also criticised on the basis of community 'control', where the 'usual suspects' can take centre stage and dominate the agenda at the expense of wider and more strategic concerns. In addition, Holden (2006) notes that due to their very consultative nature they are expensive and so resource support (human and financial) is often insufficient in the long term; bottom-up led indicators do not command the same legitimacy as top-down ones; and responsibilities for action on indicator trends are often unclear.

An emerging and third type of SIs development is represented by the hybrid or integrated approach. This model aims for a result that is greater than the sum of the top-down and bottom-up models, by adding up their strengths and cancelling out their weaknesses. However, hybrid-developed SIs are only emerging and understanding has mainly developed along three lines (Turcu, 2013):

- the development of methodologies for developing such indicators, but step-by-step guidance is not always a guarantee of things materialising in practice
- the understanding of crossing points and knowledge transfer between the top, middle and bottom levels of expertise, but the focus has mainly been the interface between top (i.e. scientists) and middle (i.e. technocrats and policy makers) and little is understood about the bottom (i.e. the public)
- the special scale (i.e. macro-mezo-micro or national/international-national/regional-local) at which such indicators are deployed; however, cascading down from the national to regional level is better understood than from the national and/or regional to local level.

One example of such integrated SIs is that developed by Turcu (2010, 2013) and presented in Figure 10.3. She develops SIs in three consecutive steps: (1) by engagement with the existing literature and drawing on five publicly acknowledged lists of indicators, in order to derive a first list of indicators; (2) via consultation with top-level 'experts' to probe into the initial list and transform it into a shortlist of indicators relevant to the context of application; and (3) through

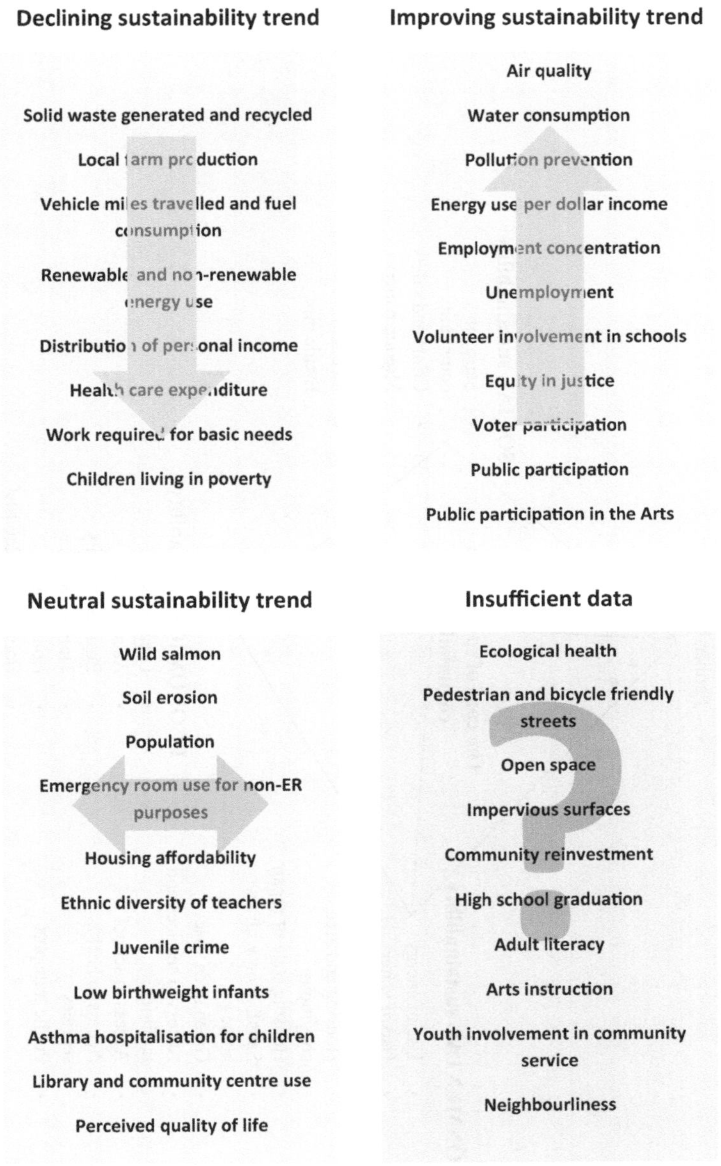

Declining sustainability trend

Solid waste generated and recycled

Local farm production

Vehicle miles travelled and fuel consumption

Renewable and non-renewable energy use

Distribution of personal income

Health care expenditure

Work required for basic needs

Children living in poverty

Improving sustainability trend

Air quality

Water consumption

Pollution prevention

Energy use per dollar income

Employment concentration

Unemployment

Volunteer involvement in schools

Equity in justice

Voter participation

Public participation

Public participation in the Arts

Neutral sustainability trend

Wild salmon

Soil erosion

Population

Emergency room use for non-ER purposes

Housing affordability

Ethnic diversity of teachers

Juvenile crime

Low birthweight infants

Asthma hospitalisation for children

Library and community centre use

Perceived quality of life

Insufficient data

Ecological health

Pedestrian and bicycle friendly streets

Open space

Impervious surfaces

Community reinvestment

High school graduation

Adult literacy

Arts instruction

Youth involvement in community service

Neighbourliness

Figure 10.2   Sustainable Seattle (S2): indicator trends in 1998

Source: Adapted from Sustainable Seattle (1998, p. 5)

consultation with bottom level key players and communities to signpost local concerns and processes and test relevance at the local level.

Turcu (2013) finds that these hybrid–developed SIs fit generally well to the context; however, new indicators tend to emerge despite the intensive consultation process at the top and bottom;

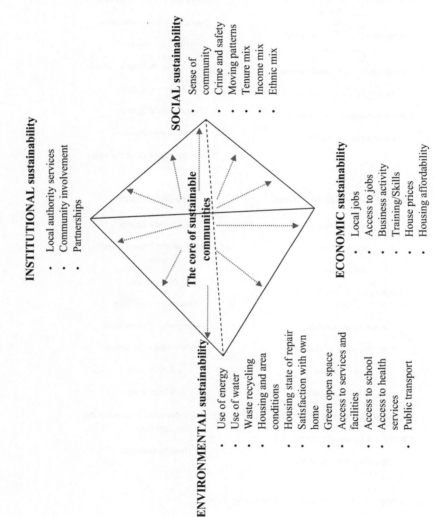

INSTITUTIONAL sustainability

- Local authority services
- Community involvement
- Partnerships

SOCIAL sustainability

- Sense of community
- Crime and safety
- Moving patterns
- Tenure mix
- Income mix
- Ethnic mix

The core of sustainable communities

ENVIRONMENTAL sustainability

- Use of energy
- Use of water
- Waste recycling
- Housing and area conditions
- Housing state of repair
- Satisfaction with own home
- Green open space
- Access to services and facilities
- Access to school
- Access to health services
- Public transport

ECONOMIC sustainability

- Local jobs
- Access to jobs
- Business activity
- Training/Skills
- House prices
- Housing affordability

Figure 10.3 A hybrid set of sustainability indicators

Source: Turcu (2013)

and some indicators are considered more important (i.e. are valued more at the bottom). The latter is little considered in indicator development to date and thus, SIs cannot be seen as final measures of sustainability, but rather as flexible ones, underlying the process of sustainability (Turcu, 2013).

Part III: certification schemes for sustainable buildings and built environment

Certification schemes for sustainable buildings and built environments are tools for assessing sustainability performance and facilitating informed decision-making in the built environment. These type of tools can be seen as the latest generation of impact assessment tools. They draw on Environment Impact Assessments (EIAs) developed in the US in the 1970s, which evolved into Strategic Environmental Assessment (SEAs) in the 1980s and Sustainability Assessments (SAs) in the 1990s. BREEAM (Building Research Establishment Environmental Assessment Method) was launched in 1990 by the UK's Building Research Establishment (BRE) and is the world's first established method of certifying sustainable buildings.

Certification schemes are usually developed by national green councils (i.e. UKGBC, USGBC, DGNB, JaGBC, GBCA, etc.) and/or other organisations (i.e. BRE, JSBC, BioRegional); they are voluntary and respond to market demand. Table 10.5 illustrates a number of such certification schemes at both the building and/or neighbourhood level. Sharifi and Murayama (2013) classifies them into two types: (1) tools for assessing sustainable buildings and spin-offs of such tools to assess sustainable neighbourhoods; and (2) tools which are the result of research projects.

They can be exported and used across different contexts (i.e. BREEAM and LEED) or nationally developed and so, specific to a country (i.e. TREES in Thailand and Miljobyggnad or CityLab in Sweden). Over the last decade they have evolved from a focus on buildings to a wider focus on neighbourhoods or larger built areas; and from an environmental focus to a more holistic one, aiming to also cover social and economic aspects of sustainability.

There is little research on the performance and efficiency of such tools. With a few exceptions (see Sharifi and Murayama, 2013), existing studies look at modest comparisons between two different certification schemes at the most (for example BREEAM and LEED); and at their 'application' to specific buildings and sites, which, per se, raises questions about the generalisation of findings, but also the transferability of lessons learnt. They are criticised on their approach to selection and weighting of indicators; and their complexity and lack in transparency, which make them difficult to understand and compare. Looking at seven tools from Australia, Europe, Japan and the US, Sharafi and Murayama (2013) find that

> most of the tools are not doing well regarding the coverage of social, economic, and institutional aspects of sustainability; there are ambiguities and shortcomings in the weighting, scoring, and rating; in most cases, there is no mechanism for local adaptability and participation; and, only those tools which are embedded within the broader planning framework are doing well with regard to applicability.
>
> (Sharifi and Murayama, 2013, p. 73)

Among sustainability certification schemes applied at a neighbourhood scale, two stand out. They are LEED-ND and BREEAM Communities. The US's LEED-ND (or LEED for Neighbourhood Development), launched in 2009 as a spin-off of LEED established in 2000, was

Table 10.5 Examples of certification schemes for sustainable buildings and/or sustainable neighbourhoods

Type	Certification scheme (scale of application, year)	Country of origin	Developed by
Tools (building level) and spin-off tools (neighbourhood/development level)	BREEAM (buildings, 1990) BREEAM Communities (neighbourhoods, 2009) www.breeam.com/	UK	Building Research Establishment (BRE)
	LEED (buildings, 2000) LEED-ND (neighbourhood development, 2009) www.usgbc.org/leed?gclid=CL-34PvYwtQCFSW17Qod3wwC_A	US	US Green Building Council (USGBC), Council for New Urbanism (CNU), Natural Resources Defence Council (NRDC)
	CASBEE Comprehensive Assessment System for Built Environment Efficiency (buildings, 2001) CASBEE-UD (urban development, 2004) www.ibec.or.jp/CASBEE/english/	Japan	Japan Green Building Council (JGBC), Japan Sustainable Building Consortium (JSBC)
	DGNB System (buildings, 2008) www.dgnb-system.de/en/system/certification_system/	Germany	German Sustainable Building Council
	Green Star (buildings, 2013) Green Star Communities (neighbourhood development, 2013) www.mygreenstarenergy.com/	Australia	Australia Green Building Council (AGBC)
	ECC Earth Craft Communities (regional/neighbourhood, 2003) www.earthcraft.org/builders/programs/	US	Greater Atlanta Home Builders Association, Atlanta Regional Commission, Urban Land Institute. Atlanta District Council and Southface
	QSAS (buildings, 2009) QSAS-NH (neighbourhood development, 2010)	Qatar	Gulf Organisation for Research and Development
	BCA Green Mark (buildings, 2005) BCA Green Mark Districts (neighbourhoods, 2009) www.bca.gov.sg/greenmark/green_mark_buildings.html	Singapore	Building and Construction Authority (BCA)

Category	Tool	Country	Organization
Project embedded tools	**Green Building Index** (buildings, n/a) **Green Neighbourhood Index** (neighbourhoods, n/a) http://new.greenbuildingindex.org/	Malaysia	Malaysian Institute of Architects (PAM), Association of Consulting Engineers Malaysia (ACEM)
	Miljobyggnad (building, 2011) www.sgbc.se/var-verksamhet/miljoebyggnad	Sweden	Sweden Green Building Council (SGBC)
	TREES Thai Rating of Energy and Environmental Sustainability (building, 2010)	Thailand	Thai Green Building Institute (TGBI)
	HQE²R Sustainable renovation of buildings for sustainable neighbourhoods toolkit (neighbourhood, 2004) www.eukn.eu/e-library/project/bericht/eventDetail/hq2er-sustainable-renovation-of-buildings-for-sustainable-neighbourhoods-1/	EU (FP5)	Research team: UK (UWE); Denmark (Cenergia); Italy (ICIE, Quasco); Germany (IOER); Spain (CAATB, IteC); Netherlands (Ambit)
	EcoDistricts (neighbourhood, 2009) https://ecodistricts.org/	US	Portland Sustainability Institute
	SPeAR Sustainable Project Appraisal Routine (neighbourhood, 2000) www.arup.com/projects/spear	UK	ARUP
	OLP One Living Planet Principles (building and neighbourhood, 2002) www.bioregional.co.uk/oneplanetliving/	UK	BioRegional, World WildlifeFund (WWF)

Source: Adapted from Sharifi and Murayama (2013)

jointly developed by the US Green Building Council (USGBC), Congress for New Urbanism (CNU) and Natural Resources Defence Council (NRDC). LEED-ND places an emphasis on the selection of the site, design and construction elements that bring buildings and infrastructure together into a neighbourhood; and relate the neighbourhood to its landscape as well as its local and regional context.

The UK's BREEAM Communities was launched in 2009 and builds on BREEAM, the very first certification scheme at the building level launched in 1990 and developed by the Building Research Establishment (BRE). BREEAM-ND aims to help planners and developers to take into the account a range of issues from the earliest stages of the development process, and to measure and independently certify the sustainability of project proposals at the planning stage of the development process.

Looking across certification schemes for sustainability in the built environment, five important observations can be made. First, they are made of indicators and so, indicators come with strengths and limitations. On the one hand, they can act as powerful decision tools; cover multiple aspects of sustainability; nurture intergenerational equity; reflect multiple stakeholder knowledge and interests; and be context specific. On the other hand, linkages between SIs are not considered; they are dominated by short-term thinking and one-off measurements; and can be potentially 'hijacked' by certain stakeholder interest groups.

Second, their measurement is determined by their 'coverage', i.e. indicators they consist of. They all take different emphases and there is an overall lack of balance between the four pillars of sustainability (i.e. environmental, economic, social and institutional/cultural). The environmental dimension (both natural and built environment) is dominant by and large; that is to say that resource- and design-related indicators take precedence over other indicators. Social indicators receive different interpretations under various certification schemes; economic indicators do not receive enough attention; and institutional indicators are little addressed.

Third, the majority of these tools are developed from the top and by the market, by sustainability experts and selected stakeholders under the auspices of formal institutions, but applied at the bottom, to buildings and urban areas. In the previous section, I argued that good SIs should reflect on multiple knowledge from both the top and the bottom. However, only little grassroots and bottom-up knowledge is involved in the development of current certification schemes with a few exceptions such as, for example, the HQE²R certification scheme and some more recent examples such as CityLab in Sweden.

Fourth, certification schemes need to fit the 'context' or locality they are applied to. While it is preferable for each country to develop its own certification scheme, this might be unattainable. In such situations, an 'adopted' tool must be adapted and customised using suitable local benchmarks and weightings to be used in the assessment framework. However, only a few tools allow for the use of local benchmarks, i.e. HQE²R. In addition, transferring a tool from the context in which it has been created to a different one is not easy. Even popular tools such as LEED and BREEAM have proved to be difficult to use outside their originator countries. For example, Sweden have tried for a number of years to adapt BREEAM to their context, to only decide more recently to design their own 'Swedernised' BREEAM tool, CityLab. In other words, one size does not fit all.

Finally, the information they present is 'sophisticated' and not always easy to 'digest' by policy makers, politicians, the general public and, sometimes, even by 'experts'. Certified projects are assigned a label or rating computed from the scores they have achieved on individual indicators. Labels and ratings are usually appealing for their simplicity, which usually work on the principle of 'at a glance' understanding and appealing visualisation. However, labels and ratings cannot be regarded as transparent assessments of sustainability as they build on integrating individual indicators and so, brushing over and/or missing in detail. Moreover, they present different levels or types of information. For example, the two examples below exemplify two approaches.

Japan's CASBEE-UD certification offers three levels of information, derived from 31 indicators (Figure 10.4). First, the BEEUD (Building Environmental Efficiency of Urban development) graph below shows how sustainable the project is, i.e. the steeper (and darker) the gradient, the more sustainable the project. Second, the 'radar chart' is indicating the performance of the six sustainability domains measured. Finally, the 'six bar charts of credits' (Qud and LRud) plot the performance of each indicator in each domain, which helps the reader to understand which indicators are doing well and which are in need of attention. This is complex and relatively detailed information which needs processing at three different levels across six established domains of sustainability.

ARUP's SPeAR certification is based on 23 individual indicators which are rated on a seven-point scale, from 'optimum' to 'worst case' on a single 'rosette' (Figure 10.5). Strong (i.e. optimum) indicators are closer to the centre of the rosette (and indicated by bright greens) while 'worrying' (i.e. worst case) indicators are further away from the centre of the rosette (and indicated by red and orange shades) – see here for a colour illustration www.arup.com/projects/spear/spear_diagram. Compared to the way the CASBEE-UD assessment communicates information, SPeAR seems less complex and more effective visually.

Conclusions

Sustainability and sustainable development are not easy to define. Thus, they are not easy to measure either. However, a number of approaches have raised to the challenge and, amongst those, the use of SIs is perhaps one of the most discussed in academia and employed in practice approaches. SIs are important tools in supporting the process and delivery of sustainable buildings and environments. This chapter has shown what the ideal characteristics of SIs are and how SIs should be developed in order to covey the diversity of issues purported by sustainable urban development.

Sets of SIs come with their strengths and limitations and serve best their context's and users' purposes. On the one hand, they cannot be comprehensive because of the range of factors involved in measuring sustainability, which is inexhaustible. They cannot be transferred easily and face the challenge of implementation in real contexts; are mainly developed by 'experts'; and offer an unbalanced view and thus, measurement of sustainability. On the other hand, they have been instrumental in raising the environmental awareness of policy makers, politicians and the general public; disseminate more widely knowledge and understanding of sustainable urban development; and support urban decision-making processes.

However, the area of built environment studies (i.e. planning and urbanism studies) have traditionally focused on the physicality of the built environment and/or urban form and so, have adopted the urban form approach to sustainability (Breheny, 1992), which is also reflected in the development of related SIs. I argue that SIs in the built environment should also focus on processes and flows. They should be dynamic and incorporate spatial as well as temporal aspects of urban development, which are, as previously discussed, intrinsic features of sustainability and sustainable urban development. This should make them relevant to real-world built environment conditions across space and time, which are dynamic, complex and ever changing.

Certification schemes in the built environment are an increasingly prominent feature of sustainable urban development or, more precisely, property-led development with sustainability/environmental claims. Scholars are not clear about the potential of these tools to lead to sustainable outcomes and have questioned, among others, their 'sophistication' which makes them

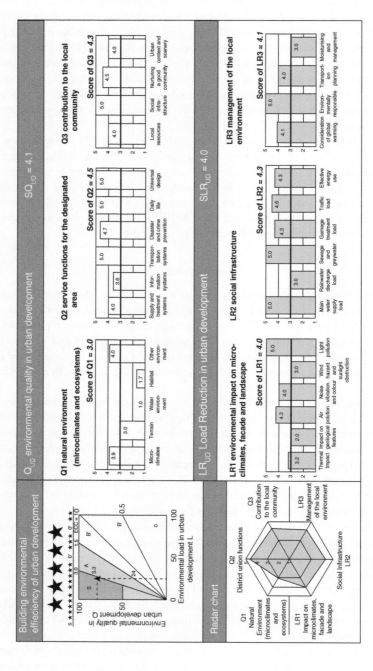

Figure 10.4   CASBEE-UD information: BEEUD chart, radar chart, and six bar charts of credits

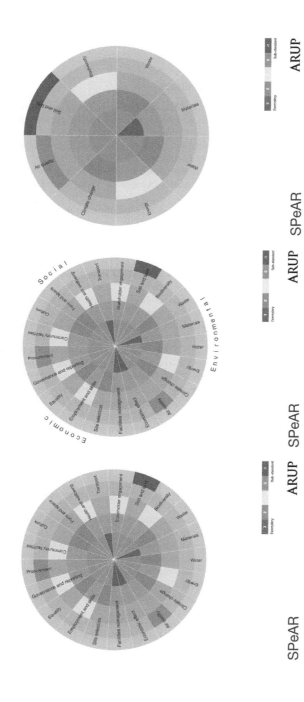

Figure 10.5 SPeAR visualisation

Source: www.arup.com/projects/spear/spear_diagram

resource-intensive and difficult to use (Elgert, 2016), but also the politics and power dynamics behind developing such schemes (Merry et al., 2015) – also see Chapter 24 in this book by Joss and Rydin. However, urban developers see them as a way of embedding sustainability in the development process, showing 'green credentials' and supporting decision-making towards sustainable buildings and neighbourhoods.

References

Adams, W. M. 2001. *Green Development: Environment and Sustainability in the Third World*. London: Routledge.
Adams, W. M. 2006. *The Future of Sustainability: Re-thinking Environment and Development in the Twenty-first Century*. Cambridge: IUCN World Conservation Union.
Atkisson, A. 1999. Developing indicators of sustainable community: Lessons from sustainable Seattle. *In:* Satterthwaite, D. (ed.) *Sustainable Cities*. London: Earthscan.
Bell, S. & Morse, S. 2003. *Measuring Sustainability: Learning from Doing*. London: Earthscan.
Brandon, P. S. & Lombardi, P. 2005. *Evaluating Sustainable Development in the Built Environment*. Oxford: Blackwell.
Breheny, M. J. 1992. *Sustainable Development and Urban Form*. London: Pion Limited.
Brugmann, J. 1997a. Is there a method in our measurement? The use of indicators in local sustainable development planning. *Local Environment*, 2, 59–72.
Brugmann, J. 1997b. Sustainability indicators revisited: Getting from political objectives to performance outcomes—a response to Graham Pinfield. *Local Environment*, 2, 299–302.
EC. 2000. *European Common Indicators: Towards a Local Sustainability Profile*. Brussels: European Commission (EC).
Eckerberg, K. & Mineur, E. 2003. The use of local sustainability indicators: Case studies in two Swedish municipalities. *Local Environment*, 8, 591–614.
Elgert, L. 2016. The double edge of cutting edge: Explaining adoption and nonadoption of the STAR rating system and insights for sustainability indicators. *Ecological Indicators*, 67, 556–564.
EU. 2008. *The Reference Framework for Sustainable Cities – A European Vision*. European Union (EU). http://www.ectp-ceu.eu/index.php/en/6-news/news/425-the-reference-framework-for-sustainable-cities
Habitat, U. 2009. *Global Report on Human Settlements 2009: Planning Sustainable Cities*. London: Earthscan.
Hardi, Peter, Stephan Barg, Tony Hodge (1997) *Measuring Sustainable Development: Review of Current Practice* (occasional Paper No 17). Winnipeg: International Institute for Sustainable Development (IISD).
Hempel, L. C. 1999. Conceptual and analytical challenges in building sustainable communities. *In:* Mazmanian, D. & Kraft, M. (eds.) *Toward Sustainable Communities: Transition and Transformations in Environmental Policy*. Cambridge, MA: MIT Press.
Hemphill, L., Berry, J. & Mcgreal, S. 2004. An indicator-based approach to measuring sustainable urban regeneration performance: Part 1, Conceptual foundations and methodological framework. *Urban Studies*, 41, 725–755.
Hemphill, L., Mcgreal, S. & Berry, J. 2002. An aggregated weighting system for evaluating sustainable urban regeneration. *Journal of Property Research*, 19, 353–373.
Holden, M. 2006. Revisiting the local impact of community indicators projects: Sustainable Seattle as prophet in its own land. *Applied Research in Quality of Life*, 1, 253–277.
Innes, J. & Booher, D. 2000. Indicators for sustainable communities: A strategy building on complexity theory and distributed intelligence. *Planning Theory and Practice*, 1, 173–186.
Karadimitriou, N., Gabrieli, T. & Turcu, C. 2016. *Measuring the Social, Economic and Environmental Effects of Property and Infrastructure Development*. London: RICS.
Kline, E. 2001. Indicators for sustainable development in urban areas. *Sustainability Assessment and the Management of Urban Environments*, 275–297.
Lave, L. & Gruenspecht, H. 1991. Increasing the efficiency and effectiveness of environmental decisions: Benefit-cost analysis and effluent fees a critical review. *Journal of the Air & Waste Management Association*, 41, 680–693.
Lele, S. M. 1991. Sustainable development: A critical review. *World Development*, 19, 607–612.
Maclaren, V. W. 1996. Urban sustainability reporting. *Journal of the American Planning Association*, 62, 184–202.
Mega, V. & Pedersen, J. 1998. *European Sustainability Indicators*.: European Foundation for the Improvement of Living and Working Conditions. Luxembourg: EUR-OP.

Merry, S. E., Davis, K. E. & Kingsbury, B. 2015. *The Quiet Power of Indicators: Measuring Governance, Corruption, and Rule of Law*. Cambridge: Cambridge University Press.

Morse, S. & Fraser, E. D. 2005. Making 'dirty' nations look clean? The nation state and the problem of selecting and weighting indices as tools for measuring progress towards sustainability. *Geoforum*, 36, 625–640.

Neuman, M. & Whittington, J. 2000. *Building California's Future: Current Conditions in Infrastructure Planning, Budgeting, and Financing*. San Francisco, CA: Public Policy Institute of California.

Owens, S. 1992. Energy, environmental sustainability and land-use planning. *In*: Breheny, M. J. (ed.) *Sustainable Development and Urban Form*. London: Pion Limited.

Parkin, S. 2000. Sustainable development: The concept and the practical challenge: Proceedings of the Institution of Civil Engineers. *Civil Engineering*, 138, 3–8.

Pinfield, G. 1996. Beyond sustainability indicators. *Local Environment*, 1, 151–163.

Pinfield, G. 1997. Sustainability indicators: A new tool for evaluation? *In*: Farthing, S. M. (ed.) *Evaluation of Local Environmental Policy*. Aldershot: Avebury.

Ravetz, J. 2000. Integrated assessment for sustainability appraisal in cities and regions. *Environmental Impact Assessment Review*, 20, 31–64.

Reed, M., Fraser, E. D., Morse, S. & Dougill, A. J. 2005. Integrating methods for developing sustainability indicators to facilitate learning and action. *Ecology and Society*, 10, r3.

Rees, W. E. 1997. Is 'Sustainable City' an oxymoron? *Local Environment*, 2, 302–310.

Rees, W. E. & Wackernagel, M. 1996. Urban ecological footprints: Why cities cannot be sustainable – and why they are the key to sustainability. *Environmental Impact Assessment Review*, 16, 223–248.

Renn, O., Goble, R. & Kastenholz, H. 1998. How to apply the concept of sustainability to a region. *Technological Forecasting and Social Change*, 58, 63–81.

Schröter, M., van der Zanden, E. H., van Oudenhoven, A. P. E., Remme, R. P., Serna-Chavez, H. M., de Groot, R. S. & Opdam, P. 2014. Ecosystem services as a contested concept: A synthesis of critique and counter-arguments. *Conservation Letters*, 7, 514–523.

Sharifi, A. & Murayama, A. 2013. A critical review of seven selected neighborhood sustainability assessment tools. *Environmental Impact Assessment Review*, 38, 73–87.

Siemens AG. 2009. *European Green City Index: Assessing the Environmental Impact of Europe's Major Cities*. Munich: Siemens AG.

Sustainable Seattle. 1998. *Sustainable Seattle Indicators of Sustainable Communities*. Seattle: Sustainable Seattle.

Turcu, C. 2010. *Examining the Impact of Housing Refurbishment-Led Regeneration on Community Sustainability: A Study of Three Housing Market Renewal in England*. PhD Thesis, London School of Economics.

Turcu, C. 2012. Local experiences of urban sustainability: Researching Housing Market Renewal interventions in three English neighbourhoods. *Progress in Planning*, 78, 101–150.

Turcu, C. 2013. Re-thinking sustainability indicators: Local perspectives of urban sustainability. *Journal of Environmental Planning and Management*, 56, 695–719.

Turcu, C. 2017. Sally Engle Merry, The seduction of quantification: measuring human rights, gender violence, and sex trafficking. *Critical Policy Studies*, 11(3): 383–385.

UN. 2016. *Report of the Inter-Agency and Expert Group on Sustainable Development Goal Indicators*. Washington: United Nations (UN) Economic and Social Council.

WCED. 1987. *Our Common Future: The Report of the Brundtland Commission*. Oxford: World Commission on Environment and Development (WCED).

Zdan, T. 1997. *Assessing Sustainable Development: Principles in Practice*. Winnipeg: International Institute for Sustainable Development.

Zeijl-Rozema, A. V. & Martens, P. 2010. An adaptive indicator framework for monitoring regional sustainable development: A case study of the INSURE project in Limburg, The Netherlands. *Sustainability: Science, Practice and Policy*, 6, 6–17.

11

MEASURING WATER SCARCITY AND WATER CONSUMPTION

Jonathan Chenoweth

Introduction

Water is essential for life, with social and economic development being completely dependent upon adequate access to water resources. All societies depend upon direct access to water resources to meet human needs with food production equally dependent upon ready access to water resources. Demand for water has grown as population has increased together with its demand for food, fibre and energy; rising living standards and changing consumption patterns have pushed up water use faster than population growth in most of the world (United Nations World Water Assessment Programme, 2015).

According to the United Nations, more than 2 billion people globally are effected by water stress and 1.8 billion are exposed to unsafe drinking water (United Nations, 2016). Access to water and sanitation was included in the United Nations Sustainable Development Goals agreed in March 2016. Goal 6 is to "ensure availability and sustainable management of water and sanitation for all" by 2030 (United Nations, 2016, p. 6). This goal goes beyond a focus only on drinking water supply and sanitation provision and seeks to address the broader issue of water resources sustainability as water supply and sanitation cannot be achieved without consideration of its broader context.

Sustainable development was defined by the Brundtland Report as development which "meets the needs of the present without compromising the ability of future generations to meet their own needs" (World Commission on Environment and Development, 1987, p. 43). Sustainable development indicators are used to measure the interaction of environmental and human systems in order to improve decision-making processes and ensure continuity and functionality of these systems (Ciegis et al., 2009; Rotz and Fraser, Chapter 6, this volume). To be useful, indicators need to be informative, relate to policy goals, be easily understandable and calculable, be reliable, be based on readily available data and should condense data without the loss of critical information (Ciegis et al., 2009). Perfect sustainability indicators are rare with most indicators involving a compromise between technical feasibility, availability of data and relevance.

Sustainability indicators focused on water are useful for a variety of purposes. At the macro level such an indicator can show whether direct and indirect human needs globally or regionally are achievable, both now and in the future, thus assisting with policy making at this level. At the micro level, water indicators can help decision-making, investment and allocation decisions, and even potentially help shape consumption choices for individuals. This paper reviews the variety of water indicators which have been developed and how effective they are at meeting these goals.

Indicators of water stress and scarcity

An index of water scarcity

Water is not scarce at the planetary scale. Annual renewable freshwater resources, the volume of surface water flow and groundwater recharge around the world, total 40,700 km^3 according to L'vovich and White (1990). The Food and Agriculture Organization's (2016a) Aquastat database suggests a total of 42,810 km^3 per year of renewable freshwater is available. With a global population of 7.55 billion (United Nations Department of Economic and Social Affairs, 2017), this equates to approximately 5,670 m^3 of water available per person per year. However, these water resources are unevenly distributed temporally and spatially and do not conform to patterns of human demand. Thus, although freshwater may be plentiful at a global level, scarcity is a critical problem in some regions.

Water scarcity is defined by UN-Water (UN-Water, 2007, p. 4), the United Nations' body responsible for coordinating on freshwater related issues, as "the point at which the aggregate impact of all users impinges on the supply or quality of water under prevailing institutional arrangements to the extent that the demand by all sectors, including the environment, cannot be satisfied fully". Water scarcity is a product of resource availability and demand. A traditional neo-Malthusian view holds that while resources are essentially fixed, demand for resources will increase with population growth (Meadows et al., 1992). This understanding underpins the most widely used indicator of water scarcity – the renewable water resources per capita indicator (Chenoweth, 2008b).

The renewable water resources per capita indicator was proposed by Falkenmark (1986) when considering the amount of water required for national food self-sufficiency in sub-Saharan Africa. According to Falkenmark (1986), a country faces water stress when its renewable per capita water resources fall below approximately 1,700 cubic metres (m^3). A country is water stressed when its per capita water resources are less than 1000 m^3, with water shortages then threatening economic development, human health and well-being. When its resources are less than 500 m^3 per capita a country faces absolute water scarcity. With a growing population a water-stressed country inevitably faces worsening scarcity (Falkenmark, 1986).

The Falkenmark water scarcity indicator is widely used for assessing whether a country is facing water stress or scarcity. Seckler et al. (1998) refer to it as the standard indicator of water scarcity while the FAO (Food and Agriculture Organization, 2000) suggests that the indicator is almost universally reported and indeed the Food and Agricultural Organisation (2003) uses it to identify water scarce countries in its *Review of World Water Resources by Country* report. The United Nations World Water Assessment Programme (2003, 2016) also refers to this indicator in its reports, with its first World Water Development Report in 2003 even suggesting that 1,700 m^3 of drinking water per capita was required for an active and healthy life, a misunderstanding of the indicator since no one could physically drink so much water in a year. This indicator is regularly referred to in the World Water Development Reports (United Nations World Water Assessment Programme, 2003, 2016).

The major shortcoming of the Falkenmark water scarcity indicator is that it does not consider differences in how water is used in different countries or the ability of countries to adapt to changing circumstances. Thus, according to this indicator a country such as Denmark with renewable water resources of 1,058 m^3 per capita is water stressed, verging on being water scarce, while Iran with 1,732 m^3 per capita is considered not at all water scarce but may become water stressed in the near future. However, with little use of irrigation in Denmark and thus only modest use of its total available water resources, there is no significant imbalance between resource availability and demand in the country and thus water scarcity does not impact upon social or economic development. In Iran, however, irrigation makes up 92% of water use, with water availability being the major constraint on further agricultural development due to the country's semi-arid climate (Food and Agriculture Organization, 2016a).

As shown by Chenoweth (2008b) in an evaluation of the Falkenmark water scarcity indicator against a wide range of indicators of national development, the per capita water resources availability of a country shows no correlation with any basic indicator of human development nor the composite Human Development Index. The lack of any significant correlation suggests that water resources availability at a national level is insignificant compared to other factors impacting upon development or the ability of a country to meet the basic water requirements of its population (Chenoweth, 2008b). As Allan (2001) has shown, countries have adapted to limited water resources by importing food to meet local food requirements while simultaneously developing their non-agricultural economies. Cereal imports made up 55% of supply in 2011 in western Asia and 52% in northern Africa, two of the most water scarce regions according to the Falkenmark indicator. Even least developed countries are now connected to global food markets, with cereal imports making up 16% of supply in such countries 2011 (Food and Agriculture Organization, 2016b). Allan (2001) describes food imports to water scarce countries as "virtual water" – rather than importing huge quantities of water to maintain local food self-sufficiency, countries import "virtual water" via bulk grains, which is far more practical and cost effective as a solution.

With food needs met through trade, the Falkenmark benchmarks do not indicate whether water scarcity is impacting upon the ability of a country to develop. As Chenoweth (2008b) shows countries have developed with far less water availability than is suggested as necessary by the Falkenmark index, with as little as 50 m^3 of water per capita per year needed to meet social and economic water needs for development. However, the Falkenmark index can be useful for identifying countries where water resources need to be carefully allocated and managed due to intense competition for available resources from potential competing uses.

Intensity of water use index

A widely used alternative to the Falkenmark index of water scarcity is the intensity of water use index suggested by Raskin et al. (1997). They proposed a water use-to-resource indicator of water stress in which they outlined that when less than 10% of available water is withdrawn from a catchment there is "no stress", 10% to 20% of water withdrawn represents "low stress", 20% to 40% of water withdrawn represents "stress", and more than 40% withdrawn represents "high stress" (Raskin et al., 1997, pp. 23–24). While Raskin et al. (1997) cite a number of references to justify the 20% threshold they outlined, no justification (or evidence) was provided for the 40% threshold. Other researchers have proposed alternative threshold levels for water scarcity. For example, Molden et al. (2007) suggest that physical water scarcity, when water resources development is approaching or has exceeded sustainable limits, occurs when more than 75% of the discharge from a river basin is withdrawn for agricultural, domestic and industrial use.

It is generally accepted that all other things being equal, the greater the proportion of water resources withdrawn from a river basin, the more ecological stress the river will face. Low flows in rivers as a result of water extraction exacerbate the impacts on aquatic ecosystems of other environmental stressors such as sedimentation and pollution, with low flows potentially creating conditions which may exceed the tolerance threshold of local ecosystems (Rolls et al., 2012). Similarly, it is also broadly accepted that the greater the proportion of available water resources which is withdrawn from the natural environment of a country, the more water stressed the country is likely to be. Thus a country like Sweden, where only 1.5% of total available renewable water resources are used each year, can be expected to be less water stressed than Denmark where it is 10.6% or Germany where it is 21.4% of available water resources. All of these countries can be expected to be much less water stressed than Syria where 84.2% of available water resources are used each year (Food and Agriculture Organization, 2015).

While the water use intensity index can be applied on a national scale, the impacts on aquatic ecosystems due to freshwater withdrawals and pollution runoff tend to be local. If all the water from a river basin is withdrawn for irrigation use so that the river no longer discharges to the sea there will be a severe impact on the local ecosystem which will in no way be balanced by more modest water withdrawals in a neighbouring river basin. Australia provides a good illustration of this point. While Australia only withdraws 3.9% of its renewable freshwater resources each year and thus as a whole the country is not classed as water stressed according to this indicator, it is clear that much of the south-east of the country is indeed water stressed. This region's major river basin, the Murray-Darling River basin covers only 14% of Australia's surface area but water use in the basin accounts for as much as half of Australia's total water use (Leblanc et al., 2012). Basin discharge is estimated to be reduced by 61% under current average conditions compared to natural conditions. Due to significant variability in precipitation, there is no discharge to the sea 40% of the time, compared to just 1% of the time under natural conditions (Leblanc et al., 2012). The ecological impacts of water withdrawals in the basin, exacerbated by associated land use changes, have been acute, particularly in the lower reaches of the basin. National averages of water withdrawals clearly do not capture real water stress since water scarcity is a local or regional environmental problem.

An alternative intensity of water use index to that of Raskin et al. (1997) has been proposed by Smakhtin, Revenga and Döll (2004). They argue that an estimation of the environmental water requirements for a river needs to consider both the baseflow and high-flow requirements of the local ecosystems. The ecosystems of river basins with highly variable flow rates are more likely to be adapted to cope with relative water scarcity and therefore will require a smaller proportion of the total average river discharge volume to maintain an acceptable ecosystem quality, whereas a larger proportion of the total average river discharge will be required to maintain ecosystem health in river basins with less variable flow (Hughes and Hannart, 2003).

To estimate the environmental water requirements of a river basin taking into account its discharge variability Smakhtin, Revenga and Döll (2004) argue that the baseflow and high-flow requirements of the river need to be calculated and satisfied if the ecology is to be maintained. Once the environmental water requirement of a river basin is known, the volume of water which can be safely extracted for human use can be calculated as the difference between the total average discharge volume of the river basin and environmental water requirements of the basin. Smakhtin et al. (2004) argue that water scarcity occurs where the water withdrawals from a river basin exceed the volume of water which can be safely extracted.

Pastor et al. (2014) reviewed five potential methods for calculating environmental flow requirements of a river basin, including the method proposed by Smakhtin et al. (2004) as well as a method they proposed which they called the Variable Monthly Flow (VMF) method. This method considers the natural variability of a river by defining its environmental flow requirements on a monthly basis but adjusts these requirements according to the flow season (Pastor et al., 2014). The VMF method suggests that a minimum of 60% of the mean monthly flow a river should remain for ecosystem needs during the low-flow season, 45% during intermediate-flow seasons, and 30% during the high-flow season. The low-flow season is defined as months with less than or equal to 40% of the mean annual flow, while high-flow months are defined as months with 80% or more of the mean annual flow.

Steffen et al. (2015) suggest using the VMF method to calculate a river basin scale boundary of water consumption to complement the planetary boundary for water that they suggest. Based on the VMF method for calculating environmental flow requirements, Boulay et al. (2017) propose the Available Water Remaining (AWARE) index. This indicator evaluates water consumption in a river basin compared to the volume of water available for use after environmental flow requirements, as calculated by the VMF method, have been met and shows how close rates of water consumption in a region are compared to the limits which permit ecological integrity of the river system to be maintained.

Water access indicators

The right to water was explicitly recognised as a human right in Resolution 64/292 of the United Nations General Assembly in 2010, with the resolution stating that access to safe water is integral to the realisation of other human rights (United Nations General Assembly, 2010). The importance of access to water had previously been recognised as an independent human right in 2002 (United Nations Committee on Economic Social and Cultural Rights, 2002) and as Brooks (2007) notes, few people argue against access to water being a basic right even if this right is not universally achieved.

Access to water as a human right clearly goes beyond basic drinking water requirements as this does not allow the fulfilment of other basic human rights. However, as noted by Chenoweth (2008a) there is no common understanding of how much water is actually required to meet human health needs, allow economic development and eradicate poverty.

Howard and Bartram (2003) suggest 7.5 litres per capita per day as the minimum water requirement for direct human consumption needs, with 2 litres of this needed for food preparation. Gleick (1996) suggests that 5 litres per person per day are required for drinking purposes in tropical climates but suggest that a minimum of 50 litres per person per day is required for human and ecological needs. This breaks down to 5 litres for drinking, 20 litres for sanitation, 15 litres for bathing and 10 litres for food preparation (Gleick, 1996). Looking beyond just direct human consumption needs, Howard and Bartram (2003) suggest that 20 litres per person per day provides basic access which will allow the meeting of only some hygiene requirements, 50 litres per person per day provides intermediate access which will allow most requirements to be met, and 100 litres per person per day provides optimum access which will allow the meeting of all requirements (Howard and Bartram, 2003).

Looking beyond basic household needs, a variety of estimates have been suggested as the minimum amount of water required for social and economic development. Chenoweth (2008a) examined water use in countries with high human development as assessed by the Human Development Index and found that as little as 85 litres per person per day could meet all household requirements while providing a high quality of life if bathing water was recycled for toilet flushing. Expanding the scope to consider the water requirements of sustaining a modern non-agricultural economy suggested that another 35 litres per person per day were required for economic uses, and additional 15 litres per person per day for system distribution losses (since nearly all water distribution systems suffer some losses, depending upon the piping technology used, maintenance regimes and local geology), thus a total of 135 litres per person per day were required to meet all domestic and economic needs (Chenoweth, 2008a).

In 2000, the United Nations Millennium Development Declaration set the goal by 2015 "to halve the proportion of people who are unable to reach or to afford safe drinking water" (United Nations, 2000, p. 5). The figure of a minimum of 20 litres per person per day within 1 kilometre of the person's dwelling was adopted as the required volume of water for meeting the Millennium Development Goal for water.

The WHO/UNICEF Joint Monitoring Programme for Water Supply and Sanitation (JMP) was established to monitor progress towards this water and sanitation Millennium Development Goal and adopted the term "use of an improved drinking water source" as the criteria for meeting the goal (WHO/UNICEF Joint Monitoring Programme for Water Supply and Sanitation, 2011, p. 10). This was adopted as a proxy for measuring access to safe drinking water as there was a lack of a reliable historic time series dataset on access to safe water (WHO/UNICEF Joint Monitoring Programme for Water Supply and Sanitation, 2011). Improved drinking water sources included piped household connections, standpipes, boreholes, protected wells and springs and rainwater collection, while unimproved sources included unprotected wells and springs, water delivered by cart or truck, bottled water and direct use of surface waters like a river or lake (WHO/UNICEF Joint Monitoring Programme for Water Supply and Sanitation, 2011).

The JMP initiated the Rapid Assessment for Drinking Water Quality approach to test water quality from drinking water sources it defined as improved. Based on a survey of five countries they found that approximately half of protected wells were providing contaminated water, as were approximately one-third of protected springs and boreholes, and one in ten piped water supplies (WHO/UNICEF Joint Monitoring Programme for Water Supply and Sanitation, 2011). Thus access to safe drinking water was likely to be far lower than estimated by the JMP in its reporting on achievement of the Millennium Development Goal for water. Despite the acknowledged flaws in the proxy indicator which the JMP was using, the JMP reported that the Millennium Development Goal for water was met in 2010, five years ahead of the target (WHO/UNICEF Joint Monitoring Programme for Water Supply and Sanitation, 2012).

Target 6.1 of the Sustainable Development Goals launched in 2015 was "By 2030, achieve universal and equitable access to safe and affordable drinking water for all" (WHO/UNICEF Joint Monitoring Programme, 2016, p. 1). The proposed indicator for this target is the percentage of population using safely managed drinking water sources, with this defined as the percentage of population using an improved drinking water source located on their premises which is available when needed and free of contamination (WHO/UNICEF Joint Monitoring Programme, 2016). The drinking water supplied must meet needs for drinking, cooking, food preparation and personal hygiene but a minimum volume does not appear to have been specified. Thus the proposed indicator for this Sustainable Development Goal target overcomes some of the key shortcomings of its equivalent Millennium Development Goal. The indicator is to be measured via household surveys to ascertain use of improved water sources, with water quality testing needed or data from regulators on compliance with drinking water quality standards. Preliminary estimates suggest that 48% of the global population used safely managed drinking water sources in 2010 (WHO/UNICEF Joint Monitoring Programme, 2016).

Water footprint indicators

Stand-alone water footprints

As previously noted, when discussing how countries manage a growing imbalance between their population and water resources Allan (2001) coined the term "virtual water" to refer to the volume of water required to produce agricultural commodities. Hoekstra and Hung (2002) then sought to quantify these virtual water flows, developing the concept of water footprints. A water footprint was defined by Hoekstra et al. (2009) as the total volume of freshwater across a supply chain that is required to produce a product, including both direct and indirect water use.

According to the water footprint indicator developed by Hoekstra and the Water Footprint Network (WFN), the global annual average water footprint of humanity is 9,087 Gm^3 per year, of which 74% is green water, 11% blue water and 15% grey water (Hoekstra and Mekonnen, 2012). Blue water refers to runoff extracted from aquifers, lakes, wetlands and reservoirs that is used in irrigation, industry and households; green water refers to precipitation which infiltrates into the soil that is consumed by directly plants in situ (Falkenmark et al., 2009). Rain-fed agriculture is thus entirely dependent on green water, with green water not directly useable by households or industry unless it enters a groundwater body or stream. Grey water is a measure of the volume of freshwater required in a receiving water body to assimilate pollutants from production in order to meet water quality standards (Mekonnen and Hoekstra, 2011). The validity of breaking down water footprints into these constituents has been questioned since blue and green water are not discrete categories (Wichelns, 2011). While blue and green water footprints are both estimates of real volumes of water consumed, a grey water footprint is not an estimate actual water consumption but of pollution impact (Witmer and Cleij, 2012).

According to the water footprinting methodology put forward by the WFN, water footprints per capita average 1,385 m^3/year around the world but vary considerably between countries (Hoekstra and Mekonnen, 2012): the US has a water footprint of 2,842 m^3/capita/year, whereas in the UK it is 1,258 m^3/capita/year and as low as 552 m^3/capita/year in the Democratic Republic of Congo. The water footprint of individual commodities also varies significantly. Beef has an estimated average water footprint of 15,415 m^3/ton, while for pork it is 5,988 m^3/ton and chicken 4,325 m^3/ton (Mekonnen and Hoekstra, 2012). Roasted coffee has an estimated average water footprint of 18,925 m^3/ton, wheat 1,827 m^3/ton, potatoes 287 m^3/ton and carrots 195 m^3/ton (Mekonnen and Hoekstra, 2011). In other words, a kilogram of beef required 15,415 times its weight in water on average for its production.

In addition to the water footprint methodology put forward by WFN, a number of alternatives have been suggested. Ridoutt and Pfister (2010) argue that green water should not be included in water footprints as the use of green water does not contribute to water scarcity. As soil moisture can only be used by plants in situ and not extracted for other uses its use should be considered via other means such as via an environmental life cycle assessment as a land use impact. Ridoutt et al. (2012) suggest an alternative water footprint which considered only consumptive use, weighting blue water use at each point of a product's supply chain according to the local level of water stress. Applying this water footprint methodology to some beef production case studies in Australia, they estimate water footprints ranging from 3.3 to 221 m^3/ton, a stark contrast to Mekonnen and Hoekstra's estimate of 15,415 m^3/ton. The WFN has argued against weighted water footprints on the grounds that the introduction of a weighting means that a water footprint ceases to represent real water volumes (Morrison et al., 2010).

A further variation on the water footprint concept is that of estimating net water footprint rather than total water footprint (SABMiller and WWF-UK, 2009). Net green water refers to the difference between the green water uptake of the crop being assessed and that of the natural vegetation which the crop displaces. Where crop farming replaces forest, the removal of deep rooted trees can lead to a decrease in evapotranspiration, resulting in more surface runoff and groundwater recharge (Ruprecht and Schofield, 1989). This means that negative net green water footprints are possible (Hastings and Pegram, 2012). Applying the WFN methodology and two different variants of the net green approach when calculating the water footprint of hydroelectric generation in New Zealand, Herath et al. (2011) produce three estimates of the water footprint per gigajoule generated: 6.05 m³/GJ using the WFN methodology, 2.72 m³/GJ when considering net consumptive water use due to land use change, and 1.55 m³/GJ when considering net consumptive water use due to land use change and precipitation occurring over the reservoir. In another example of the application of a net water footprint methodology, Deurer et al. (2011) calculated a net water footprint of negative 500 litres per tray of kiwi fruit, compared to Hoekstra et al.'s (2009) estimation of 100 litres. There are numerous methodological possibilities for calculating stand-alone water footprints, with the appropriate methodology depending upon the goal, however, as different methodologies can produce dramatically different results, the results of different studies are not necessarily comparable (Chenoweth et al., 2014). As argued by Turcu (Chapter 10, this volume), it is difficult to achieve a "one size fits all" when it comes to sustainability indicators.

A number of purposes for stand-alone water footprints have been proposed, with relatively few papers questioning the purpose of the indicator. Chenoweth et al. (2014) suggest that the proposed purposes of water footprinting can be grouped under three broad themes: as a tool to assist water resources management and deal with water scarcity, as a means of consumer empowerment and as a means of promoting equity in the use of global water resources. However, while a water footprint is a useful indicator for highlighting global or regional interdependencies, its simplicity restricts its usefulness as a water resources management tool (Chenoweth et al., 2014). As a tool for consumer empowerment its value is limited as a water footprint alone only indicates the volume of water used to produce a product but does not provide any information of the sustainability of this water use (Witmer and Cleij, 2012). Using water footprints as a tool for promoting equity of water use is problematic as water scarcity is a local or regional problem, with savings in water use in one location having little impact on water scarcity in other regions. While water scarcity is a very serious problem in some regions, as previously noted globally water is not scarce and most water is not traded but used locally. Despite methodical limitations, water footprints have been useful in stimulating discussions on the relationships between water use, food security and consumption, with the calculation of water footprints helping companies to focus upon and consider more carefully how they use water (Chenoweth et al., 2014).

Water footprints as part of Life Cycle Assessment

Life Cycle Assessment (LCA) is a tool developed to measure the combined effect of different environmental impacts across a product's supply chain – from cradle to grave (Finnveden et al., 2009). LCA did not initially include water consumption as an impact as it was initially focused on industrial products produced in humid northern North America and Europe where was scarcity was not a significant problem (Milà i Canals et al., 2009). In parallel with the development of water footprints by WFN, the LCA research community has sought to incorporate water usage as an impact category in LCA and as a result of this process has developed the international water footprint standard (ISO14046) (Pfister et al., 2017).

The ISO water footprint methodology is broadly similar to the WFN methodology in concept. Both methodologies follow a life cycle approach and use similar data collection. However, they differ in a number of key respects. Whereas the WFN methodology focused upon global water use and in particular the productivity of global water use, the ISO methodology focuses upon the environmental impact of water use. Thus water use in a supply chain is assessed via a scarcity weighted approach whereby water use in a water-rich area is considered to have a lower environmental impact than water use in a water-stressed region and the final water footprint does not represent physical units of water actually consumed in production (Pfister et al., 2017). Like with LCA generally, the ISO approach focuses upon marginal change to the environment compared to the background situation, whereas the WFN methodology aggregates marginal and non-marginal impacts together when calculating total water use. Thus, with the ISO methodology green water consumption is assessed in comparison to baseline conditions rather than the total volume evapotranspirated, unlike with the WFN methodology (Pfister et al., 2017). This avoids double counting of these impacts with land use impacts. The WFN and ISO methodologies also differ significantly in their communication of water footprints. A WFN water footprint is frequently reported as a single number stand-alone indicator whereas LCA results are reported as a set of indicators (Pfister et al., 2017). Thus, green and grey water use are accounted for via land use, toxicity and eutrophication indicators, rather than as a water volume.

Conclusions

There is no perfect sustainable water indicator. An indicator must be selected according to its purpose, with a variety of indicators having been developed to assist with a range of water resources management decision-making and policy issues. Water indicators can be grouped into those indicators which seek to assess water resources scarcity in some form, those which seek to assess household access to water and sanitation, and those which seek to assess the impact of production and consumption choices on water resources and the environment. In each of these three areas, indicators are continuing to be proposed and refined; however, there is always the constant tension between simplicity and usefulness. An indicator like the Falkenmark water scarcity index is widely cited as it is simply constructed, the required data is freely available, and the indicator is easily understood. However, at the same time it provides only limited information on the challenges a country faces meeting the water needs of its people, economy and environment. Alternative indicators of water scarcity, like those which assess water withdrawals in relation to environmental water needs are more informative but less readily understandable and are more challenging to calculate.

Water indicators are continuing to evolve and be refined, as demonstrated by the recently published ISO standard methodology for water footprints. A key current challenge in terms of water indicators is the development of a practical and effective way of assessing progress towards the Sustainable Development Goal for water and sanitation. While the proxy indicator of access to improved water and sanitation that was used for assessing progress towards the Millennium Development Goal for water and sanitation provided some measure of progress, the adoption of a similar proxy indicator for the Sustainable Development Goals for water and sanitation would be problematic if we really want to show that universal and equitable access to safe and affordable drinking water for all has been achieved.

References

Allan, T., 2001. *The Middle East Water Question: Hydropolitics and the Global Economy*. I.B. Tauris, London.

Boulay, A.M., Bare, J., Benini, L., Berger, M., Lathuillière, M.J., Manzardo, A., Margni, M., Motoshita, M., Núñez, M., Pastor, A.V., Ridoutt, B., Oki, T., Worbe, S., and Pfister, S., 2017. The WULCA consensus characterization model for water scarcity footprints: Assessing impacts of water consumption based on available water remaining (AWARE). *International Journal of Life Cycle Assessment* 23, 368–378.

Brooks, D., 2007. Human rights to water in North Africa and the Middle East: What is new and what is not; what is important and what is not. *International Journal of Water Resources Development* 23, 227–241.

Chenoweth, J., 2008a. Minimum water requirement for social and economic development. *Desalination* 229, 245–256.

Chenoweth, J., 2008b. A re-assessment of indicators of national water scarcity. *Water International* 33, 5–18.

Chenoweth, J., Hadjikakou, M., and Zoumides, C., 2014. Quantifying the human impact on water resources: A critical review of the water footprint concept. *Hydrology and Earth Systems Sciences* 18, 2325–2342.

Ciegis, R., Ramanauskiene, J., and Startien, G., 2009. Theoretical reasoning of the use of indicators and indices for sustainable development assessment. *Inzinerine Ekonomika-Engineering Economics* 63, 33–40.

Deurer, M., Green, S.R., Clothier, B.E., and Mowatt, A., 2011. Can product water footprints indicate the hydrological impact of primary production? – A case study of New Zealand kiwifruit. *Journal of Hydrology* 408, 246–256.

Falkenmark, M., 1986. Fresh water – time for a modified approach. *Ambio* 15, 192–200.

Falkenmark, M., Rockström, J., and Karlberg, L., 2009. Present and future water requirements for feeding humanity. *Food Security* 1, 59–69.

Finnveden, G., Hauschild, M.Z., Ekvall, T., Guinée, J., Heijungs, R., Hellweg, S., Köhler, A., Pennington, D., and Sangwon, S., 2009. Recent developments in Life Cycle Assessment. *Journal of Environmental Management* 91, 1–21.

Food and Agriculture Organization, 2000. *New Dimensions in Water Security*. Land and Water Development Division, Food and Agriculture Organization, Rome.

Food and Agriculture Organization, 2003. *Review of World Water Resources by Country*. Food and Agriculture Organization, Rome.

Food and Agriculture Organization, 2015. *Aquastat: Computation of Long-Term Annual Renewable Water Resources (RWR) by Country (in km3/year, average)*. Land and Water Development Division, Food and Agriculture Organization, Rome.

Food and Agriculture Organization, 2016a. *Aquastat Datasets*. Food and Agriculture Organization, Rome.

Food and Agriculture Organization, 2016b. *FAOSTAT Commodity Balances – Crops Primary Equivalent*. Food and Agriculture Organization, Rome.

Gleick, P.H., 1996. Basic water requirements for human activities: Meeting basic needs. *Water International* 21, 83–92.

Hastings, E. and Pegram, G., 2012. *Literature Review for the Applicability of Water Footprints in South Africa*. Water Research Commission, Gezina.

Herath, I., Deurer, M., Horne, D., Singh, R., and Clothier, B., 2011. The water footprint of hydroelectricity: A methodological comparison from a case study in New Zealand. *Journal of Cleaner Production* 19, 1582–1589.

Hoekstra, A.Y., Chapagain, A.K., Aldaya, M.M., and Mekonnen, M.M., 2009. *Water Footprint Manual: State of the Art 2009*. Water Footprint Network, Enschede.

Hoekstra, A.Y. and Hung, P.Q., 2002. *Virtual Water Trade: A Quantification of Virtual Water Flows Between Nations in Relation to International Crop Trade, Value of Water Research Report Series*. IHE Delft, Delft.

Hoekstra, A.Y. and Mekonnen, M.M., 2012. The water footprint of humanity. *Proceedings of the National Academy of Sciences* 109, 3232–3237.

Howard, G. and Bartram, J., 2003. *Domestic Water Quantity, Service, Level and Health*. World Health Organization, Geneva.

Hughes, D.A. and Hannart, P., 2003. A desktop model used to provide an initial estimate of the ecological instream flow requirements of rivers in South Africa. *Journal of Hydrology* 270, 167–181.

Leblanc, M., Tweed, S., Van Dijk, A., and Timbal, B., 2012. A review of historic and future hydrological changes in the Murray-Darling Basin. *Global and Planetary Change* 80–81, 226–246.

L'vovich, M.I. and White, G.F., 1990. Use and transformation of terrestrial water systems, in: Turner, B.L., Clark, W.C., Kates, R.W., Richards, J.F., Matthews, J.T., and Meyer, W.B. (Eds.), *The Earth as Transformed by Human Action: Global and Regional Changes in the Biosphere over the Past 300 Years*. Cambridge University Press, Cambridge, pp. 235–252.

Meadows, D.H., Meadows, D.L., and Randers, J., 1992. *Beyond the Limits: Global Collapse or a Sustainable Future*. Earthscan, London.

Mekonnen, M.M. and Hoekstra, A.Y., 2011. The green, blue and grey water footprint of crops and derived crop products. *Hydrology and Earth System Sciences* 15, 1577–1600.

Mekonnen, M.M. and Hoekstra, A.Y., 2012. A global assessment of the water footprint of farm animal products. *Ecosystems* 15, 401–415.

Milà i Canals, L., Chenoweth, J., Chapagain, A., Orr, S., Antón, A., and Clift, R., 2009. Assessing freshwater use impacts in LCA: Part I – inventory modelling and characterisation factors for the main impact pathways. *The International Journal of Life Cycle Assessment* 14, 28–42.

Molden, D., Frenken, K., Barker, R., de Fraiture, C., Mati, B., Svendsen, M., Sadoff, C., and Finlayson, C.M., 2007. Trends in water and agricultural development, in: Molden, D. (Ed.), *Water for Food, Water for Life: A Comprehensive Assessment of Water Management in Agriculture Edited*. Earthscan & International Water Management Institute, London, pp. 57–89.

Morrison, J., Schulte, P., and Schenck, R., 2010. *Corporate Water Accounting: An Analysis of Methods and Tools for Measuring Water Use and Its Impact*. UNEP and Pacific Institute, Oakland.

Pastor, A.V., Ludwig, F., Biemans, H., Hoff, H., and Kabat, P., 2014. Accounting for environmental flow requirements in global water assessments. *Hydrology and Earth System Sciences* 18, 5041–5059.

Pfister, S., Boulay, A.M., Berger, M., Hadjikakou, M., Motoshita, M., Hess, T., Ridoutt, B., Weinzettel, J., Scherer, L., Doll, P., Manzardo, A., Nunez, M., Verones, F., Humbert, S., Buxmann, K., Harding, K., Benini, L., Oki, T., Finkbeiner, M., and Henderson, A., 2017. Understanding the LCA and ISO water footprint: A response to Hoekstra (2016) "A critique on the water-scarcity weighted water footprint in LCA". *Ecological Indicators* 72, 352–359.

Raskin, P. Gliek, P., Kirshen, P., Pontius, G., and Strzepek, K., 1997. *Water Futures: Assessment of Long-Range Patterns and Problems*. Swedish Environment Institute and United Nations, Stockholm.

Ridoutt, B.G. and Pfister, S., 2010. A revised approach to water footprinting to make transparent the impacts of consumption and production on global freshwater scarcity. *Global Environmental Change* 20, 113–120.

Ridoutt, B.G., Sanguansri, P., Freer, M., and Harper, G.S., 2012. Water footprint of livestock: Comparison of six geographically defined beef production systems. *The International Journal of Life Cycle Assessment* 17, 165–175.

Rolls, R.J., Leigh, C., and Sheldon, F., 2012. Mechanistic effects of low-flow hydrology on riverine ecosystems: Ecological principles and consequences of alteration. *Freshwater Science* 31, 1163–1186.

Ruprecht, J.K. and Schofield, N.J., 1989. Analysis of streamflow generation following deforestation in southwest Western Australia. *Journal of Hydrology* 105, 1–17.

SABMiller and WWF-UK, 2009. *Water Footprinting: Identifying & Addressing Water Risks in the Value Chain*. SABMiller and WWF, Woking.

Seckler, D., Amarasighe, U., Molden, D., de Silva, R., and Barker, R., 1998. *World Water Demand and Supply, 1990 to 2025: Scenarios and Issues*. International Water Management Institute, Colombo.

Smakhtin, V., Revenga, C., and Döll, P., 2004. *Taking into Account Environmental Water Requirements in Global-scale Water Resources Assessments, Comprehensive Assessment of Water Management in Agriculture*. International Water Management Institute, Colombo.

Steffen, W., Richardson, K., Rockström, J., Cornell, S.E., Fetzer, I., Bennett, E.M., Biggs, R., Carpenter, S.R., de Vries, W., de Wit, C.A., Folke, C., Gerten, D., Heinke, J., Mace, G.M., Persson, L.M., Ramanathan, V., Reyers, B., and Sörlin, S., 2015. Planetary boundaries: Guiding human development on a changing planet. *Science* 347, 736.

United Nations, 2000. *United Nations Millennium Declaration*. A/RES/55/2, United Nations General Assembly, New York. http://www.un.org/millennium/declaration/ares552e.pdf

United Nations, 2016. *The Sustainable Development Goals Report 2016*. United Nations, New York.

United Nations Committee on Economic Social and Cultural Rights, 2002. *General Comment No. 15 (2002): The Right to Water (arts. 11 and 12 of the International Covenant on Economic, Social and Cultural Rights)*. United Nations Committee on Economic, Social and Cultural Rights.

United Nations Department of Economic and Social Affairs, 2017. *World Population Prospects: The 2017 Revision United Nations*. United Nations Department of Economic and Social Affairs, New York.

United Nations General Assembly, 2010. *Resolution Adopted by the General Assembly: 64/292 The Human Right to Water and Sanitation*. United Nations General Assembly, New York.

United Nations World Water Assessment Programme, 2003. *Water for People, Water for Life: The United Nations World Water Development Report*. UNESCO Publishing and Berghahn Books, Paris.

United Nations World Water Assessment Programme, 2015. *Water for a Sustainable World: The UN World Water Development Report 2015*. United Nations Educational, Scientific and Cultural Organization, Paris.

United Nations World Water Assessment Programme, 2016. *Water and Jobs: The UN World Water Development Report 2016*. United Nations Educational, Scientific and Cultural Organization, Paris.

UN-Water, 2007. *Coping with Water Scarcity: Challenge of the Twenty-First Century*. United Nations, New York.

WHO/UNICEF Joint Monitoring Programme, 2016. *Methodological Note: Proposed Indicator Framework for Monitoring SDG Targets on Drinking Water, Sanitation, Hygiene and Wastewater*. World Health Organisation/United Nations Children's Fund, Geneva.

WHO/UNICEF Joint Monitoring Programme for Water Supply and Sanitation, 2011. *Drinking Water: Equity, Safety and Sustainability*. WHO/UNICEF, Washington.

WHO/UNICEF Joint Monitoring Programme for Water Supply and Sanitation, 2012. *Progress on Drinking Water and Sanitation: 2012 Update.* WHO/UNICEF, Washington.

Wichelns, D., 2011. Virtual water and water footprints: Compelling notions, but notably flawed: Reaction to two articles regard the virtual water concept. *Gaia* 20, 171–175.

Witmer, M.C.H. and Cleij, P., 2012. *Water Footprint: Useful for Sustainability Policies?* PBL Netherlands Environmental Assessment Agency, The Hague.

World Commission on Environment and Development, 1987. *Our Common Future.* Oxford University Press, Oxford.

12

PARTICIPATORY APPROACHES FOR THE DEVELOPMENT AND EVALUATION OF SUSTAINABILITY INDICATORS

Simon Bell and Stephen Morse

Introduction

The idea of employing an element of stakeholder participation in the identification of sustainability indicators (SIs) as well as how they can best be assessed and indeed used is well established and many examples exist in the literature since the 1990s, when the concept of Local Agenda 21 was first proposed at the Rio Earth Summit. The logic is very clear; the inclusion of those who have a 'stake' (interest) in achieving what the SIs are meant to help achieve (i.e. sustainable development) would greatly enhance the chances of success. However, while the logic is clear the definition of what is meant by stakeholder has been somewhat fraught. Indeed, the very term 'stakeholder participation' has two contestable elements; just what is a stakeholder and what is participation? In this chapter, adapted from a chapter in *Resilient Participation: Saving the Human Project?* published by Earthscan, London (Bell and Morse 2012), we try to bring some clarity to the understanding of these two elements.

The context of the chapter in the *Resilient Participation* book was to provide an outline of why participation is important in sustainable development and to set out for the reader the range of approaches that have been adopted. We all know that 'participation' is something of a catchall phrase that can mean many things. After all, if we interview someone using a highly structured questionnaire then that is 'participation' of a sort; we are engaging with another human being. But we usually mean much more than that; a process by which the voices of those participating have been given greater force than merely replying to set questions. However, there are nuances here and some approaches to participation give participants a greater voice and ability to influence change than do others.

The other complication here is that those sponsoring interventions have caught the participation bug. It is hard to imagine any proposal for funding being successful unless participation is mentioned somewhere. Ironically, the danger here is that participation has to be proven. This might sound like an odd statement as surely this is not necessarily a bad thing. If funds are being devoted to paying for participation to take place then why should there not be some accountability? This sounds desirable and indeed harmless, but in practice it can mean that participation degenerates into a process of counting people who attend; with signatures, addresses, phone numbers, etc. so someone can check that they were present. Indeed, the accountability agenda can become to dominate so much that the participatory process and why it generates almost become secondary even if they are considered at all. The result is a reactionary form of participation that seeks to address the fashionable desires of funders and their desire for accountability while the benefits of participation can become lost. These are deep waters.

The chapter reproduced here has been amended from its original form. We have shortened it and added some text to bring out the link to SIs. We begin the chapter by discussing one of the most-used phrases in the sustainable development literature – stakeholders. We then move on to cover some of the approaches taken to participation and arrive at some conclusions regarding the participatory process and SIs. It is not our intention to present a 'cookbook' of how to use these methods for exploring SIs, but instead point to some questions and gaps in knowledge.

Stakeholders? Who are they?

In seeking a widely used and readily accessible definition of stakeholders, Wikipedia (accessed in 2017) provides a useful starting position in that it describes a stakeholder in seemingly broad terms as:

> anyone who has an interest in the project. Project stakeholders are individuals and organizations that are actively involved in the project, or whose interests may be affected as a result of project execution or project completion. They may also exert influence over the project's objectives and outcomes.

By this definition, a 'stakeholder' in something can be someone remote from that 'thing' or living next door to it. It could include those who may live far away from the environs of (for example) a sustainable development project, but who may take an interest. Thus, the construction of a dam in China may have little, if any, direct impact on someone living in the Bronx area of New York, but if that person takes an interest in the project, perhaps by hearing about it in the media, then according to this definition they automatically become a stakeholder. At first glance this may seem like something of a 'stretch' and hence be rather unconvincing. Why should someone living in the Bronx be a stakeholder for a project located thousands of miles away in China just because they take an 'interest' in it? Nonetheless by the first few words of the Wikipedia definition they become a stakeholder. The other two sentences in the definition suggest that there must be an 'active involvement' by an individual, including for example the exertion of an influence over the project's execution, or that the individual must be 'affected' in some way by the project. Hence, for example, the employees of the company charged with constructing the dam in China are also stakeholders as they are 'affected' in one way or another (via job retention, promotion, salary, completion bonuses, working conditions, etc.). One can reasonably assume that these stakeholders will largely be in favour of the project given that they gain financially from its construction. There is a further group of people who are stakeholders in such a project; those that commissioned it and have paid the contractor. Included here may be politicians (democratically elected or not), civil servants and parastatals but could also include other companies. These groups may have many motives for wanting (or not as the case may be) the project.

But the list of stakeholders is even longer than that set out above. After all what about those living near the dam and who may well have to be relocated or perhaps those that will find themselves living near to a new shoreline or in the path of a force of water if the dam is breeched? Feelings within this group will likely be far more diverse and not necessarily positive. Some may want the project if they see a benefit while others will not. Then there are those who will benefit from the electricity which is generated even if they live some distance (many miles) away from the dam. Finally, there are those who may not gain from the dam in any way or who may not even live in China but who will feel that it will have a negative impact on the environment. Destruction of unique habitats because of building the dam could generate serious questions as to whether this is indeed a sustainable development project at all. Included here may be neighbouring countries through to international environmental agencies and non-governmental organisations (NGOs). With the inclusion of the latter as stakeholders we can go full circle back to the Bronx as many of these international NGOs have memberships that span the globe. Hence even with this narrower definition the individual in the Bronx can still be a stakeholder in a geographically distant project provided their 'interest' is translated into 'action'. Thus, in the 'no man is an island', globalised world in which we live anyone can become a stakeholder in almost anything.

Thus, the Wikipedia definition appears to be appropriately broad precisely because a list of those having an interest in a project can also be broad. But this breadth can bring problems as not all stakeholders will share the same view as to what the project should achieve and how. Some may argue that the project should not exist at all. In the end, we are left with the familiar 'trade-offs' we often see within sustainable development and familiar conundrums as to how these 'trade-offs' should take place or whether they should take place at all. Tellingly, who makes such decisions? Should some stakeholders be allowed to have a larger voice than others? Indeed, is it right for us to ignore some voices completely?

In terms of SIs, it is highly likely that different stakeholder groups will have different ideas as to what matters in sustainable development and the SIs that should be used to assess progress (or not) towards those goals. Even within a single stakeholder group there is likely to be much diversity; although it continues to surprise us how often this is forgotten given a desire to 'include' as many groups as possible. This perspective begins with an assumption that stakeholders know what they want to see in sustainable development. This could be challenging given that sustainability can be extremely vague and even abstract. We could do this the other way around, of course, and begin by asking stakeholders what SIs they think are important and use that to help them come to an appreciation of what matters in sustainable development. In this case the SIs represent tangible ways of thinking about sustainability, and they could be used by the stakeholders to explore what they mean by sustainable development.

We could think of the first condition as 'SI-in-concept' and the second, as 'SI-in-rank'. The first term delineates a thought-out view of the SI whereas the second starts from the positon of the importance or value or rank of the SI. The latter relates most closely to what Hezri refers to as 'conceptual use' of SIs (Hezri 2004).

Getting to the stakeholder: participation in process

While participatory methods are many and diverse (see for example the participatory typology developed by Rowe and Frewer 2005), they have advantages over other forms of social research. However, there is often a significant leap to be made between participatory theory (*talking the talk*) as espoused above and participatory practice (*walking the talk*). Just how are people to be included within a participatory process? This may seem like a straightforward question, but there are many complex dimensions which are often overlooked (for example, the entire field

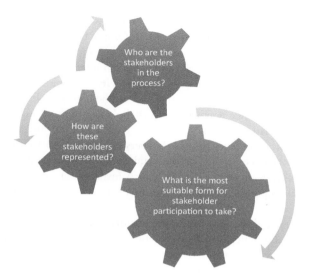

Figure 12.1 Some of the key questions in a participatory process

of culture theory which to some extent informs our thinking (Douglas 1992; Adams 1995). Let us take the following logical steps in sequence (Figure 12.1):

1   Who are the stakeholders?
2   How are stakeholders to be represented?
3   How are the stakeholders to participate?

In any one intended process of change the population which could be impacted could number thousands, if not millions, and may stretch well beyond the immediate 'place' where the activities are to be implemented. Within this population there may well be groupings of 'like-minded' individuals who share a common agenda (such as the contractor of the dam project and those doing the contracting), but as discussed above it is a mistake to assume homogeneity within groups and there can be much diversity in perspective. Hence while the term 'stakeholder' is an all-too-convenient label the identification of those to be included is not as straightforward as it may seem.

Secondly, how are the stakeholders to be represented? If the stakeholder groups can be identified, then how are they to be represented within the process and how are their views to be 'swept in'? It is often and famously difficult to get stakeholders to 'own' their stake and be included in a process! This may sound counter-factual given that they are affected in some way by the intervention, but, after all, people have busy lives and while they may care about the project there is inevitably a trade-off between devoting time to engaging within a participatory process and other priorities that they face such as getting the kids to school each day, paying the bills and making sure that there is enough food in the house. Even if the participation is intended to help with these day-to-day activities there may be a time lag so that any benefits (e.g. a new school building) may accrue for others and not necessary for those taking part. Also, of course, it simply may not be possible to include everyone except in a very limited form (in an online or postal survey for example) so it may be necessary to identify a limited number of representatives of the various stakeholder groups. But while this may be appealing in logistical terms, can all groups be adequately included? What about groups that have internal division? Should sub-groups be included as well? Sociologists often refer to the myth of community, and as noted above we often conveniently assume homogeneity within groups in order to make the process of participation easier, but such assumptions can be highly misleading. Often the desire in such workshops is to sacrifice depth within stakeholder groups in order to capture breadth between groups; but variation within stakeholder groups may be just as high, if not larger, than variation between stakeholder groups. Answers regarding who to include and why will be driven by the inevitable constraints on time and resources, but that does not diminish their importance. For any given process of change which involves stakeholders there can be many perspectives depending upon who is – and who isn't – included; who is and who isn't willing to be included.

Third, what is the 'best' (or more appropriate) form of participation? If the stakeholders can be identified and some means of representation agreed with them then the next obvious question is the form which the process of participation should take? A subsidiary question here might be; which of the processes of participation are best suited to an exploration of SIs? There are many ways in which stakeholders can be invited into and included within a process, and there are many champions of each of these approaches espousing their relative advantages over competitors. The literature is replete with participatory methods, many of which are subtle 'variations on a theme', as well as imaginative acronyms for these varied approaches and some examples will be discussed later. Each does indeed have its own set of pros and cons, including fundamental concerns such as the resources (including time) required, and there is no shortage of arguments made in favour (or against) the various methods. Indeed, it often seems as if a preference for one or the other is more linked to personal taste than anything else and some of the rhetoric used by the respective proponents of one approach or another can often sound more like evangelisation! Nonetheless, which method is 'best', if such an adjective can be employed in any meaningful sense, will depend upon context and the expertise and experience of those attempting to facilitate the participation. Bad decisions over which approach to take, and indeed a poor implementation of what should be a viable approach, can greatly reduce and even eliminate the value of including stakeholders even if steps 1 and 2 have been done well.

What one gets out of stakeholder participation will in large part depend upon how questions 1 to 3 above have been addressed and the reflexivity of the process. If they have been addressed superficially then the result may well be what can be referred to as pseudo-participation. This is when some stakeholders are included in the process thereby suggesting that participation has occurred but they may not be representative of any wider groups or have little (if any) power to influence the process. Thus, we may be able to 'twist' a so-called participatory process to derive the outputs (for example a list of SIs) that we wish to see. Indeed, there is a large difference between using the label 'participation' for a one-way process that comprises nothing more than those with power telling stakeholders what they must do and a genuine 'participatory' process founded upon genuine inclusion. In between these extremes there are many possibilities and these potential gradations in participation have long been recognised. Back in the 1960s Sherry Arnstein (1969) in the US coined the term 'ladder of participation' (Table 12.1), with rungs of the ladder representing a spectrum of participation from exploitation at one end (bottom of the ladder) to community-led initiatives at the top of the ladder where everything is controlled by the community.

Table 12.1 Sherry Arnstein's ladder of participation

Type of participation	Characteristics
Passive	People are informed about a decision, what they have to do or what has happened with no ability to influence in any way.
Functional	People have little control over what needs to be done but may have some control (albeit limited) over how it is to be done.
Consultative	People are consulted about what needs to be done, but the way in which they are consulted is controlled by external agents, and this group also controls the analysis and presentation of results.
Manipulative	People are given limited representation on a committee, board or panel charged with implementing or managing an intervention, and thus in theory they have some input throughout the process. However, in practice they are outnumbered on the committee and thus easily outvoted by other members.
Interactive	People are fully involved in the analysis of conditions, development of action plans, etc. and they do have power to bring about change. However the engagement is facilitated by 'outside' agencies.
Self-mobilisation	As for 'Interactive' above, but people mobilise themselves and initiate actions without the involvement of any external agency.

Note: Increasing participation from top to bottom of the table.

Origins of participation

Participatory studies have a long antecedence. Some say that the first book on participation/participant observation is the Anabasis by Xenophon written around 400 BC (Professor Simon Goldhill, University of Cambridge, BBC Radio 4, 26th May 2011). The story surrounds a large army of Greek mercenaries hired by Cyrus the Younger which found itself stranded behind enemy lines with most of its leaders killed. It had to fight its way back home and Xenophon relates how they had to make what we would now call participatory decisions about tactics, logistics, etc. The story provided the basis for a novel called *The Warriors* (1965) written by Sol Yurick and set in New York during the 1960s, and in turn the novel became the basis for a controversial (at the time) cult movie also called *The Warriors* and set in New York, released in 1979. The participatory dimension is far less obvious in the novel and movie but it is nonetheless amazing to think that the claim for the first book on participation became reflected in a cult movie of the 1970s.

Sadly, our own work on participation was not influenced by *The Warriors* movie but stemmed instead from a shared background in international development during the 1970s and 1980s. In this field, there are some formidable 'big beasts' of participation and participatory methods. We are thinking here of the work of Donald Schon (Schon 1983, 1987), the action learning thinking of Kolb (Kolb 1984) and, of course, Robert Chambers of the University of Sussex in the UK who provided a massive steer to the participatory literature with Rapid Rural Appraisal (RRA), Participatory Rural Appraisal (PRA) and Participatory Learning and Action (PLA) – approaches which have been heavily cited and provided the foundation for much of the participation literature in sustainable development (Chambers 1981, 1983, 1992, 1996, 1997, 2002; Biggs 1995; Biggs and Smith 1995; Biggs et al., 2003). The RRA-PRA-PLA spectrum represents a timeline in thinking from the 1970s (RRA) to the 1990s (PLA).

RRA has its origins within the international development of the 1970s, a decade or so after many African countries had achieved their independence, and was formulated as quick means of extracting information from communities in those countries as the prelude to the implementation of interventions funded by aid agencies to help them. It was meant, in part, to be an 'antidote' to the prevalent, at that time, approach of designing development projects in Washington and elsewhere and imposing them on communities who had little say in the nature of the interventions. Needless to say, many of these projects addressed the wrong priorities and often failed. The 'rural' in RRA emphasises the focus on small-scale agriculture which many development projects had at that time given that the populations were mostly in rural areas and livelihoods were underpinned by agriculture. In those days RRA was essentially an extractive process by which development project planners could get a grasp on what was needed in terms of interventions. Hence the emphasis on 'rapid' and 'appraisal'. Participation in this sense simply meant the provision of information and insight by which someone else could make decisions, but even so it was a step change from the 'top-down' planning of development that was in vogue at the time. One of the outcomes of an RRA is likely to be an idea of what matters (better yield, less labour input, sustained yield over time, better education, provision of water, etc.) and how best the achievement of this could be assessed. Therefore, while they were not called 'SIs' at the time, the outputs of RRA may well be SIs, and the approach taken in many SI projects today have much in common with the epistemology (rapid and extractive) that underpins RRA.

RRA gave way to PRA in the 1980s as development workers saw the importance of going beyond a mere extraction of information as the prelude to a project and into getting groups to help themselves. But the 'rural' remained in the title to emphasise the continuing focus on the 'place' where many of the poor were assumed to live. Here the idea was no longer to engage with people to gain information and insight but to consider and facilitate ways in which they could help themselves. It assumes, of course, that the people being engaged in the process have the power to make the changes that may emerge but more on this later. Indicators within a PRA context would exist to help the community assess its own progress towards attainment rather than being tools that only others would use.

PLA is one of the latest manifestations of this approach and has much in common with the ideas in PRA, with an emphasis on learning amongst groups and using the ideas that emerge as a prelude to action. Note how the term 'rural' has been dropped and 'appraisal' has been replaced by 'learning'.

The beauty of the RRA-PRA-PLA spectrum, but especially the thinking which emerged towards the latter end of the evolution, is that all is up for grabs, including the very meaning of 'development' as perceived by the local community. Thus, at least in theory, PLA should mean that power is located firmly in the community and they are free to set out all what needs to be achieved (what development means to them), and by whom, to help improve their lives. Thus, in Figure 12.2 the centre of the diagram represents the action or change which the community wishes to bring about. This is obviously the critical outcome and is rightly at the heart of the process. However, surrounding this focus is a series of processes that help frame the desired change or action. Included here will be learning from each other and emergent insights, and these don't just orbit the core as a remote planet orbits a star but they should have an intrinsic influence in terms of appreciating what needs to be done. With 'real' PLA the core does not exist at the start of the process and must be created by the processes that surround it.

While the RRA-PRA-PLA spectrum has been highly influential and indeed the ideas encompassed within the spectrum have been re-exported back from the developing to the developed world, it does not address the fundamental issue of uneven power that so often emerges within participatory processes. Helping a community understand its problems and what

Figure 12.2 The dynamics of participatory research

it needs to solve them does not necessarily mean that those problems will be solved. After all, they may not have the required power to bring about their desired change. Power has a notoriously unequal distribution within society. Addressing the participatory literature which emerges from the Chambers-influenced domain, in 1994 Bell produced a paper which engaged with participation as exhibited in development studies and discoursed around the idea of it as a new incarnation of Western intellectual tyranny. Building on previous critical work (Mosse 1993) Bell suggested that:

> (participatory methods) are only as untyrannical, eductive and locally sympathetic as the context and the scientist are prepared to be or, perhaps more meaningfully, are able to be given the limitations of their own culturally based view of their own methods.
>
> (Bell 1994 page 332)

By itself participation is a convenient and attractive label which can be applied in a wide variety of engagements, but it is also deceptive. The early 2000s saw the emergence of a more critical literature on participation and included some important landmark texts such as Cooke and Kothari (2001) and Mohan and Hickey 2004). Further, and particularly in the case of the Mohan and Hickey book, the notion of the critical appraisal of participation is somewhat debunked and the powerful and useful transformative capacity of much participatory method is explored. Within this past-participation literature, participation almost goes full circle; from undeniable social good, to imperial tyranny and all the way back again.

Part of the post-participation discourse relates to the point that participation is usually facilitated in some manner or form, typically by someone who is 'outside' of those doing the participation. This can matter a lot and it is possible for a facilitator to 'steer' a participatory process in a particular direction, including the nature of any SIs that emerge. The value of the facilitation process for individual, group and collective is now clearly established (Huxham and Cropper 1994; McFadzean and Nelson 1998; Morton et al., 2007) and the requisite skills and essential inputs of the facilitator in contexts of systemic interventions has been addressed in detail by authors such as Ackermann (1996) and Nutt (2002). Ironically it is an aspect that has largely been overlooked in the literature on RRA-PRA-PLA, even though for the most part these approaches are created and applied by people external to the communities they are meant to help. Given that the facilitators were often from the developed world and living under quite different conditions than the groups where they were facilitating the 'doing' of an RRA-PRA-PLA, the relative absence of much reflective analysis as to their influence is surprising. After all, the facilitators do have much power even if they do not wish to acknowledge it. We argue that the process of facilitating participation is at least as important as participation itself. Indeed, if the aim of the participatory process is to arrive at very defined and concise sets of outputs, and SIs are an example of that, then one could argue that the danger of a steered facilitation is greater compared to outputs that are more 'mission statement' in nature. It would be relatively easy for a facilitator to drop hints about SIs just by mentioning a few names (have you thought about including GDP, what about NO_x emissions?) while influencing a group's deliberation towards a mission may arguably be harder. This raises the issue of passive and unconscious, immeasurable and/or accidental development of an SI agenda by a community and, if we go on to accept that this is a real issue to the arrival at 'objective measure' then the importance of participation assessment is even more important. The value of the indicator is one thing; the transparency of the process of indicator selection is an area which we have only just begun to explore.

Participatory approaches

Some well-known examples of participatory approaches include the following. Any of these could be used to derive a set of SIs.

- Citizens' juries. As the name implies this comprises a group of stakeholders who act as a jury and are thus able to question witnesses and thus help frame an answer to a question. The process is controlled by the jury but can be time consuming as witnesses may often be questioned individually and indeed in some cases witnesses may be asked to re-appear. Hence, the process may take days to complete.
- Consensus conference. These are similar to citizens' juries in terms of process. The only difference between the two is that citizens' juries often take place behind closed doors while the 'consensus conference' takes place in public.
- Deliberative polling. This is where a stakeholder group is first 'polled' in broad terms about what they think of an issue. A small panel from this group is then convened to discuss the issue in more detail, but this time they are provided with more background and can question experts. In effect, it provides an insight into how stakeholders may change their views (or not, as the case may be) once provided with more information.
- Delphi surveys. This involves a series of 'evolved' questionnaires given to a large sample of stakeholders whereby the responses of the first are used to design the second and so on, so that the process 'narrows' down to the key issues. It is a means of achieving consensus without the problems involved in group work, but can be laborious and depends upon the willingness of the sample of stakeholders to keep completing the questionnaires. Hence, maintaining motivation can be a challenge.

- Focus group. These are relatively short sessions where a sample of stakeholders are brought together and asked to discuss a topic under the guidance of a facilitator. The advantage of this approach is its speed; each session may be as short as two hours. However, the process is unlikely to deliver depth of insight, and should be used in situations where a broad perspective is being sought.
- Planning cell. Here a small group of stakeholders are asked to act as 'consultants' in putting together a report. They are free to access any information they wish, including interviews with experts, and they may decide to divide the work between them. This provides more flexibility than the more rigid approaches of 'citizens' jury' and 'consensus conference', but much depends upon the ability of the team to work together and the process can be time consuming (perhaps taking a week or more).
- Scenario workshop. As the name implies this is a workshop where a range of participants are asked to discuss what may happen given certain conditions and come up with suggested plans for achieving a desired change. Thus, rather than having a separation of lay people, planners, technical experts, etc. as seen in some of the other methods, the categories are combined. The advantage of this approach is that it clearly focusses on what needs to be done to achieve change. However, as can be imagined this is dependent upon the mix of people involved and their expertise and knowledge of the issues.
- World café. Similar to the focus group but held in a purposely informal atmosphere (hence the use of the word 'café') and with a looser structure. Participants are divided into small groups around 'coffee tables' and asked to discuss an issue. After some time, the members of the groups are changed so as to allow an interchange between the 'tables'. At the end of the process the insights are shared in a plenary session where all members come together.

We wish to reiterate that this small sample of approaches should not be seen as suggesting that we think these are the 'best' or most appropriate for arriving at a suite of SIs. We have included them simply because they provide the reader with a taste of the range of participatory approaches. Indeed, as mentioned above, a specific 'participatory' exercise reported in the literature may include a number of these as well as at least as many variants. Hence, a focus group can be used to set out some initial ideas for what SIs could be included and these could be used to frame the start of a 'Delphi survey' that filters the SIs and creates a 'best' list. Similarly, a 'citizens' jury' approach could be employed within a 'deliberative poll' process. Much can depend upon the time and resources available. There are also some generic 'headings' which often appear in the literature to describe a mindset of the approach rather than a specific method, including for example 'action research', 'open learning' and 'participatory learning' (as in PLA). The type and form of method used in any one project will depend upon context, nature of the participants, resources available (including time) and of course the personal preferences and expertise of those facilitating the process.

The range of forms of participation are broad and can span almost the entirety of Arnstein's ladder (Table 12.1). They range at one end from people being passive recipients of information (Newson and Chalk 2004), to their taking part within deliberative processes and therefore being far more active in the entire research process (e.g. Landman et al. 2003; Banjade and Ojha 2005). Other approaches include stakeholders being engaged in cognitive mapping (Ozesmi and Ozesmi 2003; Dodouras and James 2007) and scenario building exercises (Sheppard and Meitner 2005; Gurung and Scholz 2008; Lei-Chang et al. 2010). Indeed, some of them, such as cognitive mapping and scenario building, could equally be done by an individual and are not designed solely to be used in a participatory mode. Nonetheless, these demonstrate a wide range of different forms of engagement all given the label of 'participation' in one form or another. As mentioned before, it cannot be deduced that one specific 'how' is 'right' in an absolute sense, as each of them has their own advantages and disadvantages. Rather, participatory researchers have applied just about every conceivable form of engagement to attempt to undertake participatory research in new, novel and varied manners. To demonstrate this variety, and also to underline the difficulty experienced in persuading participants to participate, a particular area of participation that emerged from 2006 onwards concerned the use of incentive payments for ecosystem services (Matta and Kerr 2006; Blackman and Woodward 2010; Petheram and Campbell 2010).

How's of participation

The 'how's of participation' is a vast subject and it is important to distinguish between what we call participatory strategy and participatory tactics. Strategies are broad statements of intent and purpose; such as we find in the RRA-PRA-PLA spectrum and indeed elsewhere. Hence terms such as RRA, PRA and PLA become shorthand for an approach but it is not enough to say 'we did an RRA with communities in Southeastern Nigeria' and leave it at that. Tactics are the specific methods; the 'how's' by which people have been engaged. In RRA-PRA-PLA we need to set out who was engaged in the process and how did that engagement take place? In our experience, the published studies where participation was employed tend to be rich on strategy but weaker on tactics; they tend to have a lack of granularity regarding the detail of 'how' the participation was achieved. Some notable exceptions to this point are provided by Halvorsen (2001), Modinger and Kobus (2005), Newig et al. (2008) and Pedzisa et al. (2010). At one level this is perhaps understandable given that the methods have been around for some time and thus may be regarded as 'routine' without any need for elaboration. There is also a tendency for a participatory process to use a number of specific methods in unison, and hence the details can perhaps be seen by the authors of the papers as too complex and messy to present in detail but there are dangers here as much can depend on the detail.

The literature also has little to say about how people working in participatory approaches arrived at the outputs they did. Put another way, if a sample of people was taken from the same 'population' of specialists or those living in the same community, and divided into small groups to provide insights into the same issue as for example with the 'scenario workshop' or 'focus group' approach mentioned earlier it is highly unlikely that all of the groups would arrive at exactly the same analysis. The same would potentially apply, of course, if the exercise was repeated with the same people but with gaps in time between the exercises. In both cases (variation across groups and variation for the same group over time) the chances are that there will be points of overlap but also many differences. But what has caused these differences and indeed do they matter? The answer to the first point is, of course, wide ranging as a host of influences may be involved. Looking at variation for the same group over time it is possible that circumstances have changed and an analysis taken at time '1' would yield a different set of issues to that taken at time '2'. In terms of variation between groups an obvious consideration is simply the group membership. It is a truism that people are not all the same and even if groups are formed from the same broad category (e.g. farmers) they will vary in gender, age, experience and so on. Hence, they will bring a quite different set of insights to the groups. Similarly, the group dynamics can be quite different; this is how members interact and share their insights as well as encapsulate them into a vision. Such factors are obviously interrelated; the nature of membership can result in certain dynamics. Thus, in a group comprising experienced members of a profession there may be a tendency for younger, less experienced members to be ignored and side-lined.

Similarly, in certain societies a group comprising both men and women may be dominated by the men and perhaps generate different outcomes to a group comprising only women. Yet for all its obvious importance these factors which can yield variation in insight are weakly covered in the literature. This is a view supported by Rowe and Frewer:

> the plethora of engagement mechanisms that have been developed and used, there are relatively few definitive accounts of their natures (and these are often contradictory), and this has limited the number of mechanisms we could classify with confidence.
>
> (Rowe and Frewer 2005 page 285)

Group membership is often simply wrapped up within what could be described as the 'sampling frame' issue; the need to make sure that those taking part are somehow representative of important groups. It is also something that experienced facilitators will be aware of and during the initial process of sample selection (or perhaps more accurately sample invitation!) and group formation they may attempt to control for it. But the influence of group dynamic is more difficult to 'control'. Nonetheless this is important as it can strongly influence what emerges from the process. As Buhler (Buhler 2002 page 3) puts it there has been:

> a neglect of the ways in which unacknowledged dynamics of participation and exclusion, both outside and within formalised instances of participation, shape the outcomes of 'participation'.

For example, in a workshop focussed on SIs there may be a tendency for a group which includes an acknowledged 'expert' on indicators to defer to that expertise and allow him/her to drive the process while other members sit back and talk amongst themselves. Perhaps even worse, the expert may simply take a textbook approach and list all of the SIs that he/she has read or written about in the literature. Indeed, this takes us to another interesting dimension of participation that has not received the attention that it should in the literature; the integration of scientific and lay knowledge. After all, the community may not know everything that might be relevant to them, and experts, even if external, can provide valuable insights. This is often formally acknowledged in methods such as 'citizens' juries' where lay participants are given a chance to question experts, but much depends upon what questions are asked and not just the answers. Indeed, one of the problems with these approaches is that the lay people might not necessarily know the best questions to ask – the sort of questions one expert might ask another. Hence our point earlier that using participatory methods to develop SIs can arguably be more open to 'abuse' then methods geared towards 'mission statement' outputs. It is easy to drop an SI name or hint into a conversation and hence steer the outputs in a particular direction. There are some critical balances to be made here between the role of expert knowledge and what can, and should, emerge organically from the groups.

Visualisation

Visualisation is often a major element of participatory processes, and indeed was a core element of the RRA-PRA-PLA spectrum. In the RRA-PRA-PLA spectrum language was often a barrier between facilitators and participants, and ideas could be represented by diagrams in the sand and the use of stones and other devices to represent numbers etc. But this is by no means limited to the RRA-PRA-PLA spectrum and its emphasis on the developing world. In the 'soft systems' approaches of Peter Checkland we have 'rich pictures' (see: Checkland 1981; Checkland and

Scholes 1990; and Checkland and Poulter 2006). Pictures paint a thousand words and it is much easier for a group to develop and indeed explain its insights to others via a pictorial representation rather than via writing and editing text. An example of a rich picture that emerged out of a participatory process in the POINT project can be found in Figure 12.3. This picture was produced during a workshop in 2009 and the group was asked to explore the use of SIs. However, the presence of SIs in this picture may not be obvious at first but they are there nonetheless. Eurostat is shown as a source of information for SIs, especially for the environmental dimension of sustainable development, and the group stressed the need for cooperation with environmental authorities at the EU and nation-state levels. In the rich picture the group makes the point that many people do not understand what SIs mean. Such indicators can be used as a help to change behaviour but the groups felt that this function does not really work. The picture also set out the importance of using the media to get information embodied by SIs out into society as a way of achieving sustainable development. Indeed, in some ways this group was ahead of its time in recognising the role of the media in the 'use' of SIs and the dangers that may be inherent within that. As we will discuss in our concluding chapter at the end of the book, this is something which has taken on a new twist with the rise of 'fake news' and 'alternative facts' that followed the election of Donald Trump in the USA. Thus, the rich picture is a qualitative analysis of what are in practice very quantitative 'things' (SIs).

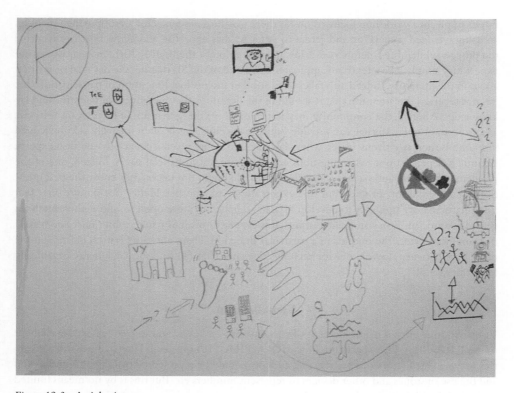

Figure 12.3 A rich picture

Some conclusions and a call to arms

Overall, we can conclude that participatory methods have been widely used for a variety of purposes, including the identification of SIs, how they may best be measured and used to set targets and monitor progress. However, there are dangers within the participatory landscape and while some of these have been well explored (e.g. identification of stakeholders and methods for the 'doing' of participation) there are others that have hardly been touched (e.g. influence of the facilitator and how process influences outputs). Some of these relatively untouched areas remain surprising to us given that the outputs from such approaches may be assumed to vary significantly depending upon the mix of participants and their dynamics and these in turn can be influenced by factors such as location, methods, skill of the facilitator and so on. Hence, the 'how' of the process is important and goes beyond a simple description of process (as so often found in the literature) but into a critical analysis of process and what effects it could have had on outputs. There appears to be a lack of reflective practice in how participatory methods are applied and this extends to a lack of reflective material on how participation is experienced. In effect, a sole focus on what comes out the process as a basis for more research or intervention may be understandable but could also be potentially misleading.

There is a danger that participatory methods become a 'black box' with the tricks of the trade only known to those who facilitate these processes. In fairness, there is some truth here as each of the approaches does require skill, although arguably this is more so for some than others. Some of the approaches (world café, focus groups) are heavily dependent upon good facilitation while others require some skill in questionnaire design and analysis (Delphi survey). Even in those that seem to be fairly 'hands off' from an external perspective such as the 'planning cell' still have significant logistical demands that need to be managed. Participation might become a political 'fix' and a perceived easy solution to all social ills and, from a practitioner point of view, questions remain concerning how participation is used and engaged with. What are the skills needed to engage in participation? Surely, not anyone can be suited to facilitate or catalyse a participatory process. Within participatory group processes it can be relatively easy for a facilitator to, consciously or unconsciously impose his/her assumptions on the work of groups. How is this guarded against and/or understood?

A further feature of the 'back box' is that no one may care what happens inside as long as something 'acceptable' comes out. Thus, participatory processes may focus almost entirely on the delivery of the 'end-product'; the new insights and solutions which the process has (hopefully) generated without worrying all that much about how these were arrived at as long as everyone enjoyed themselves, or at least were not too stressed, and felt it was worthwhile. Linked to this sometimes is a desperate seeking for the 'ideal consensus' – a process in itself which is fraught with problems (Connelly and Richardson 2004). If participants agreed together and gained new ideas or insights from each other then that is very much a bonus. All the funder of the workshop may require is the end-product, for example a listing of SIs. This may sound harsh but in our experience it is more often the case than not. The reality is often that a funding agency also has accountability to others and a key indicator is successful 'delivery' of the workshop or whatever with an agreed set of conclusions and recommendations. The report can be written, participants counted and listed and everyone can now go home. Implementation of these recommendations is for someone else to consider, and unfortunately the suggestions may be all too readily dismissed as 'unworkable' or 'unaffordable'. Hence perhaps understandably there has been little, if any, motive to unpick the black box and put time and energy into deriving an understanding as to why groups have arrived at their analyses. It is so easy to say – 'so what?' As long as I have the outputs and can wrap them up in a report to those funding the workshop then that is all that matters.

But, at a deeper level, this mindset discloses a disservice to participation. A warm buzz and a sense of making a contribution on the one hand, and the reassurance that a box has been ticked on the other. But this is gradually being called into question by the recipients and designers of participatory processes. After all, what is the point of engaging in a lengthy and expensive 'planning cell' where a team of 20 or more people question numerous experts and pour over documents and evidence if at the end of the process the report sits on a shelf and has no further influence?

References

Ackermann, F. (1996). Participant's perceptions on the role of facilitators using group decision support systems. *Group Decision and Negotiation* 5(1): 93–112.

Adams, J. (1995). *Risk.* London, UCL Press.

Arnstein, S. R. (1969). A ladder of citizen participation. *Journal of the American Planning Association* 35(4): 216–224.

Banjade, M. R. and Ojha, H. (2005). Facilitating deliberative governance: Innovations from Nepal's community forestry program: A case study in Karmapunya. *The Forestry Chronicles* 81: 403.

Bell, S. (1994). Methods and mindsets: Towards an understanding of the tyranny of methodology. *Journal of Public Administration and Development* 14(4): 323–338.

Bell, S. and S. Morse (2012). *Resilient Participation: Saving the Human Project?* Abingdon, Routledge.

Biggs, S. (1995). *Contending Coalitions in Participatory Technology Development: Challenges to the New Orthodoxy: The Limits of Participation, Intermediate Technology.* London, Intermediate Technology.

Biggs, S., D. Messerschmidt and B. Gurung (2003). *Contending Cultures amongst Development Actors: Order and Disjuncture: The Organisation of Aid and Development.* London, SOAS.

Biggs, S. and G. Smith (1995). *Contending Coalitions in Agricultural Research and Development: Challenges for Planning and Management: Evaluation for a New Century.* Vancouver, Canadian Evaluation Association and the American Evaluation Association.

Blackman, A. and R. T. Woodward (2010). User financing in a national payments for environmental services program: Costa Rican hydropower. *Ecological Economics* 69: 1626–1638.

Buhler, U. (2002). *Participation with 'Justice and Dignity': Beyond the New Tyranny.* University of Bradford Working Papers. Bradford, University of Bradford.

Chambers, R. (1981). Rapid rural appraisal: Rationale and repertoire. *Public Administration and Development* 1: 95–106.

Chambers, R. (1983). *Rural Development: Putting the Last First.* Harlow, Pearson.

Chambers, R. (1992). *Rural Appraisal: Rapid, Relaxed and Participatory.* Brighton, Institute of Development Studies.

Chambers, R. (1996). ZOPP, PCM and PRA: Whose reality, needs and priorities count? Zopp marries PRA? In: *Participatory Learning and Action: A Challenge for Our Services and Institutions.* Eschborn, Deutsche Gesellschaft für technische Zusammenarbeit.

Chambers, R. (1997). *Whose Reality Counts? Putting the First Last.* London, Intermediate Technology Publications.

Chambers, R. (2002). *Participatory Workshops: A Sourcebook of 21 Sets of Ideas and Activities.* London, Earthscan.

Checkland, P. (1981). *Systems Thinking, Systems Practice.* Chichester, Wiley.

Checkland, P. and J. Scholes (1990). *Soft Systems Methodology in Action.* Chichester, Wiley.

Checkland, P. and J. Poulter (2006). *Learning for Action: A Short Definitive Account of Soft Systems Methodology, and Its Use, Practitioners, Teachers and Students.* Chichester, Wiley.

Connelly, S. and T. Richardson (2004). Exclusion: The necessary difference between ideal and practical consensus. *Journal of Environmental Planning and Management* 47(1): 3–17.

Cooke, B. and U. Kothari, Eds. (2001). *Participation the New Tyranny.* London, Zed Books.

Dodouras, S. and P. James (2007). Fuzzy cognitive mapping to appraise complex situations. *Journal of Environmental Planning and Management* 50(6): 823–852.

Douglas, M. (1992). *Risk and Blame: Essays in Cultural Theory.* London, Routledge.

Gurung, D. B. and R. W. Scholz (2008). Community-based ecotourism in Bhutan: Expert evaluation of stakeholder-based scenarios. *The International Journal of Sustainable Development and World Ecology* 15: 397–411.

Halvorsen, K. E. (2001). Assessing public participation techniques for comfort, convenience, satisfaction, and deliberation. *Journal of Environmental Management* 28: 179.

Hezri, A. A. (2004). Sustainability indicators system and policy process in Malaysia: A framework for utilisation and learning. *Journal of Environmental Management* 73(4): 357–371.

Huxham, C. and S. Cropper (1994). From many to one – and back: An exploration of some components of facilitation. *Omega* 22(1): 1–11.

Kolb, D. (1984). *Experiential Learning: Experience as the Source of Learning and Development*. London, Prentice-Hall.

Landman, T., A. Norval, J. Pretty and H. Ward (2003). Open citizens' juries and the politics of sustainability. *Political Studies* 51: 282–299.

Lei-Chang, H., Y. Shu-Hong, G. Xun, C. Fu-Cun, F. Zheng-Qiu, W. Xiang-Rong, W. Ya-Sheng and W. Shou-Bing (2010). A sustainable landscape ecosystem design. *Annals of the New York Academy of Sciences* 1195: E154–E163.

Matta, J. and J. Kerr (2006). Can environmental services payments sustain collaborative forest management? *Journal of Sustainable Forestry* 23: 63–79.

McFadzean, E. and T. Nelson (1998). Facilitating problem-solving groups: A conceptual model. *Leadership and Organization Development Journal* 19(1): 6–13.

Modinger, J. and H. Kobus (2005). Approach and methods for the assessment of sustainable groundwater management in the Rhine-Neckar Region, Germany. *International Journal of Water Resources Development* 21: 437–451.

Mohan, G. and S. Hickey, Eds. (2004). *Participation – From Tyranny to Transformation: Exploring New Approaches to Participation in Development*. London, Zed Books Ltd.

Morton, A. F., F. Ackermann and V. Belton (2007). Problem structuring without workshops? Experiences with distributed interaction within a PSM process. *Journal of the Operational Research Society* 58: 547–556.

Mosse, D. (1993). *Authority, Gender and Knowledge: Theoretical Reflections on the Practice of PRA*. London, Overseas Development Institute.

Newig, J., H. Haberl, C. Pahl-Wostl and D. Rothman (2008). Formalised and Non-Formalised Methods in Resource Management – Knowledge and Social Learning in Participatory Processes: An Introduction. *Systemic Practice and Action Research* 21: 381–387.

Newson, M. and L. Chalk (2004). Environmental capital: An information core to public participation in strategic and operational decisions? The example of river 'Best Practice' projects. *Journal of Environmental Planning and Management* 47: 899–920.

Nutt, P. C. (2002). *Why Decisions Fail: Avoiding the Blunders and Traps That Lead to Debacles*. San Francisco, Berrett-Koehler.

Ozesmi, U. and S. Ozesmi (2003). A participatory approach to ecosystem conservation: Fuzzy cognitive maps and stakeholder group analysis in Uluabat Lake, Turkey. *Journal of Environmental Management* 31: 518.

Pedzisa, T., I. Minde and S. Twomlow (2010). An evaluation of the use of participatory processes in wide-scale dissemination of research in micro dosing and conservation agriculture in Zimbabwe. *Research Evaluation* 19: 145–155.

Petheram, L. and B. M. Campbell (2010). Listening to locals on payments for environmental services. *Journal of Environmental Management* 91: 1139–1149.

Rowe, J. and L. Frewer (2005). A typology of public engagement mechanisms. *Science, Technology and Human Values* 30(2): 251–290.

Schon, D. (1983). *The Reflective Practitioner: How Professionals Think in Action*. San Francisco, Jossey-Bass.

Schon, D. (1987). *Educating the Reflective Practitioner*. San Francisco, Jossey-Bass.

Sheppard, S. R. J. and M. Meitner (2005). Using multi-criteria analysis and visualisation for sustainable forest management planning with stakeholder groups. *Forest Ecology and Management* 207: 171–187.

13

ENVIRONMENTAL GOVERNANCE INDICATORS AND INDICES IN SUPPORT OF POLICY-MAKING

Dóra Almássy and László Pintér

One of the most complex and pressing policy challenges of the 21st century will be safeguarding natural resources and restoring the environmental sustainability of our planet. This challenge stems from increasing frequency, intensity and adverse impacts associated with global environmental change such as extreme weather events, loss of biodiversity, deforestation, rapid urbanization, the reduction in renewable freshwater resources or sea level rise. One of the most complex and enduring policy challenges of the 21st century will be safeguarding natural resources and restoring the environmental sustainability of our planet (Özkaynak et al., 2013). While since the early 1970s the international community adopted an increasing number of environmental agreements and introduced various national policies to support their implementation, there is a significant and in many cases widening gap between aspirations and actual results (UNEP, 2012). In light of the continuing or accelerating pressures on the environment and related impacts, it is imperative to assess environment-related policies and implementation mechanisms more thoroughly to understand their effectiveness and link to accountability mechanisms.

Capacity is an important aspect of environment-related policy, and required to ensure response measures are effective and warrant progress towards established goals. Over the last decades, environmental indicators were developed not only to measure pressures on and the quality of our environment. Increasingly, they are also aiming at assessing environmental governance and policy implementation capacities. With the increasing popularity of composite indicators (Becker et al., 2017) several indices have been developed that include environmental governance indicators. Despite the interest in and availability of new governance indices, however, questions are lingering regarding their methodological soundness and applicability (Gisselquist, 2014).

Aiming to provide a review of the state-of-the-art, this chapter offers an overview of existing environmental governance indices (or composite indicators) and discusses their methodological approaches, primarily based on the ten-step composite indicator development methodology of the OECD (Organisation for Economic Co-operation and Development) and the EC JRC (European Commission Joint Research Centre) (OECD and EC JRC, 2008). Moreover, it also provides insights into the applicability of such indices in policy planning, implementation, review and revision as well as an outlook to their possible future use and development.

Environmental governance indices – a brief overview

Indices as composite indicators are formed by aggregating indicators for the purpose of characterizing a multi-dimensional issue (such as sustainable development), which cannot be measured by a stand-alone indicator (OECD and EC JRC, 2008). They gain importance and attract attention when policy-makers demand simplified but meaningful information of the state and the performance of complex fields (Saisana and Saltelli, 2008), reflecting important, but possibly hidden aspects of reality, such as economic growth, societal development or environmental protection (Becker et al., 2017). Composite indicators can also enable and facilitate comparison of the performance of different, individual entities (such as countries) based on a benchmark or to each other. They can promote accountability by attracting media and public interest (Pinter et al., 2000; Paruolo et al., 2013).

Over the last decade, there has been a significant increase in the development and application of composite indicators. At the Beyond GDP conference in November 2007, in his opening speech, José Manuel Barroso, the then President of the European Commission, underlined the growing gap between available data and the tools to interpret and apply them in policy-making to promote the sustainability of societies, economies and the planet (Barroso, 2007). The 9th recommendation of the Stiglitz report (Stiglitz et al., 2009) also underlined the need for the provision or development of objective and subjective indicators, characterizing different dimensions of sustainable development and enabling the construction of composite indices. The number of search results for the term "composite indicator" using Google Scholar has also been growing exponentially, from 992 in October 2005 and 5340 in December 2010 Bandura, 2011) to 8440 in March 2013 and to almost 19,000 in December 2016.

Indices that focus on assessing the state of the environment (or one of its defined elements, such as air, water or climate change) and measuring progress towards environmental objectives (such as improved air quality, water security or GHG emission mitigation) also became more widely reported and used. A 2011 review of composite indicators (Bandura, 2011) studied 290 indices, out of which 26 – almost 10% – focused on environmental themes.

Well-known examples of environmental indices include:

- the Environment Performance Index (EPI), developed by the Yale and Columbia University in 2006, as a successor to the Environmental Sustainability Index (ESI) to benchmark

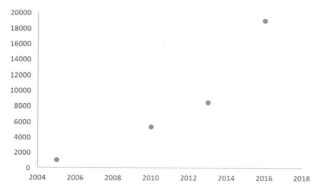

Figure 13.1 Increase in the term "composite indicators" found by Google Scholar between 2005 and 2016

Source: Authors' calculation and Bandura (2011)

environmental performance of different countries (see more in this volume about the development of and the experience with the EPI in Esty and Emerson, Chapter 5)
- the Living Planet Index (LPI), an initiative of the World Wildlife Fund (WWF) to assess the state of the world's biodiversity, distinguishing 555 terrestrials, 323 freshwater and 267 marine species (Srebotnjak, 2008; Loh et al., 2005)
- the Human Sustainable Development Index (HSDI), an updated version of the Human Development Index, complemented with an environmental dimension (for a critical review of the HSDI refer to Bravo, Chapter 18 in this volume).

Similarly to the EPI or the LPI, most environmental indices examine the quality of the environment in general or focus on some selected elements such as climate change or water resources. However, as the Oxford Martin Commission for Future Generations argues, there is also a need "to develop a Long-Term Impact Index, which would rate the effectiveness of leaders of countries, companies and international organizations in addressing longer-term challenges. . . [and] primarily assess processes and policies" (Oxford Martin Commission for Future Generations, 2013, p. 63). Although physical characteristics provide the primary basis for the assessment of the status and sustainability of the environment, the authors of this chapter argue that it is also important and possible to assess and quantitatively measure how the environment and natural resources are governed or managed to reach environmental goals.

For the purposes of this study (based on Chasek et al., 2016 and Fukuyama, 2013) we define environmental governance as the capacity of countries, regions, cities or other administrative unit to create policies and via these policies, implement environment goals. Accordingly, we consider environmental governance indices composite indicators that aim to monitor the capacities of countries to manage environmental goal implementation efforts.

Review of environmental indices with a governance component

This section provides a summary of 23 indices that focus on measuring environmental governance capacities either in a broad sense or with focus on specific environmental themes at the national, regional or municipal level. The indices selected for the review all include a capacity component. However, some of them focus entirely on environmental governance, while others consider governance only as one element of a more heterogeneous composite (e.g. together with state of the environment or environmental performance indicators).

The indices included in this review are shown in Table 13.1 with their theme, focus, general scope, publishing organization, year of introduction and frequency of updates.

Out of the 23 indices, 10 concentrated on environmental governance (shaded rows in Table 13.1), while the other 13 also covered other aspects of environmental performance that were complemented by governance indicators. For instance, 80% of the indicators in the Climate Change Performance index measured quantitative emission levels and trends, while 20% of the climate policies were based on expert opinion (Bruck et al., 2016). In the case of the Watershed Sustainability Index only one of its four components, with three indicators, focused on the management aspects of river basin protection (Chaves and Alipaz, 2007). In contrast, environmental governance aspects played a larger role in some other indices. For example, in the Green City Index 13 out of 30 indicators focused on the assessment of environmental policies and actions taken at the city level (Economist Intelligence Unit, 2012) and 60% of the indicators in the ASEM Eco-Innovation Index included focused on the capacity of a country to deploy environmental innovations (ASEIC, 2015). Representing the "Climate Accountability Subindex" of the Climate Competitiveness Index, 13 out of 26 indicators focused on measuring

Table 13.1 Environmental governance capacity indices and their attributes (compilation of the authors) – in chronological order according to the year of introduction

	Name	Theme	Focus number of indicators	Geographic scope	Developers	Year of introduction/ Frequency of updates
1.	Environmental Sustainability Index	Environment	Partially focuses on governance with 4/21 indicators	Global, 146 countries	Yale Center for Environmental Law and Policy and Columbia University	2000 Yearly between 2000–2005
2.	Water and Wetland Index	Water	Environmental governance The number of indicators is unknown	22 EU Member States, EU Accession Countries and non-EU countries	WWF	2003 One-time effort
3.	Canadian Water Sustainability Index	Water	Partially focuses on governance with 3/15 indicators	6 Canadian cities	Morin, A. (2006), Aboriginal Policy Research Consortium	2006 One-time effort
4.	Climate Change Performance Index	Climate Change	Partially focuses on governance with 2/15 indicators (20% weight)	Global, 58 countries	Germanwatch and Climate Action Network	2006 Yearly
5.	Watershed Sustainability Index	Water	Partially focuses on governance with 3/15 indicators	Brazil (SF Verdadeiro)	Chaves, Henrique M. L. and Alipaz, S.	2007 Tested in various river basins
6.	City Biodiversity Index	Biodiversity	Partially focuses on governance with 9/23 indicators	Global, self-evaluation tool for cities	National Parks Board, Singapore	2009 Applied in several cities
7.	Asia Water Governance Index	Water	Environmental governance 20 indicators	20 Asian countries	Araral, E. and Yu, D. Lee Kuan Yew School of Public Policy	2009 One-time effort
8.	Low-carbon competitiveness Index	Climate Change	Partially focuses on governance with 12/19 indicators	Global, G20 countries	Vivid Economics, commissioned by the Climate Institute	2009 and 2013

(Continued)

Table 13.1 (Continued)

	Name	Theme	Focus number of indicators	Geographic scope	Developers	Year of introduction/ Frequency of updates
9.	Climate Competitiveness Index (Climate Accountability Subindex)	Climate Change	Partially focuses on governance *with 13/26 indicators*	Global, 95 countries	AccountAbility in partnership with UNEP	2010 One-time effort
10.	Resource Governance Index	Natural Resources Management	Environmental governance *61 indicators (2017 edition)*	Global, 81 countries, rich in natural resources such as oil, gas and minerals	Natural Resource Governance Institute	2010 (pilot) 2013 and 2017 (with updated methodology)
11.	Climate Laws, Institutions and Measures Index (CLIMI)	Climate Change	Environmental governance *12 indicators*	Global, 95 countries	EBRD	2011 One-time effort
12.	Energy Trilemma Index	Energy	Partially focuses on governance *with 13/35 indicators*	Global, 129 countries	World Energy Council	2011 Yearly
13.	Sustainable Water Governance Index	Water	Environmental governance *7 indicators*	City of Salta, Argentina	Iribarnegaray, M.A. and Seghezzo, L.	2011 (pilot) One-time effort
14.	Forest, Land and REDD+ Governance Index	Forests	Environmental governance *117 indicators*	Indonesia, national and provincial level	UNDP Indonesia	2012 2014 (case study)
15.	Green City Index	Environment	Partially focuses on governance *with 13/30 indicators*	Global, 130 Major cities	Economist Intelligence Unit, sponsored by Siemens	2012 One-time effort
16.	Africa Capacity Indicators	Natural Resource Management	Environmental governance *69 indicators*	Selected African countries	African Capacity Building Foundation	2013 One-time effort
17.	Equity index in water and sanitation	Water	Partially focuses on governance *with 2/3 indicators*	Global, 56 developing countries	Luh, J, et al. (2013) The Water Institute and the Gillings School of Global Public Health at UNC	2013 One-time effort

No.	Index	Theme	Focus	Coverage	Institution	Year / Frequency
18.	ASEM Eco-innovation Index	Environment	Partially focuses on governance *with 12/20 indicators*	49 (later 51) European and Asian countries	ASEM SMEs Eco-Innovation Center (ASEIC)	2013, yearly between 2013–2015
19.	Bertelsmann Sustainable Governance Indicators	Sustainable Development	Partially focuses on environment *with 2/67 indicators*	41 EU and OECD countries	Bertelsmann Foundation	2014, Yearly
20.	Environmental Policy Stringency Index	Climate change and air pollution	Environmental governance *15 indicators*	28 OECD and 6 BRIICS countries	OECD	2014, Yearly updates
21.	Sustainability-adjusted Global Competitiveness Index	Sustainable Development	Partially focuses on environment *with 3/10 indicators in 1 of 3 components*	Global, 113 economies	World Economic Forum	2014, Yearly
22.	Environmental Democracy Index	Environment	Environmental governance *75 indicators*	Global, 70 countries	A partnership convened by the World Resource Institute	2015, One-time effort
23.	Urban water and sanitation governance index	Water	Environmental governance *18 indicators*	Cities	UN-Habitat	n.a. has not been tested

Note: The 10 indices which concentrated on environmental governance are shaded.

national leadership, strategy and coordination, investment promotion and business support as well as citizen engagement (Lee et al., 2010).

The composite indicators reviewed covered a variety of themes (Figure 13.2): 7 focused on water resources, 6 on climate change and energy, 4 on general environmental issues, 2 on natural resource management, 2 on forests and biodiversity and 2 looked at sustainable development from a broader point of view (including economic and social dimension in addition to environmental aspects). Among the 10 indices with exclusive environmental governance focus, 4 were related to water management, 3 to climate change, 2 to natural resources, 1–1 to forests and environmental protection in general.

As for geographic scale (Figure 13.3), the majority of the indices (16) compared country-level performance, 5 covered cities and 2 other governance units, such as provinces or river basins. Among the 10 indices focusing on environmental governance, 7 were developed for country comparisons, 2 for cities and 1 for the subnational level.

With regards to geographic distribution (Figure 13.4), 13 of the indices included countries or cities from several regions of the world, while 5 focused on countries from a single continent such as Europe, Asia or Africa. Four indices focused at the country level, often comparing several subnational jurisdictions or examining one subnational unit.[1] Among the environmental governance indices, 5 were global, 2 regional (focusing on Asia and Africa) and 2 focused on a single country (Indonesia) or city (in Argentina).

Most of the indices (16) were created by international or non-governmental organizations, such as the Organization for Economic Co-operation and Development (OECD), the United Nations Development Program (UNDP), and WWF. Six were developed by academia or research institutes although the Green City Index, while developed by a research institute (the Economist Intelligence Unit), was being sponsored by a private company (Siemens AG). One, the City Biodiversity Index, was launched by a national government body, the National Parks Board in Singapore (Chan et al., 2014).

The earliest identified index with an environmental governance component was the Environmental Sustainability Index, originally developed in 2000. The first index with an exclusive

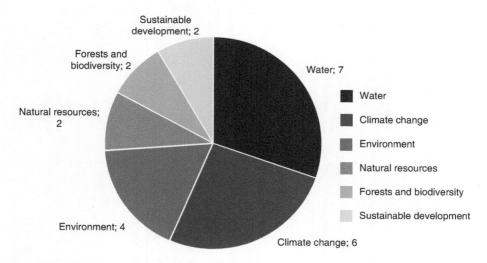

Figure 13.2 Themes covered by the composite indicators included in this review

Geographic scale

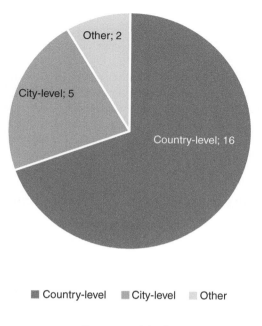

Geographic focus

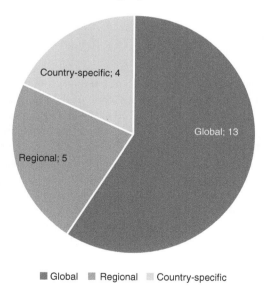

Figures 13.3 and 13.4   Geographic scale and focus of the composite indicators included in this review

focus on environmental governance capacities was the Water and Wetland Index of WWF, created in 2003. In spite of early development efforts, the majority (15) of the indices were launched only after 2010. As of 2016, 7 of the reviewed indices are or have been assessed regularly, 3 have been published twice, 2 have been tested in various places (e.g. in different cities). However, almost half of the indices (10) remained a one-off effort and one has not been tested yet.

This research also found that most of the indices that focused exclusively on environmental governance remained a one-time effort, indicating either methodological or application challenges. This may also be an indication that the maintenance and regular publishing of governance capacity-related indices itself requires ongoing capacity. With the aim to better understand the barriers of regular use and update of such indices the rest of the chapter discusses 8 environmental government indices.

Analysis of environmental governance indices

Based on the review of 23 indices with an environmental governance dimension, the following 8, focused exclusively on environmental governance have been selected for more detailed analysis[2]:

1   Africa Capacity Indicators on Natural Resource Management[3]
2   Asia Water Governance Index
3   Climate Laws, Institutions and Measures Index (CLIMI)
4   Environmental Democracy Index
5   Environmental Policy Stringency Index
6   Forest, Land and REDD+ Governance Index
7   Resource Governance Index
8   Sustainable Water Governance Index

To ensure methodological robustness and consistent interpretation of composite indicators, the guidelines of the OECD and the Joint Research Centre of the European Commission suggest a ten-step development process (OECD and EC JRC, 2008). The steps include (1) the creation of a theoretical framework as a basis for the selection and combination of the indicators; (2) the selection of the indicators; (3) the imputation of missing data through (a) case deletion, (b) single imputation or (c) multiple imputation; (4) a multivariate analysis to investigate the overall structure of the indicators; (5) normalization to render the indicators comparable; (6) weighting and aggregation according to the underlying theoretical framework and data properties; (7) sensitivity analysis of the composite indicators to identify possible sources of uncertainty; (8) disaggregation of the index to test transparency of underlying indicators or values; (9) correlation of the composite indicator with other published indicators and (10) visualization of the composite index in a clear and simple way.

In addition to these methodological consideration, another important aspect of composite indicators is the utility and replicability of results. For governance indicators, (Gisselquist, 2014) suggested a ten-question analytical framework. While many of the questions concern conceptualization and methodological issues related to index construction, it also includes considerations related to index utility such as replicability ("is the measure [including all of its sub-components] transparent and replicable?") and applicability ("does the measure allow the analyst to address key questions of interest?") (Gisselquist, 2014, pp. 522–523).

For the purposes of this analysis, the above approaches were grouped under four themes.

- Theoretical framework
- index structure and indicator selection
- coherence and soundness
- presentation and application.

The four themes are all supported by the BellagioSTAMP principles, particularly Principle 4 on Framework and Indicators and Principle 6 on Effective Communication (Pintér et al., 2012 and Pintér et al., Chapter 2).

Theoretical framework

Although research highlighted that the accurate definition of sustainability dimensions is essential to select the right indicators for an index and make the composition or system of the indicators functional (OECD EC JRC, 2008; Boulanger, 2008; Hsu et al., 2013), the importance of the theoretical foundation of composite indices seems to be often overlooked. A study by Gisselquist (2014) indicated that many governance indices are not grounded in a solid conceptual framework but provide only an operational definition for the governance concept applied.

This analysis found that many of the environmental governance indices studied explicitly identified the conceptual basis for indicator selection. The Sustainable Water Governance Index put forward a "five-dimensional sustainability concept", represented by a "sustainability triangle of "Place", "Permanence", and "Persons" (Iribarnegaray and Seghezzo, 2012, p. 2926). The Forest, Land and REDD+ Governance Index created its own conceptual framework for participatory governance assessment based on relevant principles, governance issues and actors (UNDP Indonesia, 2013). Developers of other indices refrained from defining their own framework but built on conceptual frameworks in previous scholarly work or in international conventions and guidelines. For instance, the Asia Governance Index was based on the work of Saleth and Dinar (2004) about the institutional economics of water and the concept of the Climate Laws, Institutions and Measures Index (CLIMI) was grounded in political economy theory (Steves and Teytelboym (2013). Using existing international guidelines as underlying conceptual frameworks, the Environmental Democracy Index was established on the UNEP's Bali Guidelines on public participation and access to information, while the Resource Governance Index followed the principles established by the International Monetary Fund's (IMF) 2007 Guide on Resource Revenue Transparency and the Extractive Industries Transparency Initiative (Natural Resource Governance Institute, 2013).

At the same time, the conceptual framework was less pronounced for some other indices and as Gisselquist (2014) noted, developers only provided an operational definition of the applied concept. For instance, the authors of the Africa Capacity Indicators on Natural Resource Management defined capacity as the core governance concept they focus on as "the ability of people, organizations, and society as a whole to manage their affairs successfully" (Africa Capacity-building Foundation, 2013, p. 19) while for its Environmental Policy Stringency Index, the OECD defined policy stringency "as a higher, explicit or implicit, cost of polluting or environmentally harmful behaviour" (OECD, 2014, p. 14).

Index structure and indicator selection

As expected, in each of the cases, the structure and indicator selection for the studied environmental governance indices followed the conceptual framework or operational definition. For

---

example, the Asia Governance Index covered laws, policies and administration, in line with the underlying water governance concept established by Saleth and Dinar (Araral and Yu, 2010b) and the Environmental Democracy Index includes 75 indicators based on UNEP's 23 Bali Guidelines grouped in three categories of access to information, public participation and access to justice (Worker and de Silva, 2015). Although the indicator selection appears to be more robust in the case of indices with an explicit conceptual framework, a conceptual framework was not necessarily a prerequisite to robust index structure and indicator selection. For instance, whereas no comprehensive conceptual framework was present, the components of the Environmental Policy Stringency Index were created according to the taxonomy of green growth policy instruments of de Serres et al. (2010).

As for structure, the indices included a minimum of two, maximum six components. To a varying degree, these components mostly covered the presence and quality of relevant environmental laws and policy frameworks, the implementation process and institutional capacities. Government transparency and civic involvement also appeared in some cases (Environmental Democracy Index; Forest, Land and REDD+ Governance Index; Resource Governance Index). The CLIMI covered international cooperation and the Sustainable Water Governance Index also included equity aspects. The number of indicators included in the indices varied considerably, ranging from a minimum of 7 (Sustainable Water Governance Index) to a maximum of 117 (Forest, Land and REDD+ Governance Index). Based on indicator number it appears to be two clusters: half of the indices were based on 20 or fewer indicators, while the other 4 had 50 or more included. In most cases, the indicators were not distributed evenly among the different components. An overview of the structure of the 8 indices studied in detail is shown in Table 13.2.

Table 13.2 Overview of the structure of the 8 indices studied in detail

Name of the index	Number of components	Theme of components and number of indicators per themes	Total number of indicators
Africa Capacity Indicators on Natural Resource Management	5	Policy Environment (9 indicators) Processes for Implementation (32 indicators) Development results for Natural Resource Management (19 indicators) Capacity Development Outcome (9 indicators)	69 indicators
Asia Water Governance Index	3	Legal (6 indicators) Policy (8 indicators) Administration (6 indicators)	20 indicators
Climate Laws, Institutions and Measures Index	4	International cooperation (2 indicators) Domestic climate framework (3 indicators) Significant sectoral fiscal or regulatory measures or targets (6 indicators) Additional cross-sectoral fiscal or regulatory measures (1 indicator)	12 indicators

Name of the index	Number of components	Theme of components and number of indicators per themes	Total number of indicators
Environmental Democracy Index	3	Transparency (21 indicators) Participation (15 indicators) Justice (39 indicators)	75 indicators
Environmental Policy Stringency Index	2	Market Based (10 indicators) Non-market policies (5 indicators)	15 indicators
Forest, Land and REDD+ Governance Index	6	Law and Policy Framework (24 indicators) Governance Capacity (27 indicators) Civil Society Capacity (18 indicators) Indigenous People/Community/ Women (12 indicators) Business Capacity (11 indicators) Performance (25 indicators)	117 indicators
Resource Governance Index (2017 edition)	3	Value Realization (35 indicators) Revenue Management (16 indicators) Enabling Environment (10 indicators)	61 indicators
Resource Governance Index (2013 edition)	4	Institutional and Legal Setting (10 indicators) Reporting Practices (20 indicators) Safeguards and Quality Controls (15 indicators) Enabling Environment (5 indicators)	50 indicators
Sustainable Water Governance Index	3	Access (3 indicators) Planning (3 indicators) Participation (1 indicator)	7 indicators

From a statistical point of view, indicator selection should be based on analytical soundness, measurability, country coverage, relevance and their relationship to each other (OECD and EC JRC, 2008). The most detailed description of the indicator development process was provided for the Forest, Land and REDD+ Governance Index (UNDP Indonesia, 2013), which noted that the indicators were subject to an assessment against the SMART objectives (specific, measurable, attainable, relevant and time-bound; ibid., p. 50). Iribarnegaray and Seghezzo (2012) outlined that the selection of the indicators for the Sustainable Water Governance Index was mainly influenced by "(a) coherence with the conceptual framework (b) pertinence to assess specific aspects of the governance for sustainability of the system; (c) minimum correlation between parameters at the same level; and (d) availability and reliability of local information" (p. 2936), which fulfils the criteria of (a) analytical soundness, (b) relevance, (c) relationship between the indicators and (d) coverage. While in many cases the methodological descriptions did not provide detailed information on the indicator selection process and whether they were evaluated against criteria, there usually were some hints regarding the selection process. For instance, Araral and Yu (2010b) justified the selection of the indicators for the Asia Water Governance index based on their policy robustness (*soundness and relevance*) and independence from political manipulation. Steves and Teytelboym (2013) decided to use indicators for the CLIMI which have been tested for and used in other indices as "proxies for climate change cooperation" (p. 8), thus fulfilling the criteria of measurability and country coverage.

Coherence and soundness of the indices

To ensure methodological soundness, the development of the indices should follow a sequence of steps grounded in statistical methods as described above according to the OECD and EC JRC methodology (2008). While only one index, the Asia Water Governance Index highlighted the application of a similar approach (Araral and Yu, 2010b, p. 11); relevant methodological steps can be identified for many of the other indices as well.

Indicator measurement

Indicator measurement refers to establishing a score for an indicator either by direct quantification or by assigning a score to a qualitative judgement. With regards to measurement, the indicators were mostly qualitative in nature, assessing the existence of a given governance element, resource or capacity. As such, their measurement method was also more subjective and they were assessed by the developers or independent experts on a perception scale (e.g. from 0/1–3; 0/1–5 or 0/1–100).

With regards to data imputation, the lack of data for such indices was considered "more the rule than the exception" as Iribarnegaray and Seghezzo (2012) noted it. Thus, the developers of the Sustainable Water Governance Index suggested that indicator selection should be relatively flexible to ensure measurability as these tools "are intended to help the process of decision-making by using the best available information in a given time and place" (ibid., p. 2936). In other cases, data collection for the index itself had an important policy learning function in the process, as a new type of information was collected, often with the involvement of stakeholders (e.g. in the case of the Environmental Democracy Index or the Forest, Land and REDD+ Governance Index). On the downside, we also saw that when data was missing, imputation was not always possible. For example, the Africa Capacity Indicators were not calculated for Angola and South Africa due to missing data.

As a footnote to imputation, the use or non-use of imputed values has to be tested through uncertainty and sensitivity analysis. While using imputed values may introduce elements of uncertainty with regard to the choice or reliability of the imputed values, avoiding the practice altogether may also be problematic. As shown through the analysis of the Global Innovation Index, avoiding imputation might encourage leaving out low data values and thus leading to purposeful distortion (Saisana et al., 2017). The consequence of the "no imputation" choice in an arithmetic average is that it is equivalent to replacing an indicator's missing value for a given country with the respective sub-pillar score. Hence, the available data (indicators) in the incomplete pillar may dominate, sometimes biasing the ranks up or down.

Because of the primary use of perception-based scoring of the indicators, normalization of raw data seemed not to be a major methodological issue for most of the studied indices. The Environmental Policy Stringency Index for example used normalization to "account for the different impact of nominal tax rates across countries" (OECD, 2014, p. 19). The Sustainable Water Governance Index, which used a mix of objective measurement and subjective expert evaluations noted that all indicators were normalized on a 0–100 scale (Iribarnegaray and Seghezzo, 2012).

Weighting and aggregation

Drawing from previous assessments of composite indicators for measuring sustainable development, it is important to place special emphasis on weighting and aggregation (Jesinghaus, Chapter 26 in this volume; Böhringer and Jochem, 2009). These steps are considered crucial for ensuring the objective presentation of country performance, e.g. strong and weak performances on different indicators do not balance out each other (Becker et al., 2017; Paruolo et al., 2013; Bandura, 2011 and 2008).

Five of the studied environmental governance indices applied equal weighting as they considered the different components equally important from the governance assessment point of view. However, this decision was not always straightforward. For instance, while the Environmental Democracy Index applied equal weight for its three components, two of its three components (information and participation) had a relative higher weight due to fewer guidelines under these when compared to the third component on justice (Worker and de Silva, 2015). However, in connection to this, the developers noted that they refrained from deciding whether "certain guidelines were more fundamental than others and argue in favour of weighting one pillar over another" (Worker and de Silva, 2015, p. 7). The developers of the Sustainable Water Governance Index also noted that while they considered the three components of their framework equally important, in some cases it "could be necessary to assign different weights to the categories" (Iribarnegaray and Seghezzo, 2012, p. 2939).

Meanwhile, the Asia Water Governance Index and the CLIMI chose to apply different weights to the components for various reasons. The authors of the Asia Water Governance Index used weights to "generate stochasticity" among the index components (Araral and Yu, 2010b, p. 12); for the CLIMI the weights aimed at reflecting "the contribution of each of the sectoral policy areas to possible carbon emission reductions" (Steves and Teytelboym, 2013, p. 8).

In case of the Resource Governance Index, the 2017 edition assigned equal weights to its three components. At the same time, the authors recognized that some questions, which included in those indicators that consisted of a fewer number of questions in total, had a relatively higher weight and took this into consideration when the questions of the indicators were grouped together (Natural Resource Governance Institute, 2017b). Moreover, the 2013 edition of the Index – which applied a somewhat different methodology and included 50 indicators under 4 components – assigned higher weight to the component on "reporting practices" as the authors suggested that the "actual disclosure constitutes the core of transparency" (Natural Resource Governance Institute, 2013). Related to this latter, an analysis carried out by Becker et al. (2017) confirmed that the higher weights assigned to the reporting practices in the Resource Governance Index is beneficial, "given that information about the other components is contained in" the index "through correlations" (Becker et al., 2017, p. 19).

Sensitivity and correlation analysis

As noted by Saisana and Saltelli (2008), sensitivity analysis should be carried out during the construction of composite indicators, rather than afterwards, so that its results can be reflected in the design of the index.

Out of the 8 studied indices, 4 of them carried out some sort of robustness analysis. The components of the Africa Capacity Index were selected via a hierarchical cluster analysis to ensure the relevance of the index components (Africa Capacity-Building Foundation, 2013). The developers of the CLIMI index applied sensitivity analysis to justify the weighting of components (Steves and Teytelboym, 2013). For the Asia Water Governance Index and for the

Environmental Policy Stringency Index an uncertainty test was carried out to confirm the soundness of the results (Araral and Yu, 2010b and OECD, 2014).

To further test the validity of the indices, assessing the correlation of the composite indicator with other published indicators is suggested (OECD and EC JRC, 2008). While some of the indices did not carry out such analysis, the Asia Water Governance Index was tested against the Worldwide Governance Indicators of the World Bank and the results of the Environmental Policy Stringency Index were compared against similar policy indices. In the case of the Asia Water Governance Index, a strong positive correlation was identified among the index and World Bank's Worldwide Governance indicators (Araral and Yu, 2010b). The authors of the Environmental Policy Stringency Index found strong correlation with the CLIMI and medium-level correlation with the results of the World Economy Forum's index on perceived environmental policy stringency (OECD, 2014). For analytical purposes, the CLIMI index was also correlated with indicators such as per capita income, knowledge of anthropogenic climate change and carbon-intensity (Steves and Teytelboym, 2013). Lastly, in the case of the Forest, Land and REDD+ Governance Index the Pearson-correlation method was used to identify relationships between the different components (UNDP Indonesia, 2012).

Presentation and application

Given that composite indices are mostly developed in order to summarize and communicate complex information to decision-makers and other stakeholders, an important, but often overlooked aspect of index development is its presentation and use. Presentation and communication refer to several potential aspects of the index, including language, objectivity and fairness, visual tools, storytelling and communicating the right level of complexity, as discussed by the 6th BellagioSTAMP principle (Chapter 2, Pintér, this volume).

Visual presentation

The European Commission's Competence Centre on Composite Indicators and Scoreboards at the Joint Research Centre offers a variety of visualization solutions, from a simpler tabular format through bar or linear charts to more complex options (Composite Indicators Research Group, 2016). At the same time, Albo et al. (2016) noted the lack of guidelines for visualization of composite indicators and the broad use of radar charts for presentation, without reliable empirical evidence proving its effectiveness.

As most of the studied environmental governance indices aimed at comparing country-level performance, they often used a simple, tabular format to present ranking from best to worst performers (e.g. Africa Capacity Indicators, CLIMI, Environmental Policy Stringency Index). Some other country rankings, (e.g. the Asia Water Governance Index, Environmental Democracy Index, Resource Governance Index) also used a simpler tabular or bar chart format, but also presented country rankings on a map (see Figure 13.5).

Application

The environmental governance indices studied were usually developed with a specific policy purpose in mind, including analytic support, cross-country comparisons or enhancement of policy learning. For example, the Africa Capacity Index aimed at supporting decision-makers in how to finance capacity-building objectives (ACBF, 2013) and the Forest, Land and REDD+ Governance Index offered a comprehensive approach to governance assessment and monitoring.

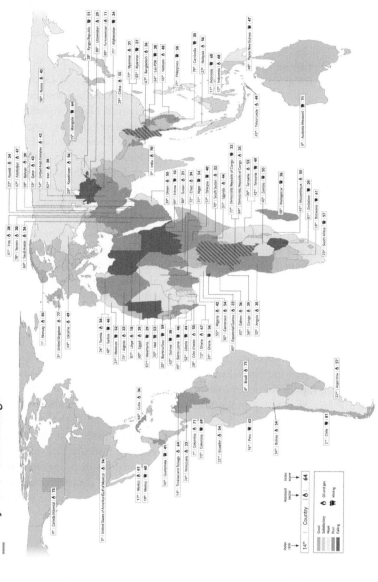

2017 Resource Governance Index
country scores and rankings

Figure 13.5 Map–based visualization of the Resource Governance Index for 2017 (Natural Resource Governance Institute, 2017a)

The CLIMI, the Environmental Policy Stringency Index and the Resource Governance Index were developed to provide an analytical tool for country-by-country comparison of climate, green growth and natural resource management policies. The Sustainable Water Governance Index applied a conceptual approach to understanding the role of "governance for sustainable development" in water management (Iribarnegaray and Seghezzo, 2012), while the Asia Water Governance Index's main objective was to support policy learning about water governance (Araral and Yu, 2010a). Directed more strongly towards the civil society and the general public, the main purpose of the Environmental Democracy Index was to raise awareness and public engagement.

Besides the stated purpose however, not much information is available about the actual use and perceived utility of the reviewed indices. Based on the number of Google search results, three of the indices – the Environmental Democracy Index, the Environmental Policy Stringency Index and the Resource Governance Index – achieved higher visibility. However, this may partially be due to the fact that these indices were developed by larger organizations, such as the World Resources Institution, which is behind the Environmental Democracy Index and the OECD, which developed the Environmental Policy Stringency Index. Nevertheless, it seems that for example the Environmental Democracy Index fulfilled its objective to some extent in raising awareness on the topic: at the time of the publication of the Index in 2015, it received considerable media attention and several national newspapers (e.g. in the UK, India and Malaysia) reported how their respective countries ranked. The Resource Governance Index also received similar media attention when published in 2013 and has been quoted in many articles, research papers and studies ever since. The 2017 edition was also promoted widely and newspapers reported about its results in many of those countries, which were included in the index. The Asia Water Governance Index also achieved some visibility as it was among the three finalists of the 2010 Suez International Water Prize and it was endorsed by the 2009 Economic Nobel Prize winner, Elinor Ostrom (Araral and Yu, 2010a).

Two other factors of use include the replicability of governance indices as shown by Gisselquist (2014) and also pointed out as "repeated measurement" in the 8th BellagioSTAMP principle on continuity and capacity (Pintér et al., 2012 and Pintér et al., Chapter 2, this volume.). While the reviewed indices delivered important information on various environmental governance topics in support of policy assessment and learning, out of the eight indices only the Environmental Policy Stringency Index is calculated annually and published in the Statistical Database of the OECD. In addition, after its first publication in 2013, the second edition of the Resource Governance Index was published in 2017 and the authors of the index also foresee further editions in the future (Natural Resource Governance Institute, 2017b). As for replicability, the Forest, Land and REDD+ Governance Index study has been repeated as a case study exercise for nine districts of Indonesia. The report of this index also explained how the results of the index can be applied to assessment and monitoring and how it can be institutionalized in Indonesia in order to ensure regular updating.

Conclusions

This study started off with a recognition that in addition to direct metrics of environmental conditions and outcomes there is significant interest in the policy literature and practice in capturing the institutional and governance dimensions of environmental sustainability. As shown by the large number of initiatives that were launched over the last several years this is a fertile field for policy research and innovation, and illustrates the need for understanding the deeper drivers of and responses to environmental change. While governance is complex and multi-dimensional, theoretical frameworks and aggregation methods allow the construction of composite indices that in principle provide a high-level overall snapshot of this dimension for a given country, thematic area or issue overall.

However, as also indicated by the examples in the chapter, despite some commonalities, there is also a great diversity of the approaches that suggests the research and policy community still approaches governance indices as experiments. Not surprisingly, most environmental governance indices remained a one-time effort.

The assessment of index development processes and their use in decision-making highlighted a number of methodological and application challenges. While detailed methodological guidance for the constructions of indices is available, index development is still wrought with dilemmas and difficulties: time and resource-consuming data collection and data update processes, weighting and aggregation of components based on established statistical methodologies as well as sensitivity and correlation analysis confirming the robustness of the indices in question, among others.

As to index use in decision-making, visual presentation in a meaningful, yet easily understandable way, the promotion of the results and the regular update of the measure to ensure the sustainability of the results were discussed. While at the technical level these are important design considerations, other factors such as the fit with policy agendas and dilemmas or inherent knowledge gaps regarding the link between a governance index performance and actual environmental sustainability outcomes are equally important (e.g. Hezri, 2004). Developing, testing and making governance indices tools of and for policy learning with the close involvement of users would be one of the avenues worth exploring.

Notes

1 One of the indices (the UN-Habitat developed Urban water and sanitation governance index) have not been applied or tested yet.
2 Two of the indices, with focus on environmental governance, were excluded from the review: the Water and Wetland Index, as the authors of this chapter could not identify its detailed methodological description and the UN-Habitat developed Urban water and sanitation governance index, as it has not been applied or tested yet.
3 One of the components of the Africa Capacity Indicators on Natural Resource Management contained some indicators that are performance-related; however the share of these indicators compared to the total number of indicators was less than 10% and thus we decided to include this composite indicator among the studied governance indices.

References

Africa Capacity-Building Foundation. (2013). *Africa Capacity Report 2013: Capacity Development for Natural Resource Management.* The African Capacity Building Foundation, Harare, Zimbabwe.

Albo, Y., Lanir, J., Bak, P., and Rafaeli, S. (2016). *Static vs. Dynamic Mapping in Radial Composite Indicator Visualization.* AVI '16 Proceedings of the International Working Conference on Advanced Visual Interfaces. pp. 264–271.

Araral, E. and Yu, D. (2010a). *Asia Water Governance Index.* Lee Kuan Yew School of Public Policy. Institute of Water Policy. URL: http://lkyspp.nus.edu.sg/iwp/wp-content/uploads/sites/3/2013/04/AWGI-brochure-IWP-LKYSPP9-10.pdf (Accessed: 1 December 2016)

Araral, E. and Yu, D. (2010b). *Water Governance: Critique, Theory and Evidence from Asia.* URL: http://www.nus.edu.sg/dpr/files/research_highlights/2012_04Apr_WaterGovernance_Critique_Theory_and_Evidence_from_Asia.pdf (Accessed: 10 March 2018)

ASEM SMEs Eco-Innovation Center (ASEIC). (2015). *ASEM Eco-Innovation Index 2015: Measuring Sustainable Future for Asia and Europe.* URL: www.aseic.org/resources/download/asei/result_2015/2015_ASEM_Eco-Innovation_Index_Final_Report.pdf (Accessed: 1 June 2017)

Bandura, R. (2008). *A Survey of Composite Indices Measuring Country Performance: 2008 Update.* Technical report, United Nations Development Programme. Office of Development Studies, New York.

Bandura, R. (2011). *Composite Indicators and Rankings: Inventory 2011.* URL: http://nebula.wsimg.com/beb0f5b0e9b6f0c298ae72e7519b22a4?AccessKeyId=EA00C1BFA208EDA3747F&disposition=0 (Accessed 15 March 2018)

Barroso, J. M. (2007). Beyond GDP – Opening Speech. In *Beyond GDP Conference.* URL: http://europa.eu/rapid/press-release_SPEECH-07-734_en.htm?locale=en (Accessed 15 March 2018)

Becker, W., Saisana, M., Paruolo, P., and Vandecasteele, I. (2017). Weights and importance in composite indicators: Closing the gap. *Ecological Indicators,* 80: 12–22. URL: www.sciencedirect.com/science/article/pii/S1470160X17301759 (Accessed: 25 May 2017)

Böhringer, C. and Jochem, P. (2009). *Measuring the Immeasurable: A Survey of Sustainability Indices.* Discussion Paper No. 06–073. Center for European Economic Research.

Boulanger, P.-M. (2008). Sustainable development indicators: A scientific challenge, a democratic issue. *S.A.P.I.EN.S.* [Online], 1(1). URL: http://journals.openedition.org/sapiens/166 (Accessed: 15 March 2018)

Bruck, J., Marten, F., and Bals, C. (2016). *The Climate Change Performance Index: Results 2016.* Germanwatch and Climate Action Network. URL: https://germanwatch.org/en/download/13626.pdf (Accessed: 1 December 2016)

Chan, L., Hillel, O., Elmqvist, T., Werner, P., Holman, N., Mader, A., and Calcaterra, E. (2014). *User's Manual on the Singapore Index on Cities' Biodiversity (also known as the City Biodiversity Index).* National Parks Board, Singapore.

Chasek, P., Downie, D. L., and Brown, J. W. (2016). *Global Environmental Politics: Dilemmas in World Politics.* Seventh Edition. Westview Press, Boulder, Colorado.

Chaves, H. M. L. and Alipaz, S. (2007). An integrated indicator based on basin hydrology, environment, life, and policy: The watershed sustainability index. *Water Resource Management* (Springer) 21: 883–895.

Composite Indicators Research Group. (2016). *Step 10: Visualization.* URL: https://composite-indicators.jrc.ec.europa.eu/?q=content/step-10-visualisation (Accessed: 1 December 2016)

de Serres, A., Murtin, F., and Nicoletti, G. (2010). *A Framework for Assessing Green Growth Policies.* OECD Economics Department Working Papers, No. 774, OECD Publishing.

Economist Intelligence Unit. (2012). *The Green City Index.* Siemens AG, Munich, Germany.

Fukuyama, F. (2013). What is governance? *Governance,* 26(3): 347–368.

Gisselquis, R. M. (2014). *Evaluating Governance Indexes: Critical and Less Critical Questions.* WIDER Working Paper No. 2013/068.

Hezri, A. A. (2004). Sustainability indicator system and policy processes in Malaysia: A framework for utilisation and learning. *Journal of Environmental Management,* 73(4): 357–371.

Hsu, A., Johnson, L. A., and Lloyd, A. (2013). *Measuring Progress: A Practical Guide from the Developers of the Environmental Performance Index (EPI).* New Haven: Yale Center for Environmental Law & Policy.

Iribarnegaray, M. A. and Seghezzo, L. (2012). Governance, sustainability, and decision making in water and sanitation management systems. *Sustainability,* 4: 2922–2945.

Lee, H., MacGillivray, A., Begley, P., and Zayakova, E. (2010). The climate competitiveness index 2010. *AccountAbility.*

Loh, J., Green, R. E., Ricketts, T., Lamoreux, J., Jenkins, M., Kapos, V., and Randers, J. (2005). The living planet index: Using species population time series to track trends in biodiversity. *Philosophical Transactions of the Royal Society B: Biological Sciences,* 360(1454): 289–295.

Luh, J., Baum, R., and Bartram, J. (2013). Equity in water and sanitation: Developing an index to measure progressive realization of the human right. *International Journal of Hygiene and Environmental Health,* 216: 662–671. doi:10.1016/j.ijheh.2012.12.007

Morin, A. (2006). *The Canadian Water Sustainability Index (CWSI) Case Study Report.* Aboriginal Policy Research Consortium International (APRCI). Paper 215. URL: http://ir.lib.uwo.ca/aprci/215 (Accessed: 15 March 2018)

Natural Resources Governance Institute. (2013). *Methodology of the Resource Governance Index.* Natural Resources Governance Institute, New York. URL: www.resourcegovernance.org/sites/default/files/rgi_2013-Methodology.pdf (Accessed: 5 February 2017)

National Resource Governance Institute. (2017a). *2017 Resource Governance Index.* URL: https://resource-governance.org/sites/default/files/documents/2017-resource-governance-index.pdf (Accessed: 5 October 2017)

National Resource Governance Institute. (2017b). *2017 Resource Governance Index*. Method Paper. URL: http://resourcegovernanceindex.org/about/methodology (Accessed: 5 October 2017)

OECD. (2014). *Measuring Environmental Policy Stringency in OECD Countries – A Composite Index Approach*. URL: www.oecd.org/officialdocuments/publicdisplaydocumentpdf/?cote=ENV/EPOC/WPIEEP(2014)3/ANN2/FINAL&docLanguage=En (Accessed: 1 December 2016)

OECD and EC JRC. (2008). *Handbook on Constructing Composite Indicators: Methodology and User Guide*. OECD, Paris, France.

Oxford Martin Commission for Future Generations. (2013). *Now for the Long Term*. Oxford Martin School and University of Oxford. URL: www.oxfordmartin.ox.ac.uk/downloads/commission/Oxford_Martin_Now_for_the_Long_Term.pdf (Accessed: 1 October 2015)

Özkaynak, B., Pinter, L., and van Vuuren, D. (2012). Chapter 16: Scenarios and Sustainability Transformation. In *UNEP, Global Environment Outlook-5*. UNEP, Nairobi, Kenya.

Paruolo, P., Saisana, M., and Saltelli, A. (2013). Ratings and rankings: Voodoo or science? *Journal of the Royal Statistical Society: Series A*, 176(3): 609–634.

Pintér, L., Hardi, P., Martinuzzi, A., and Hall, J. (2012). Bellagio STAMP: Principles for sustainability assessment and measurement. *Ecological Indicators*, 17: 20–28.

Pinter, L., Zahedi, K., and Cressman, D. (2000). *Capacity Building for Integrated Environmental Assessment and Reporting: Training Manual*. UNEP and IISD. Published by the International Institute for Sustainable Development, Winnipeg, Manitoba, Canada.

Saisana, M., Domínguez-Torreiro, M., and Vertesy, D. (2017). Annex 3: Joint Research Centre Statistical Audit of the 2016 Global Innovation Index. In Dutta, S., Lanvin, B., and Wunsch-Vincent, S. (Eds.) *The Global Innovation Index 2017*. Cornell University, INSEAD and The World Intellectual Property Organization. URL: file:///Users/laszlopinter/Downloads/gii-full-report-2017.pdf (Accessed: 15 March 2018)

Saisana, M. and Saltelli, A. (2008). Expert panel opinion and global sensitivity analysis for composite indicators. *Lecture Notes in Computational Science and Engineering*, 62: 251–275.

Saleth, R. M. and Dinar, A. (2004). *The Institutional Economics of Water: A Cross Country Analysis of Institutions and Performance*. Edward Elgar Publishing, Cheltenham.

Srebotnjak, T. (2008). *Environmental Performance Index*. Encyclopedia of Quantitative Risk Analysis and Assessment. Wiley Online Library, John Wiley & Sons, Ltd.

Steves, F. and Teytelboym, A. (2013). *Political Economy of Climate Change Policy*. Smith School Working Paper Series. Smith School of Enterprise and the Environment.

Stiglitz, J., Sen, A., and Fitoussi, J.-P. (2009). *Report by the Commission on the Measurement of Economic Performance and Social Progress*. URL: www.stiglitz-sen-fitoussi.fr/en/index.htm (Accessed: 1 March 2013)

UNDP Indonesia (2013). *Participatory Governance Assessment: The 2012 Indonesia Forest, Land and REFF+ Governance Index*. UNDP, Indonesia.

UNEP – United Nations Environment Programme. (2012). *Measuring Progress, Environmental Goals and Gaps*. UNEP, Nairobi, Kenya.

Worker, J. and de Silva, L. (2015). *The Environmental Democracy Index: Technical Note*. World Resources Institute, Washington, DC. URL: www.environmentaldemocracyindex.org/sites/default/files/files/EDI_Technical%20Note%20Final%207_9_15.pdf (Accessed: 5 February 2017)

WWF. (2003). *WWF's Water and Wetland Index: Critical Issues in Water Policy across Europe*. WWF, Madrid, Spain.

14

ENVIRONMENTALLY SUSTAINABLE NATIONAL INCOME, AN INDICATOR

Roefie Hueting and Bart de Boer

The subject matter of economics

The view that the 'environment' contrasts with 'economic interests' may for the greater part be explained by a misplaced identification of 'economics' with production. In the theory of subjective value it is the greatest possible satisfaction of wants, the maximum welfare of individuals, not the maximisation of national product, that is of primary importance. Scarcity, interpreted as the discrepancy between wants and means, now occupies a central position in the definition of the subject matter of economics and thus as an explanation of the value phenomenon. Following the above reasoning, the subject matter of economics may be defined as the problem of choice with regard to the use of scarce, alternatively applicable means for the satisfaction of classifiable wants.

This definition is an obvious widening of the earlier theory. In principle the one-sided coupling of economics to the phenomenon of production has been abandoned. In modern economic theory production is regarded as one of the means that can contribute to the satisfaction of wants – the welfare – of humans. Production thus ceases to be the central objective of economic action and is regarded as only one of the means of attaining a given end.

Of the authors who have constantly reflected on the points of departure of economic theory, P. Hennipman occupies a special position. He defines the view referred to here as the point of view that 'the common heart of the problems concerning economic science lies in the relations between relatively scarce, alternatively usable goods and the whole of the wants or purposes, whatever their nature, served by the goods' (Hennipman, 1962, p. 48; see also Hennipman, 1995). It emerges from the context of Hennipman's view that this definition contains a broad concept of goods which in fact can better be designated by the term 'means'. The ends themselves are meta-economic and are not for economists to judge. Ends or wants are given, and are discussed only insofar as their achievement or satisfaction depends on the use of scarce means. Maximising or even just increasing the size of the social product is no longer a necessary aim that can lay claim to a logical priority. All objectives desired by individuals which are in conflict with this, form a logical and complete part of economic policy. When they are given preference above production, this does not mean a sacrifice of welfare on the strength of 'non-economic' considerations.

The concept of environmental functions

In the theoretical basis for the environmentally sustainable national income (eSNI), we define the environment as the non-human-made physical surroundings, which consists of the components water, air, and soil, and further on plant and animal species, and the life-support systems (including ecosystems) of our planet, on which humanity is entirely dependent, whether producing, consuming, breathing or recreating (Hueting, 1974).

The possible uses or functions of our physical surroundings have come into being largely via processes proceeding at a geological or evolutionary pace. For the life-support systems it is unfeasible ever completely to be replaced by technology, as is shown by Goodland (1995); see also Dasgupta and Heal (1979). It is largely thanks to these life-support systems (Hueting and Reijnders, 2004), which are under threat of disruption, that indispensable (or vital) environmental functions remain available. Life-support systems are understood to mean the processes that maintain the conditions necessary for life on earth. This comes down to maintaining stable conditions within narrow margins.

A great number of possible uses (*possibilities* to use) can be distinguished, which are essential for production, consumption, breathing, et cetera, and thus for human existence. We call these *environmental functions*, or in short: functions (Hueting, 1969, 1974). As long as the use of a function does not hamper the use of another or the same function, so as long as environmental functions are not scarce, an insufficiency of labour, in this context intellect and technology, is the sole factor limiting production growth, as measured in standard NI. As soon as one use of a function is at the expense of another or the same function (by excessive use), though, or threatens to be so in the future, a second limiting factor is introduced. This *competition of functions* leads to partial or complete loss of function. An example of excessive use of one and the same function, leading to its loss, is overfishing resulting in decreased availability of the function 'water to accommodate fish species'; then the catch of some species decreases or species become extinct. Competing functions are economic goods, for more of one function means less of another.

It may be instructive to give some examples of environmental functions. As regards water, a distinction has been made between the following functions: 'water for drinking', 'water for cooling', 'water for flushing and transport', 'process water', 'water for agricultural purposes', 'water for recreation', 'water in the natural environment', 'navigable water', 'water as an element in the social environment', 'water for construction', and 'water as a medium for dumping waste'.

An environmental component (see above) always has three aspects.

1   A quantitative aspect. This relates to amounts of matter, such as resources: oil, water, ores et cetera. Quantitative competition is absolute; the part of a resource withdrawn on behalf of a certain function entirely excludes use of that part for other functions. With regard to water, this takes place by actual withdrawal of water from the environment. In the case of air, quantitative competition occurs in air traffic. In soil, quantitative competition includes the current or expected future shortage of so called non-renewable resources such as oil, metals, mineral phosphate and a renewable resource: groundwater.

2   A qualitative aspect. This relates to overburdening the function 'medium for dumping waste' by chemical, physical or biological 'agents' which cause partial or total loss of all other possible uses of the environment. Examples are the function 'resource for the production of drinking water' or 'air for physiological functioning of humans, plants and animals (breathing)'. By agent, in this context, is meant a constituent or amount of energy (in whatsoever form) which may cause loss of function either by its addition to or by its

withdrawal from the environment by man. An agent could be a chemical, plant, animal, heat, radioactivity, etc.

3   A spatial aspect. Spatial competition of functions occurs when there is not enough space for the use or intended use of the functions. Worldwide competition exists between use of space for production of food, production of bio fuels, natural ecosystems and the survival of species, road building, building of houses, traffic and possibilities for children to play and discover their surroundings. This occurs above all on soil. Especially the function 'space for the existence of natural ecosystems' is threatened. Spatial competition is probably the main cause of species extinction, through loss and fragmentation of habitats.

The decreased availability of a function may relate to each of these three aspects.

Valuation: an unsolvable problem leading to standards

A prerequisite for the eSNI is its comparability with the standard net NI; comparability is understood here to be that the figures of these quantities are expressed in the same units and can be added and subtracted: they must be additive. For this purpose the prices of environmental functions must be found which are comparable with market prices. A way to achieve this is to search for the minimum of the sum of the demand and supply curves of the functions. From this follow the shadow prices of the functions. These prices are used in the present project to estimate the costs which constitute the distance between the NI and the eSNI.

The shadow prices can only be established with the aid of data on supply and demand for environmental functions. Because functions are collective goods, they fall outside the market mechanism, and therefore a supply and a demand curve must be construed for each function. If there are no preferences for a good, its value is zero, irrespective of how important, or even indispensable, that good may be for humankind. If a good can be obtained without sacrificing an alternative, its value is likewise zero. In valuing environmental functions, both preferences and costs must be quantified. These are therefore two inseparably linked elements of the valuation of environmental functions and their loss. Valuations that are, ultimately, based on estimates of only preferences (demand) or costs (supply) are here viewed as techniques forming part of the single valuation method presented here. See also (Hueting, 1996).

Value is understood to be here price times quantity of a good, thus excluding the consumers' surplus (what one is prepared to pay above its price, whether it is a market price or a shadow price). Knowing the shadow prices of the environmental functions is necessary for knowing which production factors (labour and capital) are needed for preservation of the functions which are essential for human life, including production and consumption. The sum total of the values of the production factors equals the distance between the NI and the eSNI.

The availability of functions depends on the state of their carriers: our physical surroundings. If the latter become less suitable or unsuitable for the use of some functions by the excessive use of other functions, mostly for production and consumption, then the physical surroundings have to be restored. To what extent this has to be done depends on the urgency of the preferences for the availability of the impaired functions. The calculation of the supply and the demand curve is part of a comparative static analysis, performed for each year in which the shadow prices of the functions are needed, e.g. for the calculation of the eSNI. We construe the curves as follows. On a system of coordinates, function availability is recorded on the horizontal axis, in physical units, with the preferences and annual costs of the measures to restore functions being plotted on the vertical axis (Hueting, 1974, 1980). Going from the origin to the right, the burdening or use u of the function decreases and its availability a increases. The figure connects ecology and economics. The figure shows that an decrease of the damage D and the compensation costs C plotted on the one curve (representing the – incomplete – demand for the function) constitutes the benefits accruing from an increase of the elimination costs E (supplying the function) plotted on the other. The aim, now, is to find the availability a of the function for which the total costs $C(a) + D(a) + E(a)$ are minimal, in other words, to find the point where the difference between the benefits $-(C + D)$ and the costs E is maximal. This is achieved if [1]

$$\frac{d}{da}(C + D + E) = 0$$

We define c and d as the marginal *benefits* of the decrease of the compensation and damage *costs* C and D and e as the marginal elimination costs:

$c = -dC/da$
$d = -dD/da$
$e = dE/da$

so that the optimality condition may be written as

$c + d = e.$

The point of intersection of the marginal curves $c + d$ and e therefore corresponds to the minimum of the total cost curve $C + D + E$. If the social preferences for the function are completely expressed in the $c + d$ curve (which is not the case), this intersection point defines the optimal recovery of the function's availability, a_o. Starting from the adage that the price which reflects the social costs is equal to the marginal costs, the distance from the abscissa to the e curve or the $c + d$ curve at the optimum a_o yields the shadow price p_o of the environmental function. The shadow price of an environmental function is therefore equal to the marginal costs of elimination at optimal restoration of function.

Below it is shown how the supply curve and the demand curve are composed.

The *supply* curve in Figures 14.1A and 14.1B is built up from expenditures on measures, to be taken by whatever party from the year of investigation onwards, which increase the availability of the function. The elimination measures are arranged by increasing costs per unit of function restored. This resulting curve can be seen as a supply curve, because it supplies the function. We call this the elimination curve, because the measures eliminate the burden at the source. Except in the case of irreparable damage, the elimination costs can always be estimated by consulting environmental technical expertise. So this curve can always be constructed. The measures consist of:

1   technical measures, including process re-engineering, redesign, developing and applying (renewable) substitutes for non-renewable resources (for example solar energy, glass fibre) and rearranging space to create more space for ecosystems
2   direct shifts from environmentally burdening to less burdening activities (reallocation)
3   a decrease in the size of the population.

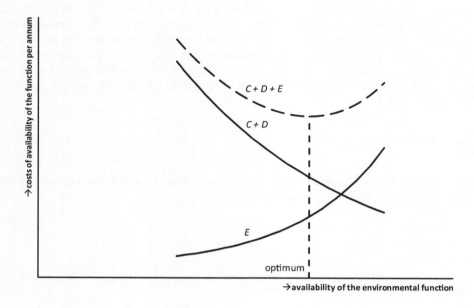

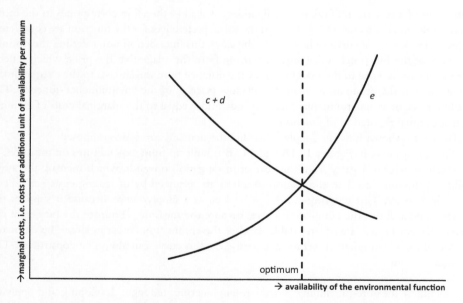

Figures 14.1 A and B Costs of elimination and revealed preferences for an environmental function; A: total curves, B: marginal curves

The *demand* curve in Figures 14.1A and 14.1B consists of all expenditures, actually made, by whatever party, resulting from loss of environmental functions. The costs actually incurred fall into two categories:

1   expenditures on measures to compensate for loss of function, such as the raising of dykes as a result of disruption of various functions regulating hydrology and climate, or on preparing drinking water as a result of overuse of the function 'dumping ground for waste'; these are the compensation costs;
2   expenditures, actually made relating to damage, such as housing damage and harvest losses caused by flooding due to loss of the function 'hydrological regulation' of forests and soil, or the restoration of damage caused by flooding due to excessively cutting forests, etc. (overuse of the function 'provider of wood', etc.) that consequently are losing their function 'regulation of the water flow' and production losses and medical costs ensuing from, say, loss of the function 'air for physiological functioning'.

All these amounts can be interpreted as expressing revealed preferences for the original functions. For category 2, this is based, strictly speaking, on the assumption that those suffering damage through loss of a function are prepared to pay at least the amount required to restore that damage in order to achieve restoration and lasting availability of the function in question. The curve has the same shape as a normal demand curve for a product. With decreasing availability of the function, progressively more compensation measures must be taken and progressively more financial damage occurs: the price (indicating the marginal utility) increases.

It can be argued that preferences for essential functions can be expressed very partially as the compensation and damage costs. As an example, there is no point in creating new forests or lakes as long as the process of acidification has not been halted by elimination measures, because without elimination at the source the process will acidify the newly created forests and lakes. Erosion-driven soil loss cannot be compensated. Much of the damage resulting from loss of functions will take place in the future; cases in point are damage due to disruption of climatic stability and to the loss of the functions of natural ecosystems such as rainforests and estuaries; no financial damage or compensation expenditures can therefore arise in the present. Choosing a discount rate, for instance the market interest, for calculating the net present value of future damage boils down to making an assumption about preferences for future environmental costs and benefits (Hueting, 1991). This does not, therefore, resolve the basic problem of preferences being unknown. We cannot base ourselves on observed individual behaviour, furthermore, given the working of the prisoners' dilemma. In practice, individuals do not switch to environmentally sound behaviour, because they doubt whether others will do the same, as a result of which the effect is thought to be negligible while the individual concerned is caused detriment. The same holds at a meso- and macro-scale. If one company takes measures to protect the environment but others do not, it will price itself out of the market. If a given country adopts measures and others do not follow, that country will suffer damage, while the effect of those measures will be insubstantial. Finally, there is a lack of information, for example about the complex nature of life-support systems and about the relation between safeguarding the environment, employment and growth. All these aforementioned factors, which make it impossible and very difficult respectively to fully express preferences for environmental functions.

It is therefore logical to look at the possibilities for retrieving the demand for functions with the aid of contingent valuation. Efforts have been made to trace these preferences by asking people how much they would be prepared to pay to wholly or partially restore lost environmental functions and to conserve them. Much research is being done on willingness to pay or to accept (contingent valuation). However, this method does not always provide reliable estimates for many reasons (Hueting, 1989 and 2011).

As the social preferences for environmental functions can be measured only partially, their shadow prices, which are defined by the intersection of the first derivatives of the constructed curves for demand and supply (see Figure 14.1B), cannot be determined. Consequently, these shadow prices – and the value of environmental functions – remain largely unknown. This means that the *correct prices for the human-made goods* that are produced and consumed at the expense of environmental functions, and on which the NI is based, remain *equally unknowable*. Consequently, to provide the necessary information, we cannot escape from making *assumptions* about the relative preferences for environmental functions and produced goods.

One of the possible assumptions is that the economic agents, individuals and institutions, have a dominant – or absolute – preference for an environmentally sustainable development. This assumption is legitimate since governments and institutions all over the world have stated support for environmental sustainability. Furthermore Hueting (1987, p. 65), referring to the ecological risks by production growth, postulates:

> Man derives part of the meaning of existence from the company of others. These oth-
> ers include in any case his children and grandchildren. The prospect of a safer future
> is therefore a normal human need, and dimming of this prospect has a negative effect
> on welfare.

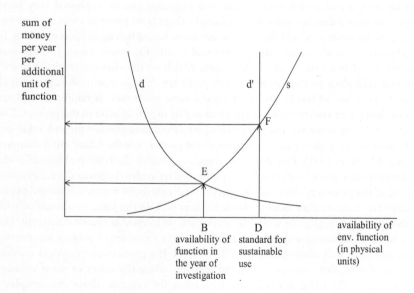

Figure 14.2   Translation of costs in physical units into costs in monetary units

s = supply curve or marginal elimination cost curve (e in Figure 14.1B); d = incomplete demand curve or marginal benefit curve based on individual preferences revealed from expenditures on compensation and damage (c + d in Figure 14.1B); d = 'demand curve' based on assumed preferences for sustainability; BD = distance that must be bridged in order to arrive at sustainable use of environmental functions; area BEFD = total costs of the loss of functions, expressed in money; the arrows indicate the way in which the loss of environmental functions recorded in physical units is translated into monetary units. The availability of the function (B) does not need to coincide with the level following from intersection point (E).

The environmentally sustainable income (eSNI), described below, is therefore based on the assumption of dominant preferences for environmental sustainability; see for example Hueting, Bosch and De Boer (1992), Hueting and Reijnders (1998). *Another* possible assumption is that the economy is currently on an optimal path that is characterised by the changes in the standard NI, exempted of so-called asymmetrical entries, abbreviated as asyms (see below).

So *both the eSNI and the standard NI are conditional* in the context of what is at issue in economic theory and statistics, namely to provide indicators of the effect of our actions on our welfare. This holds true apart from the fact that measuring NI has much smaller uncertainty margins than measuring eSNI does.

The assumed absolute social preferences for sustainable use of an (essential) environmental function become apparent as a very steep (inelastic) part of the demand curve of the function at the minimal sustainable level of its availability. The demand curve then reaches the abscissa practically vertically at that minimally sustainable availability. The steep part of the curve may be approximated by the vertical line representing the sustainability standard, defined as the minimal availability of the function.

The thus defined sustainability standards can only be established by the natural sciences, not by economists, provided the economic context of the application of the standards is clear. They are objective insofar natural sciences are objective. They must of course be distinguished clearly from the subjective preferences for whether or not they should be attained. Without standards environmentally sustainability is indeterminate.

In establishing sustainability standards, as the basic point of departure is taken the natural regeneration capacities of the concerned environmental processes: as long as these remain intact, environmental functions will remain available. These processes determine the state of the environment on which the functions and consequently the standards depend. The standards have to be chosen thus that these processes are in dynamic equilibrium; see Hueting and De Boer (2001) and Hueting and Reijnders (2004). For instance, the growth and mortality processes of algae or fish populations determine their age distribution, and consequently the availability of the function 'water as a habitat for fish'.

Environmentally sustainable national income

Environmentally sustainable national income (eSNI) is defined as the maximal attainable production level by which vital environmental functions remain available for future generations, based on the technology available at the time. Thus the eSNI provides information about the distance between the current situation (standard NI) and a sustainable situation (eSNI). The estimate of eSNI in a year is obtained by a comparative, static exercise in which time plays no role. In reality, the length of the period to bridge the distance between NI and eSNI, that is the transition period towards a sustainable situation, is limited only by the condition that vital environmental functions must not be damaged irreversibly. In combination with the standard national income (NI), the eSNI indicates whether or not the part of the production that is not based on sustainable use of the environment, is becoming smaller or greater. Because of the precautionary principle, future technological progress is not anticipated in the calculation of eSNI. When constructing a time series of eSNIs, technological progress finds expression after the event on the basis of the development of the distance between the eSNI and standard NI over the course of time. When the distance between NI and eSNI increases, society is drifting farther away from environmental sustainability; if the distance decreases, society is approaching environmental sustainability.

The theory of and the necessary statistics for an eSNI have been worked on since the mid-sixties. The method of the present calculation was proposed by Hueting, Bosch and De Boer (1992). A first rough estimate of the eSNI for the world by Tinbergen and Hueting (1991, 1992) arrives at roughly 50% of the production level of the world: the world income. The method was developed further into the model approach published by Verbruggen et al. (2001) and Hueting and De Boer (2001). Estimates for The Netherlands by a cooperation of Statistics Netherlands, the Institute of Environmental Studies and the Netherlands Environmental Assessment Agency also arrived at about 50% of the production level or national income of The Netherlands; see Verbruggen et al. (2001) and Dellink and Hofkes (2008). This corresponds with the production level in the early seventies. In the period 1990–2005 the distance between NI and eSNI increased by thirteen billion euro or 4%. The eSNI has been calculated each fifth year, because data on the cost effectiveness of the available technical measures for elimination of the emissions involved were generally updated with that frequency.

The latter estimation has been carried into effect by means of a model which traces the consequences of (1) the reactions to the change in price ratios (environment burdening activities become relatively more expensive, whereas environmentally benign activities become relatively cheaper), (2) direct shifts to environmentally less burdening activities and (3) if this is insufficient, a virtual reduction of the population. The price ratios obtained by internalising the costs of eliminating the excess burden on the environment reflect the environmentally sustainable situation. The greater the steps are to internalising the sustainability costs, the sooner an environmentally sustainable activity level will be reached. Of course there is a limit to the size of these steps. Too great steps lead to chaos: society must be able to adapt to the changes in the price ratios.

The model traces the changes in the produced quantities in reaction to the change in price ratios (see the preceding paragraph) and vice versa. The change in price ratios can be elucidated as follows. It follows from Hueting (1981), Hueting (1984) and Hueting, Bosch and De Boer (1992) that, during a long period, the bulk of national income growth has been generated by industries that caused the greatest losses of environmental functions, both in production and in consumption. The increase in productivity in these industries, measured in terms of goods produced, has been much greater than elsewhere in the economy, so the real prices of these products have decreased strongly, and, with them, the price ratio between environmentally burdening and less burdening products. As a result, any present or future shift to environmentally friendly products will have a negative impact on the volume of national income. When, as in the simulation of environmentally sustainable income, the costs for attaining environmental sustainability are internalised in the prices of environment burdening products, the real prices of the latter increase, as does the price ratio between environmentally burdening and friendly products. The latter price ratios reflect the situation in an environmentally sustainable situation. Attaining environmental sustainability without a (drastic) change in price ratios is infeasible.

The eSNI is above all intended for gauging the distance between the achieved and the sustainable level of production in the course of time. Because expenditure on a number of elimination measures and a great deal of expenditure on repairing damage and on compensation measures are booked as contributions to the NI, NI is not a good yardstick of (the development of) the level of production. During a transition to the sustainable path the distance between NI and eSNI may increase as a result, while the gap between the sustainable and the present level of production (the NI reduced by asymmetric entries, in short, NI ex asyms), which is what it is all about, decreases. Hence the gap that has to be bridged to achieve a sustainable level of production (the eSNI) is (NI ex asyms – eSNI) and not (NI – eSNI). See De Boer and Hueting (2004), and De Boer (2013) for the formal mathematical details.

The time period needed to bridge the gap will be shorter as economic policy concentrates more on this goal than on increasing the production measured in NI.

This indicator is meant to serve as information for decision making.

The eSNI is the only indicator which (1) is directly comparable with standard NI because it is estimated in accordance with the conventions of the System of National Accounts (SNA), (2) relates the measurable physical environment ('ecology') with subjective preferences (economy) as shown in Figure 14.2, (3) provides the distance between the actual (NI) and sustainable (eSNI) production level in factor costs and (4) shows the development of this distance in the course of time and thus shows whether or not society is drifting further away from environmental sustainability defined as keeping vital environmental functions available for future generations. Therefore eSNI is indispensable information for society and policy.

Acknowledgement

We thank Herman Daly for his remarks on an earlier concept.

Note

1 The second necessary condition is that the second derivative of $C + D + E$ is positive, which is satisfied because the marginal curves $c + d$ and e are convex over the whole range; see Figure 14.B.

References

Dasgupta, P.S. and G.M. Heal. *Economic Theory and Exhaustible Resources*, Cambridge University Press, Cambridge, 1979.

Boer, B. de. *Waardoor groeit het BBP?* (What Makes GDP Grow?). Unpublished paper, 2013.

Boer, B. de and R. Hueting. "Sustainable National Income and Multiple Indicators for Sustainable Development". In *Measuring Sustainable Development: Integrated Economic, Environmental and Social Frameworks*, 39–52. Organization for Economic Co-operation and Development (OECD), Paris, 2004.

Dellink, R. and M.W. Hofkes. *Sustainable National Income 2005: Analysis for The Netherlands. Trend and Decomposition Analysis of a Sustainable National Income in 2005 According to Hueting's Methodology*, Instituut voor Milieuvraagstukken, Vrije Universiteit, Amsterdam, 2008.

Goodland, R. "The concept of environmental sustainability", *Annual Review of Ecology, Evolution and Systematics* 26 (1995): 1–24.

Hennipman, P. "Doeleinden en criteria". In *Theorie van de economische politiek*.: Stenfert Kroese, Leiden, 1962.

Hennipman, P. *Welfare Economics and the Theory of Economic Policy*, Hartmolls Limited, Bodmin and Cornwall, 1995.

Hueting, R. "Correcting national income for environmental losses: Towards a practical solution". In *Environmental Accounting for Sustainable Development*, edited by Y. Ahmad, S. El Serafy and E. Lutz, The World Bank, Washington, DC, 1989.

Hueting, R. "Economic aspects of environmental accounting", *Journal of Interdisciplinary Economics* 2, no. 1 (1987).

Hueting, R. "Five ways to combat misleading information about economic growth". In *Theories and Effects of Economic Growth*, edited by Richard L. Bertrand, 1–28, Nova Science Publishers, Inc., New York, 2011.

Hueting, R. *New Scarcity and Economic Growth: More Welfare through Less Production?* Translated by Trevor Preston, North-Holland Publishing Company, Amsterdam, New York and Oxford, 1980.

Hueting, R. *Nieuwe schaarste en economische groei: Meer welvaart door minder productie?* Agon Elsevier, Amsterdam and Brussels, 1974.

Hueting, R. "Results of an economic scenario that gives top priority to saving the environment and energy instead of encouraging production growth". In *Economic Growth and the Role of Science*, edited by Sören Bergström, Holms Gårds Tryckeri, Edsbruk, 1984.

Hueting, R. "Ruimtelijke ordening en het allocatievraagstuk", *Economisch-Statistische Berichten*, May 1969.

Hueting, R. "Some comments on the report 'A low energy strategy for the United Kingdom', compiled by Leach G. et al. for the International Institute for Environment and Development (IIED)", Working Party on Integral Energy Scenarios, The Hague, May 20, 1981.

Hueting, R. "The parabel of the carpenter". In *Valuation Methods for Green National Accounting: A Practical Guide*, The World Bank, U.N. Statistical Office and Ecological Economics, Washington, DC, 1996.

Hueting, R. "The use of the discount rate in a cost-benefit analysis for different uses of a humid tropical forest area", *Ecological Economics* 12 (1991), 43–57.

Hueting, R. and B. de Boer. "Environmental valuation and sustainable national income according to Hueting". In *Economic Growth and Valuation of the Environment: A Debate*, edited by J. van der Straaten, H.R.J. Vollebergh and E.C. van Ierland, 17–77, Edward Elgar, Cheltenham, UK, Northampton, MA, 2001.

Hueting, R. and L. Reijnders. "Broad sustainability contra sustainability: The proper construction of sustainability indicators". *Ecological Economics*, 50 (2004), 249–260.

Hueting, R. and L. Reijnders. "Sustainability is an objective concept". *Ecological Economics* 27, 2 (1998), 139–147.

Hueting, R., P.R. Bosch, and B. de Boer. *Methodology for the Calculation of a Sustainable National Income*, Statistical Essays, M 44, Statistics Netherlands, SDU/Publishers, 1992. Also published as WWF International report, Gland, Switzerland, 1992.

Tinbergen, J. and R. Hueting. "GNP and market prices: Wrong signals for sustainable economic success that mask environmental destruction". In *Environmentally Sustainable Economic Development; Building on Brundtland*, edited by R. Goodland, H. Daly, S. El Serafy and B. von Droste. United Nations Educational, Scientific and Cultural Organization (UNESCO), Paris, 1991. Also published in (R. Goodland et al. (eds.)), *Population, Technology and Lifestyle: The Transition to Sustainability*, Ch. 4: 52–62. The International Bank for Reconstruction and Development and UNESCO. Island Press, Washington, DC, 1992. Also published in (R. Goodland et al. (eds.)), *Environmentally Sustainable Economic Development: Building on Brundtland*, Environment Working Paper 46, The World Bank, Washington, DC, 1991.

Verbruggen, H., R.B. Dellink, R. Gerlach, M.W. Hofkes and H.M.A. Jansen. "Alternative calculations of a sustainable national income for the Netherlands according to Hueting". In *Economic Growth and Valuation of the Environment: A Debate*, edited by J. van der Straaten, H.R.J. Vollebergh and E.C. van Ierland, 17–77, Edward Elgar, Cheltenham, UK, Northampton, MA, 2001.

15

GREEN ACCOUNTING

Balancing environment and economy[1]

Peter Bartelmus

A United Nations report on the post-2015 development agenda aims at "realizing the future we want for all" (United Nations System Task Team 2012). But what is it we all want? Is it maximum well-being or happiness, or is it just meeting our needs, as proclaimed by the popular definition of sustainable development (WCED 1987)? Happiness and development goals are, to a great extent, nonmaterial. They are also hard to define, measure, and implement. It remains to be seen if the extension of eight Millennium Development Goals and 21 targets (United Nations, no date-b) into 17 Sustainable Development Goals and 169 targets (United Nations, no date-a) will produce a more efficient implementation of the international development agenda.[2]

The commonly used national accounts focus therefore narrowly on observable market activities and economic growth. Indicators of sustainable development, well-being, human development, quality of life, or environmental sustainability seek to show that such a focus is misleading. They combine selected concerns and statistics, deemed to be representative of our broader goals in life. All these indicators are proxy measures for something bigger than what the underlying statistics suggest. Their meaning and validity need careful examination before they can be used in policy and decision making. Some indicators give equal weight to unequal issues when calculating averages of, for instance, health, education, or pollution data; other measures apply controversial money values when pricing "priceless" (see Figure 15.1) environmental services like waste disposal or the nonmarket supply of natural resources (Bartelmus 2008).

It is not surprising that national statistical offices are reluctant to include these indicators in their regular data collection programs. Nor is it a surprise that policymakers continue to focus on the economy and its established statistics and accounts. The national accounts provide the standard indicators of economic performance and – over time – economic growth. Gross domestic product (GDP) is just one of many accounting indicators but has been the focus of economic analysis and policy. It is also accused of being a misleading measure of well-being, despite national accountants arguing "against the welfare interpretation of the accounts" (European Commission et al. 2009: 12).

Figure 15.1 Pricing the priceless. A green accounting study (Bartelmus et al. 2003) estimated that in 1990 the environmental costs in West Germany were equal to 60 billion Deutschmark, about 3% of net domestic product

Source: © VisLab/Wuppertal Institute for Climate, Environment and Energy, with permission from the copyright holder

GDP bashing is not the solution

The authors of the popular Genuine Progress Indicator (GPI) – supposedly a measure of national welfare – famously asked: "Why is America down, when GDP is up?" (Cobb et al. 1995). Dismissing GDP out of hand might jump the gun, though:

- GDP was never designed as a measure of human well-being or national welfare. It is simply the total economic value of goods and services produced in a country during one year. The final use of goods and services by households, enterprises, and other countries balances their supply. GDP is thus not only a measure of national output but also of its uses as consumption, capital formation, and net exports (minus imports). As pointed out by the Stiglitz Commission: "GDP is not wrong *as such*, but wrongly used" (Stiglitz et al., no date: 8).
- The worldwide-adopted System of National Accounts (European Commission et al. 2009) defines and measures, among others, economic production, national income, final consumption, capital formation, and international trade. Accounting equations and the use of market prices provide transparent and consistent tools for adding up the results of different economic activities. Showing the results for economic sectors (households, industries, government) makes it possible to assess production and consumption patterns and the distribution of income and wealth.
- GDP bashing might throw out the baby with the bathwater, the baby being the national accounts and GDP the bathwater. There is indeed no other place where standardized measures of economic activities can be found and presented to policymakers in a meaningful

"nutshell". Individuals, corporations, and trade unions can compare information on their economic situation and prospects with those of their own country and other nations.

Seeing that the national accounts will not go away, why not go right into the accounts and adjust them? Policymakers should find it easier to accept a need for reorienting the economy when their main source of information tells them to do so. The price for this is, however, limited coverage: the national accounts include only those issues that can be readily observed, measured, and valued. Adjusting the accounts for environmental impacts may thus include the interaction between the economy and the environment, but excludes less-documented social, cultural, or institutional concerns.

Greening the national accounts

The System of integrated Environmental and Economic Accounting (SEEA) has been designed to assess the environment-economy interaction and to adjust the key economic indicators of GDP, capital, and income (Bartelmus et al. 1991). The 1992 Rio Earth Summit endorsed the original SEEA in its Agenda 21 and asked to implement it as a satellite rather than a replacement of the conventional national accounts; this could be seen as "a first step towards the integration of sustainability into economic management" (United Nations 1994: para. 8.41, 8.43).

The idea is to consider nature and its services to the economy as natural capital. The services of natural capital include, in particular, the provision of raw materials to the economy and the absorption of wastes and pollutants by environmental sinks. This allows treating the depletion of natural resources (e.g., by deforestation, mining, or overfishing) and the degradation of the environment (notably, by pollution) as capital consumption. The objective is to apply the accounting concepts of produced capital (such as roads, buildings, or machines) and capital consumption to natural capital and its depletion and degradation.

Figure 15.2 shows in the dark cells how natural capital and the cost of its consumption can be introduced into the framework of the national accounts. When measuring economic activity, the 1993 SEEA (United Nations 1993) accounts additionally for the costs of hitherto ignored environmental impacts. Measuring the costs of sustainability as capital consumption allows their deduction from *gross* indicators of economic activity, including value added, domestic product, and capital formation. The results are an environmentally adjusted *net* domestic product (EDP) and environmentally adjusted *net* capital formation (ECF).

The SEEA has now been twice revised. The latest 2012 version of the SEEA (United Nations et al. 2014) appears to reject the full adjustment of accounting aggregates, omitting in particular the cost of environmental pollution. Monetizing the impacts of pollution is considered to be a matter of research and experimentation. The SEEA seeks thus to avoid being drawn into the controversial measurement of individual happiness, welfare and welfare-based wealth, the quality of life, or the sustainability of economic growth and development. The SEEA's compatibility with the national accounts should appeal (even in its reduced form) to policymakers who wish to compare the conventionally measured and "greened" performance of the economy.

Accounting for sustainability: a practical step toward redesigning the economy

At the heart of greening the national accounts is measuring the sustainability of economic activity and its use of the natural environment. The purpose of accounting for the costs of both

OPENING STOCKS | Produced assets + Environmental assets

	PRODUCTION *(industries)*	FINAL CONSUMPTION	CHANGES IN CAPITAL STOCKS	CHANGES IN CAPITAL STOCKS	REST OF THE WORLD
SUPPLY OF PRODUCTS	Outputs				Imports
USE OF PRODUCTS	Intermediate consumption	Final consumption	Gross capital formation		Exports
PRODUCED CAPITAL USE	Capital consumption		Capital consumption		
NATURAL CAPITAL USE	Environmental cost (of natural capital consumption)			Natural capital consumption	

+ Other asset changes = Other asset changes

CLOSING STOCKS | Produced assets | Environmental assets

Figure 15.2 Outline of the SEEA. The environmental asset accounts show the stocks and flows of natural capital. They include natural capital consumption and other changes such as natural growth or the effects of natural disasters. Natural capital consumption is also shown as a cost of the use of natural capital. Expenditures for the improvement of natural capital are part of gross capital formation.

Source: Bartelmus (2001), Figure 3, modified, with permission from Eolss Publishers

produced and natural capital consumption is to retain funds for replacing used-up capital goods. Produced and natural capital maintenance is the accounting definition of the sustainability of future production and consumption, in other words, of economic growth.

A global application of the SEEA (Bartelmus 2009) can illustrate the meaning of these adjustments and their results. Data gaps and different cost concepts in the available data make this a rough first study of global sustainability. Global environmental depletion and degradation costs amounted to about three trillion U.S. dollars or 6% of world GDP in 2006. During 1990–2006, the world economy showed similar growth rates for GDP and EDP. For such short time periods, ECF paints a better picture of the *potential* sustainability of economic activity: it indicates the capacity to produce new capital after accounting for the loss of produced and natural capital.

Figure 15.3 shows large differences in the sustainability of economic growth for the world's major regions and countries. Positive ECF in industrialized countries and China shows sustainable economic growth. Negative ECF in developing countries, notably in Africa and Latin America, indicates that these countries have been living off their natural and produced capital base. Overall, the world economy appears to be sustainable, at least in terms of weak economic sustainability.

Weak sustainability maintains the overall monetary value of produced and natural capital. It implies that the different capital categories can be substituted when reinvesting for capital maintenance. This is the reason why some ecological economists prefer physical sustainability measures such as the carrying capacity of territories or the resilience of ecosystems to perturbations. The complexity and large variety of ecosystems make it difficult to apply such "ecological sustainability" at national or international levels (Bartelmus 2013: 25, 30–31).

Produced and natural capital maintenance is a narrow but operational definition of the sustainability of economic growth. It ignores other less tangible human, social, and institutional capital categories. Measurement and conceptual problems – what is capital consumption? – have so far prevented accounting for the loss and replacement of health and skills of human capital, and the networking, social cohesion, and law and order of social/institutional capital. Nonetheless, all these capital categories have been called forth as pillars of sustainable development.

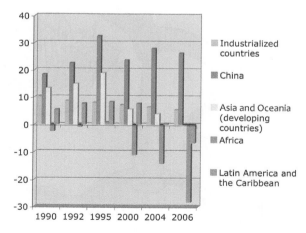

Figure 15.3 Environmentally adjusted net capital formation (ECF, percent of EDP). The world economy and industrialized countries are – weakly – sustainable. The economic performance of most African countries has not been sustainable.

Source: Bartelmus (2009), Figure 4, with permission from Elsevier (*Ecological Economics*)

International organizations use the multiple-pillar argument to explain the connections between sustainable economic growth and development. The United Nations Environment Programme's green-economy report maintains that the "transition to a green economy is to enable economic growth and investment while increasing environmental quality and social inclusiveness" (UNEP 2011: 16). The Rio+20 Earth Summit places the "green economy in the context of sustainable development and poverty eradication" (United Nations 2012: part III). The green growth strategy of the Organisation for Economic Co-operation and Development is more concrete: greened economic growth, which maintains produced and natural capital, cannot replace sustainable development but is deemed to be a measurable subset of such development; both, growth and development, can be enhanced by reducing, reusing, and recycling natural resources and other material flows (OECD 2011, 2015). In all these cases, sustainability, in terms of capital maintenance, looks like the anchor that prevents drifting off into difficult-to-measure realms of well-being or development.

The next step of actually redesigning the economy requires the allocation of the cost of environmental sustainability to those households and enterprises that caused nonsustainability by their environmental impacts. Well-known market instruments such as eco-taxes or limited-pollution permits can prompt economic agents to internalize these costs in their plans and budgets. The purpose is to make them change their environmentally harmful production and consumption styles. Delayed and weak responses might make it necessary to supplement market instruments with governmental rules and regulations. Facing a large variety of sustainability frameworks, and concepts and methods of indicators,[3] further action, beyond the environment-economy interface, has to be left for now to political negotiation.

Integrated environmental-economic accounts can provide the benchmarks for setting the level of market instruments and other tools of sustainability policies. Greening the national accounts could unleash the greening of an economy that finds the balance between economic activity and environmental quality (Figure 15.4).

Figure 15.4 Finding the balance. What are the trade-offs between economic production, consumption, and environmental quality?

Source: Bartelmus (2013), Figure 4, with permission from Arik Bartelmus and the Taylor and Francis Group

Further work

A number of open questions remain, including the following:

- *The valuation of environmental services.* Many stocks of natural resources and most sinks for pollutants are not traded in markets. They do not obtain a market price, and their economic value has to be imputed with the help of different valuation techniques. Contrary to the original SEEA, the latest revision relegates, therefore, environmental degradation – mostly from pollution – and its monetary valuation to future research and experimental ecosystem accounting. Allowing only for the depletion of economic natural resources, which are already part of the national asset accounts, looks like omitting the environment from environmental-economic accounting.[4]
- *Satellite accounts.* Agenda 21 of the 1992 Rio Earth Summit recommended implementing the SEEA "as a complement to, rather than a substitute for, traditional national accounting" (United Nations 1994: para. 8.42). Satellite accounts leave the conventional national accounts untouched, even if they ignore running down economic resource stocks of minerals, timber, or fish. Should the conventional accounts adjust their economic indicators for natural resource depletion? Do we need a satellite of the satellite accounts to include environmental degradation in the SEEA? Will satellite accounts continue to be ignored by policymakers? These are some of the questions which will determine the adoption of the SEEA by the official statistical services of countries.
- *Strong versus weak sustainability.* What is the significance of ignoring critical (i.e., essential and nonsubstitutable) natural capital in weak-sustainability accounting and policy? How can critical capital be identified in the greened physical and monetary national accounts?
- *Corporate accounting.* Corporations have shied away from accounting for the full cost of environmental impacts. Obviously, they prefer showing what they have done for the environment, i.e., their expenses for environmental protection. Can the national environmental-economic accounts serve as a model for corporate accounting? Can such linkage improve corporate social responsibility?
- *Coverage of human, social, and institutional capital.* Capital consumption of these intangible categories is difficult to imagine and even harder to measure. Can nonmonetary indicator sets adequately describe the use of intangible capital? Can these indicators be used for aggregating all capitals into holistic measures of sustainable development, well-being, or happiness? This is an important area of further research. As we all know: noncountables count.

The first 1992 Earth Summit in Rio de Janeiro called for establishing the SEEA in all member states "at the earliest date" (United Nations 1994: para. 8.42). The Johannesburg Summit in 2002 ignored green accounting and encouraged instead further work on indicators of sustainable development. As mentioned, one of the main themes of the Rio+20 Summit was the green economy in the context of sustainable development. Hopefully, this will put comprehensive environmental-economic accounting back on the international agenda of monitoring and implementing sustainable growth and development.

Notes

1 Updated reprint from *Solutions* 3 (2), June 2012, with kind permission by the editor.
2 Reijnders argues in this book (Chapter 20) that the variety of objective and subjective indicators advanced to meet these goals might prevent a definite assessment of sustainability.

3 See the contributions of Joss and Rydin (Chapter 24), and Janoušková, Hák, and Moldan (Chapter 30) to this book.
4 See Bartelmus (2014 and 2015) for a critical evaluation of the SEEA revision and its treatment of environmental degradation cost in "experimental ecosystem accounts".

References

Bartelmus, P. (2001). 'Accounting for sustainability: greening the national accounts', in Tolba, M.K. (ed.) (2001). *Our Fragile World, Challenges and Opportunities for Sustainable Development*, Eolss Publishers, Oxford.
Bartelmus, P. (2008). *Quantitative Eco–nomics: How Sustainable Are Our Economies?*, Springer, Dordrecht.
Bartelmus, P. (2009). 'The cost of natural capital consumption: Accounting for a sustainable world economy', *Ecological Economics* 68: 1850–1857.
Bartelmus, P. (2013). *Sustainability Economics: An Introduction*, Routledge, London and New York.
Bartelmus, P. (2014). 'Environmental-economic accounting, progress and regression in the SEEA revisions', *Review of Income and Wealth* 60: 887–904.
Bartelmus, P. (2015). 'Do we need ecosystem accounts?' *Ecological Economics* 118: 292–298.
Bartelmus, P., Albert, J., and Tschochohei, H. (2003). 'Wie teuer ist uns die Umwelt?' [How much for the environment?], *Zeitschrift für Umweltpolitik & Umweltrecht* 3: 333–370.
Bartelmus, P., Stahmer, C., and van Tongeren, J. (1991). 'Integrated environmental and economic accounting: Framework for a SNA satellite system', *Review of Income and Wealth* 37 (2): 111–148.
Cobb, C., Halstead, T., and Rowe, J. (1995). 'If the GDP is up, why is America down?' *The Atlantic Monthly*, October: 59–78.
European Commission, International Monetary Fund, Organisation for Economic Co-operation and Development, United Nations, and World Bank. (2009). *System of National Accounts 2008*, United Nations, New York. Online: http://unstats.un.org/unsd/nationalaccount/docs/SNA2008.pdf (accessed 9 March 2017).
Organisation for Economic Co-operation and Development (OECD). (2011). *Towards Green Growth*. doi:10.1787/9789264111318-en (accessed 9 March 2017).
Organisation for Economic Co-operation and Development (OECD). (2015). *Material Resources, Productivity and the Environment*. Online: www.oecd.org/environment/waste/material-resources-productivity-and-the-environment-9789264190504-en.htm (accessed 8 March 2017).
Stiglitz, J.E., Sen, A., and Fitoussi, J.-P. (no date). *Report by the Commission on the Measurement of Economic Performance and Social Progress*. Online: www.stat.si/doc/drzstat/Stiglitz%20report.pdf (accessed 9 March 2017).
United Nations. (no date-a). *Sustainable Development Goals*. Online: www.un.org/sustainabledevelopment/sustainable-development-goals/ (accessed 9 March 2017).
United Nations. (no date-b). *We Can End Poverty, Millennium Development Goals and Beyond 2015*. Online: www.un.org/millenniumgoals/ (accessed 9 March 2017).
United Nations. (1993). *Integrated Environmental and Economic Accounting*, United Nations, New York. Online: http://unstats.un.org/unsd/publication/SeriesF/SeriesF_61E.pdf (accessed 9 March 2017).
United Nations. (1994). *Earth Summit, Agenda 21, the United Nations Programme of Action from Rio*, United Nations, New York. Online: www.un.org/esa/sustdev/documents/agenda21/english/Agenda21.pdf (accessed 9 March 2017).
United Nations. (2012). *Resolution Adopted by the General Assembly on 27 July 2012, the Future We Want (A/RES/66/288)*. Online: www.un.org/ga/search/view_doc.asp?symbol=A/RES/66/288&Lang=E (accessed 9 March 2017).
United Nations Environment Programme (UNEP). (2011). *Towards a Green Economy: Pathways to Sustainable Development and Poverty Eradication*. Online: http://web.unep.org/greeneconomy/resources/green-economy-report (accessed 9 March 2017).
United Nations, European Commission, Food and Agriculture Organization of the United Nations, International Monetary Fund, Organisation for Economic Co-operation and Development, and the World Bank. (2014). *System of Environmental-Economic Accounting 2012, Central Framework*, United Nations, New York. Online: http://unstats.un.org/unsd/envaccounting/seeaRev/SEEA_CF_Final_en.pdf (accessed 9 March 2017).

United Nations System Task Team on the Post-2015 UN Development Agenda. (2012). *Realizing the Future We Want for All*, United Nations, New York. Online: www.un.org/millenniumgoals/pdf/Post_2015_UNTTreport.pdf (accessed 9 March 2017).

World Commission on Environment and Development (WCED). (1987). *Our Common Future*, Oxford University Press, Oxford.

16

ECOLOGICAL FOOTPRINT ACCOUNTS

Principles[1]

*Mathis Wackernagel, Alessandro Galli, Laurel Hanscom,
David Lin, Laetitia Mailhes, and Tony Drummond*

Introduction – addressing all demands on nature, from carbon emissions to food and fibres

Through the Paris Climate Agreement, nearly 200 countries agreed to keep global temperature rise to less than 2°C above the pre-industrial level. This goal implies ending fossil fuel use globally well before 2050 (Anderson, 2015; Figueres et al., 2017; Rockström et al., 2017).

The term "net carbon" in the agreement further suggests humanity needs far more than just a transition to clean energy; managing land to support many competing needs also will be crucial. If the human economy moves out of fossil fuel fast and furiously, as staying within a 2°C limit would require demand for substitutes – for instance, forest products for fuel – could place tremendous new pressures on planet Earth if improperly managed (Smeets and Faaij, 2007). The agreement also references "sustainable management of forests" (page 23) to absorb CO_2 and "aims to strengthen the global response to climate change in a manner that does not threaten food production" (page 22). This combination of forces – consumption, deforestation, food production, emissions, and population – stresses more than ever the need for comprehensive resource accounting tools like the Ecological Footprint, which tracks the competing demands on the biosphere.

The carbon Footprint is an important component of the Ecological Footprint. Yet it is one that will vanish if we put the Paris Climate Agreement into practice. The all-encompassing Ecological Footprint helps countries better understand competing needs such as reforestation for carbon sequestration, food, and timber for everything from heat, to furniture, to paper.

Humanity will succeed when we address these competing demands on our planet's ecosystems as a whole, and this is the underlying purpose of the Ecological Footprint accounts.

To this end, this chapter documents and discusses the role of Ecological Footprint accounting. It covers the purpose of the Ecological Footprint accounts, explains their role in sustainability and economic assessments, describes how the robustness and rigour of these accounts are being improved, and reveals the answers to common issues raised about the Footprint in scientific and policy literature.

Ecological Footprint accounting is driven by one key question: *How much of the biosphere's (or any region's) regenerative capacity does any human activity demand?* Or more specifically: How much of the planet's (or a region's) regenerative capacity[2] does a defined activity demand in order to provide all the ecosystem services that are competing for mutually exclusive space?

Such activities could be supporting the consumption metabolism of the humanity, a particular population, a production process, or something as small and discreet as producing 1 kg of durum wheat spaghetti. These services include provision of all the resources that the population or a process consumes and absorption of that population's or process's waste, using prevailing technology and management practice (Wackernagel, 1991; Rees and Wackernagel, 1994; Wackernagel and Rees, 1996; Wackernagel et al., 2002; Wackernagel et al., 2014). The ability of ecosystems to provide for these resources – its renewable capacity – we call "biocapacity".

As financial "profit and loss" statements track both "expenditure" and "income", or as balance sheets document "assets" and "liabilities", Ecological Footprint accounts also have two sides; demand on biocapacity (Footprint) against availability of biocapacity.

The Ecological Footprint emerged as a response to the challenge of sustainable development, which aims at securing human well-being within planetary constraints. By staying within what the planet can provide, one makes sure that biocapacity, the essential ingredient for any value chain, is available now and for future generations. This is what the "planetary boundary" community calls humanity's "safe operating space" (Rockström et al., 2009; Steffen et al., 2015). The underlying objective of Ecological Footprint accounts is to provide motivational, managerial, and monitoring capacity for assessing and dealing with biocapacity and its biophysical constraints.

Keeping humanity's Ecological Footprint within the biocapacity of the planet is a minimum threshold for sustainability. While this threshold can be exceeded for some time, exceeding it leads inevitably to (unsustainable) depletion of nature's stocks. In other words, such depletion can only be maintained temporarily.

Each ecosystem reacts differently to overuse. Forests can be overharvested significantly compared to their renewal rate, because standing stocks of a middle-aged or mature forest can easily be 50 fold of annual growth rates (FAO, 2015). With the Paris declaration that defines an upper global warming limit, the amount of additional carbon that can be added to the atmosphere becomes defined. For example, a calculator by the Mercator Research Institute on Global Commons and Climate Change, based on IPCC's 2014 Synthesis Report, concludes that at current emission rates, the carbon budget for staying within 1.5°C would be eaten up by 2021, using an upper estimate, and generously assuming that non-CO_2 greenhouse gases have no additional impact (which of course they have) (accessed 2017). Overused fisheries also can lead quite rapidly to lower yields as demonstrated for instance by the 1992 cod-fish collapse in Canada (Frank et al., 2011). These examples all underline that, while it is possible to harvest beyond regeneration, this cannot persist.

The Ecological Footprint makes apparent the gap between human demand and regeneration. In its applications, Ecological Footprint accounts typically underestimate human demand as not all aspects are measured, and overestimate biocapacity because it is difficult to measure how much of current yield is enabled by reduced future yield (for instance as in the case of overuse of groundwater, or erosion).

Therefore, Ecological Footprint accounts are metrics that merely define minimal conditions for sustainability. They do not cover all material aspects of sustainability. Ecological Footprint accounts focus on the minimal condition of living within the planet's ecosystem's regenerative capacity.

It is important to note that reducing the human Footprint to "one planet Earth" is still insufficient, since wild species compete for the fruits of the planet's biocapacity as well. E.O. Wilson, in his recent book *Half-Earth*, argues that half of the Earth should be left for wild species "to stave off the mass extinction of species, including our own" (Wilson, 2016, jacket quote, and www.half-earthproject.org/book/).

If the basic condition of human demand staying within the available biocapacity is not met, Ecological Footprint accounting becomes a metric for "unsustainability". Therefore, by providing this bottom-line condition for sustainability, Ecological Footprint accounts provide a foundation upon which many other sustainable development metrics and strategies can be built.

What Ecological Footprints do and how they are measured

When people catch more fish than fishing grounds can regenerate, fisheries eventually collapse; when people harvest more timber than forests can re-grow, they advance deforestation; when people emit more CO_2 than the biosphere can absorb, CO_2 accumulates in the atmosphere and contributes to global warming. The overuse of these and other renewable resources is called "overshoot". Biocapacity is shorthand for biological capacity, which is the ability of any ecosystem – even the whole biosphere – to produce useful ecosystem services for humans. This includes regeneration of biological materials and absorption of wastes generated by humans. Biocapacity is not fixed. It represents the availability of natural, renewable resources and waste absorption services that can be used by humanity in a given year. The abundance and productivity of natural capital changes each year.[3] For instance natural disasters such as forest fires or landslides, or human-induced degradation such as deforestation, soil loss, climatic impacts, or acidification can reduce biocapacity. On the other hand, careful agricultural and forestry management can also magnify biocapacity.

Box 16.1 The two principles underlying Ecological Footprint accounting

Life, including human life, competes for biologically productive areas. These areas represent nature's ability to renew itself. This fundamental capacity ultimately limits the material metabolism of animal species, including humans. We call this renewal capacity "biocapacity".

For instance, the amount of fossil fuel still underground is not the most limiting factor for its use. Rather, what limits fossil fuel use even more is the planet's capacity to absorb its CO_2 emissions. Also, rare elements (key metals/minerals used for industrial purposes) are not in themselves significantly limiting for the human economy. With more energy, deeper mines can be built to access them. The availability of these materials is only limited by the energy availability to concentrate these metals and minerals from more dispersed ores. Energy, in turn, cannot rely on fossil fuel sources, since the absorptive capacity for carbon is limited. While shifting away from fossil fuels could reduce CO_2 absorption needs, it could also potentially add new biocapacity demands elsewhere through the use of different energy sources. All this points to biocapacity as the materially limiting factor.

To map human dependence on biocapacity, Ecological Footprint accounting is based on two basic principles:

1   **Additivity:** Given that human life competes for biologically productive surfaces, these surface areas can be added up. The Ecological Footprint (or Footprint) therefore adds up all human demands on nature that compete for biologically productive space: providing biological resources, accommodating urban infrastructure or absorbing excess carbon from fossil fuel burning. (Surfaces that serve multiple human demands are counted only once.) The Footprint then becomes comparable to the available biologically productive space (biocapacity).

2   **Equivalence:** Since not every biologically productive surface area is of equal productivity, areas are scaled proportionally to their biological productivity. Therefore, the measurement unit for Ecological Footprint accounting, global hectares, are biologically productive hectares with world average productivity.

Both Footprint and biocapacity can be calculated at global, national, local, household, and individual levels.

There is an important debate regarding biocapacity: Are current levels of biocapacity sustainable? Can biocapacity ever reach a maximum, or is there still a lot of room to increase the biocapacity of specific land? As currently measured in national assessments based on the United Nations (UN) data, biocapacity only captures what is reported as being regenerated, not whether this level of bioproductivity – or ability to maintain its level of potential net primary productivity – can be maintained forever. If this level of bioproductivity cannot be maintained, one could consider the biocapacity to be fragile. Within the domain of Ecological Footprint research, "fragility of biocapacity" has not been researched in detail. Such research would provide deeper insight into how much of the currently assumed biocapacity may not last, for instance due to water, energy, or soil constraints. However, a preliminary investigation of this aspect (Moore et al., 2012) has revealed that the world's biocapacity could potentially rise through 2030, peaking at 12.5 billion gha (1.5 gha per capita – assuming the UN's medium population projection) because of the effects of increased availability of land suitable for agriculture (this being a result of the initial effects of climate change). As the climate warms further, soil becomes depleted, groundwater is compromised, land becomes constrained, and agricultural land would with high likelihood be given preference over forests in an attempt to fulfil the food requirements of a growing world population. As a result, world biocapacity could then decrease. One estimate is a drop to 11.7 billion gha in 2050 (1.3 gha per capita), or less if yields drop (Challinor et al., 2014).

Biologically productive regions represent the area, both land and water, that supports significant photosynthetic activity and biomass accumulation that can be utilized by humanity. To achieve sustainable development, it is crucial to have information regarding humanity's demand and material dependence on the biosphere as well as the complementary information: what the biosphere does provide, in any given year. Hence Ecological Footprint accounting compares the actual amount of biological resources produced and the wastes absorbed by the planet in a given year to the total human demand on nature for that year. This demand is defined by the biological resources humans extract and the subsequent waste generated in a given year.

This accounting can be done at any scale, from the resource demand of a single activity or a single individual, to that of a city, country, or the entire world (see "Data for National Footprint Accounts and testing results" section for more detail). Global Footprint Network's most recent national and global accounts – its National Footprint Accounts (Global Footprint Network, 2018) – show that, in 2014 (the most recent year for which UN data is available) humanity continued to be in overshoot,[4] demanding in 2014 over 68 per cent more than what the biosphere renewably provided in that year.

We emphasize that Footprint assessments are accounts, not indices, such as the Environmental Sustainability Index (Global Leaders of Tomorrow Environment Task Force, 2002), or the Dow Jones sustainable development index (www.sustainability-index.com). Accounting is systematically distinct from an index or a composite, which combines various incommensurable elements into a single number. By contrast, accounts start from a clear research question, and they use a common unit as their measurement. Therefore, accounting-based metrics are standardized and readily compared and generalizable. Each unit is comparable if not largely substitutable.[5] Examples include financial accounting, which includes GDP, where dollars are the unit, or greenhouse gas accounts, where the unit is CO_2 equivalents. In the case of Ecological Footprint accounting, the unit is global hectares.[6]

However, composite indices, such as a Mercer Quality of Life Ranking (Mercer, 2016; Mercer, 1994) which compares the liveability of cities, or the World Economic Forum competitiveness measures (WEF, 1974–2018) comparing national economies, company performances as measured by the Dow Jones Sustainable Development Index (2016), Transparency International's corruption perceptions index (Transparency International, 2015) measuring the perceived levels of public sector corruption, or the Environmental Performance Index which rates country status and performance against sustainability target (Dahl, Chapter 3; Dahl, Chapter 23; Esty and Emerson, Chapter 5; Conrad and Cassar, Chapter 19) are a somewhat arbitrary aggregation of diverse indicators into an index, with the indicators being averaged out according to a particular weighing framework. The upside of indices is that they can be as broad as their authors wish and cover various topic areas. The downside is that the results depend on the arbitrary architecture of the index, with assumed or implied trade-offs. In other words, composite indices lack a clear, method-independent research question, a prerequisite for scientific inquiry. In spite of their limited scientific robustness, indices may still serve practical functions. For instance, they can be used as alarm bells, but they cannot be used for determining the quantitative implications of trade-offs. They can also be constructed as proxies for quick or standardized assessments or diagnostics, such as those carried out in psychology or healthcare. They are helpful diagnostic short-cuts once the index is extensively tested in statistically rigorous ways against measureable outcomes. Indices in public policy typically lack the sample size needed for such statistical testing. Short of that, they are not a scientifically reliable diagnostic tool.

The underlying premise of the Footprint accounts is based on the recognition that the ecosystem services required for human activities compete for biologically productive space. Meaning, these areas support processes such as the harvest of rain, provision of nutrients, and capture of sunlight. Then, the Footprint is the sum of all the mutually exclusive areas needed for all the demanded services.

The area demanded is calculated by turning the formula for yield on its head. Since yield is defined as:

$$Yield = \frac{Amount \ per \ year}{Area \ occupied}$$

It follows that

$$Area \ occupied = \frac{Amount \ per \ year}{Yield}$$

Rather than expressing the area results in hectares, each hectare is adjusted for its respective biocapacity. These adjusted hectares are called *global hectares*. These global hectares are defined as biologically productive hectares with world average bioproductivity. They are the standard measurement units for both Ecological Footprint and biocapacity. One global hectare worth of

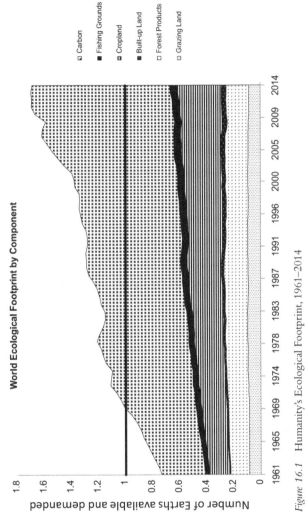

Figure 16.1 Humanity's Ecological Footprint, 1961–2014

Source: Global Footprint Network (2018)

any area is (in theory) able to produce a similar amount of biomass regeneration. It is a "similar" amount, because different hectares across the world do not provide identical kinds and amounts of biomass. Even so, hectares across biomes and vastly different plant communities – from tropical to boreal, from wet to dry – can be compared for productivity of meat, cereals, timber, or carbon sequestration capacity. The intent of the accounts is to base the comparison on the area's potential Net Primary Productivity. Because of data limitations, the national assessments provided by Global Footprint Network's National Footprint Accounts approximate measuring equivalence by using data on differences in agricultural potential as the basis for comparison. More on Net Primary Productivity is discussed below.

This graph shows the ratio between human demand and the Earth's biocapacity, and the components of the human demand, from 1961 to 2013. In other words, the Footprint in this Figure 16.1 is not expressed in global hectares, but in number of planets. It does not imply that biocapacity does not change over time – just that the number of planets available has been constant, even though the planet itself has changed over the time period.

Ecological Footprint accounts attempt to track all competing demands for biologically productive surfaces. These demands include regenerating harvested renewable resources and absorbing wastes generated by human processes, as well as accommodating urban infrastructure and roads.

These simple and visual principles make the Footprint accounts easy to communicate and understand, as for instance also explained in the example of the Ecological Footprint of one person (Box 16.2).

Box 16.2   Calculating the Ecological Footprint of Gérard Depardieu in 6 easy steps

Let's take the case of the actor Gérard Depardieu to illustrate how Footprints are calculated. Say Depardieu's coffee comes from Guatemala, the wheat to feed the chickens that lay his eggs comes from Iowa, and the wool used for his suit is from New Zealand. Thus his Footprint is spread all across the world.

To assess his Footprint, we ask:

1   How much pasture does it take to feed the cows for the dairy and meat he consumes?
2   How large are the fields needed to produce all his beans, cotton, rubber, sugar, cereals – not only for his bread and spaghetti, but also for feeding his share of chickens and pigs?
3   How much ocean area is necessary to produce the fish that he eats?
4   How much land does his home (or portion of it, if he shares his home with others), his garden, and his share of the roads, city squares, and parks occupy?
5   How much forest area is necessary to absorb the CO_2 from fossil fuel he uses – for heating and cooling his homes, producing the goods and services he consumes, driving and flying him around, etc.?
6   How much area is needed for the energy and resources used to provide Gérard's share of social expenditures like hospitals, police forces, government services, educational facilities, and military activities?

To get Gérard Depardieu's Footprint, we first translate all the areas from the above questions into the actual areas needed. Then, we translate actual areas needed into standardized "global hectares" with world average productivity or growing potential (global hectares becomes the common currency). Then we simply add them up. This is the area Depardieu occupies from the beginning to the end of his life. Of course, this area fluctuates over the years, depending on his level of consumption in each year, but also on the efficiency of production in that given year and the changing productivity of the biosphere.

Data for National Footprint Accounts and testing results

National Footprint Accounts use over one billion data points to track the Footprint and bio-capacity of 200 countries from 1961 until today. The input data for the Ecological Footprint comes from a variety of international data sets, predominantly the UN, FAO, and IEA. Therefore, the quality, i.e., accuracy and precision, of the National Footprint Accounts is dependent upon the level of accuracy and availability of these data. The primary inputs are detailed in Appendix 16.2. Of course, both the accuracy and detail of the Footprint results need further development. Global Footprint Network builds on 20 years of methodological development and continues to refine and develop the tool with inputs from its partner organizations and the advisory board.

Most of the methodological improvements are a reflection of better data becoming available. For instance, the 2016 National Footprint Accounts introduced 21 improvements, most signifi-cantly a recalculation of the world average ability of forests to absorb CO_2. The conclusion of this recalculation was that the initial absorption rate of 0.97 t C ha^{-1}yr^{-1} absorption may in light of new data be much lower, possibly as low as 0.73 t C ha^{-1}yr^{-1} (Mancini et al., 2016).

UN data limitations prevent national calculations from capturing all resource flows. Particularly on the waste side, current accounts only include CO_2 emissions from burning fossil fuel as well as energy used for managing waste. Demand on nature, i.e., the Ecological Footprint, is categorized into six different area types: cropland, grazing land, forest products, carbon Footprint, built-up land, and fishing grounds (see Figure 16.1). Biocapacity is categorized by only five categories, since forest land is used both for carbon Footprint and forest products. Forests require long-term protection from harvest in order to be used for effective carbon sequestration. Current national accounts do not distinguish or identify which portions of forests are under such protection.

Ecological Footprint accounts focus on the biosphere's annual resource flows. Fossil fuel deposits (or underground ores) are not considered to be biocapacity. Rather, they are economic assets in the lithosphere. They are similar to gold deposits in the bank's safe, with which the own-ers can buy products and services, such as biocapacity or services thereof. Lithosphere assets are thus included only to the extent that they place a demand on biosphere resources, such as in the process of mining, or when fossil fuels are burned and CO_2 is emitted. Therefore, the effects of oil exploration, refining and final use are directly accounted for.

Climate change is not directly measured by Ecological Footprint accounting. Still, loss (or gain) of biocapacity is tracked by the Footprint from year to year (as long as the input data reflect these changes). Since the accounts only measure outcome, they do not determine whether these changes are directly caused by climate change. However, predictions of climate models can be translated into estimates of biocapacity changes. Annual fluctuation in the biocapacity of coun-tries also indicates higher vulnerability to changing weather patterns.

A number of national government organizations have independently tested and reviewed the accounts. Some of the reviews are presented on Global Footprint Network's website at www.footprintnetwork.org/reviews. Some reviews suggested some methodological improvements. Many of them are now incorporated in the accounting template for all countries.

Unfortunately, underlying statistics do not identify their confidence intervals. This limits the ability to offer confidence intervals for national Ecological Footprint results. Sensitivity analyses can indicate estimated result ranges – but they cannot describe these ranges with statistical probability.

In order to prevent exaggeration of the overuse of the planet's regenerative capacity, the applied accounting method is constructed to be conservative. Therefore, the results of the National Footprint Accounts are most likely an *underestimate* of overshoot.

The approach to rather underestimate, rather than overestimate overshoot strengthens the argument for a significant and rapid reduction of the human economy's resource consumption in order to secure human well-being.

Ecological Footprint and climate change

Ecological Footprint and biocapacity results are also consistent with the 2015 Paris Agreement, which came into effect on November 4, 2016, stipulating that global temperature rise should remain well below 2°C, and possibly even below 1.5°C over pre-industrial levels.

Avoiding an increase over 2°C requires, according to IPCC reviewed climate models, less than 450 ppm CO_{2e} atmospheric concentration. Further, 450 ppm may be on the high side, particularly for Paris's postulated 2°C upper long-term limit. According to IPCC reviewed studies, there is only a 66 per cent probability that we will reach this goal (IPCC, 2014).

In 2017, the atmosphere contained 407 ppm CO_2 (and significantly higher (i.e., >450 ppm) when measured in CO_{2e}). Currently, humanity's emissions increase the CO_2 concentration by 2–3 ppm per year. In other words, humanity has less than 20 years of current emissions left to comply with Paris. Some climate assessments would even suggest that the emissions would have had to cease ten years ago to reach the Paris goal. meaning humanity should have stopped emitting ten years ago. Many conclude that humanity might well need net-negative carbon emissions to reach the Paris goal.

While the carbon assessment defines the maximum carbon we can emit while staying within the temperature goal, Ecological Footprint accounts compare the overall amount that people demand to what can be renewed. Still, both approaches come to similar conclusions, recognizing that the resource metabolism of the human economy has become too large compared to what the planet can provide continuously.

Ecological Footprint accounting complements and strengthens carbon considerations in a number of ways. First, Ecological Footprint accounts confirm Paris reduction requirements without depending on complex, dynamic, and assumption-prone climate models. With basic, widely understood scientific principles (as explained in Box 16.1), the accounts can be audited by anyone with a basic science education.

Second, the accounts support the Paris Agreement's use of net-emissions. The focus on net-emissions recognizes the fundamental link between the atmosphere and the biosphere. It is not only about carbon emissions, but also about how much of the carbon can be sequestered, by biological, technical, or other means.

Third, the focus on biocapacity becomes even more relevant once we acknowledge that fossil fuel will no longer be useable once the carbon budget is exhausted, and what will be left to power the economy is biocapacity, supplemented by energy that is generated on biologically non-productive areas, such as photovoltaics in deserts or windmills off-shore. Further, if humanity should still use fossil fuels beyond the carbon budget, the ensuing climate change would most likely reduce the planet's overall biocapacity, making it even more difficult to power the economy in the long run.

Lastly, by putting the climate challenge into the context of biocapacity, the resource security perspective becomes more obvious, possibly helping to overcome the common misperception that climate change is an inevitable "tragedy of the commons". The argument, that investing into an economy's resource security would be in that economy's self-interest, is still missing in the climate debate.

Ecological Footprint and Planetary Boundaries

The Ecological Footprint research is closely related to the concept of Planetary Boundaries (Rockström et al., 2009; Steffen et al., 2015). In simple terms, Ecological Footprint could be seen as an aggregate of Planetary Boundaries. With one important distinction: Planetary Boundaries are identified as maximum thresholds, the crossing of which would make humanity leave "the (Holocene's) safe operating zone" and bring about destructive, and potentially irreversible changes. In contrast Ecological Footprint measures demand against ecosystem regeneration. This boundary can be transgressed without immediate risks, if the transgression is time-limited and does not lead to irreversible depletion of the assets.

The Planetary Boundaries are set at a precautionary level below the threshold of lasting damage. The choice of the boundary depends on the degree of risk which decision-makers are willing to take on, which, in turn, is influenced by how resilient societies are to major environmental change. According to the authors, "normative judgements influence the definition and the position of planetary boundaries" (Rockström et al., 2009). In other words, the boundaries are also subject to human preferences and cannot be sharply and fully objectively defined. But they can be approximated scientifically.

Both Footprint and Planetary Boundary assessments would be even more useful if they also reflected how long a boundary can be transgressed before a threshold is crossed. Also note that the Planetary Boundaries describe the global situation; the Ecological Footprint is scale independent: it can be applied to any geographic scale.

Conclusion: what Ecological Footprints offer

In essence, Ecological Footprint accounting answers a very simple and fundamental question: How much of the biosphere's (or any region's) regenerative capacity does any human activity demand? Because life competes for biologically productive spaces, it is possible to add those spaces up and compare them with how much productive area is available. Further, by scaling each area proportional to its productivity, it becomes possible to calculate for each activity that requires biologically productive space, what percentage of the planet's biocapacity it occupies. Also, it becomes possible to map how much of the planet's biocapacity is located where or how much of the planet's biocapacity of the planet is located in a defined region.

While simple and transparent, the accounts also come with sophistication for more detailed assessments. More on the calculation methodology underlying Ecological Footprint accounting is available through Global Footprint Network publications, including the *Working Guidebook to the National Footprint Accounts 2016* (based on the 2016 edition) and a method paper (Borucke et al., 2013). In addition to these scientific publications, a summary of the results for the general public is presented in *Living Planet Reports*, published by WWF (the Worldwide Fund for Nature), with support from Global Footprint Network, and the Zoological Society of London (see WWF et al., 2008, 2010, 2012, 2014, 2016). The 2017 Edition of the National Footprint Accounts was launched in April, 2017, and all results that are sufficiently robust are available on an open Data Platform at http://data.footprintnetwork.org.

Each edition is accompanied by a multi-regional input-output (MRIO) analysis, which provides additional insight into the components of the overall Footprint by consumption category, more details on the geography of trade flows, and Footprint intensity per major economic sector. This MRIO analysis is based on the GTAP data set from the University of Purdue, that sheds light on 57 sectors of economies. This analysis allows to construct tables that show which consumption activities are occupying how much of the overall Ecological Footprint. Such analyses allow for more detailed assessments of components of economies.

Further, both carbon calculations and Ecological Footprint accounting make a clear case that a stable human economy requires a significant reduction in resource throughput. Ecological Footprint accounting adds to the discussion the idea that there is a biocapacity budget available to power us – only the carbon Footprint needs to go down to zero.

Yet, such throughput reductions as identified by carbon accounts and Ecological Footprint are in stark contradiction with most policies implemented today. Recognizing this contradiction, as well as the biophysical necessity to avoid staying in overshoot in order to maintain resource availability, Global Footprint Network emphasizes the need to have reliable metrics on resource demand and availability. Therefore, even in the face of current accounting limitations it is highly unlikely that humanity, or any nation, would be better off without any Footprint results. As outlined in Appendix 16.1, currently no other resource accounts exist that can comprehensively compare human demand to planetary regeneration. This makes these accounts an important complement to efforts to provide monetary assessments of the value of natural capital (Bartelmus, Chapter 15; Hueting and de Boer, Chapter 14, this volume).

The basic assessments provided by Ecological Footprint and biocapacity accounts are critical for sustainable development, because not meeting the basic condition of living within the regenerative capacity of planet Earth makes sustainable development impossible. Yet the current Ecological Footprint accounts, which most likely underestimate human demand and exaggerate long-term biocapacity document a significant global overuse of the planet's regenerative capacity. Ignoring this equates to planning for and encouraging economic and societal failure.

Notes

1 This chapter builds on Mathis Wackernagel, Gemma Cranston, Juan Carlos Morales, Alessandro Galli (2014). 'Chapter 24: Ecological Footprint Accounts: From Research Question to Application', Giles Atkinson, Simon Dietz, Eric Neumayer and Matthew Agarwala (eds.), 2014, *Handbook of Sustainable Development: second revised edition*, Edward Elgar Publishing, Cheltenham, UK.
2 The potential of the planet's surface to provide net primary productivity, powered by photosynthesis.
3 Sometimes, results are presented in terms of "number of planets". This is equivalent to showing the ratio between humanity's Footprint and the planet's biocapacity.
4 Ecological overshoot occurs when a population's demand on an ecosystem exceeds the capacity of that ecosystem to regenerate the resources it consumes and to absorb its wastes (see also Catton, 1982).
5 For no accounts are the units totally pure, or universally interchangeable. They are just reasonably good approximations of more or less interchangeable units. For example, one dollar to a low-income person may be worth much more than to a billionaire; yet, the dollar is a good approximation of a comparable unit of purchasing power. Or the last cubic metre of freshwater removed from a dry area is far more damaging than the first, or the last kilogram of fish caught causes more impact on the fish stock than the first kilogram of fish. Also, depending on the species and the respective ecosystem health, the impact of consuming 1 kg of fish can vary by magnitudes. Yet it is a meaningful and scientifically robust research question to inquire: how many kilograms of fish were removed from this lake? This and all other questions based on a commensurable unit can be answered through accounting.

6 A global hectare is a common unit that encompasses the average productivity of all the biologically productive land and sea area in the world in a given year (Galli et al., 2007; Monfreda et al., 2004). Biologically productive areas include cropland, forest and fishing grounds, and do not include deserts, glaciers, and the open ocean.

References

Anderson, K. (2015), 'Duality in climate science', *Nature Geoscience*, **8**, 898–900. doi:10.1038/ngeo2559, Published online 12 October 2015.

Borucke, M., Moore, D., Cranston, G., Gracey, K., Iha, K., Larson, J., Lazarus, E., Morales, J.C., Wackernagel, M., and Galli, A. (2013), 'Accounting for demand and supply of the Biosphere's regenerative capacity: The National Footprint Accounts' underlying methodology and framework', *Ecological Indicators*, **24**, 518–533.

Catton, W.R., Jr. (1982), *Overshoot: The Ecological Basis of Revolutionary Change*, The University of Illinois Press, Urbana, IL.

Challinor, A.J., Watson, J., Lobell, D.B., Howden, S.M., Smith, D.R., and Chhetri, N. (2014), 'A meta-analysis of crop yield under climate change and adaptation', *Nature Climate Change*, **4**, 287–291.

Christensen, V., Walters, C.J., Ahrens, R.N.M., Alder, J., Buszowski, J., Christensen, L.B., Cheung, W.W.L., Dunne, J., Froese, R., Karpouzi, V.S., Kaschner, K., Kearney, K., Lai, S., Lam, V., Palomares, M.L.D., Peters-Mason, A., Piroddi, C., Sarmiento, J.L., Steenbeek, J., Sumaila, R., Watson, R., Zeller, D., and Pauly, D. (2008), *Models of the World's Large Marine Ecosystems: Intergovernmental Oceanographic Commission Technical Series 80*, IOC, UNESCO, Paris, available at: http://unesdoc.unesco.org/images/0017/001792/179240e.pdf (accessed 28 December 2016).

Dow Jones Sustainable Development Index, results of the annual Dow Jones Sustainability Indices (DJSI) review for 2016 released on September 8, 2016, available at: www.sustainability-index.com

Figueres, C., Schellnhuber, H.J., Whiteman, G., Rockström, J., Hobley, A., and Rahmstorf, S. (29 June 2017), 'Three years to safeguard our climate', *Nature*, **546**, 593–595, doi:10.1038/546593a

Fischer-Kowalski, M., Krausmann, F., Giljum, S., Lutter, S., Mayer, A., Bringezu, S., Moriguchi, Y., Schütz, H., Schandl, H., and Weisz, H. (2011), 'Methodology and indicators of economy-wide material flow accounting: State of the art and reliability across sources', *Journal of Industrial Ecology*, **15**(6), 855–876, http://dx.doi.org/10.1111/j.1530-9290.2011.00366.x

Food and Agriculture Organization (FAO) of the United Nations. (2015), *Global Forest Resources Assessment 2015*, Desk reference, FAO, Rome, available at: www.fao.org/3/a-i4808e.pdf

Food and Agriculture Organization (FAO), IIASA (2000), 'Global Agro-Ecological Zones (GAEZ)', available at: www.fao.org/ag/AGL/agll/gaez/index.htm.

Frank, K.T., Petrie, B., Fisher, J.A.D., and Leggett, W.C. (2011), 'Transient dynamics of an altered large marine ecosystem', *Nature*, **477**. doi:10.1038/nature10285

Fritz, S., Hartley, A., Bartholomé, E., and Belward, A. (2004), 'GLC-2000: A new global database for environmental monitoring and resource management', in Veroustraete, F., Bartholomé, E., and Verstraeten, W.W. (eds.), Proceedings of the 2nd International vegetation user conference – 1998–2004: 6 years of operational activities, Office for official publications of the European Communities, Luxembourg, 423–432.

Galli, A., Kitzes, J., Wermer, P., Wackernagel, M., Niccolucci, V., and Tiezzi, E. (2007), 'An exploration of the mathematics behind the Ecological Footprint', *International Journal of Ecodynamics*, **2**(4), 250–257.

Global Footprint Network. (2018), *National Footprint Accounts 2018*, available at: http://data.footprintnetwork. org (accessed 28 April 2018).

Global Footprint Network. (2017), *National Footprint Accounts 2017*, Global Footprint Network, Oakland CA.

Global Leaders of Tomorrow Environment Task Force. (2002), *Environmental Sustainability Index*, World Economic Forum; Yale Center for Environmental Law and Policy, available at: http://sedac.ciesin.columbia.edu/theme/sustainability (accessed 28 December 2016).

Gulland, J.A. (1971), 'The fish resources of the ocean', *Fishing News*, West Byfleet.

Haberl, H., Erb, K.H., Krausmann, F., Gaube, V., Bondeau, A., Plutzar, C., Gingrich, S., Lucht, W., and Fischer-Kowalski, M. (2007), 'Quantifying and mapping the human appropriation of net primary production in earth's terrestrial ecosystems', Proceedings of the National Academy of Sciences, **104**(31), 12942–12947.

Hertwich, E.G. and Peters, G.P. (2009), 'Carbon Footprint of nations: A global, trade-linked analysis', *Environmental Science & Technology*, **43**(16), 6414–6420.

IPCC. (2001), 'Climate Change 2001: The Scientific Basis. Contribution of Working Group I to the Third Assessment Report of the Intergovernmental Panel on Climate Change', Houghton, J.T., Ding, Y., Griggs, D.J., Noguer, M., van der Linden, P.J., Dai, X., Maskell, K., and Johnson, C.A. (eds.), Cambridge University Press, Cambridge, United Kingdom and New York, NY, USA, 881pp.

IPCC. (2006), 'IPCC 2006 Guidelines for National Greenhouse Gas Inventories Volume 4: Agriculture, Forestry, and Other Landuse', OECD, Paris, 475–505.

IPCC. (2014), *Climate Change 2014: Synthesis Report*. Contribution of Working Groups I, II and III to the Fifth Assessment Report of the Intergovernmental Panel on Climate Change [Core Writing Team, R.K. Pachauri and L.A. Meyer (eds.)], IPCC, Geneva, Switzerland, 151 pp., available at: www.ipcc.ch/pdf/assessment-report/ar5/syr/AR5_SYR_FINAL_All_Topics.pdf

Kitzes, J. Galli, A., Bagliani, M., Barrett, J., Dige, G., Ede, S., Erb, K., Giljum, S., Haberl, H., Hails, C., Jolia-Ferrier, L., Jungwirth, S., Lenzen, M., Lewis, K., Loh, J., Marchettini, N., Messinger, H., Milne, K., Moles, R., Monfreda, C., Moran, D., Nakano, K., Pyhälä, A., Rees, W., Simmons, C., Wackernagel, M., Wada, Y., Walsh, C., and Wiedmann, T. (2009), 'A research agenda for improving national Ecological Footprint accounts', *Ecological Economics*, **68**(7), 1991–2007.

Krausmann, F., Erb, K.-H., Gingrich, S., Haberl, H., Bondeau, A., Gaube, V., Lauk, C., Plutzar, C., and Searchinger, T.D. (2013), 'Global human appropriation of net primary production doubled in the 20th century', *PNAS*, **110**(25), 10324–10329, http://dx.doi.org/10.1073/pnas.1211349110.

Mancini, M.S., Galli, A., Niccolucci, V., Lin, D., Bastianoni, S., Wackernagel, M., and Marchettini, N. (2016), 'Ecological Footprint: Refining the carbon Footprint calculation', *Ecological Indicators*, **61**, 390–403.

Mercator Research Institute on Global Commons and Climate Change. (n.d.) *Carbon Clock* made by MMC scientists Alexander Radebach and Tom Schulze, available at: www.mcc-berlin.net/en/research/co2-budget.html (accessed on February 2, 2017)

Mercer, C. (ed.) (1994), *Urban and Regional Quality of Life Indicators*, Institute for Cultural Policy Studies, Brisbane.

Mercer, C. (2016), *2016 Quality of Life Rankings*, available at: www.imercer.com/content/mobility/quality-of-living-city-rankings.html www.mercer.com/newsroom/western-european-cities-top-quality-of-living-ranking-mercer.html?_ga=1.109138885.1371121059.1482973651 (accessed 28 December 2016).

Monfreda, C. (personal communication) (2008), SAGE, University of Wisconsin, Madison.

Monfreda, C., Wackernagel, M., and Deumling, D. (2004), 'Establishing national natural capital accounts based on detailed ecological footprint and biological capacity assessments', *Land Use Policy*, **21**, 231–246.

Moore, D., Galli, A., Cranston, G.R., and Reed, A. (2012), 'Projecting future human demand on the Earth's regenerative capacity', *Ecological Indicators*, **16**, 3–10.

Pauly, D. and Christensen, V. (1995), 'Primary production required to sustain global fisheries', *Nature*, **374**, 255–257.

Rees, W. and Wackernagel, M. (1994), 'Ecological Footprints and appropriated carrying capacity: Measuring the natural capacity requirements of the human economy', in Jansson, A., Hammer, M., Folke, C., and Costanza, R. (eds.), *Investing in Natural Capital*, Island Press, Washington, DC.

Rockström, J., Gaffney, O., Rogelj, J., Meinshausen, M., Nakicenovic, N., and Schellnhuber, H.J., (March 23, 2017). 'A roadmap for rapid decarbonization', *Science*, **355**(6331), 1269–1271. doi: 10.1126/science.aah3443

Rockström, J., Steffen, W., Noone, K., Rerssòn, A., Chappin, F.S.I., Lambin, E., Lenton, T.M., Scheffer, M., Folke, C., Schellnhuber, H.J., Nykvist, B., De Wit, C.A., Hughes, T., Van Der Leeuw, S., Rodhe, H., Sornlin, S., Snyder, P., Constanza, R., Svedin, U., Falkenmark, M., Karberg, L., Corell, R.W., Fabry, V.J., Hansen, J., Walker, B., Liverman, D., Richardson, K., Crutzen, P., and Foley, J. (2009), 'A safe operating space for humanity', *Nature*, **461**, 472–475.

Smeets, E.M.W. and Faaij, A.P.C. (2007), 'Bioenergy potentials from forestry in 2050', *Climatic Change*, **81**: 353–390 (April 2007), doi:10.1007/s10584–10006–19163-x

Steffen, W., Richardson, K., Rockstrom, J., Cornell, S.E., Fetzer, I., Bennett, E.M., Biggs, R., Carpenter, S.R., de Vries, W., de Wit, C.A., Folke, C., Gerten, D., Heinke, J., Mace, G.M., Persson, L.M., Ramanathan, V., Reyers, B., and Sorlin, S. (2015), 'Planetary boundaries: Guiding human development on a changing planet', *Science*, **347**(6223). doi:10.1126/science.1259855

Transparency International. (2015), *Transparency International's Corruption Perceptions Index*, available at: www.transparency.org/cpi2015/

UNECE/FAO (2000), 'Forest resources of Europe, CIS, North America, Australia, Japan and New Zealand: contribution to the global Forest Resources Assessment 2000', Geneva Timber and Forest Study Papers No. 17. New York and Geneva, UN. www.unece.org/trade/timber/fra/pdf/contents.htm

Wackernagel, M. (1991), *Using "Appropriated Carrying Capacity" as an Indicator: Measuring the Sustainability of a Community*. Technical Report to the UBC Task Force on Healthy and Sustainable Communities, Vancouver.

Wackernagel, M., Cranston, G., Carlos M.J., and Galli, A. (2014), 'Chapter 24: Ecological Footprint Accounts: From Research Question to Application', in Atkinson, G., Dietz, S., Neumayer, E., and Agarwala, M. (eds.), *Handbook of Sustainable Development, second revised edition*, Edward Elgar Publishing, Cheltenham, UK.

Wackernagel, M. and Rees, W.E. (1996), *Our Ecological Footprint: Reducing Human Impact on the Earth*, New Society Publishers, Gabriola Island, BC.

Wackernagel, M., Schulz, N.B., Deumling, D., Linares, A.C., Jenkins, M., Kapos, V., Monfreda, C., Loh, J., Myers, N., Norgaard, R., and Randers, J. (2002), 'Tracking the ecological overshoot of the human economy', *Proceedings of the National Academy of Sciences*, **99**, 9266–9271.

Wilson, E.O. (2016), *Half-Earth: Our Planet's Fight for Life*, Liveright Publishing Corporation, New York.

World Economic Forum (WEF). (2018), *The Global Competitiveness Report 2017–2018*, World Economic Forum, Geneva. http://www3.weforum.org/docs/GCR2017-2018/05FullReport/TheGlobalCompetitivenessReport2017%E2%80%932018.pdf (accessed March 5, 2018) [this is an annual report since 1974]

WWF International, Global Footprint Network, ZSL Zoological Society of London. (2008, 2010, 2012, 2014, 2016), *Living Planet Report 2008, 2010, 2014, 2016*, WWF, Gland, Switzerland, available at: http://wwf.panda.org/about_our_earth/all_publications/lpr_2016/ (accessed 28 December 2016).

Appendix 16.1

COMPARING THE FOOTPRINT ACCOUNTS WITH SIMILAR APPROACHES (AFTER GALLI ET AL. 2016)

Concept	Footprint and biocapacity	Planetary Boundaries	Mass flow analysis (also called "material footprint")	Carbon Footprint	WAVES/ Genuine saving	Inclusive wealth	Genuine Progress Indicator (GPI or ISEW)	Human Appropriation of Net Primary Productivity (HANPP)	TEEB
Organizations	Global Footprint Network	Stockholm Resilience Centre	Wuppertal Institute	IEA/IPCC	World Bank	UN University	Herman Daly, John and Cliff Cobb, Redefining Progress, others	Systems Ecology – UNEP Austria	
What research question is being answered?	How much of the regenerative capacity of the biosphere is occupied by human demand? (Plus, where does demand originate, and how is the biocapacity distributed on the planet?)	What are Planetary Boundaries, and for each one of them, how close is humanity to those limits?	How much mass moves through an economy?	How much CO_2 from fossil fuel is released within a country? Also by a lifestyle or activity.	How much net wealth does a country have? How does it change year to year? (focus on natural capital)	How much wealth is in a country? How does it change year to year?	What is the net income of a country, including non-market benefits, and excluding defensive expenditures?	How much net primary production is appropriated by human economies from the ecosystems within their region?	What is the economic value of ecosystem services?

How is this question relevant to understanding a country's (or other entity's) risk and opportunity exposure?	In the 21st century, biocapacity is increasingly a limiting factor for the human economy. It is essential to know how much you have, how much you use, and what the trends are.	Makes a scientific global case for a number of dimensions. Adds credibility to the possibility of global overshoot. May not be easily applicable at local scale. Not clear what trade-offs are among boundaries.	More mass flow is a proxy for the overall amount of resources being used.	Future climate treaties could put a limitation on this emission, through prices, or regulations. To set targets and monitor progress, metrics are needed.	Is overall wealth (measured in monetary value) building up per capita? If not, this is a risk to income generation in the future.	Is overall wealth (measured in monetary value) building up per capita? If not, this is a risk to income generation in the future.	GPI adjusts GDP for aspects that subtract from well-being, and adds those that are missing, making the measure a more realistic assessment of what the true annual income of a nation is.	How intensively are they using their own ecosystems? Higher usages, in combination with high net imports, put countries at risk. High usages could also lead to degradation.	How big are ecological benefits compared to economic benefits? Are there hidden costs that overshadow benefits? Are there both economically and ecologically better options for development?
Metric Unit Key websites	global hectares www.footprint network.org Wackernagel et al. 2014	kg/yr/kg/yr www.stockholm resilience.org Rockström et al. 2009	kg/year www.wupper inst.org www.material flows.net Fischer-Kowalski et al 2011	kg/year www.ipcc.ch Hertwich and Peters, 2009	$ www.wavepart nership.org see website for reports	$ inclusivewealth index.org see website for reports	$ rprogress.org/ sustainability/ indicators/ genuine_progress_ indicator.htm	kg biomass/year www.uni-klu. ac.at/socec/ inhalt/1.htm Krausemann et al. 2013	$/yr www.teebweb. org see website for reports
Strengths	Provides the bottom-line answer to a central question: Is there enough biocapacity to maintain the metabolism of the economy? Area is relatively easy to understand – it is like a farm. Has been tested by 12 national governments.	Each one of the Planetary Boundaries can easily be communicated and are known to most publics. Can build on independent robust scientific assessments in each domain.	Kg easy to understand, directly links to tracked mass flows of categories. Some statistical offices now track mass flows.	There is a scientific effort behind carbon accounting. Public is starting to be more sensitive to basic climate science.	Dollars speak loudly to traditional economic analysts.	Dollars speak loudly to traditional economic analysts.	Dollars speak loudly to traditional economic analysts. GPI relates clearly to GDP, possibly the most prominent policy indicator.	Biophysical assessment.	Powerful case stories. Applicable to business and policy contexts.

Appendix 16.1 (Continued)

Concept	Footprint and biocapacity	Planetary Boundaries	Mass flow analysis (also called "material footprint")	Carbon Footprint	WAVES/ Genuine saving	Inclusive wealth	Genuine Progress Indicator (GPI or ISEW)	Human Appropriation of Net Primary Productivity (HANPP)	TEEB
Weaknesses	Many details could be improved beyond the current accounts that use 6,000 data points per country and year. The accounts, however, are constantly being refined. There is currently no direct link to financial figures, which makes it harder to communicate to finance oriented audiences. However, numbers can be interpreted for them.	Some boundaries are global (CO_2), others are local (water, nitrogen). Difficult to understand trade-offs among them. Difficult to apply at sub-planetary scale.	Mass flow accounts are at the basis of Footprint accounts. But it is less clear what question they answer. One kg of gravel has different demand on nature than one kg of wood. (Apart from weight, in what way are they ecologically equal?) How do mass flows link to supply? Which mass flows are included and which ones not, and why? While having good material statistics is fundamental, result interpretation (or how to use them to guide policy) is not as obvious.	CO_2 in isolation is hard to tackle since self-interest for those reducing their emission is not obvious or may be absent. Just focusing on CO_2 may detract from all other environmental pressures.	Dollars are unstable predictors of the future. Prices can fluctuate by magnitudes. They only show current human preferences in the market, not ecological necessities.	Dollars are unstable predictors of the future. Prices can fluctuate by magnitudes. They only show current human preferences in the market, not ecological necessities. Results are counterintuitive, and suggest that natural capital has extremely low value.	Dollars are unstable predictors of the future. Prices can fluctuate by magnitudes. They only show current human preferences in the market, not ecological necessities, or resource limits. What is added or subtracted from GDP to get GPI can be arbitrary, a problem which could be overcome with clear and widely accepted accounting standards for GPI calculations.	Tool cannot establish clear ecological limits to demand. Does not deal with trade.	Not comprehensive yet. Also mostly based on financial value assessments.

Appendix 16.2

FUNDAMENTAL SOURCES AND DESCRIPTION FOR DATA USED WITHIN THE NATIONAL FOOTPRINT ACCOUNTS

Data set	Source	Description
Production of primary agricultural products	FAO ProdSTAT	Data on physical quantities (tonnes) of primary products produced in each of the considered countries.
Production of crop-based feeds used to feed animals	Feed from general marketed crops data is directly drawn from the SUA/FBS from FAOSTAT. Data on crops grown specifically for fodder is drawn directly from the FAO ProdSTAT	Data on physical quantities (tonnes) of feeds, by type of crops, available to feed livestock
Production of seeds	Data on crops used as seeds is calculated by Global Footprint Network based on data from the FAO ProdSTAT	Data on physical quantities (tonnes) of seed
Import and export of primary agricultural and livestock products	FAO TradeSTAT	Data on physical quantities (tonnes) of products imported and exported by each of the considered countries.
Livestock crop consumption	Calculated by Global Footprint Network based upon the following data sets: • FAO Production for primary Livestock • Haberl et al. (2007). Quantifying and mapping the human appropriation of net primary production in Earth's terrestrial ecosystems.	Data on crop-based feed for livestock (tonnes of dry matter per year), split into different crop categories.
Production, import, and export of primary forestry products	FAO ForeSTAT	Data on physical quantities (tonnes and m³) of products (timber and wood fuel)[a] produced, imported, and exported by each country.

(Continued)

Data set	Source	Description
Production, import, and export of primary fishery products	FAO FishSTAT	Data on physical quantities (tonnes) of marine and inland fish species landed as well as import and export of fish commodities.
Carbon dioxide emissions by sector	International Energy Agency	Data on total amounts of CO_2 emitted by each sector of a country's economy.
Built-up/infrastructure areas	A combination of data sources is used, in the following order of preference: 1. CORINE Land Cover 2. FAO ResourceSTAT 3. Global Agro-Ecological Zones (GAEZ) Model 4. Global Land Cover (GLC) 2000 5. Global Land Use Database from the Center for Sustainability and the Global Environment (SAGE) at University of Wisconsin.	Built-up areas by infrastructure type and country. Except for data drawn from CORINE for European countries, all other data sources only provide total area values.
Cropland yields	FAO ProdSTAT	World average yield for 164 primary crop products.
National yield factors for cropland	Calculated by Global Footprint Network based on cropland yields and country-specific un-harvested percentages.	Country-specific yield factors for cropland.
Grazing land yields	Chad Monfreda (personal communication). (2008), SAGE, University of Wisconsin, Madison.	World average yield for grass production. It represents the average above-ground edible net primary production for grassland available for consumption by ruminants.
Fish yields	Calculated by Global Footprint Network based on several data including: • Sustainable catch value (Gulland, 1971) • Trophic levels of fish species (Christensen et al., 2008) • Data on discard factors, efficiency transfer, and carbon content of fish per tonne wet weight (Pauly and Christensen, 1995).	World average yields for fish species. They are based on the annual marine primary production equivalent.

Data set	Source	Description
Forest yields	World average forest yield calculated by Global Footprint Network based on national Net Annual Increment (NAI) of biomass. NAI data is drawn from two sources: Temperate and Boreal Forest Resource Assessment – TBFRA (UNECE and FAO, 2000). Global Fiber Supply Model – GFSM (FAO, 1998).	World average forest yield. It is based on the forests' Net Annual Increment of biomass. NAI is defined as the average annual volume over a given reference period of gross increment less that of neutral losses on all trees to a minimum diameter of 0 cm (d.b.h.).
Carbon uptake land yield	Calculated by Global Footprint Network based on data on terrestrial carbon sequestration (IPCC, 2006) and the ocean sequestration percentage (IPCC, 2001). Further details can be found in Kitzes et al., (2009, p. 69).	World average carbon uptake capacity. Though different ecosystems have the capacity to sequester CO_2, carbon uptake land is currently assumed to be forest land only by the Ecological Footprint methodology.
Equivalence Factors (EQF)	Calculated by Global Footprint Network based on data on land cover and agricultural suitability. Data on agricultural suitability is obtained from Global Agro-Ecological Zones (GAEZ) (FAO and International Institute for Applied Systems Analysis, 2000). Land cover data drawn from ResourceSTAT.	EQF for crop, grazing, forest and marine land. Based upon the suitability of land as measured by the Global Agro-Ecological Zones model (FAO, 2000).

Note: [a] In Global Footprint Network's national accounts, "wood fuel" is not considered to be a derived product because fuel wood productivity is higher than timber productivity since more of a tree can be used for fuel than for timber. It is treated in a same manner as the primary products in the Footprint calculation. Therefore, it is covered under primary products in the MRIO model.

PART III

Agency experience

17

GOVERNING BY NUMBERS

China, Viet Nam, and Malaysia's adaptation of the Environmental Performance Index

Angel Hsu

Introduction

As environmental problems have grown in number and severity in the past half-century, nations have increasingly strived to implement and evaluate efforts to address these hazards. Information disclosure and data-based approaches to environmental decision-making have led to a proliferation of quantitative tools for assessing environmental policy performance (Tietenberg, 1998; Florini, 2007; Case, 2001, p. 10774; Mol, 2006). The use of indicators has increased, with performance tracking and reporting now "widespread across the public sector in many industrialized and industrializing countries" (Taylor, 2007, p. 341).

Indicators are commonly used to describe real-world outcomes of public policy. As Davis et al. (2012; p. 9) highlight, an indicator, by setting a particular standard, implies a certain normative framing:

> embedded within them [indicators] . . . a much more far-reaching theory – which some might call an "ideology" – of what a good society is, or how governance should ideally be conducted to achieve the best possible approximation of a good society or good policy.

Indicators can provide a scientific basis for political decision-making, enhancing public awareness, informing the conceptual framing of environmental problems, and influencing the processes used to develop solutions (Merry et al., 2015). Many indicators and indices, including the UN Development Programme's Human Development Index, the World Bank's World Governance Indicators, and the UN's Millennium Development Goals, are used to show "good governance" and to inform decisions on aid allocation (Davis et al., 2012). These tools are attractive to policymakers who present indicators as "efficient, consistent, transparent, scientific, and impartial" (Davis et al., 2012). This impartiality is particularly appealing for decision-makers whose legitimacy or power is contested (Porter, 1996).

In East and Southeast Asia the use of indicators in public policy is closely associated with late industrialization and economic development characterized by strong, often authoritarian state power. Centralized state power has largely driven the region's remarkable economic expansion, lending authoritarian regimes legitimacy and entrenching their rule in some countries.

For these regimes to retain power they must maintain "performance legitimacy", which has historically depended upon economic development and rising living standards (Beeson, 2010). Governments in Asia – notably in Taiwan, Hong Kong, and Singapore – have implemented performance measurement systems and Key Performance Indicators (KPIs) largely through top-down initiatives as a way to attract public and media attention to beneficial policy outcomes (Taylor, 2007).

Evidence-based policy evaluation has recently emerged as a new form of environmental political legitimacy in China and other countries in East and Southeast Asia. Wang (2013) asserts that this form of environmental performance legitimacy is distinct from theories of eco authoritarianism, the proponents of which argue that authoritarian governments are superior to democratic regimes in managing the environment. In the new mode, environmental protection is a "tool for delivering on the central components" of a regime's performance legitimacy, which, for China and Southeast Asian governments, rests on continued economic growth and social stability (Wang, 2013). Environmental goals become intertwined in a government's priorities in as much as they help a country attain economic and social goals. Beeson (2010) suggests that the interlinkage of environmental outputs and regime mandates creates an "environmental authoritarianism" that likely entrenches or encourages a return to authoritarian rule.

In China and Viet Nam, environmental issues have become issues of social stability. China's Ministry of Environmental Protection (MEP) 2014 State of Environment Report identified 712 cases of "abrupt environmental incidents", including protests about environmental issues, a 31 percent increase from the previous year (MEP, 2014). Chinese citizens have also increasingly voiced displeasure about environmental issues through official channels – MEP's established complaint hotline registered 38,689 cases in 2015 alone (MEP, 2016). Meanwhile, more than three-quarters of Chinese people surveyed in 2015 described pollution as a "big" or "very big" problem (Gao, 2015). "Air pollution in China", writes Jane Nakano with the Center for Strategic and International Studies, "has turned into a major social problem and its mitigation has become a crucial political challenge for the country's political leadership" (Nakano, 2014). Viet Nam's government faced widespread opposition in 2008 from elites, activists, and environmental scientists when it approved plans for a bauxite mine in cooperation with a Chinese company while foregoing an environmental impact assessment. The plan incited nationwide protest and presented, according to Thayer (2010), a new public challenge to state authority. "For the first time", reports Thayer, "the competency of the government to decide on large-scale development projects was called into question by a broad national coalition of mainstream elites including environmentalists, scientists, economists, social scientists, and retired officials" (Thayer, 2010). In April 2016, tens of millions of fish washed ashore along a 200-km stretch of Viet Nam's central coastline, all killed by toxins illegally released into the ocean by a foreign-owned steel factory. Considered one of the country's worst-ever environmental disasters, the fish-kill sparked lawsuits and protests among Vietnamese citizens, and the social unrest has continued to today, as protesters – mostly fishermen who have not been compensated – clashed with police as recently as February 2017. Illustrating a new and potent source of unrest, these cases exemplify the convergence of environmental degradation, economic development, and performance legitimacy in many East Asian nations.

In the new paradigm of environmental performance legitimacy, governments often develop data-driven policy tools to demonstrate environmental achievement. In this chapter, I examine the cases of China, Malaysia, and Viet Nam – three Asian countries that have adapted the Environmental Performance Index (EPI) as a mechanism to guide subnational environmental policy. The EPI, jointly developed by Yale and Columbia Universities, is among the longest-standing environmental country rankings, since its initial iteration as the Environmental Sustainability Index (ESI) in 2000 (YCELP and CIESIN, 2000). Why have these three countries decided to develop subnational EPIs and for what policy aims? This chapter will focus on the motivations, policy rationale, and practical challenges in each case. I aim to identify motivations and underlying themes that explain why these countries have chosen to use the global EPI framework to measure and track subnational environmental implementation. And I discuss how these cases speak to the broad use of environmental indicators and ranking systems in real-world contexts.

The Environmental Performance Index (EPI)

Created in 2006, the Environmental Performance Index (EPI) (in this volume see also Esty and Emerson, Chapter 5 for a detailed history of the EPI and Conrad and Cassar, Chapter 19 for a critique of the EPI) is a biennial ranking of national environmental performance produced by Yale and Columbia Universities in partnership with the World Economic Forum (WEF) – the EPI's results are announced at WEF's Annual Meeting in Davos. A composite index, the EPI features 20 indicators among nine policy issues, ranging from air and water quality to fisheries and forestry management (Figure 17.1). These indicators and policy issues are grouped into two overarching policy objectives: reducing human-health hazards from environmental pollution and harm; and natural resource management. The 2016 EPI includes 180 countries, representing 99 percent of the global population, 98 percent of global GDP, and 97 percent of global land area (Hsu et al., 2016).

Targets are identified either through international treaties or Conventions (e.g., the Convention on Biological Diversity or CBD establishes national protected area targets for terrestrial and marine habitats) or scientific thresholds (e.g., the World Health Organization has identified an average exposure to fine particulate matter limit). The application of a universal set of targets to gauge national environmental performance allows for easy comparison as raw data are consistently transformed on a scale of 0 to 100, with 0 representing a low performance benchmark or worst performer and 100 the best performer or countries that achieve the defined policy target (refer to Hsu et al., 2016 for full methodological details).

Scholars have referred to the EPI as the "most ambitious effort to measure national environmental performance" (Fiorino, 2011). The EPI has inspired the creation of similar indices for ocean health (The Ocean Health Index) and gender and environment (IUCN's Gender and Environment Index) among others. Several countries have adopted the EPI framework according to national priorities and developed indicators and datasets to evaluate environmental performance at the subnational scale. Besides the three countries discussed in this chapter, Abu Dhabi in the United Arab Emirates, the Basque Country – contested region in Spain – and several other nations and subnational jurisdictions have conducted EPI studies.

Subnational EPIs in China, Malaysia, and Viet Nam

China

China's meteoric economic growth since market reforms began in 1978 has come with severe environmental costs. The country is today the world's largest energy consumer and emitter of greenhouse gases, and air pollution in its cities regularly exceeds the World Health Organization's

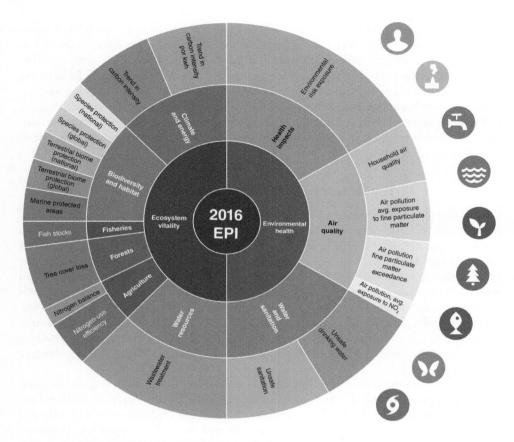

Figure 17.1   The 2016 Environmental Performance Index framework

Source: Hsu et al. (2016)

recommended safe thresholds (Greenpeace, 2015). China's Ministry of Environmental Protection (MEP), in its 2015 State of the Environment Report, found 60 percent of water sources unfit for human consumption (MEP, 2015).

Since 1953, China's government has used five-year plans to lay out blueprints and establish targets for the country's social and economic development. The plans are "key indicators of the directions and changes in development philosophy" of the state and ruling Chinese Communist Party (CCP) (Fan, 2006) and lay out broad guiding principles for society (e.g., *shengtai wenmin* or ecological civilization, a principle outgoing Party Secretary Hu Jintao introduced at the 17th National People's Congress meeting in 2007) as well as specific targets for various aspects of growth and development. Beginning with the 10th Five-Year Plan (2001–2005), the plans have included an increasing number of environment and energy-related indicators and targets. The 12th Five-Year Plan – referred to as the "greenest" five-year plan to date due to the number of energy and environment-related targets included (Seligsohn and Hsu, 2011) – for the first time made these metrics mandatory (*yueshuxing zhibiao*) and deemphasized aspirational economic growth targets (*yuqixing zhibiao*). Environment and energy targets were also added to local leaders' performance evaluation systems to elevate their importance in promotion and review processes (Hsu, 2013). China's 13th Five-Year Plan (2016–2020) further ingrained the country's burgeoning environmental ethic in its national development outlook. This most recent Plan sets a limit on China's total energy consumption, a first, and broadens the government's pollution concerns beyond air, setting goals to improve water and soil quality.

Recognizing the environmental toll of China's relatively unfettered industrialization and economic growth, the Chinese Academy for Environmental Planning (CAEP) in 2004 began an exercise called "Green GDP" to calculate the economic cost of China's pollution. The Green GDP results were not released due to opposition from some provincial leaders who did not want to be identified for sub-par performance and thus held responsible for the country's environmental hazards (Li, 2007; Liu and Ansfield, 2008). Government officials have considered reviving Green GDP calculations, particularly in response to President Xi Jinping's urging of alternative progress measures to GDP (Wang, 2016; Liu, 2015), and amidst a global movement to "green" national accounts – to consider natural resources and environmental goods as assets on government balance sheets (Bartelmus, Chapter 15, this volume). Yet an official Green GDP calculation has not been released to date.

Seeking alternatives to the Green GDP, a team of researchers at Yale University, Columbia University, City University of Hong Kong, and the CAEP in 2008 evaluated the feasibility of building a provincial Environmental Performance Index in China based on the global EPI framework. Some of the very same provincial leaders in China who had opposed the Green GDP's release were invited to a series of stakeholder workshops held between September 2008 and June 2009 to provide input on the index framework design and indicator selection. This stakeholder outreach made the index development process transparent and inclusive, and researchers hoped that by garnering buy-in from provincial officials the subnational EPI would avoid the Green GDP's fate (Hsu et al., 2012).

Data transparency and availability proved to be insurmountable challenges for implementing the provincial China EPI. Raw data, particularly on air and water quality, was inaccessible and considered too politically sensitive for public release. Information about public environmental health and many ecosystem-related indicators, including surface water and soil quality, were also unavailable. International researchers were unable to independently verify any of the official statistics provided by CAEP, calling into question the veracity of calculated indicators. CAEP also expressed reservations about utilizing data other than officially reported (but unverifiable) statistics and did not wish to use satellite data to create proxy indicators for air quality, which were presented in the final report only as a research exercise (YCELP and CIESIN, 2011). In 2011, the researchers concluded that poor data availability and transparency prevented the construction of a robust environmental index at the provincial level (Hsu et al., 2012). The international team never completed a comprehensive provincial-level EPI in China.

Researchers at CAEP, Nanjing University, Nankai University, and the Chinese University of Hong Kong have continued, since 2011, to develop a provincial EPI for China independent of Yale and Columbia universities. The first iteration of the report was published in April 2016 and evaluated provincial environmental performance from 2006 to 2010. The index included 47 indicators derived from China's Statistical Yearbook, which is produced annually and is publicly accessible (Figure 17.2). The initial report was opened for public comment from China's 31 provinces, with comments collected through the MEP's Department of Policies, Laws, and Regulations. The public can view and interact with the

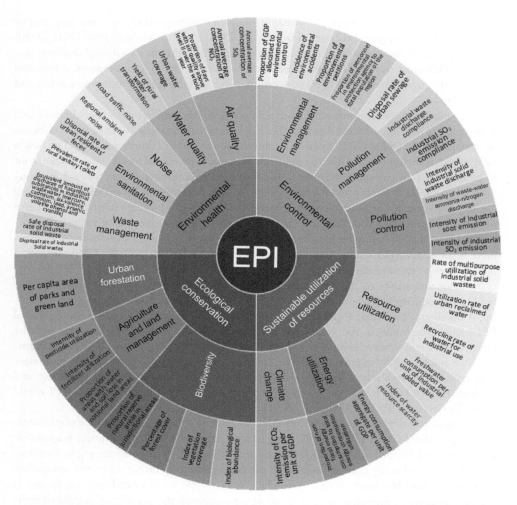

Figure 17.2 The China EPI indicator framework with 39 indicators; the more recent report increased the number of indicators to a total of 47

Source: Adapted and translated from CAEP's China EPI

report's data and indicators via a new website, demonstrating CAEP's commitment to make the information accessible.[1] A second version including data from 2004 to 2013 is under development. Lead author Dong Zhanfeng, a researcher at CAEP, says he hopes the China EPI will facilitate policy decisions and inform the Chinese public on the progression and shortfalls of regional environmental management. The ranking will help regional governments understand their performance relative to their neighbors and other subnational jurisdictions in China. The provincial EPI also provides constructive recommendations to local governments to help them achieve environmental policy targets proposed in China's 13th Five-Year Plan (2016–2020) (Yan, 2016).

Malaysia

Rich in natural resources, including tin, timber, and the arable land left by forestry operations, Malaysia built its economy in the 20th century on resource extraction. The country's extraordinary forests were razed for timber, agricultural development, and human settlements in the early 1900s and the clearing intensified in intermittent spurts throughout the century. Malaysian states at times derived an average of one- to two-thirds of their budgets solely from timber. The Federal Land Development Authority (FELDA), formed in 1956 with the mission to eradicate poverty through oil palm and rubber development, carried out the vast majority of deforestation, logging 3.4 million hectares of forest in Peninsular Malaysian by 1977 (Hezri and Nordin Hasan, 2006).

Beginning in the 1970s, Malaysia's economic structure shifted from resource extraction and agriculture to manufacturing-based output, although this shift occurred primarily in Peninsular Malaysia, not in Sabah and Sarawak, Malaysia's two states in Borneo. The country's manufacturing sector's share of GDP grew from 14% in 1970 to more than 31% in 1994 (Hezri and Nordin Hasan, 2006). The service sector, meanwhile, has steadily expanded its share of Malaysia's economy and now accounts for more than half of its GDP (World Bank, 2017). The country's economic maturation has coincided with rapid urban expansion. Between 1970 and 2000, the urban population quadrupled, and today more than three out of five Malaysians live in urban areas (Hezri and Nordin Hasan, 2006). Malaysia's rapid urbanization and its transformation from an economy based solely on natural resource extraction and agriculture to a broader sectoral mix including industrial manufacturing and services has brought with it a shifting landscape of environmental destruction and degradation. Ecological loss and hydrological disruptions associated with land clearing are now compounded by acute air, soil, and water contamination as unmitigated development diminishes biodiversity and threatens human health.

Malaysia has a long history of environmental governance extending back to the 19th century and British colonial rule, yet its environmental laws historically aimed to promote the "wise use" and "sustainable yield" of resources, and have not sought environmental protection (Sani, 1993). These regulations, like the 1935 Forests Enactment and 1965 National Land Code, are fragmented and generally inconsistent with one another. The country's federal system – the only one of its kind in Southeast Asia – complicates national efforts at environmental management, as Malaysia's Constitution gives each state control over its land use (Hezri and Nordin Hasan, 2006).

In the past two decades, however, Malaysia's environmental laws have improved and an awareness of the need for national sustainability measures has taken root. The country's economic and geopolitical openness have helped spur its environmental awakening. Foreign states have influenced Malaysia's environmental governance and sustainable development planning to a greater degree than they have in China and Viet Nam. Beginning in 1994, the Danish Cooperation for Environment and Development (DANCED), for instance, helped improve Malaysia's environmental planning and policy processes, instilling a culture of government and civil society connectedness through government-to-government intervention (Hezri and Nordin Hasan, 2006).

Despite improvements in Malaysia's environmental governance, the country has continued to develop forested lands for agricultural uses – mostly palm oil production – at a rate that many international groups have decried as unsustainable (Pak, 2015). The nation's greenhouse gas emissions have reached record levels, hitting 433 million tons carbon dioxide equivalent in 2012, largely driven by forest conversion to palm oil plantations (WRI, 2017). Malaysia's struggle to balance industrial and agricultural development, resource exploitation, and economic restructuring with sustainability commitments, urbanization, and human health concerns has created demand from both government and civil society for new tools to measure and manage the country's environment.

Seeing their ranking drop in the global EPI, from 9th out of 133 countries in 2006 to 26th out of 149 in 2008 to 54th out of 163 in 2010, Malaysia's government sought to understand the underlying causes for the drop and to improve subnational performance (Hawkins, 2014). The government recognized granular data were needed to determine the root of their country's worsening performance in the global EPI. In 2010, the Ministry of Natural Resources and the Environment (NRE) approached the University of Teknologi – Malaysia (UTM), asking researchers there to develop a state-level EPI for the country. The state-level EPI would have several major goals: to highlight environmental problems and identify high-priority issues; to track pollution control and natural resource management trends at the local and national levels; to identify best practice policies that achieve positive environmental results; to weed out ineffective efforts from which resources can be reallocated; to develop baselines for inter-state performance comparison; to facilitate benchmarking; and to spotlight linkages between environmental policies and co-benefits, including public health and resource efficiency (NRE and UTM, 2014).

The development of better environmental decision-making tools available to policymakers was another key impetus for creating a provincial EPI in Malaysia. Prior to the Malaysia EPI, Rahmalan bin Ahamad, professor at UTM and the director of the Malaysia EPI, said,

> the Air Pollution Index (API) and Water Quality Index (WQI) were the only indicators established to provide decision making tools for immediate and medium term response to environmental concerns. Since both the API and WQI are limited in scope, the EPI represents a more comprehensive reporting system that provides a decision making tool for medium and long term policy implementation at the federal, state and local government levels.
>
> (Hawkins, 2014)

Like the provincial China EPI feasibility study, Malaysia elected to add socioeconomic sustainability as a third objective to its state-level EPI in order to capture resource use efficiency and governance indicators, including environmental awareness and behavior. The authors also included indicators on waste management, urban green space, and food safety – all innovations on the global EPI framework.

After the 2010 pilot assessment was completed, the Malaysia EPI team set out to calculate the country's subnational EPI. In 2012 the group released a pilot version of the Malaysia EPI (MyEPI[2]) and in 2014 released a second version comparing that year's results at both a subnational and national scale. MyEPI finds a small overall improvement nationally from 2012 to 2014, reporting an index score of 71.8 out of 100 in 2014, up from 68.8 in 2012. The project assessed 16 Malaysian states using 33 measures, finding overall improvements in the country's environmental burden of disease, agriculture and land use, resource efficiency, and environmental governance categories. The 2014 MyEPI introduced a star-rating system – subindicators that divide Malaysian states into five color-coded categories, with corresponding star ratings, according to each state's index score. Most states achieved a three-star rating, corresponding to EPI scores of 60.0–79.9, and were assigned a yellow color code. One state, Pahang, earned a five-star rating in the socioeconomic sustainability category and was coded blue (Hsu, 2015). Malaysia's state-level sub-indicators exemplifies how nations strive to specialize the EPI to their particular governance systems. In this case, MyEPI uses an easy-to-understand ranking of states to highlight best and worst actors and spur competition among its subnational jurisdictions.

The 2012 and 2014 MyEPI launch events included state-level government officials and members of more than 50 national ministries and departments who oversee data collection and monitoring for particular environmental issues. This stakeholder buy-in and partnership has been key to MyEPI's successful development, yet members of MyEPI have pointed to the difficult challenges local leaders face trying to implement policies to improve performance (Hsu, 2015). Local leaders seek policies that can be adopted to address weak spots identified through the MyEPI and similar metric systems, yet time lags in data collection, policy monitoring, and evaluation, and the geophysical nature of many environmental issues prevent real-time diagnosis and policy learning. MyEPI metrics helps local leaders identify areas of needed improvement, but the onus is on these leaders to create policies and management programs to address pressing issues. Local officials often face political and financial constraints that hinder their ability to implement solutions to environmental problems, even when MyEPI makes the hazards known to the government and public.

Viet Nam

Viet Nam's real GDP has grown 5 to 9 percent annually for more than two decades, propelling the country from abject poverty to a modern economy. Dubbed the fifth Asian Tiger, Viet Nam is today a global industrial hub with competitive labor rates in textile and electronics markets. The nation's GDP per capita has quadrupled since 1985 – growth accompanied by improvements in the quality of life for many of the country's nearly 90 million people. Concurrent with this period of economic expansion, Viet Nam has experienced rapid urbanization clustered in the country's two urban cores: Hanoi in the north and Ho Chi Minh City in the south (World Bank, 2012).

This economic and industrial development has, however, come at a cost. Industrialization and increased consumption have degraded environmental quality in Viet Nam, diminishing some of the nation's gains in quality of life. In the global EPI, Viet Nam's ranking has hovered just above the lowest quartile. In 2006 it ranked 99th out of 133 countries and most recently 131st out of 180 countries in the 2016 EPI. Nearly half the country's people are exposed to unsafe levels of air pollution, toxins released into the atmosphere mostly by factories, power plants, and motorized vehicles (Hsu et al., 2016; Wai et al., 2017). Poorly planned urban development and industrial activities have also negatively impacted biodiversity, wildlife habitat, and Viet Nam's forests.

Viet Nam's societal trends in the last three decades – economic growth, industrialization, urbanization, and environmental degradation – have corresponded with shifts in policy and governance. Beginning with the Đổi Mới Policy in 1986, Viet Nam has moved from a communist economy to what the government has called a "socialist-oriented market economy" (Quitzow, Bär, and Jacob, 2013). As the government loosened restrictions on private ownership and opened trade with the West, environmental risk entered mainstream policy discussions. Following the 1985 National Conservation Strategy, which was never officially adopted, Viet Nam's leadership announced its National Plan for Environment and Sustainable Development in 1991. This policy set legislative goals and established Viet Nam's National Environment Protection Agency, followed soon after by the creation of the Ministry of Science, Technology and Environment (MOSTE) (changed in 2002 to the Ministry of Natural Resources and Environment [MONRE]) and the Vietnamese Environment Agency (VEA) (now the Vietnam Environment Administration). In 1993 the National Law on Environmental Protection was passed, and several other laws were enacted in the following years designed to protect and regulate various natural resources including the country's land, water, minerals, and forests (Quitzow, Bär, and Jacob, 2013).

Despite transitioning to a market-driven economic model, Viet Nam's government has never relinquished its centralized command-and-control system of governance. Many of the environmental laws of the 1990s claimed overlapping and contradictory authority and went largely unenforced (Mitchell, 2006). Friction between the VEA and local Departments of Natural Resources and Environment (DONRE), which are accountable to local People's Committees whose goals are primarily economic development, erodes the government's already weak capacity for enforcement of environmental regulations (World Bank, 2008). In the past decade, however, Viet Nam's government has shown itself increasingly responsive to societal pressures, reacting to the country's environmental crises and legislative shortcomings with efforts to enhance institutional capacity, transparency, and performance accountability.

The government revised the Law of Environmental Protection in 2005, broadening the law's scope and strengthening the country's environmental legal framework. The revised law also created specific policy instruments, a structure for environmental impact assessment, and an environmental protection fund (Quitzow, Bär, and Jacob, 2013). Viet Nam's institutional capacity to enforce environmental laws and standards is limited by its sparse environmental monitoring. The country first created a national environmental quality monitoring system in 1995, yet publicly available environmental data remains meager more than 20 years later. Incidental, place-based sampling and monitoring is the main source of environmental information in Viet Nam (Mol, 2009).

Formal civil society is a weak institution in Viet Nam due to sustained government efforts to stifle public criticism and dissent (Abuza, 2015). Yet citizen participation influences government decision-making in Viet Nam, as it has for decades (Nguyen, Le, Tran, and Bryant, 2015) (Coe, 2015). The country's economic growth and urbanization have complicated civic involvement, as capital interests are, for the first time, able to crowd out the voices of people in a society where wealth inequality has become a concern. Nonetheless, the internet has democratized information in Viet Nam to a greater degree than in China, and the potential for environmental data dissemination has never been greater (Nguyen, Le, Tran, and Bryant, 2015).

Although environmental protection strategy, policy, and law is formulated at the national level, implementation is allocated to Viet Nam's provincial governments. There are few robust environmental performance metrics at this level, according to the UN Development Programme (UNDP) (UNDP, 2014). The country's national reporting requirements are not sufficiently detailed to allow for comparisons between provinces, which would foster competition among local officials to improve environmental performance. A 2010 Environmental Assessment Report undertaken by the Institute on Policy and Strategy (ISPONRE), a government-sponsored research institute, in consultation with a number of stakeholders and government agencies, identified seven major environmental concerns for Viet Nam, including inland surface water pollution, urban air pollution, forest degradation, biodiversity loss, climate change impacts, solid waste management, and land degradation (UNDP, 2014). The government developed a set of indicators to assess these issues at the national level, yet the UNDP determined that the indicators were not detailed enough to inform local authorities' agendas and resource allocation for environmental policies. This gap prompted the UNDP to initiate a feasibility study to scope a provincial-level EPI that would help inspire a competitive "green race" among Viet Nam's provinces. The UNDP's Public Administration Performance Index (PAPI), a joint effort initiated in 2009 with the Center for Community Support and Development Studies and several other institutions, had spurred a similar "green race". PAPI reflects input and feedback from nearly 75,000 citizens in Viet Nam and was met with strong support from civil society and various government institutions in Viet Nam that welcomed the index as a tool to measure the performance of public administration officials and governance at the provincial level (UNDP, 2012). Another major impetus in Viet Nam's decision to adapt the EPI was the inclusion of an "Environmental Sustainability Index", modeled after the EPI, as an indicator in its National Statistical Indicators System (NSIS). With the Prime Minister's adoption of Decision Number 43/2010/QD-TTg in June 2010, the NSIS was established to include 24 environmental indicators, one of which was modeled after the ESI (UNDP, 2015).

UNDP commissioned the Yale EPI team in 2014 to partner with ISPONRE and a group of local consultants to produce a feasibility study for a provincial EPI in Viet Nam. The study included the development of an indicator framework (Figure 17.3) formed in consultation with ISPONRE and other external stakeholders; a data gap analysis whereby provincial-level data for each indicator issue was determined; and preliminary calculation of indicators where complete data were available in all of Viet Nam's 64 provinces (e.g., only forestry, access to water, and access to sanitation) (Hsu and Zomer, 2015). The feasibility study found that the major barrier preventing Viet Nam's government from developing and implementing a provincial EPI was data availability. Data for only three out of the 18 indicators identified in the framework were available at the provincial level. Data availability was identified as the major obstacle preventing the Viet Nam EPI's calculation, so Hsu and Zomer (2015) made several recommendations for how these gaps could be remedied, including the use of satellite-derived proxies for air pollution exposure and forest cover.

Since the feasibility study was completed, Viet Nam has worked closely with the Malaysia EPI team to create proxy datasets in lieu of reported data, with the aim of piloting a provincial EPI. From late 2016 to June 2017, the Universiti Teknologi Malaysia (UTM), which comprises the Malaysia EPI team, worked with UNDP Viet Nam and local partners to construct a pilot Viet Nam provincial index. Due to limited data availability, the pilot Viet Nam EPI assesses performance in only three policy categories and five indicators: Population-weighted average fine particulate concentration ($PM_{2.5}$), Population-weighted average nitrogen dioxide (NO_2) concentration for Air Quality (Impacts on Human Health), Forest cover and Tree cover loss in the Forestry category, and a Water Quality Index that combined data for several water pollutants to assess the Water-Ecosystems category. These indicators were selected based on data availability and weighted evenly (e.g., each indicator within the three policy categories comprised 50 percent of a province's score, with the Water Quality Index comprising 100 percent; while each of the three policy categories comprised one-third of a province's score) to produce the pilot Viet Nam EPI score (Wai et al., 2017).

Viet Nam's provincial EPI's initial results reveal that most provinces perform poorly. The Viet Nam EPI utilized the same star-rating system employed in the Malaysia EPI, with the following distinctions on a scale from 0 to 100 for proximity-to-target (PTT) scores: Excellent ($90.0 \leq PTT \leq 100.0$), Good ($80.0 \leq PTT < 90.0$), Fair ($60.0 \leq PTT < 80.0$), Poor ($40.0 \leq PTT < 60.0$), and Very Poor ($0 \leq PTT < 40.0$). Only five provinces (Tra Vinh, Dong Thap, Can Tho, An Giang, and Dak Lak) achieved an Excellent score; while most provinces (32 out of 64) had a score of Fair, and 17 provinces received a Poor rating with a score of 60 and below. The pilot effort found regional differences, with provinces located in the country's Central Highlands (no provinces received a score lower than 73) and Mekong Delta (four out of five provinces in this region achieved an Excellent rating) regions performing better than other regions (Wai et al., 2017). UTM identified the lack of industrialization and emphasis on agricultural activities as primary reasons for these regions' high performance. The authors observed poorer performance

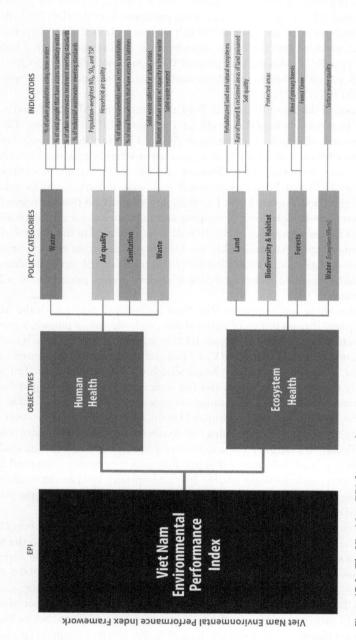

Figure 17.3 The Viet Nam EPI framework

Source: Hsu and Zomer (2015)

in provinces in the Red River Delta Region, including worst-performer Hung Yen, due to these provinces' heavy industrial activity and manufacturing.

The forestry category stands out as one where provinces in Viet Nam generally perform well. In 1943 approximately 43 percent of Viet Nam's total land area was forested, but heavy deforestation due to agricultural land conversion, poor forest management, and overexploitation resulted in forest coverage rates of only 10 to 12 percent during the 1990s (Nguyen et al., 2010). In Viet Nam pilot EPI, many provinces have demonstrated their ability to dramatically increase forest cover based on targets set by the national governments. Dong Thap and Thai Binh provinces, for instance, have been able to increase their forest cover by more than 400 percent, although in both cases the overall starting hectares of forest were modest (11.50 and 1.40 hectares, respectively).

Discussion

China, Malaysia, and Viet Nam's adoption of the global EPI framework is indicative of several trends that have key implications for other developing countries. First, these national EPIs exemplify a broad governance shift towards the use of data-driven tools for environmental management. Technological innovation has, in recent decades, created vast flows and repositories of information – including data on environmental characteristics of all kinds, behavioral trends of individuals and societies, and effects from policies tracked over time. Following the private sector's lead, governments are more and more using contemporaneous information to guide policy creation and evaluation (Keegan, 2015). Second, a common motivation in each case is the need for better tools to gauge subnational policy implementation, as states and provinces are primarily responsible for executing national policy directives. Officials from the three focal countries all pointed to a lack of subnational metrics needed to evaluate and compare local environmental policy achievements as a primary reason for adapting the global EPI. Third, the countries explored in this chapter all recognize the value of aligning internal policy with international movements.

The three focal countries faced many challenges in constructing their subnational EPIs – accurately assessing policy performance is challenging even in data rich countries. The dearth of subnational data in each case, a problem most severe in Viet Nam, has proved to be a stumbling block in realizing the EPI's full potential for these nations. China and Viet Nam are deemed by scholars as "information-poor" environments, characterized as countries in which information and informational processes are marginalized or suppressed for a variety of reasons ranging from economic, political, institutional, or cultural-ideological constraints (Mol, 2009). China and Viet Nam, according to Mol (2009), exhibit at least three of these information-poor environmental typologies: economic constraints that limit the capacity to invest in environmental monitoring – an issue clearly seen in the case of Viet Nam's sparse air quality monitoring network; political restrictions on the free flow of information, which is pronounced in the Chinese government's restriction and censorship of information and cordoning off of data deemed for "official" use – a limitation that hampered the China EPI; and institutional organizational constraints that impact the collection, handling, processing, and dissemination of information. Operating with top-down, vertically nested institutional structures, both China and Viet Nam's attempts to collect and manage high-quality data from provincial and local counterparts have proven challenging (Hsu et al., 2012; Hsu, 2013; Mol, 2009). Malaysia, on the other hand, has benefited from cooperation from more than 50 government agencies for data collection, avoiding some of the data availability problems that obstruct China and Viet Nam's efforts.

As these nations' experiences with building national EPIs has shown, environmental management poses many challenges beyond data collection, indicator development, and index creation. Even when an issue or policy is rigorously evaluated, governments must innovate policy fixes and build public support for governance solutions. This issue of public support is more and more important in developing nation contexts. Indices and rankings have proven effective tools to command public attention and spur governments into action, especially in matters of human and environmental health (Rotberg, 2004). In East Asia, where meritocratic ideals and quantitative evaluation form the bedrock of modern social stratification, rankings strike a chord in the public consciousness (Poocharoen and Brillantes, 2013). This study's focal nations' leaders sought an index that used analytical "best practices", and the EPI's association with the World Economic Forum and biennial release at the Annual Meeting in Davos helped to cement its reputation as the international gold standard of environmental indices. The EPI's launch in conjunction with the World Economic Forum is explicitly mentioned several times in the 2014 MyEPI Introduction (UTM and NRE, 2015).

One of the EPI's most prominent effects is the "race to the top", or "California effect" (Vogel, 1997), that countries undertake as they try to out-compete each other and climb the EPI's rankings (Porter and van der Linde, 1995). This competition demonstrates EPI's role as a mechanism of policy diffusion and convergence (Bennett, 1991), a phenomenon occurring when states emulate policies of peers through "ideational" competitiveness (Tews and Busch, 2002). EPI is also an instrument of policy learning, a tool that states, organizations, and other actors use to transfer knowledge, programs, and policies from one setting to another (Dolowitz and Marsh, 1996). Policy learning is dependent upon a multiple events, including the generation and incorporation of information (e.g., data) into policy decisions, yet the precise channels and diffusion processes are not always clear (Sabatier and Jenkins-Smith, 1993). The EPI identifies national and global benchmarks, facilitating policy learning and diffusion processes through the creation of international norms that define "strong" and "weak" environmental performance and performers, spotlighting leading countries to whom others can look for examples of effective policy implementation. Policy diffusion is evident in this study's three cases, particularly in Malaysia's addition of an economic resource efficiency category, which mirrored China's subnational framework. We saw direct policy learning in action when the Malaysia EPI's team assisted Viet Nam's government with knowledge sharing and capacity building, helping its fellow Southeast Asian country develop a provincial EPI of its own.

The advent of evidence-based environmental governance is part of a broader trend of increased government accountability, a paradigm of which the EPI is a key part. Environmental outcomes have become closely tied to government performance legitimacy, a quality which had in previous decades depended solely on economic output and social stability. Citizens of nations throughout the world demand greater transparency today than a decade ago and are less satisfied with economic growth that degrades the environment. This growing dissatisfaction with poor quality growth explains why Malaysia's government has explicitly described its commitment to a New Economic Model that embraces sustainable growth (UTM and NRE, 2015), and Malaysia's EPI has shown an increase in environmental awareness among surveyed participants (MyEPI, 2014). China's citizens too have demonstrated growing concern about environmental issues, with particular focus on air and water pollution as well as food safety (Pew, 2013). The China and Malaysia EPI's websites allow for public access to environmental data and indicators that previously were scattered across multiple sources and not presented in easily understandable formats. The China EPI's solicitation of citizen feedback on indicators and the resulting analysis are significant steps towards enhanced transparency and public participation in the policymaking process – moves that were emphasized in the 2013 revisions to China's Environmental Protection Law (Wubbecke, 2014).

These indicator systems' influence on the policy processes in China, Malaysia, and Viet Nam is in flux, and it is too early to assess their long-term effects. While environmental measurement and policy evaluation help build institutional capacity, governments must respond appropriately to realize the benefits that indicator systems can bring. These systems are potent tools to help governments improve their environments at all levels of society, yet nations must intelligently invest in adequate data infrastructure to collect and analyze information that accurately reflects environmental conditions. Indicator systems and subnational indices will be prominent components of sound environmental governance this century. In the coming years, it is up to government and civil society institutions to create the conditions for their successful deployment.

Notes

1 China's Provincial Environmental Performance Assessment System can be accessed at http://118.123.13.161:9009/Home
2 Malaysia's EPI (MyEPI) can be accessed at www.epi.utm.my/v4/

References

Abuza, Z. (2015). Stifling the public sphere: Media and civil society in Vietnam. *Media and Civil Society in Egypt, Russia, and Vietnam*, 37. Available: http://www.ned.org/wp-content/uploads/2015/10/Stifling-the-Public-Sphere-Media-Civil-Society-Egypt-Russia-Vietnam-Full-Report-Forum-NED.pdf.

Beeson, M. (2010). The coming of environmental authoritarianism. *Environmental Politics*, 19(2), 276–294.

Bennett, C. J. (1991). What is policy convergence and what causes it? *British Journal of Political Science*, 21(2), 215–233.

Case, D. (2001). The law and economics of environmental information regulation. *Environmental Law Reporter*, Vol. 31, p. 10773.

Coe, C. A. (2015). 'Civilized city': How embedded civil society networks frame the debate on urban green space in Hanoi, Vietnam. *Asian Journal of Communication*, 25(6), 617–635.

Davis, K. E., Kingsbury, B., and Merry, S. E. (2012). Introduction: Global governance by indicators. *Governance by Indicators*, 3–28. Oxford University Press: Oxford, UK.

Dolowitz, D. and Marsh, D. (1996). Who learns what from whom: A review of the policy transfer literature. *Political Studies*, 44(2), 343–357.

Fan, C. C. (2006). China's eleventh five-year plan (2006–2010): From 'getting rich first' to 'common prosperity'. *Eurasian Geography and Economics*, 47(6), 708–723.

Fiorino, D. J. (2011). Explaining national environmental performance: Approaches, evidence, and implications. *Policy Sciences*, 44(4), 367–389.

Florini, A. (2007). Introduction: The battle over transparency. In *The Right to Know: Transparency for an Open World* (pp. 1–16), edited by Ann Florini. New York: Columbia University Press.

Gao, G. (2015). *As Smog Hangs over Beijing, Chinese Cite Air Pollution as Major Concern*. Pew Research Center. Available: www.pewresearch.org/fact-tank/2015/12/10/as-smog-hangs-over-beijing-chinese-cite-air-pollution-as-major-concern/

Greenpeace. (2015). *New Data Shows Beijing Air Pollution Improving, but Rest of China Still Suffering – Greenpeace*. Available: www.greenpeace.org/eastasia/press/releases/climate-energy/2015/air-ranking-2015-Q1/

Hawkins, N. (2014). *Malaysia's Environmental Performance Index: The Environmental Performance Index*. Yale University: New Haven, CT. Available: http://epi.yale.edu/indicators-in-practice/malaysias-environmental-performance-index-0

Hezri, A. A. and Nordin Hasan, M. (2006, February). Towards sustainable development? The evolution of environmental policy in Malaysia. In *Natural Resources Forum* (Vol. 30, No. 1, pp. 37–50). Blackwell Publishing Ltd.: Oxford, UK.

Hsu, A. (2013). Limitations and challenges of provincial environmental protection bureaus in China's environmental data monitoring, reporting and verification: Environmental reviews and case studies. *Environmental Practice, 15*(3), 280–292.

Hsu, A. (2015). *MyEPI: Malaysia Launches 2014 Environmental Performance Index.* Yale University: New Haven, CT. Available: http://epi.yale.edu/myepi-malaysia-launches-2014-environmental-performance-index

Hsu, A. et al. (2016). *The 2016 Environmental Performance Index.* Yale University: New Haven, CT. Available: www.epi.yale.edu

Hsu, A., de Sherbinin, A., and Shi, H. (2012). Seeking truth from facts: The challenge of environmental indicator development in China. *Environmental Development, 3*, 39–51.

Hsu, A. and Zomer, A. (2015). *Final Report: Feasibility Study for a Provincial Environmental Performance Index in Viet Nam.* UNDP: Hanoi. Available: www.vn.undp.org/content/vietnam/en/home/library/environment_climate/feasibility_study_for_a_provincial_environmental_performance_index.html

Keegan, M. (2015). *From Data to Decisions to Action – The Evolving Use of Data and Analytics in Government.* IBM Center for the Business of Government. Available: www.businessofgovernment.org/article/data-decisions-action%E2%80%94-evolving-use-data-and-analytics-government

Li, L. (2007). *China Postpones Release of Report on 'Green' GDP Accounting.* Worldwatch Institute. Available: www.caep.org.cn/english/ReadNewsEN.asp?NewsID=1069.

Liu, J. (2015). China restarts study on 'green GDP'. *China Dialogue,* March 3. Available: www.chinadialogue.net/blog/7821-China-restarts-study-on-green-GDP-/en

Liu, M. and Ansfield, J. (2008). Where poor is a poor excuse: Beijing's brass lags behind leaders of nations with similar incomes. *Newsweek,* July 7–14. Available: www.newsweek.com/id/143693?tid=relatedclS

Merry, S. E., Davis, K. E., and Kingsbury, B. (Eds.). (2015). *The Quiet Power of Indicators: Measuring Governance, Corruption, and Rule of Law.* Cambridge University Press: Cambridge.

Ministry of Environmental Protection (MEP), China. (2016). *2015 State of the Environment Report.* Available: http://www.mep.gov.cn/hjzl/zghjzkgb/lnzghjzkgb/201606/P020160602333160471955.pdf.

Ministry of Environmental Protection (MEP), China. (2015). *2014 State of the Environment Report.* Available: http://english.sepa.gov.cn/Resources/Reports/soe/soe2011/201606/P020160601592064474593.pdf

Ministry of Natural Resources and the Environment (NRE) Universiti Teknologi Malaysia (UTM) (2014). *Environmental Performance Index for Malaysia 2014.* Available: www.epi.utm.my/v3/download.php

Mitchell, C. L. (2006). Beyond barriers: Examining root causes behind commonly cited Cleaner Production barriers in Vietnam. *Journal of Cleaner Production, 14*(18), 1576–1585.

Mol, A. P. J. (2006). Environmental governance in the information age: The emergence of informational governance. *Environment and Planning C: Government and Policy, 24*, 497–514.

Mol, A. P. J. (2009). Environmental governance through information: China and Vietnam. *Singapore Journal of Tropical Geography, 30*(1), 114–129.

Nakano, J. (2014). *China's War on Pollution and the Uncertain Fate of "King Coal".* Center for Strategic and International Studies. Available: www.csis.org/analysis/china%E2%80%99s-war-pollution-and-uncertain-fate-%E2%80%9Cking-coal%E2%80%9D

Nguyen, T. T., Siegfried, B., and Holm, U. (2010). Land privatisation and afforestation incentive of rural farms in the Northern Uplands of Vietnam. *Forest Policy and Economics, 12*(7), 518–526.

Nguyen, T. V., Le, C. Q., Tran, B. T., and Bryant, S. E. (2015). Citizen participation in city governance: Experiences from Vietnam. *Public Administration and Development, 35*(1), 34–45.

Pak, J. (2015). Is Malaysia's palm oil worth the cost? *BBC News.* Available: www.bbc.com/news/world-asia-33729763

Pew. (2013). *Environmental Concerns on the Rise in China.* Pew Research Center. Available: www.pewglobal.org/2013/09/19/environmental-concerns-on-the-rise-in-china/

Poocharoen, O. O. and Brillantes, A. (2013). Meritocracy in Asia Pacific: Status, issues, and challenges. *Review of Public Personnel Administration, 33*(2), 140–163.

Porter, M. E. and van der Linde, C. (1995). Toward a new conception of the environment-competitiveness relationship. *The Journal of Economic Perspectives, 9*(4), 97–118.

Porter, T. M. (1996). *Trust in Numbers: The Pursuit of Objectivity in Science and Public Life.* Princeton University Press: Princeton, NJ.

Quitzow, R., Bär, H., and Jacob, K. (2013). Environmental governance in India, China, Vietnam and Indonesia: A tale of two paces. *Environmental Policy Research Centre FFU Report,* 1–2013.

Rotberg, R. I. (2004). Strengthening governance: Ranking countries would help. *Washington Quarterly, 28*(1), 71–81.

Sabatier, P. and Jenkins-Smith, H. C. (1993). *Policy Change and Learning: An Advocacy Coalition Approach.* Westview Press: Boulder, CO.

Sani, S. (1993). Economic development and environmental management in Malaysia. *New Zealand Geographer, 49*(2), 64–68.

Seligsohn, D. and Hsu, A. (2011). *What to Look for in China's 12th Five-Year Plan.* World Resources Institute (March 2, 2011). Available: www.wri.org/stories/2011/03/what-look-chinas-12th-five-year-plan.

Taylor, J. (2007). The usefulness of key performance indicators to public accountability authorities in East Asia. *Public Administration and Development, 27*(4), 341–352.

Tews, K. and Busch, P. O. (2002). Governance by diffusion? Potentials and restrictions of environmental policy diffusion. In *Global Environmental Change and the Nation State: Proceedings of the 2001 Berlin Conference on the Human Dimensions of Global Environmental Change* (pp. 168–182). Potsdam Institute for Climate Impact Research: Potsdam.

Thayer, C. A. (2010). Political legitimacy of Vietnam's one party-state: Challenges and responses. *Journal of Current Southeast Asian Affairs, 28*(4), 47–70.

Tietenberg, T. (1998). Disclosure strategies for pollution control. *Environmental & Resource Economics, 11,* 587–588.

UNDP. (2012). *The Vietnam Provincial Governance and Public Administration Performance Index (PAPI) 2011: Measuring Citizen Experience.* United Nations Development Programme: Hanoi.

UNDP. (2014). *Procurement Notice for an International Consultant for Development of a Feasible Proposal for Applying an Environmental Performance Index (EPI) at Provincial Level in Viet Nam.* Available: http://procurement-notices.undp.org/view_file.cfm?doc_id=31177

UNDP. (2015). *Procurement Notice for Consultant to Enhance Capacity for Implementing Rio Conventions.* UNDP: Hanoi. Available: http://procurement-notices.undp.org/view_file.cfm?doc_id=70575

UTM and NRE, Malaysia. (2015). *Introduction to the MyEPI.* Universiti Teknologi: Malaysia. Available: www.epi.utm.my/v4/wp-content/uploads/2015/05/03-C1-Introduction.pdf

Vogel, D. (1997). Trading up and governing across: Transnational governance and environmental protection. *Journal of European Public Policy, 4*(4), 556–571.

Wai, C.W., Noor, Z. Z., and N.H. Mohamed (2017). *Viet Nam Provincial Environmental Performance Index.* UNDP VietNam: Hanoi.

Wang, A. L. (2013). The search for sustainable legitimacy: Environmental law and bureaucracy in China. *Harvard Environmental Law Review, 37,* 365–589.

Wang, J. (2016). Environmental costs: Revive China's green GDP programme. *Nature, 534*(7605), 37.

World Bank. (2008). *Review and Analysis of the Pollution Impacts from Vietnamese Manufacturing Sectors.* Washington, DC: EASRE, The World Bank.

World Bank. (2012). *Corruption from the Perspectives of Citizens, Firms, and Public Officials: Results of Sociological Surveys.* World Bank: Hanoi.

World Bank. (2017). *Services, etc., value added (% of GDP).* Available: http://data.worldbank.org/indicator/NV.SRV.TETC.ZS?locations=MY

WRI. (2017). *CAIT Climate Data Explorer.* Available: http://cait.wri.org/

Wubbecke, J. (2014). The three-year battle for China's new environmental law. *China Dialogue.* Available: www.chinadialogue.net/article/show/single/en/6938-The-three-year-battle-for-China-s-new-environmental-law

Yan, C. (2016). *China's Environmental Performance Index: The Environmental Performance Index.* Yale University: New Haven, CT. Available: http://epi.yale.edu/content/chinas-provincial-environmental-performance-index

YCELP and CIESIN. (2000). *Pilot Environmental Sustainability Index.* Available: http://epi.yale.edu/sites/default/files/2000_pilot_esi_report_0.pdf

YCELP and CIESIN. (2011). *Towards a China Environmental Performance Index.* Yale Center for Environmental Law and Policy: New Haven, CT. Available: www.ciesin.org/documents/china-epi-report.pdf

18

THE HUMAN SUSTAINABLE DEVELOPMENT INDEX[1]

Giangiacomo Bravo

Introduction

The *Human Sustainable Development Index* (HSDI) has been proposed as a way to amend the "iconic" United Nations' *Human Development Index* (HDI) by adding an environmental dimension.[2] In a 2011 *Nature* commentary, its creator Chuluun Togtokh argued that "[with] the current HDI, developed nations and oil-rich countries are placed highly without regard to how much their development paths cost the planet and imperil humanity's future development" and that "[the UN] should change the way it calculates the HDI. The revised index should include each nation's per capita carbon emissions, and so become a Human Sustainable Development Index" (Togtokh 2011, 269). In the years that followed the publication of Togtokh's paper, the use of the HSDI has slowly gained traction. I previously published two updates of Togtokh's original calculations, along with the formal description of the procedure to produce the index starting from publicly available data (Bravo 2014, 2015). Other authors that recently discussed the HSDI include Estoque and Murayama (2014), Comes (2015), Diaconu and Popescu (2016), Hein (2016), and Borgnäs (2017).

This chapter aims to critically review the HSDI and to explore its relation with other prominent environmental indicators. The remaining of the chapter is structured as follows. The next section will define the HSDI and present a formal description of the procedure to compute it. The third section will introduce the 2015 HSDI, based on recently available UN data. The fourth section will critically assess its relation with other environmental indicators. The last section will summarize and discuss the results.

HSDI definition

The rationale behind the HSDI is to add an environmental dimension to the HDI – which already covers two of the three dimensions of sustainability, namely the social and the economic ones – to build a true sustainable development index (see Goodland 1995). The HDI includes three different series of data: life expectancy at birth, education (mean years of schooling and expected years of schooling), and income (Gross National Income *per capita*). Following the technical notes of the *Human Development Report* (UNDP 2015), each of these "dimensions" is represented by a specific sub-index (I_{dim}) computed as

$$I_{dim} = \frac{x - \min}{\max - \min}$$
(1)

where x is the observed value for a given country, maxima are computed as "aspirational values" (usually highest observed or projected values), and minima refer to somewhat arbitrarily defined "subsistence values", equal or below the minimum observed values. In practice, the minima used in the 2015 *Human Development Report* are 20 years of life expectancy, zero years of both expected and mean schooling, and 100 PPP Dollars of income. Maxima are 85 years of life expectancy, 18 expected years of schooling, 15 years of mean schooling, and 75,000 PPP Dollars of income (UNDP 2015, technical notes). The three dimension indexes are first separately estimated, then the HDI is computed as their geometric mean. Since all three dimension indexes fall by construction between zero and one, the HDI is limited in the same interval with greater values indicating higher development levels.

The HSDI adds an environmental dimension to the HDI, namely *per capita* CO_2 emissions. The corresponding index is computed by taking the complement to one of equation (1) to reflect the fact that higher emissions mean a poorer environmental performance. In formulae,

$$I_{emissions} = 1 - \frac{x - \min}{\max - \min} = \frac{\max - x}{\max - \min}$$
(2)

with the maximum corresponding to the highest observed value in the 2000–present period and the minimum set to zero, i.e., representing a fully decarbonized economy. Then, in analogy with the HDI, HSDI values are computed as

$$HSDI = (I_{life} \cdot I_{education} \cdot I_{income} \cdot I_{emissions})^{1/4}$$
(3)

or, alternatively,

$$HSDI = HDI^{3/4} \cdot I_{emissions}^{1/4}$$
(4)

All four dimensions hold the same weight in the HSDI, which ranges in the [0, 1] interval with higher values meaning both a higher standard of living and lower emissions.

The 2015 HSDI

Previous HSDI calculations were updated using the data included in the 2015 *Human Development Report* (UNDP 2015), along with the latest available emission figures. HDI data refer to 2014 and were downloaded from the UNDP database (http://hdr.undp.org/en/statistics/hdi/). Data on CO_2 emissions stemming from the burning of fossil fuels and the manufacture of cement are measured in metric tons *per capita* and refer to 2013. They were downloaded from the World Bank database (http://data.worldbank.org/indicator/EN.ATM.CO2E.PC).

The 2015 HSDI was computed using the procedure above and resulted in 186 observations covering most world countries.[3] The data presented from now on refer to the outcome of equation (4) calculations. All data and the R code used to generate them are available in https:// linnaeus.academia.edu/GiangiacomoBravo. The country with the highest HSDI is Switzerland (0.93), while the one showing the lowest value is Niger (0.45). The average is 0.74 and the index distribution is significantly left skewed ($G_1 = -0.49$).[4] Geographically, most of the top-20 HSDI countries are European ones (Figure 18.1). Noteworthy exceptions to this rule are Hong Kong, New Zealand, Singapore, Israel, and Australia. Impressively, all but one bottom-20 countries in the HSDI rank are Sub-Saharan Africa ones, the only exception being Afghanistan.

Despite the introduction of the environmental dimension, the HSDI remains highly correlated with the HDI (Figure 18.2). The correlation is almost perfect for HDI values below 0.7 ($r = 0.998$), with poor, low-emission countries improving their HDI scores at the same pace they increase CO_2 emissions. More "noise" exists above this threshold ($r = 0.876$), showing the existence of different development trajectories once basic needs are satisfied (Figure 18.2, upper-left scatterplot).

It is worth noting that the three socio-economic dimensions of the HDI (and hence of the HSDI) are strongly and positively correlated and that CO_2 emissions correlate with income as well, although less strictly. As a consequence, the emission index *negatively* correlates with all other dimensions (Figure 18.2), which means that a trade-off exists between the human and the environmental dimensions of the HSDI. The developed countries that better succeeded in reducing this trade-off (e.g., Switzerland, Denmark, and Sweden) are the ones scoring better on the new index, while some of the HDI leaders, having economies heavily dependent on fossil fuel consumption, fell way down the rankings (e.g., Luxembourg, USA, and most oil-producing countries).

Comparison with other indicators

To asses how the HSDI captures the environmental dimension of sustainability, we compared it with a number of environmental indicators commonly estimated at the country level. For all variables, the most recent estimates at the time of writing were used.

- The *Ecological Footprint* (EF) estimates the burden on natural systems of consumption processes (see also Wackernagel et al.'s contribution in Chapter 16). The EF is measured in global hectares (gha) *per capita*. EF data include 172 observations, refer to 2012 and were downloaded from the Global Footprint Network website (Global Footprint Network 2016).

- The *biocapacity* estimates the biological productivity of natural and man-managed systems. More specifically, biocapacity is a measure of the amount of bioproductive land available, where "bioproductive" refers to land and water areas that support significant photosynthetic activity and accumulation of biomass (Ewing et al. 2010). The biocapacity is measured in gha *per capita*, just as the EF. Data include 172 observations, refer to 2012 and were downloaded from the Global Footprint Network website in conjunction with the EF data.

- The 2016 *Environmental Performance Index* (EPI) is a composite indicator ranking countries' performance in the realization of the United Nations' Sustainable Development Goals (Hsu et al. 2016).[5] The index is compiled by Yale and Columbia University in collaboration with the World Economic Forum. The EPI index summarizes 20 indicators using a 0 to 100 score, where 100 indicates a better performance. Data refers to 2016 and include 178 observations.

HSDI

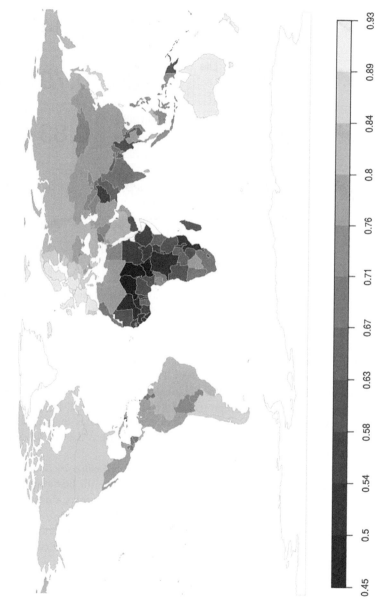

0.45   0.5   0.54   0.58   0.63   0.67   0.71   0.76   0.8   0.84   0.89   0.93

Figure 18.1   Geographical distribution of the 2015 HSDI

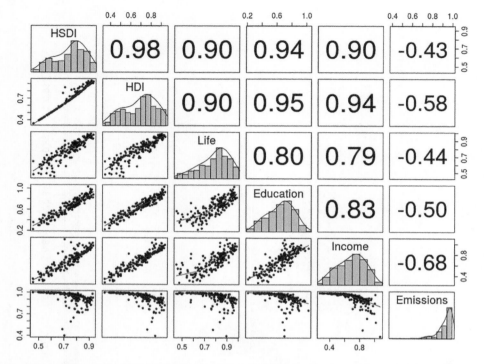

Figure 18.2 Binary correlations between the HSDI and HDI, and between all sub-indexes with corresponding scatterplots. The diagonal panels present the distribution of each index or sub-index

- *Terrestrial and marine protected area* data measure the totally or partially protected areas of at least 1,000 hectares in a given country. The index is compiled by the United Nations Environmental Program and the World Conservation Monitoring Centre and encompasses areas enjoying different levels of protection (see Bertzky et al. 2012). Data refer to 2014 and report the percentage of protected area in each country. They include 86 observations and were downloaded from the World Bank database (http://data.worldbank.org/indicator/ER.PTD.TOTL.ZS).
- The *Global Environment Facility* (GEF) *benefits index for biodiversity* is a comprehensive indicator of national biodiversity. For each country, it includes the best available and comparable information on four relevant dimensions: represented species, threatened species, represented eco-regions, and threatened eco-regions (Pandey et al. 2006). The GEF index ranges from 0 to 100, with 100 indicating the highest biodiversity. Data refer to 2008, include 184 observations and were downloaded from the World Bank database (http://data.worldbank.org/indicator/ER.BDV.TOTL.XQ).
- *Forest area* data simply report the proportion (in percent terms) of the country area covered by forest in each country. Data refer to 2015, include 185 observations and were downloaded from the World Bank database (http://data.worldbank.org/indicator/AG.LND.FRST.ZS).

Figure 18.3 presents the binary correlations between the HSDI and all other indicators. The HSDI positively correlates with the EF and EPI, while no significant correlation exists

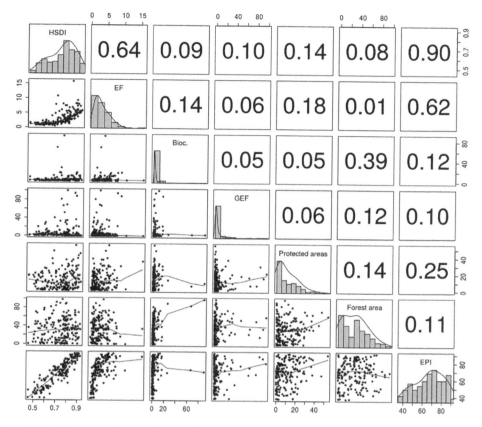

Figure 18.3 Binary correlations between the HSDI and all other indicators with corresponding scatter-plots. The diagonal panels present the distribution of each variable

with the other indicators. In particular, both the extension of protected areas and the GEF index hold no relation with the HSDI. This highlights the difficulties of the HSDI in evaluating sustainability at the local level and, more specifically, in taking into account the extent and effects of conservation activities. On the other hand, the correlation with the EF and EPI is positive and highly significant. The reasons behind this results will be analyzed in the next two sections.

Relation with the Environmental Footprint

The positive correlation between the HSDI and the EF implies that high-ranked countries consume, on average, *more* of the Earth's natural capital than low-ranked ones. This correlation is even stronger using Spearman's ρ instead of Pearson's r ($\rho = 0.79$), which suggests that the relation between the HSDI and the EF is not perfectly linear, although monotonic (see also the upper-left scatterplot in Figure 18.3). More specifically, the EF slowly grows from low to medium HSDI values but rapidly increases for high-HSDI countries. This is similar to the relation that the HSDI holds with the Gross Domestic Product (GDP), which is little surprising since the EF itself strongly correlates with the GDP (Bagliani et al. 2008).

It is worth noting that all top 20 HSDI countries have an EF of at least 4.9 gha/cap.,[6] which is almost three times the sustainable level of 1.7 gha/cap. given by Earth's total biocapacity (see Ewing et al. 2010). No country with an EF ≤ 1.7 gha/cap. actually has a HSDI above 0.8 except Sri Lanka and Georgia, which are the only two falling in the "sustainable" area delimited by high or very high HSDI and a *per capita* footprint below the global average biocapacity (Figure 18.4). Among the countries scoring relatively well on both indexes are Argentina (HSDI = 0.84, EF = 3.1 gha/cap.), Hungary (HSDI = 0.85, EF = 2.9 gha/cap.) and Spain (HSDI = 0.89, EF = 3.7 gha/cap.).

Things are somewhat different by considering local biocapacity, since some of the top 20 countries in the HSDI ranking – specifically Sweden, Norway, New Zealand, and Australia – are low-populated ones with large biological resource availability, which led to a biocapacity reserve despite high EF levels. Nevertheless, all other top 20 countries have a large biocapacity deficit, showing the difficult trade-off between social and environmental goals when a large population is present.

Relation with the Environmental Performance Index

Special consideration concerns the strong positive correlation between the HSDI and the EPI. This is somewhat surprising as the EPI is a much more complex index, including nine issue areas and based on over 20 individual indicators (Hsu et al. 2016). Nevertheless, the relation between the EPI and all the environmental indicators considered in this chapter is surprisingly similar to the HSDI one, up to the point that the two indexes seem to capture almost equally well the same underlying dimension of sustainability. In addition, its relatively strong correlation with the EF means that the EPI suffers from some of the same issues discussed in the previous

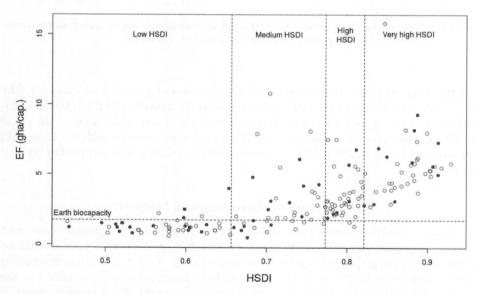

Figure 18.4 HSDI and Ecological Footprint by country. Empty circles indicate countries with an EF higher than the local biocapacity, filled ones countries with an EF lower than the local bio-capacity. Vertical dashed lines mark the quartiles of the HSDI distribution. The horizontal dashed line indicates the available world biocapacity in *per capita* terms.

section, including the fact that all top-ranked EPI countries are not sustainable in terms of consumption of the world's natural capital.

To better understand the two indexes, it is worth checking the relation between the HSDI and the different components forming the EPI. First, the EPI can be split into two "overarching objectives", namely ecosystem vitality and environmental health. The relation with the former is stronger ($r = 0.90$), mainly because it includes several indicators directly affecting human health and life quality, such as exposure to pollution and access to safe drinking water. The relation with the latter index looks weaker ($r = 0.64$) despite one of the issue areas included in it, namely climate and energy, looks similar to the HSDI emission index. However, the indicators included in this area represent trends in carbon intensity, not absolute emissions, which explains the fact that the correlation between these two elements is not significant ($r = 0.14, p = 0.146$). More generally, the EPI issue areas that more strongly correlate with the HSDI are water and sanitation ($r = 0.94$), health impacts ($r = 0.89$), and water resources ($r = 0.77$). These issues areas are actually linked to the three dimensions of the HDI and drive much of the relation with the HSDI as well.

Conclusion

The HSDI was proposed as a way to promote sustainable development by amending the HDI in order to put a stop to the "celebration" of "gas-guzzling developed nations" (Togtokh 2011). This promise has been only partially fulfilled by the new index, which, although bringing some added value, looks as a relatively small step ahead of the current state of affairs. On the negative side, the HSDI remains too much correlated with the HDI and far from reliably representing environmental sustainability. More specifically, it completely overlooks the systemic dimension of social-ecological systems, introducing a single pressure indicator instead of trying to analyze how the different parts of the system interact or to focus on potential equilibrium shifts in response to environmental pressures (e.g., Holling 2001, Gallopin's Chapter 22 in this book). This makes the HSDI largely uncorrelated with most environmental and conservation indicators, like the extension of protected areas or the biodiversity index, while it positively correlates with the Ecological Footprint, which implies an overall higher impact on natural systems for top-ranked HSDI countries. From this point of view, the HSDI cannot be considered a true indicator of environmental sustainability.

On the other hand, the HSDI strongly correlates with the Environmental Performance Index, which suggests that it is able to capture at least some of the dimensions underlying the latter indicator. Taking into account that, unlike the EPI, the HSDI can be easily computed from publicly available data sources, it can be thought as a "fast and frugal" way to capture in a single indicator some relevant dimensions underlying human (sustainable) development. The fact that not much information is lost (in comparison with a much more comprehensive indicator like the EPI) actually suggests that the HSDI is quite efficient in capturing some significant dimensions of human development and its relation with environmental health.

In addition, the HSDI holds a certain merit in highlighting the intrinsic difficulties of simultaneously pursuing socio-economic and environmental goals. In his *Nature* commentary, Togtokh (2011, 269) argued that "emissions are positively and strongly correlated with income; less so with the HDI; and not at all with health and education", indirectly suggesting that the latter two goals could be achieved without increasing income and emissions. Despite its intuitive validity, our analysis showed that this argument is not correct, as health and education correlate with income even more than emissions (Figure 18.2). A better interpretation could be that the current development path implies a trade-off between social and environmental goals, at least when the overall pressure on natural systems is taken into account, e.g., by using CO_2 emissions or the EF as indicators. This is not an inescapable doom and some countries, especially European ones, are better than others in limiting this trade-off, which translates in a position in the HSDI rank higher than in the HDI one. Still, wealthy countries as a whole score well in the HSDI even if they are responsible for most cumulated greenhouse gas emissions (Monastersky 2009) and consumption of natural capital (Global Footprint Network 2016), which cast doubts on the ability of the indicator to really capture the environmental dimension of sustainability (see Goodland 1995).

To sum up, the HSDI is a small step ahead from currently prevailing indexes such as the HDI. From a "little is better than nothing" point of view, I can only agree with Togtokh's argument that an environmental dimension should be added to the way the UN assess human development and hope that the UN will follow his advice and include CO_2 emissions in their standard index. Nevertheless, the current balance of socio-economic vs. environmental dimensions in the HSDI clearly favours the former set of indicators and, if not further amended, it will continue to equate the overuse of natural resources with welfare. In previous works, I presented several possible amendments to the HSDI, including (1) a "strong" HSDI equally weighting the human and environmental dimensions of each country (Bravo 2015) and (2) the introduction of further environmental measures in the HSDI Bravo (2014).

Any index inevitably is the product of a number of more or less arbitrary choices (not only scientific ones, since politics often plays a major role). At the same time, in a rapidly changing planet the need of better indicators is greater than ever, so even a small step in the right direction should be welcomed. Devising new indicators is a slow, cumulative process. On the one hand, they must be clear, reliable, and able to inform citizens and policy makers in their efforts to address human development. On the other, they need to include all the relevant environmental dimensions. What is clear is that, without their guidance, the overshooting of the planetary boundaries representing the "safe operating space" for humanity (Rockström et al. 2009, Steffen et al. 2015) could become even more likely, as we would not even realize that the danger is approaching.

Notes

1 This chapter revises and updates the article "The Human Sustainable Development Index: New calculations and a first critical analysis" originally published in the *Ecological Indicators* journal (37: 145–150, 2014). Contents reproduced under Elsevier license n. 3971920601921.
2 See also Costanza et al. critique to current prosperity indicators in Chapter 7.
3 Note that, due to the rounding of the values of the dimension indexes in HDR tables, equations (3) and (4) can actually produce slightly different values. The data presented from now on refer to the outcome of equation (4) calculations. All data and the R code used to generate them are available in https://linnaeus.academia.edu/GiangiacomoBravo.
4 All statistical analyses were performed using the R platform, version 3.2.3 (R Core Team 2015).
5 The EPI is also discussed by Esty and Emerson in Chapter 5, Hsu in Chapter 17, and Conrad and Cassar in Chapter 19.
6 Note that no EF estimations exist for smaller countries such as Hong Kong, Iceland, and Liechtenstein.

References

Bagliani, M., G. Bravo, and S. Dalmazzone. (2008). A consumption-based approach to environmental Kuznets curves using the ecological footprint indicator. *Ecological Economics* 65(3), 650–661.
Bertzky, B., C. Corrigan, J. Kemsey, S. Kenney, C. Ravilious, C. Besançon, and N. Burgess. (2012). *Protected Planet Report 2012: Tracking Progress Towards Global Targets for Protected Areas*. Cambridge: UNEP-World Conservation Monitoring Centre.

Borgnäs, K. (2017). Indicators as circular argumentation constructs? An input-output analysis of the variable structure of five environmental sustainability country rankings. *Environment, Development and Sustainability 9*(3), 769–790.

Bravo, G. (2014). The human sustainable development index: New calculations and a first critical analysis. *Ecological Indicators 37*(Part A), 145–150.

Bravo, G. (2015). The human sustainable development index: The 2014 update. *Ecological Indicators 50*, 258–259.

Comes, C.-A. (2015). HSDSI analysis for EU 28 countries. *Procedia Economics and Finance 32*, 154–159.

Diaconu, L. and C.C. Popescu. (2016). Human capital – a pillar of sustainable development: Empirical evidences from the EU states. *European Journal of Sustainable Development 5*(3), 103–112.

Estoque, R.C. and Y. Murayama. (2014, August). Social-ecological status index: A preliminary study of its structural composition and application. *Ecological Indicators 43*, 183–194.

Ewing, B., D. Moore, S. Goldfinger, A. Oursler, A. Reed, and M. Wackernagel. (2010). *The Ecological Footprint Atlas 2010*. Oakland: Global Footprint Network.

Global Footprint Network. (2016). *The National Footprint Accounts*, 2016 edition. Oakland, CA: Global Footprint Network.

Goodland, R. (1995). The concept of environmental sustainability. *Annual Review of Ecology and Systematics 26*, 1–24.

Hein, W. (2016). Entwicklung messen: Ein überblick über verschiedene indikatoren und ihre grenzen. In K. Fischer, G. Hauck, and M. Boatcă (Eds.), *Handbuch Entwicklungsforschung*, pp. 155–168. Wiesbaden: Springer Fachmedien Wiesbaden.

Holling, C.S. (2001). Understanding the complexity of economic, ecological and social systems. *Ecosystems 4*, 390–405.

Hsu et al. (2016). *2016 Environmental Performance Index*. New Haven, CT: Yale University.

Monastersky, R. (2009). A burden beyond bearing. *Nature 458*, 1091–1094.

Pandey, K.D., P. Buys, K. Chomitz, and D. Wheeler's. (2006). *Biodiversity Conservation Indicators: New Tools for Priority Setting at the Global Environment Facility*. The World Bank, World Development Indicators 2006. Washington, DC, USA: The International Bank for Reconstruction and Development.

R Core Team. (2015). *R: A Language and Environment for Statistical Computing*. Vienna, Austria: R Foundation for Statistical Computing.

Rockström, J., W. Steffen, K. Noone, Åsa Persson, F.S. Chapin, E.F. Lambin, T.M. Lenton, M. Scheffer, C. Folke, H.J. Schellnhuber, B. Nykvist, C.A. de Wit, T. Hughes, S. van der Leeuw, H. Rodhe, S. Sörlin, P.K. Snyder, R. Costanza, U. Svedin, M. Falkenmark, L. Karlberg, R.W. Corell, V.J. Fabry, J. Hansen, B. Walker, D. Liverman, K. Richardson, P. Crutzen, and J.A. Foley. (2009). A safe operating space for humanity. *Nature 461*, 472–475.

Steffen, W., K. Richardson, J. Rockström, S.E. Cornell, I. Fetzer, E.M. Bennett, R. Biggs, S.R. Carpenter, W. de Vries, C.A. de Wit, C. Folke, D. Gerten, J. Heinke, G.M. Mace, L.M. Persson, V. Ramanathan, B. Reyers, and S. Sörlin. (2015). Planetary boundaries: Guiding human development on a changing planet. *Science 347*(6223), 736.

Togtokh, C. (2011). Time to stop celebrating the polluters. *Nature 479*, 269.

UNDP. (2015). *Human Development Report 2015: Work for Human Development*. New York: United Nations.

19

THE ENVIRONMENTAL PERFORMANCE INDEX

Does this reflect reality?

Elisabeth Conrad and Louis F. Cassar

Introduction

As repeatedly discussed in this volume, sustainability indicators have played and continue to play a crucial role in monitoring progress towards sustainable development, with the emergence of a veritable 'indicator industry' (Bell and Morse, Chapter 1, this volume). From the wide range of sustainability indicators developed, of particular popularity have been aggregate or composite indicators (CIs) that are able to synthesize and summarize information on multiple environmental, economic, and/or social aspects. Examples include the Living Planet Index, Environmental Sustainability/Performance Index, Human Development Index, and Environmental Vulnerability Index, several of which are discussed elsewhere in this publication. Rogge (2012) identifies multiple reasons for the boost in popularity of CIs, including their ability to simplify complex issues into a single index, their ease of interpretation by the media and the public, and the fact that they help decision-makers assess performance and trends and identify priority issues. Notwithstanding this popularity, however, some authors have expressed concerns about the robustness of such indices, highlighting fundamental scientific flaws in their construction and issues with the weighting of variables, and suggesting that the results of such indices may be inconsistent, if not outright misleading (Böhringer and Jochem, 2007).

In this chapter, we focus specifically on one such composite indicator – the Environmental Performance Index (EPI). This has already been discussed elsewhere in this volume (Esty and Emerson, Chapter 5) but for the benefit of readers, we will provide a brief recap of its main characteristics here. The EPI is a proximity-to-target indicator (Figure 19.1), i.e., it evaluates a country's performance relative to a defined policy target, based on an expert consensus-based framework. Scores are aggregated at several levels. First, national-level data for 24 indicators is standardized and transformed, with indicators selected on the basis of six criteria – relevance to countries under a wide range of circumstances, performance orientation, basis in established scientific methodology, quality of data, time series availability, and completeness of global and temporal coverage (Hsu et al., 2016). Second, data from these indicators is aggregated into nine core issue categories, with one–six indicators in each. Weighting of indicators within these issue categories is based on data quality and indicator relevance. Finally, scores for the overarching environmental health and ecosystem vitality categories are calculated; these are then weighted

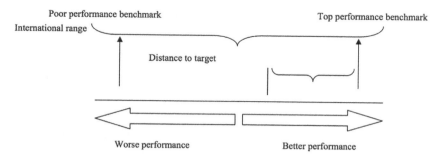

Figure 19.1 EPI – a proximity-to-target indicator

equally (50% each) for calculation of a country's total EPI score based on their arithmetic mean. Potential values of the EPI range from 0 to 100.

The top performers, as ranked in the 2016 EPI report, were Finland, Iceland, and Sweden, countries renowned for their environmental credentials. Finland, for example, is Europe's most forested country, while Iceland obtains all its energy from renewable sources. The top ten also included countries whose placement is perhaps more surprising, including the small island state of Malta (in 9th place). Malta measures just 316 km^2 in area but supports a population of over 434,000, giving it a population density amongst the highest in the world. This exerts significant environmental pressures in a context of limited space and few natural resources. Indeed, Malta has one of the highest rates of urban land-take in the EU and the highest proportion of artificial land amongst 27 EU countries – at 32.6%, this is close to eight times the European average of 4.1% (Eurostat, 2016). This is not related solely to the country's high population density but also to poor efficiency of land use; by way of example, as of 2005, 22.4% of dwellings were reported to be permanently vacant (NSO, 2007). Notwithstanding, urbanization continues at a very rapid pace. The country is also distinguished by its high rate of car ownership and use, with an estimated 852 vehicles per 1,000 population (NSO, 2017), one of the highest rates in the world. Malta furthermore faces the constraints of a semi-arid climate and limited annual rainfall, exacerbated by the absence of any perennial surface freshwater bodies of significant extent; it is therefore heavily reliant on the use of desalination technology to meet potable freshwater demand. The country derives its energy primarily from imported fossil fuels, with no oil, coal, or gas reserves of its own. It has next to no natural forest coverage, having been deforested several centuries ago, and agriculture remains largely reliant on chemical inputs, with limited adoption of organic methods. Given the above, Malta's high EPI score of 88.48 and ranking in 9th place was met with surprise and even incredulity, at least in some quarters. To put this result into context, Malta's result places it above France, the United Kingdom, Australia, Switzerland, Austria, and Germany, to name just a few.

In this contribution, we take a closer look at Malta's 2016[1] EPI results within each of the nine issue categories, with a view to evaluating the extent to which these scores accurately reflect the environmental state-of-affairs. We consider whether indicators selected within each category sufficiently and correctly reflect broad on-the-ground conditions within each sector, drawing comparisons with other data sources where relevant. We then compare the EPI scores with the results of a survey conducted among residents of Malta, gauging their personal assessment of the country's environmental performance. Finally, we discuss what these results indicate about the utility of the EPI as a measure of country performance.

A review of Malta's EPI results

Malta's positive performance in the 2016 EPI was based on above-average results in all but one target area (Tables 19.1 and 19.2). Its 9th-place ranking was a significant improvement from its positioning in 34th place two years prior (Hsu et al., 2014) and its 87th place finish in 2012 (Emerson et al., 2012). Malta received the maximum possible score of 100 for 13 of the 24 indicators measured. Of the remaining eleven indicators, three received scores >90, three between 80–90, two between 70–80, with only three <70, indicating largely positive performance throughout. In terms of its relative performance, Malta was ranked as the top performer, i.e., in first place (singularly or jointly with other states) for no less than 14 of 24 indicators measured. In the next sections, we take a closer look at Malta's performance within the two main EPI priority areas of ecosystem vitality and environmental health.

Ecosystem vitality

The ecosystem vitality score is based on six criteria: (1) water resources, (2) agriculture, (3) forests, (4) fisheries, (5) biodiversity and habitats, and (6) climate and energy (Table 19.1).

Water resources: The single indicator used for EPI calculations in this target area is wastewater treatment, i.e., the proportion of wastewater collected and produced by households, municipalities, and industry that is treated, weighted by the population covered by the sewage network. Malta's high score reflects the significant advances that the country has made in wastewater treatment in recent years, with 100% of the population now connected to urban wastewater treatment plants (Eurostat, 2015). However, although the indicator is taken as representative of *water resources* more broadly, other statistics paint a different picture of Malta's water situation. Among EU countries, Malta is considered to have the lowest proportion of freshwater resources per inhabitant (Eurostat, 2015) and to have the highest possible ranking of water stress (Gassert et al., 2013). Freshwater is estimated to be over-extracted from aquifers at a rate of 11 million m^3 per annum (Spiteri et al., 2015), with a water exploitation index in 2014 of 46.5%,[2] an increase of more than 10% from 2005 values. The country's external water dependency is estimated at 92% (Hoekstra and Mekonnen, 2012). Even though its performance in the wastewater treatment field has been very promising, Malta nevertheless faces sustainability issues even in this sector, with all sewage sludge from wastewater treatment currently disposed of in landfills and with the operation of a number of treatment plants repeatedly interrupted in recent years due to farm waste clogging the works (resulting in the direct discharge of untreated sewage into the sea). Given the above, it is clear that while the EPI indicator is based on accurate data, there are issues with its scope, and it is a far from sufficient reflection of the state of water resources.

Agriculture: The EPI assessment is based on two indicators of agricultural performance: nitrogen-use efficiency (NUE), measuring the ratio of nitrogen inputs to outputs in crops, and nitrogen balance (NBALANCE), measuring excess nitrogen released to the environment as a result of overuse of fertilizers. Malta performs below average for both these indicators, scoring 66 for NUE and just 2 for NBALANCE. The 2016 EPI report notes that it is difficult to calculate environmental degradation resulting from agricultural inputs, also explaining that computation of results was constrained by data availability. Despite these shortcomings and although differences in calculation methodologies render a direct comparison difficult, this score appears broadly reflective of national-level data indicating that nearly all crops are over-fertilized with nitrogen (NSO, 2008), even if it is worth noting that the 2016 EPI figures are based on data that extends only up to 2010. The issue of excessive nitrogen use is a particular concern in Malta given the risk of pollution of groundwater bodies (noted above), with the entire territory of

Table 19.1 EPI 2016 indicator scores for Malta (on a scale of 0–100) for **ecosystem vitality**, compared to average scores across 180 states, and ranking of Malta's performance relative to other states. The superscript ★ indicates that Malta's performance was above average for the indicator/area in question.

Weighting (%)	Target area/indicator	Malta's score	Average score	Malta's relative ranking
Ecosystem vitality★		84.13	62.13	14
25	**Water resources★**	89.37	48.97	29
100	Wastewater treatment★	89.37	48.97	29
10	**Agriculture**	49.75	78.62	141
75	Nitrogen-use efficiency	65.56	80.17	128
25	Nitrogen balance	2.3	73.99	137
10	**Forests**	NA	52.53	NA
100	Tree cover loss	NA	52.53	NA
5	**Fisheries★**	82.36	48.01	6
100	Fish stocks★	82.36	48.01	6
25	**Biodiversity and habitats★**	93.98	74.74	29
20	Terrestrial protected areas (national biome weights)★	100	77.13	1
20	Terrestrial protected areas (global biome weights)★	100	77.42	1
20	Marine Protected Areas	69.38	70.20	85
20	Species protection (national)★	100	72.78	1
20	Species protection (global)★	100	74.79	1
25	**Climate and energy★**	84.79	72.56	29
75	Trend in carbon intensity★	79.72	69.73	56
25	Trend in CO_2 emissions per KwH★	100	86.61	1
NA	Access to electricity★	100	85.07	1

the Maltese Islands designated a Nitrate Vulnerable Zone, and with fertilizers, manure, and soil cultivation all identified as possible sources of nitrate pollution (Heaton et al., 2012).

Also not reflected in this indicator are broader issues relating to excessive chemical use in agriculture. A report of the European Food Safety Authority found that, based on 2015 data, locally grown produce is more than twice as likely to exceed acceptable pesticide levels as the EU average, with 5.6% of samples analyzed exceeding maximum residue levels; this was the worst result amongst the 30 countries analyzed (EFSA, 2017). In February 2017, a local newspaper reported that 13% of fruits and vegetables sold at the farmers' market in 2012 were found to contain excessive and illegal levels of pesticides, with a later report asserting that one in five locally grown greens has residues above acceptable limits. These data point to significant issues with the environmental sustainability of agriculture, with widespread and significant implications, including for human and ecosystem health.

Forests: The Forests category of the EPI is based on the single measure of tree cover loss between 2000 and 2014. The indicator is measured only for countries that have at least 2% of their total area covered by 30% canopy. Given that Malta does not meet this criterion, it did not receive a score, implying that this is not a relevant consideration; however, this is disputable. Malta was historically considerably more forested than it is at present, with extensive deforestation having occurred following human settlement and with a significant dearth of trees at present. The continued dearth of trees arguably represents an environmental failing, especially when considering that several other Mediterranean states have for decades invested in programmes of afforestation and reforestation, and have consistently recorded a positive rate of change in recent years (FAO, 2015). The same FAO report found that only a handful of states (such as Gibraltar, Monaco, and San Marino) have fewer trees than Malta relative to size, with the country having had no recorded increase in forest area between 1990 and 2015 (FAO, 2015). The need to increase tree cover has been repeatedly acknowledged at policy level in recent years, with lack of access to green and recreational spaces even identified as a public health concern (Vincenti and Braubach, 2013). Malta has seen a number of attempts to implement afforestation programmes; however, in general, these have had limited success, with many planned projects not completed or not even initiated (Cassar and Conrad, 2014), for a variety of reasons. Considering the EPI as a 'proximity-to-target' indicator, and given the failure to meet targets set, Malta would therefore likely score low on this criterion.

Fisheries: The Fish Stocks indicator measures the proportion of a country's total catch (within its Exclusive Economic Zone) that comes from overexploited or collapsed fish stocks. Malta's high score of 82 is significantly above the average (48). This is perhaps because Maltese fisheries are typically artisanal and economically marginal, with a fishing fleet that is tiny in comparison to that of other states. Malta has also made considerable strides in the establishment of Marine Protected Areas (MPAs). Nevertheless, the country has featured prominently in discussions of fishery sustainability in the Mediterranean, largely because it has been rapidly carving out a niche for itself in the field of aquaculture and particularly tuna ranching, especially since the 1990s (Said et al., 2016). While it would be unfair to evaluate the performance of an entire sector based only on one sub-activity, tuna ranching has come to play a role that is significant enough to at least merit some further consideration. Between 2015 and 2016, Blue Fin Tuna (BFT) landings almost doubled, with an increase in wholesale value of 69% over this same time period (NSO, 2016a). However, there has been concern over the state of BFT fisheries in the Mediterranean, resulting in 2006, in the International Commission for the Conservation of Atlantic Tunas (ICCAT) adopting a 15-year recovery plan for the species and imposing a quota system. Although recent indications have been positive and quotas have therefore been increased, there have been claims that actual catches far exceed Total Allowable Catches, that catching of immature tuna and use of illegal fishing practices are common, and that several countries hide or falsify data (Greenpeace, 2006), making a realistic assessment of the state of sustainability of this fishery difficult and leading to calls for cautious interpretation of statistics because of these uncertainties (WWF, 2016). Similar claims that global marine fisheries catches are underreported were made just last year (Pauly and Zeller, 2016). The EPI includes a 'penalty' score to reflect poor data quality, but ranks Malta's fisheries data as being of high to very high quality. It is also worth considering other environmental issues arising from commercial fisheries, including negative impacts of bottom trawling leading to a consistent decline in the biomass index of a number of species, and depletion of incidental catch species (Nature Trust Malta, 2015). Although data uncertainties limit this evaluation, it is possible and even likely that there may be at least some overestimation of Malta's fisheries score.

Biodiversity and habitats: The EPI score for biodiversity and habitats is based on five equally weighted indicators (Table 19.1). Malta received the maximum possible score of 100 for the two indicators measuring terrestrial habitat protection. The country has indeed made significant strides in extending coverage of terrestrial protected areas over recent years, with these now covering nearly a quarter of the country's land area (UNEP-WCMC, 2017), well above the Aichi target-based EPI threshold of 17% protection of terrestrial habitat. Conversely, and notwithstanding the progress made in establishing MPAs (as discussed above), Malta's coverage of Marine Protected Areas remains lower than the corresponding target of 10% (at 6%) (UNEP-WCMC, 2017), with a consequently lower score.

The EPI report notes that these indicators gauge national performance but acknowledges that "there is no guarantee that the increase of protected areas will prevent species and biodiversity loss" (Hsu et al., 2016, p. 94), also noting the need to emphasize efforts to better manage, rather than expand, protected areas. We argue that this latter point calls into question the ability of the selected indicators to provide any sort of realistic assessment of the state-of-health of biodiversity and habitats, particularly given the well-documented phenomenon of 'paper parks'. In a global review looking at how effective protected areas are in meeting their conservation targets, Leverington et al. (2010) found that the overall mean score for effectiveness was 0.53 out of a maximum possible score of 1, with only 22% of areas considered to be in the sound management range. An assessment of Marine Protected Areas across the Mediterranean reached a similar conclusion that management is insufficient (Gabrié et al., 2012). These concerns are also relevant to protected areas in Malta. For example, it was only in December 2016 that management plans and conservation orders for many of the country's Natura 2000 sites were formally approved, and implementation in many of these sites is completely absent or still lacking. A number of other sites have management plans that are significantly outdated. Past reviews of the state of protected areas in Malta have revealed not only shortcomings related to management planning, financing, and threat management, but also the absence of adequate review, evaluation, and adaptive management safeguards (Conrad, 2008; Galea, 2015; Zammit, 2015). The small island of Comino, a Natura 2000 site in its entirety, can be used to illustrate the significant gap between paper plans and reality. Objectives listed in the management plan include management of tourism activities at the island's most popular bathing site (known as the Blue Lagoon), ensuring that rural tourism and outdoor recreation are practiced in harmony with the site's conservation status, restoration of a derelict pig farm site, and establishment of a daily patrol schedule, among others. At the time of writing, none of these were even close to being achieved and as of late 2016, the island was still subject to largely uncontrolled tourism pressures, with widespread trampling, a recent notable increase in vehicular traffic within the island, no realistic plans for reuse of the derelict pig farm, and no effective wardening/patrol system in place.

Malta also received maximum scores for indicators measuring the degree of overlap between protected areas and species habitat ranges, based on data provided by Yale's Map of Life. However, a closer examination of the source data used for these indicators shows that scale may be a significant limiting factor for such an assessment in a country as small as Malta, given that the entire land territory of Malta falls within a single pixel. Because of the resolution of spatial data, this indicator therefore provides little useful insight into possible gaps between within-country coverage of protection and species ranges. What data does exist from other sources suggests that this overlap has improved but is nevertheless not reflective of the EPI score of 100. Bonanno (2013), for example, estimates 63% overlap between endemic distributional areas and protected surfaces within the Sicilian floristic territory, including Malta. Of relevance, concerns have recently been expressed about the potential loss of such overlap within Mediterranean areas in the light of projected future climate conditions (Barredo et al., 2016).

Climate and energy: The two indicators used for calculation of a climate and energy score are trend in carbon intensity and trend in CO_2 emissions per KwH. Trend in carbon intensity measures the degree of decoupling between a country's GDP and CO_2 emissions (with Malta scoring 79). Although differences in methodologies render a direct comparison difficult, other analyses have shown that although CO_2 emissions and GDP continue to broadly mirror each other, there are some indications of relative decoupling (Conrad and Cassar, 2014; Malta Environment and Planning Authority, 2012). Trend in CO_2 emissions per KwH measures the extent of decarbonization in electricity and heat production. Malta is one of 52 countries that was automatically assigned the maximum score of 100, on the basis that they already have a low level of CO_2 emissions per KwH. However, an energy efficiency report for Malta notes the following: "Emissions for power generation are quite high. The average CO_2 emission factor for power generation decreased from 1,600 gCO_2/Kwh in 1990 to < 1,000 g/CO_2kWh in 1995. . . [and] has remained roughly stable since then" (Enerdata, 2011, p. 6); the same report ranks Malta as "among countries with lowest performances" on this criterion (p. 1). National data indicates fluctuations from year to year but with a significant decrease from 2014 to 2015, largely due to Malta's connection to the Italian Transmission Network via a Malta-Sicily submarine power cable. While there therefore does appear to be a trend towards decreased emissions, the blanket assignment of a maximum score does not appear justified. It is also of note that the EPI assessment is based on data extending only to 2012, over which time period CO_2 emissions per kwH actually increased (from 1,914 CO_2 equivalent kilotons in 2011 to 2,028 in 2012) (NSO, 2016a).

A third indicator (access to electricity) was not used for calculation of composite scores.

Environmental health

The environmental health score takes into account three criteria: (1) health impacts, (2) air quality, and (3) water and sanitation (Table 19.2).

Health impacts: Health impacts are determined on the basis of a single indicator – environmental risk exposure, data for which is derived from the Institute for Health Metrics and Evaluation's Global Burden of Diseases, Injuries, and Risk Factors study. Malta's score of 83.68 places it in 52nd position; according to the source data, the largest cause of premature death in Malta is ischemic heart disease, followed by lung cancer, cerebrovascular disease, and Alzheimer's (Institute for Health Metrics and Evaluation, 2015). The risk factors that most significantly drive death and disability combined are dietary risks, high systolic blood pressure, and high body-mass index, among others. Malta also has rates of ischemic heart disease, congenital defects, neonatal

Table 19.2 EPI 2016 indicator scores for Malta (on a scale of 0–100) for **environmental health**, compared to average scores across 180 states, and ranking of Malta's performance relative to other states. The superscript ★ indicates that Malta's performance was above average for the indicator in question.

Weighting (%)	Target area/indicator	Malta's score	Average score	Malta's relative ranking
Environmental health★		92.83	72.62	20
33	**Health impacts★**	83.68	66.41	52
100	Environmental risk exposure★	83.68	66.41	52
33	**Air quality★**	94.81	77.93	11
30	Household air quality★	95	71.75	1
	Household air quality – risk exposure★	100	75.83	1
30	Air pollution – average exposure to $PM_{2.5}$★	100	90.28	1
	Air pollution – average exposure to $PM_{2.5}$★ (risk exposure)	72.87	66.7	87
30	Average $PM_{2.5}$ exceedance★	100	82.03	1
10	Average exposure to NO_2★	96.25	76.36	11
33	**Water and sanitation★**	100	73.51	1
50	Access to sanitation★	100	74.67	1
	Unsafe sanitation – risk exposure★	100	72.21	1
50	Access to drinking water★	100	75.29	1
	Unsafe drinking water quality – risk exposure★	100	71.88	1

preterm birth, and diabetes that are significantly higher than in comparable countries (Institute for Health Metrics and Evaluation, 2015).

Water and sanitation: Water and sanitation are assessed on the basis of four indicators – access to sanitation, risk of exposure to unsafe sanitation, access to drinking water, and risk of exposure to unsafe drinking water. On all four criteria, Malta scores the maximum possible 100. These indicators generally accurately reflect Malta's high level of human development. However, as noted earlier, nitrate pollution has been shown to potentially impact on the quality of drinking water and consequently on human health; this is not reflected under this target area, which only takes into account access to improved water sources (i.e., primarily those protected from faecal contamination).

Air quality: Air quality is assessed on the basis of six indicators, collectively assessing household air quality, exposure to $PM_{2.5}$, and exposure to NO_2. Malta has an overall high score of 95, reflecting generally positive national trends of decreasing levels of the measured pollutants. However, national-level data and the evaluation of selected pollutants only obscure the fact that air pollution remains a localized concern in some areas. For example, while national data shows a decline in NO_2 concentrations between 2009 and 2011, with levels well below EU and WHO limit values, above-limit levels were recorded at 18 (of 131) sites. In the case of particulate matter, limit values at one traffic-dominated site were exceeded on 80 of 340 days (Malta Environment and Planning Authority, 2012). The EPI assessment is also limited to the two selected pollutants, which are not necessarily the most relevant. Indeed, Malta's Air Quality Plan (MEPA, 2010) identifies PM_{10} as the main pollutant of concern. It is also of note that air quality has repeatedly been recorded to be a key public concern; in one assessment, 13.9% of the population reported major problems with local air quality and 31.9% reported moderate problems, indicating a perception of air quality much worse that the EU average (where 75.6% report no problems), especially among low-income populations (Vincenti and Braubach, 2013). This was also confirmed in this present study (see the next section).

Public assessment of environmental performance

In this section, we consider the extent to which the EPI assessment reflects the views of those living in Malta, based on the results of a public survey, a brief overview of which is given in Table 19.3. This was administered over the phone to a sample of 389 individuals aged 18 and over, stratified by gender and age and representative of the demographics of the Maltese population (at a 95% confidence level and with a 5% margin of error). Relevant key findings are reviewed below.

When asked to rate Malta's overall environmental performance on a scale of 1 to 10 (with 1 being the lowest value and 10 being the highest), respondents' answers ranged across the full spectrum of possible values, with an average score of 5.6. Over 25% of respondents ranked Malta's overall performance as poor (score of 0–4); 55% considered performance to be mid-range (score of 5–7), while some 19% of respondents provided a score of 8 or higher. Among the most significant environmental issues identified were air pollution (cited by 54% of respondents), urbanization (48%), waste generation (38%), habitat loss (26%), and marine pollution (21%).

When asked to rate Malta's performance within each of the seven EPI priority areas, respondents' assessments again varied widely, with mean values ranging between 5 and 7. Overall, Malta's performance was judged to be strongest in the energy field, with the lowest-ranked areas being air quality and climate change. Over 50% of respondents ranked performance in the air quality sector as being ≤ 5; similarly, over 50% of respondents ranked performance relating to water resources to be ≤ 6. Finally, respondents were given an explanation of Malta's 9th place ranking in the 2016 EPI and asked to give a rating to reflect how accurately they feel this represents Malta's actual environmental performance. Results varied, with a mean value of 6. Some 30% of respondents considered the EPI report to be of poor accuracy (score of 0–4), 37% of moderate accuracy (score of 5–7), and 34% of high accuracy (score of 8–10).

These results provide several insights of relevance. First, it is evident that there is no single predominant opinion on Malta's environmental performance across the population; views vary widely, as do levels of awareness, knowledge, and interest. Some considered Malta's 9th place ranking to be ludicrous and completely unfounded in reality, while others felt this was a fair reflection of the progress the country has made in the environmental field. It is of note that the

Table 19.3 Overview of survey exploring public perceptions of environmental quality in Malta

Target respondents: Residents of Malta aged 18 and over
Sample size: 389
Margin of error: 5%
Sampling method: Random stratified sampling
Survey administration: Telephone survey
Main survey questions:

1. On a scale of 1–10★, how would you rank Malta's environmental performance in general?
2. What do you consider to be the three most significant environmental issues that Malta currently faces?
3. Please rank Malta's environmental performance within each of the specified sectors [EPI priority areas] on a scale of 1–10.
4. A study published in January 2016 ranked Malta 9th out of 180 countries on the basis of its environmental performance. How accurately do you think this ranking reflects Malta's actual environmental performance (on a scale of 1–10)?

★ Whenever a question required respondents to provide a ranking, an explanation of the spectrum of scores from 1 to 10 was provided.

subject of environmental performance was prone to be policitized by several respondents, with their answers seen to be extolling or disparaging the virtues of the political party presently in government. This should be borne in mind as a constraint that prejudices interpretation of the results. In general, however, it appears unlikely that the EPI's strongly positive overall evaluation is shared by a majority of the population. Second, survey results show that several environmental issues considered to be most significant by respondents are either: (1) not included within EPI target areas (e.g., urbanization) or (2) if incorporated (directly or indirectly), the EPI assessment does not appear to fully or accurately the present state-of-affairs as per public opinion (e.g., air pollution, habitat loss). In the case of an issue like urbanization, this itself comes with a myriad of related concerns ranging from noise pollution to local air quality to the availability of public space – several relevant aspects are discussed at length in Chapter 10 (Turcu). Third, respondents' relative rankings of performance in different sectors do not tally with the relative rankings given in the EPI. For example, respondents ranked Malta's performance in biodiversity and air quality quite poorly overall, but both these areas received above-average rankings in the EPI.

Discussion and conclusions

It was not the intention of this contribution to cast Malta's environmental performance in a bad light. Malta has made substantial strides in the environmental field in recent decades across different sectors, even if considerable challenges remain. It is however, our firm belief that if indicators are truly going to contribute to environmental decision-making in a constructive manner, then they need to be *useful* and *relevant*, allowing accurate gauging of a situation at a given point in time. Similarly, in the introduction to this volume, Bell and Morse talk of *resilient* and *honest* measures. It is in this spirit that we set out to take a critical look at Malta's EPI ranking. The question we ask is, does Malta's EPI rating represent reality or, in other words, is the EPI providing a relevant and honest assessment of environmental performance in Malta?

Based on the above review, our answer would appear to be 'not quite'. It is evident that the EPI has at least some shortcomings in terms of its ability to accurately portray Malta's environmental performance. Indeed, Börhringer and Jochem's (2007) concern that the results of such indices may be inconsistent or misleading appears to be relevant. This is especially the case with the *ecosystem integrity* score, which seems to be strongly distorted and to give a false impression of very positive performance. This distortion appears due to a combination of factors including excessive reliance on indicators that reflect 'paper' progress rather than actual progress (e.g., in the case of biodiversity), a misleading assessment of priority areas due to exclusive focus on one or few dimensions of it (e.g., use of wastewater treatment as the sole indicator of water resources), blanket assignment of high scores not based on analysis of country-level data (e.g., trend in CO_2 emissions per KwH), omission of criteria that ought to be relevant (e.g., forests), and the failure to include priority areas that are of national relevance (e.g., urbanization). While recognizing that the EPI is designed to reflect performance across a diverse range of countries with a wide range of circumstances and that its ability to fully reflect the performance of any one single country may therefore be imperfect, it is nevertheless worrying when the metric paints a picture that is poorly reflective of reality.

This review also suggests that the EPI may especially struggle to accurately document the environmental performance of small or marginal territories with a unique set of circumstances (as in the case of small island states like Malta). This is not surprising when considering that the index needs to cater for countries ranging from the size of Malta to the size of Russia, > 54,000 times larger. The use of broader-scale data that makes possible assessment of these larger territories unfortunately leads to a loss of data resolution for smaller territories that may render such assessment largely meaningless. Furthermore, the considerable data demands required for calculation of the EPI also create a time lag of several years that may misrepresent results – many of the datasets used for calculation of 2016 EPI indicators are at least several years old, effectively meaning that this is not assessing the present state-of-affairs but the situation some years back. This may be especially significant for small territories, where change, positive or negative, can cascade through a system rapidly. This also highlights a danger of such CIs, which have the benefit of wide visibility but the downside that results are often presented in popular media without detailed explanation of the nature or time-frame of the data from which they are derived.

We also argue that despite being presented as a gauge of policy performance, assessing how close countries are to meeting targets set, the EPI does not really serve this function effectively because of two key limitations. First, it has limited capability to consider, in the first place, the appropriateness and adequacy of policy targets. In the case of Malta, for example, aiming to increase coverage of protected areas is all well and good but largely meaningless as long as many of these remain poorly and/or inadequately managed. A much more relevant target would be to increase the extent and effectiveness of management of these sites but this is harder to measure in a way that is quantifiable and that would be applicable worldwide. Second, the EPI has little capacity to assess actual effectiveness of policies. Indicators should arguably also serve an ex post evaluation function, providing insight into the ability of policies to, for example, change the state of the environment, to address underlying driving forces of change, to be cost-effective, and to produce lasting results.

Based on the above, it must be concluded that the EPI fails to perform adequately on several key principles that have been highlighted elsewhere in this volume. In Chapter 2, for example, Pintér et al. refer to the Bellagio STAMP principles of *adequate scope* and *transparency*. While certainly not due to intentional design, Malta's EPI calculations are flawed in both respects, lacking the temporal and geographical scale of consideration that would render results meaningful, and with flaws of transparency that are arguably inevitable given the loss of detail in communication of aggregated indicators. An environmental performance indicator is treated as such by the public and often also by policymakers, and a score for *biodiversity* or *water* is often take at face value to be a comprehensive assessment of that particular sector. The various provisos that are clearly highlighted by the authors of the EPI in methodological material unfortunately tend to be lost when a headline proclaiming that Malta has the 9th best environmental performance worldwide presents itself. There are also flaws relating to the *relevance* and *reliability* criteria highlighted by Janoušková, Hák, and Moldan (Chapter 30), as has already been discussed above. Finally, the very pertinence of proximity-to-target methods certainly merits some reflection, particularly with reference to Jesinghaus's (Chapter 26) insightful observations regarding the political motivation behind chosen targets.

As a report card of country performance, the EPI can therefore be considered to have some but limited utility; it provides a general indication of a country's performance in different sectors and relative to other states, but cannot be used as an objective basis for gauging the success of policy. However, the index has the potential to be more useful if better calibrated, or smart-scaled, to specific regions or sectors. Several examples already exist, with modified versions of the EPI for specific areas or sectors (e.g., Hawkins, 2014; Spawn, 2015; Zomer, 2014). A similar exercise could be carried out to create a European version of the EPI that takes into account the priority objectives of the 7th Environment Action Programme, including objectives such as waste generation and use of freshwater resources that do not feature in the EPI but that are highly relevant regionally. For a country like Malta, this would be one step closer to providing a meaningful gauge of environmental performance.

Acknowledgements

We gratefully acknowledge Mr. Paul Galea, Mr. Mekonen Birhane, and Ms. Chantelle Dimech, for survey data collection.

Notes

1 Since this contribution was written, a new edition (2018) of the EPI has been published; this now places Malta in an even higher 4th position, behind Switzerland, France, and Denmark. The analysis in this chapter is based exclusively on the 2016 results; however, the observations made regarding the accuracy of this ranking remain pertinent also in view of the 2018 report conclusions.
2 According to the European Environment Agency, value > 40% indicates severe water stress.

References

Barredo, J.I., Caudullo, G. & Dosio, A. 2016, "Mediterranean habitat loss under future climate conditions: Assessing impacts on the Natura 2000 protected area network", *Applied Geography*, vol. 75, pp. 83–92.
Böhringer, C. & Jochem, P.E.P. 2007, "Measuring the immeasurable – A survey of sustainability indices", *Ecological Economics*, vol. 63, no. 1, pp. 1–8.
Bonanno, G. 2013, "Adaptive management as a tool to improve the conservation of endemic floras: The case of Sicily, Malta and their satellite islands", *Biodiversity and Conservation*, vol. 22, no. 6, pp. 1317–1354.
Cassar, L.F. & Conrad, E. 2014, *An Outline Strategy for Implementation of a National Restoration and Afforestation Project in the Maltese Islands*. Report prepared for the Ministry of Sustainable Development, the Environment, and Climate Change. Available: https://msdec.gov.mt/en/Documents/Downloads/Afforestation_Restoration%20Ecology_Cassar.pdf
Conrad, E. 2008, "Conservation planning in a cultural context – an island perspective: The case of the Maltese Islands", *Journal of Environmental Consumerism*, vol. 4, nos. 7–8, pp. 37–42.
Conrad, E. & Cassar, L.F. 2014, "Decoupling economic growth and environmental degradation: Reviewing progress to date in the small island state of Malta", *Sustainability*, vol. 6, no. 10, pp. 6729.

Emerson, J.W., Hsu, A., Levy, M.A., de Sherbinin, A., Mara, V., Esty, D.C. & Jaiteh, M. 2012, *2012 Environmental Performance Index and Pilot Trend Environmental Performance Index*, Yale Center for Environmental Law and Policy, New Haven, CT.

Enerdata. 2011, *Malta Energy Efficiency Report*. Available: https://library.e.abb.com/public/559f269d9ff2f48 5c12578dc002dcce6/Malta.pdf

European Food Safety Authority. 2017, "The 2015 European Union report on pesticide residues in food", *EFSA Journal*, vol. 15, no. 4, doi:10.2903 /j.efsa.2017.4791

Eurostat. 2015, *Water Statistics*. Available: http://ec.europa.eu/eurostat/statistics-explained/index.php/ Water_statistics

Eurostat. 2016, *Land Cover, Land Use and Landscape*. Available: http://ec.europa.eu/eurostat/statistics-explained/index.php/Land_cover,_land_use_and_landscape

Food and Agriculture Organization (FAO). 2015, *Global Forest Resources Assessment 2015*, FAO, Rome.

Gabrié, C., Lagabrielle, E., Bissery, C., Crochelet, E., Meola, B., Webster, C., Claudet, J., Chassanite, A., Marinesque, S., Robert, P., Goutx, M. & Quod, C. 2012, *The Status of Marine Protected Areas in the Mediterranean Sea*, MedPAN and Rac/SPA, Marseille.

Galea, P. 2015, *The financial sustainability of a number of Natura 2000 sites in Malta*, B.Sc. (Hons), Earth Systems dissertation, University of Malta.

Gassert, F., Reig, P., Luo, T. & Maddocks, A. 2013, *Aqueduct country and river basin rankings: A weighted aggregation of spatially distinct hydrological indicators*, Working paper, World Resources Institute, Washington DC.

Greenpeace. 2006, *Where have all the tuna gone? How tuna ranching and pirate fishing are wiping out Bluefin Tuna in the Mediterranean Sea*, Greenpeace International, Amsterdam.

Hawkins, N. 2014, May 22, "Malaysia's environmental performance index: Yale Environmental Performance Index", *Indicators in Practice*.

Heaton, T.H.E., Stuart, M.E., Sapiano, M. & Micallef Sultana, M. 2012, "An isotope study of the sources of nitrate in Malta's groundwater", *Journal of Hydrology*, vol. 414–415, pp. 244–254.

Hoekstra, A.Y. & Mekonnen, M.M. 2012, "The water footprint of humanity", *Proceedings of the National Academy of Sciences of the United States of America*, vol. 109, no. 9, pp. 3232–3237.

Hsu, A. et al. 2016, *Environmental Performance Index*, Yale University, New Haven, CT.

Hsu, A., Emerson, J., Levy, M., de Sherbinin, A., Johnson, L., Malik, O., Schwartz, J. & Jaiteh, M. 2014, *The 2014 Environmental Performance Index*, Yale Center for Environmental Law & Policy, New Haven, CT.

Institute for Health Metrics and Evaluation. 2015, *Malta*, Institute for Health Metrics and Evaluation. Available: www.healthdata.org/malta

Leverington, F., Lemos Costa, K., Pavese, H., Lisle, A. & Hockings, M. 2010, "A global analysis of protected area management effectiveness", *Environmental Management*, vol. 46, no. 5, pp. 685–698.

Malta Environment and Planning Authority (MEPA). 2010, *The Air Quality Plan for the Maltese Islands*. Available: www.mepa.org.mt/file.aspx?f=4367

Malta Environment and Planning Authority (MEPA). 2012, *The Environment Report: Indicators 2010–2011*, MEPA/NSO, Floriana.

National Statistics Office (NSO). 2007, *Census of Population and Housing 2005: Volume 2 Dwellings*, NSO, Valletta.

National Statistics Office (NSO). 2008, *Gross Nitrogen Balance for Malta 2007*, NSO, Valletta.

National Statistics Office (NSO). 2016a, *Agriculture and Fisheries 2014*, NSO, Valletta.

National Statistics Office (NSO). 2016b, *News Release 162/2016: Electricity Generation 2006–2015*, NSO, Valletta.

National Statistics Office (NSO). 2017, *News Release 011/2017: Motor vehicles: Q4/2016*, NSO, Valletta.

Nature Trust Malta. 2015, *Current and Future Impacts on the Marine Environment: Challenge to Achieve Good Environmental Status*, Malta Report, MedTrends Project.

Pauly, D. & Zeller, D. 2016, "Catch reconstructions reveal that global marine fisheries catches are higher than reported and declining", *Nature Communications*, vol. 7, pp. 10244.

Rogge, N. 2012, "Undesirable specialization in the construction of composite policy indicators: The environmental performance index", *Ecological Indicators*, vol. 23, pp. 143–154.

Said, A., Tzanopoulos, J. & MacMillan, D. 2016, "Bluefin tuna fishery policy in Malta: The plight of artisanal fishermen caught in the capitalist net", *Marine Policy*, vol. 73, pp. 27–34.

Spawn, A. 2015, April 2, "From global to regional: The Abu Dhabi EPI", Yale Environmental Performance Index, *The Metric*.

Spiteri, D., Scerri, C. & Valdaramidis, V. 2015, "The current situation for the water sources in the Maltese Islands", *Malta Journal of Health Sciences*, vol. 2, no. 1, pp. 22–25.

UNEP-WCMC. 2017, January, *Protected Area Profile for Malta from the World Database of Protected Areas*. Available: www.protectedplanet.net

Vincenti, K. & Braubach, M. 2013, *Environmental Health Inequalities in Malta*, Environmental Health Policy Coordination Unit.

World Wildlife Fund (WWF). 2016, *Position Paper: East Atlantic and Mediterranean Bluefin Tuna: Towards the Full Recovery of the Stock*. Available: http://d2ouvy59p0dg6k.cloudfront.net/downloads/wwf_s_position_on_bluefin_tuna_2016.pdf

Zammit, T. 2015, *Basic resilience assessment principles with reference to the Pembroke Natura 2000 site*, B.Sc. (Hons), Earth Systems dissertation, University of Malta.

Zomer, A. 2014, December 9, "Improving environmental data and performance in Vietnam", Yale Environmental Performance Index, *The Metric*.

20

SUSTAINABILITY-RELATED INDICATORS DEVELOPED FOR GOVERNMENTS

L. Reijnders

Introduction

When I was a young boy, one of my favorite books was about a professor doing complex arithmetic to solve problems. He did so when his wife disappeared. He multiplied the name of his wife by the words cuckoo clock, as this clock was also gone. In this way he found the name of place where his abducted wife was held. This came back to me when I read the paper *Sustainability Index for Taipei* by Lee and Huang (2007). To replace a set of 48 sustainability indicators in the plan for the sustainable development of this Taiwanese city, Lee and Huang selected 51 sustainability indicators, based on discussions with experts, scholars and government departments. The indicators proposed by Lee and Huang (2007) include the percentage of public places with wireless internet connections, the per capita floor area of private dwellings, the number of bicycle kickstands and the per capita pedestrian walkway index.

A 1915 Canadian Commission on Conservation, cited in the same paper, stated that sustainability means that natural capital should not be reduced. Natural capital includes abiotic goods (e.g. minerals, water), abiotic services (e.g. flows of energy), ecosystem goods (e.g. forestry products) and ecosystem services (e.g. protection against soil erosion) (Terama et al. 2016). Deriving the conservation of natural capital from such indicators as the number of bicycle kickstands and the percentage of public places with wireless internet connections, as proposed by Lee and Huang (2007), would seem to require the complex arithmetic of my children's book professor. The loss of phosphate resources linked to the feeding of Taipei is significant to the conservation of natural capital as the depletion of phosphate rock resources may strongly restrict the number of people that can be fed in the future (Reijnders 2016). However, an indicator reflecting the loss of phosphate resources is not included in the 51 indicators proposed by Lee and Huang. Also, the loss of copper from the economy might matter as it may contribute to losing natural capital, more specifically reducing the ability to supply copper for essential uses to future generations (Reijnders 2003). However, among the 51 indicators proposed by Lee and Huang (2007) there is no indicator for copper loss from the economy. The absence of indicators for losses of phosphorus and copper resources is all the more remarkable as the Taiwanese economy is heavily dependent on the import of natural resources (Chen et al. 2009).

One might argue that, given current political settings, in constructing sustainability indicators the focus should not be on sustainability but on sustainable development as coined in the aftermath of *Our Common Future* (World Commission on Environment and Development 1987). This argument would probably seem farfetched to Lee and Huang (2007) as they state that sustainable development should lead to sustainability. Furthermore, the first time that 'sustainable development' was used in a worldwide policy forum, in the 1980 World Conservation Strategy of the International Union for the Conservation of Nature (IUCN), this was in the phrase 'Living resource conservation for sustainable development'. This World Conservation Strategy stated: 'sustainable utilization is a simple idea: we should utilize species and ecosystems at levels and in ways that allow them to go on renewing themselves for all practical purposes indefinitely'. The World Conservation Strategy (IUCN 1980) was in the tradition that the conservation of natural capital is a *prerequisite* for a social and economic development that is sustainable. This is at variance with the view that environment is a *dimension* of sustainability taken by Lee and Huang (2007).

On the other hand, one may argue that a set of sustainability-related indicators made for governments should fit the political context. So, it would seem useful to go back to the origin of government action in the field of indicators for sustainability or sustainable development. This is the publication *Our Common Future* of the World Commission on Environment and Development (1987). *Our Common Future* defines sustainable development as: 'a pattern of development that meets the needs of the present generation without jeopardizing the ability of future generations to meet their own needs'. Indeed Lee and Huang (2007) refer to the work on sustainable development indicators by the Commission on Sustainable Development (CSD) of the United Nations, which builds on this definition. Though the definition of sustainable development given by the World Commission on Environment and Development (1987) is ambiguous, it is clear that justice between the generations is a central issue in sustainable development as defined in *Our Common Future*. Rawls (1999) has written in *A Theory of Justice* that justice between the generations should lead to decision making as if decision makers do not know to which generation they belong (under the 'veil of ignorance'). This would give equal weight to present and future generations and would seem preferable to the practice of economists, who tend to use discounted utility in allocating weight to future generations (e.g. Pezzey 1992).

In view of the centrality of intergenerational justice to sustainable development as defined in *Our Common Future* an important issue in constructing sustainability-related indicators for governments is: does this set reflect the ability of future generations to meet their needs? The set of indicators proposed by Lee and Huang (2007) includes motorcar- and motorcycle-ownership rates. These indicators would seem relevant to justice between the generations as increasing ownership rates for cars and motorcycles reflect increasing depletion rates for mineral oil resources, increasing losses of metal resources and increasing long-term loads of pollutants (Chester and Horvath 2009; Nakamura et al. 2014), which can negatively affect future generations. However, Lee and Huang state that an *increase* in motorcar and motorcycle ownership has a *positive* effect on sustainable development. The assignation of a positive value would seem to follow from the view of Lee and Huang that sustainability should apply to four equally weighted dimensions: environment, (social) equity, economy and institutions (including politics). Because increased ownership of cars and motorcycles is felt by Lee and Huang to positively contribute to economic sustainability, such increased ownership is also supposed to contribute positively to sustainable development. From the way Lee and Huang (2007) deal with increasing ownership rates of cars and motorcycles one may conclude that neither intergenerational justice nor the conservation of natural capital as a prerequisite to sustainable development is central to the set of indicators they proposed.

This contribution will consider the question whether the set of sustainability indicators proposed by Lee and Huang (2007) for use by the Taipei government has exceptional characteristics.

For this purpose first other sets of local and regional sustainable development indicators made for governments (and their agencies) will be considered. Subsequently indicator sets proposed within the framework of the United Nations (UN) and a number of indicator sets prepared for national governments will be surveyed. From this survey conclusions will be drawn as to the character of indicator sets for sustainability or sustainable development made for governments.

Local and regional government indicator sets

The first two sets of local and regional indicators to be considered here also come from Asia. The first set regards Chongming County, Shanghai (China), for which Yuan et al. (2003), using a consultation process, proposed a set of sustainability indicators. No definition of sustainability (or sustainable development) was given. Seventeen indicators were selected by Yuan et al. (2003). Eight indicators regarding the economic condition were selected. This was found to be in line with China's Agenda 21 which emphasized economic development (Yuan et al. 2003). Three out of the 17 indicators (waste treatment and management, environmental quality and ecological protection) were in the realm of natural capital. Other indicators included: level of crime and resident satisfaction with participation. Differently from Lee and Huang (2007), Yuan et al. (2003) did not propose an aggregate indicator to be derived from the 17 indicators selected.

Hai et al. (2014) proposed an expert-consultation based set of sustainability indicators for Thai Bin Province in Vietnam. No definition of sustainability or sustainable development was given. In total 69 indicators were selected. Ordered by themes, 15 related to economic development, 9 to health, 7 to poverty, 7 to land, 5 to the atmosphere, 4 to education, 4 to production and consumption patterns, 3 to demography, 3 to fresh water, 2 to natural hazards and 1 to global economic partnership. Hai et al. (2014) did not propose an aggregate indicator to be derived from the 69 indicators which they selected.

The indicator sets constructed by Yuan et al. (2003), Lee and Huang (2007) and Hai et al. (2014) are similar in that neither justice between the generations nor the conservation of natural capital as a prerequisite to sustainable development is central to their construction. In other respects they show much variety.

There have been efforts to limit variety in local and regional sustainability-related indicator sets (see also Chapter 17 by Hsu in this Handbook). China has developed an indicator set for urban application across the country (Michael et al. 2014). This set can be used to calculate an Urban Sustainability Index and has four categories or dimensions: society, environment, economy and resource utilization. The 2011 version of this indicator set includes 17 indicators and the 2013 version thereof 34 indicators (Michael et al. 2014). Indicators included in the 2013 version include: number of doctors per capita, pension security coverage, industrial SO_2 discharged per unit of gross national product (GDP), disposable income per capita, per capita government investment in research and development and total energy consumption per unit of GDP. Malaysia developed a set of common indicators to be applied by Malaysian city governments (Michael et al. 2014; Ibrahim et al. 2015). The 2012 version thereof includes: the percentage of Grade A public toilets, the Happiness Index, the number of tourist attractions and recreation centers and the growth rate of private investment (Michael et al. 2014). Sets of common sustainable development indicators for use by local governments have also been developed in France, Italy, Lebanon, Portugal, Spain and the United Kingdom (Mascarenhas et al. 2010; Moreno Pires et al. 2014). Pintér et al. (2005) noted that in spite of efforts to establish common sustainability indicators for cities, the diversity of urban sustainable development indicators increased. Moreno Pires et al. (2014) who investigated the fate of common local indicators in Portugal found limited support and use of such indictors. Thus it should not come as a surprise that when one surveys publications regarding local and regional sustainability-related indicator sets (Brugman 1997; Mascarenhas et al. 2010; Tanguay et al. 2010; Shen et al. 2011; Michael et al. 2014; Moreno Pires and Fidélis 2015; Science for Environment Policy 2015; Pupphachai and Zuidema 2017), one is struck by their very large variety. Tanguay et al. 2010 attribute this to divergent interpretations of sustainable development, the wide range of objectives to be met and differences in accessible data.

The availability of reliable data has been reported to be a serious problem in the construction (and application) of local and regional sustainability-related indicator sets (Cassar et al. 2013; Science for Environment Policy 2015). Regarding the interpretation of sustainable development, Mascarenhas et al. 2010, Tanguay et al. (2010) and Shen et al. (2011) note a considerable number of cases in which sustainable development is interpreted in terms of quality of life for the present generation. There are also sets of indicators that only deal with environmental performance (Brugman 1997; Mascarenhas et al. 2010). Rather often the indicator sets have social, economic, environmental and governance dimensions, without capturing the linkages between these domains (Science for Environment Policy 2015). Aggregated and weighted indexes for sustainable development are apparently rather uncommon. I have been unable to find a sustainability-related indicator set made for a local or regional government in which intergenerational justice and conservation of natural capital as a prerequisite to sustainable development are central.

UN indicator sets

The work on sustainable indicators at the United Nations (UN) is in this Handbook also discussed by Dahl, Chapter 23, and by Rotz and Fraser, Chapter 6. The, now disbanded, Commission on Sustainable Development (CSD) of the UN has developed guidance documents for the construction of governmental indicator sets for sustainable development, the most recent one dating from 2007 (UN Commission on Sustainable Development 2007). The CSD guidance document of 2007 proposes a core set of 50 indicators and a larger set of 96 indicators for sustainable development, to be based on available objective statistical data. The core set has indicators in the social, economic, environmental and institutional domains and also includes a number of 'cross-cutting' themes such as natural hazards and poverty. Examples of core indicators are the percentage of the population living in coastal areas and the contribution of tourism to gross national product. The guidance document states that 'the overall progress towards sustainable development' can be monitored by using these indicators, but notes that 'given the complexity and the continuing limits of understanding sustainable development definite answers are unlikely' (UN Commission on Sustainable Development 2007).

A problem with the indicators proposed by the CSD regards the availability and quality of data regarding proposed indicators (cf. Constanza et al. 2016; SDG Collaborators 2016). Also the measurement of indicators may be subject to political entanglement, which may lead to distorted estimates (SDG Collaborators 2016). The absence of reliable data can limit indicator use and usefulness.

The CSD guidance document of 2007 refers to sets of sustainability of sustainable development indicators for governments and agencies, 'which to a large extent follow the guidance of the UN Commission on Sustainable Development' (UN Commission on Sustainable Development 2007). However, Smits and Hoekstra (2011) noted that nearly all countries have sustainable development indicator sets that are very different from the indicator set proposed by the CSD.

In September 2015 the General Assembly of the United Nations has moved the goal posts by adopting *Transforming Our World. The 2030 Agenda for Sustainable Development.* This document contains 17 Sustainable Development Goals (SDG) and 169 targets for 2030 (UN General Assembly 2015; Hák et al. 2016). Examples of the 169 targets are in Box 20.1.

Box 20.1   Examples of targets in *Transforming Our World. The 2030 Agenda for Sustainable Development*

Source: UN General Assembly (2015)

Target 1.2 By 2030, reduce at least by half the proportion of men, women and children of all ages living in poverty in all its dimensions according to national definitions.

Target 4.4 By 2030, substantially increase the number of youth and adults who have relevant skills, including technical and vocational skills, for employment, decent jobs and entrepreneurship.

Target 8.5 By 2030, achieve full and productive employment and decent work for all women and men, including for young people and persons with disabilities, and equal pay for work of equal value.

Target 11.2 By 2030, provide access to safe, affordable, accessible and sustainable transport systems for all, improving road safety, notably by expanding public transport, with special attention to the needs of those in vulnerable situations, women, children, persons with disabilities and older persons.

Target 12.5 By 2030, substantially reduce waste generation through prevention, reduction, recycling and reuse.

As pointed out by Weitz et al. (2016) most of the 169 proposed targets leave significant scope for interpretation.

The 17 goals included in *Transforming Our World. The 2030 Agenda for Sustainable Development* are in Table 20.1. Each goal has a set of indicators proposed within the UN framework in 2016 (Inter-Agency and Expert Group on Sustainable Development Goal Indicators 2016a, b, c). Examples of such indicators are also in Table 20.1. The total number of indicators for the Sustainable Development Goals 2030 proposed in 2016 is 230 (Inter-Agency and Expert Group on Sustainable Development Goal Indicators 2016c). Eighty-nine thereof have been designated as Tier I indicators by the Inter-Agency and Expert Group on SDG Indicators, for which 'an established methodology exists and data are already widely available' (UN Economic and Social Council 2016a; Inter-Agency and Expert Group on Sustainable Development Goal Indicators 2016c).

The political declaration accompanying the 2030 Sustainable Development Goals clarifies that countries are expected to make a national interpretation thereof, setting their own goals and targets in view of their conditions and capabilities (Weitz et al. 2016). This is likely to lead to a divergence from the indicators proposed within the UN framework. Indeed, in an official reaction from China, Weibo (2016) stated that China suggests priority for nine key areas, including 'innovation-driven development strategies and generating momentum for sustainable, healthy and stable economic growth', which will impact indicator choice. And a report of the German Federal Government (2016 p. 13, 14) noted that 'not all targets and international indicators are to be incorporated in the National Sustainable Development Strategy partly because not all are appropriate . . . and partly because Germany's own objectives and targets in some areas are further-reaching and more ambitious'.

Table 20.1 2030 Sustainable Development Goals in *Transforming Our World. The 2030 Agenda for Sustainable Development*

Goal	Example of indicator
1. End poverty in all its forms everywhere	Proportion of the population living below the international poverty line (disaggregated)
2. End hunger, achieve food security and improved nutrition and promote sustainable agriculture	Prevalence of stunting among children under 5 years of age
3. Ensure healthy lives and promote well-being for all at all stages	Under 5 mortality rate
4. Ensure inclusive and equitable quality education and promote lifelong learning opportunities for all	Percentage of children under 5 years of age on } | track in health, learning and psychosocial well-being (by sex)
5. Achieve gender equality and empower all women and girls	Proportion of women and girls aged > 15 subjected to sexual violence by persons other than intimate partner in the previous 12 months, by age and place of occurrence
6. Ensure availability and sustainable management of water and sanitation for all	Change in the extent of water related ecosystems over time
7. Ensure access to affordable, reliable, sustainable and modern energy for all	Proportion of population with primary reliance on clean fuels and technology
8. Promote sustained, inclusive and sustainable economic growth, full and productive employment and decent work for all	Number of commercial bank branches and automated teller machines (ATMs) per 100000 adults
9. Build resilient infrastructure, promote inclusive and sustainable industrialization and foster innovation	Proportion of the rural population living within 2 km of an all-season road
10. Reduce inequality within and among countries	Growth rates of household expenditure or income per capita among the bottom 40% of the population and the total population
11. Make cities and human settlements inclusive, safe, resilient and sustainable	Proportion of the population that has convenient access to public transport (disaggregated)
12. Ensure sustainable consumption and production patterns	Number of companies publishing sustainability reports
13. Take urgent action to combat climate change and its impacts	Mobilized amount of US$ per year starting in 2020 accountable towards the 100 billion US$ commitment
14. Conserve and sustainably use the oceans, seas and marine resources for sustainable development	Average marine acidity (pH) measured at agreed suite of representative sampling stations
15. Protect, restore and promote sustainable use of terrestrial ecosystems, sustainably manage forests, combat desertification and halt and reverse land degradation and halt biodiversity loss	Proportion of land that is degraded over total land area
16. Promote peaceful and inclusive societies for sustainable development, provide access to justice for all and build effective, accountable and inclusive institutions at all levels	Percentage of children aged 1–17 years who experienced any physical punishment and/or psychological aggression by care givers, in the past month
17. Strengthen the means of implementation and revitalize the global partnership for sustainable development	Proportion of individuals using the Internet

Sources: UN General Assembly (2015) and examples of indicators (Inter-Agency and Expert Group on Sustainable Development Goal Indicators 2016a, b, c)

Though there have been substantial efforts to improve the availability of statistics, the absence of reliable national data remains a serious problem for making indicators operational in the short and medium term (Constanza et al. 2016; Dunning and Kalow 2016; UN 2016). For instance, regarding the Tier I indicator from Table 20.1 'Percentage of the population living below the international poverty line', Dunning and Kalow (2016) found that 37 of the UN member states had no publicly available relevant data since 2000. The three next indicators from Table 20.1 refer to children under 5 years. The first two thereof are categorized as Tier I (Inter-Agency and Expert Group on Sustainable Development Goal Indicators 2016c). It is estimated that worldwide 1 in 4 children under the age of 5 are not recorded (and thus do not turn up in objective statistical data) so the three indicators referring to children under 5 years suffer (UN Economic and Social Council 2016b). The problem of missing data also applies to other proposed indicators. The *Sustainable Development Goals Report 2016* (p. 47) (UN 2016) notes that over the period 2010–2014 death registration data, which are essential to constructing basic health statistics, were available for 145 out of 230 countries. Of these 145 countries 128 had death registration data that were at least 75% complete. Also, the informal settlements like urban slums tend to escape existing objective statistics and so do informal economic activities in many high-income countries (Arfvidsson et al. 2017). In evaluating the measurement of the 2030 Sustainable Development Goals in the Netherlands, it was found that only 33% of the indicators proposed within the UN framework statistical information was available (Centraal Bureau voor de Statistiek 2016).

There is no indication in the UN documents discussed here that there was a 'veil of ignorance' over the question to which generation their authors belong (also: Horton 2014; Spaiser et al. 2016). Nor is the conservation of natural capital as a prerequisite to sustainable development central to the CSD indicator set of 2007 (UN Commission on Sustainable Development 2007). Two of the 17 2030 Sustainable Development Goals regard biotic natural capital; so do two indicators for Goal 2 and one for Goal 6 (UN Economic and Social Council 2016a; Inter-Agency and Expert Group on Sustainable Development Goal Indicators 2016b). However, apart from water availability, marine pH (acidity) and limiting climate change (Goal 13), abiotic natural capital is not covered. Within the UN framework the conservation of natural capital has not been viewed as a prerequisite to sustainable development. Rather 'the state of the environment' has been viewed as an aspect or a dimension of sustainable development goals. Overall, the indicator sets proposed within the UN context would seem to aim at what one might call a rather responsible good life for the present generation.

Indicator sets for national governments

As noted by Smits and Hoekstra (2011), national governmental sustainable development indicator sets have much diverged from guidance by the United Nations (e.g. UN Commission on Sustainable Development 2007). To illustrate this divergence, sets of indicators will be considered developed for national governments that do not have a major problem with the availability of data.

A first example of divergence between guidance by the United Nations and actual *national* sustainable development indicator sets is the Dashboard on Sustainable Development, developed for the French government (Ayong Le Kama et al. 2004; Nourry 2008). The development of the Dashboard started out from previous work of the CSD (134 indicators divided into the domains economic, social, environmental and institutional). The actual Dashboard has, however, a set of 45 indicators in three domains (economic, environmental, social-health) and 12 themes. Indicators include artificial surface, the consumption of alcohol and tobacco, fertility, suicide rate among the young, labor productivity and the development of bird populations.

Another example of the difference between UN guidance and actual indicator sets is the 2001 set of 30 sustainable development indicators for Sweden (Statistics Sweden 2001). *Our Common Future* and the work of the CSD are acknowledged but the structure chosen is different from the CSD proposals. The indicators are ordered under themes which may combine economic, social and environmental elements. The themes are: Efficiency, Contribution and Equality, Adaptability and Values and Resources for Future Generations. Indicators include prevalence of allergic asthma among school children, women's salaries as a percentage of men's salaries, electoral participation and exploitation of the Baltic herring. The history of sustainable development indicators in Finland is described elsewhere in this Handbook (Rosenström, Chapter 21).

In line with the guidance of the CSD, no aggregation was proposed for the French and Swedish indicator sets. Neither the conservation of natural capital as a prerequisite to sustainable development nor justice between the generations as operationalized by Rawls (1999) were central to indicator construction in the indicator sets for the French and Swedish governments.

Interestingly, the first theme in the German governmental set of 38 sustainable development indicators is intergenerational equity (Statistisches Bundesamt 2014). This theme includes social, economic and environmental issues. The consumption of natural resources is included. This is not done not in terms of the *conservation* of natural capital, but in terms of resource *productivity*. Improved resource productivity has as a first-order effect a reduced depletion rate of resources generated by slow geological process. However, as a second-order effect the economy may be impacted in such a way that resource consumption may be stimulated (e.g. by lower resource costs) (e.g. Dahmus 2014). Other themes in the set of German governmental indicators are quality of life, social cohesion and international interdependence. Indicators include: frequency of obesity all-day care for children and differences in the salaries of men and women. There is no aggregate indicator.

Differences between indicator sets may follow from definitions of sustainable development which would seem at variance with the definition given in *Our Common Future*. For instance, the US Interagency working group on sustainable development defined in 1998 sustainable development as: 'an evolving process that improves the economy, the environment and society for the benefit of current and future generations' (Berry 1998). This US Interagency working group published an experimental set of sustainable development indicators. This set has indicators in the social, economic and environmental domains, based on objective statistical data. Proposed indicators include participation in arts and recreation, inflation and home ownership. Conservation of natural capital as a prerequisite to sustainable development and justice between the generations, as defined by Rawls (1999), are not central to the proposed indicators. The Interagency working group felt that using their set of indicators could provide 'no single answer regarding progress in sustainable development' (Berry 1998).

Van Vuuren and de Kruijf (1998) reviewed progress regarding sustainable development indicators in the Netherlands. They used a definition which is different from that in *Our Common Future*: 'aiming at a balance between economic, social and environmental goals, which can be potentially maintained for a long time'. Van Vuuren and de Kruijf (1998) stated that 'the concept (of sustainable development) is strongly related to views on nature, culture or economy' and that 'values vary from place to place and over time'. The further development of sustainable development indicators in the Netherlands has however returned to the definition of sustainable development in *Our Common Future* (Smits and Hoekstra 2011). Indicators are conceptualized with three dimensions ('here and now', 'later' and 'elsewhere'). There are 82 indicators, categorized under 20 themes in the proposed long list and 30 indicators in the short list. The latter include time spent on recreation, R&D expenditures and the number of victims from burglary and assault. The indicators are partly based on objective statistical data (e.g. time spent on recreation) and partly on subjective data (e.g. satisfaction with family life). Gross capital formation and financial capital (assets minus liabilities) are included in the short list of indicators. Natural capital is represented by the indicators per capita land area, biodiversity, climate, energy reserves, surplus phosphorus in soils, chemical and biological water quality and exposure to PM10 (particulate matter with a diameter < 10 micrometer). Justice between the generations, as operationalized by Rawls (1999), is not central to indicator construction, but impacts on future generations are considered. The indicators used allowed the 2014 Monitor Sustainable Netherlands to conclude that the quality of life in the Netherlands is high but that the costs thereof are partially shifted to future generations and that natural capital related to the Dutch economy is reduced (Centraal Bureau voor de Statistiek 2014).

The divergence from CSD guidance that applies to individual member states of the European Union also holds for the European Union as such. Eurostat (the statistical office of the European Union) monitors sustainable development in the European Union. Indicators are allocated to 10 themes (Eurostat 2013) (see Box 20.2) and based on objective statistical data. Sustainable development is not defined. There is no aggregate index and results are reported in a disaggregated way. So, in the 2013 report for instance states that there is a 'muted recovery of the labor market', that there are 'improvements in waste treatment and pollutant emissions' and that 'the gender pay gap is substantially reduced'. Indicators related to natural capital are limited to the common bird index, fish catches and water usage. Intergenerational justice, as operationalized by Rawls, is not central to the Eurostat indicator construction.

Box 20.2 Themes used by Eurostat for monitoring sustainable development

Source: (Eurostat 2013)

Socioeconomic development
Sustainable consumption and production
Social inclusion
Demographic changes
Public health
Climate change and energy
Sustainable transport
Natural resources
Global partnership
Good governance

Still another interesting example of deviation from CSD guidance regards Bhutan. Bhutan has shifted its efforts in the field of sustainability indicator construction away from the use of available objective statistics to the construction of indicators for the Gross National Happiness Index, for which data are gathered on the basis of dedicated questionnaires put to a section of the population considered to be representative (Center for Bhutan Studies & GNH Research 2015). The Gross National Happiness Index is based on the view that sustainable development 'should take a holistic approach towards notions of progress and give equal importance to non-economic aspects of wellbeing' (Center for Bhutan Studies & GNH Research 2015). The Gross National Happiness Index covers nine equally weighted domains: psychological well-being, health, education, living standards, time use, good governance, cultural diversity and resilience, community vitality and ecological diversity and resilience (Center for Bhutan Studies & GNH Research 2015). For the Gross National Happiness Index 33 indicators have been constructed and the Gross national Happiness Index ranges from 0 to 1.

There has been major effort aiming at the harmonization of national sustainable development indicators beyond the work of the CSD. This effort has focused on indicator construction considering economic, human, natural and social capital, measured in terms of stocks. Reports reflecting this effort (Schoenaker et al. 2015) have been:

- *Measuring Sustainable Development* (Working Group on Statistics for Sustainable Development 2008)
- *Report by the Commission on the Measurement of Economic Performance and Social Progress* (Stiglitz et al. 2009)
- *Conference of European Statisticians Recommendations on Measuring Sustainable Development* (Task Force on Measuring Sustainable Development 2014).

The *Conference of European Statisticians Recommendations on Measuring Sustainable Development* (Task Force on Measuring Sustainable Development 2014) distinguished three conceptual dimensions of sustainable development:

- the human well-being of the present generation in one particular country
- the well-being of future generations
- the well-being of people living in other countries.

A set of 60 indicators along the lines of these three conceptual dimensions was proposed. Also the *Conference of European Statisticians Recommendations on Measuring Sustainable Development* (Task Force on Measuring Sustainable Development 2014) published a long list with a set of 90 thematic indicators and a short list with 24 thematic indicators covering fields such as nutrition, physical safety, leisure, trust and mineral resources (excluding coal and peat).

This major harmonization effort has had a limited success. The indicator construction at the UN regarding the 2030 Sustainable Development Goals has not been in line with the *Conference of European Statisticians Recommendations on Measuring Sustainable Development* (2014). At the beginning of 2017 only Belgium and the Netherlands were confirmed users of the framework recommended in the *Conference of European Statisticians Recommendations on Measuring Sustainable Development* (2014).

As to the sets of national governmental sustainability indicators reviewed here: apart from the absence of central roles for intergenerational justice as defined by Rawls and the conservation of natural capital as a prerequisite to sustainable development there seems to be another common characteristic. Their construction so far apparently mainly aims at monitoring developments in view of what might be considered a more or less responsible good life of the present generation. Also one may note that there has been a trend towards the inclusion of subjective data into indicator construction, which has been reversed by the indicators for the 2030 Sustainable Development Goals proposed within the UN framework in 2016 (Inter-Agency and Expert Group on Sustainable Development Goal Indicators 2016a, b, c).

Concluding remarks

There is a very wide variety in proposed governmental indicator sets for sustainability and sustainable development. This is in line with the point of view that sustainability is a subjective concept (Bell and Morse 2008). The set of sustainability indicators proposed by Lee and Huang (2007) for use by the Taipei government is mainstream among the indicator sets discussed here in that justice between the generations and the conservation of natural capital as a prerequisite to sustainable development are not central to their construction. On the other hand the aggregated and weighted sustainability index for Taipei presented by Lee and Huang (2007) would seem rather uncommon. Among the indicator sets reviewed here in some detail, only Bhutan (Gross National Happiness Index) and China (Urban Sustainability Index) also have aggregated and weighted indexes. This appears to be in line with the findings of Schoenaker et al. (2015) who reviewed 55 national indicator sets and concluded that such indicators became less popular after 1992.

The national implementation of the 2030 Sustainable Development Goals is likely to lead to indicator sets diverging from the indicators proposed within the UN framework in 2016 (Inter-Agency and Expert Group on Sustainable Development Goal Indicators 2016a, b, c). The latter indicator set is not in line with intergenerational justice as operationalized by Rawls (1999) and the conservation of natural capital as a prerequisite for sustainable development. This would seem to be a good reason for refocusing on these aspects of sustainability (also: Terama et al. 2016).

Acknowledgment

The valuable comments of Dr. R. Hoekstra on an earlier version of this chapter are gratefully acknowledged.

References

Arfvidsson, H., Simon, D., Oloko, M., and Moodley, N. (2017). "Engaging with and measuring informality in the proposed urban sustainable development goal". *African Geographical Review, 36*: 100–114.

Ayong Le Kama, A., Lagrenne, C., and Le Lourd, P. (eds.) (2004). *Indicateurs nationaux du developpement durables: lesquels retenir?* Ministère de l'Écologie et du Développement Durable, Paris (France) (236p).

Bell, S. and Morse, S. (2008). *Sustainability Indicators: Measuring the Unmeasurable?* 2nd edition, Earthscan, London (UK).

Berry, D. (ed.) (1998). *Sustainable Development in the United States: An Experimental Set of Indicators.* A progress report prepared by the U.S. Interagency Working Group on Sustainable Development Indicators, Washington DC (USA), December.

Brugman, J. (1997). "Is there a method in our measurement? The use of indicators in local sustainable development planning". *Local Environment, 2*: 59–72.

Cassar, L.F., Conrad, E., Bell, S., and Morse, S. (2013). "Assessing the use and influence of sustainability indicators at the European periphery". *Ecological Indicators, 35*: 52–61.

Center for Bhutan Studies & GNH Research. (2015). *Bhutan's 2015 Gross National Happiness Index.* Thimpu (Bhutan) (8p).

Centraal Bureau voor de Statistiek. (2014). *Monitor Sustainable Netherlands (Monitor Duurzaam Nederland) 2014.* Indicatoren Rapport, Den Haag (the Netherlands).

Centraal Bureau voor de Statistiek. (2016). *Meten van SDGs: een eerste beeld voor Nederland.* Den Haag (the Netherlands).

Chen, Y.K., Chen, C., and Hsieh, T.F. (2009). "Establishment and applied research on environmental assessment indicators in Taiwan". *Environmental Monitoring and Assessment, 155*: 407–417.

Chester, M. and Horvath, A. (2009). *Life Cycle Energy Emissions Inventories for Motorcycles, Diesel Automobiles, School Buses, Electric Buses, Chicago Rail and New York City Rail.* UC Berkeley Center for Future Urban Transport, University of California, Berkeley (USA) (106p).

Constanza, R., Daly, L., Fioramonti, L., Giovannini, E., Kubiszewski, I., Mortensen, L.F., Pickett, K.E., Ragnarsdottir, K.V., de Vogli, R., and Wilkinson, R. (2016). "Modelling and measuring sustainable wellbeing in connection with the UN Sustainable Development Goals". *Ecological Economics, 130: 350–355.*

Dahmus, J.B. (2014). "Can efficiency improvements reduce resource consumption?" *Journal of Industrial Ecology, 18: 883–897.*

Dunning, C. and Kalow, J. (2016). *SDG Indicators: Serious Gaps Abound in Data Availability.* Center for Global Development, Washington, DC and London. Available at: http://cgdev.org.nlog.sdg-indicators-serious-gaps-abound-data-availablity (Accessed at 2-9-2016).

Eurostat. (2013). *Sustainable Development in the European Union: 2013 Monitoring Report of the EU Sustainable Development Strategy.* Publications Office of the European Union, Luxembourg.

German Federal Government. (2016). *Report to the High-Level Political Forum on Sustainable Development 2016.* Berlin (Germany) (59p).

Hai, L.T., Hai, P.H., Ha, P.T.T., Ha, N.M., Dai, L.Y., Hoa, P.V., Huan, N.C., Cam, L.V. (2014). "A system of sustainability indicators for the province of Thai Binh, Vietnam". *Social Indicator Research, 116: 661–679.*

Hák, T., Janousková, S., and Moldan, B. (2016). "Sustainable development goals: A need for relevant indicators". *Ecological Indicators, 60: 565–573.*

Horton, R. (2014). "Why the sustainable development goals will fail". *The Lancet, 383: 2196.*

Ibrahim, F.I., Omar, D., and Mohamad, N.H.N. (2015). "Theoretical review of sustainable city indicators in Malaysia". *Procedia – Social and Behavioral Sciences, 202: 322–329.*

Inter-agency and Expert Group on Sustainable Development Goal Indicators. (2016a). *Goal Indicators: Provisional Proposed Tiers of Global SDG Indicators 2016 as of March 24.* Mexico City, Mexico.

Inter-agency and Expert Group on Sustainable Development Goal Indicators. (2016b). *Introduction to Provisional Tiers of Global SDG Indicators & Provisional Proposed Tiers of Global SDG Indicators.* Third Meeting 30 March–1 April, Mexico City, Mexico.

Inter-agency and Expert Group on Sustainable Development Goal Indicators. (2016c). *Tier Classification of Global SDG Indicators.* Fourth Meeting November 2016, Geneva, Switzerland.

IUCN (International Union for the Conservation of Nature). (1980). *World Conservation Strategy.* Geneva (Switzerland).

Lee, Y. and Huang, C. (2007). "Sustainability index for Taipei". *Environmental Impact Assessment Review, 27: 505–521.*

Mascarenhas, A., Coelho, P., Subtil, E., and Ramos, T.B. (2010). "The role of common local indicators in regional sustainability assessment". *Ecological Indicators, 10: 646–656.*

Michael, F.L., Noor, Z.Z., and Figueroa, M.J. (2014). "Review of urban sustainability indicators assessment – Case study between Asian countries". *Habitat International, 44: 491–500.*

Moreno Pires, S., Fidélis, T., and Ramos, T.B. (2014). "Measuring and comparing local sustainable development through common indicators: Constraints and achievement in practice". *Cities, 39: 1–9.*

Moreno Pires, S. and Fidélis, T. (2015). "Local sustainability indicators in Portugal: Assessing implementation and use in governance contexts". *Journal of Cleaner Production, 86: 289–300.*

Nakamura, S., Kondo, Y., Kagawa, S., Matsubae, K., Nakajima, K., and Nagasaka, T. (2014). "MaTrace: Tracing the fate of materials over time and across products in open-loop recycling". *Environmental Science & Technology, 48: 7207–7214.*

Nourry, M. (2008). "Measuring sustainable development: Some empirical evidence for France from eight alternative indicators". *Ecological Economics, 67: 441–456.*

Pezzey, J. (1992). *Sustainable Development Concepts an Economic Analysis.* World Bank Environmental Paper 2. The World Bank, Washington, DC (USA) (14p).

Pintér, L., Hardi, P., and Bartelmus, P. (2005). *Sustainable Development Indicators: Proposals for a Way Forward.* International Institute for Sustainable Development, Winnipeg (Canada).

Pupphachai, U. and Zuidema, Z. (2017). "Sustainability indicators: A tool to generate learning and adaptation in urban sustainable development". *Ecological Indicators, 72: 784–793.*

Rawls, J. (1999). *A theory of justice.* Harvard University Press, Cambridge, MA (USA).

Reijnders, L. (2003). "Recovery of dissipated copper and the future of copper supply". *Resources, Conservation and Recycling, 38: 59–66.*

Reijnders, L. (2016). "Phosphorus in agriculture: A limited resource". *CAB Reviews, 2016: 26* (9p).

Schoenaker, N., Hoekstra, R., and Smits, J.P. (2015). "Comparison of measurement systems for sustainable development at the national level". *Sustainable Development, 23: 285–300.*

Science for Environment Policy. (2015). *Indicators for sustainable cities: In-depth report 12.* Available at: http://ec.europa.eu/science-environment-policy (Accessed 8-11-2016) (24p).

SDG Collaborators. (2016). "Measuring the health-related Sustainable Development Goals in 188 countries: A baseline analysis from the Global Burden of Disease Study 2015". *The Lancet, 388: 1813–1850.*

Shen, L., Ochoa, J.J., Shah, M.N., and Zhang, X. (2011). "The application of urban sustainability indicators – A comparison between practices". *Habitat International, 35: 17–29.*

Smits, J.P. and Hoekstra, R. (2011). *Measuring Sustainable Development and Societal Progress; Overview and Conceptual Approach.* Statistics Netherlands, Den Haag (the Netherlands).

Spaiser, V., Ranganathan, S., Swain, R.B., and Sumpter, D.J.T. (2016). "The sustainable development oxymoron: Quantifying and modelling the incompatibility of sustainable development goals". *International Journal of Sustainable Development & World Ecology*, doi: 10.1080/13504509.2016.135624 (15p).

Statistics Sweden. (2001). *Sustainable Development Indicators for Sweden – a First Set.* Stockholm (Sweden) (64p).

Statistisches Bundesamt. (2014). *Nachaltige Entwicklung in Deutschland: Indikatorenbericht 2014.* Wiesbaden (Germany) (81p).

Stiglitz, J.E., Sen, A., and Fitoussi, J.P. (2009). *Report by the Commission on the Measurement of Economic Performance and Social Progress.* Paris, France.

Tanguay, G.A., Rajaonson, J., Lefebvre, J., and Lanoie, P. (2010). "Measuring the sustainability of cities: An analysis of the use of local indicators". *Ecological Indicators, 10: 407–418.*

Task Force on Measuring Sustainable Development. (2014). *Conference of European Statisticians Recommendations on Measuring Sustainable Development.* United Nations, New York (USA) and Geneva (Switzerland).

Terama, E., Milligan, B., Jimenez-Aybar, R., and Mace, G.M. (2016). "Accounting for the environment as an asset: Global progress and realizing the 2030 Agenda for Sustainable Development". *Sustainability Science, 11: 945–950.*

UN. (2016). *The Sustainable Development Goals Report.* United Nations, New York (USA).

UN Commission on Sustainable Development. (2007). *Indicators of Sustainable Development: Guidelines and Methodologies.* United Nations, New York (USA).

UN Economic and Social Council. (2016a). *Report of the Inter-Agency and Expert Group on Sustainable Development Goal Indicators.* E/CN.3/2016/2/Rev1.19–12–2016. United Nations, New York (USA).

UN Economic and Social Council. (2016b). *Progress Towards the Sustainable Development Goals.* Report to the Secretary General. E/2016/75 June 3. United Nations, New York (USA).

UN General Assembly. (2015). *Transforming Our World: The 2030 Agenda for Sustainable Development.* United Nations, New York (USA).

Van Vuuren, D.P. and de Kruijf, H.A.M. (1998). *Compendium of Data and Indicators for Sustainable Development in Benin, Bhutan, Costa Rica and the Netherlands.* RIVM, Bilthoven (the Netherlands) (176p).

Weibo, H. (2016). *Executive Summary of China's Actions on the Implementation of the 2030 Agenda for Sustainable Development.* Available at: https://sustainable development.un.org/ (Accessed at 12-11-2016).

Weitz, N., Persson, A., Nilsson, M., and Tenggren, S. (2016). *Sustainable Development Goals for Sweden: Insights on Setting a National Agenda.* Stockholm Environment Institute, Stockholm (Sweden) (58p).

World Commission on Environment and Development. (1987). *Our Common Future.* Oxford University Press, Oxford (UK).

Working Group on Statistics for Sustainable Development. (2008). *Measuring Sustainable Development.* United Nations, New York (USA).

Yuan, W., James, P., Hodgson, K., Hutchinson, S.M., and Shi, C. (2003). "Development of sustainability indicators by communities in China: A case study of Chongming County, Shanghai". *Journal of Environmental Management, 68: 253–261.*

21

SUSTAINABLE DEVELOPMENT INDICATORS, FINLAND

Going from large descriptive sets to target-oriented actively used indicators

Ulla Rosenström

Introduction

The "hype" surrounding sustainable development indicators (SDI) began in the early 1990s, but by the beginning of the next decade many researchers had started questioning whether the supposed link between the indicators and policy actually existed (e.g. Bell and Morse 2001; Gudmundsson 2003; Hezri 2004). Indeed, if the number of SDI sets reflected the state of the sustainability of the earth, we would be in good hands. However, melting glaciers, increasing numbers of extinct species and dense pollution in megacities suggest that the numerous SDIs have neither succeeded in their task to raise awareness among citizens nor have they guided decision-makers to make better decisions (e.g. Lyytimäki 2014). The indicators in themselves have been in focus, not their use and impact on decision-making. In fact, it seems that most effort has been made on the development process of indicators and agreement on what makes a good set. Despite all the work, there is no universally agreed set of SDIs (Lehtonen et al. 2016).

The history of efforts to get SDIs utilized is long and the reasons for their scant utilization have remained largely the same: the sets are often too large and vague to give clear policy guidance, while poor data availability and time lags further contribute to weak interest by the intended users (Rosenström and Lyytimäki 2006). Finland has been among the forerunners in developing SDIs since the late 1990s, and has made special efforts to enhance their use. The unique location of the leadership of indicator work, first at the Ministry of the Environment and, from the beginning of 2016, at the Prime Minister's Office, has enabled experimentation and innovative approaches that have increased the use and influence of the indicators.

This article concentrates on the production and communication of indicator sets and not on the qualities of specific indicators. Individual indicators (especially indices), can be created and promoted by single individuals, but an SDI set is normally developed through a process that involves at least experts but sometimes also the wider public and policymakers through participatory processes. The article describes efforts made to improve the appeal of the indicator sets and to create more opportunities for their use in Finland. The agency experience described in this paper is written from the point of view of a civil servant and is not a scientific analysis of the indicators or their use.

Use is largely considered in this paper as direct use. Certainly, sustainable development indicators can be and are used in other ways. In fact, the early descriptive indicators were mostly used conceptually in raising awareness and their influence has materialized perhaps much later (Lyytimäki 2014). And as we are dealing with interest groups and politicians, political use for persuading others and legitimizing personal views is probably common as well. However, for a practitioner (the person in charge of leading an indicator project), the clearest objective is to aim for direct instrumental use by the foreseen users. Use might lead to influence but this is not always the case.

In Finland, the efforts and outcomes can be divided into four phases, although they may overlap: Phase I (1996–2000): large sets that measured what experts thought relevant for sustainable development (SD). Phase II (2001–2008): tailoring of smaller indicator sets to be used for specific purposes (the leaflets). Phase III (2009–2016): www.findicator.fi online service that included more than just national SDIs. In the Findicator service the indicators were updated automatically and a Google search was optimized, which emphasized timeliness and accessibility. Phase IV (2017–today): the Findicator service needs to be renewed and the national SDIs moved to a new location with stronger emphasis on use.

Four phases of indicator development in Finland

Phase I: 1996–2000 large and comprehensive indicator sets

Many researchers identify the beginning of the SDI work with the adoption of Agenda 21 at the UN 1992 Conference on the environment and development in Rio (see Boulanger in Chapter 8). Finland became involved with the global SDI community in 1996 by agreeing to test the UNCSD indicators (United Nations 1996). The exercise involved collecting data and assessing the relevance of the 134 suggested indicators to both our national and more general, global needs. Twinning with South Africa helped to identify the global perspective, i.e. although some indicators were irrelevant to Finland they were important for others and hence had to be kept on the list (Rosenström and Muurman 1997).

The testing exercise paved the way for the development of national sustainable development indicators that would measure the impacts of the national strategy for sustainable development (Ministry of the Environment 1998). Although the considerable work done to prepare the UNCSD indicator set – notably in compiling data and finding experts to analyze the indicators – had not led to much use in Finland or elsewhere (Pintér et al. 2005), the national SDIs were developed in a largely similar manner as an exhaustive and expert-driven exercise (Rosenström and Palosaari 2000).

However, although this was a large set, the Finnish SDIs had some communicative elements that were new at the time. For example, the smaller size of the publication and an Internet version (not just a pdf) where individual indicators were linked with each other (showing, for instance, whether GDP appeared to influence emissions). Furthermore, the indicators were actively promoted to two parliamentary committees in their meetings by the authors and analyzed in the country's largest national newspaper in a weekly column for half a year.

Despite the communication efforts, the indicators were not very successful if measured by how much the foreseen users (members of two Finnish parliament committees) knew about them when interviewed (Rosenström 2006). According to the interviews, the main reason for the low interest was that the indicators really did not bring to light anything new or sensational (Rosenström 2009).

In hindsight, the main value of the SDI set was that it made sustainable development more concrete, especially to those involved in the selection process. It also laid a foundation for the subsequent national work by identifying data sources and national experts (already started in the

UNCSD indicator testing). The indicators were descriptive in nature and not associated with any measurable targets due to the nature of the national sustainable strategy. They barely influenced policymaking, at least in the short term, as very few of the interviewees could remember using them (Rosenström 2006). As mentioned, the main influence was among the sectoral experts that participated in the selection process. The experts, for example, learned what data was available and also became more acquainted with the sustainable development issues. Policymakers themselves were not involved in the development process.

Phase II: 2001–2008 tailoring of smaller indicator sets to be used for specific purposes

As it became apparent, after interviewing several members of the parliament (Rosenström 2006), that large SDI sets served in the conceptualization of SD but were too vague for politicians to grasp, new efforts to improve the indicators were undertaken by civil servants and researchers working with the FNCSD (the Finnish National Sustainable Development Commission). Moreover, updating large sets was becoming burdensome. Simultaneously with research efforts, politicians both in Finland and elsewhere (e.g. the French president Sarkozy) became interested in a smaller number of indicators, scoreboards and even indices that would provide more direct answers on how countries performed.

Furthermore, statisticians were also starting to take a larger role in developing the indicators with the leadership of the OECD statistical division and its enthusiastic director Enrico Giovannini. The international conferences with focus on "better measures for better policies" organized by the OECD since 2004 also involved policymakers across world. The focus was not on measuring sustainable development but societal progress and later well-being. The work has many parallels to the sustainable development indicator work, although the environmental dimension is weaker.

The Finnish SDIs were updated in 2005 along with the adoption of the new SD strategy, and the number of indicators was reduced remarkably. Although the link to the new strategy was strengthened, as compared with the earlier SDI set, there was no mechanism to genuinely promote the use of the indicators in decision-making or regular monitoring of the strategy.

The most successful indicator product during this phase in Finland was a so-called "leaflet" that was prepared for the meetings of the FNCSD. It contained up to eight indicators fitted onto an A4-sheet folded in three. The inspiration came from the DG Environment and British DEFRA, which had produced similar leaflets in the early 2000s.

The leaflets supported FNCSD meetings directly. From 2003 to the early 2010s each meeting of the commission had a special theme (e.g. forestry, transport) and the leaflet rather successfully presented indicators of that theme from the different pillars of the SD. The production time was about four weeks and the leaflets were used by the key ministers and other decision-makers of the FNCSD during the meetings. The Prime Minister of Finland often pointed to the indicators as the chairperson of the meeting. In hindsight, it would have been a good idea for the experts to give a five-minute presentation of the indicators at the beginning of the meetings to make full use of the opportunity of having the attention of such high-level members of the FNCSD.

Towards the end of the decade, new types of indicators, subjective indicators of progress and well-being, were introduced and promoted most visibly by the Stiglitz commission (Stiglitz et al. 2010). Later, similar work was taken up in Finland by Prime Minister Mari Kiviniemi in 2010 with a working group to advise the government whether GDP could be replaced by one or more indicators (Prime Minister's Office 2011).

Phase III: 2009–2016 tackling timeliness with online indicator service

While the national SDIs were sporadically updated as part of the FNCSD work by the Ministry of the Environment, the Finnish Prime Minister's Office (PMO) launched a web-based indicator portal called www.findicator.fi in 2009. It is still in use today and is an online service with about 100 indicators including a special subset of SDIs. In the Findicator service, the indicators are updated automatically from a database and the interpretations adhered to the indicators are mostly generated automatically from press releases when the data is published.

The trigger for monitoring societal progress came from the aforementioned OECD Global Forums. Civil servants from the PMO attended the conference and felt the government needed such indicators to support evidence-based policymaking. Advised by the national SDI experts, the starting point for the development of the Findicator service was the observation that despite all the efforts to reduce the size of indicator sets and new communicating tools, the time lags were still a big obstacle. Therefore, the indicators should be online. The idea was to have a selected set of about 100 existing indicators concerning all aspects of the society, with easy-to-use graphs and interpretations. The selection process of the indicators involved both experts and potential users such as politicians, but the process was not as exhaustive as it had been with the earlier SDIs. As the indicators had to have existing data sources, the first draft was based on existing national and international indicator sets.

Although the data production time per se was not shortened, the indicators were updated automatically as soon as new data was entered into the database. Furthermore, the users were provided with information next to the indicator graph about the last update and the next update. Hence, the users could better trust that they had the most up-to-date indicators, which seems to be important for politicians (Rosenström 2006).

The Findicator service also enables the users to download the data and to copy-paste or embed the graphs for their own uses. Therefore, the dissemination and use of the indicators was greatly increased as people could use the graphs. Although the graphs were automatically generated, their appearance was made as easy to read as possible. The use of the Findicator.fi service has been monitored from the beginning and the analytics have shown a steady increase in the number of visitors and visits.

The national SDIs were added later to the Findicator service. The decision to include them was only partly successful. The SDIs were simply listed on one page with links to data sources that were not updated very often. Furthermore, the SDIs were not accompanied with interpretations unless the link led to a page with interpretation. Some of the indicators that were part of the actual Findicator set were given broader interpretation that also took sustainable development into consideration. However, Statistics Finland wanted to remain neutral and not take a stand on whether the indicators portrayed good or bad development. For users, especially politicians, this would have been important.

The PMO ended its cooperation with Statistics Finland on the Findicator service at the end of 2016. There were many reasons for this due to the PMO's changed priorities and resources. Statistics Finland will continue to maintain the service at least during 2017, and perhaps 2018 as well. The SDIs will be moved to a new website during the summer of 2017.

Although the Findicator service did not considerably increase the use of SDIs it had many other merits. According to Statistics Finland (personal communication 12.1.2017), the Findicator service forced the statistical office to really consider the user needs for the first time and to optimize its services for web search engines, which people nowadays use to search for information, instead of using portals. Furthermore, the Findicator service brought together different data producers that had not cooperated previously. It also highlighted the need to develop common database solutions and to streamline data storage.

In summary, having indicators and especially the SDIs online solved some problems related to updating but it did not contribute to the use of indicators as tools to analyze sustainable development. The trade-off between automatically updated indicators and influential indicators was apparent: it was only possible to have indicators that had an electronic source and these were either automatically updated or someone actually had to do the updating. In other words, potentially useful indicators that were not available in such format were excluded. Therefore, it seems that in order to reach politicians or policymakers (political advisors or civil servants) there must be a clear demand for the indicators and just having them readily available on the internet is not enough. It would be good to have the indicators constantly updated online but this requires large resources. For Statistics Finland, this kind of service may serve to increase the use of statistics but in order for the Prime Minister's Office to be involved, the link to policy issues would have to be stronger. Or if the set of indicators does not have a strong link to an existing set of targets or strategy, the number of indicators would have to be large so that users would really find something that meets their needs.

Phase IV: 2017–today current linking indicators to use and creating opportunities for use

One of the greatest virtues of the Findicator service is that it directs people searching for information to official data. The Google optimization was one of the key elements. However, it does not help people to understand complex issues any better, or contribute much to sustainable development policies when interpretation is largely missing and policy advice is not given. In order to have instrumental use of SDIs, the indicators must be anchored to the sustainable development goals or strategies and the real use points in time of the indicators determined. The key to such use is to engage the users.

The Finnish National Sustainable Development Commission has been chaired by the Prime Minister almost continuously throughout its existence. However, the secretariat was held by the Ministry of the Environment until the beginning of 2016 when it was moved to the Prime Minister's Office to be closer to the Prime Minister, who is the chairperson. The new location also highlights the cross-sectoral nature of sustainable development.

Currently, the FNCSD secretariat is working on the implementation plan for the Agenda 2030, which is done largely through the national Society's Commitment to Sustainable Development. The commitment is a long-term, shared objective for the future of Finland. Instead of a traditional strategy, the commission has agreed on eight goals and all actors in society are invited to make concrete commitments to reach one or more of these goals. The commitments are public and those who make promises are held accountable for them (https://commitment2050.fi/).

The Findicator service includes indicators designed to monitor the state of the sustainable development in Finland relating to those eight goal areas. As previously mentioned, the indicators are merely listed, not analyzed or interpreted. At the end of 2016, work was started to update these indicators and to find a concrete use for them.

The update is carried out as a multi-stakeholder exercise and will lead to about 30–40 indicators. Besides traditional statistics, other sources, such as barometer data or subjective indicators, will be considered. An online service perhaps restricted too much what was feasible as an indicator when the data had to come from a database. The new SDIs will be more open to new ideas although data must be available.

The aim is that the secretariat itself will actively use the indicators to analyze and communicate the indicators in a planned annual *State of the Sustainable Development of Finland* event. There will also be an annual cycle of highlighting a certain indicator each month of the year. To engage stakeholders, it will be possible to comment on each indicator in a moderated website.

To summarize, the road to forever develop and improve indicators and to communicate and disseminate them has been travelled. Now it is time to determine when, where and how the indicators will be used and then use them to actually influence the way the citizens and policy-makers act. To mitigate misuse, the annual events will provide a platform to analyze the state of SD in the light of the indicators.

Conclusions

It is probably safe to say that much more effort has been put into developing and publishing indicators than actually analyzing the state of the sustainable development using the indicators. In fact, few indicator sets have lasted very long and most of them have been so-called "one-timers" without subsequent updates. The use of indicators is still a vague concept and the blame for the lack of use is often attributed to difficulties in updating and low policy relevance. Relevance is discussed comprehensively by Janoušková et al. in Chapter 30 of this book.

Table 21.1 summarizes the different phases identified in this article. It shows that over the past twenty years there has been a shift from a long list of descriptive sustainable indicators available in the background to shorter lists that are considered as tools for decision-making. There have been trials and errors as well as side tracks.

Table 21.1 Comparison of the different phases

	I Descriptive set 1996–2000	*II Smaller sets, leaflets 2001–2008*	*III Online Findicator service 2009–2016*	*IV 2017–today Strenghtening use*
Development process	Technocratic, expert driven	Specific expert groups	Wide consultation of potential users, experts, use of existing work	Technocratic, interest groups
Coverage	Wide coverage, defined sustainable development	Specific to chosen themes, indices constructed with limited number of variables	Society at large, web-based portal did not limit the number of indicators	Limited to the eight goals of the "Finland we want", aim 30–40 indicators
Target audience	Unclear, wide	Clear, only those attending specific meetings of the FNCSD, disseminated later in the web	Very wide	Specific purpose, open to all
Communication	Press release and event with Minister of the Environment, website, later newspaper series	Handed to the meeting participants, downloadable from the FNCSD website	Vigorous marketing of the service (Facebook campaign, pens), later Google optimization	Used visibly at different occasions, emphasis on analysis and influence

The development process of SDIs has been mostly expert-driven and technocratic in all cases. The reality is that the engagement of policymakers (as most often the target audience or foreseen users) is difficult. Experts on the other hand are usually eager to participate – especially those from special interest groups are very keen to get their voices heard. One could say that generally the largest interest in the SDIs is usually during the development process but once they are published the interest wanes dramatically. This can also be problematic if the interest groups are needed to cooperate further in providing data in the updates but they do not have the interest or resources. For them the indicators are not about monitoring sustainable development in the long term but for defining sustainable development. In other words, their conviction is that "we measure what we value and value what we measure". Bell and Morse discuss the challenges of stakeholder participation further in Chapter 12 of this book.

The coverage of the SDIs in the different phases varied considerably from a wide descriptive set of about 100 indicators (both I and III) to a very specific theme. The current SDIs that measure the Finnish Society's goals of the commitment represent a midway point. A large set always requires a lot of resources for updating, interpreting and publishing. More tailored and smaller indicator sets have seemed more useful in terms of getting the attention of the intended users and having the resources to compile, publish and distribute them. The Finnish Government currently uses 30 performance indicators to monitor progress towards the targets mentioned in the Government Programme. From a personal experience, this number is an absolute maximum that can be presented to a government in an internal meeting.

As seen in the table, the target audience has always been quite wide and unclear to some degree. Only the theme-specific indicator leaflets had a clear target and use. Besides having a clear user in mind, the target or the platform for use should be known or created. With so much different information available, no one can rely on simply publishing indicators and hoping they will be used. It is important to create opportunities for the use.

The field of communication has changed immensely in twenty years. The opportunities that social media provides for communication (and also as a source of information) are huge. The citizens and the politicians use social media more than the experts in their capacity as experts. The information we provide competes with ever-growing amounts of other information. When the SDI work began in Finland, information on the internet was still scarce, whereas today, merely having something available in the internet is not enough to generate impact. The current FNCSD secretariat uses social media for general communication and will use it to promote the updated indicators as well. Before the Findicator service, such communication was very scarce and even the Findicator tweets and Facebook updates were either automatically generated or otherwise very mechanic as it was not considered necessary to spend much time on social media.

Lack of timeliness of the indicators still remains one of the biggest challenges for direct use and this problem is not likely to be overcome soon. This calls for other solutions by the practitioners, such as using estimates and forecasting together with the indicators when presenting them. If data is 2–3 years old, the interpretation must be able to show what the current situation is and where we are likely to head. This naturally requires a lot of work and supports the idea of having fewer but better indicators.

Lastly, it is somewhat surprising how little digitalization has improved data timeliness or created new opportunities to measure sustainable development. Too much of the data is still presented on an annual basis when more real-time databases could be created. The pace of things gets faster all the time and people want information faster as well. As previously mentioned, more creativity is needed to communicate sustainable development to policymakers.

The research of indicators and the improvement of their quality are essential in improving governmental decision-making. However, good indicators are of little influence and importance if they are not used in any way. Although use does not guarantee the desired influence, aiming at use is well argued for. Hence efforts to create opportunities for use and disseminating information remain crucial.

References

Bell, S. and Morse, S. (2001). Breaking through the glass ceiling: Who really cares about sustainability indicators? *Local Environment* 6(3), pp. 291–309.

Gudmundsson, H. (2003). The policy use of environmental indicators – Learning from evaluation research. *The Journal of Transdisciplinary Environmental Studies* 2(2), pp. 1–12.

Hezri, A. (2004). Sustainability indicators system and policy processes in Malaysia: A framework for utilisation and learning. *Journal of Environmental Management* 73, pp. 357–371.

Lehtonen, M., Sébastien, L., and Bauler, T. (2016). The multiple roles of sustainability indicators in informational governance: Between intended use and unanticipated influence. *Current Opinion in Environmental Sustainability*, 18, pp. 1–9.

Lyytimäki, J. (2014). Communicating sustainability under increasing public budget constraints. *Latin American Journal Management for Sustainable Development* 1(2-3), pp. 137–145.

Ministry of the Environment. (1998). *Finnish Government Programme for Sustainable Development*. Council of state decision-in-principle on the promotion of ecological sustainability. The Finnish Environment Institute. Helsinki: Ministry of the Environment, 261.

Pintér, L., Hardi, P., and Bartelmus, P. (2005). *Sustainable Development Indicators: Proposals for the Way Forward*. Prepared for the United Nations Division for Sustainable Development (UN-DSD). International Institute for Sustainable Development.

Prime Minister's Office. (2011). *BKT ja kestävä hyvinvointi: Yksi luku ei riitä suomalaisen yhteiskunnan tilan kuvaamiseen*. (GDP and Sustainable Wellbeing: One Measure Is Not Enough to Monitor Finnish Society). Reports of the Prime Minister's Office 12/2011, 34.

Rosenström, U. (2006). Exploring the policy use of sustainable development indicators: Interviews with Finnish politicians. *The Journal of Transdisciplinary Environmental Studies* 5(1–2), Available at: www.journal-tes.dk/ [Accessed 8 June 2017].

Rosenström, U. (2009). Sustainable development indicators: Much wanted, less used? *Monographs of the Boreal Environment Research* No. 33, 74.

Rosenström, U. and Lyytimäki, J. (2006). The role of indicators in improving timeliness of International environmental reports. *European Environment* 16(1), pp. 32–44.

Rosenström, U. and Muurman, J. (1997). *Results from Testing CSD Indicators of Sustainable Development in Finland*. Helsinki: Finnish Environment Institute, 249.

Rosenström, U. and Palosaari, M. (Eds.). (2000). *Signs of Sustainability: Finland's Indicators for Sustainable Development 2000*. Helsinki: Finnish Environment, Environmental Policy, 122.

Stiglitz, J., Sen A., and Fitoussi, J. (2010). *Mismeasuring Our Lives: Why GDP Doesn't Add Up*. The Report by the Commission on the Measurement of Economic Performance and Social Progress. New York and London: New Press, 292.

United Nations. (1996). *Indicators of Sustainable Development Framework and Methodologies*. United Nations, New York.

22

THE SOCIO-ECOLOGICAL SYSTEM (SES) APPROACH TO SUSTAINABLE DEVELOPMENT INDICATORS

Gilberto C. Gallopin

Introduction

The approach for sustainable development indicators presented here was developed by the author of this article in the context of the Project ESALC (Evaluation of the Sustainability of Latin America and the Caribbean) within the Economic Commission for Latin America and the Caribbean (ECLAC). The project was coordinated by Gilberto Gallopin, with the collaboration of Martina Chidiak, Hernan Dopazo, Carlos Gho, David Manuel-Navarrete, Cecilie Modvar, Laura Ortiz, María Luisa Robleto, Andrés Schuschny, and Rodolfo Vilches.

The project produced a comparative analysis of the sustainability of the majority of the countries of Latin America and the Caribbean. The approach was officially adopted by Argentina for its National System of Indicators of Sustainable Development (http://estadisticas.ambiente.gob.ar/?idarticulo=13486) and by the Region of Catalonia, Spain (ISC 2008). The approach is considered to be universally applicable.

The United Nations defines sustainable development as development that meets the needs of the present without compromising the ability of future generations to meet their own needs (www.un.org/issues/m-susdev.html). This apparently simple concept is actually quite complex, combining the term "development", which implies a directional and progressive change (a quantitative but above all qualitative progress) with the term "sustainable" that has to do with the permanence in time; sustainable development implies, then, a process of change (improvement) that can be maintained over time. Some of the chapters of this book (e.g. Chapter 10, Turcu; Chapter 20, Reijnders) focus on sustainability and others (e.g. Chapter 2, Pintér et al.; Chapter 9, Spangenberg) on sustainable development, both in its general conception as used by the U.N., and in its restricted version of environmentally sustainable development (e.g. Chapter 17, Wackernagel et al.).

At first glance, this concept of "maintenance of change" may seem paradoxical, but it is precisely here that the difference between the concepts of sustainable development and sustainability lies. Sustainability is a term that denotes the ability to maintain a situation or condition over time, such as when we talk about the sustainable exploitation of a forest, or a sustainable city. But the concept of development implies precisely the change of a current situation or condition, not its maintenance.

A process of change can be sustainable or unsustainable; for example, a process of continued growth of material consumption is not sustainable over the long term in a finite world, but a development process defined in terms of improving the quality of life of human beings can be sustainable if it focuses on the deployment of the social, cultural, and psychological human potential rather than material consumption (once a basic threshold of material consumption has been reached).

In this chapter, the basic concepts of sustainable development and related indicator frameworks, and indicators of sustainable development will be presented and discussed, including their concrete application to the country of Honduras, and a comparison with the whole of Latina America and The Caribbean.

The basic dimensions of sustainable development

It is widely accepted that the fundamental dimensions of sustainable development are environmental, economic, and social (the latter being broadly conceived, including cultural, social, political, demographic, and institutional). However, in many cases (such as the United Nations Commission on Sustainable Development), the institutional dimension is highlighted separately, which makes operational sense, since it contains the structures and processes that allow a society to regulate its actions in pursuit of its objectives. This shows that sustainable development is a systemic concept, not a sectoral one. The four dimensions must be improved, and this in a sustainable way, to truly obtain sustainable development. A society that preserves its natural resources at the cost of increasing the poverty level of its population could eventually be called *environmentally sustainable*, but in no way could we talk about *sustainable development* in this case.

Sustainability and sustainable development

The notions of sustainability and sustainable development are often employed interchangeably, but they are quite distinct concepts. Sustainability, like sustainable development, has been defined in many different ways. However, using a systemic framework, sustainability can be reduced to its essential elements in accordance with the following formula (Gallopín, 2003, Gallopín et al., 2014):

$$V\left(S_{t+1}\right) \cong V\left(S_t\right)$$

$$for\, t_0 \le t \le t_f$$

(1)

This general definition includes the fundamental aspects of the special definitions in the literature. In equation (1), V is the valuation function of the state of the system (S), or of its outputs or products. In other words, a system is sustainable (within the interval between the initial time – t_0 – and the time horizon or final time being considered – t_f) when the net "value" (not necessarily defined in economic terms) of the system or the product obtained remains approximately the same over time (t). This formulation applies to V and does not necessarily imply that the system S remains in a stationary or constant state. Indeed, all systems open to exchanges with their environment maintain their identity through permanent dynamic adjustments, adaptations, and self-organization.

Any assignation of value entails a subjective component and, in consequence, the specification of the function V (and the choice of the system's variables and products that are of interest) may vary widely depending on the range of perceptions and points of view regarding the relations between nature and society. For example, for some, S is nothing more than the total stock of capital and V a monetary measure of that capital. For others, V is some type of aggregate function of well-being, and S can be divided into natural, manufactured, and social capital. Or else V may be a valuation function that includes some ethical priorities for the conservation of all living species and is expressed in non-monetary units. Many of the discrepancies concerning the meaning of sustainability and sustainable development manifest themselves precisely in the explicit or implicit specification of the function and the reasoning supporting it.

The concept of sustainable development is very different from that of sustainability, as the word "development" clearly points to the idea of change, in the direction of "improvement". It is therefore a normative concept, in contrast to the concept of sustainability, which can contain also cases of undesirable sustainability[1] (e.g. sustainable poverty, sustainable tyrannies).

In sustainable development what is being sustained, or ought to become sustainable, is the process of improvement of the human condition (or rather, of the socio-ecological system [see "An integrative analytical framework: the socio-ecological system" section]) in which human beings participate), a process that does not necessarily require (and indeed is incompatible with) the indefinite growth in consumption of energy and materials. In symbolic terms the definition of sustainable development is:

$$V\left(S_{t+1}\right) > V\left(S_t\right)$$
$$for\, t_0 \leq t \leq t_f \tag{2}$$

Strictly speaking, the expression (2) denotes a sustained increase in value over time between t_0 and t_f; to call it sustainable, it needs to be shown that this increase can be maintained indefinitely over time or, in practice, for very long periods (t_0 to t_f).

In addition to the *valuation function* employed, another source of confusion in the use of the concepts of sustainability and sustainable development lies in the *subject* of sustainability implied. At one end of the spectrum are those who pay attention only to the sustainability of the social or socioeconomic system and, at the other, those who prioritize only the sustainability of nature.

However, the only option that makes sense in the long-term is to seek the sustainability of the whole socio-ecological system. The rationale for considering the whole system is based upon the existence of important causal interlinkages between society and nature.

Frameworks for indicators

The concept of indicator has been defined in many different, sometimes contradictory, ways. However, in its most general sense, an indicator is a *sign*. In semiotics (the general theory of signs), a sign is defined as something which stands for something to somebody in some respect or capacity.

At a more concrete level, it has been shown (Gallopín 1996, 1997) that indicators are *variables* (not "values", as they are sometimes called). A variable is an operational representation of an attribute (quality, characteristic, property) of a system. Contrary to the usual definitions, an indicator could be either a qualitative (nominal) variable, a rank (ordinal) variable, or a quantitative variable (Gallopín 1996).

The *pragmatic* interpretation of a particular variable as indicator is usually made on the basis that such a variable conveys information on the condition and/or trend of an attribute(s) of the system considered that is relevant for decision-making.

Indicators do not provide explanations; they only point to situations or trends that contribute to a description of what is happening to the system, a description that is expected to support decision-making.

This chapter focuses on indicators (as in Chapter 21 by Rosenström), rather than on aggregated indices (single numbers generated by combining two or more variables – see Chapter 13 by Almássy and Pintér, Chapter 14 by Hueting and de Boer, Chapter 15 by Bartelmus, Chapter 16 by Wackernagel et al., Chapter 17 by Hsu, Chapter 18 by Bravo, Chapter 19 by Conrad and Cassar). Wall et al. (1995) note that the development of highly aggregated indicators is confronted with the dilemma that, although a high level of aggregation is necessary in order to intensify the awareness of problems, the existence of disaggregated indicators is essential in order to draw conclusion for possible courses of action.

Indicators are chosen to provide relevant information for making decisions. But isolated indicators are not very useful. Indicators are much more helpful if they are organized in some kind of coherent framework than if they are selected haphazardly as a collection of disparate items.

Frameworks organize individual indicators or sets of indicators in a coherent manner. But they have several additional uses (UNEP-DPCSD 1995): They can guide the overall data and information collecting process. They are useful communication tools to decision-makers, summarizing key information derived from many different sectors. They suggest logical groupings for related sets of information, promoting their interpretation and integration. They can help identify important issues for which adequate information is lacking. Indicator frameworks can help to spread reporting burdens, by structuring the information collection, analysis, and reporting process across the many issues and areas that pertain to sustainable development. Conversely, the absence of conceptual frameworks may generate incompatible data, difficult-to-use information, and the multiplication of sets of indicators that are difficult to adjust (Segnestam et al. 2000).

Indicator frameworks are particularly relevant in the case of sustainable development, because the latter embraces many issues and dimensions.

Different analytical frameworks (Geniaux et al. 2009, Moldan and Billharz 1997, Hák et al. 2007) have been used to identify, develop, and communicate indicators. In the particular case of *environmental indicators*, several approaches have been used including: the "media approach" (air, water, land, and living resources); the "goals approach", used to select indicators according to legal and administrative mandates; and the "sector approach", examining indicators of environmental impact from the perspective of economic sectors (transportation, industry, urbanization, agriculture, and so on).

In the field of *environment and development* some of the major frameworks are:

- integrated environmental-economic accounting systems or other national accounts-based recordings of stocks and flows of natural resources and environmental services, in most cases expressed in monetary terms
- frameworks of environmental statistics, such as the United Nations Framework for the Development of Environmental Statistics (FDES), which lists statistical variables in a systematic manner but without attempting to establish accounting or functional relationships among those variables. The contents of the FDES are "statistical topics", or those aspects of environmental and related socioeconomic concerns that are amenable to statistical description and analysis
- ad hoc nomenclatures or listings of environmental indicators, using selected "themes", "issues", or "subsystems".

A framework that gained international prominence is the "Pressure-State-Response" (PSR) framework (OECD, 1993) derived from the stress-response framework applied to ecosystems (Friend and Rapport 1979). However, as shown by Gallopin (1997) this framework, originally devised for environmental indicators, is not meaningful for indicators of sustainable development. The same objection holds for the different variations of it, such as the "driving force-pressure-state-impact-response" (DPSIR) and others. The PSR, is best perceived as a taxonomy for ordering indicators, but without an underlying functional causality.

Other ordering frameworks have been used by different institutions and countries, involving ordering of indicators along different pillars, axes, or dimensions of interest for sustainable development (Hass et al. 2002, Quiroga 2001). Examples include: economic, environmental, and social (or cultural) (many countries); economic, environmental, social, and institutional; efficiency, contribution and equality, adaptability, and values and resources for coming generations; economic growth, critical capital stocks, local/global interface, current needs, and future needs; socio-cultural, financial-economic, and ecological-environmental factors cross-referenced to "here and now", "here and later", and "elsewhere, now and later"; long-term endowments and liabilities, processes, and current results, subdivided into economy, environment, and society; social solidarity, economic efficiency, and environmental responsibility; produced, natural and human capital; current quality of life, changes in natural capital, in human capital, in physical capital, and in social capital.

Systemic frameworks

The UN Commission for Sustainable Development (CSD) recognized (UN 2001, p. 27) very early that "A successful framework should reflect the connections between dimensions, themes, and sub-themes. It should implicitly reflect the goals of sustainable development to advance social and institutional". However, the CSD never adopted a systemic framework. It started with the four basic "pillars" of sustainable development divided into themes and sub-themes; it changed thereafter into just themes and sub-themes, and currently the sustainable development goals (SDG) constitute the official UN framework (see Chapter 23 by Dahl).

Balaton group

A systemic framework for sustainable development indicators has been proposed by the "Balaton Group" (Meadows 1998), based on the "Daly Triangle" relating natural wealth to ultimate human purpose through technology, economics, politics, and ethics. According to Meadows, indicators can be derived from each level of the triangle separately, but the most important indicators will reflect the connections between one level and another. In this framework, the three most basic aggregate measures of sustainable development are the *sufficiency* with which ultimate ends are realized for all people, the *efficiency* with which ultimate means are translated into ultimate ends, and the *sustainability* of use of ultimate means.

Bossel

Another interesting systemic framework was produced by H. Bossel. After critically reviewing a number of approaches previously used, Bossel (1999) concluded that none of these are adequate. The specific critiques regarding the use of lists of indicators covering the problem area under investigation (exemplified by the approaches of the UNCSD and of the World Bank) are that (1) they are derived ad hoc, without a systems-theoretical framework to reflect the operation and viability of the total system; (2) they always reflect the specific expertise and research interests of their authors; (3) as a consequence they are overly dense in some areas (multiple indicators for essentially the same concern), and sparse or even empty in other important areas.

In Bossel's view, the total system for which indicators are sought is composed by six sub-systems (aggregated in the three major subsystems defined as the human system, the support system, and the natural system).[2]

Based on widespread theories of dynamical systems, he posited that there are just three general types of indicators: indicators corresponding to *states*, *rates*, and *converters*. The first type provides information of system states (stocks or levels); the second monitors the rates of change of system state; the third type is derived from the others, and provides information obtained by appropriate conversion of state and rate information. The choice of representative indicators therefore boils down to identifying states and rates that provide relevant information about system viability.

Sets of indicators of sustainable development about a given system are determined by two distinct requirements. They have to provide essential information about (1) the state (and cor-responding viability) of the system itself and (2) about its position with respect to individual and societal goals.

Bossel's contribution is founded upon orientors theory, developed to understand and analyze the diverging visions of the future and normative interests of different societal actors, and to define criteria and indicators for sustainable development (Bossel 1977, 1996, 1998).

Briefly, orientors are categories representing the essential system needs, or interests, that have to be fulfilled to some minimum degree to ensure a system's viability and sustainable development.

Orientors can be used as a checklist of what is important in and for systems, i.e. basic system needs (Bossel 1996). For Bossel, indicators must be selected to reflect the state of satisfaction of the basic orientors. Moreover, the choice of indicators must reflect important characteristics of dynamic systems as well as ethical concerns.

The basic system orientors proposed by Bossel (1999) are defined by two sets of questions: (1) What is the viability[3] of the affecting system (or subsystems)? (i.e. satisfaction of each basic orientor of that system) and (2) How does each affecting system (subsystem) contribute to the viability (the basic orientors) of the affected systems (subsystems)? In other words, indicator sets are determined by (1) the system itself (its state and viability) and (2) the interests, needs, or objectives of the system(s) depending on them.

The approach can be applied to systems at different scales; examples are provided ranging from a city to an unspecified global region.

Switzerland's Monet model

The Swiss model represents a rare instance of a systemic framework actually used by a country. Switzerland defined the so-called Monet stock-flow model (SFSO et al. 2001) as a framework to classify indicators. The model has similarities to the "driving force-pressure-state-impact-response" model but it differs in that is also applicable to social and economic issues, in addition to the environmental ones.

The stock-flow model contains levels, capital, input/output flows, defining criteria, and responses. *Levels* are defined as the extent to which the needs of the individuals and society are met (mostly in *per capita* terms). *Capital* represents the status and potential of (environmental, economic, and social) resources available to satisfy the needs; capital indicators estimate stock and its accumulation or decline (but not consumption). Capital may be represented as absolute values (drinking water supply) or relative values (proportion of threatened species, hospital beds per capita). *Input/output* variables are flows originating from "capital" in order to meet the needs described under "level", together with appreciation or depreciation of "capital" (e.g. through capital investment or pollutant emissions). Measurement relates to continuous consumption (flow) but not accumulation of decline of capital stock. *Defining criteria* refer to the assessment of "input/output" relative to (economic, social, and environmental) efficiency and of disparities in the meeting of needs ("level") or in the provision of "capital". They deal with the issue that particular needs may be met to varying degrees of sustainability, depending on the form taken by the "inputs/outputs". *Responses* represent the social and political measures aimed at influencing input/output.

An integrative analytical framework: the socio-ecological system

The concept of sustainable development denotes a process that has to be sustainable along the economic, social, and environmental dimensions. This multidimensional nature of the concept makes it necessary to use a conceptual framework for understanding and assessing progress that is integrated and systemic, rather than sectorial and lineal.

It is becoming more and more evident that society and nature operate as interacting entities or functionally coupled systems, and as such, mutually determined. In other words, it is not possible to understand the sustainability of the whole system including both society and nature without including into the analysis their mutual interdependencies.

The concept of *socio-ecological system* (SES) denotes any system including both ecological (or biophysical) and human components, ranging in scale from the household to the planet.[4] The term has been coined by Gallopín et al. (1989) and formally defined by Gallopín (1991). The major generic interlinkages between the components of a socio-ecological system have been identified in detail by Gallopín (1994) and further refined by Gallopín and Christianson (2000). The concept is similar (but not identical) to other terms coined, such as coupled human-environment systems (Turner, Kasperson et al. 2003; Turner, Matson et al. 2003) or social-ecological systems (Berkes and Folke 1998).

Thus, the fundamental unit of analysis for the purposes of understanding, assessing, and acting in sustainable development is not the environment, the economy, or the society; it is the whole system including the social, economic, and environmental subsystems as well as the interlinkages among them. Indeed, it has been proposed (Gallopín et al. 2001) that the SES is the natural unit of analysis for sustainable development research. It is the socio-ecological system itself that must develop sustainably, and that requires a harmonization in all of the central dimensions.

The SES framework as it has been defined by the project ESALC is a stylized version of the detailed descriptions mentioned above, and it distinguishes four main subsystems: social, economic, institutional, and environmental; these subsystems correspond to the four basic categories proposed by the United Nations Commission on Sustainable Development (UNCSD 1995, UN 2001) and also to the basic pillars of sustainable development (these pillars were also used by Jesinghaus in Chapter 26).

The normative criterion underlying this conceptual framework is the sustainable improvement of the quality of life of the population, which depends on the harmonic interplay between the elements of the SES.

The first subsystem is the social, broadly defined as including variables of the quality of life (satisfaction of material and non-material needs of the human being), income and its distribution,[5] and demographic aspects. The economic subsystem includes the production and consumption of goods and services, trade, the general state of the economy, infrastructure and human settlements (the built environment), and wastes generated by consumption and production. The institutional subsystem contains formal and informal institutions of society, laws and regulations, and policies, and also includes the main societal structures and processes (sociopolitical agents, political processes, power structures, etc.) and the knowledge and the values of society. The environmental subsystem includes the natural environment in its aspects of natural resources, ecological processes, life-support processes, and biodiversity.

The main functional flows, interrelationships or couplings between the subsystems of a socio-ecological system at the national level can be represented as in Figure 22.1. The two short arrows from and to the large box representing the total system indicate interactions between the system and its external world (e.g. international trade, inputs and outputs of energy and materials, etc.).

The interrelationships have been selected to be as neutral and as universal as possible, not requiring the user to adopt any theoretical or philosophical stance or world view (see Chapter 9 by Spangenberg – other than the notion of the integrated and interconnected nature of the unit of analysis for sustainable development).

They belong to two basic types: on the one hand, the flows of matter and/or energy between some of the subsystems (e.g. waste that leaves the economy or the natural resources that enter it). On the other hand, information, control signals, and/or actions that generate changes in the variables and organization of the receiving subsystems (e.g. financial flows, regulations and taxes, protected natural areas).

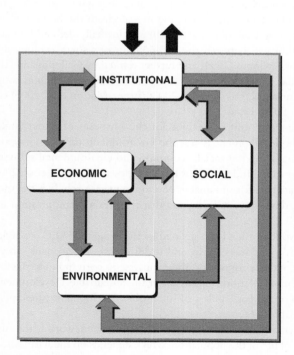

Figure 22.1   A representation of the socio–ecological system at the national scale as a framework for defining indicators of sustainable development

The arrows between the economic and institutional subsystems represent functional linkages such as policies, economic instruments, and pricing, in one direction, and monetary flows (such as money from taxes) in the other. The arrows between the economic and environmental subsystems include, among others, flows of environmental goods and services (such as natural resources) into economic production or into direct consumption, and in the other direction, wastes generated by consumption and production flowing into the environment.

The arrows between the economic and social subsystems include the effects of consumption on the quality of life, the supply and demand of employment, the impacts of the urban environment on the quality of life.

The arrows from the environmental to the social subsystem include interrelations as the impacts of the quality of the natural environment on human health.

The arrows between the institutional and social subsystems include the effects of the institutional subsystem on the social environment of people (education, security, value system) and the impact of quality of life on institutions (influence of the growth of poverty on social demands).

Finally, the arrows between the institutional and environmental subsystems include causal influences such as the direct institutional and political impacts on the environmental subsystem (protected areas, environmental impacts of military and some terrorist actions).

Most arrows between subsystems represent reciprocal influences between them, and therefore are bidirectional. The exception are the interrelations between the both institutional and social subsystems with the environmental one.

The institutional subsystem has a direct effect on the environmental, but the reciprocal is not true: the scheme assumes that changes in the environmental subsystem only influence the institutional subsystem via its reverberations through the social subsystem (e.g. impact of pollution on human health) or through the economic subsystem (e.g. impacts of soil degradation on agriculture).

In the case of the social subsystem, the effects of the environmental subsystem on the social are emphasized, but there are no direct effects in the opposite direction, since as stated above, in this conceptualization the influences of the social subsystem on the environment are channeled through the consumption processes, included within the economic subsystem.

In addition to the relevant information provided by each indicator individually, the set of indicators allow a panoramic view of the trajectory of the national socio-ecological system in its most important dimensions. Sustainable development indicators, collectively, measure the desirability of the trajectory (the "development" component) and its sustainability.

For example, the simultaneous look at the indicators of the subsystems makes it possible to detect whether the development of the national system (or regional or local according to the scale to which it is applied) is harmonious in its social, economic, environmental, and institutional dimensions or whether it appears to be happening at the expense of, or accompanied by deterioration of, some of other the subsystems.

The examination of the interrelationships between subsystems can show, for example, that energy production is becoming increasingly insufficient to cover domestic consumption, or that the volume of marine fishing is falling, giving signs of possible sources of unsustainability (or at least pointing to supply problems) of some subsystem, such as economic, which may reverberate across the whole SES.

In other words, indicators of sustainable development, considered under the SES organizing framework, can help to provide a holistic view of the sustainability of the development of the national SES, as well as that of its various subsystems, and also identify some of the interrelations that are becoming problematic through time.

The sustainable development indicators of the SES system

For the original application of the SES approach and for reasons of usability and international comparability, only indicators that are easily accessible from international sources for as many countries as possible and are documented through time were used.

Since the term "sustainable development" includes two different concepts, development and sustainability, it is not easy to find indicators that individually provide information on the two faces of sustainable development. It is thus more appropriate to identify a system of indicators that *collectively* provides the required information. In the SES approach, for each subsystem indicators of two types are defined:

- of *development or performance* (e.g. life expectancy at birth, GDP growth, natural resource endowments)
- of *sustainability* (e.g. fiscal deficit as % of GDP, demographic dependency ratio, change in forest area/total forest area)

No attempt was made to define indicators of development for the environmental subsystem, because it was judged to be very controversial and confusing.

Many of the sets of sustainable development indicators currently utilized nationally or internationally (e.g. the UN indicators of the Sustainable Development Goals – SDG –) do not distinguish between the two categories, which makes it difficult to interpret trends and identify policy implications.

Variations in the values of development indicators represent a step forward (or backward) clear in normative terms, but not necessarily informing about sustainability. For example, a reduction in the rate of poverty is clearly desirable, but says nothing about the sustainability of such reduction; it is an indicator of the component "development" of sustainable development, but not of the component "sustainability".

On the other hand, the indicator "total emissions of carbon dioxide" does not have a direction of change inherently desirable, but it provides important information about the contribution of the country to global sustainability. An indicator of sustainability must say something about the capacity for maintenance in time, or the risk of falling into an irreversible situation, for the factor or process that is representing.

Exceptionally, some indicators can be used to show trends in both components of sustainable development. One of those few is income inequality (Gini Index or other) which indicates increased risk of increasing conflicts and social tensions and thus the sustainability of society; in addition, such an increase is also normatively undesirable.

In addition to the indicators of subsystems, a small number of indicators of flows or interrelationships between subsystems are identified, such as the generation of hazardous waste (flow from the economy to the environment), or timber production (flow from the environment to the economy).

Finally, indicators of intensity or efficiency (some of which correspond to the so-called indicators of "decoupling") were identified, basically of two types: economic intensity (per unit of GDP) such as the energy intensity of the economy (joules/GDP/year), and demographic (or per capita) intensity, such as consumption of energy per capita-year.

The complete set of proposed quantitative indicators appears in Table 22.1.

Table 22.1 Indicators of Sustainable Development (IDS)

SUBSYSTEMS:

SS Social

Of Development:

- life expectancy at birth (number of years)
- labor force with secondary education (% of total labor force)
- persistence to grade 5, total or survival ratios (%) to 5th grade primary (% of cohort)
- percent of population living below poverty line (%)
- population with access to improved drinking water sources (% of total population)
- population with access to improved sanitation (% of total population)
- ratio of average female wage to male wage (%)
- adult literacy rate (% of total adult)
- mortality rate under 5 years old (rate for each 1000 born alive)
- Happiness Index (Score 0–10)

Of Sustainability:

- GINI Index (%)
- demographic dependency ratio (%)
- population growth rate (%)
- Relation between the 20% most rich and the 20% most poor of the income distribution (%)

SS Institutional

Of Development:

- Internet users (number of users per 1000 persons)
- number of telephone lines (telephone lines per 1000 people)

Of Sustainability:

- Corruption Perception Index (Score 0–10)
- expenditure on R&D (% of GDP)

SS Economical

Of Development:

- Gross Domestic Product Per Capita
- Gross Domestic Product (annual growth rate)
- Gross Domestic Product
- labor productivity (constant 1995 US$ per economically active population)

Of Sustainability:

- gross capital formation (% of Gross National Income)
- overall Budget Deficit, including grants (% of Gross National Income)

SS Environmental

Of Development:

Of Sustainability:

- forested land area (% of total area)
- total forest area, percent change (%)
- annual withdrawals of ground and surface water (% of total renewable water)

INTERLINKAGES

Between the SES and its external environment

- ozone-depleting CFCs consumption (ozone-depleting potential [ODP], metric tons)
- current account balance (% of Gross Domestic Product)
- total CO_2 emissions (metric tons)
- total debt (% of Gross National Income

(*Continued*)

Table 22.1 (Continued)

SUBSYSTEMS:

Between SS Economical and SS Institutional
- VAT (value added tax) compliance (% of potential collect)

Between SS Institutional and SS Social
- government effectiveness (point estimate)
- total social public expenditure (% of Gross Domestic Product)

Between SS Economical and SS Social
- labor demand (unemployment [annual average rate])
- total population (thousand persons)
- Growth National Income (GNI) per capita, PPP (Current US$)

From SS Institutional and SS Environmental
- protected area (% of total area)

From SS Economical to SS Environmental
- forest plantations (% of total forest area)
- use of fertilizers (kilograms per hectare)
- use of pesticides (kilograms per hectare)

From SS Environmental to SS Economical
- share of consumption of renewable energy resources (%)
- forest industrial roundwood (thousand cubic meters)
- forest wood fuel (thousand cubic meters)
- marine annual fish catch (metric tons)
- consumption/energy production (%)
- annual withdrawals of ground and surface water (cubic meters)

From SS Environmental to SS Social
- percentage of the value of the production (U$S 1987) of the most polluting industrial sectors with respect to the total value of industrial production (%)
- number of vehicles per capita
- deaths for respiratory causes (number of people deaths for respiratory causes)
- organic water pollutant emissions (kilograms per day)

INTENSITIES OR EFFICIENCIES

Economic
- intensity of energy use (mega joules as % of Gross Domestic Product [constant 1995 US$])
- CO_2 Emissions (kilograms per constant 1995 US$ of GDP)

Demographic
- arable and permanent crop land area (thousand hectares per person)
- CO_2 emissions (tons per habitant)
- household final consumption expenditure (constant 1995 US$ per capita)
- total renewable resources water (cubic meters per capita)
- energy consumption (giga joules per habitant)

Results for Honduras and for Latin America and the Caribbean

This section includes a presentation of the results of the applications of the indicators for the case of a country (Honduras) and its comparison with the overall results for Latin America and the Caribbean (Gallopín 2006).

An accepted standard or a norm that shows that a value of the indicator is desirable or undesirable is available for only very few indicators. For this reason, time trends, rather than absolute values of the indicators, were used for the application to concrete nations. In general it is easy to decide if an indicator is improving or deteriorating. The criterion used is: when the change was in the desirable direction and the variation in the value of the indicator was 10% or greater, it was defined as an improvement, and similarly for the deterioration. If the variation was less than 10% in either direction, no significant change was assumed.

Space precludes showing many of the results. Figure 22.2 shows a synthesis of the evolution of the indicators during the decade from 1990 to 2000. Due to the scarcity of indicators available for Honduras, the figure is based on a smaller set of indicators than those shown in Table 22.1. Nevertheless, as an illustration, it can be noted that the major problem areas regarding sustainable

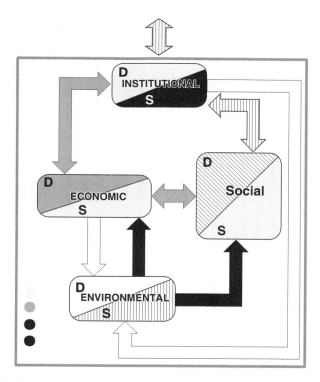

Figure 22.2 Trends of IDS for Honduras, years 1990–2000. Red (represented in black) = deterioration, green (light gray) = improvement, and yellow (dark gray) = maintenance. Gradient colors indicated combinations of trends between different indicators of the same subsystem or interlinkage; vertical hatch = green and red), diagonal hatch (green and yellow). "D" and "S" denote development and sustainability, respectively. The small circles correspond to the indicators of efficiency or intensity.

Source: Gallopín (2006)

Table 22.2 Comparison between the evolution in the available indicators for Honduras and the values for Latin America and the Caribbean

THEME	INDICATORS	NAME	1990–2000s	LAC	G:R:Y	countries
Economic subsystem	Of development	Gross Domestic Product per capita			22:1:9	32
		Labor productivity (constant 1995 US$ per economically active population)			8:4:8	20
	Of sustainability	Gross Capital Formation (% of Gross National Income)			12:9:9	30
Social subsystem	Of development	Percent of population living below poverty line (%)			4:1:4	9
		Mortality rate under 5 years old (rate for each 1000 born alive)			21:0:9	30
	Of sustainability	Income inequality: relation between the 20% most rich and the 20% most poor of the income distribution (%)			2:3:4	9
		Demographic dependency ratio (%)			14:0:6	20
Environmental subsystem	Of sustainability	Forested land area (% of total area)			3:12:23	38
		Annual withdrawals of ground and surface water (% of total renewable water)			6:7:4	17
Institutional subsystem	Of development	Number of telephone lines (telephone lines per 1000 people)			40:0:1	41
	Of sustainability	Corruption Perception Index (Score 0–10)			2:3:3	8
National/International		Ozone-depleting CFCs consumption (ozone-depleting potential [ODP], metric tons)			17:5:3	25
		Current account balance (% of Gross Domestic Product)			12:17:4	33
		Total CO_2 emissions (metric tons)			0:30:3	33
		Total debt (% of Gross National Income			15:12:2	29

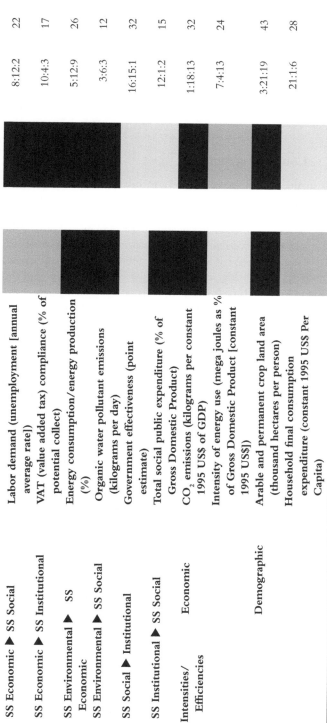

				G:R:Y	
SS Economic ▶ SS Social	Labor demand (unemployment [annual average rate])			8:12:2	22
SS Economic ▶ SS Institutional	VAT (value added tax) compliance (% of potential collect)			10:4:3	17
SS Environmental ▶ SS Economic	Energy consumption/energy production (%)			5:12:9	26
SS Environmental ▶ SS Social	Organic water pollutant emissions (kilograms per day)			3:6:3	12
SS Social ▶ Institutional	Government effectiveness (point estimate)			16:15:1	32
SS Institutional ▶ SS Social	Total social public expenditure (% of Gross Domestic Product)			12:1:2	15
Intensities/ Efficiencies	Economic	CO$_2$ emissions (kilograms per constant 1995 US$ of GDP)		1:18:13	32
		Intensity of energy use (mega joules as % of Gross Domestic Product [constant 1995 US$])		7:4:13	24
	Demographic	Arable and permanent crop land area (thousand hectares per person)		3:21:19	43
		Household final consumption expenditure (constant 1995 US$ Per Capita)		21:1:6	28

Notes: p = incomplete series; LAC = Latin America and the Caribbean

G:R:Y = number of countries with green, red, or yellow trends

Light gray = green (improvement); dark gray = yellow (stagnation); black = red (deterioration)

Source: Gallopín 2006

development of the country (in the time period considered) referred more to the issues of sustainability than those of development, and they are concentrated mainly in the institutional and environmental subsystems. The diagram provides an holistic vision of the trends, and helps to focus on the problematic issues.[6]

Table 22.2 shows a comparison between the evolution in the available indicators for Honduras and the values for Latin America and the Caribbean. A more complete set of indicators exists for most countries of the region. The color allocated to the trends in LAC is the color exhibited by the majority of countries for the indicator, without any weighting. In the three cases where a tie existed, the two attributed colors are depicted.

Concluding remarks

The set of indicators organized in the SES framework allows to interpret the trends of the national socio-ecological system and pinpoint where the critical areas lie, both in relation to the aspects of development and of sustainability.

In this sense, the system makes possible a first general overview, a panoramic photo, of the sustainability of development of a country. As with any holistic perspective, it does not replace but complements further detailed sectoral analysis bases on additional indicators and studies, but it provides a more meaningful understanding of the evolution of the country than any of the commonly used aggregated indices.

While the SES ordering framework is appropriate for any country, the particular set of sustainable development indicators used for the region (listed in Table 22.1) was specially selected in order to include indicators that are available for most countries. This is particularly important for developing countries, and also for the purposes of international comparison. The contents of the set of indicators may be changed by a country that wants to adapt it to its particular conditions and problematique, and is not looking for international comparison; this is what was done by Argentina and by Catalonia in Spain, by replacing some of the proposed indicators by others considered more relevant for their situation, and adding some indicators that were not available for other countries.

As with any holistic view, it is important to be parsimonious with the inclusion of indicators, in order to avoid missing the forest for the trees.

One of the most important benefits of the SES as an organizing framework for indicators of sustainable development is its highlighting of the existence of causal, dynamic interlinkages between the social, economic, institutional, and environmental subsystems (see Chapter 29, Grabowsky et al. and Chapter 6, Rotz and Fraser). Those functional links are rarely considered in the different systems of indicators. A case in point is the UN SDG and targets: the lack of explicit identification and analysis of the interlinkages is likely to result in policies with a major risk of overall failure (a typical instance of suboptimization).

A successful approach for sustainable development at the global level will require the identification of the critical linkages and the careful consideration of the potential synergies and antagonisms between the goals as well as between the targets, and an integrated strategy to avoid the pitfalls. Given that linear thinking is still dominant in most institutions (including governments), the outlook is rather pessimistic, at least in the short and medium term.

Notes

1 Similarly to Rotz and Fraser's discussion of resilience in Chapter 6.
2 Bossel is using the terms system and subsystem flexibly here; normally, one would talk about the human, support, and natural subsystems, and would refer to the six components as sub-subsystems.

3 For Bossel, sustainable development is a property of viable systems: if a system is viable in its environment, it will be sustainable; viability implies sustainability (and vice versa); both terms are used interchangeably (Bossel 1999, p. 24).

4 However, the scales of primary interest for the present purposes are the national, regional (supranational), and regional (sub-national) ones.

5 Obviously, the consumption processes could have been included, within the social subsystem; their inclusion within the economic subsystem is equally defendable and results in greater graphical simplicity.

6 The original diagrams are in color (green, yellow, red, and gradations among them when some indicators of an element changed in different directions; this provides a vivid overall impression of the situation of the whole country. Unfortunately, color printing is not available for this book.

References

Berkes, F. and Folke, C., (eds.), 1998, *Linking Social and Ecological Systems: Management Practices and Social Mechanisms for Building Resilience*, Cambridge University Press, Cambridge.

Bossel, H., 1977, 'Orientors of nonroutine behaviour', in H. Bossel (ed.), *Concepts and Tools of Computer-assisted Policy Analysis*, Birkhäuser, Basel, 227-265.

Bossel, H., 1996, 'Deriving indicators of sustainable development', *Environmental Modeling and Assessment* 1(4), 193–218.

Bossel, H., 1998, *Earth at a Crossroads: Paths to a Sustainable Future*, Cambridge University Press, Cambridge.

Bossel, H., 1999, *Indicators for Sustainable Development: Theory, Method, Applications*. A Report to the Balaton Group, International Institute for Sustainable Development, Winnipeg, Canada.

Friend, A. and Rapport D., 1979, *Towards a Comprehensive Framework for Environment Statistics: A Stress-Response Approach*, Statistics Canada, Ottawa, Canada.

Gallopín, G.C., 1991, 'Human dimensions of global change: Linking the global and the local processes', *International Social Science Journal*, 130, 707–718.

Gallopín, G.C., 1994, *Impoverishment and Sustainable Development: A Systems Approach*. International Institute for Sustainable Development, Winnipeg, Canada.

Gallopín, G.C. 1996. 'Environmental and Sustainability Indicators and the Concept of Situational Indicators. A Systems Approach'. *Environmental Modelling & Assessment* 1(3), 101–117.

Gallopín, G.C., 1997, 'Indicators and their use: Information for decision-making, Part I-Introduction', in B. Moldan and S. Billharz (eds.), *Sustainability Indicators: A Report on the Project on Indicators of Sustainable Development*, SCOPE 58, Wiley, Chichester, 13–27.

Gallopín, G.C., 2003, 'A systems approach to sustainability and sustainable development', *Serie medio ambiente y desarrollo No. 64, Sustainable Development and Human Settlements Division*, ECLAC, Santiago, Chile (also in Spanish as "Sostenibilidad y desarrollo sostenible: un enfoque sistémico").

Gallopín, G.C., 2006, *Sostenibilidad del Desarrollo en América Latina y el Caribe: cifras y tendencias. Honduras*, LC/W.104, División de Desarrollo Sostenible y Asentamientos Humanos, CEPAL, Santiago de Chile.

Gallopín, G.C. and Christianson, K., 2000, *Sustainable Development, Society and the Environment: A Conceptual Framework for Tracking the Linkages*, Stockholm Environment Institute, Stockholm.

Gallopín, G.C., Funtowicz, S., O'Connor, M., and Ravetz, J., 2001, 'Science for the 21st century: From social contract to the scientific core', *International Journal Social Science* 168, 219–229.

Gallopín, G.C., Gutman, P., and Maletta, H., 1989, 'Global impoverishment, sustainable development and the environment, a conceptual approach', *International Social Science Journal* 121, 375–397.

Gallopín, G.C., Jiménez Herrero, L.M., and Rocuts, A., 2014, 'Conceptual frameworks and visual interpretations of sustainability', *International Journal of Sustainable Development* 17(3), 298–326.

Geniaux, G., Bellon, S., Deverre, C., and Powell, B., 2009, *Sustainable Development Indicator Frameworks and Initiatives*, Report no. 49, Seamless, INRA, France.

Hák, T., Moldan, B., and Dahl, A.L., 2007, *Sustainability Indicators: A Scientific Assessmen*, SCOPE 67, Island Press, Washington.

Hass, J.L., Brunvol, F., and Høie, H., 2002, *Overview of Sustainable Development Indicators Used by National and International Agencies*, OECD Statistics Working Paper 2002/1, STD/DOC(2002)2, OECD, Paris.

ISC, 2008, *Informe de Sostenibilitat a Catalunya 2006*, Generalitat de Catalunya, Spain.

Meadows, D., 1998, *Indicators and Information Systems for Sustainable Development*. A Report to the Balaton Group, the Sustainability Institute, Hartland Four Corners, VT, USA.

Moldan, B. and Billharz, S., (eds.), 1997, *Sustainability Indicators: A Report on the Project on Indicators of Sustainable Development*, SCOPE 58, Wiley, Chichester.

OECD, 1993, *Organization for Economic Cooperation and Development Core Set of Indicators for Environmental Performance Reviews*. A Synthesis Report by the Group on the State of the Environment, OECD, Paris.

Quiroga, R.M., 2001, Indicadores de sostenibilidad ambiental y de desarrollo sostenible: Estado del arte y perspectivas. (LC/L.1607-P), serie Manuales 149, CEPAL, United Nations, Santiago de Chile.

Segnestam, L., Winograd, M., and Farrow, A., 2000, *Developing Indicators: Lessons Learned from Central America*, World Bank, Washington, DC.

SFSO (Swiss Federal Statistical Office), SAEFL (Swiss Agency for the Environment, Forests and Landscape) and ARE (Federal Office for Spatial Development), 2001, *Structure of Indicator System and Selection of Indicators*, Consultation document, Provisional version, September 2001, Neuchâtel.

Turner II, B.L., Kasperson, R.E., Matson, P.A., McCarthy, J.J., Corell, R.W., Christensen, L., Eckley, N., Kasperson, J.X., Luers, A., Martello, M.L., Polsky, C., Pulsipher, A., and Schiller, A., 2003, 'Science and technology for sustainable development special feature: A framework for vulnerability analysis in sustainability science', *Proceedings of the US National Academy of Sciences* 100(14), 8074–8079.

Turner II, B.L., Matson, P.A., McCarthy, J.J., Corell, R.W., Christensen, L., Eckley, N., Hovelsrud–Broda, G.K., Kasperson, J.X., Kasperson, R.E., Luers, A., Martello, M.L., Mathiesen, S., Naylor, R., Polsky, C., Pulsipher, A., Schiller, A., Selin, H., and Tyler, N., 2003, 'Illustrating the coupled human – environment system for vulnerability analysis: three case studies', *Proceedings of the U.S. National Academy of Sciences* 100(14), 8080–8085.

UNCSD (United Nations Commission on Sustainable Development), 1995, *Work Programme on Indicators of Sustainable Development of the Commission on Sustainable Development*, ID:2129634260, United Nations Department for Policy Coordination and Sustainable Development, New York.

UNEP-DPCSD, 1995, *The Role of Indicators in Decision-Making*, Discussion Paper prepared by UNEP for the Indicators of Sustainable Development for Decision Making Workshop, 9–11 January, Ghent, Belgium.

United Nations, 2001, *Indicators of Sustainable Development: Guidelines and Methodologies*, Second Edition, September 2001, United Nations, Division for Sustainable Development, New York.

Wall, R., Ostertag, K., and Block, N., 1995, *Synopsis of Selected Indicator Systems for Sustainable Development*. Report for the research project, 'Further development of indicator systems for reporting on the environment' of the Federal Ministry of the Environment, Fraünhofer Institute for Systems and Innovation Research, Karlsruhe.

23

UNEP AND THE CSD PROCESS FOR SUSTAINABLE DEVELOPMENT INDICATORS

Arthur Lyon Dahl

Introduction

The adoption of Agenda 21, the global action plan for sustainable development, at the United Nations Conference on Environment and Development (UNCED), the Rio Earth Summit, in 1992, was a high point in international efforts to address the challenges of planetary sustainability. It called for new levels of cooperation and collaboration at the international level, among them the development of indicators of sustainable development. This paper explores the ways in which the international community, and particularly the United Nations (UN), organised to respond to this mandate, as seen from the perspective of the United Nations Environment Programme (UNEP, now UN Environment) and the UN System-wide Earthwatch. I had been named by UNEP to coordinate Earthwatch in early 1992, after serving in the UNCED secretariat and contributing to the drafting of Agenda 21, so I was directly responsible to oversee the implementation of this mandate, becoming task manager responsible for Chapter 40 of Agenda 21, Information for Decision-making, in reporting to the UN Commission on Sustainable Development (CSD). This is the story of how an international civil servant, with a broad responsibility but essentially no resources, responds to such a challenge at the science-policy interface. A separate paper describes in parallel the intellectual history of the evolving concept of indicators of sustainable development (Dahl, Chapter 3, this volume).

The Earthwatch coordination function was itself quite unique in the UN system. It originated in the UN Conference on the Human Environment in Stockholm in 1972 (UN 1973) which named the environmental assessment part of its action plan "Earthwatch", and became the responsibility of UNEP. It was reinforced by UN General Assembly resolutions, mentioned explicitly as a coordination function in Agenda 21, and confirmed by the Advisory Committee on Coordination made up of the heads of all UN agencies. Yet it was a function without clear definition and not answerable to anybody beyond UNEP management, leaving room for considerable creativity in carrying out its responsibilities. It could convene meetings of all relevant parts of the UN system, and took advantage of the emerging Internet to use its web site as a principal means of information sharing (www.un.org/earthwatch/ and archival web site at http://yabaha.net/dahl/earthw.html). With broad responsibility for environmental assessment at the global level, it covered data collection and management including global observing systems,

347

environmental assessments and reporting, scientific advisory processes, and the whole science-policy interface. Indicators were a logical part of this mandate.

The organisations of the UN family, like many institutions, do not like to be coordinated, especially by an upstart like UNEP. It is a bit like naming yourself an orchestra conductor, inviting musicians to join you, trying to convince the players to play a single work together, and setting the rhythm, in the hope that they will produce something harmonious. Building trust and respect is important, with a focus on showing everyone's efforts in a good light, providing strategic vision, and identifying areas where many see the advantages of cooperation. It helped that the UN System-wide Earthwatch Coordination office was so small (myself and a half-time secretary) and thus represented no threat of empire-building.

The indicators agenda

With respect to indicators, the mandate from Rio was clear (Boulanger, Chapter 9). Chapter 40 of Agenda 21 states: "Indicators of sustainable development need to be developed to provide solid bases for decision-making at all levels and to contribute to a self-regulating sustainability of integrated environment and development systems" (UN 1992 §40.4). "Within the organs and organizations of the United Nations system and relevant international organizations, data-collection activities, including those of Earthwatch and World Weather Watch, need to be strengthened" (UN 1992 §40.8).

> Institutional capacity to integrate environment and development and to develop relevant indicators is lacking at both the national and international levels. Existing institutions and programmes such as the Global Environmental Monitoring System (GEMS) and the Global Resource Information Database (GRID) within UNEP and different entities within the system-wide Earthwatch will need to be considerably strengthened. Earthwatch has been an essential element for environment-related data. While programmes related to development data exist in a number of agencies, there is insufficient coordination between them. The activities related to development data of agencies and institutions of the United Nations system should be more effectively coordinated, perhaps through an equivalent and complementary "Development Watch", which with the existing Earthwatch should be coordinated through an appropriate office within the United Nations to ensure the full integration of environment and development concerns.
>
> (UN 1992 §40.13)

This development watch was never created, but Earthwatch interpreted its responsibility as including all the dimensions of sustainable development.

Assembling the principal stakeholders

The first step was to identify the key stakeholders and experts who could contribute to the process of indicator development, both in the United Nations itself and in the scientific community. The World Resources Institute (WRI) started the process by organising a Workshop on Environmental Indicators in Washington, D.C., 7–8 December 1992, bringing together 21 indicator experts from international organisations (FAO, OECD, UNDP, UNEP Earthwatch, UN University, World Bank), national governments (Canada, Japan, Mexico, Netherlands, USA), and research institutes and universities in Argentina, Canada, England, India, and USA. The workshop concluded on the importance of focussing on the needs of policymakers; the needs of developing countries; developing a minimum set of indicators, not more than 3 or 4 in terms of composite indicators; and the need for rapid development of candidate indicators (Tunstall et al. 1994). Some of the experts present, including Albert Adriaanse of the Dutch Ministry of Environment, Allen Hammond of WRI, Jeff Tschirley (FAO), Manuel Winograd, and myself, continued in the indicators process in varying capacities. This was a first opportunity to share concepts and experience, with background papers from the participants, and opportunities to plan future cooperation. It marked the beginning of a community of sustainable development indicator practitioners.

The United Nations also needed to define how it would take the indicators agenda forward at the interface between science and policy. I organised together with Peter Bartelmus of UNSTAT (UN Statistical Division) the UNEP/UNSTAT Consultative Expert Group on Environment and Sustainable Development Indicators in Geneva on 6–8 December 1993 (UNEP/UNSTAT 1993) with 20 organisations represented from inside and outside the UN system. We invited Bedřich Moldan, first Minister of Environment in the Czech Republic, a vice president of the Commission on Sustainable Development, and Director of the Environment Center at Charles University in Prague, to chair the meeting, as he was a scientist, diplomat, and policymaker. He continued to be a key player in the development of indicators, and we have collaborated on many occasions. Some other experts who remained with the core group continuing after this meeting included Jan Bakkes of RIVM (Rijksinstituut voor Volksgezondheid en Milieu) and John O'Connor of the World Bank. The meeting consulted on a process leading to a common framework for a set or sets of indicators and elements of a work plan on environmental indicators and indicators of sustainable development for national and international use. After the meeting, UNEP and UNSTAT tried to maintain the consultative group as an informal network to continue discussion on indicators. By July 1994, there were 35 members in the list, but it proved difficult to sustain networking on the different issues identified.

One outcome of the meeting was the recognition that a scientific process was needed to stimulate research on sustainable development indicators in support of the intergovernmental process. Professor Moldan was also active in the Scientific Committee on Problems of the Environment (SCOPE) of the International Council of Scientific Unions (ICSU, now the International Council for Science). He therefore organised a SCOPE project in collaboration with UNEP to develop highly aggregated indicators of sustainable development (1994–1997) with a scientific committee in which I participated.

The process that went ahead focussed mostly on biophysical, social, and institutional indicators. Despite the efforts of Peter Bartelmus at UNSTAT to link the CSD indicators to the development of a System for Integrated Environmental and Economic Accounting (SEEA) (UNSTAT 1993), no real connection was made. His significant effort *Towards a Framework for Indicators of Sustainable Development* (Bartelmus 1994) could not overcome the basic dichotomy of monetary accounting versus physical indicator development. Bartelmus contributed to the development of green accounting, and the UN Statistical Division maintained a programme to compile environmental statistics and indicators, but without real cooperation with the CSD indicators work programme.

Inter-agency coordination

As part of the effort to implement Agenda 21, the UN created an Inter-Agency Committee on Sustainable Development (IACSD) to coordinate efforts within the UN system and to allocate responsibilities as task managers for the chapters of Agenda 21 in reporting to the Commission on Sustainable Development (CSD). As Task Manager for Earthwatch, I frequently served as UNEP representative on the IACSD, and soon became Task Manager as well for Agenda 21, Chapter 40: Information for Decision-making, continuing until 2001. This included preparing the Secretary-General's reports to the CSD when chapter 40 was on the agenda (UN 1995).

At a more technical level, the UN System-wide Earthwatch Coordination function of UNEP could logically initiate consultations on a coherent approach to this mandate, as well as providing guidance and coherence to the larger effort to use science for decision-making in the UN system, and to assess and improve scientific advisory processes. The Earthwatch web site linking the efforts of all the UN system partners became a primary tool for communications and coordination, with a special section on indicators. Earthwatch also contributed to the development of the Global Observing Systems, and supported the Integrated Global Observing Strategy Partnership with the space agencies that led to the creation of the intergovernmental Group on Earth Observations (GEO).

After the Rio Earth Summit, and following on from the successful working parties of experts from within and outside the UN system that had contributed to preparing Agenda 21, we initiated an annual inter-agency Earthwatch Working Party from 1994 to 2002 to which all the UN agencies and relevant scientific bodies were invited to send experts. Indicators and the data systems to support them became part of the agenda. The First Meeting of the Earthwatch Inter-Agency Working Party (Geneva, 1–2 June 1994) brought together representatives of UN-Habitat, UNCTAD, UNDP, UNDPCSD (now UNDESA), UNFPA, UNHCR, UNSTAT, UNEP, FAO, IAEA, IOC, UNESCO, WHO, and WMO. It adopted terms of reference for Earthwatch and agreed on the modalities for continuing cooperation. With reference to the proposal in Agenda 21 for a "Development Watch" parallel to Earthwatch, the meeting recommended that Earthwatch be expanded to include the information requirements for assessment and reporting on sustainable development (UNEP 1994). This provided a mechanism not only for inter-agency coordination on indicators work, but also for sharing responsibility for the necessary supporting infrastructure of data collection and reporting from which indicators could be derived. While UNDP and others continued to discuss a possible Development Watch in the UN system for a few years, it never took off.

Indicators, of course, are only useful if the data are available to calculate them, and many indicator projects fall short because of this. Everyone was also conscious that proposals for indicator methodologies needed to be accompanied by data collection systems. The UN system agencies mobilised to address many of these supporting challenges both individually for indicators within their areas of expertise and collectively through Earthwatch.

In my function as Coordinator of the UN System-wide Earthwatch 1992–2000, I organised or co-organised many UN inter-agency meetings, participated in the CSD expert groups on indicators, represented UNEP in the scientific efforts of the SCOPE projects on indicators, and was often a major session speaker at the meetings, even replacing the Director of the UN Division for Sustainable Development (UNDSD) in chairing one of their expert group meetings. With my frequent stays in New York for the CSD and other events, I was fully integrated into the UNDSD team in providing secretariat support to the meetings and writing the reports when necessary. However, by 2000 UNEP lost interest in Earthwatch coordination and I was moved to other responsibilities before retiring in 2002. This did not, however, affect my involvement in indicators in the SCOPE project and elsewhere.

Preparing the CSD indicators work programme

The UN Division for Sustainable Development (UNDSD) in the Department for Policy Coordination and Sustainable Development (UNDPCSD, later the Department of Economic and

Social Affairs – UNDESA) initially led by Joke Waller-Hunter, was the secretariat for the Commission on Sustainable Development (CSD). It had lead responsibility for the programme on sustainable development indicators.

When the CSD first met in 1993, there was considerable interest in indicators, but when the second session in 1994 considered suggestions for a CSD work programme to implement the Agenda 21 recommendation for indicators of sustainable development, there was some opposition from developing countries. They feared that such indicators would be used as a tool for green conditionality in development financing and to control what they were doing. Support for the programme came from OECD and other countries working on indicators.

Meanwhile, the UNDSD began preparations for the indicators programme (see Table 23.1 for chronology). A Task Force on Indicators for Sustainable Development was established

Table 23.1 Brief chronology of the CSD work programme on indicators

Dates	Organiser	Title	Location
7–8 December 1992	World Resources Institute	Workshop on Environmental Indicators	Washington, D.C.
6–8 December 1993	UNEP, UNSTAT	Consultative Expert Group on Environment and Sustainable Development Indicators	Geneva
22–23 September 1994	World Bank	Workshop on Indicators of Sustainable Development	Washington, D.C.
9–11 January 1995	UNEP, SCOPE Costa Rica, Belgium	Workshop on Indicators of Sustainable Development for Decision-Making	Ghent, Belgium
14–15 February 1995	UNDSD	1st Expert Group Meeting on Indicators for Sustainable Development	New York
28 April 1995	UN	3rd Commission on Sustainable Development approved work programme	New York
25–26 July 1995	UNDSD	2nd Expert Group Meeting on Indicators of Sustainable Development	New York
15–17 November 1995	SCOPE, UNEP, Germany	2nd Scientific Workshop on Indicators of Sustainable Development	Wuppertal, Germany

(Continued)

351

Table 23.1 (Continued)

Dates	Organiser	Title	Location
19 January 1996	UNDSD/UNEP	Meeting on Common/ Compatible Systems of Access to Data	New York
6–8 February 1996	UNDSD	UN Expert Meeting on Methodologies for Indicators of Sustainable Development	Glen Cove, Long Island, New York
23 September 1996	UNDSD, UN System-wide Earthwatch	3rd Expert Group Meeting on Indicators of Sustainable Development	Geneva
24 September 1996	UNDSD/UNEP	Workshop on Information for Sustainable Development and Earthwatch	Geneva
September 1996	UN	*Indicators of Sustainable Development Framework and Methodologies* published	
20–22 November 1996	UNDSD, Belgium	Second International Workshop "Launching the testing of Sustainable Development"	Ghent, Belgium
23–24 October 1997	UNDSD	4th Expert Group Meeting on Indicators of Sustainable Development	New York
19–21 January 1998	SCOPE, Czech Republic	4th International Workshop on Indicators of Sustainable Development	Prague
7–8 April 1999	UNDSD	5th Expert Group Meeting on Indicators of Sustainable Development	New York
7–9 December 1999	UNDSD	International Workshop on CSD Indicators of Sustainable Development	Barbados
25–28 September 2000	UNDSD, UNEP, Canada	International Expert Meeting on Information for Decision Making and Participation	Aylmer, Quebec

Dates	Organiser	Title	Location
September 2001	UN	*Indicators of Sustainable Development: Framework and Methodologies* 2nd edition published	
10–14 May 2004	SCOPE, UNEP, IHDP, EEA	Assessment of Sustainability Indicators Workshop	Prague
13–15 December 2005	UNDSD	6th Expert Group Meeting on Indicators of Sustainable Development	New York
3–4 October 2006	UNDSD	7th Expert Group Meeting on Indicators of Sustainable Development	New York
2007	UN	*Indicators of Sustainable Development: Guidelines and Methodologies* 3rd edition published	
5–16 October 2008	UNDSD	Expert Group Meeting on Climate Change & Sustainable Development: The Role of Indicators	New York
17–19 September 2009	UNDSD	Expert Group Meeting on Institutionalizing Sustainable Development Indicators for Measuring Progress of National Strategies	Bridgetown, Barbados

consisting of Hermann Habermann (Director), Peter Bartelmus and Reena Shah from the UN Statistical Office (UNSTAT), and Joke Waller-Hunter (Director), Kenneth Ruffing, Lars Hyttinen, Mary Pat Williams Silveira, and Lars Mortensen from UNDSD. I was asked to join it as the UNEP representative at its third meeting on 21 September 1994, when we reviewed a draft list of 75 key national indicators for sustainable development including pressure, state and response indicators developed by UNDPCSD and UNSTAT. The list as revised by the task force was presented at a World Bank Workshop on Indicators of Sustainable Development on 22–23 September 1994 in Washington, D.C., with many experts and some governments participating. After further revision based on comments received, the provisional list and an accompanying paper were presented to the Bureau of the CSD on 20 October 1994, and then circulated to agencies to invite contributions to the development of specific indicators and to participate in the work programme. A note on the results of this process was circulated to governments on 22 November 1994, and a draft Work Programme on Indicators of Sustainable Development was issued on 20 December 1994 in preparation for the third session of the CSD. The actors responsible for developing each indicator were identified, with the aim of preparing methodology sheets and producing a manual by 1996.

To unblock the diplomatic situation at the CSD, UNEP and SCOPE partnered with the governments of Costa Rica and Belgium to organise a Workshop on Indicators of Sustainable Development for Decision-Making in Ghent, Belgium, on 9–11 January 1995, as a high-level stakeholder consultation (Bell and Morse, Chapter 12). The workshop brought together representatives and diplomats from the CSD, including its President, Klaus Töpfer of Germany and Vice-Chairman, Ministers from Belgium and Costa Rica, and delegations from Barbados, Belgium, Brazil, Canada, China, Costa Rica, France, Germany, India, Namibia, Norway, Philippines, Poland, and USA. Intergovernmental organisations represented included the European Commission, European Environment Agency (EEA), EUROSTAT, OECD, UNDPCSD, UNDP, UNEP, and WHO. The SCOPE project scientific committee chaired by Professor Moldan included Albert Adriaanse (Netherlands), Peter Bartelmus (UNSTAT), myself (Earthwatch), Allen Hammond (WRI), Donella Meadows (Dartmouth), Aromar Revi (TARU, India), and Manuel Winograd (Argentina), assisted by Philippe Bourdeau, Secretary-General of SCOPE. Non-governmental organisations represented were WWF, New Economics Foundation and IUCN. UNEP and UNDPCSD presented a joint working paper which I drafted (Dahl 1995a), SCOPE presented the scientific issues, and options were reviewed. I represented both UNEP and SCOPE on the organising committee for the workshop and gave the closing talk on the way ahead. The workshop succeeded in building trust and confidence between the scientists and the policymakers, and it was agreed that an indicators programme that provided the tools for national governments to assess their own sustainable development according to their own criteria, and that would not be used for comparisons and rankings between countries, would be politically acceptable. We had succeeded in creating a close working relationship between science, policymaking, and government implementation for the indicators programme, with scientists who understood diplomacy and diplomats who appreciated the science. The report of the workshop (Gouzee et al. 1995) was officially submitted by the governments of Belgium and Costa Rica to the CSD at its third session in April 1995 when Chapter 40 of Agenda 21 was on the agenda (UN 1995).

To carry the planning process forward, UNDSD convened a first Expert Group Meeting on Indicators for Sustainable Development in New York on 14–15 February 1995 to finalise the work programme and get commitments from actors, mainly UN-system organisations, who would implement the work programme by further developing the indicators and underlying methodologies, and to analyse data availability.

The CSD indicators programme

The work programme on indicators of sustainable development was approved by the Commission on Sustainable Development at its third session in April 1995. The CSD praised the SCOPE results and called for SCOPE to coordinate scientific efforts on the identification of interlinkages, the development of aggregated indicators, further development of indicators, and work on frameworks.

To follow up this decision, UNDSD convened a second Expert Group Meeting on Indicators of Sustainable Development in New York on 25–26 July 1995 to approve an implementation plan, which was distributed on 4 August. These annual Expert Group Meetings were the principal guiding mechanism for the CSD work programme on indicators, complemented by workshops on more specific topics (Table 23.1). A roster of experts from governments, international organisations, and non-governmental organisations was developed to contribute to programme implementation. Preparation of the draft methodology sheets for each indicator was a major inter-agency effort for the remainder of 1995, with consultations at multiple levels within and between agencies.

After running an Earthwatch Working Party 3 in New York on 17–18 January 1996, I helped to organise a UNDPCSD/UNEP Meeting on Common/Compatible Systems of Access to Data (New York, 19 January 1996), which discussed sharing UN system information, common core data sets, and a UN system home page for Sustainable Development (UNEP 1996a), all of which would help to support the indicators process.

UNDSD organised a UN Expert Meeting on Methodologies for Indicators of Sustainable Development 6–8 February 1996 in Glen Cove, Long Island, New York, with 48 experts from 29 governments, plus agencies and some research centres, to provide a detailed review of all the draft methodology sheets, to review country experience with indicators and discuss national pilot testing of the indicators, and to make recommendations on the further development of the programme of work on indicators. Country reports were submitted by Australia, Belgium, Brazil, Canada, China, Costa Rica, Germany, Hungary, India, Japan, Korea, Malaysia, Mexico, Morocco, Netherlands, Nigeria, Philippines, Ukraine, USA, and Venezuela. One recommendation was for the SCOPE/UNEP project to explore linkages and to develop highly aggregated indicators based on different themes of sustainability. The methodology sheets were then submitted as a background paper to the fourth session of the CSD in April–May 1996, which approved decisions supporting the programme of work on indicators.

The 3rd Expert Group Meeting on Indicators was organised by UNDSD and the UN System-wide Earthwatch on 23 September 1996 in Geneva, Switzerland, to report on the status of the revised methodology sheets, start the pilot testing phase in a few testing countries, and prepare regional meetings in implementation of the CSD 4 decision. This was followed immediately on 24 September by the UNDPCSD/UNEP Workshop on Information for Sustainable Development and Earthwatch (UNEP 1996b).

The first "blue book" of *Indicators of Sustainable Development Framework and Methodologies* was published in October 1996 (UN 1996). Most of the 134 indicator sheets, with details of how to calculate the indicator, were prepared by the relevant UN agencies.

The programme then moved into the three-year country testing phase. This began with a Second International Workshop "Launching the testing of Sustainable Development" in Ghent, 20–22 November 1996 with 60 participants, organised by Belgium and Costa Rica as a CSD intersessional event. Twelve countries committed to participate in the testing phase: Belgium, Bolivia, Brazil, China, Costa Rica, Czech Republic, Finland (Rosenström, Chapter 21), Germany, Morocco, South Africa, Venezuela, and UK. I introduced the indicator methodologies and explained environmental indicators. By March 1997 there were 15 testing countries, and 22 by the end of the testing phase.

One innovation was the pairing of governments between an industrialised country with more experience, and a developing country. For example, Finland paired with South Africa, Belgium with Costa Rica, Germany with Brazil, and France with Tunisia. The process itself led to more integration at the national level. In South Africa, the process stimulated closer collaboration between ministries and the creation of an inter-ministerial mechanism. Belgium had to legislate to make it possible to combine data from the Flemish and Walloon provinces and generate indicators at the federal level. In practice, most governments selected about 50 of the CSD indicators as relevant to their sustainable development, plus another 50 to cover other dimensions of their specific situation.

The UN system also organised activities in the field to help countries take up the indicators. These started with the ESCAP Regional Consultative Meeting on Environmentally Sound and Sustainable Development, Bangkok, 26–29 November 1996 (UN ESCAP 1996), followed by the Regional Workshop for Latin America and the Caribbean, San Jose, Costa Rica, 10–12 March 1997 (UN 1997a), and the Africa Regional Capacity 21/UNDPCSD Workshop: Indicators of Sustainable Development in Africa, in Accra, Ghana, 3–6 June 1997, where I was a facilitator and speaker.

The Fourth Expert Group Meeting on Indicators of Sustainable Development in New York, 23–24 Oct 1997, reviewed the status of the testing programme and the results of the regional workshops. A major theme was harmonisation with other indicator programmes including those of UN specialised agencies and conventions. Another item on the agenda was current status and approaches to aggregation and linkages (UN 1997b).

Country experience during the testing phase was reviewed at the Fourth International Workshop on Indicators of Sustainable Development, Prague, Czech Republic, 19–21 January 1998 (UN 1998a) and reported to the CSD in E/CN.17/1998/15 §21–24. It followed the workshops in Ghent, Wuppertal and Glen Cove (USA), and provided the first opportunity to share the experience of testing countries. I provided a briefing on recent developments in linkages and aggregation, including the work of the Consultative Group on Sustainable Development Indicators (see below, International Institute for Sustainable Development).

UNDSD also organised a Workshop on Indicators of Consumption and Production Patterns to fill a gap in the indicators framework. The results were shared at the CSD-6 Intersessional Ad Hoc Working Group in New York, 2–3 March 1998 (UN 1998b) and published (UN 1998c). The Caribbean SIDS organised their own Caribbean Regional Workshop on Sustainable Development Indicators in Barbados, 22–23 October 1998, adapting the CSD indicators to their own situation (Crowards et al. 1998).

The Fifth Expert Group Meeting on Indicators of Sustainable Development, New York, 7–8 April 1999 (UN 1999a) reviewed the results of the national testing of indicators in 22 countries, and a study commissioned by UNDSD on linkages and aggregation (Guinomet 1999), and proposed a thematic framework as more policy relevant, with a more limited core set for all countries, plus optional indicators as relevant. UNDSD asked me to chair the meeting after the opening session.

UNDSD convened an International Workshop on CSD Indicators of Sustainable Development, Barbados, 7–9 December 1999 upon finalisation of the testing process so that the testing countries could exchange experiences and best practices, and ensure the integration of results into the revised indicator framework and methodologies (UN 1999b). It reviewed the proposed thematic framework and core indicators.

A Progress Report on the Implementation of the CSD Work Programme on Indicators of Sustainable Development was submitted to the Eighth Session of the Commission on Sustainable Development (24 April–5 May 2000) as Background Paper No. 7 (UN 2000). The Government of Canada, UNDESA, and UNEP organised an International Expert Meeting on Information for Decision Making and Participation in Aylmer, Quebec, 25–28 September 2000, for which I prepared a background paper (UNEP 2000), and the report was submitted to CSD 9 (UN 2001f).

After consideration at a CSD Intersessional Working Group on Information for Decision-making for which I was part of the secretariat, the second edition of the CSD indicators *of Sustainable Development: Framework and Methodologies* was submitted as Background Paper No. 3 and approved at the 9th Session of the Commission on Sustainable Development in April 2001. It was published shortly after as another "blue book" (UN 2001a). It contained a new set of 56 core indicators. The CSD also considered a Report on the Aggregation of Indicators of Sustainable Development prepared by UNDSD as Background Paper No. 2 (UN 2001g). The Secretary-General reported to the Commission on Information for Decision-Making and

Participation (UN 2001b) with an addendum on the CSD Work Programme on Indicators of Sustainable Development (UN 2001c), and on the Report of the Ad Hoc Inter-sessional Working Group on Information for Decision-making and Participation and on International Cooperation for an Enabling Environment (UN 2001d). The CSD also acted as the preparatory committee for the World Summit on Sustainable Development (WSSD), which also considered information and institutions for decision-making (UN 2001e). However the WSSD outcome document only made a few brief references to indicators at the national level.

The next few years saw a number of regional meetings focussed on implementation of the indicators. The ECLAC Seminar on Sustainable Development Indicators in Latin America and the Caribbean, Santiago, Chile, 29–30 November 2001, analysed and exchanged regional experiences on the construction of sustainability indicators, discussed the obstacles to implementation and strategies for overcoming them, and started a regional network of sustainable development indicators (UN ECLAC 2001). For SIDS, there was a Resource Persons Meeting on Using Information in Decision-Making for Sustainable Development in Small Island Developing States, St. Lucia, 27–28 May 2003; a Training Workshop on Methodologies, Tools and Best Practices for Managing Information for Decision-making on Sustainable Development in Caribbean SIDS, Trinidad and Tobago, 27–31 October 2003; and a Regional Caribbean Workshop on National Sustainable Development Strategies and Indicators of Sustainable Development, Castries, St. Lucia, 14–15 January 2004 (UN 2004a). ESCAP organised a workshop on National Sustainable Development Strategies for Asia and the Pacific which included a component on indicators of sustainable development, Bangkok, Thailand, 29–31 October 2003 (UN ESCAP 2003). The UNDSD held an Arab Regional Workshop on National Sustainable Development Strategies (NSDS) and Indicators of Sustainable Development, Cairo, Egypt 12–14 December 2004 (UN 2004c).

In 2004, the Secretary-General reported to the CSD on Progress in implementing the decisions of the Commission on Sustainable Development related to improvements in national reporting and further work on indicators of sustainable development (UN 2004b).

The time had come to revisit the CSD indicators again, both scientifically by SCOPE and in their application by UNDSD. The UN commissioned an assessment of recent developments and activities in 2004 (Shah 2004) which was reviewed at the SCOPE/UNEP/IHDP/EEA Assessment of Sustainability Indicators (ASI) project, ASI Workshop 10–14 May 2004, Prague, Czech Republic. Another commissioned paper from IISD looked at ways forward, including experience with the CSD's role in sustainable development indicators, its general mandate and role, an overview of the CSD's indicator process, national level uptake and experience, areas of sustainable development inadequately covered in the current indicator core set, and the potential, advantages, and limitations of a common global sustainable development indicator framework (Pintér et al. 2005). It was a working paper for the next UNDSD Expert Group Meeting, restarted after six years.

The Expert Group Meeting on Indicators of Sustainable Development in New York, 13–15 December 2005, reviewed the interim revised set of indicators, the suitability of frameworks, and future areas of work (UN 2005). It agreed on a revised interim list of 99 indicators. The meeting also agreed to remove the explicit division of indicators into four "pillars" (social, environmental, economic, institutional). It further agreed to distinguish indicators into core indicators relevant for most countries, and non-core indicators that either provide additional information to core indicators or cover issues that are relevant for many but not most countries. The thematic framework was to be retained, but with modified themes and sub-themes. It also discussed other indicator frameworks under development and possible options for future work on indicators (UN 2006b §5).

The fourteenth session of the CSD in 2006 considered a background paper on Global Trends and Status of Indicators of Sustainable Development (UN 2006a). A final Expert Group Meeting on Indicators of Sustainable Development was convened in New York, 3–4 October 2006, to finalise the review process. It placed the indicators in fourteen themes: poverty; governance; health; education; demographics; natural hazards; atmosphere; land; oceans, seas and coasts; freshwater; biodiversity; economic development; global economic partnership; and consumption and production patterns (UN 2006b).

The third edition of *Indicators of Sustainable Development: Guidelines and Methodologies* was published in 2007, with 98 indicators including 50 core indicators (UN 2007). The indicators were related to Agenda 21, the Johannesburg Plan of Implementation and the MDG indicators.

While this basically concluded the CSD Programme of Work on Indicators of Sustainable Development, UNDSD did organise two follow-up meetings. An Expert Group Meeting on Climate Change & Sustainable Development: The Role of Indicators, was held in New York, 15–16 October 2008 (UN 2008), and a regional Expert Group Meeting on Institutionalizing Sustainable Development Indicators for Measuring Progress of National Strategies was organised in Bridgetown, Barbados, 17–19 September 2009, for the Small Island Developing States (SIDS) of the Caribbean (UN 2009).

Complementary processes

Alongside the intergovernmental indicators programme at the CSD, there were supporting efforts from the scientific community organised by some of the same experts assisting the UNDSD.

SCOPE projects on indicator science

As mentioned above, the Scientific Committee on Problems of the Environment (SCOPE) of the International Council for Science organised a SCOPE project with UNEP support to explore the science of indicators of sustainable development in 1994–1997. The scientific committee for the project, headed by Professor Moldan, included some of the same experts supporting the CSD process including myself representing UNEP. After the Ghent workshop addressing the policy issues in January 1995, the SCOPE project organised a second Scientific Workshop on Indicators of Sustainable Development at the Wuppertal Institute in Germany on 15–17 November 1995 (Billharz and Moldan 1996) where leading researchers considered all the key issues. I was on the organising committee, gave an opening address for UNEP, presented a paper on various concepts for indicators of sustainability (Dahl 1995b), and made the closing remarks at the end of the thematic sessions.

The first SCOPE project ended with the publication of a book on the state of the art in sustainable development indicators (Moldan et al. 1997) which was distributed to all delegations at the Rio+5 session of the General Assembly in 1997. I contributed a review of comprehensive approaches (Dahl 1997a) and examples of vector-based indicators (Dahl 1997b).

With the very rapid development of the science and practice of indicators, and their growing importance in policymaking, Bedřich Moldan with SCOPE decided to organise a second project on assessment of sustainability indicators (2003–2007) to make a scientific assessment of the remaining conceptual and methodological challenges and the need to ensure their policy relevance (Janoušková et al., Chapter 30). Papers were commissioned from many experts, 64 of whom gathered at a workshop in Prague in May 2004. The results of the deliberations were assembled in a book highlighting both what had been accomplished and the many challenges still ahead (Hak et al. 2007). I chaired the working group on conceptual challenges, co-authored the overview chapter with Bedřich Moldan (Moldan and Dahl 2007), contributed another chapter on integrated assessment and indicators (Dahl 2007), and co-edited the resulting volume.

International Institute for Sustainable Development

One useful initiative during this period was the organisation by Peter Hardi of the International Institute for Sustainable Development (IISD) of a Conference on Principles of Sustainable Development Performance Measurement, held in Bellagio, Italy, in November 1996. Rather than considering the content of indicators, the expert group in which I participated looked at lessons learned about the processes of creating and implementing an indicators programme, and produced the "Bellagio Principles" of good practice in indicator development (Hardi and Zdan 1997) which became a standard reference.

Another outcome of the meeting in Bellagio was the creation by a small number of key indicator experts of a Consultative Group on Sustainable Development Indicators (CGSDI 1996–2005) as a virtual think-tank. Following its creation at Bellagio, it worked primarily over the Internet until IISD organised a meeting in Middleburg, Virginia, on 9–11 January 1998. Initial members were Alan AtKisson, David Berry, Gilberto Gallopin (until September 1999), Allen Hammond, Peter Hardi, Jochen Jesinghaus, Donella Meadows, John O'Connor, Ismail Seragel-din, Robert B. Wallace, and myself. Three more members were added in September 1999: Edgar Gutierrez (University of Costa Rica), Yuchi Moriguchi (National Institute for Environmental Studies, Japan), and Adil Najam (Boston University). Bedřich Moldan was added in 2001 when Donella Meadows passed away.

The CGSDI's initial focus was on approaches to highly aggregated indices of sustainable development. Based on the CGSDI discussion, and with contributions from other members, Jochen Jesinghaus created the Dashboard of Sustainability to present complex indicator data sets in an easy-to-understand graphic form, while making it possible to burrow down for the details for those who were interested. The CSD indicator set was loaded into the Dashboard of Sustainability for demonstration at a side event at CSD 9 in 2001. Trend analysis was added in time for presentation of the Dashboard in side events at the World Summit on Sustainable Development in Johannesburg in 2002, including one I organised through the International Environment Forum. With the multiplication of indicator initiatives, including more than 400 loaded into the Dashboard, and a few final exchanges on the future of indicators work, the CGSDI wound down by 2006.

The "Bellagio Principles" were updated in 2011 at a second meeting in Bellagio. The *Bellagio Sustainability Assessment and Measurement Principles* (BellagioSTAMP) revised the original Principles through a similar expert group process. The new BellagioSTAMP includes a complete set of eight principles: (1) Guiding vision; (2) Essential considerations; (3) Adequate scope; (4) Framework and indicators; (5) Transparency; (6) Effective communications; (7) Broad participation; and (8) Continuity and capacity (Pintér et al. 2012, Chapter 2).

Wider outreach

In order to clarify my own thinking on sustainable development from an integrated perspective, I wrote a book, *The Eco Principle: Ecology and Economics in Symbiosis* with my own synthesis of the issues around sustainability and the need for a systems approach (Dahl 1996). It seemed important to keep the scientific community informed of progress, so I published a paper in 2000 on recent methodological and conceptual developments in sustainability indicators (Dahl 2000) in addition to my contributions through the CSD process and SCOPE. In 2002, through the

International Environment Forum, I organised a Dialogue on Indicators for Sustainability in the Forum on Science, Technology and Innovation for Sustainable Development at the World Summit on Sustainable Development, Johannesburg, on 27 August 2002, with speakers including Bedřich Moldan, Jochen Jesinghaus from EUROSTAT/JRC, and an expert from UNDSD. My paper was on the *Usefulness of Indicators for Sustainability* (Dahl 2002). In 2006, UNESCO asked me to prepare the first of a series of UNESCO-SCOPE Policy Briefs on *Indicators of Sustainability: Reliable Tools for Decision Making* (Dahl 2006) which was distributed at the CSD. A special issue of *Ecological Indicators* on sustainability indicators that I co-edited in 2012 included my general review of achievements and gaps in indicators for sustainability (Dahl 2012).

In 2007, UNEP commissioned me to review all national reports on the state of the environment and sustainability since the Rio Earth Summit in 1992, and to prepare for the UNEP Governing Council in 2009 an overview of the environmental assessment landscape and state-of-the-environment reporting at the national level (Dahl 2008). One conclusion of this review was that 66 countries were using indicators in their national reports, a significant impact at least partly due to the CSD indicators programme.

In conclusion, it took 15 years and a variety of formal and informal mechanisms between the UN secretariat and agencies, governments and the scientific community, with the guidance and approval of the UN Commission on Sustainable Development, to evolve a policy-relevant, scientifically validated set of indicators of sustainable development. However, despite repeated requests from governments, reviews of progress, and the best efforts of the scientific community, no consensus emerged on highly aggregated indices (Dahl, Chapter 3, this volume).

A number of key experts were involved across the different processes, especially in the early years, providing both vision and coherence as the programme moved forward. While the Commission on Sustainable Development has been replaced, the progress made in its indicator programme enshrined indicators as important policy tools to move towards sustainability in many national processes. Today, with the new UN 2030 Agenda and its Sustainable Development Goals and indicators, a whole new scale of indicator activity is under way, which could well benefit from some of the lessons learned and experience acquired over the past 25 years.

References

Bartelmus, Peter. 1994. *Towards a Framework for Indicators of Sustainable Development.* Department for Economic and Social Information and Policy Analysis, Working Paper Series No. 7. New York: United Nations.

Billharz, Suzanne and Bedřich Moldan (eds.). 1996. *Scientific Workshop on Indicators of Sustainable Development,* Wuppertal, Germany, 15–17 November 1995. Report. Scientific Committee on Problems of the Environment (SCOPE). Prague: Charles University Environmental Center.

Crowards, Tom, Sophie van der Meeren and Leise Perch. 1998. *Report of the Caribbean Regional Workshop on Sustainable Development Indicators,* Barbados, 22–23 October 1998. Barbados: Caribbean Development Bank.

Dahl, Arthur Lyon. 1995a. The role of indicators in decision-making (Discussion paper by UNEP and DPCSD), p. 11 and Annex III. In Nadine Gouzee, Bernard Mazijn and Suzan Billharz (eds.), *Indicators of Sustainable Development for Decision-Making.* Report of the Workshop of Ghent, Belgium, 9–11 January 1995, submitted to the UN Commission on Sustainable Development. Federal Planning Office of Belgium, Brussels.

Dahl, Arthur Lyon. 1995b. Opening address, pp. 25–26; summary of presented paper "Towards indicators of sustainability", pp. 50–51; and Framework of sustainability issues from Agenda 21, pp. 57–58. In Suzanne Billharz and Bedřich Moldan (eds.), *Report of the SCOPE Scientific Workshop on Indicators of Sustainable Development,* Wuppertal, Germany, 15–17 November 1995. Charles University Environment Centre, Prague. Towards indicators of sustainability (full paper): https://iefworld.org/ddahl95b.htm

Dahl, Arthur Lyon. 1996. *The Eco Principle: Ecology and Economics in Symbiosis*. London: Zed Books Ltd, and Oxford: George Ronald.

Dahl, Arthur Lyon. 1997a. The big picture: Comprehensive approaches – introduction, Chapter 2, pp. 69–83. In Bedřich Moldan, Suzanne Billharz and Robyn Matravers (eds.), *Sustainability Indicators: A Report on the Project on Indicators of Sustainable Development*. Scientific Committee on Problems of the Environment, SCOPE 58. John Wiley and Sons, Chichester.

Dahl, Arthur Lyon. 1997b. From concept to indicator: Dimensions expressed as vectors, Box 2H, pp. 125–127. In Bedřich Moldan, Suzanne Billharz and Robyn Matravers (eds.), *Sustainability Indicators: A Report on the Project on Indicators of Sustainable Development*. Scientific Committee on Problems of the Environment, SCOPE 58. John Wiley and Sons, Chichester.

Dahl, Arthur Lyon. 2000. Using Indicators to Measure Sustainability: Recent Methodological and Conceptual Developments. *Marine and Freshwater Research* 51(5): 427–433.

Dahl, Arthur Lyon. 2002. *Usefulness of Indicators for Sustainability*. Paper presented at the Dialogue on Indicators for Sustainability, Forum on Science, Technology and Innovation for Sustainable Development, World Summit on Sustainable Development, Johannesburg, 27 August 2002. https://iefworld.org/ddahl02a.htm

Dahl, Arthur Lyon. 2006. *Indicators of Sustainability: Reliable Tools for Decision Making*. UNESCO-SCOPE Policy Briefs No. 1, May 2006. Paris: UNESCO-SCOPE. http://unesdoc.unesco.org/images/0015/001500/150005e.pdf

Dahl, Arthur Lyon, 2007. Integrated assessment and indicators, Chapter 10, pp. 163–176. In Tomas Hak, Bedřich Moldan and Arthur Lyon Dahl (eds.), *Sustainability Indicators: A Scientific Assessment*. SCOPE Vol. 67. Washington, DC, Island Press.

Dahl, Arthur Lyon. 2008. *Overview of Environmental Assessment Landscape at National Level: State of State-of-the-Environment Reporting*. Note by the Executive Director. UNEP/GC.25/INF/12/Add.1, 45 p. www.unep.org/gc/gcss-x/download.asp?ID=1015

Dahl, Arthur Lyon. 2012. Achievements and gaps in indicators for sustainability. *Ecological Indicators* 17: 14–19. June 2012. http://dx.doi.org/10.1016/j.ecolind.2011.04.032

Gouzee, Nadine, Bernard Mazijn and Suzan Billharz. 1995. *Indicators of Sustainable Development for Decision-Making*. Report of the Workshop of Ghent, Belgium, 9–11 January 1995, submitted to the UN Commission on Sustainable Development. Brussels: Federal Planning Office of Belgium.

Guinomet, Isabelle. 1999. *The Relationship between Indicators of Sustainable Development: An Overview of Selected Studies*. Background paper for the Fifth Expert Group Meeting on Indicators of Sustainable Development, New York, 7–8 April 1999. 183 p.

Hak, Tomas, Bedřich Moldan and Arthur Lyon Dahl (eds.). 2007. *Sustainability Indicators: A Scientific Assessment*. SCOPE Vol. 67. Washington, DC, Island Press, 413 p.

Hardi, Peter and Terrence Zdan. 1997. *Assessing Sustainable Development: Principles in Practice*. Winnipeg: International Institute for Sustainable Development. www.iisd.org/pdf/bellagio.pdf

Moldan, Bedřich, Suzanne Billharz and Robyn Matravers (eds.). 1997. *Sustainability Indicators: A Report on the Project on Indicators of Sustainable Development*. Scientific Committee on Problems of the Environment, SCOPE 58. Chichester: John Wiley and Sons.

Moldan, Bedřich and Arthur Lyon Dahl. 2007. Challenges to sustainability indicators, Chapter 1, pp. 1–24. In Tomas Hak, Bedřich Moldan and Arthur Lyon Dahl (eds.), *Sustainability Indicators: A Scientific Assessment*. SCOPE Vol. 67. Washington, DC, Island Press.

Pintér, László, Peter Hardi and Peter Bartelmus. 2005. *Sustainable Development Indicators: Proposals for a Way Forward*. Prepared for the United Nations Division for Sustainable Development (UN-DSD). Winnipeg: International Institute for Sustainable Development. www.iisd.org/sites/default/files/publications/measure_indicators_sd_way_forward.pdf

Pintér, László, Peter Hardi, André Martinuzzi and Jon Hall. 2012. Bellagio STAMP: Principles for sustainability assessment and measurement. *Ecological Indicators* 17: 20–28. http://dx.doi.org/10.1016/j.ecolind.2011.07.001

Shah, Reena. 2004. *CSD Indicators of Sustainable Development – Recent Developments and Activities*. SCOPE/UNEP/IHDP/EEA Assessment of Sustainability Indicators (ASI) project, ASI Workshop 10–14 May 2004, Prague, Czech Republic. New York: United Nations. https://sustainabledevelopment.un.org/content/documents/scopepaper_2004.pdf

Tunstall, Dan, Allen Hammond and Norbert Menninger. 1994. *Developing Environmental Indicators*. Washington, DC: World Resources Institute.

UN. 1973. *Report of the United Nations Conference on the Human Environment*, Stockholm, 5-16 June 1972. A/CONF.48/14/Rev.1. New York: United Nations. http://www.un-documents.net/aconf48-14r1.pdf

UN. 1992. *Agenda 21*. Adopted at the United Nations Conference on Environment & Development, Rio de Janeiro, Brazil, 3–14 June 1992. New York: United Nations. https://sustainabledevelopment.un.org/content/documents/Agenda21.pdf

UN. 1995. *Information for decision-making and Earthwatch*. Report of the Secretary-General, UN Commission on Sustainable Development, Third Session, 11–28 April 1995. E/CN.17/1995/18.

UN. 1996. *Indicators of Sustainable Development Framework and Methodologies*. New York: United Nations. 428 p.

UN. 1997a. *Regional Workshop on Indicators of Sustainable Development for Latin America and the Caribbean Region*, Costa Rica, 10–12 March 1997. https://sustainabledevelopment.un.org/content/dsd/dsd_aofw_ind/ind_ws0397.shtml

UN. 1997b. *Fourth Expert Group Meeting on Indicators of Sustainable Development*, New York, 23–24 October 1997. https://sustainabledevelopment.un.org/content/dsd/dsd_aofw_ind/ind_egm1097.shtml

UN. 1998a. *Report of the Fourth International Workshop on Indicators of Sustainable Development*, Prague, Czech Republic, 19–21 January 1998. E/CN.17/1998/15. New York: United Nations. www.un.org/ga/search/view_doc.asp?symbol=E/CN.17/1998/15%20&Lang=E

UN. 1998b. *Workshop on Indicators of Consumption and Production Patterns*, New York, 2–3 March 1998. Available in the CSD-6 Inter-sessional Ad Hoc Working Group documents page www.un.org/documents/ecosoc/cn17/1998/background/ecn171998-mccpp59text.htm

UN. 1998c. *Measuring Changes in Consumption and Production Patterns: A Set of Indicators*. Department of Economic and Social Affairs ST/ESA/264. New York: United Nations. www.un.org/documents/ecosoc/cn17/1998/background/ecn171998-mccpp59text.htm

UN. 1999a. *Fifth Expert Group Meeting on Indicators of Sustainable Development*, United States, 7–8 April 1999. https://sustainabledevelopment.un.org/content/dsd/dsd_aofw_ind/ind_egm0499.shtml

UN. 1999b. *International Workshop on CSD Indicators of Sustainable Development*, Bridgetown, Barbados, 7–9 December 1999. https://sustainabledevelopment.un.org/content/dsd/dsd_aofw_ind/ind_ws1299.shtml

UN. 2000. *Progress Report on the Implementation of the CSD Work Programme on Indicators of Sustainable Development*. Background Paper No. 7, Commission on Sustainable Development, Eighth Session, New York, 24 April-–5 May 2000.

UN. 2001a. *Indicators of Sustainable Development: Guidelines and Methodologies*. Second Edition. New York: United Nations. 320 p. https://sustainabledevelopment.un.org/content/documents/indisd-mg2001.pdf

UN. 2001b. *Report of the Secretary-General on Information for Decision-Making and Participation*. Commission on Sustainable Development, Ninth session, 16–27 April 2001 E/CN.17/2001/4. https://documents-dds-ny.un.org/doc/UNDOC/GEN/N00/811/77/PDF/N0081177.pdf?OpenElement

UN. 2001c. *Report of the Secretary-General on Information for Decision-Making and Participation. Addendum – The CSD Work Programme on Indicators of Sustainable Development*. Commission on Sustainable Development, Ninth session, 16–27 April 2001. E/CN.17/2001/4/Add.1. https://documents-dds-ny.un.org/doc/UNDOC/GEN/N00/811/93/PDF/N0081193.pdf?OpenElement

UN. 2001d. *Report of the Ad Hoc Inter-sessional Working Group on Information for Decision-making and Participation and on International Cooperation for an Enabling Environment*. Commission on Sustainable Development, Ninth session, 16–27 April 2001. E/CN.17/2001/17. https://documents-dds-ny.un.org/doc/UNDOC/GEN/N01/308/63/PDF/N0130863.pdf?OpenElement

UN. 2001e. *Information and Institutions for Decision-making*. Commission on Sustainable Development acting as the preparatory committee for the World Summit on Sustainable Development, Organizational session, 30 April–2 May 2001. E/CN.17/2001/PC/3. https://documents-dds-ny.un.org/doc/UNDOC/GEN/N01/274/63/PDF/N0127463.pdf?OpenElement

UN. 2001f. *Report of the International Expert Meeting on Information for Decision Making and Participation*, Commission on Sustainable Development, Ninth session, 16–27 April 2001, Background Paper No. 1. E/CN.17/2001/BP/1.

UN. 2001g. *Report on the Aggregation of Indicators for Sustainable Development*. Commission on Sustainable Development, Ninth session, 16–27 April 2001, Background Paper No. 2. E/CN.17/2001/BP/2.

UN. 2004a. *Regional Caribbean Workshop on National Sustainable Development Strategies and Indicators of Sustainable Development*, Castries, St. Lucia, 14–15 January 2004. www.un.org/esa/sustdev/natlinfo/nsds/Report_Caribbean04.pdf

UN. 2004b. *Report of the Secretary-General on Progress in Implementing the Decisions of the Commission on Sustainable Development Related to Improvements in National Reporting and Further Work on Indicators of Sustainable Development*. Commission on Sustainable Development. E/CN.17/2004/17. www.un.org/ga/search/view_doc.asp?symbol=E/CN.17/2004/17%20&Lang=E

UN. 2004c. *Arab Regional Workshop on National Sustainable Development Strategies (NSDS) and Indicators of Sustainable Development*, Cairo, Egypt, 12–14 December 2004. www.un.org/esa/sustdev/natlinfo/nsds/cairo_rpt.pdf

UN. 2005. *Expert Group Meeting on Indicators of Sustainable Development*, New York, 13–15 December 2005. www.un.org/esa/sustdev/natlinfo/indicators/egmIndicators/report.pdf and documents: https://sustainabledevelopment.un.org/content/dsd/dsd_aofw_ind/ind_egm1205.shtml

UN. 2006a. *Global Trends and Status of Indicators of Sustainable Development*. Background Paper No. 2. Commission on Sustainable Development, Fourteenth Session, New York, 1–12 May 2006. www.un.org/esa/sustdev/csd/csd14/documents/bp2_2006.pdf

UN. 2006b. *Expert Group Meeting on Indicators of Sustainable Development*, New York, 3–4 October 2006. www.un.org/esa/sustdev/natlinfo/indicators/egmOct06/report.pdf and documents: https://sustainabledevelopment.un.org/content/dsd/dsd_aofw_ind/ind_egm1006.shtml

UN. 2007. *Indicators of Sustainable Development: Guidelines and Methodologies*. Third Edition. New York: United Nations. 93 p. and methodology sheets 398 p. https://sustainabledevelopment.un.org/content/documents/guidelines.pdf and https://sustainabledevelopment.un.org/content/documents/methodology_sheets.pdf

UN. 2008. *Expert Group Meeting on Climate Change & Sustainable Development: The Role of Indicators*. New York, 15–16 October 2008. https://sustainabledevelopment.un.org/content/dsd/dsd_aofw_ind/ind_egm1008.shtml

UN. 2009. *Expert Group Meeting on Institutionalizing Sustainable Development Indicators for Measuring Progress of National Strategies*, Bridgetown, Barbados, 17–19 September 2009. https://sustainabledevelopment.un.org/content/dsd/dsd_aofw_ind/ind_pdfs/egm0909/REPORT_final.pdf and documents: https://sustainabledevelopment.un.org/content/dsd/dsd_aofw_ind/ind_egm0909.shtml

UN ECLAC. 2001. *Seminar on Sustainable Development Indicators in Latin America and the Caribbean*, Chile, 29–30 November 2001. www.un.org/esa/sustdev/natlinfo/indicators/eclac2001eng_indicators.pdf

UNEP. 1994. *Report of the First Meeting of the Earthwatch Inter-Agency Working Party*, Geneva, 1–2 June 1994. www.un.org/earthwatch/about/docs/Ewwp1rpt.htm

UNEP. 1996a. *DPCSD/UNEP Meeting on Common/Compatible Systems of Access to Data*, New York, 19 January 1996. UNEP/DEIA/MR.96–92. www.un.org/earthwatch/about/docs/comacc1.htm

UNEP. 1996b. *DPCSD/UNEP Workshop on Information for Sustainable Development and Earthwatch*, Geneva, 24 September 1996. Report UNEP/DEIA/MR.96–12. www.un.org/earthwatch/about/docs/wisderp3.htm

UNEP. 2000. *Background Paper, International Expert Meeting on Information for Decision Making and Participation*, Canada, 25–28 September 2000. www.un.org/earthwatch/about/docs/ottawabk.htm

UNEP/UNSTAT. 1993. *Consultative Expert Group Meeting on Environmental and Sustainable Development Indicators*, Geneva, 6–8 December 1993. www.un.org/earthwatch/about/docs/consind.htm

UN ESCAP. 1996. *Regional Consultative Meeting on Environmentally Sound and Sustainable Development Indicators*, Bangkok, 26–29 November 1996. https://sustainabledevelopment.un.org/content/dsd/dsd_aofw_ind/ind_rcm1196.shtml

UN ESCAP. 2003. *National Sustainable Development Strategies for Asia and the Pacific* (which included a component on indicators of sustainable development), Thailand, 29–31 October 2003. www.un.org/esa/sustdev/natlinfo/nsds/Report_Bangkok03.pdf

UNSTAT. 1993. *Integrated Environmental and Economic Accounting*, Interim version. Handbook of National Accounting, Studies in Methods, Series F, No. 61. Statistical Division, Department of Economic and Social Information and Policy Analysis, Statistics Division. New York: United Nations.

24

PROSPECTS FOR STANDARDISING SUSTAINABLE URBAN DEVELOPMENT

Simon Joss and Yvonne Rydin

Introduction

The 'New Urban Agenda', adopted at the landmark UN-Habitat III conference in 2016, not only reaffirmed urbanisation as a key policy issue at the highest international level, but also underlined the continuing – indeed growing – reliance on indicators, standards and similar tools for implementing urban policy and guiding practice on the ground (UN-Habitat III 2016). The adoption of the Sustainable Development Goal 11 (short, SDG11), with its headline definition of 'mak[ing] cities inclusive, safe, resilient and sustainable' (UN Development Program 2016), is significant both in that cities have for the first time been afforded their own category in the official set of UN development goals and that, consequently, the 'New Urban Agenda' has come to be defined through a collection of specific targets and indicator metrics. This rightly draws critical attention to the expanding role of indicators in contemporary urban policy and planning. Apart from prompting empirical questions about how the translation of high-level targets and standardised indicators into variegated local contexts works and what new governance processes and practices result from this, the 'New Urban Agenda' also raises more normative questions about the city as a measurable entity. The observation that SDG11 renders cities a 'development tool' (Biron and Scruggs 2015) reflects a wider trend to conceptualise 'the urban' in terms of assessment techniques, control measures and operating systems (Joss 2015). For Caprotti *et al.* (2017: 2), the 'New Urban Agenda' thus reinforces 'the increasing focus on the city as a "measurable" entity, reducible to data streams and controllable through a range of new technologies', which risks producing a reductionist urban agenda with the potential to privilege some discourses and practices while sidelining others.

Beyond a narrow technical – and already well-established – discussion of how urban sustainability indicators should be constructed (e.g. Bell and Morse 2008; Munier 2011; Pinter *et al.* 2012; Boyko *et al.* 2012), there is then a wider need to consider how these are deployed, and for what purpose, by various practice communities. This highlights the significance of indicators, standards and related frameworks as governance tools: they variously act as interventions in governing processes for urban sustainability (e.g. Rydin 2007; Elgert and Krueger 2012; Joss *et al.* 2012; Lehtonen 2015; Elgert 2016; Lehtonen *et al.* 2016). As such, consideration needs to be given to how the application of indicators and standards on the ground involves complex mechanisms of knowledge co-production, collaborative planning, assessment and networking among heterogeneous actors. This also focuses attention on how indicators and standards as governing process relate to, and impact on, particular spatial settings. Furthermore, beyond the local contexts of application, consideration needs to be given to the growing number of diverse organisations driving the design and promotion of urban indicator sets and standards. This reveals differing motivations for, and approaches to, sustainable urban development which, in turn, helps explain the sheer variety of frameworks currently on offer. It also highlights that, while the application of urban sustainability indicators and standards necessarily has to be analysed within particular local settings, at the same time it requires attention to wider governance dynamics resulting from the intervention of external actors and the fashion for cross-comparative 'best practice' performance assessment and benchmarking.

Altogether, these aspects not least also prompt close consideration of the diverse users of these frameworks: from those creating the frameworks in the first place to those adopting them for specific practice purposes, and in between those variously engaged in a mediating and translating role. Here, not only is it key to understanding the particular motivations driving individual actors, but also paying attention to how (well) actors' diverse roles, interests and motivations align and interact around particular framework applications and how, in turn, this shapes and produces urban sustainability practices.

Building on these governance perspectives, this chapter seeks to appraise the emergent theory and practice of urban sustainability frameworks in the following four parts: first, definitional groundwork is laid by outlining key characteristics of frameworks. Second, a global overview is given of the variety of frameworks and standards having emerged in recent years, with particular focus on their different emphasis on governance functions. Third, an analysis is provided of the kinds of issues that can be expected to emerge when frameworks are applied in particular local practice contexts. From this, fourth, some recommendations are offered about the prospects for standardising sustainable urban development. The following discussion is informed *inter alia* by comparative research conducted as part of the Leverhulme Trust-funded International Network *Tomorrow's City Today* (see Joss *et al.* 2015) and more recent work on city standards.

Key dimensions of urban sustainability frameworks

The term 'urban sustainability framework' is used here as an analytical category, to consider and compare a variety of approaches to standardising the design, assessment and implementation of sustainable urban development initiatives. While the overall picture of emergent policy and practice is one of plurality and diversity, nevertheless some common features are apparent: in particular, frameworks are defined by the interaction of four key dimensions.

First, these replicable frameworks each combine multiple urban sustainability aspects and criteria; as such, they differ from the more conventional approach to defining single indicators in a more fragmentary manner. By bundling together a spectrum of urban sustainability dimensions and related indicators, these frameworks seek to interconnect individual dimensions, thereby prompting a more cohesive approach to sustainable urban development. This emphasis on the integrative relationship of multiple indicators, and thus on a 'whole-system' approach to sustainable urbanism, in itself underscores governance as a core aspect of frameworks. It should also be noted, however, that in some instances frameworks rather mechanistically present long lists of indicators (predictably grouped into 'environmental', 'economic' and 'social' sustainability categories) without much information on their symbiotic interdependence and combined practice applicability. This is countered by some frameworks that innovatively articulate the mutually reinforcing relationship between multiple indicator groups. The *Community Capital Tool* (Roseland 2012) and *One Planet Living Framework* (Bioregional undated) are examples of the latter; they each reach beyond the basic triple bottom-line approach to sustainability by, for example, emphasising the linkage between economic development and social equity and the close interrelationship between environmental resource consumption and urban form. It is also worth noting that, reflecting varying underlying conceptual assumptions or organisational purposes, there can be considerable differences in thematic weight: some frameworks – such as the *Climate Positive Development Program* with its focus on carbon neutral urban development (C40 Cities undated) or the *City Biodiversity Index* with its emphasis on urban biodiversity (National Parks Board undated; Chan *et al.* 2014) – include a more focused set of indicators, while others opt for a more all-encompassing range.

The second dimension concerns the inclusion of various process criteria aimed at guiding the design, planning, implementation and evaluation of urban sustainability initiatives. This may work at two levels: frameworks typically include a set of governance-themed indicators – a unique feature – alongside various environmental, economic and social criteria. For example, the aforementioned *City Biodiversity Index* features nine (out of 23) indicators relating to governance and management. Moreover, frameworks frequently offer step-by-step guidance on how to implement sustainability initiatives. The *Climate Positive Development Program* includes a multi-stage engagement process, which entails collaborative planning followed by implementation and periodic evaluation, and eventually leading to certification where a programme has been successfully accomplished. *Eco² Cities* (World Bank 2010; Suzuki *et al.* 2010) is another example of a framework which places great emphasis on the process aspect of sustainable development (arguably more so than on specific indicator content), thereby allowing for the alignment of high-level goals and local engagement with a strong social learning element. This process dimension again highlights the often close interrelationship at work between framework proposer and adopter.

The third dimension relates to the spatial configuration which the framework articulates and seeks to affect. Some frameworks are tailored towards well-delineated spatial arrangements; for example, the *Climate Positive Development Program* exclusively deals with urban infill developments at neighbourhood level. While this serves to ringfence a given urban sustainability initiative, in practice it nevertheless often requires complex boundary work with the surrounding wider areas (Joss 2015: 222–227). In contrast, other frameworks are defined flexibly for multi-scalar adaptation. The *One Planet Living Framework*, for example, comes in several versions for use at community, city and city-regional levels; and it has even been adapted for use by businesses across different sites (Joss 2015: 227–231). This dimension underscores the frameworks' potential for aligning governance approaches with particular spatial configurations.

Finally, the fourth key dimension is the project-nature at the heart of frameworks. By adopting a framework for use in a particular practice context, urban sustainability initiatives become defined as distinct projects. This typically entails sequential development phases (vision-making, design, planning, implementation, evaluation, etc.) and tailor-made organisational structures and management processes. This reflects a wider trend of 'projectification' in urban development (e.g. Book *et al.* 2010; Joss 2011), one which is particularly common in the context of public-private partnerships and has been associated with the corporatisation of urban development practices (and as such is often subject to a neoliberal critique). Positively, a project approach can contribute to improved governance capacity by assembling diverse policy priorities and heterogeneous actors around programmatically structured, spatially delineated sustainability initiatives. At the same time, such an approach has its own risks of creating new boundary problems and unintentionally decontextualising sustainable development from its wider urban context, thus causing novel governance challenges of its own (Joss 2015: 163–201).

Global trends

International interest in the prospect for standardising and replicating sustainable urban development is a relatively recent phenomenon. One global survey, conducted in 2013, counted over 40 diverse frameworks which, with a few exceptions, have all emerged since the millennium and mostly within the last decade (Joss *et al.* 2015). (For comparison, a similar survey identified over 50 urban sustainability rating tools; see Criterion Planners 2014.) This development mirrors the more general trend of growing interest in sustainable urbanism as a topic of research, policy and practice (De Jong *et al.* 2015).

Some of the diversity among current urban sustainability frameworks is apparent from the range of organisations – from international organisations to local government networks, and from professional bodies to social enterprises – involved in their promotion. Notably, international or national agencies only account for a minority of framework promoters (though their reach and influence may be great). In contrast, there is a striking preponderance of professional bodies and non-governmental organisations. Frameworks promoted by professional bodies have in many cases evolved out of standards designed for individual (green) buildings and, therefore, tend to have a relatively technical character, with prescriptive procedures and fixed assessment rationale. On their part, frameworks proposed by social enterprises tend to be defined more obviously by the particular organisational mission – for example, espousing a strong community agenda – and they frequently involve the social enterprises as co-producers of knowledge and practices in close collaboration with local adopters. Altogether, the large proportion of non-governmental organisations of one kind or another, featuring alongside international and national agencies, suggests a burgeoning competitive market for urban sustainability frameworks and prompts attention to the different governance arrangements at work.

From this global picture, four main clusters of frameworks can be identified according to their dominant governance modalities, as follows (for details of the underlying methodology and results, see Joss *et al.* 2015). Representative examples for each are listed in Table 24.1:

'Performance assessment' frameworks

The prominence of this type of framework is perhaps unsurprising, since conventionally indicators have been defined mainly quantitatively for the purpose of calculations and testing. Hence, frameworks here entail the measurement of the sustainability of particular places and developments using set criteria, with a view to tracking progress over time and/or enabling comparisons with other initiatives. Such assessments, then, often serve the purpose of allowing cities to benchmark themselves competitively against others, thereby providing a knowledge base for policy-making. The *City Biodiversity Index*, which was initiated in 2008 by the government of Singapore (hence, also *Singapore Index*) and subsequently endorsed by the UN Convention of Biological Diversity, provides a typical example of this type of framework. It is a tool designed for cities to assess and monitor progress on biodiversity conservation over time. It stipulates a methodology for each participating city to assess itself on 23 categories and related indicators, with scores reported alongside a contextual 'city profile' including information such as the city's size, population and natural features. Apart from its use by Singapore itself, the framework has to date been adopted by over 70 cities around the world and has been used to draw up the scoring criteria for the European Capitals of Biodiversity award scheme.

The *Green City Index* (Siemens 2012) is an example of a industry-based performance assessment framework aimed at facilitating cross-city comparison. The indicator set varies for each global region, to reflect differing conditions and data availability, but typically includes

Table 24.1 Exemplars of urban sustainability frameworks categorised according to key governance functions

Performance assessment	Certification	Design and planning	Standardisation
– CASBEE for Urban Development/Cities – City Biodiversity Index ('Singapore Index') – CityGrid – Eco-City Development Index System – European Common Indicators – Global City Indicators Facility – Global Urban Indicators – Green Cities Challenge – Green City Index – International Ecocity Framework and Standards – REAP for Local Authorities – Sustainable Cities Index	– BREEAM Communities – Climate Positive – EcoDistricts – EcoQuartier – Estidama Pearl Community Rating System – Enterprise Green Communities – IGBC Green Townships Rating System – LEED ND – Living Building Challenge – One Planet Living – Star Community Rating – Sustainable Communities	– ASEAN ESC Model Cities – Biosphere Eco-City – Community Capital Tool – Eco² Cities – Green Climate Cities – Green Communities – Urban Sustainability Indicators – Reference Framework for Sustainable Cities	– ISO 37100 Sustainable Cities and Communities – ISO 37120 Sustainable Development of Communities – ISO 37122 Indicators for Smart Cities – ISO 37123 Indicators for Resilient Cities – Related national standards by e.g. AENOR (ES), AFNOR (FR), BSI (UK), DIN (DE)

Source: Joss *et al.* (2015)

approximately 30 variables across nine thematic categories (CO_2 emissions, energy, land use, environmental governance, etc.). Around half the indicators are quantitative; the others require qualitative assessments of policies. To date, using this framework, Siemens has accumulated data for over 120 large cities across five continents; and building on this, the company has developed the *City Performance Tool*, which allows cities to simulate and model the likely environmental and economic impacts of introducing new technologies.

The focus on assessment in this category highlights the importance of auditing, measurement and benchmarking as a means of capturing, verifying and, thus, improving sustainability performance. This function relates to assessment both internally within a municipal governance setting, and externally between cities for the purpose of comparison and competitive benchmarking.

'Certification' frameworks

This second cluster also typically features performance assessment, but this is geared towards certification or endorsement (see also Turcu, this volume, Chapter 10). Certification schemes normally involve a membership-based multi-stage accreditation process, typically against some fee payment. They can be adopted at the building scale but increasingly also for new city neighbourhoods (Sullivan *et al.* 2014). They appeal to developers and utility companies since the formal accreditation process may assist both in securing third-party investment and in market-ing the development with a sustainability 'kitemark'. In this sense, they respond to the needs of actors seeking to promote urban developments or cities externally. As one might expect, these schemes are mainly championed by professional bodies (e.g. green building councils) and social enterprises, and less so by international government agencies or local authorities. A prominent example in this cluster is *LEED ND* ('Neighborhood Development'), which was launched in 2010 by the US Green Building Council (undated). Alongside *BREEAM Communities*, which was introduced by BRE (formerly Building Research Establishment) in 2008 and re-launched in 2012 (BRE undated; BRE Global 2013), *LEED ND* illustrates the evolution of indicator frameworks over time, from a concern with individual buildings to more integrated assessments of urban districts as a whole. It is used to certify developments at different stages, with a focus on green buildings, smart growth and urbanism, including green infrastructure, integrated transport and liveable community. In its multi-stage approach, it is intended to have a strong shaping influ-ence on urban development from the early planning phase onwards.

The *Climate Positive Development Program* mentioned earlier also exemplifies this cluster well. It has been applied in cooperation with development partners in 17 projects across six conti-nents. This is also a multi-stage accreditation scheme, but with a more singular focus on net carbon emissions, focusing in particular on energy, transport and waste. The use of this high-level 'output' indicator, rather than a complex set of prescriptive ones, allows the means of imple-mentation to be determined locally. As such, this also potentially allows it to be used alongside other complementary frameworks, as illustrated by Menlyn Maine, a new-build development in Pretoria, South Africa, which concurrently uses the *Green Star South Africa* (GSSA) framework as well as *LEED NC* ('New Construction') and *LEED ND* (see Joss 2012: 16).

Two certification schemes promoted by social enterprises – namely, the *One Planet Living Framework*, and *Sustainable Communities* (Audubon International, undated) – blend certification with a strong element of community engagement. In order to facilitate social learning, both of these frameworks are relatively prescriptive in terms of the process of certification (including benchmark measurements, stakeholder workshops, action plans and periodic evaluation), but relatively flexible in the precise indicators used. The *One Planet Living Framework* also includes an open-access version alongside the formal (paid for) accreditation scheme.

Interestingly, certification has more recently also been incorporated into several frameworks by national agencies, including France's *EcoQuartier*, Brazil's *Selo Casa Azul Caixa*, and the UAE's *Estidama Pearl Community Rating System* (see Table 24.1).

'Design and planning' frameworks

Frameworks in this cluster (which is less prominent than the previous two) have as their main feature the provision of guidance on the *processes* of sustainability planning: here governance orientation is towards supporting the establishment of 'design communities' of different types, with strong emphasis on collaborative decision-making and interactive learning. They normally also incorporate an element of performance assessment, and they may additionally place strong emphasis on community engagement. Notable examples of the latter are the *Community Capital Tool*, UNESCO's *Biosphere Eco-City Programme* and the US Environmental Protection Agency's *Green Communities* (see Table 24.1).

There is a tendency for such frameworks to prescribe broad principles for sustainability assessment rather than mandate detailed, concrete targets. The *Biosphere Eco-City*, for example, sets only overarching parameters for the types of indicators which participants might consider including. The World Bank's *Eco² Cities* framework deliberately moves away from prescribing specific indicators, on the basis that every city has a unique set of pre-existing economic, social, cultural, institutional and environmental challenges and opportunities. Its key aim instead is to facilitate a process whereby local stakeholders themselves decide and act on priority issues (while also recommending that participant cities adopt a recognised framework of more pre-scribed indicators alongside this process, depending on their specific requirements). As part of this 'city-based decision support system', it guides local adopters to implement collabora-tive design and decision processes based on a shared, integrated framework and using various small-scale 'catalyst' pilot projects prior to scaling-up to city-wide adaptations. This and similar participatory, design-based approaches may be particularly relevant in urban settings with lim-ited pre-existing governance capacities, such as rapidly developing urban centres in the Global South. Indeed, the initial pilot cities using the *Eco² Cities* framework are all located in South East Asia (Indonesia, the Philippines, Vietnam).

'Standardisation' frameworks

A more recent innovation still is represented by formal standards for sustainable urban develop-ment. This category refers in particular to work undertaken by both national and international standardisation bodies. For example, the International Standardization Organization (ISO) has since 2014 issued a suite of *Sustainable Cities and Communities* standards, with sets of indica-tors accompanied by descriptive frameworks and practical implementation manuals (see ISO/TC268, undated). Several national agencies, such as the British Standards Institution (BSI) and Spain's standards agency AENOR have published their own sets of standards for domestic appli-cation, in close interaction with efforts at international level. These formal standards appear to pursue two distinctive functions: on one hand, they signal the efforts by both national and international bodies to seek to achieve more systematised and regulated guidance on sustainable urban development practice; on the other, they are indicative of a more recent shift towards link-ing the sustainability agenda with the emergent smart city agenda, by emphasising the impor-tance of (digital) data and information as basis for sustainable development. A case in point is the recent report *Standardized City Data to Meet UN SDG Targets* published by the World Council on City Data (Patava 2017).

In summary, presently the field of urban sustainability frameworks remains open and varied, both in terms of the actors involved and the intended governance functionality. For now, there is no strong evidence of marketplace consolidation in any one direction, but there are pres-sures for standardisation as different frameworks compete for attention with regard to offering governance solutions for sustainable urban development. It is possible in the future that particu-lar schemes will come to dominate different specialist niches; various types of 'gold standard' may emerge which each respond to a particular type of sustainability-related goal. Alternatively, frameworks with more holistic remits may prove to be more successful, depending on their abil-ity to deliver practical innovations and tangible sustainability outcomes on the ground. Either way, the challenges need to be considered arising from the varied experience of implementing frameworks in particular urban contexts.

Governance challenges

The application of a framework in a local context should not be expected to be a straightfor-ward process. After all, as an instrument designed to be replicable for use in multiple settings, the framework's generic guidance – relating to substantive and procedural sustainability aspects – requires local adaptation and integration. This necessitates various processes of negotiation as local actors work to translate a framework into context-specific actions and practices. The following identifies some of the challenges likely to occur in the application of frameworks on the ground and that, therefore, need to be worked through if realistic local engagement with given frameworks is to be achieved.

Boundary work

The way that a governance tool, such as an assessment framework, operates will be influenced by a number of features: the way that it defines the scope of its application, how it demarcates the spatial area to be assessed or transformed, the particular activities assessed, the defined timeframes and the specified participating actors and institutions. This can give the impression that the operation of a framework is rather tightly constrained by its format.

Yet in practice, this bounded construct, however internally consistent, has to engage with wider external structures and processes resulting in complex boundary work. For example, the spatial boundaries of a framework's application will be porous: air quality, traffic conditions or economic success, for instance, may depend primarily on what happens elsewhere. Similarly, the operational and jurisdictional dimensions of wider infrastructure or regulatory systems involved may jar against the approach embodied by the framework. Participating organisations may not all work to similar timescales. Thematic or procedural prescriptions may conflict with existing regulatory requirements at different scales.

Consequently, resolving such tensions may necessitate ongoing active boundary work, whereby collaborations or divisions of labour are agreed upon, compromises are reached, and innovative design solutions negotiated. In short, if a given framework is to be an effective governance tool, it needs to be flexible enough to accommodate local adaption. At the same time, it needs to maintain a certain robustness and consistency, to ensure its integrity as a replicable, standardising mechanism for sustainable urban development.

Above all, a framework needs to be legible in different domains. It does not just 'do work' at the boundary but also travels across that boundary. A classification scheme such as BREEAM Communities will be the focus of discussions in planning authorities (amongst both local politicians and professional planners), in project team meetings where a wide range of professionals will be present, and in the economic decision-making of the developer concerned with the cost and value implications of a specific rating. The framework must be an active, workable document and process in these different locations. It can thus function as a 'boundary object' or, in the terminology of Actor-Network Theory, an immutable mobile (see e.g. Star and Griesemer 1989; Holden 2013; Schweber 2013; Schweber and Haroglu 2014).

Community engagement

The urban arena is one where many stakeholders interact (see also Bell & Morse, this volume, Chapter 12, and Domingues et al., this volume, Chapter 25). Given the wide range of actors involved in any particular local context, a framework may need to speak several 'languages'. Those frameworks adopting the more technical discourse of policy-makers, planners, urban designers or property developers may fail to engage wider local communities. This is problematic insofar as initiatives which do not take account of local community needs and aspirations often fail to gain traction. Then again, the alternative approach of following principles of simple language and conceptual accessibility, which some frameworks espouse, may fail to motivate sufficiently private-sector actors or municipal authorities seeking to promote urban initiatives based on recognised technical certification.

The difficulties inherent in communicating simultaneously with professional actors and the wider community may be one reason for the emergence of parallel strands of frameworks: some choose to emphasise technical requirements, while others focus more on facilitating inclusive collaborative social learning. Overall, the former currently appear to occupy a stronger position in practice, due to the fact that many have evolved from technical index and certification systems (such as green building codes) and the fact that social and cultural aspects of sustainability are still frequently underrepresented in comparison with more technical environmental and economic aspects.

Even for frameworks which are generally considered advanced in terms of embracing social sustainability, the communicative dimension may prove challenging. Community engagement may be well-intentioned and integrated in the framework's governance process, but it can easily result in perfunctory 'thin' participation if insufficient time and resources are made available. What is more, what constitutes substantive, 'thick' participation may be difficult to prescribe, not least also because of different cultural meanings and traditions of community engagement.

Furthermore, the requirement to incorporate a community engagement dimension may result in a top-down approach, where the promoters of the project, development or framework seek to encourage such engagement. It does not leave space or necessarily recognise the importance of bottom-up initiatives which have been so significant within the urban sustainability movement (see Roseland 2012), particularly during the earlier years of Local Agenda 21, but also now with the growth of urban experimentation in alternative urban sustainability pathways (e.g. Baccarane *et al.* 2014; Evans *et al.* 2016; Scholl and Kemp 2016). Given the role of frameworks as a form of knowledge claim, the potential for citizen science initiatives to interface with more expert-led assessment should not be underestimated either. These points emphasise that the practice and potential of community engagement may often go beyond the more limited forms encouraged and envisaged by the frameworks discussed here.

Partnership facilitation

If frameworks anticipate the needs of particular key audiences and imply certain relationships between them, they cannot fully determine the nature and qualities of these relationships. Frameworks, in other words, neither sit neutrally outside local governance arrangements, nor determine them, but work more dynamically as co-producers of relatively unpredictable partnerships between their promoters, adopters and other variously empowered local actors. The nature of such partnerships not only differs from case to case, but may shift over time between the different phases of a project (and depending on changes in the political or commercial context). However, a common feature seems to be the necessity of a framework champion working across the partnership relationships.

The importance of such a champion can be understood as a response to the complexity of these partnerships and the networks they represent (see Rydin *et al.* 2003; Rydin 2013). There are transactions costs involved in operating across such networks; these transactions costs rise with the number of actors that are involved, their heterogeneity and how diffuse – as opposed to clustered – that the networks are. A champion can be considered as a network manager, facilitating communication across the network and the commitment to action by various actors. They can reduce transactions costs provided they are centrally located in the network and actively seek to promote collective action, in this case towards the implementation of a framework.

Frameworks offering a 'fixed' template or protocol may appear to promise greater certainty by mandating particular relationships, though there is no guarantee that such relationships will be constructive ones. Instead, a more flexible approach in which relationships are negotiated on an ongoing basis among those involved may result in more effective cooperation and practice learning. Then again, such fluid, organic partnership-building may risk obfuscating the relationship between framework champion and adopter, not least where the framework champion acts in a dual role of co-developer and certifier. In response, this suggests the need for an explicit articulation of the framework champion-adopter relationship, and the boundaries between shared and separate responsibilities among actors involved.

Robustness of assessment and endorsement

The fluid hybridity resulting from negotiated partnerships may lead to divergent outcomes, depending on the motivations and resources available to the actors involved at different stages of the process. Although the negotiations and problem solving involved may be viewed in a positive light as fundamental goals of social learning and innovation, they simultaneously raise questions about transparency over decision-making. Rather than based on some agreed, open methodology, the actions emanating from a framework implementation may be more the result of closed discussions and informal negotiations between framework champion and local adopters. This is problematic insofar as it challenges the principle of like-for-like comparison central for performance assessment, benchmarking and certification; and as such could undermine the claim of replicability and standardisation associated with urban sustainability frameworks.

The challenge of marrying the facilitative role of frameworks with the need for robust, standardised assessment may be a further reason why a clustering of frameworks, rather than a unidirectional process of standardisation, appears to be occurring globally. However, the challenge of ensuring robust assessment is not automatically met where frameworks prescribe fixed, technical indicators and detailed methodologies for assessment. The relatively rigorous assessment possible at, say, the building level is much more difficult to replicate at city-wide level, given the complexity and diversity of non-technical issues at play; and data capture, monitoring and measurement may not be as systematic and accurate in practice as posited in principle.

Altogether, the emergent practice experience of framework application suggests caution against overestimating the potential of standardisation; instead the choice of frameworks currently available points to substantive local adaptation and innovation. The parallel challenges of managing boundaries, engaging communities while motivating public- and private-sector actors, facilitating constructive partnerships and ensuring robust assessment procedures even raise the possibility that a universal standard would in fact have limited value. On the other hand, further fragmented growth of the field raises its own set of problems. An unlimited 'pick and mix' approach may imply a 'race to the bottom', with a tendency for less demanding frameworks to be adopted.

In contexts where there are costs involved in adopting a specific framework, there also has to be a demonstrable benefit to the adopter. Ideally competition between alternative frameworks will be based on such benefits, rather than just reduced complexity and costs. Ultimately, though, the viability of individual frameworks may depend increasingly on their demonstrable ability to overcome the challenges of translating abstracted principles into effective transformative action.

Policy and practice lessons

The varied experience of urban sustainability frameworks to date suggests that recommending a one-size-fits-all approach would at this stage be inappropriate. The following points, therefore, are intended as broad recommendations in support of further critical work on how frameworks of one kind or another can be conceptualised, designed and developed in practice.

Benefit of variety

Within the last decade, numerous new urban sustainability frameworks have cropped up, promoted by a heterogeneous group of organisations and applied in diverse urban settings and policy contexts. Based on this trend, it may be realistic to expect ongoing variety, not least for the following two reasons: first, conceptually, sustainable urban development is far from a settled matter, with continuous differences in thematic accentuations and priorities; and second, in practice, the multitude of contexts in which sustainable urbanism is applied suggests the persistence of variability. There may, therefore, yet be limitations to the scope for standardisation of urban sustainability, at least when understood rather narrowly as uniformity of content and process. The prospect of continuous diversity, however, need not necessarily be viewed as problematic. On the contrary, it can be embraced positively as a process of collective, experimental innovation and learning. This should helpfully contribute to the growing body of knowledge about sustainable urban development. From a policy perspective, therefore, what at this stage is arguably less needed is a push for uniform standardisation, and instead more of a stance which allows for a plurality of approaches to be accommodated flexibly in the interest of knowledge innovation and social and policy learning.

Clarity of purpose

Within this context of variety, however, those in the business of designing urban sustainability frameworks and those adopting them in practice should strive to be clear about the frameworks' intended contributions to governance processes. This should also help make explicit the motivations of various actors in deploying these frameworks. Concerning the 'performance assessment' cluster of frameworks, these have a comparatively more circumscribed, technical functionality rooted in standardised methods and techniques for measuring and appraising particular sustainability dimensions. While this makes for ready integration into a variety of policy and governance contexts, nevertheless careful attention needs to be paid to questions about the robustness and reliability of the methods and techniques in local application contexts. On its part, the 'certification' cluster merits close consideration of how accreditation mechanisms interact with (local) planning and regulations, as well as of the relationship arising between the certifier and the local adopter; neither of these points can be assumed as given. In the case of frameworks in the 'design/planning' cluster, a critical issue is how participants can be effectively incorporated in these broad processes; another is again the ability to align the activities generated by the application of a framework in the wider policy and planning cycles. Depending on these varying governance functions, different communication efforts are required; in any case, communication is a central consideration, from explicating the particular conceptual understanding underpinning the framework to specifying its particular substantive and procedural elements in principle as well as in practice.

A matter of context

While it is essential to probe into how frameworks themselves are internally constructed, it is ultimately to their practice application in particular contexts that one has to turn: it is here that full insight can be gained into their actual contributions to sustainable urban development processes and outcomes. Empirical analysis points to the complex, multiple interactions arising from the application of frameworks in specific urban settings. If one considers the use of a framework as an intervention in governance, then this focuses attention to questions, among others, about:

the appropriate moment in the planning and policy process when the chosen framework should be introduced; the mobilisation of relevant existing networks of actors, or the need for convening new networks; the integration of the processes and outcomes generated by the framework into wider planning and policy-making; and the need for oversight and accountability. In short, these and related questions draw our attention to the inevitable boundary work involved as part of the process of applying frameworks in urban governance contexts, and alert us to issues of social and political agency and power, some of the effects of which may well be unintentional, and hence also to the potential for conflict. If using a framework is to be more than a technocratic process, then these governance issues should be considered of central importance in application practice, and they can be expected to co-determine sustainable development outcomes.

Commitment to openness

Given the still relatively nascent state of the theory and practice of urban sustainability frameworks, and ongoing debates about the value of standardising city governance, a commitment to openness seems called for, in the interest of generating relevant knowledge and fostering shared learning. From the conceptual approach to framework design to the selection criteria for framework application, and from the documentation of framework outputs to the evaluation of processes and outcomes, the field would greatly benefit from open source and access commitments to foster innovation and diffusion. Even in the more sensitive areas of commercial applications and certification, there are notable examples of organisations practising a culture of information transparency and knowledge exchange. However it needs to be recognised that many frameworks operate as a commercial product and that the organisations promoting them need a robust business model to survive. This need not prevent transparency and openness provided the requirement of maintaining viability are also recognised.

Conclusions

The application of replicable urban sustainability frameworks in particular local contexts is designed as an intervention in governance processes: they serve to provide strategic and technical guidance on how sustainable city initiatives are defined, facilitate collaboration and networking among relevant stakeholders, assist with performance assessment, and obtain endorsement, among other functions. The interactions arising from such intervention may inevitably cause some tension concerning what is defined generically, 'top down' as part of a replicable framework, and what is fashioned locally, 'bottom up' reflecting the particular conditions on the ground. What constitutes an appropriate balance between the standard aspects of urban sustainability frameworks and the local variation of particular applications remains an open discussion in need of ongoing conceptual and practical exploration. One way of considering this interaction would be to postulate that replicable frameworks should enshrine global standards pertaining to substantive aspects of urban sustainability: this could, for example, be grounded in the principles of Ecological Footprint or zero-carbon emissions (as in the case of the *One Planet Living* and *Climate Positive Program* frameworks). Based on these absolute, outcome-oriented global standards, the process-oriented implementation could be defined flexibly by the frameworks, reserved for local determination and adaptation. This would also allow room, depending on individual circumstances, for additional locally relevant sustainability dimensions to be integrated into the overarching global framework. For example, the United Nations Environment Programme recommends such an approach, in what it calls a 'two-layered, nested model combining local and global assessments' (UNEP 2012: 5). Similarly, Williams *et al.* (2012: 12) suggest that 'developing a set of very few core indicators, supported by city-specific non-core indicators, presents a practical solution to the issue of compatibility and standardised evaluation'. The advantage of such an approach is that urban sustainability frameworks would be defined by absolute, global standards; however, this would require international agreement on what these should be – in the case of environmental dimensions most likely relating to the world's ecological carrying capacity (footprint) and/or carbon emission reduction targets.

Another way of considering the interaction would be to forgo any attempt to standardise substantive aspects of sustainable development and instead centre the definition of frameworks upon procedural dimensions. This would be based on the argument that there exists too much variation concerning what constitutes sustainable urban development across vastly different cities and global regions to be able to expect to arrive at global standards that are meaningful and practical. Instead, the focus should be on facilitating 'good practice' concerning institutional, organisational and social processes to enable actors on the ground – especially in situations with limited existing governance capacity – to engage effectively with sustainable urban development. The strength of this approach is its ability to promote knowledge transfer and common practice learning across different settings; its weakness, arguably, is that it leaves untouched the essential question of what the minimum standards for global urban sustainability should be.

However exactly the balance ends up being struck between the standard aspects of urban sustainability frameworks and the local variation of particular applications – an important but as yet not fully exhausted discussion – the implications of using replicable frameworks within specific local contacts need careful consideration. At present, most of the frameworks are too recent and their applications in practice only at pilot stage to allow a more definitive verdict based on empirical evidence. What is clear, though, is that as practical experience accumulates, these frameworks require closer, in-depth examination to determine their potential and actual contribution to sustainable urban innovations – and the importance of critically reflecting on this development will only grow if certain frameworks come to dominate the field in the future. Far from being a peripheral concern, standardisation looks set to become a major – even a decisive – factor shaping the outcomes of sustainable city initiatives, the relationships among various actors, and the process of generating and translating knowledge about urban sustainability.

Acknowledgements

We are grateful to Dr Nancy Holman (London School of Economics), and Dr Elizabeth Rapoport (Urban Land Institute), for their thoughtful comments on an earlier version of this paper. We would also like to acknowledge the contributions by our colleagues in the international research network 'Tomorrow's City Today' (supported by Leverhulme Trust grant IN-2012–2102), on which this article is based.

References

Audubon International. (Undated). *Sustainable Communities Program*. URL: www.auduboninternational.org/sustainable-communities-program [accessed 31 January 2017]

Baccarne, B., Mechant, P., Schuurma, D., De Marez, L. and Colpaert, P. (2014). Urban socio-technical innovations with and by citizens. *Interdisciplinary Studies Journal*, 3 (4): 143–156.

Bell, S. and Morse, S. (2008). *Sustainability Indicators: Measuring the Immeasurable?* 2nd edition. London and Sterling, VA: Earthscan.

Bioregional. (Undated). *One Planet Living Framework*. URL: www.bioregional.co.uk/oneplanetliving/ [accessed 31 January 2017]

Biron, C.L. and Scruggs, G. (2015). Goal 11: The opportunities of the urban SDG. *Devex International Development News*, 25 September 2015. URL: www.devex.com/news/goal-11-the-opportunities-of-the-urban-sdg-86980 [accessed 25 January 2017]

Book, K., Eskilsson, L. and Khan, J. (2010). Governing the balance between sustainability and competitiveness in urban planning: The case of the Orestad model. *Environmental Policy and Governance*, 20: 382–396.

Boyko, C.T, Gaterell, M.R., Barber A.R.G., Brown J., Bryson J.R., Butler D., Caputo S., Caserio M., Coles R., Cooper R., Davies G., Farmani R., Hale J., Hales A.C., Hewitt C.N., Hunt D.V.L., Jankovic L., Jefferson I. and Rogers C.D.F. (2012). Benchmarking sustainability in cities: The role of indicators and future scenarios. *Global Environmental Change*, 22: 245–254.

BRE. (Undated). *BREEAM Communities Technical Standard*. URL: www.breeam.com/communities [accessed 31 January 2017]

BRE Global. (2013). *BREEAM Communities: Integrating Sustainable Design into Masterplanning*. Watford, England: BRE Global Ltd. URL: www.breeam.com/filelibrary/BREEAM%20Communities/Introduction_to_BREEAM_Communities.pdf [accessed 30 May 2017]

C40 Cities. (Undated). *Climate Positive Development Program*. URL: www.c40.org/networks/climate-positive-development-program [accessed 31 January 2017]

Caprotti, F., Cowley, R., Datta, A., Castan Broto, V., Gao, E., Georgson, L., Herrick, C., Odendaal, N. and Joss, S. (2017). The new urban agenda: Key opportunities and challenges for policy and practice. *Journal of Urban Research and Practice*. Published online 9 January 2017. http://dx.doi.org/10.1080/17535069.2016.1275618

Chan, L., Hillel, O., Elmqvist, T., Werner, P., Holman, N., Mader, A. and Calcaterra, E. (2014). *User's Manual on the Singapore Index on Cities' Biodiversity (also known as the City Biodiversity Index)*. Singapore: National Parks Board.

Criterion Planners. (2014). *A Global Survey of Urban Sustainability Rating Tools*. URL: http://crit.com/wp-content/uploads/2014/11/criterion_planners_sustainability_ratings_tool.pdf [accessed 31 January 2017]

De Jong, M., Joss, S., Schraven, D., Zhan, C. and Weijnen, M. (2015). Sustainable – smart – resilient – low carbon – eco – knowledge cities, making sense of a multitude of concepts promoting sustainable urbanization. *Journal of Cleaner Production*, 109: 25–38.

Elgert, L. (2016). The double edge of cutting edge: Explaining adoption and nonadoption of the STAR rating system and insights for sustainability indicators. *Ecological Indicators*, 67: 556–564.

Elgert, L. and Krueger, R. (2012). Modernising sustainable development? Standardisation, evidence and experts in local indicators. *Local Environment: The International Journal of Justice and Sustainability*, 17 (5): 561–571.

Evans, J., Karvonen, A. and Raven, R. (eds.). (2016). *The Experimental City*. Abingdon: Routledge.

Holden, M. (2013). Sustainability indicator systems within urban governance: Usability analysis of sustainability indicator systems as boundary objects. *Ecological Indicators*, 32: 89–96.

ISO/TC268. (undated). *Sustainable Cities and Communities*. Standards catalogue. International Standardization Organization (Technical Committee 268). URL: www.iso.org/iso/iso_catalogue/catalogue_tc/catalogue_tc_browse.htm?commid=656906

Joss, S. (2011). Eco-city governance: A case study of Treasure Island and Sonoma Mountain Village. *Journal of Environmental Policy and Planning*, 13 (4): 331–348.

Joss, S. (ed.). (2012). *Tomorrow's City Today: Eco-city Indicators, Standards & Frameworks: Bellagio Conference Report*. London: University of Westminster (International Eco-Cities Initiative).

Joss, S. (2015). *Sustainable Cities: Governing for Urban Innovation*. London: Palgrave Macmillan.

Joss, S., Cowley, R., de Jong, M., Müller, B., Park, B.-S., Rees, W., Roseland, M. and Rydin, Y. (2015). *Tomorrow's City Today: Prospects for Standardising Sustainable Urban Development*. London: University of Westminster (International Eco-Cities Initiative).

Joss, S., Tomozeiu, D. and Cowley, R. (2012). Eco-city indicators: Governance challenges. *WIT Transactions on Ecology & the Environment*, 155: 109–120.

Lehtonen, M. (2015). Introduction: Indicators as governance tools. In: *The Tools of Policy Formulation: Actors, Capacities, Venues and Effects* (Jordan, A.J. and Turnpenny, J.R., eds.). Cheltenham: Edward Elgar.

Lehtonen, M., Sébastien, L. and Bauler, T. (2016). The multiple roles of sustainability indicators in informational governance: Between intended use and unanticipated influence. *Current Opinion in Environmental Sustainability*, 18: 1–9.

Munier, N. (2011). Methodology to select a set of urban sustainability indicators to measure the state of the city, and performance assessment. *Ecological Indicators*, 11 (5): 1020–1026.

National Parks Board. (Undated). *Singapore Index on Cities' Biodiversity*. Singapore: Singapore Government. URL: www.nparks.gov.sg/biodiversity/urban-biodiversity/the-singapore-index-on-cities-biodiversity [accessed 31 January 2017]

Patava, J. (2017). *WCCD ISO 37120 Standardized City Data to Meet UN SDG Targets*. Report presented at UN World Data Forum, 15 January 2017. Toronto: World Council on City Data. URL: https://undataforum.org/WorldDataForum/wp-content/uploads/2017/01/TA2.13_Patava.City-Data-for-SDGs-Cape-Town-Presentation-NO-VIDEO.pdf [accessed 22 June 2017]

Pinter, L., Hardi, P., Martinuzzi, A. and Hall, J. (2012). Bellagio Stamp: Principles for sustainability assessment and measurement. *Ecological Indicators*, 17: 20–28.

Roseland, M. (2012). *Toward Sustainable Communities: Solutions for Citizens and Their Governments*. 4th edition. Gabriola Island, BC: New Society Publishers.

Rydin, Y. (2007). Indicators as a governmental technology? The lessons of community-based sustainability indicator projects. *Environment and Planning D: Society & Space*, 25: 610–624.

Rydin, Y. (2013). The issue network of zero carbon built environments: A quantitative and qualitative analysis. *Environmental Politics*, 22 (3): 496–517.

Rydin, Y., Holman, N. and Wolff, E. (2003). Local sustainability indicators. *Local Environment*, 8 (6): 581–589.

Scholl, C. and Kemp, M. (2016). City labs as vehicles for innovation in urban planning processes. *Urban Planning*, 1 (4): 89–102.

Schweber, L. (2013). The effect of BREEAM on clients and construction professionals. *Building Research and Information*, 41 (2): 1–17.

Schweber, L. and Haroglu, H. (2014). Comparing the fit between BREEAM assessment and design processes. *Building Research and Information*, 42 (3): 300–317.

Siemens. (2012). *The Green City Index*. A summary of the Green City Index research series. Munich: Siemens.

Star, S. L. and Griesemer, J. R. (1989). Institutional ecology, 'translations' and boundary objects: Amateurs and professionals in Berkeley's Museum of Vertebrate Zoology, 1907–1939. *Social Studies of Science*, 19 (3): 387–420.

Sullivan, L., Rydin, Y. and Buchanan, C. (2014). *Neighbourhood Assessment Frameworks: A Literature Review*. UCL USAR Working Paper. URL: www.ucl.ac.uk/usar/wps/USARWPS01-Sullivan-Neighbourhoods-PDF [accessed 31 January 2017]

Suzuki, H., Dastur, A., Moffatt, S., Yabuki, N. and Maruyama, H. (2010). *Eco² Cities: Ecological Cities as Economic Cities*. Washington, DC: The World Bank.

UN Development Program. (2016). *Sustainable Development Goal 11: Sustainable Cities and Communities*. URL: www.undp.org/content/undp/en/home/sustainable-development-goals/goal-11-sustainable-cities-and-communities.html [accessed 25 January 2017]

UN Environment Program. (2012). *Working Paper: Framework Elements for Assessing Urban Environmental Performance*. URL: www.unep.org [accessed 27 June 2014]

UN-Habitat III. (2016). *The New Urban Agenda*. URL: https://habitat3.org/the-new-urban-agenda [accessed 25 January 2017]

US Green Building Council. (Undated). *LEED v4 Neighbourhood Development Guide*. URL: www.usgbc.org/guide/nd [accessed 31 January 2017]

Williams, C., Zhou, N., He, G. and Levine, M. (2012). *Measuring in All the Right Places: Themes in International Municipal Eco-City Index Systems*. Pacific Grove, CA: American Council for an Energy-Efficient Economy.

World Bank. (2010). *Eco² Cities Brochure*. URL: http://siteresources.worldbank.org/INTEASTASIAPACIFIC/Resources/Eco2_Cities_Brochure.pdf [accessed 9 January 2014]

25

STAKEHOLDER-DRIVEN INITIATIVES USING SUSTAINABILITY INDICATORS

Ana Rita Domingues, Rodrigo Lozano, and Tomás B. Ramos

Introduction

Sustainability indicators (SIs) have been extensively used, for instance by biologists, and have become a key tool to operationalise sustainability (Bell and Morse 2008). SI allows to measure and communicate the state and progress of sustainability aspects. Despite different methods and tools that exist to assess sustainability, indicators is one of the approaches most widely used (Ramos 2009). Indicators have been used over time as symbolic representations (Moldan and Dahl 2007). For instance, as a way of measuring and comparing sustainability performances of local-regional territories (Mascarenhas et al. 2010), and improve the dialogue with stakeholders (Ramos and Moreno Pires 2013) through the creation of new communication channels in sustainability debates. SI are also considered important tools in decision-making (Waas et al. 2014). Several guidelines and models that have appeared to ground the development of indicators can be found in other chapters of this book (e.g. Pintér et al., Chapter 2; Dahl, Chapter 3; Spangenberg, Chapter 9).

Three main clusters can describe the potential users of indicators types (adapted from Rickard et al. 2007): (1) voters, non-specialist media, decision-makers (who need very simple and structured information); (2) local government, policy implementers and checkers, non-governmental organisations (NGO), research funding bodies, and industry (who need intermediate level of detail and simplicity); and (3) academics and some NGO (who need technical information). Nevertheless, reality may be more complex, for example decision-makers need more technical information and policy-makers may want clearer and simpler information.

SI cover robust, less bureaucratic, and more meaningful information to a variety of stakeholders than other similar tools (such as life cycle assessment that is specific for experts). This characteristic has increased the use of SI. Stakeholders are any group or individual who influences or can be influenced by the achievement of a specific purpose (Freeman et al. 2010). According to Freeman (1984), because stakeholders have the capacity to influence decisions and other stakeholders, and thus assure the legitimacy of the process, they need to be involved in the decision-making processes so mutual interests can be accomplished.

Stakeholder engagement increases the quality of the environmental decisions because information inputs taken into account are more comprehensive, and the type of participation process influences the quality of stakeholder decisions (Reed 2008). The type of engagement depends on the goals of the initiative and availability of stakeholders. In some cases, any social actor could be a potential stakeholder to be integrated with the suitable training and education; in other situations only specific groups of stakeholders should be integrated. This depends on the aim, scope, and context of the initiative. Potentially any stakeholder could be integrated in sustainable development related processes, including vulnerable groups (WCED – World Comission on Environment and Development 1987).

Stakeholders should be represented in a balanced manner, but many times some may be over-represented. This happens especially in some cultural and political contexts, including gender, age, culture, and experience gaps between stakeholders, which constitutes a characteristic of sustainability analysis processes, even if the sample of participants is representative of a society (Bell and Morse 2008). Different groups should be represented in a proportional way to avoid some parts to hijack the process. An example on how stakeholder groups could be selected can be found in Dahl, Chapter 23. One (or more) facilitator(s) will have a key role (Bell and Morse, Chapter 12) namely in managing the flow of ideas, achievement of consensus, and clarification of conflicts using additional tools such as the nominal group technique.

Despite the aforementioned arguments, involving stakeholders may not be an easy task. A group of people that is motivated for a common goal is needed to achieve such goal (Ramos et al. 2014). Specific issues need to be decided for each environmental and sustainability indicator initiative: (1) which groups of stakeholders to be engaged (among employees, suppliers, customers, financiers, communities); (2) what type of inputs from stakeholders are relevant; and (3) what are the thematic areas and indicators relevant for the stakeholders' empowerment process. Some suggestions include creating a positive dialogue with stakeholders (Forrest 1998) and establishing a degree of engagement of stakeholder groups taking into account their specific characteristics (Luyet et al. 2012).

Participation can be described by the following typologies based on: (1) different degrees of participation from passive dissemination of information to active engagement; (2) the nature of participation according to the direction of communication flows (communication, consultation, or participation); (3) theoretical basis (normative and/or pragmatic participation); and (4) objectives for which participation is used (e.g. empowering stakeholders, building consensus) (Reed 2008). An overview on how participation takes place in sustainable development contexts can be seen in the work of Bell et al. (2012) and Bell and Morse (Chapter 12), including the type of participation (from passive to self-mobilisation), the subject, stakeholder groups, type of activities and methods employed (e.g. citizens' jury, consensus conference, deliberative polling, Delphi surveys, focus group).

New approaches have appeared to enhance the interactive role of stakeholders in environmental and sustainability indicator initiatives, beyond a one-way dialogue or passive "consultation" role. The aim of this chapter is to provide insights on voluntary and collaborative stakeholders' initiatives using SI as an evaluation and communication tool. A literature review considering scientific and grey literature was conducted, using Scopus and Google. Qualitative content analysis was conducted to review the selected documents. Some examples of initiatives where stakeholders have an active role are explored, mainly (1) selecting, developing, and evaluating SI; (2) participating actively in the collection of data in the monitoring phase of sustainability-related initiatives; and (3) using technology.

Stakeholder-driven initiatives can be defined as any event where stakeholders (as volunteers) have (Reed 2008) (1) an active engagement (degree of participation); (2) active participation (nature of the communication flow); (3) normative (based on the benefits for a democratic society, citizenship, and equity) and pragmatic theoretical basis (higher quality and durable decisions are assumed to be made); and (4) empowerment (as the objective). The term "stakeholder-driven" is used since the examples described represent proactive individuals and communities. Although these are interactive initiatives where facilitators have a key role, without an active role of the society, "stakeholder-driven initiatives" would not be possible. Thus, the key to these initiatives are stakeholders. Empowerment of stakeholders for sustainable development include inclusiveness, transparency, and accountability (Singh and Titi 2001). The strategy for empowerment is multi-faceted and multi-dimensional and involves the mobilisation of resources and stakeholder's capacities towards change.

Stakeholder-driven initiatives: enhancing the interactive process

An interactive participation (see Bell and Morse, Chapter 12, for details on types of participation) can help to achieve more comprehensive results since stakeholders are incorporated into the decision-making process in order to be taken into account by policy-makers and other stakeholders (Fraser et al. 2006). These authors suggest that the lack of empowerment of stakeholders has led to solutions that do not fit the specific characteristics of the environment (specifically in the context of evaluation of environmental impacts of plans). This happens due to lack of specific knowledge and support from the community for policy changes. Hunsberger, Gibson, and Wismer (2005) highlighted that an environmental assessment follow-up monitoring process is improved by the engagement of the community because it allows the integration of local needs. The engagement allows the inclusion of local knowledge, better assessment of cumulative impacts, and response to specific concerns. In the context of sustainable development initiatives, this suggests that the engagement of stakeholders in the selection, development, and evaluation of SI could have a significant value to create more meaningful indicators.

Mascarenhas et al. (2014) highlighted that participatory SI can be used to evaluate the strengths and weaknesses of formal assessments and draw conclusions about its overall utility and societal value. A feedback effect of increasing public awareness can have benefits to the overall sustainability assessment, such as enhancing to cope with changes. Information could be better understood since stakeholders are integrated in the process. Information flows easier and it is more transparent since the community is closer to the decision-making. In their study for assessments based on SI, Marques et al. (2013) acknowledged a shortage of efforts to integrate stakeholders' knowledge, perceptions, feelings, or their own evaluations in more technical assessments. They found that volunteer programmes can provide high-quality, reliable data to supplement government agencies' own monitoring programmes. Stakeholders involved in participatory initiatives should see how their contributions have affected the strategic or operational actions (Marques et al. 2013). In addition, the voluntary content of the initiative can potentially decrease costs associated to the monitoring phase. Voluntary programmes empower stakeholders to become more active and familiar with functions and values of resources (EPA 2000). This process increases stakeholder knowledge on the drivers, pressures, state, impact, and responses of resources towards a more acknowledgeable society.

The following sections explore selected examples of stakeholder-driven initiatives that use SI as the main tool to empower the participation of stakeholders in integrated processes (i.e. where stakeholders have an active role) specifically: (1) in the selection, development, and evaluation of SI; (2) collecting data in the monitoring phase of sustainability-related initiatives; and (3) in technology-based initiatives. In the literature, different terms used for this purpose were collected by Estrella and Gaventa (1998): "participatory evaluation", "participatory monitoring", "participatory assessment, monitoring and evaluation", "participatory impact monitoring", "process monitoring", "self-evaluation", "auto-evaluation", "stakeholder-based evaluation", and "community monitoring". The terms "evaluation" and "assessment" are often used as synonymous despite their different meaning. Thus, terms such as "self-evaluation" can be also found in the literature as "self-assessment" (e.g. Mascarenhas et al. 2014; Ramos and Caeiro 2010). All these terms were used to find literature for this research.

Selecting, developing, and evaluating indicators

The selection of SI suitable to the goals of each initiative is one of the most complex phases of the process of stakeholder groups' empowerment. The selection of SI from guidelines such as the Global Reporting Initiative (GRI) has been one of the barriers in the sustainability-reporting processes (Domingues et al. 2017), leading to a cherry-picking of indicators (Guthrie and Farneti 2008), and a tendency to compartmentalise sustainability issues (Lozano and Huisingh 2011). Stakeholders should be integrated as part of the team that conducts the selection, development, and evaluation (one may consider also validation) of SI to be used in different phases of the sustainability-related assessments. This could include not only triple-bottom-line indicators as presented in most sustainability-reporting guidelines, but also inter-linked issues and dimensions as suggested by Lozano and Huisingh (2011). The importance of the integration of stakeholders in the selection, development, and evaluation of SI by stakeholders as been highlighted by Mascarenhas, Nunes, and Ramos (2014) and Marques et al. (2013).

In a preliminary phase, the selection of SI should be flexible since only in practice one can be sure which indicators are most adequate for different groups of stakeholders (Abbot and Guijt 1998). Indicators should be submitted to a preliminary evaluation by the stakeholders that will use them (Mascarenhas et al. 2014, 2015). Some guidelines on the active role of stakeholders in the evaluation and selection process can be found in the White Paper of Sanz et al. (2014).

The engagement of stakeholders in the selection and development of indicators is crucial to include their opinions, values, concerns, and common goals (Beratan et al. 2004; Valentin and Spangenberg 2000). In accordance with the model proposed by Cloquell-Ballester et al. (2006), key stakeholders need to be informed during the process about: (1) the objective of the initiative; (2) the method of validating the final set of indicators; (3) the typology of participants in the validation process and the criteria used for their selection; (4) the number of proposals and the estimated time to perform the task; and (5) the potential use of the information obtained.

The selection and development of indicators need to consider the methods of collection and interpretation of data that will be used. The collection of data depends on what is being measured, the field, the frequency of measurement, and the cost (Danielsen et al. 2005). Each indicator can be evaluated according to a qualitative stakeholder's assessment, using a scoring procedure that can cover different criteria such as comprehensibility, relevancy, and feasibility (Donnelly et al. 2007; Ramos et al. 2004, 2007). Comprehensibility refers to the ability of the indicator to communicate the information to an appropriate level for decision-making and the general public; relevancy is related to the technical significance to assess the indicator as well as to support decision-making (for more details see Janoušková et al., Chapter 30); feasibility addresses the ability to implement and maintain the indicator operated.

Some examples of inclusion of stakeholders in the preliminary phases to select and develop indicators include: (1) identification and selection of SI for strategic monitoring of regional spatial plans in Algarve (Portugal) (Mascarenhas, Nunes, and Ramos 2015); (2) Kalahari rangeland condition and degradation in Botswana (Reed and Dougill 2002); (3) well-being in the coastal British Columbia (Canada), Kalahari rangeland early degradation in Botswana and Guernsey's sustainable development (UK) monitoring (Fraser et al. 2006); (4) assessment, management, and reporting in Marine Protected Areas (Marques et al. 2013); and (5) Local Agenda 21 in Iserlohn

(Germany) (Valentin and Spangenberg 2000). Similar processes of indicators' selection can be guided by criteria defined by Niemeijer and Groot (2008); Cloquell-Ballester et al. (2006); Donnelly et al. (2007); Reed et al. (2006), among others.

Indicators should then be evaluated, and validated by stakeholders. Performance indicators can be evaluated based on three essential issues (Cloquell-Ballester et al. 2006): (1) conceptual coherence: correct relationship between the measuring instrument (indicator) and the measurement object (e.g. environmental and social quality); (2) operational coherence: correct definition of the international operations of the measuring instrument; and (3) utility: applicability of the indicator in the assessment. Please see Ramos and Caeiro (Chapter 32) for more details on this.

In order to make a transition to more sustainable societies, a scientific based information and an individual approach is not enough. Indicators need to represent also "non-traditional" angles of sustainability, including non-material values, cultural, and ethical aspects related to sustainability (Dahl 2012; Ramos 2009); and collaboration needs to be one of the elements of the initiative, including communication and engagement of the actors (Lozano 2007). When sustainability-oriented stakeholders are part of the staff that select and develop indicators, the process could boost the development of value-based indicators since their values will be represented in the indicators (Mascarenhas et al. 2014). A collaborative approach can reduce conflicts (Lozano 2008) and criticism when combined with an improvement on sustainability performance (Hörisch, Schaltegger, and Windolph 2015).

Stakeholder engagement has closer ties to stakeholders interested in corporate sustainability performance (Hörisch, Schaltegger, and Windolph 2015). These authors suggest that stakeholder engagement in the sustainability performance could be a complement to sustainability reporting as communication of information is not enough. Some authors have suggested an increase on the interaction and dialogue between stakeholders and organisations (Hörisch et al. 2015; Higgins and Coffey 2016), beyond communication of results. Sustainability reporting has been one of the main drivers of stakeholder dialogues (Lozano, Nummert, and Ceulemans 2016). This is in line with the suggestions of enhancement of a more active role of stakeholders in sustainability-reporting processes (e.g. Domingues et al. 2017; Higgins and Coffey 2016).

Stakeholders need to be informed and empowered in order to contribute to the construction of mutual interests in organisations (Hörisch, Schaltegger, and Windolph 2015). A framework has been suggested by Perrini and Tencati (2006) in order to engage stakeholders in the assessment and communication of corporate performance, including SI.

Other examples, like the Leadership Council of the Sustainable Development Solutions Network (SDSN), involve stakeholders both in the selection of indicators and in the monitoring phase. The SDSN has developed indicators and a monitoring framework for the Sustainable Development Goals (SDGs) (SDSN 2015). The framework is a result of a participatory process with the SDSN Thematic Groups. It represents a list of SI to monitor the progress on the achievement of the SDGs and respective targets at different levels, including local and regional contexts.

Monitoring phase

Arts and Nooteboom (1999) define the monitoring phase as being characterised by a longitudinal and repetitive observation, measurement, and recording of variables and operational parameters for a specific purpose. In environmental and sustainability-related processes, some research has been done to investigate how stakeholders could actively collaborate in the monitoring phase of initiatives through a community/locally based approach (e.g. Savan et al. (2003) on the Citizens' Environment Watch initiative; Gouveia et al. (2004) on data collection by citizens using Information and Communication Technology (ICT); Danielsen et al. (2005) on locally based monitoring approaches; Measham and Barnett (2007) on the motivations and modes of environmental volunteering; Conrad and Daoust (2008) and Conrad and Hilchey (2011) on community-based monitoring frameworks). These examples show that it is possible to conduct stakeholder-driven initiatives in sustainability-related fields using SI as the common language.

According to Danielsen et al. (2005), voluntary schemes conducted by stakeholders can be as reliable as those derived from professional evaluation and monitoring. Informal and sporadic actions of environmental and sustainability data collection and evaluation, conducted by stakeholders can cover different phases of environmental and sustainability processes (Ramos and Caeiro, Chapter 32; Ramos et al. 2014). Informal actions in the sense that they are conducted by volunteers, and not by someone that is directly related to the formal/conventional process, such as a technical team. Informal data can complement data gathered by the formal/conventional sustainability assessment processes (Mascarenhas et al. 2014; Fraser et al. 2006; Ramos and Caeiro, Chapter 32). A fair balance between data quantity and quality is essential to guarantee data accuracy (Hochachka et al. 2012). Data voluntarily collected and evaluated by stakeholders can complement spatial and temporal failures of conventional monitoring systems and promote training and education of specific issues among volunteers (Silvertown 2009). This could be an incentive to pursue stakeholder-driven initiatives. Coutinho et al. (2017) developed a stakeholder-driven sustainability assessment framework that can be used to collect and evaluate performance data by employees in a public sector organisation, based on perceptions, individual practices, and voluntary monitoring indicators.

Some countries, such as Australia, Canada, the United States of America (USA), and the United Kingdom (UK) have been implementing volunteer monitoring systems in the last decades (at least since the '90s e.g. EPA 1991; EPA 1996). Such countries have used voluntary initiatives to monitor environmental-related issues at the local and regional level. The United States Environmental Protection Agency (EPA) is an example of entities that in the '90s developed a voluntary monitoring system to track nonpoint sources of pollution.[1] EPA developed guidelines for general water monitoring and specifically for lakes, estuaries, and wetlands (EPA 2006; EPA 1997a; EPA 2000; EPA 1997b; EPA 1991; EPA 1996). Such guidelines combine checklists and indicators with open- and close-ended questions to be filled by stakeholders. Some of the common monitoring activities are shoreline surveys (field observations like potential sources of pollutants), measurement of physical characteristics (e.g. stream flow, turbidity or sedimentation in streams, water clarity), and identification of exotic species (presence/absence or mapping or other quantitative methods). For instance, water characteristics are important indicators measured in terms of: (1) clearness, colourless or transparent, milky, foamy, turbid, dark brown among other colours; and, (2) odour, no smell or a natural odour, sewage, chlorine, fishy, rotten eggs. Other indicators can be the frame of the stream bank which may include vertical or undercut bank, steeply sloping, gradual sloping (EPA 1997b). These indicators are measured by trained citizens that can jointly work with or without experts, while the process is monitored by one or more supervisors that is/are responsible for the management of the monitoring activities (as suggested by Bell and Morse, Chapter 12). All these data collected collaboratively by volunteers and agencies is available online (Waterqualitydata.us. 2017). These data are reported and any monitoring results that are not according to the expected standards are managed in order to fulfil the necessary requirements in terms of e.g. environmental quality. These initiatives are conducted at local and regional levels (Epa.gov 2017a) and they are deeply related to political drivers. EPA is a federal governmental agency, its administration is appointed by the USA's president and approved by the Congress.

Some initiatives (in countries such as Portugal, Ireland, Spain, USA, and UK) have taken place to assess at local level and compare results from different places worldwide since they use the same indicators. Some examples include: the (1) Coastwatch to monitor coastal resources (Coastwatch.org 2017); (2) Florida Lakewatch to monitor lakes in the State of Florida (USA) (Lakewatch.ifas.ufl.edu 2017); (3) Earthwatch Institute with different initiatives from archaeology to wildlife (Eu.earthwatch.org 2017); (4) Citizens' Environmental Watch, similar to the previous one (Savan, Morgan, and Gore 2003); (5) Christmas Bird Count to monitor birds (Audubon 2017) (one of the oldest initiatives of citizen-based/citizen-led monitoring science); and (6) the British Trust for Ornithology that feeds the database of the National Biodiversity Network with data collected by volunteers about birds (Bto.org 2017).

Such initiatives assign responsibility to different parts of the civil society. Issues related to these initiatives are more understood (there's an increase of awareness (Fernandez-Gimenez, Ballard, and Sturtevant 2008)) and stakeholders feel more integrated. Internal trust and external credibility are created (Fernandez-Gimenez et al. 2008). According to Cook (1995), if stakeholders feel they are included as partners they will do their best to make the initiative work. The importance of the stakeholder's role is directly equivalent to the complexity of the study, specifically when conclusions are not achieved only with scientific facts but value-based judgement is also needed (Rickard et al. 2007).

Many initiatives in the monitoring phase can be found in scientific and grey literature. This shows how stakeholders have had an active role in the collection and evaluation of data associated to SI.

Technology-based initiatives

According to Gouveia et al. (2004), technology has emerged as a promoter of the use of data collected by volunteers and a facilitator of communication between them. ICT has gained an important role in supporting a collaborative system with tools and methods to collect, evaluate, and validate data. ICT promotes public engagement in initiatives such as environmental monitoring (Gouveia et al. 2004). These authors present different examples of initiatives using ICT-based tools for data collection such as multimedia data acquisition, user interface for data input and communication, and collaborative virtual environment.

Technology, such as GPS devices, cameras, and other sensors, can support the collection of high amounts of information and knowledge (Ramos et al. 2014; Painho et al. 2013). Another example is the use of Public Participation Geographic Information Systems (PPGIS) to empower social interactions on urban planning-related initiatives (Bugs et al. 2010). This bottom-up approach faces different challenges since it needs infrastructures able to store, analyse, display, and share data collected and monitored by citizens in order to be discussed by stakeholder groups.

An example of the spread on the use of ICT on collaborative initiatives is the increased number of apps available that any citizen can download in order to participate through mobile crowd-sensing. Some examples of apps available on online stores of mobile devices are (CaBA 2016): (1) "PlantTracker", to identify invasive non-native plant species (Planttracker.org.uk 2017); (2) "RiverObstacles", to identify natural or human barriers to fish migration (River-obstacles.org.uk 2017); (3) "AquaInvaders", to report and track invasive non-native aquatic species (Brc.ac.uk 2017); and (4) "FreshWaterWatch", to collect freshwater quality data for the global EarthWatch programme (Earthwatch FreshWater Watch 2017). Additionally, Coastwatch has been developing a "Micro-litter" app to identify the presence of micro-litter, including the shore position and type of material (Coastwatch Europe 2017). These initiatives encompass indicators that are user-friendly to most stakeholders, allowing any social actor to actively participate in the monitoring process after reading simple instructions available on the apps. This enables a collective collection of information by citizens.

ICT can boost stakeholder-driven initiatives since it can increase the number of potential participants and simplify the process. A unique system adopted worldwide allows to compare results; however, technical and governance challenges need to be overcome, namely through an increase or improvement of platforms available for knowledge sharing and improvement of the SI available on these platforms. After all, people have busy lives and being integrated in a proactive process like the ones described involves time and responsibility as discussed by Bell and Morse (Chapter 12). In addition, decision-makers also argue that they do not have time to consider other "opinions". Apps could be one of the options that could facilitate engagement, but the representative of the groups may be narrow.

These cases show that the empowerment of stakeholders has been mainly at the monitoring phase of environmental and sustainability assessment initiatives but there are also some examples of their empowerment to select and develop indicators. Despite these initiatives being mainly at the community/local level, they can be used as examples and be adapted to other contexts, namely through the use of technology. Technology acts as an important key to increase and reach a larger number of stakeholders involved in environmental and sustainability-related initiatives.

Conclusions

This chapter shows a variety of stakeholder-driven initiatives established and that have taken place. These allow the integration of stakeholders as part of the team that selects, develops, and evaluates indicators and as part of the team that collects data in the monitoring phase of assessment initiatives. These approaches involve an active participation of stakeholders in one or more phases of environmental and sustainability indicator initiatives. The cases described have a common ground of inclusiveness, transparency, and accountability. These are mostly at local and regional level, including some whose results can be compared between countries. They have been mainly managed by governmental entities and NGO (except for the technology-based initiatives).

Stakeholder-driven initiatives are a voluntary opportunity that can run in parallel but interactively with formal sustainability evaluation and monitoring processes. Formal/conventional, and voluntary processes can use similar SI in order to evaluate the same issues but in different ways, taking into account the different background of the social actors and including the use of checklists or similar approaches; this can then be used to triangulate and complement data. SI can be a useful evaluation and communication tool in this context, being used as the common language. An increase of interaction between experts and non-experts could enhance transparency of sustainability-related initiatives.

Despite the aforementioned, such initiatives are still a complex process involving different individuals and groups who are integrated to achieve a common goal. Decision-makers and practitioners often claim that they do not have resources, such as time to consider stakeholders' contributions. At the same time, some stakeholders may claim that they are not available to participate. Consequently, it is possible that some stakeholders are over-represented. It is crucial to guarantee the representativeness of different groups, especially vulnerable groups, in order to have a well-represented diversity, including gender, age, cultural, and political aspects. Technology can play an important role to boost the representativeness of distinct stakeholder groups, the diversity of the people represented within the groups, and to enhance participation among them.

It is important to empower different stakeholders that are suitable to participate and be involved in data collection, evaluation, and other decisions to improve the quality and use of SI. This is part of the essential work towards a more integrated and inclusive decision-making process, especially because environmental and sustainability-related initiatives are many times combined with political decisions. Integrating stakeholders in the end, where decisions are mostly already made, allows decisions to be made based on unclear criteria and jeopardising environmental and social long-term goals.

Many stakeholders desire to be part of the environmental and sustainability-related initiatives since they have become more aware and educated about these aspects. Stakeholders should then be represented and have a significant impact. Stakeholder-driven initiatives increase, for instance, the knowledge of different stakeholder groups, legitimacy, and co-responsibility of the decisions. The interactive nature of these initiatives can also increase social ties, communication between different stakeholder groups, and enhance the feedback mechanism due to the proximity between the formal, conventional, and voluntary components of the sustainability initiatives.

Different types of empowerment approaches should be studied, including the type of stakeholders to integrate in different initiatives, which SI are more suitable, and what practices could guide the use of SI beyond selection and voluntary data gathering. It is important to create a network of stakeholders that could work together using SI for a specific goal. This chapter aims to contribute to the transition to a more sustainable society, as SI can have a key role as evaluation and communication tools to enhance an analytical and joint reflection on environmental and sustainability processes.

Acknowledgments

The authors would like to acknowledge Alexandra Polido, André Mascarenhas, and Sandra Caeiro for the joint discussions on this topic.

Note

1 Nonpoint source pollution can result from different diffuse sources. It is caused by rainfall or snow-melt moving over and through the ground, which picks up and carries away natural and human-made pollutants deposing them into lakes, rivers, wetlands, coastal waters, and ground waters (Epa.gov 2017b).

References

Abbot, J. and I. Guijt. 1998. "Changing Views on Change: Participatory Approches to Monitoring the Environment". *SARL Discussion Paper No.2* 2: 1–96.

Arts, J. and S. Nooteboom. 1999. "Environmental Impact Assessment Monitoring and Auditing". In *Handbook of Environmental Impact Assessment*, edited by J. Petts, 229–251. Oxford: Blackwell Science.

Audubon. 2017. "Christmas Bird Count". [Online] Available at: http://www.audubon.org/conservation/science/christmas-Bird-Count [Accessed 15 January 2017].

Bell, S. and S. Morse. 2008. *Sustainability Indicators: Measuring the Immeasurable?* Second Edition. London and Sterling, VA: Earthscan. doi:10.1016/S0743–0167(99)00036–00034

Bell, S., S. Morse, and R. A. Shah. 2012. "Understanding Stakeholder Participation in Research as Part of Sustainable Development". *Journal of Environmental Management* 101: 13–22. Elsevier Ltd. doi:10.1016/j.jenvman.2012.02.004

Beratan, K., S. J. Kabala, S. M. Loveless, P. J. S. Martin, and N. P. Spyke. 2004. "Sustainability Indicators as a Communicative Tool: Building Bridges in Pennsylvania". *Environmental Monitoring and Assessment*, 94: 179–191. doi:10.1023/B:EMAS.0000016887.95411.77

Brc.ac.uk. 2017. "Home | Aqua Invaders". [Online] Available at: http://www.brc.ac.uk/aquainvaders/ [Accessed 15 January 2017].

Bto.org. 2017. "Welcome to the BTO | BTO – British Trust for Ornithology". [Online] Available at: https://www.bto.org/ [Accessed 15 January 2017].

Bugs, G., C. Granell, O. Fonts, J. Huerta, and M. Painho. 2010. "An Assessment of Public Participation GIS and Web 2.0 Technologies in Urban Planning Practice in Canela, Brazil". *Cities* 27 (3): 172–181. doi:10.1016/j.cities.2009.11.008

CaBA. 2016. *Citizen Science and Volunteer Monitoring.* The Rivers Trust, Defra & Environment Agency, Catchment Partnership Fund and the EU LIFE Programme as Part of the WaterLIFE Project.

Cloquell-Ballester, V.-A., V.-A. Cloquell-Ballester, R. Monterde-Díaz, and M.-C. Santamarina-Siurana. 2006. "Indicators Validation for the Improvement of Environmental and Social Impact Quantitative Assessment". *Environmental Impact Assessment Review* 26: 79–105. doi:10.1016/j.eiar.2005.06.002

Coastwatch Europe. 2017. "Microlitter". [Online] Available at: http://coastwatch.org/europe/microlitter/ [Accessed 15 January 2017].

Coastwatch.org. 2017. [Online] Available at: http://coastwatch.org [Accessed 15 January 2017].

Conrad, C. C. and K. G. Hilchey. 2011. "A Review of Citizen Science and Community-Based Environmental Monitoring: Issues and Opportunities". *Environmental Monitoring and Assessment* 176: 273–291. doi:10.1007/s10661-010-1582-5

Conrad, C. T. and T. Daoust. 2008. "Community-Based Monitoring Frameworks: Increasing the Effectiveness of Environmental Stewardship". *Environmental Management* 41: 358–366. doi:10.1007/s00267-00007-09042-x

Cook, J. 1995. "Empowering People for Sustainable Development". In *Managing Sustainable Development in South Africa*, edited by P. Fitzgeral, A. McLennan, and B. Munslow. Cape Town: Oxford University Press.

Coutinho, V., A. R. Domingues, S. Caeiro, M. Painho, P. Antunes, R. Santos, N. Videira, R. M. Walker, D. Huisingh, and T. B. Ramos. 2017. "Employee-Driven Sustainability Performance Assessment in Public Organisations". *Corporate Social Responsibility and Environmental Management* 25: 29–46. doi: 10.1002/csr.1438

Dahl, A. L. 2012. "Achievements and Gaps in Indicators for Sustainability". *Ecological Indicators* 17 (June): 14–19. Elsevier Ltd. doi:10.1016/j.ecolind.2011.04.032

Danielsen, F., N. D. Burgess, and A. Balmford. 2005. "Monitoring Matters: Examining the Potential of Locally-Based Approaches". *Biodiversity and Conservation* 14: 2507–2542. doi:10.1007/s10531-005-8375-0

Domingues, A. R., R. Lozano, K. Ceulemans, and T. B. Ramos. 2017. "Sustainability Reporting in Public Sector Organisations: Exploring the Relation Between the Reporting Process and Organisational Change Management for Sustainability". *Journal of Environmental Management* 192 (May): 292–301. doi:10.1016/j.jenvman.2017.01.074

Donnelly, A., M. Jones, T. O'Mahony, and G. Byrne. 2007. "Selecting Environmental Indicator for Use in Strategic Environmental Assessment". *Environmental Impact Assessment Review* 27 (2): 161–175. doi:10.1016/j.eiar.2006.10.006

Earthwatch FreshWater Watch. 2017. "Download Our Apps". [Online] Available at: https://freshwaterwatch. thewaterhub.org/content/download-Our-Apps [Accessed 15 January 2017].

EPA. 1991. *Volunteer Lake Monitoring: A Methods Manual.* Washington, DC: United States Environmental Protection Agency, Office of Water, Office of Wetlands, Oceans, and Watersheds.

EPA. 1996. *The Volunteer Monitor's Guide to Quality Assurance Project Plans.* Washington, DC: United States Environmental Protection Agency, Office of Wetlands, Oceans and Watersheds.

EPA. 1997a. *Volunteer Lake Monitoring.* Vol. 17. Washington, DC: United States Environmental Protection Agency, Office of Water.

EPA. 1997b. *Volunteer Stream Monitoring: A Methods Manual.* Washington, DC: United States Environmental Protection Agency, Office of Water.

EPA. 2000. *Volunteer Wetland Monitoring: An Introduction and Resource Guide.* Washington, DC: United States Environmental Protection Agency, Office of Water, Office of Wetlands, Oceans and Watersheds.

EPA. 2006. *Volunteer Estuary Monitoring: A Methods Manual.* Washington, DC: The Ocean Conservancy, United States Environmental Protection Agency, Office of Wetlands, Oceans and Watersheds.

Epa.gov. 2017a. "Wetland Volunteer Monitoring Programs | Wetlands Protection and Restoration | US EPA". [Online] Available at: https://www.epa.gov/wetlands/wetland-Volunteer-Monitoring-Programs [Accessed 15 January 2017].

Epa.gov. 2017b. "What Is Nonpoint Source? | Polluted Runoff: Nonpoint Source Pollution | US EPA". [Online] Available at: https://www.epa.gov/nps/what-Nonpoint-Source [Accessed 15 January 2017].

Estrella, M. and J. Gaventa. 1998. "Who Counts Reality?" *Participatory Monitoring and Evaluation: A Literature Review* 5: 73.

Eu.earthwatch.org. 2017. "Earthwatch Expeditions". [Online] Available at: http://eu.earthwatch.org/ [Accessed 15 January 2017].

Fernandez-Gimenez, M. E., H. L. Ballard, and V. E. Sturtevant. 2008. "Adaptive Management and Social Learning in Collaborative and Community-Based Monitoring: A Study of Five Community-Based Forestry Organizations in the Western USA". *Ecology and Society* 13 (2): 4.

Forrest, C. J. 1998. "Demystifying Public Environmental Concerns: Implementing Community Assessments". *Environmental Quality Management*, 55–68. doi:10.1002/tqem.3310070307

Fraser, Evan D. G., A. J. Dougill, W. E. Mabee, M. Reed, and P. McAlpine. 2006. "Bottom up and Top down: Analysis of Participatory Processes for Sustainability Indicator Identification as a Pathway to Community Empowerment and Sustainable Environmental Management". *Journal of Environmental Management* 78 (2): 114–127. doi:10.1016/j.jenvman.2005.04.009

Freeman, R. E. 1984. *Strategic Management: Stakeholder Approach*. Boston, MA: Pitman.

Freeman, R. E., J. S. Harrison, A. C. Wicks, B. L. Parmar, and S. De Colle. 2010. *Stakeholder Theory*. Cambridge: Cambridge University Press.

Gouveia, C., A. Fonseca, A. Câmara, and F. Ferreira. 2004. "Promoting the Use of Environmental Data Collected by Concerned Citizens through Information and Communication Technologies". *Journal of Environmental Management* 71: 135–154. doi:10.1016/j.jenvman.2004.01.009

Guthrie, J. and F. Farneti. 2008. "GRI Sustainability Reporting by Australian Public Sector Organizations". *Public Money & Management* 28 (6): 361–366. doi:10.1111/j.1467–9302.2008.00670.x

Higgins, C. and B. Coffey. 2016. "Improving How Sustainability Reports Drive Change: A Critical Discourse Analysis". *Journal of Cleaner Production* 136: 18–29. Elsevier Ltd. doi:10.1016/j.jclepro.2016.01.101

Hochachka, W. M., D. Fink, R. A. Hutchinson, D. Sheldon, W. K. Wong, and S. Kelling. 2012. "Data-Intensive Science Applied to Broad-Scale Citizen Science". *Trends in Ecology and Evolution* 27 (2): 130–137. Elsevier Ltd. doi:10.1016/j.tree.2011.11.006

Hörisch, J., S. Schaltegger, and S. E. Windolph. 2015. "Linking Sustainability-Related Stakeholder Feedback to Corporate Sustainability Performance: An Empirical Analysis of Stakeholder Dialogues". *International Journal of Business Environment* 7 (2): 200–218. doi:10.1504/IJBE.2015.069027

Hunsberger, C. A., R. B. Gibson, and S. K. Wismer. 2005. "Citizen Involvement in Sustainability-Centred Environmental Assessment Follow-up". *Environmental Impact Assessment Review* 25: 609–627. doi:10.1016/j.eiar.2004.12.003

Lakewatch.ifas.ufl.edu. 2017. "Lakewatch". [Online] Available at: http://lakewatch.ifas.ufl.edu/ [Accessed 15 January 2017].

Lozano, R. 2007. "Collaboration as a Pathway for Sustainability". *Sustainable Development* 15: 370–381. doi:10.1002/sd.322

Lozano, R. 2008. "Developing Collaborative and Sustainable Organisations". *Journal of Cleaner Production* 16: 499–509. doi:10.1016/j.jclepro.2007.01.002

Lozano, R. and D. Huisingh. 2011. "Inter-Linking Issues and Dimensions in Sustainability Reporting". *Journal of Cleaner Production* 19 (2–3): 99–107. Elsevier Ltd. doi:10.1016/j.jclepro.2010.01.004

Lozano, R., B. Nummert, and K. Ceulemans. 2016. "Elucidating the Relationship Between Sustainability Reporting and Organisational Change Management for Sustainability". *Journal of Cleaner Production* 125: 168–188. Elsevier Ltd. doi:http://dx.doi.org/10.1016/j.jclepro.2016.03.021

Luyet, V., R. Schlaepfer, M. B. Parlange, and A. Buttler. 2012. "A Framework to Implement Stakeholder Participation in Environmental Projects". *Journal of Environmental Management* 111: 213–219. Elsevier Ltd. doi:10.1016/j.jenvman.2012.06.026

Marques, A. S., T. B. Ramos, S. Caeiro, and M. H. Costa. 2013. "Adaptive-Participative Sustainability Indicators in Marine Protected Areas: Design and Communication". *Ocean & Coastal Management* 72 (February): 36–45. doi:10.1016/j.ocecoaman.2011.07.00

Mascarenhas, A., P. Coelho, E. Subtil, and T. B. Ramos. 2010. "The Role of Common Local Indicators in Regional Sustainability Assessment". *Ecological Indicators* 10 (3): 646–656. doi:10.1016/j.ecolind.2009.11.003

Mascarenhas, A., L. M. Nunes, and T. B. Ramos. 2014. "Exploring the Self-Assessment of Sustainability Indicators by Different Stakeholders". *Ecological Indicators* 39 (April): 75–83. doi:10.1016/j.ecolind.2013.12.001

Mascarenhas, A., L. M. Nunes, and T. B. Ramos. 2015. "Selection of Sustainability Indicators for Planning: Combining Stakeholders' Participation and Data Reduction Techniques". *Journal of Cleaner Production* 92 (January): 295–307. doi:10.1016/j.jclepro.2015.01.005

Measham, T. G. and G. B. Barnett. 2007. "Environmental Volunteering: Motivations, Modes and Outcomes". *Socio-Economics and the Environment in Discussion CSIRO Working Paper Series* 2007–2003.

Moldan, B. and A. L. Dahl. 2007. "Challenges to Sustainability Indicators". In *Sustainbaility Indicators – A Scientific Assessment*, edited by A. L. Dahl, T. Hák, and B. Moldan. Scientific Committee on Problems of the Environment (SCOPE) Series. Washington: Island Press.

Niemeijer, D. and R. S. Groot. 2008. "A Conceptual Framework for Selecting Environmental Indicator Sets". *Ecological Indicators* 8 (1): 14–25. doi:10.1016/j.ecolind.2006.11.012

Painho, M., T. H. Moreira de Oliveira, and L. Vasconcelos. 2013. "Governance of Marine Protected Areas: An Approach Using Public Participation Geographic Information Systems – The MARGov Project". *Journal of Environmental Science and Engineering B 2*: 25–35.

Perrini, F. and A. Tencati. 2006. "Sustainability and Stakeholder Management: The Need for New Corporate Performance Evaluation and Reporting Systems". *Business Strategy and the Environment* 308 (15): 296–308. doi:10.1002/bse.538

Planttracker.org.uk. 2017. "Home | Plant Tracker". [Online] Available at: Http://www.planttracker.org.uk/ [Accessed 15 January 2017].

Ramos, T. B. 2009. "Development of Regional Sustainability Indicators and the Role of Academia in This Process: The Portuguese Practice". *Journal of Cleaner Production* 17 (12): 1101–1115. doi:10.1016/j.jclepro.2009.02.024

Ramos, T. B., I. Alves, R. Subtil, and J. J. de Melo. 2007. "Environmental Performance Policy Indicators for the Public Sector: The Case of the Defence Sector". *Journal of Environmental Management* 82: 410–432. https://doi.org/10.1016/j.jenvman.2005.12.020

Ramos, T. B. and S. Caeiro. 2010. "Meta-Performance Evaluation of Sustainability Indicators". *Ecological Indicators* 10 (2): 157–166. doi:10.1016/j.ecolind.2009.04.008

Ramos, T. B., S. Caeiro, and J. J. de Melo. 2004. "Environmental Indicator Frameworks to Design and Assess Environmental Monitoring Programs". *Impact Assessment and Project Appraisal* 20 (1): 47–62. http://dx.doi.org/10.3152/147154604781766111

Ramos, T. B., I. P. Martins, A. P. Martinho, C. H. Douglas, M. Painho, and S. Caeiro. 2014. "An Open Participatory Conceptual Framework to Support State of the Environment and Sustainability Reports". *Journal of Cleaner Production* 64 (February): 158–172. doi:10.1016/j.jclepro.2013.08.038

Ramos, T. B. and S. Moreno Pires. 2013. "Sustainability Assessment: The Role of Indicators". In *Sustainability Assessment Tools in Higher Education Institutions: Mapping Trends and Good Practices Around the World*, edited by S. Caeiro, W. Leal Filho, C. Jabbour, and U. M. Azeiteiro, 81–99. Berlin: Springer International Publishing Switzerland.

Reed, M. S. 2008. "Stakeholder Participation for Environmental Management: A Literature Review". *Biological Conservation* 141 (10): 2417–2431. doi:10.1016/j.biocon.2008.07.014

Reed, M. S. and A. J. Dougill. 2002. "Participatory Selection Process for Indicators of Rangeland Condition in the Kalahari". *The Geographical Journal* 168 (3): 224–234. doi:10.1111/1475–4959.00050

Reed, M. S., E. Fraser, and A. Dougill. 2006. "An Adaptive Learning Process for Developing and Applying Sustainability Indicators with Local Communities". *Ecological Economics* 59 (4): 406–418. doi:10.1016/j.ecolecon.2005.11.008

Rickard, L., J. Jesinghaus, C. Amann, G. Glaser, S. Hall, M. Cheatle, and A. A. Le Kama. 2007. "Ensuring Policy Relevance". In *Sustainbaility Indicators – A Scientific Assessment*, edited by A. L. Dahl, T. Hák, and B. Moldan. Scientific Committee on Problems of the Environment (SCOPE) Series. Washington: Island Press.

River-obstacles.org.uk. 2017. "River Obstacles | Helping to Improve the Connectivity of Our River Network". [Online] Available at: https://www.river-Obstacles.org.uk/ [Accessed 15 January 2017].

Sanz, F. S., T. Holocher-Ertl, B. Kieslinger, F. Sanz García, and C. G. Silva. 2014. *White Paper on Citizen Science for Europe*. European Commission: Socientize, Citizen Science Projects.

Savan, B., A. J. Morgan, and C. Gore. 2003. "Volunteer Environmental Monitoring and the Role of the Universities: The Case of Citizens' Environment Watch". *Environmental Management* 31 (5): 561–568. doi:10.1007/s00267–00002–02897-y

SDSN. 2015. *Indicators and a Monitoring Framework for the Sustainable Development Goals: Launching a Data Revolution for the SDGs*. A Report to the Secretary-General of the United Nations by the Leadership Council of the Sustainable Development Solutions Network.

Silvertown, J. 2009. "A New Dawn for Citizen Science". *Trends in Ecology & Evolution* 24 (9): 467–471. doi:10.1016/j.tree.2009.03.017

Singh, N. C. and V. Titi. 2001. *Empowerment for Sustainable Development: Towards Operational Strategies – Engaging Stakeholders in Support of Sustainable Development Action: Decision-Makers Summary*. Winnipeg, Manitoba, Canada: International Institute for Sustainable Development.

Valentin, A. and J. H. Spangenberg. 2000. "A Guide to Community Sustainability Indicators". *Environmental Impact Assessment Review* 20: 381–392. doi:10.1016/S0195–9255(00)00049–00044

Waas, T., J. Hugé, T. Block, T. Wright, F. Benitez-Capistros, and A. Verbruggen. 2014. "Sustainability Assessment and Indicators: Tools in a Decision-Making Strategy for Sustainable Development". *Sustainability* 6 (9): 5512–5534. doi:10.3390/su6095512

Waterqualitydata.us. 2017. "Water Quality Data Home". [Online] Available at: Https://www.waterquality-data.us/ [Accessed 15 January 2017].

WCED – World Comission on Environment and Development. 1987. *Our Common Future*. Oxford: Oxford University Press.

26

HOW EVIL IS AGGREGATION? LESSONS FROM THE DASHBOARD OF SUSTAINABILITY

Jochen Jesinghaus

My story starts 25 years ago, when I got my first job at Eurostat, the European Union's Statistical Office. The job description was simple: "Build a system for collecting environmental expenditure statistics". After some weeks of reflection, I told my superiors "expenditure statistics are completely useless, because you cannot know if a government spends a lot a) because they care for their citizens' health or b) because the country is excessively polluted. Instead, we should measure the *pressures* on the environment, like *waste* or *land use* or CO_2 *emissions*, and we should publish a *pressure index* using some reasonable method of aggregation".

In hindsight, it is surprising that I was not immediately shown the door. Instead, my Head of Unit sent me to Brussels, and I could present my strange ideas to then President Jacques Delors's inner circle of advisors. They liked my idea (so did DG Environment), and many months later I had a fairly big project at Eurostat, composed of ten teams from universities, six from National Statistical Institutes (NSI), and three assistants. Some years later, we had data for 60 indicators (the most difficult part), and weighting coefficients for each of them, obtained through a survey among 2,300 environmental scientists, of which 660 actually answered our *real paper* questionnaire.

What we did not have in our calculations was the heavy resistance of the entire statistical community against any form of aggregation. Both Eurostat and the OECD maintain so-called Working Groups composed of statisticians from the NSIs. The great majority of members were strictly against aggregating CO_2 or PM_{10} emissions with *waste per capita* or *habitat loss*. It was a heroic fight, and I will be eternally grateful for the excellent training I got in these debates; but in the end we lost, and so we were not allowed to publish any aggregated data, not even at the lower level of ten environmental themes. The title of the official publication, "Towards Environmental Pressure Indicators" (Eurostat 1999), made it crystal clear that the EU's Statistical Office would restrict the information to the level of physical indicators.[1]

Why do the clients at the political level love the idea of an overall index, while the data providers are so strictly against?

I should mention at this point that the idea to construct an environmental pressure index was not mine: Albert Adriaanse at the Dutch RIVM published in 1993 a comprehensive assessment of the environmental situation in the Netherlands, including a full-fledged index of pressures on the environment. Here are two graphs (Figure 26.1) based on his results:

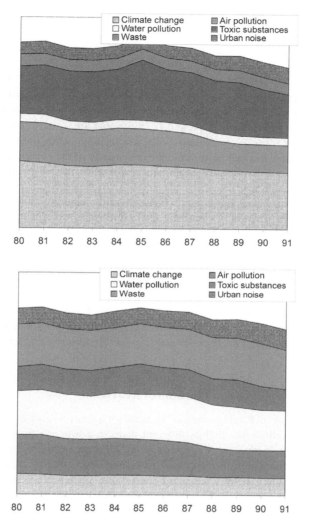

Figure 26.1 Environmental pressures in the Netherlands. Political targets (left), Sustainability targets (right)

They show that environmental pressure in the Netherlands decreased after a peak in 1985, caused inter alia by higher-than-usual toxic emissions. So far, so good – but why *two* graphs?

And here we are in the middle of the controversy: Nobody had *one* convincing answer to the question "what's the weight of water pollution as compared to climate change?" Adriaanse used the "distance to target" approach, meaning basically "we give more weight to issues that are far away from a target". The idea has its merits, and one problem: There is not only *one* target around, as the graphs demonstrate. *Political* targets may differ from "*sustainability*" targets defined by scientists. And scientists close to Greenpeace might believe in different targets than those who are close to the coal industry. In the late nineties, the European Environment Agency (EEA) collected targets for their STAR database; if I remember well, they froze the project after having found about 5,000 "targets", for just a handful of environmental issues. The scientific value of hand-picking **one** from such a collection for defining the political weight of e.g. CO_2 emissions is evidently low.

Many ideas for finding the weighting coefficients for environmental indices have been promoted since.

Using the distance to political targets is perhaps the most popular one. I have always been outspoken on this point; in my humble opinion, politicians are intelligent people, and will therefore allow only two types of political targets: (1) those that are so soft that no additional efforts or costs to the voters are needed, and (2) those that are so hard that, in order to avoid painful consequences for the electorate and/or the involved industries, they get "promoted" to a sufficiently distant future, i.e. well beyond the life expectancy of the current government.[2] Both types are obviously not a scientifically sound basis for defining the weight (i.e. the seriousness) of an environmental problem.

One of the most intriguing approaches (I won't cite the source, but searching for "benefit of the doubt" might help) argues to use "revealed preferences". Imagine an index composed of CO_2 emissions and life expectancy: A country with high life expectancy but a bad score on CO_2 emissions would thus "reveal" that they place a high weight on long life but a low weight on preventing climate change; accordingly, their *individual* country-level index would be calculated using a high weight for life expectancy, and a low weight for CO_2. The promoters claim, and rightly so, that countries will be more likely to accept an index if their weights for "bad" index components are lowered. The rankings I saw published, typically among OECD countries, looked reasonable and plausible, but I have always asked myself why poor Africans would reveal such a high preference to save the climate, and such a low desire to live longer.

The fans of AC/DC

A propos life, and its value: Placing a monetary value on a (lost) human life has been a popular topic in such debates, albeit in a slightly different context. While one fraction was chasing the mysteries of weighting coefficients for environmental (and sustainability) indices, a second one declared *money* as the ideal unit to compare apples and oranges. Interestingly enough, National Statistical Offices were less shy on that front because, after all, their flagship statistics, GDP and its databases, are already expressed in euros and dollars. So for them it seemed natural to calculate the relative damage done by CO_2 vs. PM_{10} emissions vs. waste per capita or habitat loss in monetary units.

Two related but different approaches emerged from that debate:

1 Avoidance Costs (AC)

The idea behind this approach is that calculating damages from emissions is close to impossible, but there is an indirect workaround. The logic here is: If society decides that the *optimal* level of a car's NOx emissions (i.e. the level where costs for installing filters and bad health are balanced) is x microgram per km, then the *cost* of achieving this goal equals the *damage* avoided. Assuming that "society" takes rational decisions, this logic (promoted in particular by Roefie Hueting) of estimating damages "indirectly" is correct. There are minor problems, though, with calculating this cost: Some claim that e.g. the *macro-economic* cost of reducing CO_2 emissions by 20% is *negative* (which would imply, in the logic of the AC approach, that CO_2 emissions are "beneficial"), others believe that "society" (represented by elected politicians who must care for their electorate) has significant problems with establishing clear limits for phenomena that exert their impact in the far future (e.g. 2100) in far countries (e.g. Bangladesh).

2 Damage Costs (DC)

Given these difficulties with AC, the second fraction among the monetizers preferred to calculate the costs of environmental pressures directly, as "damage costs". Among others, the EC-US Fuel Cycle Costs project (later called ExternE) developed sophisticated methods to estimate environmental damages, based mainly on Willingness-To-Pay (WTP) and Willingness-To-Accept (WTA). Inter alia, the group brought the enormous damage from PM_{10} emissions to the attention of the public. However, while WTP/WTA may work for well-studied local and immediate problems, people may have difficulties to imagine the consequences of problems that are uncertain and/or will happen in the far future (2100) in far countries (Bangladesh). Besides, while in theory WTP ("how much are you willing to pay for a clean environment?") and WTA ("how much are you willing to accept as a compensation for a dirty environment?") *should* yield the same results, in practice WTA is a factor three higher than WTP – and there is no scientifically sound rule to decide which one is more correct (see Figure 26.2).

A key problem both for the distance-to-X and the monetary approaches is that scientists from different personal and/or political backgrounds may arrive at different results.

For example, an industry expert, when asked to comment on diesel cars, would probably rebut "show me one single case where somebody died from NOx emissions"; the other side would pull out a Global Health Sciences article claiming that many thousands will die prematurely from diesel car emissions. Who is "right"?

Likewise, the perceived consequences of climate change (picking arbitrarily one element of "the environment"[3]) will differ, depending on the attitude of the respondent:

A climate change "denier" may claim that

- the contribution of man-made CO_2 emissions to climate change is unproven
- in case it exists, it will only affect a few people in countries like Bangladesh
- Canada and Siberia can produce more food, and send it to Bangladesh

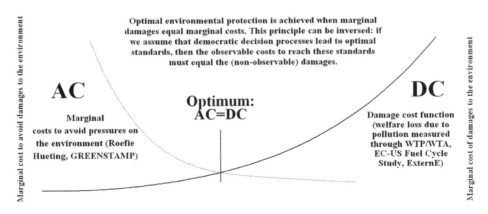

Figure 26.2 Avoidance vs. Damage Costs

- the damage should be calculated based on value of life estimates for the *victims'* countries (which typically are very low, corresponding to their low incomes and low life expectancy)
- future damages should be discounted at a high rate (for which some "scientific" justification can certainly be found in the literature).

Instead, a climate change "activist" would claim that

- the United Nations has declared that CO_2 emissions cause climate change
- it will kill millions all over the world;
- Canada and Siberia will produce more food, okay – but eat it themselves
- the damage should be calculated based on value of life estimates for the countries which *caused* climate change (which typically are very high. . .)
- damages should not be discounted at all (for "obvious" moral and ethical reasons).

My favourite quote by Stephen Wiel of the EC-US Fuel Cycle Study team:

Reasonable people find electricity externalities from 0.001¢/kwh to over 10¢/kwh, a range of four orders of magnitude.[4]

Nothing works, so what could we do?

It is when the hidden decisions are made explicit that the arguments begin. The problem for the years ahead is to work out an acceptable theory of weighting.
— Garrett Hardin, half a century ago[5]

The author didn't become a fan of AC/DC, and could not be convinced of distance-to-target and other magical approaches to aggregation. Besides, I developed some respect for the insistence of Statistical Offices to focus on "physical" indicators, and to leave the nasty valuation part to private initiatives;[6] which does *not* imply that I share this attitude, because measuring and publishing the *importance*[7] of a phenomenon through defining its weight in a given context can and should be part of the services that official statistical services are meant to deliver to society. But how could they do it?

In the late eighties I had made a very special survey among scientists, in a research faculty of the University of Mannheim called "Forschungsstelle für Gesellschaftliche Entwicklungen" (FGE): We had approached 400 German scientists with a questionnaire on environmental problems. The survey was designed so that we knew their political background, i.e. whether they were "industry" experts, or "environmentalists".[8] Not surprisingly, we found dramatic differences in their overall attitudes: industry experts thought everything was under control, environmentalists believed that everything was *out* of control. There wasn't even the tiniest indication of a common intersection between the two groups.[9] The difference might be visualized as two "cakes" whose diametres represent the importance of "the environment" as perceived by the two groups of experts (see Figure 26.3).

Apologies for the low quality graphics – this is 1991. What strikes the eye, though, is that the "cakes" are not just circles: they are subdivided into eight policy themes, i.e. Water and Air, Climate Change, etc.

Indeed, in one question to the 400 experts, we had asked them to distribute a "budget" of 100 points on the items of a list of eight themes. The diametre of the cake ("overall importance

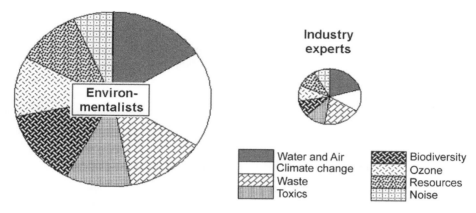

Figure 26.3 The "Cake Share Model"

of environmental problems") was thus irrelevant, but the contributions to this cake had to be judged under the aspect of *relative* importance of its pieces. And here comes the big surprise: *the opposed groups came to almost identical results!*

This has major consequences for the attempt to construct an environmental pressure index, for two reasons:

- Technically speaking, the budget question matches exactly what is needed: the shares can be used as weighting coefficients without any further intransparent and difficult-to-justify transformations.
- For the public and scientific acceptance of an index, consensus about the weights, among otherwise opposed groups, is the most precious ingredient one could imagine.

Why is it so important to have a transparent methodology that allows to demonstrate that opposed groups can come to similar conclusions?

And what is the difference between the "scientific" methods (distance to x, monetary valuation) and expert surveys or opinion polls?

As Archimedes wrote over 2200 years ago: "Give me a place to stand and I will move the earth". We don't want to move Planet Earth, but protecting it from man-made damages is already difficult enough, and expensive, so it would be fair to ask: Are our methods solid enough to serve as a "place to stand", and to help politicians decide on how to spend billions in a major policy area?

As long as the answers of scientists are orders of magnitude apart, depending on their affiliation: certainly not. But if we (plausibly) assume that the budget of policy area X is fixed, and we *can* get agreement on the *shares* of sub-policies a, b, c, then the method will be robust enough to guide the minister.

The good news: We can aggregate apples and oranges! But why should we?

So throwing apples and oranges into one basket and calling it "fruit salad" is technically feasible; but are there any good reasons to do that? Since citing the United Nations is always a good idea:[10] "the need for aggregation has been recognized in order to avoid being lost in a sea of information". At the time of the Ghent workshop, we were not yet flooded with 134 CSD indicators, 80+ MDG indicators, or 230 SDG indicators (see Chapters 3 and 23 for the details); and "big data" as a buzz word was still 20 years ahead. But even with "only" 60 environmental pressure indicators, as foreseen in the Eurostat project, the question was evidently how users could digest such a rich source of information.

For the community of scientists and activists who grew up in the Agenda 21 & UN CSD context, one major driver for indicators was obviously the desire to get more attention for Sustainable Development. We wanted to measure progress towards SD, and we wanted naming and shaming of the governments responsible for the lack of progress; and we knew that neither ordinary citizens nor journalists would be impressed by huge batteries of indicators with cryptic titles.

The CGSDI and the dashboard of sustainability

It is against this background that in 1996 the International Institute for Sustainable Development (IISD) launched the Consultative Group on Sustainable Development Indicators (CGSDI), composed of a dozen leaders of indicator programmes in various institutions.[11] I had the honour to represent the European Commission in the group.

The CGSDI chased the Holy Grail of Sustainable Development initially via email, then we met occasionally face to face. After some years, we had an understanding on basic concepts and rules – holistic, integrative, participative, etc. – that eventually led to the Bellagio Principles (see Arthur Dahl's essay in Chapter 3, Contributions to the evolving theory and practice of indicators of sustainability). Consensus emerged also that there would be a hierarchy of goals that could be represented as concentric circles, with a "Sustainable Development" circle in the middle, and (taking Agenda 21 as a model) economic, social, environmental and institutional sub-segments contributing to the central goal. Dana Meadows floated the idea that like the instruments in a car, citizens merit a *Dashboard* of Sustainable Development to understand whether their government is on the right track.

For years, the CGSDI was a rich source of intelligent ideas and philosophical exchanges. This changed around 2000, when member John O'Connor, former leader of the World Bank's indicator programme with access to a wealth of databases, took a long and energetic look at the 134 indicators proposed by the United Nations Commission on Sustainable Development. When he had finished that look, he mailed me a *spreadsheet* with data for all UN countries – and knowing that my hobby was computing, he asked, innocently: "can you translate that into a dashboard, Jochen?" I could not resist – a big mistake. ;-)

Two years later, Peter Hardi and myself presented the UN CSD Dashboard at the 2002 World Summit on Sustainable Development in Johannesburg, on behalf of the CGSDI. Its central view presented two or more countries side by side, each with a concentric "SD index" circle in the middle, and segments displaying the relative position of these countries regarding the four "pillars" of Agenda 21. The original software uses a colour scale ranging from deep red ("horrible", dark in the screenshot below) over yellow ("average") to deep green ("perfect", light in the screenshot). See Figure 26.4.

As you can see, you cannot see much; with respect to this view, the eternal argument against aggregation, "you are losing information", seems valid: We would certainly get *more* information if we looked at the 67 columns and 263 rows of the original spreadsheet. But showing the user over 17,000 cells of data has little to do with *communicating* information: What really counts is the content that can be correctly processed by the user's brain, and will eventually trigger correct judgements. For example, a citizen from the Philippines might wish to go beyond the boring grey image above, and access the underlying data. With a simple right mouse click into the central "Sustainable Development Index" circle, the user would see the disaggregated data as follows in Figure 26.5.

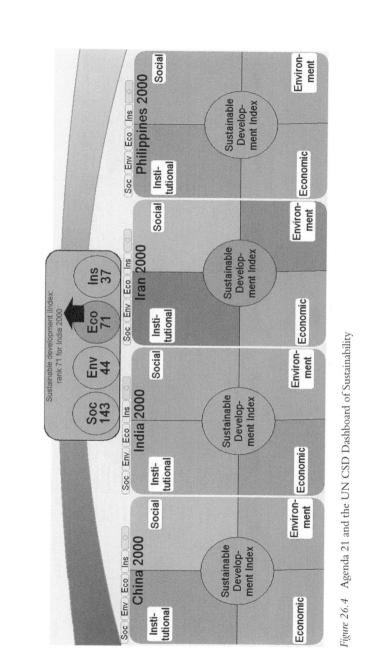

Figure 26.4 Agenda 21 and the UN CSD Dashboard of Sustainability

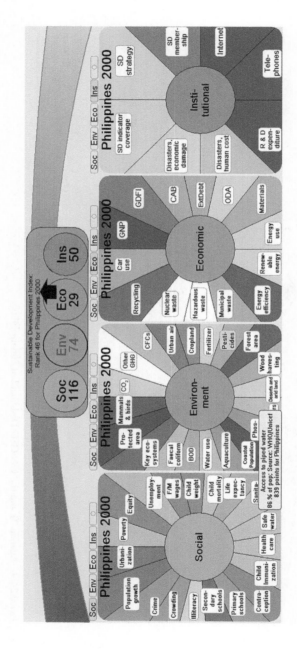

Figure 26.5 CSD Dashboard, disaggregated

Dark is bad, light is good, white means "no data". And when hovering with the mouse over, for example, "Safe water", the dashboard software would show "Access to piped water: 86% of pop; Source WHO/Unicef", as shown above; showing the data source is perhaps not *that* important for the average citizen, but statisticians insist on correct attributions.[12]

Notes on the methodology

Finally, the little box says "839 points for Philippines", calculated as linear interpolation between the best (1000) and worst (0 points) performer in the group as follows: *points = 1000*current value/(best value − worst value)*

Over time, we added many bells and whistles to the tool, but the guiding principle remained simply that every *issue* can be decomposed into contributing elements; and every element can be described in terms of

1   its share (weight, relative importance) and
2   its performance in comparison to a peer group.

This works for measuring government performance, for measuring the quality of life in your city,[13] for choosing the next car (power, consumption, comfort, prestige. . .), for deciding on a house to buy, or even to pick the best candidate for a team of researchers (academic background, publication list, teamwork capacity, social background. . .).

And it would not be limited to only two levels of aggregation. For example, a "welfare" index (pick any title that sounds right: well-being. . .) could be composed of several level II clusters; its environment cluster could be split into climate, waste, etc.; its waste sub-sub-cluster could be composed of household, toxic, and industrial waste; and the toxic sub-sub-sub-cluster might be split again into physical indicators − organic, inorganic, radioactive, etc. See Figure 26.6.

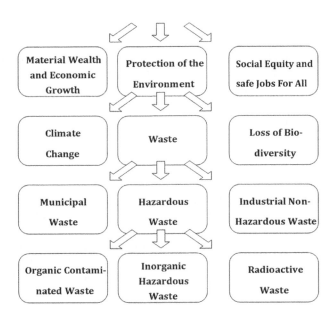

Figure 26.6   A hierarchy of "welfare"

To obtain sound weighting coefficients for each level, the "budget" question described earlier should be asked to the right experts: There is no point in asking a layperson how to distribute "importance points" to the indicators underlying "hazardous waste". Likewise, a specialist for, say, biodiversity should not be asked how much importance should be given to the main environment pillar, as compared to social and economic issues.

Note that in a democratic society, the top-level "expert" is the voter: Ordinary citizens should decide how much weight governments should give to "the" environment or "the" economy.

From the beginning, we tried to make the software flexible and easy to use. A simple interface to standard spreadsheet software allowed to translate other indicator sets into the dashboard visualization. For example, the 2005 CIESIN & Yale Environmental Sustainability Index (ESI)[14] has its own dashboard, colour-coded world map, and indicator tree included (see Figure 26.7).

Same for its successor, the Environmental Performance Index (EPI), the Environmental Vulnerability Index portrayed in Arthur Dahl's essay in Chapter 3, Chapter 33 (see Wackernagel et al. in this TK volume), and many more. Sadly, only a handful of them, namely Italy's "Ecosistema Urbano" and the UN Millennium Development Goals, had enough underlying data to allow time series.

It's time to abandon GDP!

With growing experience, the goal to replace GDP growth in its detrimental role as policy lead indicator seemed close. Awareness of GDP's shortcomings rose, and we had the right tool. The European Commission launched "Beyond GDP", and prominent politicians took strong stances:

> Among those convinced that official statisticians should join in is Nicolas Sarkozy, the French president. On September 14th a commission he appointed last year, comprising 25 prominent social scientists, five with Nobel prizes in economics, presented its findings. Joseph Stiglitz, the group's chairman and one of the laureates, said the 292-page report was a call to abandon "GDP fetishism".[15]

What was needed to advance towards a comprehensive welfare index?

Some years ago I formulated a few essential steps (Figure 26.8) towards the ultimate welfare index that would force politicians to abandon GDP and take the citizens' needs more seriously. At the end of the process, I imagined a welfare index showing the four pillars of Agenda 21, each with seven sub-indices composed of seven[16] indicators each; i.e. a total of 4*7*7=200 indicators, roughly the number that Eurostat promoted at the time as "core indicators".

Note that in my introduction to the Holy Grail of Weighting, I only covered the last two steps. Using surveys among experts for the respective sub-indices, this seems feasible – so where is the perfect Welfare Index today?

Something went wrong. Indeed, ten years after the Beyond GDP conference,[17] eight years after Joseph Stiglitz urged to abandon "GDP fetishism", we are still stuck at stage 1 of the process: Should it be three issues, economic/social environmental? Or maybe four, Agenda 21 style? Or 11, as in OECD's Better Life Index?[18]

The good news: *There is no lack of ideas.* Over the years, the author has received quite a number of datasets for translation into a dashboard, currently a bit more than 300. *Three hundred* different visions on how to measure progress. Not all of them were titled "well-being", of course; researchers want to measure each and every aspect of life, but an important lesson from the dashboard process is that there are *too many* ideas around: At expert level, there is no chance to reach an agreement on *one* set of issues and indicators.

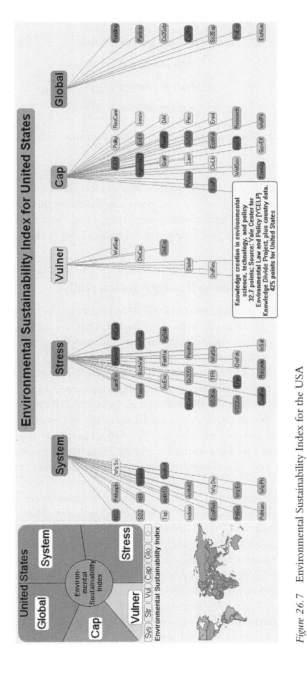

Figure 26.7 Environmental Sustainability Index for the USA

Figure 26.8   Essential steps to create a Policy Performance Index

Does it look any better at the level of politics? Agenda 21 and the UN CSD set are things of the past, the MDGs are still around but have been substituted by the SDGs, the "Better Life Index" is an OECD-only exercise, Bhutan measures "happiness", and the European Commission has a "Beyond GDP" website that is full of good ideas. *Different* ideas, of course – the EU has currently 28 member states.

So, how evil is aggregation really?

Back to the original question: Is aggregation evil? With respect to the hundreds of indices that I have personally translated into dashboards, certainly not: They are fully transparent, no information gets lost; on the contrary, visualization through aggregation has often helped researchers to *better* understand their own data.

So far the good news. The bad news is that it seems impossible to reach a consensus on how to measure true progress/better life/welfare/well-being/happiness – we cannot even find a title. And yet, there seems to be a consensus that we must go *beyond "GDP fetishism"*, to quote Stiglitz.

Everybody agrees on that point. Even Simon Kuznets, the father of Gross Domestic Product, warned against its use as a welfare indicator. You had an accident? Good for the economy. You had to organize a funeral? Even better . . . we all know the arguments. GDP aggregates every transaction on the basis of a monetary unit, regardless of its value for society. *That is evil aggregation!*

Unfortunately, the *evil aggregate* GDP drives politics. No government can survive if GDP points downwards, even if they manage to make everybody happy. That sounds paradox and illogical, but as long as journalists write more about GDP growth than about true progress, people will think "personally, I am quite happy, but it seems the economy is going down the drain – time to vote for another government".

There are reasons why GDP growth is still being used by the media, in particular: It has been around for a while (to my knowledge, the oldest environmental index is the Italian Ecosistema Urbano,[19] published yearly since 1994; in contrast, GDP dates back to World War II). Longevity of indicators is a crucial factor: Politicians know the difference between an index produced *once* by a team of researchers (no action required, just a few friendly promises) and a number that will be around for a long time (cannot be ignored, may threaten re-election, we must spend money).

Besides, GDP measures something that matters to economists: the business cycle, and it does so *reliably* because the statistical services spend enormous resources on it. GDP is perhaps the only indicator whose values are accepted "as is": We argue about the "1% growth is not enough" message, but we don't argue about the *correctness* of the number itself. Even the unemployment rate, #2 on the political agenda, is not considered as reliable as GDP.

The dirtiest marketing trick ever, though, was to link GDP growth with the jobs argument (Jesinghaus 2012):[20]

> its growth rate almost never gets interpreted as "2% growth means we got on average 2% richer". When introduced in the first half of the 20th century, GDP was used as a measure of the overall economic power of a nation, as a kind of wealth and welfare indicator. This usage has been replaced by a narrow focus on GDP growth as a *predictor of labour market problems*, expressed as the formula recession = unemployment. There is a strong logic behind this altered use of GDP: people are not scared of eating 2% less, but they *do* fear losing their jobs. What the simplistic "growth = jobs" formula ignores is the time horizon. It is certainly true that in the short run, an economic boom creates jobs: companies cannot improve quickly enough their infrastructure, and therefore hire more labour to fully exploit their current capacity. What economists and journalists alike rarely mention is that a few years after, the boom is over, and companies use their improved infrastructure to produce the same output with *less* labour. The common misuse of the short-sighted "growth means jobs" logic has prevented politics to address the true, *structural* causes of unemployment.

If GDP mattered only to economists, it would be harmless; but by introducing the *false* link to losing jobs, it became important to the whole population.

GDP won't go away, and true welfare won't come; what can we do?

Aggregation is evil when it gives mediatic power to numbers that do not deserve it: The media presence of the GDP growth rate forces governments to act against the interests of their population. There is little hope to replace it with an equally powerful index based on social, economic, cultural, and environmental indicators, and aggregated in a scientifically sound way – not because it would be overly difficult, but because the political will is lacking.

If we cannot provide a better alternative, then we might at least try to *restrict* GDP to its legitimate use as a business cycle indicator. Let companies use it for their planning, but let us convince journalists that the ordinary citizen needs to know that there is absolutely *no* mid- or long-term link between jobs and GDP growth, and that an *average* increase of x% does *not* mean that every citizen is better off by x%. Let us demand from the statistical services that they concentrate on income and wealth *inequality* rather than on GDP per capita, and on predictors of *long-term* employment rather than on short business cycles. Shrinking the influence of GDP may not satisfy the numerous statisticians and scientists who believe in the value of indicators for saving the environment, but there will be no better solution in the near future.

Notes

1 Eurostat 1999: "Towards Environmental Pressure Indicators", Publications Office of the European Union, ISBN 92-828-4978-3, published: 1999-06-03.
2 In the light of recent events, it is tempting to add a third kind: "targets based on technical specifications that can easily be cheated".
3 As Bravo writes in Chapter 18 in this volume, the Human *Sustainable* Development Index extends the HDI by adding CO_2 emissions per capita as "the" environmental component; so 100% to CO_2, simple

and clear but in great contrast to e.g. the Yale EPI, which gives only 12.5% to CO_2, encrypted as three indicators of "trends" in carbon intensity.

4 Stephen Wiel. *The Science and Art of Valuing Externalities: A Recent History of Electricity Sector Evaluations*, 1995, Lawrence Berkeley National Laboratory, www.osti.gov/scitech/servlets/purl/503480

5 Garrett Hardin, "The tragedy of the commons", *Science*, Vol. 162, December 1968.

6 See Bartelmus in Chapter 15 in this volume: "the national accounts include only those issues that can be readily observed, measured, and valued".

7 Closely related but different: relevance, see Janoušková, Hák, and Moldan in Chapter 30 in this volume.

8 The respondents were divided in six groups: environmentalists, journalists, public administration, politicians (i.e. members of parliament), scientists and industry experts. It was a big *quantitative* exercise in "stakeholder participation" – but check its meaning against Bell & Morse in Chapter 12 in this volume.

9 Spangenberg distinguishes "modificationists" and "transformationists" in his "World Views" essay in Chapter 9 of this book.

10 *United Nations Commission for Sustainable Development*, Third Session, April 1995, E/CN.17/1995/1: Workshop on Indicators of Sustainable Development, Ghent, 9–11 January 1995, Annex: Conclusions, point 4.

11 Members and their affiliations (around 1996): Alan AtKisson (Redefining Progress), David Berry (Director of the Interagency Working Group on Sustainable Development Indicators, U.S. Government), Arthur L. Dahl (Coordinator, UN System-wide Earthwatch, UNEP), Edgar E. Gutierrez-Espeleta Director of the Development Observatory at the University of Costa Rica), Allen Hammond (Director of the Indicator Program at the World Resources Institute, WRI), Peter Hardi (Director of IISD Indicators Program, CGSDI Co-ordinator), Jochen Jesinghaus (European Commission, Eurostat & JRC), the late Donella H. Meadows (lead author of *Limits to Growth*, the 1972 report to the Club of Rome), Bedřich Moldan (Chairman UN CSD-9 and former Czech Republic Environment Minister), Yuichi Moriguchi (Head, Resources Management Section, Social and Environmental Systems Division, National Institute for Environmental Studies, Japan, Adil Najam (Boston University, Associate Director of the MIT-Harvard Program on Public Disputes at the Program on Negotiation, Pakistan/USA), and John O'Connor (former Head of the World Bank's indicator team).

12 The trained eye will also notice the dark colour of "Coastal Population" – the dashboard is not to blame, the data is real, and a group of distinguished experts pushed this one into the CSD set. Despite the dark red colour, it is unlikely that the Philippine government will move coastal cities into the mountains.

13 See Turcu in Chapter 10 of this volume.

14 Yale CELP and CIESIN, http://epi.yale.edu/ and http://sedac.ciesin.columbia.edu/data/collection/epi

15 "Measuring what matters", *The Economist*, September 17th 2009, www.economist.com/node/14447939 (retrieved 30 March 2017)

16 According to George Miller, the human mind can handle about seven stimuli with acceptable precision. George Miller A. "The magical number seven, plus or minus two: Some limits on our capacity for processing information", *Psychological Review*, Vol. 63 (2) 1956: 81–97.

17 European Commission: Beyond GDP, http://ec.europa.eu/environment/beyond_gdp/background_en.html

18 OECD: Better Life Index, www.oecdbetterlifeindex.org/

19 Legambiente: Ecosistema Urbano 2017, www.legambiente.it/contenuti/dossier/ecosistema-urbano-2017

20 Jochen Jesinghaus: "Measuring European environmental policy performance", *Ecological Indicators*, Vol. 17 (2012): 29–37.

27

CRITERIA AND INDICATORS TO AUDIT THE PERFORMANCE OF COMPLEX, MULTI-FUNCTIONAL FOREST LANDSCAPES

Dwi Amalia Sari, Chris Margules,
Agni Klintuni Boedhihartono and Jeffrey Sayer

Introduction

There is a long history of forest science aimed at measuring timber volumes and yields, mean annual increments, profitability and water yields from forests. The techniques for these measurements are the stock in trade of the professional forester. However the demands that global and local societies place upon forest lands are diversifying and increasing. Forests today are managed for local, national and global public and private goods. Management must encompass objectives ranging from carbon stocks and biodiversity to local supplies of non-timber forest products and employment in timber industries (Sayer and Campbell, 2005). Countries have committed to global agreements to mitigate climate change and preserve biodiversity and they seek to meet these targets in forests where local people gain their livelihoods, industries drive economies, watersheds protect hydrological functions and urban people seek recreation. Forest landscapes are geographic limited areas that are implicitly being managed to deliver on most of the dimensions of the Sustainable Development Goals. Forest management is confronted with the need to meet these diverse goals in the short term but also to ensure long-term sustainability – thus keeping options open for the future.

There are several decades of experience with attempts to integrate conservation and development and to achieve multi-functional forest management over large spatial scales (Sayer et al., 2007a). The multiple goals inherent in such approaches always require trade-offs. More timber may mean less biodiversity or water, short-term profitability may conflict with long-term sustainability, local community benefits often conflict with national economic objectives or global environmental goals. Increasingly governments, international development agencies, conservation and development NGOs and corporations are investing in management programmes that seek to optimise the balance between these diverse and often conflicting objectives. Ecosystem approaches were widely advocated in the 1980s and 1990s (Sayer et al., 2007b). At present there is a wave of interest in "landscape approaches" that seek to achieve multiple objectives at the landscape scale (Reed et al., 2016; Sayer et al., 2013). All of these integrative interventions with multiple objectives have been beset with difficulties in assessing their effectiveness (McShane et al., 2011; McShane and Newby, 2004). Conventional measures of delivery of outcomes and impacts do not address the problems of trade-offs between conflicting goals. In addition integrated approaches must deal with the fact that human societies change their objectives over time so that there is a need to adapt management systems not only to deal with trade-offs between conflicting objectives but also to address the fact that the objectives may change over time. As a society grows richer it may attach more importance to forest recreation and less to non-timber forest products; it may favour climate change mitigation over timber harvests, etc. Criteria and indicators to assess these complex situations have to both measure outcomes and impacts and also measure the effectiveness of the governance regime in adapting management to deal with changing priorities. In the past, these challenges of assessment applied largely to discrete fixed-duration project interventions, but today a large proportion of the budgets of government forest management agencies, development banks, conservation NGOs and corporations managing estate crops are invested in landscape approaches. At present there are no agreed standards against which such investments can be audited (Sayer et al., 2016).

The adoption of the United Nations agenda 2030 and the Sustainable Development Goals in 2015 recognises the globally agreed need to pursue inclusive and sustainable development. The 17 SDGs cannot be seen in isolation – they interact and in some cases are complementary but in other cases they compete and trade-offs exist amongst them. The SDGs will have to be achieved in landscapes and forests will usually be part of those landscapes. We believe that the SDGs provide a useful conceptual framework against which to audit the performance of a landscape. Is that landscape delivering on the SDGs in an optimal way?

Forest certification as practised at present clearly does not meet the need of assessing the overall performance of a forest in meeting the needs of societies as expressed in the SDGs. Certification schemes such as those of the Forest Stewardship Council (FSC) and the Programme for the Harmonisation of Forest Certification (PEFC) do not attempt to assess effectiveness and cannot be a basis for audits. They are largely concerned with verifying compliance with laws and safeguards and avoiding adverse social and environmental impacts. They largely ignore economic performance of the forest landscape even though one might expect that governments and aid agencies might require evidence that economic benefits are achieved and that they are flowing to an appropriate mix of stakeholders and to the state. Certification assessment methodologies fail to address the issues of whether a given investment in integrated forest land management is yielding higher returns than alternative potential investments. Audits must address issues not only of performance but of efficiency. Audits must especially address the issue of equity in the distribution of costs and benefits.

The case of integrated forest management units in Indonesia

The government of Indonesia has committed to investing a large proportion of its forestry budget in integrated forest management units (KPH) which seek to optimise the contributions of the forests to Indonesian society and also to fulfil Indonesia's commitments under the United Nations Framework Convention on Climate Change and the Convention on the Conservation of Biodiversity. The KPH will need to be the key places where the SDGs are achieved in rural Indonesia. No auditing methods exist today that allow for assessment of management in achieving a satisfactory balance between all these potentially conflicting objectives. Very large amounts of money are being invested in KPH and other landscape schemes for which no satisfactory auditing methodology exists. We do not know if these ambitious approaches to integrate all dimensions of the management of forest landscapes are providing value for tax-payers' money.

The case of the forest management units in Indonesia illustrates the dilemma faced by auditing bodies. The official government criteria against which the KPH are to be assessed are:

1   Area stability – is the forest extent increasing or decreasing?
2   Forest use planning – does an agreed spatial plan exist?
3   Management plan – does a forest management plan exist?
4   Organisational capacity – is there institutional capacity to regulate forest activities?
5   Inter-strata relations within government and regulations – is competition between sectors and competing interests properly regulated?
6   Investment mechanism – is investment occurring and is it producing profits?
7   Availability of access and community rights – are land rights clear and subject to cadastral systems, especially for local and indigenous peoples?
8   Forestry dispute settlement mechanism – is there a functional mechanism for resolving disputes?

All of these except the first are process measures, only the first – area stability – is an outcome measure. Metrics upon which investments in the other seven criteria could be audited would be difficult to develop and no effort to do this has yet been attempted. None of the criteria are explicit about the benefits to society or the environment that the KPH will deliver. Will the KPH that cover 60% of rural Indonesia deliver on the SDGs? Similar issues of measurement of effectiveness exist in a number of countries where ambitious multi-objective management is being attempted. In Cameroon, Forest Management Units are the main objective of investments in sustainable forestry and conservation and they face the same problems of audit as the KPH in Indonesia.

National budgets in many countries lack methods to audit investments in multi-functional forest landscape initiatives. Aid agencies and international NGOs that support forest conservation and sustainable management programmes are faced with the same dilemma. Sayer et al. (2016) estimate that several billion dollars are invested each year in integrated landscape projects in tropical developing countries and that we have little ability to judge whether these investments are justified – or whether the same funds could be invested in different ways to achieve the same objectives. In Indonesia interventions labelled as landscape approaches are supported by the United States Agency for International Development, the World Bank, aid agencies of Germany, United Kingdom, Korea and international conservation NGOs such as World Wildlife Fund, Conservation International, the Nature Conservancy and Birdlife International. Several large corporations in the forestry sector are adopting landscape approaches to prove to their customers that their supply chains are socially and environmentally sustainable. These investments amount to tens of millions of dollars per year in Indonesia alone and at present are not subject to comprehensive performance audits. No one knows if they are achieving their objectives in a cost effective way and in many cases their objectives are stated in such general terms that any assessment of their impact is problematic. We have no way of knowing if these integrated approaches are contributing to the delivery of the SDGs.

Potential ways forward

Several studies have documented approaches to measuring the impact of integrated interventions (Sandker et al., 2009; Sandker et al., 2012; Endamana et al., 2010; Sayer et al., 2007b; Bossel et al., 2003). These studies have shown that comprehensive assessments of benefit delivery are difficult to achieve and maintain (Sayer et al., 2016). Assessment methods exist to measure environmental benefits but have proved difficult to apply to measuring social and economic development benefits. We are not aware of any integrated landscape or forest management initiatives that have succeeded in comprehensively measuring the sort of human development gains that the SDGs aspire to. The assessment systems in use can indicate whether funds were effectively spent on the objectives for which they were intended but they do not allow for auditing in the sense that the money spent was used as effectively as possible and that the objectives targeted were the appropriate ones. They tell us little about whether other ways of investing resources might have achieved the same objectives at lower cost. Terborgh (2004) and others have argued persuasively that "old fashioned" investments in guns and fences approaches to protected areas deliver more benefits than the modern generation of landscape and integrated approaches – at present there is no body of data against which this hypothesis can be tested. Assessment systems based upon criteria and indicators for outcomes tell us what was achieved but not whether the achievements were the best outcomes for the expenditure. They do not tell us whether the balance between the objectives of different stakeholders was appropriate.

The currently sector-based assessment systems seemed to have misled the public into underestimating the underlying conflicted interests among stakeholders. Different inspectorate generals under each ministry related to forestry sectors such as agriculture, mining and tourism, are responsible for auditing just their own ministerial goals. Likewise, Supreme Audit Institutions (SAI) the highest auditing bodies in a country are also required to conduct audits on particular issues or sectors rather than multi-sectoral benefit delivery (ISSAI, 2016b). Under these premises, the audit report of palm oil investments in a particular landscape might report a favourable financial gain whilst that of deforestation rate in the same area failed the environmental sustainability test. Likewise, in the private sector, the Rainforest Alliance (RA) concerned with the sustainability of rainforests, might give a different perspective on a landscape that has been certified satisfactorily by the Roundtable on Sustainable Palm Oil (RSPO). The Rainforest Alliance and the RSPO have divergent and contradictory interests in natural forest values. Even within the same sector, endorsement has different motivations. The Forest Stewardship Council (FSC), a council that brings together NGOs and forest industries, aims to broaden the scope of certification to include social and community aspects of sustainability (Kalonga et al., 2015; Newsom et al., 2006; Karmann et al., 2016). In contrast, internationally accredited certification by industries and/or landowners such as the Programme for the Endorsement of Forest Certification (PEFC) prioritises the financial aspects of sustainability and facilitates the agenda of businesses (Giessen et al., 2016; Overdevest, 2010; Burger and Zusammenarbeit, 2005; Atyi and Simula, 2002). Government-endorsed local certification, such as Lembaga Ecolabel Indonesia (LEI), assesses sustainability at the local level for the purpose of aligning practices more closely with government regulation (Chen et al., 2010, Gulbrandsen, 2005) but does not assess societal benefits.

Some authors in this book propose different approaches of measuring sustainability. Pintér et al. (Chapter 2) suggested newly improved Bellagio STAMP principles of assessing sustainability whilst Bell and Morse (Chapter 12) recommend participatory methods in generating indicators for such assessment. Likewise, Turcu (Chapter 10) introduces hybrid expert-citizen led methods for generating indicators. These suggestions support the importance of auditing as a mechanism in sustainability assessment.

We propose that one approach to a broad-based audit of the performance of a forest landscape should be based upon auditing forest landscape governance. Governance is the process by which societies organise themselves to take and implement decisions. If governance is effective and fair then the flow of benefits from the landscape might be expected to be optimal and to contribute to broad societal goals such as the SDGs. An audit would need to ensure that governance was effective in balancing the interests of multiple actors with different sectoral interests. Polycentric governance describes the situation where the decision-making of different bodies is aligned to achieve a balance that is acceptable to society. A polycentric governance system would ensure that objectives are achieved in ways which meet criteria of economic performance, efficiency and effectiveness (Ostrom, 1990; ISSAI, 2016b). Audit objectives are to assess whether or not the existing systems, operations, programmes, activities and organisations are *economically* optimising benefits whilst minimising resource consumption and cost. Effective polycentric governance should lead to the *efficient* generation of as many outputs as possible and *effectively* achieve sustainable impacts such as those expressed in the Sustainable Development Goals (SDG) (Hamilton-Hart, 2015; Elad, 2001; Ruysschaert and Salles, 2014).

Nevertheless, multi-sector landscape audits will still inevitably be massive in scale and complexity.

We argue that landscape auditing should utilise the existing audit activities by governance actors in each sector, as preliminary data for auditing a multi-sectoral landscape. We illustrate the challenges by exploring the case of Indonesia. Most business actors and governments already employ routine *internal auditing* and *inspections* as a mechanism to monitor their compliance during implementation of certain Standard Operating Procedures (SOPs) or regulations (Sharifi and Hussin, 2004). Examples are internal audits on Corporate Social Responsibility (CSR) for companies and forest monitoring by Forest Management Units (KPH) or by the Inspectorate General for public institutions. These business and government institutions most likely have implemented *external audits* by independent second party auditors, such as public accountants for the business sector and ministerial inspectorate generals (BPKP) in the public sector. This regular audit is designated to provide more independent recommendations about the company to their stakeholders — investors, suppliers, publics, creditors, debtors, or tax office — (Gray, 2000; Bommel et al., 2016; Power, 1997b; Ramanan, 2014; Andon et al., 2015). An example of an external audit is a sustainability audit by KPMG (a top-listed public accountant firm). Some companies and institutions may even go the extra mile by voluntarily opening their governance for public scrutiny as a means to assess the brand image and positioning. Companies or government institutions assign a *certification* body to give mandates to the nominated auditors to verify and certify outcomes. Examples of these certifications are FSC and RSPO (Elad, 2001; Perego and Kolk, 2012; Silva-Castañeda, 2012; Bommel et al., 2016; Nsenkyiere and Simula, 2000). A *landscape audit* would require these sporadic assessments to be integrated as components of auditing a multi-sectoral governance system in a landscape (Figure 27.1).

Supreme Audit Institutions (SAI) need to pioneer the auditing of multi-sector landscapes, regardless that their audit mechanisms are determined by the organisational relationships between the government institutions and SAI (Pollitt and Summa, 1997; Blume and Voigt, 2007; Pollitt and Summa, 1996). SAI in some countries is under the control of either the parliament or the country's leader having its audit mandate limited to responding to requests from either the head of state or the parliament (Asare, 2009; INTOSAI WGEA, 2013). By contrast, SAI in a decentralised government tends to have more authority and independence, having a comprehensive mandate to audit almost all public affairs, including the parliament and the head of state themselves (Pollitt and Summa, 1997; Azuma, 2003). While auditing mandates are relatively unchangeable, the audit mechanism should maintain the reliability of its reports through improving its audit designs. Despite its mandate limitation, SAIs are the only audit bodies in the current governance system that have the authority to conduct audits and reassess findings from each audit report by governance actors in different sectors.

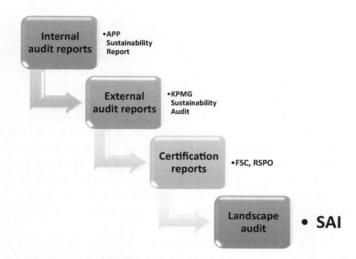

Figure 27.1 The multi-layered audit mechanism, in which reports from internal audits within the organisation, external audits by audit firms/institutions and certifications by third-party certification bodies are utilised to conduct landscape audits by Supreme Audit Institutions

Such an audit of sustainable performance of landscape governance would need to be conducted in four stages (ISSAI, 2016c). *Planning* is the most crucial step of the whole audit process. It is when the audit mechanism is designed and provides the framework to assess auditability. This is followed by *conducting* the audit designed in the planning phase. Any variation is subjected to amendment in the audit design matrix. *Reporting* communicates the results of the audit to the users. This requires translating the evidence into a standard user-friendly form, issuing the report and distributing it to the participating governance actors. A *follow-up* stage can allow for providing constructive feedback on audit reports and giving recommendations to improve the economic, efficiency and effectiveness of these services. Follow-up provides a mechanism to monitor improvement plans and to give suggestions on how recommendations can be operationalised. We only discuss the planning and conduct phase of a landscape audit, as those are the most critical.

Planning the landscape audit

Planning is the most important stage of the whole audit system. This early stage of auditing aims at establishing the overall approach for the performance audit. There are two stages: first selecting and focussing on what the topics and design will be, then identifying criteria for how to obtain data.

An Audit Design Matrix (ISSAI, 2016a) as in Figure 27.2 overarches the process of an audit. It starts with determining a broad audit objectives regarding economy, efficiency and effectiveness issues. This objective will be refined and specified into researchable audit questions. Once the questions are set, auditors established benchmarks as their audit criteria or indicators upon which the assessment will be carried out. After setting up the audit standards, appropriate audit techniques will be applied to gain audit evidence. Audit evidence is data and information that has been validated by auditors using audit methods. This evidence will need to be measured

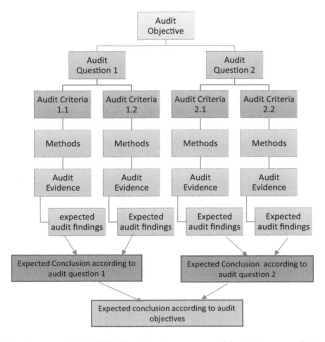

Figure 27.2 Audit Design Matrix (ISSAI) showing the process of designing an audit. It starts with determining audit objectives (economy/efficiency/effectiveness), then specifically formulates more detailed objectives into audit questions, establishing audit criteria or indicators upon which the assessment will be conducted. Methods are audit techniques to be applied in gaining audit evidence, upon which criteria will be measured. Audit findings are the gap between the expected criteria with audit evidence. Auditors then draw their professional conclusions as to whether the findings have answered the audit questions and met the audit objectives.

Source: http://pscintosai.org/data/files/5B/C5/A6/F5/3ABF6510C0EA0E65CA5818A8/issai_3200_psc.pdf

against the audit criteria. Audit findings are the gap between the expected criteria and the validated audit evidence. Auditors then draw their professional conclusion as to whether the findings have answered the audit questions and whether the audit objectives were satisfied.

Audit objectives: building a consensus on goals

A variety of participatory techniques have been widely used to engage stakeholders in the process of agreeing on landscape-level goals (Boedhihartono, 2012; Boedhihartono and Sayer, 2012). Rich pictures and drawings of landscape scenarios can be used to elicit the preferences of stakeholders on best-case and worst-case landscape outcomes. Experience with scenario drawing and rich pictures has shown that poor rural communities consistently indicate that jobs, access roads, schools and health care are their highest priority. Auditing approaches that fail to recognise this reality and focus exclusively on environmental safeguards are surely unacceptable – they can come to represent a tyranny of rich world stakeholders over very poor local people who are struggling to survive (Boedhihartono et al., 2015). See Figure 27.3.

Participatory building of simulation models to explore landscape functions has proven a valuable tool for building consensus on desirable change (Sandker et al., 2010; Collier et al., 2011).

Figure 27.3   Rich picture made by men and women group in SE Cameroon

Models can allow us to explore the relations between the different flows of benefits and can help identify interventions that will lead to desired outcomes. Models can also be used to support negotiations amongst stakeholders as they make assumptions explicit and can incorporate real quantitative data. However we have found limited use of models in less-developed countries where the issues of trade-offs are often most acute. Modelling skills are scarce and development practitioners have little faith in approaches that they perceive as academic. The conclusions of modelling exercises can be contested if they do not align with politically correct thinking on issues (Sayer et al., 2016). Sandker et al. (2007) used a model to argue that converting a small proportion of the landscape in Indonesian Kalimantan to oil palm could provide an effective way of improving local livelihoods whilst sparing forest land for conservation. The conclusions of this model were strongly contested by environmentalists who were ideologically opposed to oil palm expansion. Sayer et al. (2012b) also argued that oil palm is a desirable crop and less environmentally problematic than many alternatives but this analysis has failed to convince environmental ideologists. Sarkar et al. (2017) showed how these dilemmas might be resolved using multi-criteria analysis in a case study from Merauke, Indonesia where indicator sets were developed that could measure both environmental and development costs and benefits. Audit objectives therefore are to objectively assess which claims are valid, using indicators of economy, efficiency and effectiveness.

Audit criteria: indicators for auditing landscape-scale governance

Unfortunately, comprehensive indicator sets of this kind are not yet generally available or are not widely applied in developing countries. Audit systems such as those provided by the Forest Stewardship Council, the Programme for the Endorsement of Forest Certification and the Roundtable for Sustainable Palm Oil remain resolutely focussed on environmental and social safeguards (Dahl, Chapter 3, this volume). They largely ignore any social, economic or even environmental benefits that might flow from forestry or oil palm development activities (Rotz and Fraser, Chapter 6, this volume). This is clearly a very unsatisfactory state of affairs. It leads to a situation where an investment activity that yields significant economic benefits and generates employment opportunities for people may be restricted because it fails to meet criteria to safeguard environmental benefits that accrue to distant stakeholders in the rich world. Long-term global environmental benefits emerge as having more significance than short-term, local economic benefits – even in locations where local people live in extreme poverty.

The recent adoption of the Sustainable Development Goals (2015–2030) by the United Nations Security Council suggests options for broader ranging indicators that might be used to assess both safeguard measures and benefit flows in landscapes (Camacho, 2015). The SDGs have been endorsed by most governments and considerable investments have been made in identifying 169 indicators to assess progress in achieving the 17 goals. The SDGs and their indicators were intended to allow assessments at the level of nation states and to apply to all countries, rich and poor, but many countries are now applying the SDGs at a sub-national level. In most cases the sub-national application is at the level of provinces or districts and data is collected by local and national statistical offices. We argue that since the SDGs place heavy emphasis on alleviation of poverty, improvement of food security, improvements in education and health care and in greater equity in the distribution of benefits from economic growth, they should be a useful template for the development of indicator sets for integrated forest and landscape investments.

We find that the existing audit mechanisms have not yet included all these SDGs into their audit principles and criteria (Table 27.1). The 17 goals each have several targets designated to provide guidelines to countries wishing to embrace SDG principles in sustainable development (Nilsson et al., 2016). The UN recommended that such broad indicators be implemented into more detailed programmes or activities within a country (Nilsson et al., 2016). However, the practice of auditing the entire goals of 17 SDGs has not yet been implemented by governments or business entities. In the public sector, the International Organisation of Supreme Audit Institutions (INTOSAI) has recommended that each goal of the SDGs should be audited separately (ISSAI, 2016d; INTOSAI WGEA, 2013). In the business sector, internal/external audits and multi-sector certifications have only partially accommodated the SDGs into their auditing standards. Our reviews have shown that internal (*APP Sustainability Reports*) and external audits (KPMG), or certification (FSC for forestry sector and the Roundtable on Sustainable Palm Oil [RSPO for agriculture sector] have adopted some goals of SDG 15, Life on Land; SDG 11, Sustainable Cities and Communities and SDG 8, Decent Work/Economic Growth (Ruysschaert and Salles, 2014; United Nations, 2017; Asia Pulp and Paper, 2014; Roundtable on Sustainable Palm Oil, 2013; KPMG, 2015; Forest Stewardship Council, 2015). Yet, other goals requiring interactions with other actors and different sectors such as SDG 1, No Poverty; SDG 2, Zero Hunger; SDG 4, Quality Education; SDG 5, Gender Equality; SDG 7, Affordable and Clean Energy; SDG 10, Reduced Inequality; SDG 14, Life below Water; and SDG 17, Partnerships for the Goals are excluded (Flückiger and Seth, 2016; Colchester, 2016; Nilsson et al., 2016; Stewart, 2015).

Table 27.1a shows a detailed comparison of the inclusion of Sustainable Development Goal indicator numbers 1–9 in the auditing standards of Forest Stewardships Committee (FSC), the Roundtable for Sustainable Palm Oil (RSPO), Asia Pulp and Paper (APP) Sustainability Reports 2014, and an independent third-party audit firm KPMG. The shaded rows are the goals among goal numbers 1–9 not yet accommodated into those audit bodies under any other headings. Those are SDG 1 No Poverty; SDG 2 Zero Hunger; SDG 3 Good Health and Wellbeing, SDG 4 Quality Education; SDG 5 Gender Equality; SDG 7 Affordable and clean energy.

Table 27.1b shows a detailed comparison of the inclusion of Sustainable Development Goal indicators number 10–17 in the auditing standards of Forest Stewardships Committee (FSC), the Roundtable for Sustainable Palm Oil (RSPO), Asia Pulp and Paper (APP) Sustainability Reports 2014, and an independent third-party audit firm KPMG. The shaded rows are the goals among goals number 10–17 not yet accommodated into those audit bodies under any other headings. Those are SDG 10 Reduce inequalities; and SDG 17 Partnerships for the Goals.

Unclear definition and interconnectedness amongst SDG indicators may be the cause of such omission in real audit practices. Some terms such as "quality education", "modern energy" and "equal employment" are ambiguous, as different countries have different interpretations of what "equal/modern/quality" are. Some others such as "end poverty" and "zero hunger" are not specific and relate to almost all other goals (Camacho, 2015). The absence of integration between sustainability and economic goals has left the SDG indicators unhelpful as audit criteria (Stewart, 2015). To be able to serve as criteria, indicators need to be relevant to the audit topic, understandable and unambiguous, objective and testable. They must be able to be verified through a series of audit tests (ISSAI, 2016a). An audit design matrix needs to be developed by the multi-party audit network to enable synthesising the SDG general indicators into landscape perspective (Dutra, 2016).

Conducting landscape audits: audit methods and evidence

Multi-sector auditing relies on reliable audit evidence. Audit reports from internal, external and third-party certifications need to be validated, synchronised and reanalysed, to qualify as reliable audit evidence (ISSAI, 2016b). Audit mechanisms established the techniques and methods used by auditors to verify and test the data (Mautz and Sharaf, 1961; Power, 1997a). These validated data are usually obtained in four types of evidence (ISSAI, 2016a):

1   *Documentary evidence* is obtained through both official and non-official documents such as online materials. Any documentary data needs to be corroborated to assure its validity

Table 27.1a Adoption of SDGs into Sustainability Auditing Standard Practice, numbers 1–9

No	UN Sustainable Development Goals	Inclusion in existing audits			
		Certification (FSC)	Certification (RSPO)	Internal Audit (APP)	External Audit (KPMG)
1	No Poverty				
2	Zero Hunger				
3	Good Health and Wellbeing				
4	Quality Education				
5	Gender Equality				
6	Clean Water and Sanitation				
	By 2030, implement integrated water resources management at all levels, including through transboundary cooperation as appropriate		Integrated Waste Management		
	By 2020, protect and restore water-related ecosystems, including mountains, forests, wetlands, rivers, aquifers and lakes		Water Conservation		
	By 2030, improve water quality by reducing pollution, eliminating dumping and minimising release of hazardous chemicals and materials, halving the proportion of untreated wastewater and substantially increasing recycling and safe reuse globally			improve management of water used	
7	Affordable and Clean Energy				
8	Decent Work and Economic Growth				
	By 2030, achieve full and productive employment and decent work for all women and men, including for young people and persons with disabilities, and equal pay for work of equal value	Workers' Rights and Employment Conditions	Fair Treatment Working Condition for Workers		

Note: The shaded rows are the goals among goal numbers 1–9 not yet accommodated into those audit bodies under any other headings.

(Continued)

Table 27.1a (Continued)

No	UN Sustainable Development Goals	Inclusion in existing audits				
		Certification (FSC)	Certification (RSPO)	Internal Audit (APP)	External Audit (KPMG)	
	Protect labour rights and promote safe and secure working environments for all workers, including migrant workers, in particular women migrants, and those in precarious employment		Occupational Health and Safety	Zero fatalities for workers and contractors	Responsible Practices in Our Work Places	
	Take immediate and effective measures to eradicate forced labour, end modern slavery and human trafficking and secure the prohibition and elimination of the worst forms of child labour, including recruitment and use of child soldiers, and by 2025 end child labour in all its forms					
	Sustain per capita economic growth in accordance with national circumstances and, in particular, at least 7% gross domestic product growth per annum in the least developed countries					
9	Industry, Innovation and Infrastructure					
	By 2030, upgrade infrastructure and retrofit industries to make them sustainable, with increased resource-use efficiency and greater adoption of clean and environmentally sound technologies and industrial processes, with all countries taking action in accordance with their respective capabilities				Long-Term Sustainability	

Note: The shaded rows are the goals among goal numbers 1–9 not yet accommodated into those audit bodies under any other headings.

Table 27.1b Adoption of SDGs into Sustainability Auditing Standard Practice, numbers 10–17

No	UN Sustainable Development Goals	Inclusion in existing audits			
		Certification (FSC)	Certification (RSPO)	Internal audit (APP)	External audit (KPMG)
10	Reduced Inequalities				
11	Sustainable Cities and Communities				
	Support positive economic, social and environmental links between urban, peri-urban and rural areas by strengthening national and regional development planning	Community relations			
	By 2030, enhance inclusive and sustainable urbanisation and capacity for participatory, integrated and sustainable human settlement planning and management in all countries		Community Relations		Proactive support of local communities
	Strengthen efforts to protect and safeguard the world's cultural and natural heritage				Respect the Rights of Indigenous Peoples and Communities
12	Responsible Consumption and Production				
	By 2020, achieve the environmentally sound management of chemicals and all wastes throughout their life cycle, in accordance with agreed international frameworks, and significantly reduce their release to air, water and soil in order to minimise their adverse impacts on human health and the environment	Management Planning	Soil Management and Conservation	Controlled Emission	

(Continued)

Table 27.1b (Continued)

No	UN Sustainable Development Goals	Inclusion in existing audits			
		Certification (FSC)	Certification (RSPO)	Internal audit (APP)	External audit (KPMG)
	By 2030, achieve the sustainable management and efficient use of natural resources	Monitoring and assessment	Integrated Crop Management		
13	Climate Action				
	Strengthen resilience and adaptive capacity to climate-related hazards and natural disasters in all countries				Peatland management
	Integrate climate change measures into national policies, strategies and planning	Management Planning			Continuous reduction of carbon Footprint
14	Life Below Water				
	14.1 By 2025, prevent and significantly reduce marine pollution of all kinds, in particular from land-based activities, including marine debris and nutrient pollution			Wastewater Management	
15	Life on Land				
	15.2 By 2020, promote the implementation of sustainable management of all types of forests, halt deforestation, restore degraded forests and substantially increase afforestation and reforestation globally	Benefits from the forest	Social and Environmental Management System		
	Take urgent and significant action to reduce the degradation of natural habitats, halt the loss of biodiversity and, by 2020, protect and prevent the extinction of threatened species	High conservation value	Wildlife Protection	Preserved protection areas and the population of endangered species	

Goal	Target	Environmental values and impacts	Ecosystem Conservation	Conservation and biodiversity	Forest Protection and Conservation
	By 2020, ensure the conservation, restoration and sustainable use of terrestrial and inland freshwater ecosystems and their services, in particular forests, wetlands, mountains and drylands, in line with obligations under international agreements				
	15.a Mobilise and significantly increase financial resources from all sources to conserve and sustainably use biodiversity and ecosystems				
	15.c Enhance global support for efforts to combat poaching and trafficking of protected species, including by increasing the capacity of local communities to pursue sustainable livelihood opportunities	Implementation of management activities; Indigenous peoples' rights			
16 Peace, Justice, and Strong Institutions	16.7 Ensure responsive, inclusive, participatory and representative decision-making at all levels			Conflict resolution procedures	
	Develop effective, accountable and transparent institutions at all levels				
	Promote the rule of law at the national and international levels and ensure equal access to justice for all	Compliance with Laws			
17 Partnership for the Goals					Good Corporate Governance, Verification and Transparency; Legal Compliance and Certification

Note: The grey lines are the goals among goals number 10–17 not yet accommodated into those audit bodies under any other headings.

and reliability. Corroboration comes from cross-checking with other documents, physical examination or observation, statements by non-biased actors or analytical evidence.

2   *Physical examination* includes on-site observations. Likewise, any physical evidence must be corroborated with either documents, additional physical examinations, statements or analytical evidence, to assure its validity and reliability.

3   *Testimonial evidence* are the statements obtained from interviews surveys, questionnaires, focus group discussions and reference groups. Interviews are needed to understand perceptions and to confirm other sources of evidence, or to obtain preliminary understanding of issues which then need to be examined through other evidence sources.

4   *Analytical evidence* is obtained from analysing the relationships of data and inferencing new analytical information. This evidence will utilise software programmes to conduct analyses such as Gephi, for simple social network analysis, nViVo for more complex data analysis. These software programmes will minimise subjectivity and improve the validity of the evidence produced.

In auditing the goals of the SDGs additional data and information need to be obtained from all relevant governance actors. Governance in a landscape is inevitably polycentric with multiple actors – government agencies, companies, local communities and NGOs – operating at multiple levels –– district, national and international – from different sectors – agriculture, forestry, mining, infrastructure – all interacting with each other (Nagendra and Ostrom, 2012). Understanding the networks and thus the persons behind each role will make the process of corroborating data and information less challenging.

We argue that the governance audit mechanism can assess whether the outcome of a landscape-scale intervention is meeting the requirements of the people who are impacted by its outcomes – the stakeholders. We advocate the use of a variety of participatory techniques both in establishing the goals of the intervention and in allowing for stakeholders themselves to contribute to auditing the outcomes. We recognise that reaching agreement amongst all stakeholders on the desirable future of a landscape is likely to be a difficult task. Landscape-scale interventions are often adopted precisely because there is conflict over objectives or competing claims on land. One of the process indicators of the Indonesian KPH scheme is the extent to which conflicts are resolved. Balint et al. (2011) have argued that stakeholder views in landscape projects in the US forests are often so polarised that reaching unanimous agreement on outcomes is impossible – he argues that the problems are "wicked" and not amenable to resolution by consensus. We have argued elsewhere (Sayer et al., 2008) that forest landscape futures cannot be subject to conventional spatial planning but rather require a process of muddling through – a process of continuous adjustment, adaptation and learning. Conclusions such as these are problematic for a financial auditor – to what extent can the very large sums of money involved be justified? Can decisions be left to the discretion of the local forest administrator? How can one ensure that best practice is being respected and that funds are being used in the best interests of society?

The landscape governance mapping – and auditing – will provide more realistic argumentation on reaching agreeable objectives and later criteria. In economic audits, for example, the ultimate limitation is cheaper prices, or lower expenses, or more revenues. In efficiency audits, the goal is to produce more outputs, and in audits of effectiveness, the target is to create sustainable outcomes. Any activity by one actor needs to contribute to at least one of these three objectives. How can and will each governance actor's decision-making impact others in the same interrelated landscape? Thus, a KPH (Forest Management Unit) needs to establish its roles as an intermediary in determining mutually agreed objectives and criteria.

Conclusions

The Sustainable Development Goals can inspire generic principles for auditing complex forest landscapes. The SDGs provide a useful normative statement of the issues that a comprehensive auditing process would need to embrace. However, the indicators will vary depending on the context of each landscape. As countries develop and their societies evolve the choice of indicators will change. The FSC and PEFC have global indicators which can be applied anywhere but even these have to be adapted or nuanced depending on the conditions of the target country. The RSPO recognises more explicitly the divergences in conditions in countries and delegates make final determination of indicators at the country level. International auditing bodies such as KPMG develop indicators to address the needs of their clients. The indicators of a KPMG audit of a large forest landscape in Indonesian Sumatra were developed in consultation with a stakeholder advisory body established by the company. The indicators were inspired by the SDGs but reflected the feedback that the company and its advisory committee was receiving from local stakeholders and international activists.

Several commercial and non-governmental certification and auditing bodies are now developing assessment frameworks for large multi-functional forest landscapes. The Supreme Audit Agency in Indonesia is developing audit procedures to enable comprehensive performance audits of complex development initiatives – with a strong focus on sustainability. Sayer et al. (2016) have argued that there must be a hierarchy of steps in these auditing processes. First there must be an audit of the process by which landscape-scale decisions are made. The process audit requires that inventories of resources are compiled, stakeholder engagement is effective and equitable, scenarios are explored and long-term goals for the landscape are agreed. Since agreement may be difficult to achieve, processes must be in place to resolve conflicts. The process metrics must be subject to effective governance and normally a governmental institution will have to be the final arbiter. We therefore concur with Balint (Balint et al., 2011) that simple facilitation of a multi-stakeholder process will probably not be enough. In any situation there will inevitably be conflicting interests and legitimate differences in perspectives amongst local and more distant actors. In the complex situations of large forest industry companies in Indonesia these divergences are manifest. The companies want to make a profit, government wants to receive taxes, local people want jobs and social infrastructure and international activists want to conserve biodiversity and maximise carbon in the landscape as a climate change mitigation measure. There is no single right answer to where the balance between all of these claims lies.

The role of criteria and indicator processes in these complex and contested situations is perhaps more to allow a structuring of the debate than to provide a set of boxes to be ticked. Auditors and assessors have to ensure that the interests of all stakeholders have been taken into account. They have to ensure that laws are obeyed and procedures followed. The main benefit of an assessment process in the Sangha Tri National Landscape in Cameroon, Central African Republic and Congo was to open up a debate about the full range of options that existed for the landscape and enable a debate about the benefits to all stakeholders of different courses of action (Endamana et al., 2010; Sayer et al., 2016). A review of the lessons learnt from a decade of tracking change in that landscape showed that external macro-economic forces had more influence on local peoples' livelihoods and on the environment than direct interventions within the landscape (Sayer et al., 2012a). Ultimately the existence of democratic governance and competent institutions are essential prerequisites for success. Debates around desired scenarios and the criteria and indicators that would inform debate about progress in achieving these scenarios may be a fundamental contribution to the emergence of good governance and better institutions.

References

Andon, P., Free, C. & O'Dwyer, B. 2015. Annexing new audit spaces: Challenges and adaptations. *Accounting, Auditing & Accountability Journal*, 28, 1400–1430.

Asare, T., 2009. Internal auditing in the public sector: Promoting good governance and performance improvement. *International Journal on Governmental Financial Management*, 9(1), 15–28.

Asia Pulp and Paper. 2014. *APP sustainability reports*. Available: www.asiapulppaper.com/system/files/app_sustainability_report_2014.pdf

Atyi, R. E. A. & Simula, M. 2002. *Forest certification: Pending challenges for tropical timber*, (No. 19). Yokohama, Japan: International Tropical Timber Organization.

Azuma, Nobuo. 2003. The role of the supreme audit institution in NPM: International trend. *Government Auditing Review*, 10(1), 85–106.

Balint, P. J., Stewart, R. E., Desai, A. & Walters, L. C. 2011. *Wicked environmental problems: Managing uncertainty and conflict*, Washington, Island Press.

Boedhihartono, A. K. 2012. *Visualizing sustainable landscapes: Understanding and negotiating conservation and development trade-offs using visual techniques*, Gland, Switzerland, InUCN.

Boedhihartono, A. K., Endamana, D., Ruiz-Perez, M. & Sayer, J. 2015. Landscape scenarios visualized by Baka and Aka Pygmies in the Congo Basin. *International Journal of Sustainable Development & World Ecology*, 22, 279–291.

Boedhihartono, A. K. & Sayer, J. 2012. Forest landscape restoration: Restoring what and for whom? *Forest Landscape Restoration*, Dordrecht, Springer.

Blume, L. and Voigt, S., 2007. Supreme Audit Institutions: Supremely Superfluous? A Cross Country Assessment. ICER-International Centre for Economic Research.

Bommel, V. S., Turnhout, E. & Cook, W. C. 2016. Inside environmental auditing: Effectiveness, objectivity, and transparency. *Current Opinion in Environmental Sustainability*, 18, 33–39.

Bossel, H., Campbell, B. M. & Sayer, J. A. 2003. Assessing viability and sustainability: A systems-based approach for deriving comprehensive indicator sets. *Conservation Ecology*, 5(2), 33–63.

Burger, D. & Zusammenarbeit, D. G. F. T. 2005. *Forest Certification: An innovative instrument in the service of sustainable development?*, Eschborn, Deutsche Gesellschaft für Technische Zusammenarbeit.

Camacho, L. 2015. Sustainable development goals: Kinds, connections and expectations. *Journal of Global Ethics*, 11, 18–23.

Chen, J., Innes, J. L. & Tikina, A. 2010. Private Cost-benefits of voluntary forest product certification. *International Forestry Review*, 12, 1–12.

Colchester, M. 2016. Do commodity certification systems uphold indigenous peoples' rights? Lessons from the Roundtable on Sustainable Palm Oil and Forest Stewardship Council. *Policy Matters*. Available: www.researchgate.net/profile/Denis_Ruysschaert/publication/308008089_The_impact_of_global_palm_oil_certification_on_transnational_governance_human_livelihoods_and_biodiversity_conservation/links/57d6988708ae0c0081ea3f5c.pdf#page=151

Collier, N., Campbell, B. M., Sandker, M., Garnett, S. T., Sayer, J. & Boedhihartono, A. K. 2011. Science for action: The use of scoping models in conservation and development. *Environmental Science & Policy*, 14, 628–638.

Dutra, P. H. 2016. SDGs audit results framework. *International Journal of Government Auditing*, 43, 12.

Elad, C. 2001. Auditing and governance in the forestry industry: Between protest and professionalism. *Critical Perspectives on Accounting*, 12, 647–671.

Endamana, D., Boedhihartono, A., Bokoto, B., Defo, L., Eyebe, A., Ndikumagenge, C., Nzooh, Z., Ruiz-Perez, M. & Sayer, J. 2010. A framework for assessing conservation and development in a Congo Basin Forest Landscape. *Tropical Conservation Science*, 3, 262–281.

Flückiger, Y. & Seth, N. 2016. Sustainable development goals: SDG indicators need crowdsourcing. *Nature*, 531, 448.

Forest Stewardship Council. 2015. *FSC International Standards: FC principles and criteria for forest stewardship*. Available: https://ic.fsc.org/en/what-is-fsc-certification/principles-criteria

Giessen, L., Burns, S., Sahide, M. A. K. & Wibowo, A. 2016. From governance to government: The strengthened role of state bureaucracies in forest and agricultural certification. *Policy and Society*, 35, 71–89.

Gray, R. 2000. Current developments and trends in social and environmental auditing, reporting and attestation: A review and comment. *International Journal of Auditing*, 4, 247–268.

Gulbrandsen, L H. 2005. The effectiveness of non-state governance schemes: A comparative study of forest certification in Norway and Sweden. *International Environmental Agreements: Politics, Law and Economics*, 5(2), 125–149. doi:10.1007/s10784-004-1010-1019.

Hamilton-Hart, N. 2015. Multilevel (mis)governance of palm oil production. *Australian Journal of International Affairs*, 69, 164–184.

INTOSAI WGEA. 2013. *Sustainability reporting: Concepts, frameworks and the role of Supreme Audit Institutions*, Copenhagen, INTOSAI.

ISSAI. 2016a. *Guidelines for performance auditing process (No. 3200)*, Copenhagen, INTOSAI.

ISSAI. 2016b. *Guidelines on central concepts for performance auditing (No. 3100)*, Copenhagen, INTOSAI.

ISSAI. 2016c. *Standard for Performance Auditing (No. 3000)*, Copenhagen, INTOSAI.

ISSAI. 2016d. *Sustainable development: The role of Supreme Audit Institutions (No. 5130)*, Copenhagen, INTOSAI.

Kalonga, S. K., Midtgaard, F. & Eid, T. 2015. Does forest certification enhance forest structure? Empirical evidence from certified community-based forest management in Kilwa District, Tanzania. *International Forestry Review*, 17, 182–194.

Karmann, M., Miettinen, P. & Hontelez, J. 2016. Forest stewardship council indicators: Development by multi-stakeholder process assures consistency and diversity. *Policy Matters*. Available: https://portals.iucn.org/library/sites/library/files/documents/Policy%20Matters%20-%20Issue%2021.pdf#page=126

KPMG. 2015. *KPMG sustainability reporting*. Available: www.google.com.au/url?sa=t&rct=j&q=&esrc=s&source=web&cd=2&cad=rja&uact=8&ved=0ahUKEwimhuXCs9XUAhWMmJQKHSvDAhwQFggtMAE&url=https%3A%2F%2Fassets.kpmg.com%2Fcontent%2Fdam%2Fkpmg%2Fae%2Fpdf%2Fsustainability_report_digital.pdf&usg=AFQjCNFxMABnfvzB6zFL0r6KTerFf48fUA

Mautz, R. K. & Sharaf, H. A. 1961. *The philosophy of auditing.* American Accounting Association. Monograph No. 6. Sarasota, FL: American Accounting Association, Minnesota.

McShane, T. O., Hirsch, P. D., Trung, T. C., Songorwa, A. N., Kinzig, A., Monteferri, B., Mutekanga, D., Thang, H. V., Dammert, J. L., Pulgar-Vidal, M., Welch-Devine, M., Brosius, J. P., Coppolillo, P. & O'Connor, S. 2011. Hard choices: Making trade-offs between biodiversity conservation and human well-being. *Biological Conservation*, 144, 966–972.

McShane, T. O. & Newby, S. A. 2004. Expecting the unattainable: The assumptions behind ICDPs. *In:* McShane, T. O. & Wells, M. P. (eds.) *Getting biodiversity projects to work: Towards more effective conservation and development*, New York, Columbia University Press.

Nagendra, H. & Ostrom, E. 2012. Polycentric governance of multifunctional forested landscapes. *International Journal of the Commons*, 6(2), 104–133.

Newsom, D., Bahn, V. & Cashore, B. 2006. Does forest certification matter? An analysis of operation-level changes required during the SmartWood certification process in the United States. *Forest Policy and Economics*, 9, 197–208.

Nilsson, M., Griggs, D. & Visbeck, M. 2016. Map the interactions between sustainable development goals. *Nature*, 534, 320–322.

Nsenkyiere, E. & Simula, M. 2000. *Comparative study on the auditing systems of sustainable forest management.* Yokohama, Japan, International Tropical Timber Organization.

Ostrom, E. 1990. *Governing the commons: The evolution of institutions for collective action*, Cambridge, Cambridge University Press.

Overdevest, C. 2010. Comparing forest certification schemes: The case of ratcheting standards in the forest sector. *Socio-Economic Review*, 8, 47–76.

Perego, P. & Kolk, A. 2012. Multinationals' accountability on sustainability: The evolution of third-party assurance of sustainability reports. *Journal of Business Ethics*, 110, 173–190.

Pollitt, C. and Summa, H., 1996. Performance audit and evaluation: Similar tools, different relationships?, *New Directions for Evaluation*, 1996(71), 29–50.

Pollitt, C. and Summa, H., 1997. Reflexive watchdogs? How supreme audit institutions account for themselves. *Public Administration*, 75(2), 313–336.

Power, M. 1997a. *The audit society: Rituals of verification*, New York, Oxford University Press.

Power, M. 1997b. Expertise and the construction of relevance: Accountants and environmental audit. *Accounting, Organizations and Society*, 22, 123–146.

Ramanan, R. N. V. 2014. Corporate governance, auditing, and reporting distortions. *Journal of Accounting, Auditing & Finance*, 29, 306–339.

Reed, J., Van Vianen, J., Deakin, E. L., Barlow, J. & Sunderland, T. 2016. Integrated landscape approaches to managing social and environmental issues in the tropics: Learning from the past to guide the future. *Global Change Biology*, 22, 2540–2554.

Roundtable on Sustainable Palm Oil. 2013. *Principles and criteria for the production of sustainable palm oil.* Available: www.rspo.org/publications/download/224fa0187afb4b7

Ruysschaert, D. & Salles, D. 2014. Towards global voluntary standards: Questioning the effectiveness in attaining conservation goals: The case of the Roundtable on Sustainable Palm Oil (RSPO). *Ecological Economics*, 107, 438–446.

Sandker, M., Campbell, B. M., Nzooh, Z., Sunderland, T., Amougou, V., Defo, L. & Sayer, J. 2009. Exploring the effectiveness of integrated conservation and development interventions in a Central African forest landscape. *Biodiversity and Conservation*, 18, 2875–2892.

Sandker, M., Campbell, B. M., Ruiz-Perez, M., Sayer, J. A., Cowling, R., Kassa, H. & Knight, A. T. 2010. The role of participatory modelling in landscape approaches to reconcile conservation and development. *Ecology and Society*, 15(2), 13 [online] URL: http://www.ecologyandsociety.org/vol15/iss2/art13

Sandker, M., Ruiz-Perez, M. & Campbell, B. M. 2012. Trade-offs between biodiversity conservation and economic development in five tropical forest landscapes. *Environmental Management*, 50, 633–644.

Sandker, M., Suwarno, A. & Campbell, B. M. 2007. Will forests remain in the face of oil palm expansion? Simulating change in Malinau, Indonesia. *Ecology & Society*, 12(2), 37.

Sarkar, S., Dyer, J.S., Margules, C., Ciarleglio, M., Kemp, N., Wong, G., Juhn, D. and Supriatna, J., 2017. Developing an objectives hierarchy for multicriteria decisions on land use options, with a case study of biodiversity conservation and forestry production from Papua, Indonesia. *Environment and Planning B: Urban Analytics and City Science*, 44(3), 464–485.

Sayer, J., Bull, G. & Elliott, C. 2008. Mediating forest transitions: 'Grand design' or 'Muddling through'. *Conservation and Society*, 6, 320.

Sayer, J. & Campbell, B. 2005. *The science of sustainable development: Local livelihoods and the global environment*, Cambridge, UK, Cambridge University Press.

Sayer, J., Campbell, B., Petheram, L., Aldrich, M., Perez, M. R., Endamana, D., Dongmo, Z. L. N., Defo, L., Mariki, S. & Doggart, N. 2007. Assessing environment and development outcomes in conservation landscapes. *Biodiversity and Conservation*, 16, 2677–2694.

Sayer, J., Endamana, D., Boedhihartono, A., Ruiz Pérez, M. & Breuer, T. 2016. Learning from change in the Sangha Tri-national landscape. *International Forestry Review Special Issue: Valuing the Cameroonian Forest*, 18(S1), 139–139.

Sayer, J., Endamana, D., Ruiz-Perez, M., Boedhihartono, A., Nzooh, Z., Eyebe, A., Awono, A. & Usongo, L. 2012a. Global financial crisis impacts forest conservation in Cameroon. *International Forestry Review*, 14, 90–98.

Sayer, J., Ghazoul, J., Nelson, P. & Boedhihartono, A. K. 2012b. Oil palm expansion transforms tropical landscapes and livelihoods. *Global Food Security*, 1(2), 114–119.

Sayer, J., Sunderland, T., Ghazoul, J., Pfund, J.-L., Sheil, D., Meijaard, E., Venter, M., Boedhihartono, A. K., Day, M. & Garcia, C. 2013. Ten principles for a landscape approach to reconciling agriculture, conservation, and other competing land uses. *Proceedings of the National Academy of Sciences*, 110, 8349–8356.

Sayer, J. A., Maginnis, S. & Laurie, M. 2007. *Forests in landscapes: Ecosystem approaches to sustainability*, New York, Earthscan.

Sayer, J. A., Margules, C., Boedhihartono, A. K., Sunderland, T., Langston, J. D., Reed, J., Riggs, R., Buck, L. E., Campbell, B. M. & Kusters, K. 2016. Measuring the effectiveness of landscape approaches to conservation and development. *Sustainability Science*, 12(3), 465–476.

Sharifi, M. A. & Hussin, Y. 2004. Development of effective information systems supporting monitoring and certification process of production forest in Indonesia: Concept and progress. *International Archives of the Photogrammetry, Remote Sensing and Spatial Information Sciences – ISPRS Archives*, 35, 347–351.

Silva-Castañeda, L. 2012. A forest of evidence: Third-party certification and multiple forms of proof – a case study of oil palm plantations in Indonesia. *Agriculture and Human Values*, 29, 361–370.

Stewart, F. 2015. The sustainable development goals: A comment. *Journal of Global Ethics*, 11, 288–293.

Terborgh, J. 2004. *Requiem for nature*, Washington, Island Press.

United Nations. 2017. *Revised list of global sustainable development goal indicators*. Available: https://unstats.un.org/sdgs/indicators/indicators-list

28

THE DEVIL IS IN THE DETAIL!

Sustainability assessment of African smallholder farming

Wytze Marinus, Esther Ronner, Gerrie W. J. van de Ven,
Fred Kanampiu, Samuel Adjei-Nsiah, and Ken E. Giller

1. Introduction

Indicators for sustainability of agricultural systems are a topical and widely debated issue. The Sustainable Development Goals (SDGs) have 230 indicators for sustainability, of which only 21 can be directly linked to agriculture (United Nations – Economic and Social Council 2016). The indicator 'proportion of agricultural area under productive and sustainable agriculture' (SDG 2, indicator 2.4.1, United Nations – Economic and Social Council 2016), directly raises the question as to the meaning of 'productive and sustainable agriculture'. To meet SDG2 – Zero Hunger and Sustainable Food Systems – agricultural productivity must increase substantially, particularly in sub-Saharan Africa (SSA), to keep pace with the burgeoning population (Van Ittersum *et al.* 2016). The sustainable intensification of agriculture is seen as a key pathway to meet these future food demands (e.g. Tilman *et al.* 2011; SDSN 2013; The Montpellier Panel 2013). Sustainable intensification aims at producing more food with a more efficient use of all inputs in the long term, while reducing environmental damage and building resilience, natural capital, and the flow of environmental services (The Montpellier Panel 2013). The debate on what comprises sustainable intensification (Garnett *et al.* 2013; Kuyper and Struik 2014; Rockström *et al.* 2016), is often based on implicit assumptions, values, and norms. Making them explicit would help to structure the discussion on the type of agricultural systems we want and need to feed future generations (Struik *et al.* 2014). So how can we measure progress towards achieving SDG2? What indicators are required to monitor whether the intensification of agriculture is achieved while achieving social and economic goals and without compromising the environment?

As part of a wider effort to document, evaluate, and compare different pathways for sustainable intensification (the PROIntensAfrica Project – see www.IntensAfrica.org), we conducted a case study on the role of grain legumes in sustainable intensification in contrasting farming systems (Part 2). Grain legumes are seen as an important vehicle towards sustainable intensification in SSA (Vanlauwe *et al.* 2014). Legumes fix nitrogen (N_2) from the air, they provide nutritious grain, which often has a high market value; they contribute additional N to the soil and enhance soil fertility in the long term (Giller *et al.* 2013).

We developed an indicator framework to assess the influence of legumes on different aspects of sustainability with an 'amoeba' or spider web diagram. In this chapter, we highlight the steps taken and the struggles we faced in developing and applying the indicator framework. In Part 3 we describe the steps we took to develop the framework. In Part 4 we interpret the outcomes, assessing the variability in results at different levels (field, farm household, community). The questions raised during development of the indicator framework are summarized as the main outcome in Box 28.1. In short, we illustrate that the many steps taken in the development of an indicator framework are subjective and results of indicator frameworks for sustainability can only be meaningful if all steps and the underlying assumptions and decisions are made transparent (Box 28.1). The chapter as a whole can serve as a guide for those who wish to conduct a sustainability assessment, and to guide critical assessment of frameworks for assessing sustainability.

2. A case study in sustainable intensification: the N2Africa project

We evaluated the sustainability of farms containing grain legumes in western Kenya and northern Ghana, two action sites of the N2Africa project. N2Africa is a large-scale, science-based 'research-in-development' project focused on 'Putting nitrogen fixation to work for smallholder farmers growing legume crops in Africa' (www.N2Africa.org). Western Kenya and northern Ghana were selected from the 11 countries where N2Africa is active, as they present contrasting agro-ecological and socio-economic conditions. Diversity in population density, market access, and agro-ecological condition are the main drivers influencing agricultural development (Pender *et al.* 1999), and we used these as selection criteria for the study locations within each region (Table 28.1). The research sites together showed a wide range of population densities (56–1200 inhabitants per km²), market access (0.5–5.0 hours),

Table 28.1 General characteristics of the selected N2Africa action sites

	Northern Ghana		Western Kenya	
	Bawku West	*Savelugu*	*Vihiga*	*Migori*
Population density (inhabitants per km²)	56–103	61–70	1200	300
Access to urban markets (h)	1–3	0.5	0.5	5
Rainfall pattern	Uni-modal	Uni-modal	Bi-modal	Bi-modal
Annual rainfall (mm)	700–1100	800–1200	1800	1360
Important legumes	Soyabean, cowpea, groundnut	Soyabean, cowpea, groundnut	Bush bean	Bush bean, groundnut, soyabean

Source: Franke *et al.* (2011)

and agro-ecological conditions (uni-modal and bi-modal rainfall patterns and mean annual rainfall of 900–1800 mm). In the remainder of this chapter we refer to western Kenya and northern Ghana as case study countries and use the sub-location or county to refer to the case study communities within the countries. Surveys were done during the dry season in December 2015 and early May 2016 in northern Ghana and in March 2016 in Kenya.

3. Developing an indicator framework

In this section we describe the steps we took in developing an indicator framework for sustainability. These steps comprise the questions we encountered on our journey (Box 28.1). The questions are referred to by their number in Box 28.1, i.e. #2 for question 2.

Box 28.1 Important questions that must be addressed when developing a framework for indicators for sustainability

This is a list of questions and hurdles we encountered when developing our framework for indicators to assess sustainability of smallholder African farms at household level. We aimed to be open about where we made which decisions and what the reasoning was by listing the questions and addressing them in the different sections of this book chapter. The questions below can guide critical assessment of the decisions made in developing a framework for analysing sustainability.

Although the numbering of the questions below partly represents the order in which they were addressed, some questions were asked several times in an iterative cycle to arrive at the final indicator framework (possible links between questions are indicated in parentheses). The numbering below is also used in the text to indicate where questions were addressed.

#1 Which indicators to select? Using a participatory method or other framework for selection (i.e. principles, criteria, and indicators)? Why should some indicators be included and others not?

#2 How to make explicit why certain decisions (i.e. answering the questions in this box while reporting on your study) were made and how they influence the results?

#3 What is your research object and what should be compared in your indicator study? i.e. Are these households within the same farming system? Or, should households be compared across farming systems or even countries? (this may influence #1)

#4 At what level should the indicators be assessed and, if this is not at the same level as the other indicators or at the level that you want to present your results, how is this then aggregated to the same level, i.e. different fields to farm level? (this may influence #3)

#5 If, for instance, results of different countries are compared, how are results aggregated from household to country level? How is variation between households shown and what is the importance of this variation?

#6 Are all indicators equally important for sustainability when creating a composite indicator for a higher level, i.e. principles? Or should there be a different weight for each indicator? What process should be used for determining the weights? Who decides? How does weighting of the indicators influence the outcome at the level of principles?

#7 What does a score of 0 mean, and a score of 10 (assuming 0 is the lowest possible score in the framework and 10 the highest)? Is 10 acceptable or the maximum? And if it is the maximum, is it relative to the sample, or some other maximum? (this may depend on #3)

#8 What is your sampling strategy (i.e. a random sample, or the extremes for a proof of concept) and how large should the sample size be? (this may depend on #3 and #9)

#9 How can the indicators be assessed, i.e. through a survey or through measuring? How reliable is your method of assessment and does it fit within your research context? (this may influence #1)

Frameworks for selecting indicators for sustainability

An abundance of methods to select indicators for sustainability can be found in the literature. Apart from the 'three pillars' environment, social and economic sustainability, many frameworks have been developed for selecting, structuring, and analysing indicators for sustainability of agricultural systems. Such frameworks often have overarching concepts like domains, capitals, attributes, or principles, which aim to cover the different aspects of sustainability. For example, the MESMIS approach uses five attributes: productivity, stability, reliability, resilience, and adaptability (López-Ridaura *et al.* 2002, 2005); the AfricaRISING project uses five domains, productivity, economic sustainability, environmental sustainability, human well-being, social sustainability (Grabowski *et al.*, Chapter 29; Smith *et al.* 2017); the Sustainable Livelihoods Framework uses five capitals, human, natural, financial, social, and physical (DFID 1999); and Florin *et al.* (2012) base their analysis on five overarching principles: productivity, acceptability, security, protection, and viability.

The principles presented by Florin *et al.* (2012) are part of a hierarchical approach of principles, criteria, and indicators. This approach aims to structure and clarify indicator selection (Van Cauwenbergh *et al.* 2007; Florin *et al.* 2012): thus "Principles are overarching ('universal') attributes of a system. Criteria are the rules that govern judgement on outcomes from the system and indicators are variables that assess or measure compliance with criteria" (Florin *et al.* 2012, p. 109). Box 28.2 describes the use of principles, criteria, and indicators. It includes a detailed example on how the reasoning for selecting an indicator belonging to a criterion can be clarified by indicating what the (assumed) driver is for each indicator.

Box 28.2 Selecting indicators through a hierarchical framework of principles, criteria, and indicators

Principles, criteria, and indicators

The use of principles and criteria as a framework for selecting indicators originates from responsible forestry management (i.e. Lammerts van Bueren and Blom 1996) and is widely embraced in certification schemes (i.e. RSPO 2013; FSC 2015; RSB 2016). It was applied to agricultural systems for the first time by Van Cauwenbergh *et al.* (2007). Based on the critique of Niemeijer and de Groot

---

(2008), Florin *et al.* (2012) included *drivers* to describe the causal relationship between criteria and indicators. Describing the assumed drivers not only opens the debate on why the specific indicators are selected, it also helps to identify meaningful indicators (Niemeijer and de Groot 2008; Florin *et al.* 2014). Schut *et al.* (2014) used a similar hierarchy of principles, criteria, and indicators as well as additional 'verifiers', in a multi-actor process for developing a national governance framework for sustainable biofuels in Mozambique. They argue that their approach supported and structured transparent discussions in a participatory setting. Using principles and criteria, together with drivers, to select indicators, may therefore fit the call of Struik *et al.* (2014) to be clear and open on the underlying assumptions when analysing sustainability of agricultural systems.

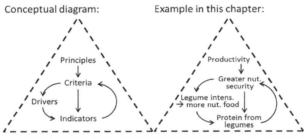

A conceptual diagram of the causal relationships among principles, criteria and indicators (after Florin *et al.* 2014) using an example from this chapter.

From the principle productivity to one of its indicators – an example

A principle often has multiple criteria and each criterion can have several indicators. We used five principles for this study – *productivity, viability, resilience, social well-being,* and *environment* – to cover the multiple aspects of sustainability of agricultural systems. Here we explain for one indicator how it was derived from the principle of productivity and what assumptions and decisions we made to do so. The *Vision of Success* of N2Africa describes how the project should lead to, amongst other things, "greater food and nutrition security", which was therefore adopted as a criterion in this case study. Some criteria (including "*greater nutrition security*") could belong to more than one principle (also to *social well-being* in this case, for instance). We noted this where applicable, following Florin *et al.* (2014), in a separate column of the table listing all indicators (Table 28.3). "*Greater nutrition security*" is to be achieved through sustainable intensification of legume cultivation, resulting in increased legume production (which is why we linked "*greater nutrition security*" to *productivity*). Legumes are rich in proteins, including essential amino acids for human growth (De Jager 2013). The assumed driver in this case was therefore that legume intensification would lead to more nutritious food being available through increased production (driver). This could be assessed as the amount of *protein from legumes* produced on farm (indicator). Although we acknowledge that the causal relations in reality may be more complex (as for instance described by FAO 2016), we consider the amount of *protein from legumes* is a good indicator for sustainability in this case study. It should, however, be assessed in the light of the other, related, indicator outcomes (i.e. *food self-sufficiency, farm gross margin, maize yield gap,* and *food security*) in order to make this single indicator relevant. This need for analysing indicator outcomes in the light of other indicators shows the need for assessing indicators as part of a framework, like principles, criteria, and indicators.

Using principles and criteria to select indicators for sustainability (#1, #2)

We used the approach of Florin *et al.* (2012) with the aim of being explicit about the decisions made in selecting indicators. Together with the other case study coordinators within PROIntensAfrica, we agreed on a common set of five principles – *productivity, viability, resilience, social well-being,* and *environment* – to enable comparisons among the case studies within PROIntensAfrica. At this stage it became clear that convergence among the case studies at the indicator level was not possible due to the wide range of agricultural systems selected (e.g. livestock systems, cocoa agroforestry systems). Convergence was possible however at the 'principle' level.

Next, we selected criteria and indicators. N2Africa focuses mainly on indicators related to productivity (legumes and subsequent crops, soil fertility), viability (household income, sustainable access to input and output markets), and social well-being (nutrition, gender equality). Our aim was to assess the wider impact of legumes on sustainability of the smallholder farms. We therefore based our choice of criteria and indicators on both N2Africa project documents and on commonly used criteria and indicators from the literature (Smith *et al.* 2017). An example of the criteria and indicators belonging to productivity is presented in Table 28.2. A detailed description of how the criteria for other principles were linked to indicators is given by Marinus *et al.* (2016a) and an overview of all indicators is provided in Table 28.3. Bell and Morse (1999) suggest that indicators should be selected using participatory methods, engaging with local stakeholders. In our case, however, we required a single framework to assess contrasting smallholder farms in two different countries. Stakeholder workshops were held, but at a later stage. In each country we reflected together with local stakeholders on the framework and the study outcomes (detailed reports of the stakeholder workshops are available: see Marinus *et al.* (2016b) and Marinus *et al.* (2016c).

Systems analysis: levels and aggregation (#3, #4, #5)

The next step was to develop the indicators and methods to assess them. An important first question was: At what level should indicators be assessed? We decided to develop an indicator framework at farm household level. This is the level at which decisions are made and therefore it is at this level where new technologies should have an impact. The impact could, for instance, be on food self-sufficiency, as many smallholders prioritize production for their own food supply. Management decisions, such as use of inputs (organic manure, fertilizers, and plant protection

Table 28.2 An example of criteria and indicators for the principle of productivity. All criteria for this example come from the N2Africa *Vision of Success* and objectives which are quoted in italics.

Principle	Criteria	Causal links: Grain legume intensification	Indicators
Productivity	*"Greater food and nutrition security"* *"Close yield gaps"*	increases availability of (nutritious) food reduces legume yield gaps and thereby eventually also maize yield gaps	Protein from legumes Food self-sufficiency Legume yield gap[1] Maize yield gap[1]

[1] Legume yield gaps and maize yield gaps were assessed at field level and aggregated to farm level to derive a farm household level indicator.

Table 28.3 Indicators collected in the household level survey and their units for the different principles. The second column identifies possible other principles under which an indicator could fit. A brief summary of the units used per indicators and their scaling is given here, more details can be found in Annex II of Marinus *et al.* (2016c).

Indicators	Possible other principles	Units	Scaling	
			0	*10*
Productivity				
Protein from legumes	*Social well-being*	% of protein required in diet	0	100
Food self-sufficiency	*Social well-being*	months year^{-1}	0	12
Legume yield gap		%	100	0
Maize yield gap		%	100	0
Viability				
Farm size		ha	0	5
Farm gross margin		100× (US$ per adult / minimum wage)	0	100
Legume intensity		% of cultivated area	0	50
Valuable assets	*Resilience*	score	From Njuki *et al.* (2011)	
Livestock owned	*Resilience*	TLU	0	10
Resilience				
N input from N$_2$-fixation		kg N ha^{-1} farm area	0	50
Agro-diversity		Simpson's diversity index crop species	No diversity	High diversity
Price variability		score	Very variable	Stable
Yield variability		score	Very variable	Stable
Social well-being				
Share of women's labour in agriculture		%	75	0
Women empowerment		score	0	10
Food security		months year^{-1}	0	12
Post-harvest storage	*Viability*	score	No protection	Several measures
Market access	*Viability*	minutes	120	0
Frequency of extension services	*Viability*	score	> 1 year ago	Weekly
Environment				
Crop protection use		score	No use	Use, no measures
N-surplus		kg N ha^{-1}	Traffic light indicators (EU Nitrogen Expert Panel 2015)	
Nitrogen-use efficiency	*Resilience, viability*	%		
Erosion control		score	No measures	Erosion not likely

chemicals) and type of feed, differ among arable fields or types of livestock on a farm. For several indicators it was necessary first to assess them at field or 'production unit' level; for instance, legume or cereal crop yield gaps, N-use efficiency, N-surplus, legume intensity, erosion control measures. Field level results were then aggregated to a farm level indicator. See Box 28.3 for a detailed example of how N-use efficiency was assessed at field scale and aggregated to farm scale.

Aggregation inevitably results in loss of information. A key question is to what extent indicators can be aggregated before vital information is lost? In Part 4 we discuss this in more detail.

Box 28.3   An example of developing an indicator: nitrogen-use efficiency

Nitrogen (N)-use efficiency for all fields containing grain crops in the previous season was calculated as:

$$Nitrogen\ use\ efficiency_{field} = \frac{\left(N\ in\ grain + N\ in\ stover\ out\ of\ field\right)}{\left(N\ mineral\ fertilizer + N\ manure + N_2\ fixed\right)}$$

N-use efficiency at farm level was calculated using a weighted (based on field size) average across all fields for which the N-use efficiency was calculated. The 'traffic light indicator' scheme (table below) for nitrogen-use efficiency of cropping systems as developed by Brentrup and Palliere (2010) and the EU Nitrogen Expert Panel (2015) was adopted for this indicator value (graph below).

Interpretation	N-use efficiency (%)
Soil N mining	> 100
Risk of soil N mining	90–100
Balanced N fertilization	70–90
Risk of N losses	50–70
High risk of N losses	< 50

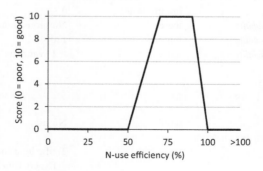

The indicator score for different nitrogen use efficiencies.

Weighting of indicators for creating composite indices for each principle (#6)

We gave all indicators an equal weighting when presenting them in an amoeba diagram and when aggregating to a higher level. Yet indicators describe different aspects of sustainability – so how to aggregate to one value? Or, some issues might be perceived to be more (or less) important than others for sustainability. Weighting of indicators can compensate for such differences. As an example, for the principle of productivity some might find the indicator legume yield gap less important than the maize yield gap. When calculating the (weighted) average score for the principle productivity, maize yield gap could then be given a heavier weighting (i.e. 1.0) than legume yield gap (i.e. 0.6). The decision to weight or not is subjective and strongly influences the outcomes at the level of principles. Arguments for weighting and aggregating need to be stated explicitly.

Scaling of indicators (#7)

Indicators can be expressed in their regular units of measurement, e.g. yield kg per ha or fertilizer use per ha, but that often complicates the comparison between them and prevents the use of composite indices. Therefore, scaling is a common approach in sustainability assessments (see for instance De Olde *et al.* (2016) for their comparison of indicator frameworks, all using scaling of indicators). However, the scaling of indicators greatly influences the outcome of a sustainability assessment. We scaled all indicators from 0 to 10. For each indicator a choice has to be made of what to consider as a minimum (0 score) and a maximum (10 score). We chose a score of 0 as a fully insufficient value of the indicator and a score of 10 a good value of the indicator related to sustainability. This is a highly subjective process, which requires full transparency of the underlying assumptions. The valuation from 'fully insufficient' to 'good' for our case study is reported in Annex II in the report of Marinus *et al.* (2016a). The values selected are also determined by the case studies themselves: for instance a maximum value for legume yield (the attainable yield, resulting in a score of 10) in a given area was determined as the 90th percentile of grain yields in N2Africa agronomic trials in that area. So for example, the attainable yield for soybean was 1990 kg ha^{-1} for western Kenya, while for northern Ghana this was 3610 kg ha^{-1}.

Here we give two additional examples on how scaling of indicators results in a loss of information and can be highly subjective. The N-use efficiency is defined as the ratio between the N output in useful product and the inputs to the system (Box 28.3). We used the 'traffic light indicator' scheme (Brentrup and Palliere, 2010; EU Nitrogen Expert Panel, 2015) to classify and scale the values of N-use efficiency (Box 28.3). Application of the traffic light indicator to derive a score of 0–10 resulted in a loss of information on the actual N-use efficiency. For instance, a score of 0 can refer to a N-use efficiency of 25%, but also 100% (Box 28.3). An N-use efficiency of 25% would however be the result of over-fertilization with a risk of N losses to the environment, while an N-use efficiency of 100% would be the effect of too small N inputs with a risk of soil mining. Both situations need completely different management measures to improve sustainability, while they both have the same low indicator score. An option to differentiate for this could be to have two separate sub-indicators, one for *risk of soil mining* and one for *risk of N losses*. This would however result in five more indicators to be included in the already full amoeba diagram if this was done for all indicators having a similar type of scaling as N-use efficiency. Moreover, the original indicator N-use efficiency would be represented by two (sub-)indicators and receive more visual attention in the amoeba diagram compared to other ones with a linear scaling and no sub-indicators.

The second example is the indicator 'share of women's labour in agriculture' (belonging to the principle of social well-being), which is an example where scaling is value-laden. This indicator compares the share of women's labour used for production of the most important crops to that of men. To cover the labour women often devote to domestic activities, an unequal scale was used in which 75% of labour or more done by women resulted in a score of 0 (Figure 28.1). This is based on an assumption that both men and women should spend equal labour hours, irrespective for what purpose, such as agricultural work, domestic activities, and off-farm activities. Stakeholders with different cultural backgrounds are likely to have divergent opinions on what a balanced gender contribution would be.

Assessing indicators (#8)

The assessment methods used depend on the available time and budget. Measuring all fields within a farm, for instance, is often considered too laborious for surveys. Yet this inevitably influences the accuracy and degree of detail of the indicator. Using farmer-estimated farm size can for instance result in considerable systematic errors (Carletto *et al.* 2013). We assessed indicators through a detailed household survey (two visits of 1–2 hours each per farm household) collaborating with experienced translators (e.g. elderly extension agents in Ghana and a field assistant that had been working for N2Africa for the past five years). In addition, we measured the individual fields of the farm as several indicators were strongly linked to field and farm size.

Some indicators were adjusted after the initial survey, as the information required was hard to retrieve from the surveys. For instance, the indicator for the use of crop protection agents, 'crop protection use', was initially to be based on the active ingredient and dose applied. Farmers were often not able to recall the name of the crop protection agent, let alone the active ingredient. Even more confusing was that 'DDT' was a common name for all insecticides, whilst DDT was not used in the area. The fact that most farmers were unable to recall the name of the crop protection agent indicates that they were unaware of the health risks in handling and application. This was an important result of the survey. Inspired by a 'test' that was used with village-based contract sprayers in northern Nigeria (CropLife Africa Middle East 2015), questions around the (safe) use of and knowledge on crop protection agents were developed as the basis for a new indicator. This example shows that although sometimes it might be difficult to apply a pre-designed questionnaire and indicators, it is possible to adapt indicators to the local situation to derive meaningful output. In areas where more knowledge on crop protection agents and their use is available, a more discriminating indicator definition based on active ingredient and dose applied could be used.

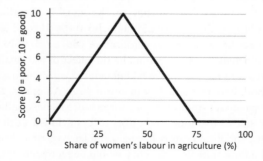

Figure 28.1   Indicator score for the share of women's labour in agriculture, calculated for the most important grain crops

Selecting households (#9)

In each case study area, ten farm households were selected from earlier N2Africa surveys: the baseline survey for western Kenya (Franke and Wolf 2011) and the early impact survey for northern Ghana (Stadler *et al.* 2016). We aimed to derive a representative sample of the distribution of the widely divergent types of farm households in the study areas (e.g. see Hengsdijk *et al.* 2014). Characteristics used to select the households were farm size, livestock owned, and valuable goods (assets) owned. For western Kenya a distinction was made between dairy cows and other livestock based on the importance of dairy for household income.

4. What do aggregated results tell us?

Aggregation of results from lower spatial scales is necessary to compare at higher levels, such as from the field to the farm household level, but with each aggregation step, (important) information is lost. We will discuss the difficulties and usefulness of aggregation at different spatial scales in this section.

Aggregating indicators from field to farm household level – an example of indicators for nitrogen use efficiency and nitrogen surplus

N-use efficiency and N-surplus were two indicators assessed at field level which had to be aggregated to derive a farm household level indicator score. We used an area-related weighted average across all fields containing grain crops per household. Comparing the outcomes for the field level N-use efficiency indicator (Figure 28.2A) and the farm household level (Figure 28.2B) average reveals why it is important to assess N inputs and outputs at the field level. A large percentage of fields had an N-use efficiency that highlighted the risk of soil mining, whereas this was masked at farm household level (Figure 28.3). Importantly, Fig. 28.2A shows that this was mainly caused by fields that receive no or very little N inputs, resulting in unequal distribution of N inputs across the farm. Earlier studies showed that such an unequal distribution of inputs to the different fields within a farm is common in the area. Tittonell *et al.* (2005) described for different areas in western Kenya how preferential input use for fields closer to the homestead results in soil fertility gradients with more fertile fields closer to the homestead and poorer fields further away from the homestead. Such continual lack of inputs can result in development of strong gradients of declining soil fertility culminating in non- or poorly responsive soils in the farthest fields. Non-responsive soils need major investments to become productive, which may not be feasible for smallholder farmers (Vanlauwe *et al.* 2010) and therefore result in a poverty trap (Tittonell and Giller 2013). To provide insight into this aspect of sustainability, assessment of N inputs and outputs and calculated N-use efficiencies and N-surplus therefore needs to be done at the field level in our systems in western Kenya. This may then also be used to develop management interventions. If the aim is purely to assess which farm households are more sustainable, in systems where N input use is more homogeneous across the farm for instance, this assessment can be done at farm household level.

In some cases indicators are interdependent. For example, Figure 28.2 illustrates how three indicators can be combined. The interaction between three indicators – N-use efficiency, N-surplus, and a desired minimum productivity – is captured in one graph (Figure 28.2). All three indicators are important for sustainability. Meaningful conclusions concerning sustainable intensification related to each of these indicators can only be drawn when analysed in the light of the other two indicators. For example, high productivity can be sustained only when

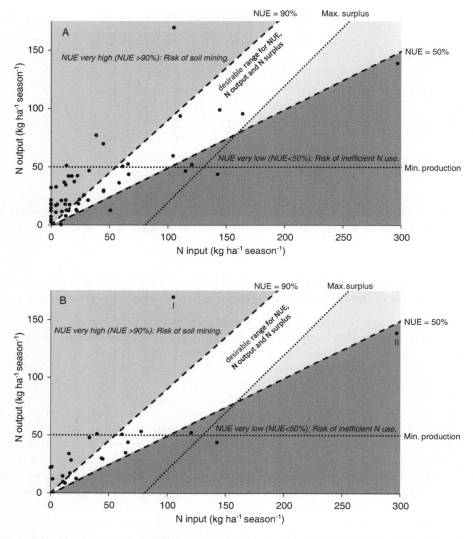

Figure 28.2 Nitrogen input and output at field (A, n=58) and farm level (B, weighted averages across fields per farm) for each of the 20 farms studied in Kenya. Layout of the figure is adapted from EU Nitrogen Expert Panel (2015). The dotted line for minimum production was adjusted from 80 kg N ha^{-1} season^{-1} (for European systems) to 50 kg N ha^{-1} season^{-1} as a more realistic target for cropping systems in SSA. This adjusted minimum production level would be equal to approximately 3000 kg maize grain ha^{-1} season^{-1}. The dotted lines for minimum production and maximum surplus are proposed target values and can be adjusted where needed.

the N-use efficiency is neither too high nor too low, and with a small N-surplus. This can be readily observed in Figure 28.2 and directly highlights the change in management required (e.g. greater N-input use or more efficient N-input use). The relatively large N-input (Figure 28.2B, point I) and N-output (point II) highlight a further difficulty when using farmers' reported data. Although field size was measured, other variables used for calculating the N budgets, e.g. nutrient inputs (manure, inorganic fertilizers) and grain yield, were farmers' estimates. This makes it

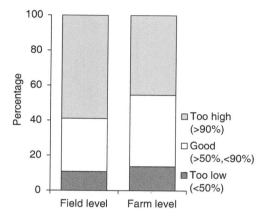

Figure 28.3 The percentage of field level and farm level (average across fields) nitrogen–use efficiency indicator outcomes that was either too high (NUE > 90%), good (NUE > 50%, < 90%), or too low (< 50%)

difficult to conclude whether points I and II are measurement errors or whether they are indeed exceptionally high values.

Aggregating indicators from farm household to community level

Comparisons of differences in sustainability between communities or regions are typically based on average outcomes of indicators per location. Although average indicator values give a quick insight in some of the differences between both locations in a country, it is important to consider the underlying variation in results as well. In western Kenya, between the two communities Vihiga and Migori for instance, the indicators farm size, number of livestock, protein from legumes, and food self-sufficiency all gave clearly higher scores for Migori (Figure 24.4A). These differences fitted well with findings from the literature and were in line with the general view in the stakeholder workshops that there is still more space for farming in Migori, resulting in larger farms and more viable opportunities for farming (Marinus *et al.* 2016c). The more positive score for the maize and legume yield gaps (meaning a smaller yield gap) for Vihiga were discussed and explained by the participants as a possible result from the greater input use in Vihiga than in Migori. The reasoning was, as farm size is smaller in Vihiga, farmers would use more inputs on a hectare basis resulting in larger yields. Looking closer at the variation in results within Vihiga and Migori, however, revealed that the results for legume and maize yield gap scores were largely overlapping and did not show clear differences (Figure 28.5).

Average results presented in amoeba diagrams mask a lot of underlying variation. An overlap in the box and whisker plots for indicator results between Vihiga and Migori was also found for indicators that would be considered different based on averages in the amoeba diagrams alone (e.g. women's empowerment, post-harvest storage, N-surplus, N-use efficiency). The box and whisker plots shown for Vihiga and Migori also highlight the variation in indicator values among households. The minimum and maximum scores differed by at least five points for 13 of the 23 indicators in both locations. Thus the averages depicted in the amoeba diagrams should be presented with some indication of the inherent variability among farm households (i.e. box and whisker plots). Only by knowing the variation can one understand what differences in averages (e.g. between case study areas) mean.

A

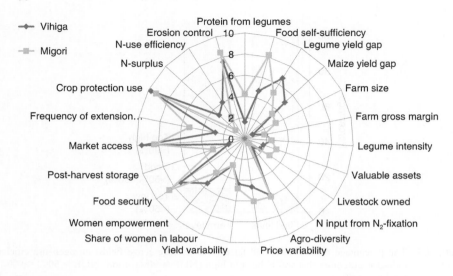

B

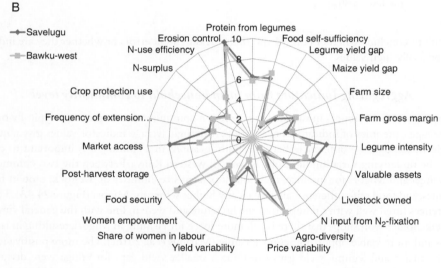

C

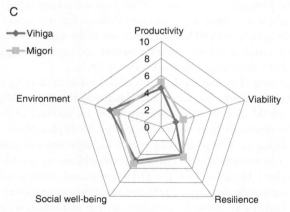

Figure 28.4 Average results across all households per research site in western Kenya (C, A) and northern Ghana (D, B). Indicators for sustainability were aggregated on the level of principles using equal weighing for the outcomes of each indicator (C, D). Outcomes for all indicators for sustainability are shown in A and B.

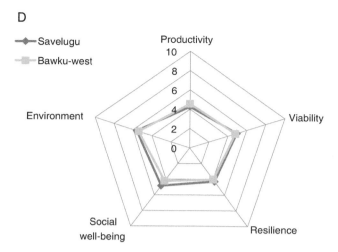

Figure 28.4 (Continued)

Indicator outcomes for northern Ghana were very similar between the communities Savelugu and Bawku West for most indicators (Figure 28.4B). Only legume intensity and market access seemed to result in a higher score for Savelugu based on the averages in the amoeba diagram. Of these two, legume intensity showed considerable overlap in the box and whisker plots (not shown). A similar variation between farm household level results per indicator within this case study area was found as in western Kenya.

Results could also be used as a basis for discussion with farmers in the community on the causes and effects of this variation, leading to an understanding of which (technology) options could work for which households (Vanlauwe *et al.* 2016). Moreover, the results on variation could give insight in the potential improvements in sustainability within the community: farmers performing well on a particular indicator show the level that is currently feasible within the community (i.e. Figure 28.6A), and we could consider the steps that need to be taken by farmers who currently perform poorly (i.e. Figure 28.6B) to improve to the same level.

Composite indices – from indicators to principles

When the individual indicators were summarized at the level of principles, nearly all underlying differences disappeared and scores for most principles averaged out to values between 5 and 6 (Figure 28.4C and D), resulting in an important loss of discriminating power among different farming systems. The principle productivity for instance, was characterized by four indicators: protein from legumes, food self-sufficiency, maize yield gap, and legume yield gap. As the average was taken across all four, the positive score for food self-sufficiency in Migori in western Kenya was evened out by lower scores of the other indicators. This is an important loss of information if the outcomes of individual indicators are important such as food self-sufficiency. An alternative is to plot the overall score for productivity but to retain also the individual value for a key indicator such as food self-sufficiency.

When comparing western Kenya and northern Ghana, only the principle viability showed any difference. A higher score for viability for northern Ghana was caused by higher outcomes for all underlying indicators (farm size, farm gross margin, legume intensity, valuable assets, and

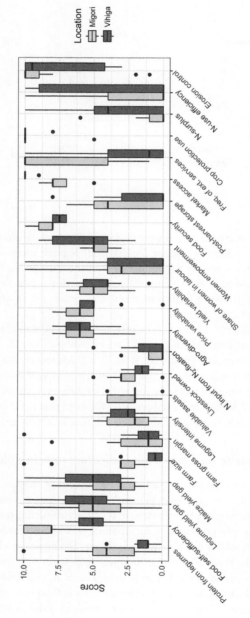

Figure 28.5 Box and whisker plots of indicator results for Migori and Vihiga, Kenya

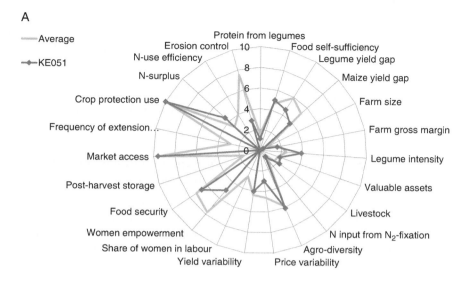

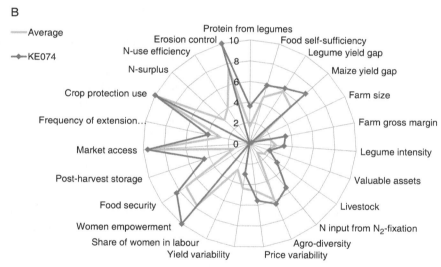

Figure 28.6 Example of individual household outcomes on the level of indicators for a household that scored poorly on most indicators (A) and a household that scored well on most indicators (B) when compared with the average for the case study area, Vihiga. Results for all households can be found in Marinus *et al.* (2016a).

livestock owned). For the other principles there were considerable differences for underlying indicators between the two case study countries, even though the average outcomes for the composite indices per principle were similar. These differences for underlying indicators were even larger than the differences between the case study areas within countries as discussed above. The effect of evening out differences seen among indicators, when creating composite indices for principles was even more pronounced when comparing between countries.

Averages summarized in composite indices per principle at best give a quick overview of the differences between areas and case study countries. Our results however, suggest that comparison of composite indices for principles provides little insight. At worst, the same average values for principles may mask important differences in the underlying indicators between countries or areas. Only for viability was it valid to compare composite indices per principle between the two case study countries, as the underlying indicator results were fully in line with the results for the composite indices per principle. Average scores as summarized in composite indices per principle provided few insights. Further, to derive measures for improvement of farm systems requires scores at the level of indicators as these give more insights in what causes low and high scores for sustainability.

Another way of comparing results – what can we say about households with high or low legume intensity?

An objective of conducting this sustainability evaluation of N2Africa was to assess possible relationships between legume cultivation and sustainability at farm household level. We selected 'legume intensity' as an indicator for sustainability as cropping systems containing legumes can have several positive effects related to sustainability such as increased (free) N inputs and reduced pest and disease pressure. Legume intensity was defined as the proportion of legumes as part of the total cultivated area. We scored a linear increase from 0 to 10 for legume intensity from 0% to 50% of cultivated land area. We assumed a legume intensity of 50% to be equivalent to a 1:1 rotation of legumes and other crops, i.e. maize (for more details see Annex II, Marinus *et al.* 2016a). No strong relationships were found between legume intensity score and other indicators for sustainability (Figure 28.7). In Kenya this was most likely due to the relatively low legume intensity for all farm households as the maximum score was 4 for both locations studied. In Ghana there were mixed results for both locations. Households with a larger proportion of legumes seem to score better on most indicators in Bawku West. In Savelugu however, there was no clear relationship between legume intensity and other indicators. Only some indicators (farm size, share of women's labour in agriculture, and N-use efficiency) had higher scores for farm households with a higher legume intensity while other indicators (valuable assets, crop protection use, N-surplus) had a lower score. Due to these small differences and small samples size (ten households per case study area), we cannot draw any conclusions about possible causal relations between indicators for sustainability and legume intensity. Purposely selecting households with larger difference in legume intensity and sampling a larger number of farm households are needed to test for such relationships between legume intensity and other indicators for sustainability.

5. Concluding remarks

A hierarchical framework of principles, criteria, and indicators proved to be a useful tool for assessing sustainability. Our main objective for using this framework was to be explicit about why certain indicators were selected in an indicator study across different farming systems. Selecting indicators, however, was only the first of several steps in which subjective decisions had to be made on how indicator results relate to sustainability as well as how they should be scaled. Only by being explicit on the steps taken and decisions made can one develop an indicator framework with meaningful outcomes that can be critically evaluated by others.

Although the amoeba diagram is a convenient tool for communication of indicator results, we should be aware of the underlying variability in indicator scores. For crucial indicators, variability can be shown in other ways. For example, we used the N-use efficiency figure for N-related indicators and box and whisker plots for other indicators. Displaying the variability reveals to what extent there is an inconvenient truth behind the average outcomes shown by indicators in amoeba diagrams. Questioning the meaning of average indicator results is important not only when analysing amoeba diagrams, but also for overall outcome of the sustainability assessment. Apart from questioning the meaning of the indicator 'percentage under sustainable agricultural land' for SDG2, it is important to consider how variation among farms can be taken into account when developing methods to assess such indicators.

Aggregation of indicators to the level of principles showed few added benefits and a major loss of important information. Comparing outcomes at the level of principles, for instance between two areas, seems therefore only useful if all or the majority of the underlying indicators

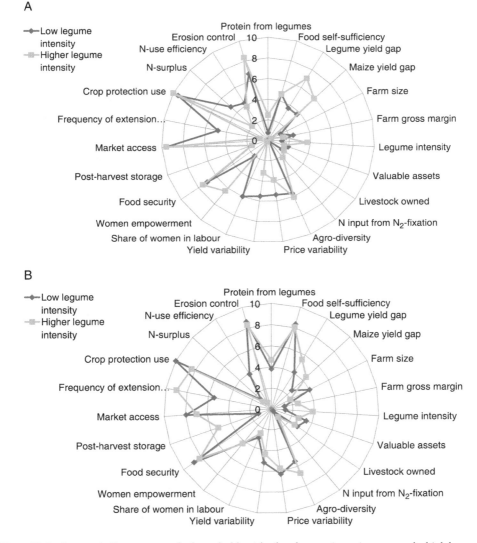

Figure 28.7 Average indicators scores for households with a low legume intensity score and a high legume intensity score (averages across respectively the 50% of the households with the lowest and highest legume intensity) in Vihiga (A) and Migori (B) in western Kenya and Savelugu (A) and Bawku West (B) in northern Ghana

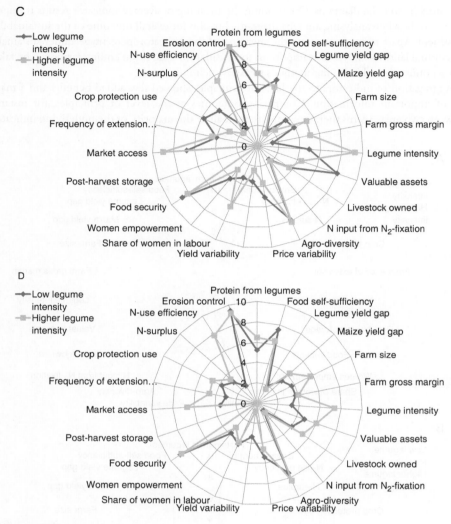

Figure 28.7 (Continued)

score higher (or lower) for one of the areas. If this is not the case, as it was in this study, it is better not to aggregate to the level of principles or criteria.

Finally, the sustainability of farming systems is by nature multi-dimensional. Some small but important details are hard to assess (i.e. the active ingredient in crop protection agents used), while others are difficult to aggregate to higher levels without losing important information (i.e. N-use efficiency at field level). Assessing the sustainability of smallholder farming systems remains therefore a balancing act, in which transparency and attention to detail are required.

Acknowledgements

We thank the Bill & Melinda Gates Foundation for funding the project N2Africa: Putting Nitrogen Fixation to Work for Smallholder Farmers in Africa (www.N2Africa.org) through a grant to Wageningen University. We also thank the European Union for funding and commissioning the case studies described in this chapter through the PROIntensAfrica project, which received funding from the European Union's Horizon 2020 research and innovation programme under grant agreement No 652671. We are grateful to Philip Grabowski and Cheryl Palm for their critical reading of an earlier draft of this chapter.

References

Bell, S. and Morse, S., 1999. *Sustainability Indicators: Measuring the Immeasurable?* Earthscan, London.

Brentrup, F. and Palliere, C., 2010. Nitrogen use efficiency as an agro-environmental indicator. In: *OECD Workshop: Agri-environmental Indicators: Lessons Learnt and Future Directions*. 23–26 March 2010. 1–9.

Carletto, C., Gourlay, S., and Winters, P., 2013. *From Guesstimates to GPStimates: Land Area Measurement and Implications for Agricultural Analysis.* The World Bank, Washington, DC, No. 6550, 29 pp.

CropLife Africa Middle East, 2015. *Assessment of Contract Sprayers in Borno State, Nigeria.* Report N2Africa project, www.N2Africa.org, Wageningen University, Wageningen, The Netherlands, 54 pp.

De Jager, I., 2013. *Literature study: Nutritional benefits of legumes consumption at household level in rural areas of sub-Saharan Africa.* Report N2Africa project, www.N2Africa.org, Wageningen University, Wageningen, The Netherlands, 95 pp.

De Olde, E.M., Oudshoorn, F.W., Sorensen, C.A.G., Bokkers, E.A.M., and De Boer, I.J.M., 2016. Assessing sustainability at farm-level: Lessons learned from a comparison of tools in practice. *Ecological Indicators,* 66, 391–404.

DFID, 1999. *Sustainable Livelihoods Guidance Sheets 2.1.* Department for International Development, London, 26 pp.

EU Nitrogen Expert Panel, 2015. *Nitrogen Use Efficiency (NUE) – an Indicator for the Utilization of Nitrogen in Agriculture and Food Systems.* Wageningen University, Alterra, Wageningen, the Netherlands, 47 pp.

FAO, 2016. *Compendium of Indicators for Nutrition-sensitive Agriculture.* Food and Agriculture Organization of the United Nations, Rome, 60 pp.

Florin, M.J., van de Ven, G.W.J., and van Ittersum, M.K., 2014. What drives sustainable biofuels? A review of indicator assessments of biofuel production systems involving smallholder farmers. *Environmental Science & Policy,* 37, 142–157.

Florin, M.J., van Ittersum, M.K., and van de Ven, G.W.J., 2012. Selecting the sharpest tools to explore the food-feed-fuel debate: Sustainability assessment of family farmers producing food, feed and fuel in Brazil. *Ecological Indicators,* 20, 108–120.

Franke, A.C., Rufino, M.C., and Farrow, A., 2011. *Characterisation of the Impact Zones and Mandate Areas in the N2Africa Project.* Report N2Africa project, www.N2Africa.org, Wageningen University, Wageningen, The Netherlands, 50 pp.

Franke, A.C. and Wolf, J.J. De, 2011. *N2Africa Baseline Report.* Report N2Africa project, www.N2Africa.org, Wageningen University, Wageningen, The Netherlands, 127 pp.

FSC, 2015. *FSC Principles and Criteria for Forest Stewardship.* Forest Stewardship Council, Bonn, Germany, 32 pp.

Garnett, T., Appleby, M.C., Balmford, A., Bateman, I.J., Benton, T.G., Bloomer, P., Burlingame, B., Dawkins, M., Dolan, L., Fraser, D., Herrero, M., Hoffmann, I., Smith, P., Thornton, P.K., Toulmin, C., Vermeulen, S.J., and Godfray, H.C.J., 2013. Sustainable intensification in agriculture: Premises and policies. *Science Magazine,* 341, 33–34.

Giller, K.E., Franke, A.C., Abaidoo, R., Baijukya, F., Bala, A., Boahen, S., Dashiell, K., Kantengwa, S., Sanginga, J.-M., Sanginga, N., Simmons, A., Turner, A., De Wolf, J., Woomer, P., and Vanlauwe, B., 2013. N2Africa: Putting nitrogen fixation to work for smallholder farmers in Africa. In: B. Vanlauwe, P. van Asten, and G. Blomme, eds. *Agro-ecological Intensification of Agricultural Systems in the African Highlands.* London: Routledge, pp. 156–174.

Hengsdijk, H., Franke, A.C., van Wijk, M.T., and Giller, K.E., 2014. *How Small Is Beautiful? Food Self-sufficiency and Land Gap Analysis of Smallholders in Humid and Semi-arid Sub Saharan Africa.* Plant Research International, part of Wageningen UR, Report No. 562, Wageningen, The Netherlands, 68 pp.

Kuyper, T.W. and Struik, P.C., 2014. Epilogue: Global food security, rhetoric, and the sustainable intensification debate. *Current Opinion in Environmental Sustainability,* 8 (1), 71–79.

Lammerts van Bueren, E., and Blom, E., 1996. *Hierarchical Framework for the Formulation of Sustainable Forest Management Standards.* Tropenbos Foundation, Wageningen, The Netherlands, 97 pp.

López-Ridaura, S., Masera, O., and Astier, M., 2002. Evaluating the sustainability of complex socio-environmental systems: The MESMIS framework. *Ecological Indicators*, 2 (1–2), 135–148.

López-Ridaura, S., Van Keulen, H., Van Ittersum, M.K., and Leffelaar, P.A., 2005. Multiscale methodological framework to derive criteria and indicators for sustainability evaluation of peasant natural resource management systems. *Environment, Development and Sustainability*, 7 (1), 51–69.

Marinus, W., Ronner, E., and Adjei-Nsiah, S., 2016b. *The Role of Legumes in Sustainable Intensification – Priority Areas for Research in Northern Ghana, Stakeholder Workshop Report*. Report N2Africa project, www. N2Africa.org, Wageningen University, Wageningen, The Netherlands, 33 pp.

Marinus, W., Ronner, E., and Kanampiu, F., 2016c. *The Role of Legumes in Sustainable Intensification – Priority Areas for Research in Western Kenya, Stakeholder Workshop Report*. Report N2Africa project, www.N2Africa. org, Wageningen University, Wageningen, The Netherlands, 31 pp.

Marinus, W., Ronner, E., van de Ven, G.W.J., Kanampiu, F., Adjei-Nsiah, S., and Giller, K.E., 2016a. *What Role for Legumes in Sustainable Intensification? – Case Studies in Western Kenya and Northern Ghana for PROIntensAfrica*. Report N2Africa project, www.N2Africa.org, Wageningen University, Wageningen, The Netherlands, 66 pp.

The Montpellier Panel, 2013. *Sustainable Intensification: A New Paradigm for African Agriculture*. Agriculture for Impact, London, 36 pp.

Niemeijer, D. and de Groot, R.S., 2008. A conceptual framework for selecting environmental indicator sets. *Ecological Indicators*, 8 (1), 14–25.

Njuki, J., Poole, J., Johnson, N., Baltenweck, I., Pali, P., Lokman, Z., and Mburu, S., 2011. *Gender, Livestock and Livelihood Indicators*. International Livestock Research Institute, Nairobi, Kenya, 40 pp.

Pender, J., Place, F., and Ehui, S., 1999. *Stagies for Sustainable Agricultural Development in the East African Hihglands*. International Food Policy Research Institute, Washington DC, No. 41.

Rockström, J., Williams, J., Daily, G., Noble, A., Matthews, N., Gordon, L., Wetterstrand, H., DeClerck, F., Shah, M., Steduto, P., de Fraiture, C., Hatibu, N., Unver, O., Bird, J., Sibanda, L., and Smith, J., 2016. Sustainable intensification of agriculture for human prosperity and global sustainability. *Ambio*, 46 (1), 4–17.

RSB, 2016. *RSB Principles and Criteria*. Roundtable on Sustainable Biomaterials, Geneva, Switzerland, 50 pp.

RSPO, 2013. *Principles and Criteria for the Production of Sustainable Palm Oil*. Roundtable on Sustainable Palm Oil, Kuala Lumpur, Malaysia, 70 pp.

Schut, M., Cunha Soares, N., van de Ven, G., and Slingerland, M., 2014. Multi-actor governance of sustainable biofuels in developing countries: The case of Mozambique. *Energy Policy*, 65, 631–643.

SDSN, 2013. *Solutions for Sustainable Agriculture and Food Systems – Technical Report for the Post-2015 Development Agenda*. Sustainable Developement Solutions Network – United Nations, New York.

Smith, A., Thorne, P.W., Snapp, S.S., Thamaga-Chitja, J.M., Hendriks, S., Ortmann, G., Green, M., McDermott, J.J., Staal, S.J., Freeman, H.A., Herrero, M., Van de Steeg, J.A., Zurek, M., Keenlyside, P., and Brandt, K., 2017. Measuring sustainable intensification in smallholder agroecosystems : A review. *Global Food Security*, 12, 127–138.

Stadler, M., Van den Brand, G., Giller, K.E., and Adjei-Nsiah, S., 2016. *N2Africa Early Impact Survey Ghana*. Report N2Africa project, www.N2Africa.org, Wageningen University, Wageningen, The Netherlands, 51 pp.

Struik, P.C., Kuyper, T.W., Brussaard, L., and Leeuwis, C., 2014. Deconstructing and unpacking scientific controversies in intensification and sustainability: Why the tensions in concepts and values? *Current Opinion in Environmental Sustainability*, 8, 80–88.

Tilman, D., Balzer, C., Hill, J., and Befort, B.L., 2011. Global food demand and the sustainable intensification of agriculture. *Proceedings of the National Academy of Sciences*, 108 (50), 20260–20264.

Tittonell, P. and Giller, K.E., 2013. When yield gaps are poverty traps: The paradigm of ecological intensification in African smallholder agriculture. *Field Crops Research*, 143, 76–90.

Tittonell, P., Vanlauwe, B., Leffelaar, P.A., Shepherd, K.D., and Giller, K.E., 2005. Exploring diversity in soil fertility management of smallholder farms in western Kenya: II: Within-farm variability in resource allocation, nutrient flows and soil fertility status. *Agriculture, Ecosystems & Environment*, 110 (3), 166–184.

United Nations – Economic and Social Council, 2016. Report of the inter-agency and expert group on sustainable development goal indicators. In: *Statistical Commission, Forty-seventh Session*. New York, 62 pp.

Van Cauwenbergh, N., Biala, K., Bielders, C., Brouckaert, V., Franchois, L., Garcia Cidad, V., Hermy, M., Mathijs, E., Muys, B., Reijnders, J., Sauvenier, X., Valckx, J., Vanclooster, M., Van der Veken, B., Wauters, E., and Peeters, A., 2007. SAFE-A hierarchical framework for assessing the sustainability of agricultural systems. *Agriculture, Ecosystems and Environment*, 120 (2–4), 229–242.

Van Ittersum, M.K., Bussel, L.G.J. van, Wolf, J., Grassini, P., Wart, J. van, Guilpart, N., Claessens, L., Groot, H. de, Wiebe, K., Mason-D'Croz, D., Yang, H., Boogaard, H., Oort, P.A.J. van, Loon, M.P. van, and Cassman, K.G., 2016. Can sub-Saharan Africa feed itself? *Proceedings of the National Academy of Sciences*, 113 (52), 14964–14969.

Vanlauwe, B., Bationo, A., Chianu, J., Giller, K.E., Merckx, R., Mokwunye, U., Ohiokpehai, O., Pypers, P., Tabo, R., and Shepherd, K.D., 2010. Integrated soil fertility management operational definition and consequences for implementation and dissemination. *Outlook on Agriculture*, 39 (1), 17–24.

Vanlauwe, B., Coyne, D., Gockowski, J., Hauser, S., Huising, J., Masso, C., Nziguheba, G., Schut, M., and Van Asten, P., 2014. Sustainable intensification and the African smallholder farmer. *Current Opinion in Environmental Sustainability*, 8, 15–22.

Vanlauwe, B., Coe, R., and Giller, K.E., 2016. Beyond averages: New approaches to understand heterogeneity and risk of technology success or failure in smallholder farming. *Experimental Agriculture*, 1–23.

PART IV

Critique of sustainability indicators and indices

29

SUSTAINABLE AGRICULTURAL INTENSIFICATION AND MEASURING THE IMMEASURABLE

Do we have a choice?

Philip Grabowski, Mark Musumba, Cheryl Palm and Sieglinde Snapp

1. Introduction

Indicators play a key role in the research for sustainable development process, as they allow performance to be monitored and policy recommendations to be developed. Indeed, effective efforts to deliver on the United Nation's Sustainable Development Goals (SDGs) requires utilizing appropriate indicators. In this chapter, we consider indicators in relationship to sustainable agricultural intensification (SAI). A rising demand for food is encountered around the world, from population growth, and from the buying power of a rising middle class (Valin et al., 2014). How can this be met in a safe, and sustained manner, one that empowers smallholder farmers and participants in the entire agri-food system? A growing consensus has emerged that SAI is critical to the achievement of a balanced approach to production of food, fuel and fiber, while keeping within safe boundaries of global environmental change and contributing towards human development (Pretty, 2008; Tilman et al., 2011).

The concept of "Sustainable Intensification" originated in the 1990s to address the issue of improving yields over the long term in fragile environments of Africa (Pretty, 1997; Reardon et al., 1995). The concept has since been more broadly embraced and seen as key to achieving many of the Sustainable Development Goals (SDSN, 2013; Rockström et al., 2017). Nevertheless, other experts debate the usefulness or even feasibility of "sustainable intensification" (Tittonell, 2014; Cook et al., 2015; Godfray, 2015; Petersen and Snapp, 2015). The term has been used loosely to describe any type of agricultural intensification that focuses on productivity increases with reduced negative environmental consequences (Godfray, 2015; Haileselassie et al., 2016; Mahon et al., 2017). Sustainable agricultural intensification (SAI) is a conceptual framework that helps guide discussions on achieving balanced outcomes from intensification (Garnett and Godfray, 2012). Many recent efforts have expanded sustainable intensification to include human well-being (income, nutrition) as well as social and gender dimensions (Loos et al., 2014; Vanlauwe et al. 2014; Smith et al., 2017). A plethora of sustainable intensification indicators have also been proposed as means for assessing and comparing the 'relative degree' of sustainability of different cropping systems and interventions (Barnes and Thomson, 2014; Zurek et al., 2015; Kanter et al., 2016) with the outcomes used to guide research, development and policies. Fewer efforts have put these indicators to use.

In this chapter, we outline a framework for selecting and assessing objective-oriented indicators across five domains of SAI (productivity, economic, environmental, human condition and social). The indicators are objective oriented following Olsson et al. (2009) and their contribution of how a goal-oriented framework can be used for selecting indicators based on objectives across sustainability dimensions. The framework was developed in response to the challenges of applying sustainability indicators to agricultural intensification, especially in the research for development context. It provides practical guidance for agricultural research and development actors to assess innovations for their relative contribution towards sustainable intensification compared to current practice or future scenarios. It was developed and is being tested in collaboration with several programs funded by the United States Agency for International Development (USAID) including the project titled "Africa Research for Sustainable Intensification for the Next Generation" (AfricaRISING) and the Sustainable Intensification Innovation Lab (SIIL). In Part 2 we outline some of the key lessons learned from the literature and our recent experiences applying sustainability indicators to agriculture. In Part 3 we summarize several important challenges that make it difficult to operationalize a system of indicators for sustainable agricultural intensification. We also document where our efforts have met the challenges and indicate where further work remains.

2. Sustainability indicators and the intensification of agri-food systems

For the concept of SAI to have meaning, specific sustainability objectives that link to appropriate indicators and metrics are required. Such indicators are needed to allow assessment of agricultural technologies, interventions and policies based on how they contribute towards multiple goals. The use of indicators is also important to track synergies, neutral interactions and tradeoffs (Garbach et al., 2017; Smith et al., 2017). Defining measurable indicators for sustainable agriculture has been a contentious issue for decades, in large part due to competing ideas regarding the scope of sustainability (Thompson, 2007; Struik et al., 2014).

Defining the appropriate scope for SAI is the topic of an emerging debate, resulting in a rapidly growing body of literature. Agriculture and development interventions to date have often focused on the intensification goal, using gains in crop yield as a principal metric of success, with few other indicators (Evenson and Gollin, 2003). This was a challenge reported in a recent assessment of SAI technologies from sub-Saharan Africa; in an assessment of fifty published studies that meet the selection criteria of being conducted in Africa over multiple site-years, only seventeen presented performance parameters beyond yield (Droppelmann et al., 2017). Indeed, many authors report productivity front and center, and neglect the consequences for profitability, equity (gender, age, class) or the environment.

Given the calamities associated with the Anthropocene, attention is urgently needed on how agriculture impacts finite resources, land use conversion, greenhouse gas emissions, loss of biodiversity and resource quality declines (Rockström et al., 2017). Assessment of various environmental goals are often combined with an assessment of yields and efficiency. For example, Pittelkow et al. (2016) present data showing that increased rice yields over 20 years in Uruguay were associated with improved energy and water use efficiency but greater nitrogen losses and greater pesticide contamination risks. We need more of these integrated, systems approaches, but now they also need to include socio-economic effects in order to avoid bias of weighting environmental aspects over other domains (Groot et al. 2012; Kanter et al. 2016).

Productivity, environment and economics have been the core domains of SAI considered in many influential calls for global attention to transforming agriculture (Baulcombe et al., 2009; Tilman et al., 2011). A review found broad agreement in the literature on the importance of simultaneously monitoring impact on production, economics and environment (Smith et al., 2017). Nevertheless, effectively integrating economic analysis can be challenging. The study by Pittelkow et al. (2016), mentioned above, acknowledged the importance of economic and social aspects of intensification but stated that, "Due to the limited scope of this study, socioeconomic indicators were not considered" (p. 17). This recognition of the value of multidisciplinary analysis is common, though its actual implementation is rare. Laudable instances of holistic assessments include analyzing linkages between socio-economic factors and climbing bean yields in Rwanda (Franke et al., 2016) and modeling the economic and biophysical tradeoffs in crop residue management (Giller et al., 2011). Unfortunately, the disciplinary nature of scientific training continues to reinforce limitations in the scope of analysis; agricultural scientists are rarely comfortable carrying out an economic analysis of the innovations they develop and economists are not trained to set up or properly interpret agronomic experiments.

Many argue that it is necessary to expand the scope of SAI to include various aspects of social sustainability (Garnett and Godfray 2012; The Montpelier Panel, 2013; Loos et al., 2014; Gunton et al., 2016). The social pillar of sustainability typically has the least developed indicators in sustainability assessments of agriculture, many of which are qualitative in nature (Diazabakana et al., 2014, Smith et al., 2017). Industrialized economies have very different social concerns relating to agriculture than economies that are primarily agricultural. For example, Gaviglio et al. (2016) present indicators for the social pillar of sustainability in the context of Italy and focus on issues related to product quality, direct-marketing, employment in agriculture, agri-tourism and animal welfare. In contrast, the issues of justice, gender equity, food security and nutrition are more prominent social issues related to agricultural change in the context of smallholder farming (Loos et al., 2014; Herforth and Harris, 2014; Rao, 2016). There is contestation regarding the inclusion of these later domains in SAI, with many authors pointing out that the ethical considerations for these social elements bring to the foreground the competing economic and political perspectives associated with agricultural change (e.g. organic inputs vs. chemical inputs, industrialized agriculture vs. small-scale farms, etc., Godfray, 2015; Gunton et al., 2016). Godfray (2015) notes that these debates should have their place but should be framed explicitly and not "fought through proxies" (p. 205) and confused with technical agronomic recommendations.

Environmental aspects of sustainability assessment also requiring making ethical decisions about which components of the environment are worth monitoring. Many environmental indicators are well defined, but the environmental pillar of sustainability involves such a large area of inquiry that there is considerable disagreement regarding the scope, and which indicators are appropriate. Diazabakana et al. (2014) note that "the environmental pillar has undergone an 'indicator explosion', due to the multitude of themes covered" (p. 10). Determining the environmental impacts of SAI technologies often depends upon the scale considered, e.g. where systems boundaries are drawn over space and time. Consider for example the widely differing indicators required to assess a farm- and landscape-level focus on conserving quality and quantity of resources for future generations compared to a global focus on issues such as land use conversion, climate change and loss of biodiversity.

In contrast to this debate on social and environmental indicators, those associated with production and economics are more generally agreed upon. Net primary productivity, grain and biomass for fodder or fuel have well-established measurement methods. Likewise, the economic indicators related to profitability and resource use efficiency (labor productivity, returns to ferti-lizer, etc.) have clear procedures for monitoring and deriving associated metrics. But challenges still exist in collecting reliable data to generate indicators in the economic and productivity domains. For example, there has been insufficient attention to assessing the quality of grain and feed production together with its quantity.

We consider here an integrated set of indicators and metrics that address five domains (pro-ductivity, economic, environment, social and human condition). These domains were developed over several meetings by scientists working on sustainable intensification (Glover, 2016; Smith et al., 2017). Further details about the domains and their indicators can be found in the Guide for Sustainable Intensification Indicator Assessment Framework (SIIL website: www.k-state. edu/siil/resources/index.html). The human condition domain and social domain contain the elements typically under the social pillar of sustainability. The human condition domain focuses on the individual's or household's food security, nutrition, health, capacity, etc. The social domain focuses on those aspects that are inherently relational (collective action, conflict resolution, women's empowerment, etc.). Considering all five domains is critical if we are to assess how an innovation is likely to impact the spectrum of development goals (Figure 29.1).

3. Challenges (and responses) in developing indicators of SAI

In this section, we summarize three groups of challenges to assessing SAI through indicators and we outline how our framework of objective-oriented indicators aims to address each set of challenges. At the same time, we summarize the process for selection and implementation of indicators across the five domains in our conceptual framework of SAI.

The first challenge is that the impacts from a change in agriculture depend on biogeochemi-cal and social processes, which occur at different spatial and temporal scales. For spatial scales, a

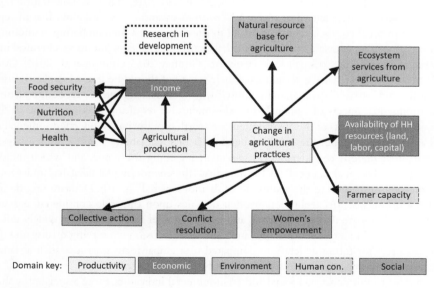

Figure 29.1   Direct and indirect effects from a change in agriculture across all five domains

Source: Guide for Sustainable Intensification Assessment – www.k-state.edu/siil/resources/index.html

new agricultural technology can affect, for example, the soil nutrient flows of the plot, the welfare accumulation of the household and the ecosystem services (such as water purification) of the landscape. Furthermore, the heterogeneity of agro-ecological and socio-economic conditions in smallholder farming systems make aggregation of data from lower scales problematic for revealing the different situations and therefore locally relevant indicators and solutions. Likewise, the high levels of temporal variability in key drivers, such as rainfall, necessitate measuring temporal system properties, which can be difficult in the short term. Where to draw systems boundaries over space and time and how to effectively collect data and link them across those scales is a crucial challenge.

Our framework of indicators addresses the first challenge by organizing metrics into categories of spatial scales and by providing a menu of indicators that can be selected based on their relevance to the context. Less work has been done but is definitely needed to develop indicators for measuring the temporal aspects of system properties.

The second challenge is that the goals of sustainable intensification are broad, spanning gender equity, improved nutrition, enhanced soil quality, poverty alleviation and increased land productivity, among others. Interdisciplinary work is essential. Furthermore, the causal links from a change in agriculture to these goals can be lengthy, which makes detecting empirical contributions towards these goals a formidable task. There may also be complex interactions and feedbacks across the processes being altered to achieve these goals, both as tradeoffs and synergies.

Our framework addresses the second challenge by outlining methods of varying levels of complexity for each of the indicators, which facilitates the affordable collection of relevant data across all domains. We also outline how to identify and quantify tradeoffs and synergies within and across these domains.

A third challenge comes from the diversity of values and priorities among agricultural stakeholders. The selection of indicators requires making value-laden decisions, as well as decisions that have potentially different impacts at and conflicts among field, household, landscape scales, especially in the environmental and social domains.

Our framework addresses the third challenge by outlining participatory methods for identifying and collecting locally specific results for many of the indicators. The goal is that the knowledge generated from the research will be useful for problem-solving because it is produced collaboratively with the stakeholders who will be affected (Speelman et al., 2007). We suggest utilizing a participatory process for indicator selection, though recognizing the time and effort it takes to operationalize that. Ideally assessment of SAI innovations will be part of an iterative co-learning approach by a group of stakeholders, guided by indicators to work towards sustainability.

The following sections provide a summary of the literature related to these challenges and details of our efforts to address those challenges. We document where our efforts have met the challenges and summarize remaining difficulties that require further work and possible approaches for improving the framework.

3.1 Challenge 1: establishing relevant spatial and temporal boundaries for the assessment

Evaluation of sustainable agricultural intensification in a given context requires carefully considering the spatial and temporal scale to ensure that the indicators selected are relevant, linked to the objectives, and sensitive in order to capture the dynamics within the system. There are different processes and stakeholders affected by an innovation over space and time and this affects which indicators are relevant to assess tradeoffs and synergies (Rodríguez et al., 2006). Identifying the spatial and temporal scale enables the scientist to focus on the process, means, outcomes and effects of the innovation ensuring that biophysical, ecological, social and economic linkages and outcomes are accounted for (Dale and Polasky, 2007; Kanter et al., 2016). The SAI assessment framework we present here is an objective-oriented framework. Such frameworks require scientists to choose indicators across multiple domains, which may create scale mismatch (Rodríguez et al., 2006).

Spatial mismatch occurs because different process and outputs are observed at different scales and in addition most studies are constrained by cost (cost of collecting data on multiple scales and expertise to collect data on multiple domains). For example, the biophysical process of crop and animal productivity can be examined at the field or farm level, while the management, consumption of goods and services, social and economic aspects are observed or measured at higher scales (household, landscape level). This requires multi-indicator and multi-scale data collection protocols. In addition, the unintended effects (synergies and tradeoffs) of given technologies may be observed at spatial scales beyond the field scale (Rodríguez et al., 2006). For example, use of fertilizer to improve bio-fortified maize yields may increase productivity at the field scale, improve nutrition at the household level, but may reduce water quality at the landscape level. If assessment of the technology is restricted to one scale without examining the effects of the innovation at other spatial scales, the possibility of instituting changes to mitigate tradeoffs (water quality) or improve synergies (improved school performance due to better nutrition) may be missed. If one takes data at a more aggregated scale, such as regional crop yields, they may not be of sufficient resolution to characterize the heterogeneity of yields at the local scales – thus making links to household-level indicators somewhat questionable or at least diminishing the utility of the links to these coarser resolution yields.

In addition, there is spatial heterogeneity in terms of biophysical conditions that may affect production and management. Soil properties may vary across different parts of field and lead to different levels of productivity (Lobell et al., 2009; Giller et al., 2011). This variability makes it difficult or impossible to assess the 'average' effect of an innovation at a broad spatial scale, especially given the heterogeneity of field-level conditions and the importance of field-level management (Marinus et al., Chapter 28). Disaggregating by soil type, farm typologies, etc. can be used for a more detailed assessment of the performance of an innovation within the broader context. Alternatively, indicator results from lower levels and their variability can be presented together with results at a broader spatial scale.

In SAI assessment, it is important to also consider the temporal sensitivity of indicators to management, biophysical, socio-economic and policy drivers (de Olde et al., 2016). In agricultural research, some processes may take place slowly, others rapidly and their respective indicators may require observations over different time periods to obtain a reliable indicator estimate. For example, obtaining an average water-limited potential yield from field experiments may require a number of years of experimentation since climatic conditions may change and yields from any one season may not be indicative of the potential yield for a given crop under good climatic conditions. Models may facilitate the estimation of trends of these indicators.

The SAI assessment framework may be used to address some of the spatial and temporal challenges as follows:

1   The assessment framework has a core list of indicators across multiple domains that guides the scientist in the project planning, monitoring and evaluation stage with information on what indicators are scale dependent (spatially) and scale independent (see www.k-state.edu/siil/resources/index.html for details). In addition, the tables of metrics by spatial scale provide an indication of how units of analysis of an indicator may change across scale and what methods of data collection may be used at these scales to generate the indicators (Table 29.1). For example, assessing gender equity at the plot level could be measured by

Table 29.1 Examples of two indicators with metrics for each spatial scale

Indicator	Field-/plot-level metrics	Farm-level metrics	Household-level metrics	Community/ landscape + metrics	Measurement method
Nutrition	Protein production (g/ha) [a,b] Micronutrient production (g/ha) [a,b]	Total protein production (g/ha) [a,b] Total micronutrient production (g/ha) [a,b] Availability of diverse food crops [a]	Access to nutritious foods [a] Dietary diversity [a] Food consumption score [a] Nutritional status (underweight, stunting, wasting) [c] Uptake of essential nutrients [d]	Market or landscape supply of diverse food [e,f] Dietary Diversity [a] Rate of underweight, stunting and wasting [c] Average birthweight [c]	[a] Survey [b] Look up tables [c] Anthropometric measurements [d] Blood tests [e] Survey of marketed foods [f] Participatory mapping
Food security	Food production (Calories/ha) [a,b]	Food production (Calories/ha) [a,b]	Food availability [a] Food accessibility [a] Food utilization [a] Food security composite index [a] Months of food insecurity [a] Rating of food security [c]	Total food production [a] % population food secure [a]	[a] Survey [b] Look up tables [c] Participatory assessment

Source: Guide for Sustainable Intensification Assessment – www.k-state.edu/siil/resources/index.html

gendered-rating of an innovation. At the household level, gender equity could be measured by gender gaps in access to resources related to the innovation, gender gaps in control over managing the innovation and gender gaps in who benefits from the production/sales. At the community level gender equity could be measured by documenting which types of men and women are benefiting and how the innovation is affecting gendered power dynamics in the community.

2 The framework also provides tools in the planning process. There is a worksheet to identify objectives of the innovation across the domains. On that worksheet, the appropriate scale at which sub-objectives or outcomes are linked to the innovation for each domain can be noted. This makes it easier to identify where proxies may be needed to match the scale of assessment. For example, if the field scale is the scale of assessment of the innovation, and food security is a sub-objective of the innovation (which is usually assessed at the household level), this may create a scale mismatch. Where possible, proxy indicators are provided in the framework; for example, at the field or farm level a metric of production of calories per hectare is provided as a proxy for food security illustrating the 'potential' available calories from the innovation. Ideally an SAI assessment will measure the household-level effect of a plot-level change, but often such effects come long after a project is over, leaving no alternative but a proxy indicator. The SAI indicator manual (www.k-state.edu/siil/resources/index.html) has also provided information on the limitations of such proxy

indicators and how to present them to avoid misrepresentation and miscommunication where scale mismatch may be an issue. Continuing the example above, the SAI indicator manual points out the importance of not equating an increase in potential available calories (from a field-level assessment) with household food security. This is done by pointing out the intervening factors between production and consumption (such as sales, theft and storage) and by pointing out the scale limitation – that higher potential calories on one plot may come at the expense of some other activity that contributes to food security.

3   In addition, the framework also provides a pre-planning exercise to assess potential trade-offs and synergies (see Part 3.2 for details and Part 3.4 for a full example) where scientists can assess the baseline consequences and benefits of the conventional technology and a scenario in which the innovation is implemented. This exercise enables the stakeholders (scientists, extension agents, etc.) to identify objectives, outcomes, tradeoffs and synergies. In the process, they can also indicate at which time steps given outcomes may be observed. If some process like land rehabilitation may take longer than improvement in yield, these are indicated in the planning exercise.

For any given objective, it is important to consider various temporal properties. The MESMIS framework of peasant natural resource management indicators (López-Ridaura et al., 2002; López-Ridaura et al., 2005) is a seminal work that provides a useful categorization of temporal system properties drawing from ecological terminology. Any particular goal or objective can be assessed in terms of if it is productive (is the level acceptable), reliable (is it potentially stable), stable (is the variability and risk acceptable), resilient (can it recover quickly and completely from a shock) and adaptable (can the system respond to permanent changes to meet the goal). This approach is powerful since systems properties are relevant across systems but it can be challenging to effectively characterize agricultural systems according to these properties. Table 29.2 provides some examples of specific objectives and what data would be needed to assess these temporal system properties.

These temporal attributes are critical for sustainability assessment but can be difficult to measure directly over the typical three-year project cycle. Unless an unforeseeable event happens during the project, the resilience and adaptability of the system will not be observed. Scenario planning and modeling can be used to estimate the potential for the system to rebound from a shock or adapt to a permanent change in driving forces. Further work is needed to develop specific indicators that can more effectively and directly capture the temporal aspects of sustainability.

3.2 Challenge 2: complex tradeoffs, synergies and unintended consequences

A second challenge is dealing with the complex interactions across the processes being altered by an innovation with the aim of achieving the broad goals associated with SAI. These interactions come as both tradeoffs and synergies, and the indirect links among indicators, and feedbacks, cuts across domains and are often not recognized due to 'disciplinary' biases in the application of indicators to assess sustainable agricultural intensification.

A major focus of assessing indicators across these five domains is to evaluate potential tradeoffs and synergies. The five domains in the SAI assessment framework provide a distinct assessment of key issues such as equity and collective action indicators in the social domain, and nutritional and food safety concerns in the human condition domain – which in most framework may be overlooked during indicator selection. If predictions are to be made regarding

Table 29.2 Examples of indicators and potential proxy indicators of system properties for specific objectives, many of which highlight temporal variability

Domain:	Productivity	Human well-being	Economic
Spatial Scale:	Plot	Household	Farm
System properties	Objective = increased crop productivity	Objective = improved nutrition	Objective = poverty reduction
Productive: **Stable: (potentially reliable)**	Yield Trends in nutrient flows and water availability	Nutritional status Trends in diet diversity and access to health care	Profitability Trends in asset and input availability
Reliable: **(normal fluctuations)**	Yield stability *Proxy:* Yield variability, or probability of low production	Malnutrition rate stability	Profit stability
Resilient: (extreme fluctuations)	Yield during and after shocks; *Proxy:* Crop and varietal diversity	Malnutrition rates during and after shocks; *Proxies:* Livelihood diversity	Profits during and after shocks *Proxies:* Diversity of buyers, diversity of uses of product
Adaptable: **(permanent changes)**	Productivity before and after systemic shift; *Proxies:* Farmer capacity; availability of alternative crops or livelihoods	Malnutrition rates through systemic shift; *Proxies:* Nutrition awareness	Profits before and after systemic shift; *Proxies:* Education level, potential for value addition, etc.

agricultural technologies' contributions to sustainable development goals and policies, this is essential. By emphasizing tradeoffs and synergies across five domains, this systems perspective also helps anticipate barriers to adoption and unintended negative consequences from agricultural innovations.

The analysis of tradeoffs and synergies can be especially difficult because the causal links from a change in agricultural practices to indicators are often indirect with many intermediary factors. This makes detecting empirical contributions from an innovation towards various indicators and goals tricky. For example, the complex links between a change in production and nutrition are illustrated in the Pathways Model of Nutrition Sensitive Agriculture (Figure 29.2). Our framework includes indicators and metrics for the different steps in the pathways between the innovation and the goal (e.g. protein production, diet diversification, stunting and gender equity). Other critical factors for improved nutrition can easily be added for a specific project wanting to carefully document all steps along the pathway, such as changes in caregiving practices, access to health care and improved sanitation.

Identifying the key context-specific causal pathways associated with specific interventions is helpful in selecting the indicators most relevant to project objectives for each domain. Continuing with the example of agriculture-nutrition linkages, imagine a project aiming to improve nutrition through improved bean production. If it is learned that farmers are primarily selling their bean harvest and buying food (e.g. eggs and dairy) then a change in nutrient composition

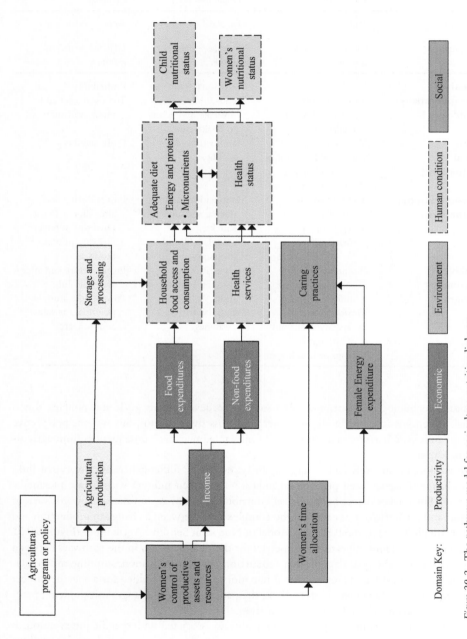

Figure 29.2 The pathways model for agriculture–nutrition linkages

Sources: Chung et al. (2015), adapted from Herforth and Harris (2014) with boxes coded to the five domains of SAI following Figure 29.1.

Domain Key: Productivity   Economic   Environment   Human condition   Social

of the crop (for example a bean with lower iron content) may be less important factor in the farming household's nutritional status than the marketability of that bean variety.

Carrying out an ex ante assessment can help agricultural researchers avoid negative unintended consequences or mitigate negative tradeoffs (Dury et al., 2015). For example, research partners in Ethiopia described an irrigation project aiming to improve nutrition through vegetable production. Contrary to those goals the vegetables were instead sold and the cash was controlled by men, so the nutritional benefits did not materialize, though benefits to income may have been substantial. Similarly, research has documented the commercialization of milk having negative nutritional impacts in India, Rwanda and Ethiopia (Dury et al., 2015). Identifying these unintended tradeoffs and impediments to achieving sustainability with intensification can assist in modifying interventions and policies that could lead to more inclusive outcomes.

Indeed, integrated, holistic use of indicators will allow assessment of win-win, win-neutral and win-lose interactions (Garbach et al., 2017). A few key examples are highlighted here from the literature. Tradeoffs associated with SAI technologies often involve production (and income derived from production) versus environmental services (Dropplemann et al., 2017). This is illustrated by agro-diversification with legumes, including many forms of agroforestry and conservation agriculture technologies. Grain yield potential of a legume is often inversely related to the ability of the nitrogen-rich crop residues to rehabilitate soil fertility, conserve moisture and soil, and in some cases, mitigate greenhouse gas emissions. In East and Southern Africa, studies with tropical multiuse legumes and agroforestry have consistently shown this tradeoff (Rao and Mathuva, 2000; Snapp et al., 2002; Rogé, et al., 2016). Interestingly, there are also innovative proposals to lessen competition and tradeoffs in resource use by expanding biomass production, through crop-livestock integration or other ways of translating sunlight into carbohydrates and growth (Baudron et al., 2014).

Our framework addresses this second challenge of incorporating tradeoffs and synergies by providing a causal loop diagram exercise as part of the indicator selection process. The goal of the exercise is to have researchers imagine the possible direct and indirect consequences that could be associated with changes from their innovations and to identify the relevant indicators. Building awareness of the possible linkages (and multiple causes for these links) is an initial step. The exercise consists of a list of indicators organized by domain. First, stakeholders circle the most direct effect from the innovation and then draw arrows representing the direct linkages with indicators with and across domains using plus and minus signs to represent synergies and tradeoffs, respectively. It is useful to go through lists of these indicators and discuss if and why there may be linkages. The next step is then to explore possible indirect and feedback linkages among indicators. Even without getting into the details of identifying metrics to operationalize the indicators, this process creates a safe opportunity to discuss linkages outside of a disciplinary focus. The exercise can best be done by an interdisciplinary team of stakeholders to explore the multiple pathways and domains.

We had positive feedback from researchers in all five countries where we facilitated the use of this exercise. It was interesting to note that the teams readily identified positive links, or synergies, between indicators. Eliciting possible negative links, or tradeoffs, required further prodding and inquiry. Questions that relate to possible tradeoffs can be developed to facilitate the discussions – but may require expertise from outside the teams.

These types of tradeoff discussions lead to the identification of indicators from the various domains that may need to be added to researchers' initial selection. Interdisciplinary teams then need to determine feasible methods for collecting data from these disparate domains and tools for robust tradeoff analysis and interpretation. These indicators and methods will be refined iteratively as described in Part 3.3, (see also Marinus et al., Chapter 28).

For example, a researcher working on soil and water conservation in Ethiopia identified an important issue through the use of this exercise. The objective of the innovation technology was to improve food security through landscape-based integrated water and land management. A focus of the project was water harvesting strategies that would include stream diversions and boreholes. Two direct goals were to improve water availability and improve crop productivity which in turn would lead to food security. The exercise helped the researcher realize that the potential for conflict over the water resources on diversion and use of water in the community would, among other things, hurt their productivity by harming their cooperative sourcing of inputs. To resolve such an issue, the scientists indicated that community committees could be formed to anticipate and resolve water-related conflicts. The researcher also noted that increased irrigation due to the implementation of the project may lead to salinization but this may be observed after the life of the project. Such potential effects should be stressed and where possible measures put in place to mitigate them.

This example also highlights aspects of the first challenge; the consideration of issues that may occur at higher and lower spatial scales of the study are important to account for when considering the indirect and direct effects of an innovation. Specifically, this case shows how an innovation at the landscape level can have effects on lower spatial scales and that this has a temporal dimension with indirect effects that may occur after the life of the project.

These are but a few examples of how analyzing tradeoffs and synergies through objective-oriented indicators related to development goals can be used to support sustainable trajectories in agriculture and associated food systems.

3.3 Challenge 3: diverse values and priorities

A third challenge comes from the diversity of stakeholders' priorities and values that may cause conflicts in implementing sustainable agricultural intensification initiatives. In addition to the biophysical environmental complexity mentioned in challenge 1, there is socio-economic complexity, including the political context for any given agri-food system (Mahon et al., 2017). The heterogeneity of agro-ecological and socio-economic conditions in smallholder farming systems pose difficulties for researchers to understand which interventions, technologies or institutional changes are of interest to different actors, which have potential to be adopted and what the barriers are (Vanlauwe et al., 2014; Descheemaeker et al., 2016).

Our framework addresses the third challenge through directed stakeholder dialogue about objectives and indicator selection, and participatory action research processes (PAR). Sets of SAI indicators are critical to the successful use of PAR in research design, data collection and synthesis of findings for specific contexts, providing a foundation for iterative co-learning (SIIL website: www.k-state.edu/siil/resources/index.html). The goal is to provide locally specific results and feedback that improves the relevance of research. We contend that PAR can be improved through the use of indicators and metrics that enhance understanding of SAI trajectories, support local adaptation and adoption, and help form policy initiatives.

Farmers and other stakeholders are becoming widely recognized for their importance to the innovation process (Campbell et al., 2016; Pound and Conroy, 2017). The process of co-learning in support of innovation is supported by a sequence of steps including: plan, action, assess/reflect and further planning through collaborative, iterative consideration of next steps (Figure 29.3).

This iterative process is based on Kolb's learning cycle (Kolb, 1984): abstract concepts to plan, test in new situations, concrete/lived experience, observations and reflections. This is from the discipline of experiential education, as illustrated for PAR as applied to agro-ecology (Kolb, 1984; Moncure and Francis, 2011). Further, it draws upon action research approaches developed

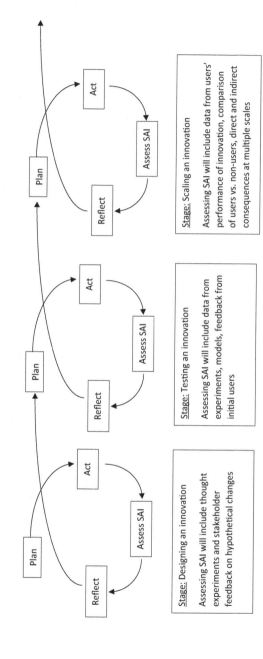

Boxes within diagram:

Stage: Designing an innovation

Assessing SAI will include thought experiments and stakeholder feedback on hypothetical changes

Stage: Testing an innovation

Assessing SAI will include data from experiments, models, feedback from initial users

Stage: Scaling an innovation

Assessing SAI will include data from users' performance of innovation, comparison of users vs. non-users, direct and indirect consequences at multiple scales

Figure 29.3 Diagram of iterative co-learning cycle over time (a spiral) with several rounds of SAI assessment and the stages of development of an innovation labeled

Source: Guide for Sustainable Intensification Assessment – www.k–state.edu/siil/resources/index.html

in the mid-1950s by social scientists who saw themselves as change agents, with a focus on collaborative solving of problems with stakeholders (Argyris and Schön, 1989). The stakeholders involved can be farmers, and other community members, but they can also be policymakers or private-sector decision-makers, as the PAR process can be carried out at district or country scale, as well as local. The calls for greater use of PAR are growing in urgency, as climate change and globalization are sources of increasing complexity and shocks to systems, that many would say requires the engagement of stakeholders, and co-learning (Campbell et al., 2016). We make the case here that the effective use of sustainability indicators can support and enhance this PAR process.

Stakeholder involvement is important in each step of the innovation and dissemination process. Participation is critical for the indicator selection process so that the assessment includes the perspectives of all stakeholders, not just a select subset of stakeholders. It is important to be aware of the power dynamics across stakeholder groups and to anticipate potential value conflicts. Consensus is often difficult but compromise through a deliberation process can be facilitated.

In general, participatory assessment involving SAI indicators is an underdeveloped area of research. There is a large body of literature related to involving farmers and others in developing indicators for participatory management of natural resources (Guijt, 1999; Speelman et al., 2007); however, other steps in the PAR process, such as farmer testing and assessment of SAI performance through indicators, are not well documented. Another aspect that requires research is developing a systematic process for choosing stakeholders to be involved in the PAR process and indicator selection. Value conflict is a challenge to the PAR process, as stakeholders often will have different priorities, and these may be highly divergent. At the same time, the value conflicts inherent in sustainable development are a key motivation for carrying out PAR and developing indicators, so that tradeoffs that represent different values can be elucidated (Batie, 2008) and discussions held for how to address them.

In the Soil, Food and Healthy Community (SFHC) in Northern Malawi, collaboration among farmers, local leaders and educators from a nearby hospital (http://soilandfood.org/) has supported the identification of indicators with local resonance, including food security, soil fertility and family health (Bezner Kerr et al., 2007). In addition to focus groups, where discussion about SAI indicators was initiated, over a thousand farmers have conducted participatory experimentation and local assessments, in an iterative process that promoted innovation and adoption of novel crops, and SAI practices. As shown in Figure 29.3, this innovation process involves multiple iterations of SAI assessment, and can address complexity and changing goals. Such cycles of action and reflection are foundational to participatory action research (Kolb, 1984; Moncure and Francis, 2011) and have been used successfully for sustainability assessments (López-Ridaura et al., 2005). The SFHC project is an example of a PAR evolutionary process, with its beginnings in 1999 as primarily an agro-ecology project, whereas today SFHC tackles such intersecting challenges as gender inequity, climate change and agricultural-health interactions (Bezner Kerr et al., 2016).

Reaching hundreds of thousands of individuals and scaling countrywide is difficult through PAR approaches. Participatory implies a level of personal engagement; thus, it is inherently expensive to scale out in terms of human resources (Snapp and Heong, 2003). A way forward may be campaigns that encourage local experimentation rather than fixed recommendations, so that farmers are encouraged to test for themselves the value of technical advice and innovations. For example, farmer groups in Ethiopia were trained in participatory experimentation without technical training in agricultural practices and were able to improve their yields through systematic experimentation with fertilizer application rates (Kraaijvanger et al., 2016).

SAI indicators can play an important role in assessing the success of such approaches. An example is provided by the "Three Reductions, Three Gains" participatory extension campaign in Vietnam that was shown to not only improve farmer profits, but also to lead to substantial reductions in pesticide use, as well as improvements in farmer capacity to experiment and observe (Heong et al., 2010). Assessing success of management guides for pesticide use in rice production in this case was placed directly in the hands of farmers, who used their own criteria and indicators (Huan et al., 2005). In addition, societal interests, such as biodiversity of arthropods, and biocontrol of potential pest outbreaks, could be considered in combination with farmer-defined indicators (Gurr et al., 2012).

Examples such as the "Three Reductions, Three Gains" illustrate how the third challenge can be addressed through a PAR process, as well as how SAI indicators can be integrated throughout to promote co-learning. The planning process benefits from the co-development of indicators, and a framework of systematic assessment supports an iterative, evolutionary process that considers multiple dimensions of sustainability.

3.4 Example of ex ante SAI assessment with enset in Ethiopia

The iterative process of assessment and action in the above figure highlights the importance of reflecting on the implications of the sustainability assessment and making adjustments. In this section, we present an example of the first step in this process as applied to a real-world complex SAI innovation in Ethiopia. Our goal is to highlight how reflecting on the three challenges above (defining spatial and temporal scales, considering tradeoffs of any synergies across domains and understanding diverse priorities) can be used to effectively guide decision-making for SAI.

The example comes from our interactions in November 2015 with researchers from AfricaRISING working to improve food security through the crop enset in Upper Gana and Jawe Kebeles, in the region of Southern Nations, Nationalities and Peoples, Ethiopia.

Enset (*Ensete ventricosum*), also known as the false banana, is a native food crop of Ethiopia. Like a banana plant it is tall with large fleshy leaves. Rather than fruits like banana however, the part of enset consumed by humans is the short, fleshy underground root (corm). The corm is cooked like a potato and the stem is squeezed and the output fermented and then baked to form a thin bread and other food products (Mohammed et al., 2013). Enset is drought tolerant and improves food security in drought-prone areas of Ethiopia. Other benefits derived from enset include: leaves as animal fodder during droughts, fiber from the stem to make ropes and strings, leaves as mulch to improve soil fertility and moisture (canopy cover) and stems to make glue (Negash et al., 2013). Enset has cultural medicinal uses and ownership of a field of enset is prestigious in some communities since it is an indication of high social economic status. Cooking and preparing enset is labor intensive, with the majority of the work done by women.

The AfricaRISING project is working with communities to improve the productivity of enset through disease control, crop management and improved genetics. The primary goal is to improve food security (both directly through enset consumption and indirectly through improve animal feed availability) with indirect benefits such as soil fertility enhancement. The project is also working to improve marketing of enset, which has a high market value to produce sacks, glue, glucose (syrup) and food products.

The potential for improved enset production to contribute to sustainable intensification is compelling for a variety of reasons. First, the crop matures over several years and its harvest is less susceptible to annual rainfall fluctuations, such as the 2015–2016 El Niño droughts that reduced cereal production by 20% in Ethiopia (Tefera, 2016). The need for resilient staple food production is an important strategy for disaster risk reduction and food security. The potential for commercializing multiple products from enset (which is not yet fully exploited) could also contribute to resilient income. These risk reductions strategies may be just as important considerations as effects on annual net income.

Second, enset and livestock are synergistic and land productivity can be very high. Enset produces feed that can be harvested throughout the year which can help overcome dry season feeding constraints, which allows herd size to increase and manure production to increase. The animal manure in turn is used to fertilize enset. This synergistic relationship may have complex consequences (positive or negative) on the landscape. Positively, enset production can reduce pressure in pasture land during the dry season, however it could also enable higher stocking rates, which may actually increase pressure on pasture lands.

Local project staff explained that enset production has been in decline over the past decade for several reasons. Enset production is a long-term investment as the primary harvest occurs seven to ten years after planting. With increased market linkages, farmers are looking for higher and more immediate returns. One response to this has been increased effort to develop commercial use of enset products, e.g. starch for glue and fiber for ropes. Another important issue is that a severe bacterial wilt has been killing enset plants. Farmers were asking for a quick chemical solution to the disease, but bacterial plant infections often require prevention through careful management (Yemataw, 2014). The bacteria may be spread through cutting tools and through the manure of animals which are fed the infected material, which is a common use for diseased plants. Areka Agricultural Research Center is carrying out research to address this important constraint to enset production.

Using the information that we obtained from discussion with the site team, we developed a tradeoff diagram to explore the current enset production system across the five domains (Figure 29.4). Enset production provides food during drought, regular feed for animals and some income. The improved soil fertility is a delayed effect mentioned by farmers who stated that they do not need to fertilize a field for several years after enset is harvested, probably due to the manure application during the enset production years as well as the accumulation of decomposed enset roots and residues. We also assume there is some erosion prevention (compared to annual crops) due to the year-round leaf cover and living root system. There are mixed effects on the social domain – high labor requirements for women but also high social prestige for households with larger plots of enset.

Next we considered changes that might occur if the research efforts to improve market linkages and to control the bacterial wilt were successful (referred to as 'scenario'; Figure 29.5). This exercise provides an avenue for stakeholders to discuss the context, objectives and indicators that may be needed to assess performance of the innovation holistically (across all domains). In addition, linkages are identified across indicators to assess tradeoffs and synergies. It emerged during this exercise that gains in production were expected to positively correlate with market orientation and food security. A key learning was the need to avoid unintended consequences for gender such as high labor requirements for post-production processing, perhaps by shifting towards an emphasis on mechanization. The project should consider possible interventions to reduce the demands on female labor both for the cropping and processing. This highlights how this exercise can help identify tradeoffs and select a complete set of indicators for SAI assessment. Furthermore, it opens discussions on possible additional interventions that are needed to reduce tradeoffs and enhance synergies. It is important to have these discussions prior to implementation in case there may not be obvious interventions that would mitigate tradeoffs.

The next step from this exercise would be to then transfer the selected indicators to a planning form to assess: (1) which metrics are most suitable for each indicator, (2) how the data will

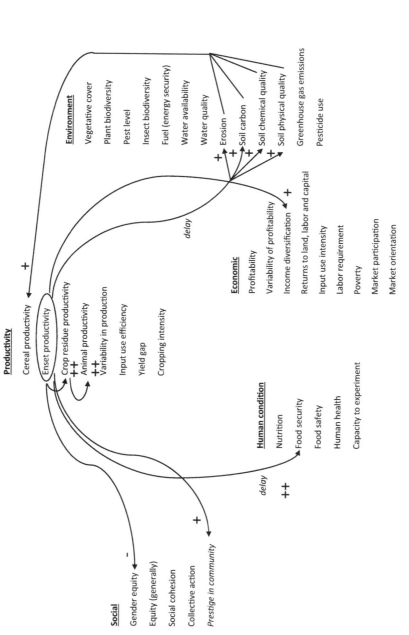

Figure 29.4 Baseline diagram of tradeoffs and synergies for enset (false banana) in Ethiopia

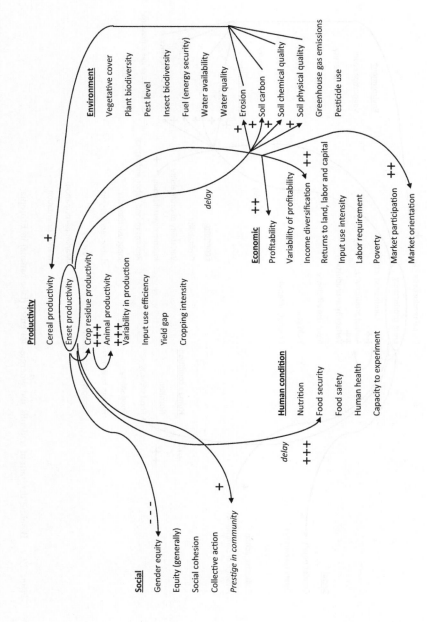

Figure 29.5 Diagram of tradeoffs and synergies for enset for the scenario of successful productivity and marketing research

be collected, (3) who will collect it, (4) what resources (money or expertise) is needed and then (5) the feasibility of the SAI assessment from the project standpoint.

As the research to improve enset production moves forward it will benefit from operationalizing a participatory approach like that described in Figure 29.2. For example, women and men should give early feedback on any new varieties as well as any mechanization efforts. This will provide a chance to mitigate unforeseen tradeoffs and to strengthen potential synergies. In addition to gendered perspectives from producers, feedback may need to be obtained from stakeholders across the value chain, especially if new varieties have different fiber or starch qualities affecting their commercial use. Such an approach would strengthen research for SAI in Ethiopia.

This example of the use of the framework is largely conceptual because it was carried out at an early stage of developing a potential SAI intervention. A more quantitative application of the framework for assessing legume intercrops with maize in Malawi is also available (Snapp et al., 2018).

4. Next steps for SAI indicator assessment

Metrics become an indicator when they are used for decision-making by comparing them to a criterion or goal. The value of any framework of indicators depends on how well the use of those indicators contribute to sound decision-making. The framework of indicators and exercises that we have developed was designed to support effective decision-making about SAI innovations by creating a structured but flexible approach to indicator selection, measurement and analysis. Further details on the process and worksheets supporting its use are available at www.k-state.edu/siil/resources/index.html. This effort is certainly a work in progress and we see several important areas for continued improvement in the future.

First, decision-making will be enhanced if SAI assessments can be reported with context-specific thresholds and/or targets for each indicator. For example, a study in India developed upper and lower thresholds for soil quality parameters in long-term rice-rice sequenced fields (Biswas et al., 2017). These values are necessarily context specific. Reference values can also be developed locally, such as a study in Cambodia on the effect of management practices on soil carbon, which used natural vegetation as a reference value, which can also be seen as a high-level target (Hok et al., 2015).

Next, sustainability indicators related to risk and variability need to be further developed. We highlight here the need for indicators that can be estimated in the timespan of a typical project, and that are practical to implement. Many of these may also be context specific but general approaches could be further developed to effectively operationalize measuring properties such as those developed by the MESMIS framework (López-Ridaura et al., 2005). Innovations that support resilience and adaptability at multiple scales are likely to be prioritized, both by farmers and policymakers, especially if the innovations reduce the risk of losses. Effectively identifying short-term proxy indicators for this will require creative research that utilizes historical data to assess why some innovations contributed to resilience while others did not.

Finally, researchers need to be supported to implement participatory processes like those described above. A clear starting point is training researchers to facilitate participatory indicator selection and to utilize participatory data collection methods for estimating indicators. Our framework provides guidance on a participatory process for indicator selection and summarizes the literature on several key participatory data collection methods (see documents at www.k-state.edu/siil/resources/index.html). However, participatory agricultural research also requires a different set of funding and incentives from typical research. Long-term relationships between communities and researchers are needed, and one way to support this is to strengthen relationships between development organizations and research centers. Research in development projects face the challenge of balancing how to meet project objectives while also satisfying scientific criteria for research.

It should also be noted that there is a risk that SAI assessment will become a donor-driven exercise divorced from the reality or priorities of on-the-ground decision-makers. During our interactions with researchers while developing this framework, their questions frequently focused on how the donor will use the assessment to evaluate their project, which was not the primary purpose of developing the indicators. Project evaluation requires a wider focus than what we have described here, which aims to specifically assess technologies or other innovations for their contribution towards SAI. Instead of trying to force this assessment into a monitoring and evaluation framework, we suggest projects developing innovations for SAI to simply have an output indicator such as "number of innovations assessed across all five domains". Research projects make valuable contributions to the scientific body of knowledge even when the innovations under research do not transform the sustainability of agriculture. It is also valuable to find out which innovations are not suitable for widespread promotion in their current form, as such information can guide technological adaptations, highlight the need for policy change or focus promotional efforts.

5. Conclusion

Developing an effective set of indicators for assessing sustainable agricultural intensification poses a number of important challenges. The key challenges include defining relevant system boundaries in terms of spatial and temporal scale, understanding the interactions across multiple objectives and how to manage them, and making the analysis relevant for stakeholders in heterogeneous landscapes and complex socio-economic environments. We have tried to address the challenges through developing a SAI framework systems approach moving beyond reductionist approaches. We have collated indicators, provided exercises and advice on their use, while resisting pressures to narrow the list to a minimum mandatory set, nor do we proscribe which are the best for different objectives. We believe that field practitioners and other users of this SAI framework are in the best place to judge which indicators and exercises are most useful. The aim of the SAI indicator framework is to help scientists, citizens and policymakers work towards diverse goals across productivity, economic, environmental, human condition and social domains. Sustainability is a difficult concept to measure, yet if we are to see a future with nature preserved and fewer hungry and disempowered men, women and youth, then we have no choice but to measure and assess progress and make mid-course corrections to alter trajectories towards the multiple goals of sustainability.

Acknowledgements

The work to develop the SAI assessment framework was made possible through funding from the United States Agency for International Development (USAID) under Cooperative Agreement No. AID-OAA-L-14–00006, Feed the Future Innovation Lab for Sustainable Intensification. We would like to thank the steering committee for that project for their many insights guiding our efforts: Gundula Fischer, Bruno Gerard, Jerry Glover, Fred Kizito, Generose Nziguheba, Vara Prasad, Peter Thorne and Bernard Vanlauwe. We would also like to thank the many researchers from AfricaRISING, SIIL and CIALCA projects for their feedback as we developed the framework.

References

Argyris, C. and Schön, D.A. 1989. Participatory action research and action science compared: A commentary. *American Behavioral Scientist*, 32(5), pp. 612–623.

Barnes, A.P. and Thomson, S.G. 2014. Measuring progress towards sustainable intensification: How far can secondary data go? *Ecological Indicators*, 36, pp. 213–220.

Batie, S. 2008. Wicked problems and applied economics. *American Journal of Agricultural Economics*, 90(5), pp. 1176–1191.

Baudron, F., Jaleta, M., Okitoi, O., and Tegegn, A. 2014. Conservation agriculture in African mixed crop-livestock systems: Expanding the niche. *Agriculture, Ecosystems & Environment*, 187, pp. 171–182.

Baulcombe, D., Crute, I., Davies, B., Dunwell, J., Gale, M., Green, N., Jones, J., Mee, S., Pretty, J., Simpson, A., Stilgoe, J., Sutherland, W., and Toulmin, C. 2009. *Reaping the Benefits: Science and the Sustainable Intensification of Global Agriculture*. London: The Royal Society.

Bezner Kerr, R., Chilanga, E., Nyantakyi-Frimpong, H., Luginaah, I., and Lupafya, E. 2016. Supporting emergent masculinities: Integrated agriculture programs to address malnutrition in northern Malawi. *BMC Public Health*, November 11.

Bezner Kerr, R., Snapp, S.S., Chirwa, M., Shumba, L., and Msachi, R. 2007. Participatory research on legume diversification with Malawian smallholder farmers for improved human nutrition and soil fertility. *Experimental Agriculture*, 43, pp. 437–453.

Biswas, S., Hazra, G.C., Purakayastha, T.J., Saha, N., Mitran, T., Roy, S.S., Basak, N., and Mandal, B. 2017. Establishment of critical limits of indicators and indices of soil quality in rice-rice cropping systems under different soil orders. *Geoderma*, 292, pp. 34–48.

Campbell, B.M., Vermeulen, S.J., Aggarwal, P.K., Corner-Dolloff, C., Girvetz, E., Loboguerrero, A.M., Ramirez-Villegas, J., Rosenstock, T., Sebastian, L., Thornton, P.K., and Wollenberg, E. 2016. Reducing risks to food security from climate change. *Global Food Security*, 11, pp. 34–43.

Chung, K., Cashin, K., Isaacs, K., and Grabowski, P. 2015. *An Introduction to Nutrition-Sensitive Agricultural Programming*. Online course. Washington, DC: USAID's FANTA Project at FHI 360. https://agrilinks.org/sites/default/files/nutrition-training/module1part1/index.htm

Cook, S., Silici, L., Adolph, B., and Walker, S. 2015. *Sustainable Intensification Revisited*. IIED Issue paper. London: IIED.

Dale, V.H. and Polasky, S., 2007. Measures of the effects of agricultural practices on ecosystem services. *Ecological economics*, 64(2), pp. 286–296.

de Olde, E.M., Moller, H., Marchand, F., McDowell, R.W., MacLeod, C.J., Sautier, M., Halloy, S., Barber, A., Benge, J., Bockstaller, C., and Bokkers, E.A. 2016. When experts disagree: The need to rethink indicator selection for assessing sustainability of agriculture. *Environment, Development and Sustainability*, pp. 1–16.

Descheemaeker, K., Ronner, E., Ollenburger, M., Franke, A.C., Klapwijk, C.J., Falconnier, G.N., Wichern, J., and Giller, K.E. 2016. Which options fit best? Operationalizing the socio-ecological niche concept. *Experimental Agriculture*, pp. 1–22.

Diazabakana, A., Latruffe, L., Bockstaller, C., Desjeux, Y., Finn, J., Kelly, E., Ryan, M., and Uthes, S. 2014. *A Review of Farm Level Indicators of Sustainability with a Focus on CAP and FADN*. http://www3.lei.wur.nl/flint/downloads/reports/FLINT

Droppelmann, K.J., Snapp, S.S., and Waddington, S. 2017. Sustainable intensification technologies for smallholder maize-based farming systems in Sub-Saharan Africa. *Food Security*, 9, p. 133. doi:10.1007/s12571-016-0636-0

Dury, S., Alpha, A., and Bichard, A. 2015. The negative side of the agricultural-nutrition impact pathways: A literature review. *World Food Policy*, 2(1), pp. 78–100.

Evenson, R.E. and Gollin, D. 2003. Assessing the impact of the green revolution, 1960–2000. *Science*, 300, pp. 758–762.

Franke, A.C., Baijukya, F., Kantengwa, S., Reckling, M., Vanlauwe, B., and Giller, K.E. 2016. Poor farmers – poor yields: Socio-economic, soil fertility and crop management indicators affecting climbing bean productivity in northern Rwanda. *Experimental Agriculture*, pp. 1–21.

Garbach, K., Milder, J.C., DeClerck, F.A., Montenegro de Wit, M., Driscoll, L. and Gemmill-Herren, B. 2017. Examining multi-functionality for crop yield and ecosystem services in five systems of agroecological intensification. *International Journal of Agricultural Sustainability*, 15(1), pp. 11–28. http://dx.doi.org/10.1080/14735903.2016.1174810

Garnett, T. and Godfray, C. 2012. Sustainable intensification in agriculture; navigating a course through competing food system priorities. *Food Climate Research Network and the Oxford Martin Programme on the Future of Food*, p. 51. Oxford, UK: University of Oxford.

Gaviglio, A., Bertocchi, M., Marescotti, M.E., Demartini, E., and Pirani, A. 2016. The social pillar of sustainability: A quantitative approach at the farm level. *Agricultural and Food Economics*, 4(1), p. 15.

Giller, K.E., Tittonell, P., Rufino, M.C., Van Wijk, M.T., Zingore, S., Mapfumo, P., Adjei-Nsiah, S., Herrero, M., Chikowo, R., Corbeels, M., and Rowe, E.C. 2011. Communicating complexity: Integrated assessment of trade-offs concerning soil fertility management within African farming systems to support innovation and development. *Agricultural Systems*, 104(2), pp. 191–203.

Glover, J. 2016. *An Indicator Framework for Sustainable Intensification Assessment*. Presentation at "Meeting on Indicators for the Sustainable Intensification of Agriculture", Michigan State University, December 14, 2016.

Godfray, H.C.J. 2015. The debate over sustainable intensification. *Food Security*, 7, pp. 199–208. doi:10.1007/s12571-015-0424-2

Groot, J.C.J., Rossing, W.A.H., Dogliotti, S., and Tittonell, P. 2012. *The COMPASS Framework – Navigating Agricultural Landscapes for Science-Based Innovation*. Conference of the European Society of Agronomy, 20–24 August 2012, Helsinki, Finland.

Guijt, I. 1999. *Participatory Monitoring and Evaluation for Natural Resource Management and Research*. Chatham, UK: Natural Resources Institute.

Gunton, R.M., Firbank, L.G., Inman, A., and Winter, D.M. 2016. How scalable is sustainable intensification? *Nature Plants*, 2, pp. 1–4. doi:10.1038/NPLANTS.2016.65

Gurr, G.M., Heong, K.L., Cheng, J.A., and Catindig, J. 2012. Ecological engineering against insect pests in Asian irrigated rice. In: Gurr, G.M., Wratten, S.D., and Snyder, W.E. (Eds.). *Biodiversity and Insect Pests: Key Issues for Sustainable Management*, pp. 214–229. Oxford, UK: Wiley-Blackwell.

Haileselassie, A., Craufurd, P., Thiagarajah, R., Kumar, S., Whitbread, A., Rathor, A., Blummel, M., Ericsson, P., and Kakumanu, K.R. 2016. Empirical evaluation of sustainability of divergent farms in the dryland farming systems of India. *Ecological Indicators*, 60, pp. 710–723.

Heong, K.L., Escalada, M.M., Huan, N.H., Chien, H.V., and Quynh, P.V. 2010. Scaling out communication to rural farmers: Lessons from the "Three Reductions, Three Gains" campaign in Vietnam. *Research to Impact: Case Studies for Natural Resource Management for Irrigated Rice in Asia*, pp. 207–220.

Herforth, A. and Harris, J. (2014). *Understanding and Applying Primary Pathways and Principles*. Brief #1. Improving Nutrition through Agriculture Technical Brief Series. Arlington, VA: USAID/Strengthening Partnerships, Results, and Innovations in Nutrition Globally (SPRING) Project.

Hok, L., de Moraes Sá, J.C., Boulakia, S., Reyes, M., Leng, V., Kong, R., Tivet, F.E., Briedis, C., Hartman, D., Ferreira, L.A., and Magno, T. 2015. Short-term conservation agriculture and biomass-C input impacts on soil C dynamics in a savanna ecosystem in Cambodia. *Agriculture, Ecosystems & Environment*, 214, pp. 54–67.

Huan, N.H., Thiet, L.V., Chien, H.V., and Heong, K.L. 2005. Farmers' evaluation of reducing pesticides, fertilizers and seed rates in rice farming through participatory research in the Mekong Delta, Vietnam. *Crop Protection*, 24, pp. 457–464.

Kanter, D.R., Musumba, M., Wood, S.L., Palm, C., Antle, J., Balvanera, P., Dale, V.H., Havlik, P., Kline, K.L., Scholes, R.J., and Thornton, P. 2016. Evaluating agricultural trade-offs in the age of sustainable development. *Agricultural Systems*. In press.

Kolb, D. 1984. *Experiential Learning*. Englewood Cliffs, NJ: Prentice Hall Publications.

Kraaijvanger, R., Veldkamp, T., and Almekinders, C. 2016. Considering change: Evaluating four years of participatory experimentation with farmers in Tigray (Ethiopia) highlighting both functional and human – social aspects. *Agricultural Systems*, 147, pp. 38–50.

Lobell, D.B., Cassman, K.G., and Field, C.B. 2009. Crop yield gaps: Their importance, magnitudes, and causes. *Annual Review of Environment and Resources*, 34(1), p. 179.

Loos, J., Abson, D.J., Chappell, M.J., Hanspach, J., Mikulcak, F., Tichit, M., and Fischer, J. 2014. Putting meaning back into "sustainable intensification". *Frontiers in Ecology and the Environment*, 12, pp. 356–361. doi:10.1890/130157

López-Ridaura, S., Masera, O., and Astier, M. 2002. Evaluating the sustainability of complex socio-environmental systems: The MESMIS framework. *Ecological Indicators*, 2(1), pp. 135–148.

López-Ridaura, S., van Keulen, H., van Ittersum, M.K., and Leffelaar, P.A. 2005. Multiscale methodological framework to derive criteria and indicators for sustainability evaluation of peasant natural resource management systems. *Environment, Development and Sustainability*, 7(1), pp. 51–69.

Mahon, N., Crute, I., Simmons, E., and Islam, M.M. 2017. Sustainable intensification – "oxymoron" or "third-way"? A systematic review. *Ecological Indicators*, 74, pp. 73–97.

Mohammed, B., Gabel, M., and Karlsson, L.M. 2013. Nutritive values of the drought tolerant food and fodder crop enset. *African Journal of Agricultural Research*, 8(20), pp. 2326–2333.

Moncure, S. and Francis, C. 2011. Foundations of experiential education as applied to agroecology. *NACTA Journal*, 55(3), pp. 75–91.

The Montpelier Panel. 2013. *Sustainable Intensification: A New Paradigm for African agriculture*. London: Agriculture for Impact.

Negash, M., Starr, M., and Kanninen, M. 2013. Allometric equations for biomass estimation of Enset (Ensete ventricosum) grown in indigenous agroforestry systems in the Rift Valley escarpment of southern-eastern Ethiopia. *Agroforestry Systems*, 87(3), pp. 571–581.

Olsson, J.A., Bockstaller, C., Stapleton, L.M., Ewert, F., Knapen, R., Therond, O., Geniaux, G., Bellon, S., Correira, T.P., Turpin, N., and Bezlepkina, I. 2009. A goal oriented indicator framework to support integrated assessment of new policies for agri-environmental systems. *Environmental Science & Policy*, 12(5), pp. 562–572.

Petersen, B. and Snapp, S. 2015. What is sustainable intensification? Views from experts. *Land Use Policy*, 46, pp. 1–10. doi:10.1016/j.landusepol.2015.02.002

Pittelkow, C.M., Zorrilla, G., Terra, J., Riccetto, S., Macedo, I., Bonilla, C., and Roel, A. 2016. Sustainability of rice intensification in Uruguay from 1993 to 2013. *Global Food Security*, 9, pp. 10–18.

Pound, B. and Conroy, C. 2017. The innovation systems approach to agricultural research and development. In: Snapp, S.S. and Pound, B. (Eds.). *Agricultural Systems: Agroecology and Rural Innovation for Development*. Second Edition. Cambridge, MA: Academic Press.

Pretty, J.N. 1997. The sustainable intensification of agriculture. *Natural Resources Forum*, 21, pp. 247–256.

Pretty, J.N. 2008. Agricultural sustainability: Concepts, principles and evidence. *Philosophical Transactions of the Royal Society B*, 363, pp. 447–466.

Rao, M.R. and Mathuva, M.N. 2000. Legumes for improving maize yields and income in semi-arid Kenya. *Agriculture, Ecosystems & Environment*, 78(2), pp. 123–137.

Rao, S. 2016. *Indicators of Gendered Control over Agricultural Resources: A Guide for Agricultural Policy and Research*. Working Paper No. 1. CGIAR Gender and Agriculture Research Network, CGIAR Consortium Office and International Center for Tropical Agriculture (CIAT). Cali, Colombia. 75 p.

Reardon, T., Crawford, E.W., Kelly, V.A., and Diagana, B.N. 1995. *Promoting Farm Investment for Sustainable Intensification of African Agriculture*. Food Security International Development Papers No. 54053. Michigan State University, Department of Agricultural, Food, and Resource Economics, East Lansing, MI USA.

Rockström, J., Williams, J., Daily, G., Noble, A., Matthews, N., Gordon, L., Wetterstrand, H., DeClerck, F., Shah, M., Steduto, P., and de Fraiture, C. 2017. Sustainable intensification of agriculture for human prosperity and global sustainability. *Ambio*, 46(1), pp. 4–17.

Rodríguez, J., Douglas Beard, T. Jr, Bennett, E., Cumming, G., Cork, S., Agard, J., Dobson, A., and Peterson, G. 2006. Trade-offs across space, time, and ecosystem services. *Ecology and Society*, 11(1):28.

Rogé, P., Snapp, S.S., Kakwera, M.K., Mungai, L., Jambo, I., and Peter, B. 2016. Ratooning and perennial staple crops in Malawi: A review. *Agronomy for Sustainable Development*, 36, p. 50. doi:10.1007/s13593-016-0384-8

SDSN. 2013. *Solutions for Sustainable Agriculture and Food Systems – Technical Report for the Post-2015 Development Agenda*. New York: Sustainable Development Solutions Network – United Nations.

Smith, A., Snapp, S.S., Chikowo, R., Thorne, P., Bekunda, M., and Glover, J. 2017. Measuring sustainable intensification in smallholder agroecosystems: A review. *Global Food Security*, 12, pp. 127–138.

Snapp, S.S., Grabowski, P., Chikowo, R., Smith, A., Anders, E., Sirrine, D., Chimonyo, V. and Bekunda, M., 2018. Maize yield and profitability tradeoffs with social, human and environmental performance: Is sustainable intensification feasible?. *Agricultural Systems*, 162, pp.77–88.

Snapp, S.S. and Heong, K.L. 2003. Scaling up: Participatory research and extension to reach more farmers. In: Pound, B., Snapp, S.S., McDougal, C., and Braun, A. (Eds.). *Uniting Science and Participation: Managing Natural Resources for Sustainable Livelihoods*, pp. 67–87. Canada, UK and IRDC: Earthscan.

Snapp, S.S., Rohrbach, D.D., Simtowe, F., and Freeman, H.A. 2002. Sustainable soil management options for Malawi: Can smallholder farmers grow more legumes? *Agriculture, Ecosystems and Environment*, 91, pp. 159–174.

Speelman, E.N., López-Ridaura, S., Colomer, N.A., Astier, M., and Masera, O.R. 2007. Ten years of sustainability evaluation using the MESMIS framework: Lessons learned from its application in 28

Latin American case studies. *The International Journal of Sustainable Development & World Ecology*, 14(4), pp. 345–361.

Struik, P.C., Kuyper, T.W., Brussaard, L., and Leeuwis, C. 2014. Deconstructing and unpacking scientific controversies in intensification and sustainability: Why the tensions in concepts and values? *Current Opinion in Environmental Sustainability*, 8, pp. 80–88. doi: http://dx.doi.org/10.1016/j.cosust.2014.10.002

Tefera, A. 2016. *Ethiopia Grain and Feed Annual Report: Global Agricultural Information Service Report ET1608*. USDA Foreign Agricultural Service. www.fas.usda.gov/data/ethiopia-grain-and-feed-annual-0

Thompson, P.B. 2007. Agricultural sustainability: What it is and what it is not. *International Journal of Agricultural Sustainability*, 5(1), pp. 5–16.

Tilman, D., Balzer, C., Hill, J., and Befort, B.L. 2011. Global food demand and the sustainable intensification of agriculture. *Proceedings of the National Academy of Sciences of the United States of America*, 108, pp. 20260–20264.

Tittonell, P. 2014. Ecological intensification of agriculture-sustainable by nature. *Current Opinion in Environmental Sustainability*, 8, pp. 53–61. doi:10.1016/j.cosust.2014.08.006

Valin, H., Sands, R.D., van der Mensbrugghe, D., Nelson, G.C., Ahammad, H., Blanc, E., Bodirsky, B., Fujimori, S., Hasegawa, T., Havlik, P., and Heyhoe, E. 2014. The future of food demand: Understanding differences in global economic models. *Agricultural Economics*, 45(1), pp. 51–67.

Vanlauwe, B., Coyne, D., Gockowski, J., Hauser, S., Huising, J., Masso, C., Nziguheba, G., Schut, M., and Van Asten, P. 2014. Sustainable intensification and the African smallholder farmer. *Current Opinion in Environmental Sustainability*, 8, pp. 15–22. doi:10.1016/j.cosust.2014.06.001

Yemataw, Z. 2014. *The Africa RISING Enset Research Initiative in Ethiopia: Enhancing the Productivity of Farming Systems*. Africa RISING Brief 10. Nairobi, Kenya: International Livestock Research Institute.

Zurek, M., Keenlyside, P., and Brandt, K. 2015. *Intensifying Agricultural Production Sustainably: A Framework for Analysis and Decision Support*. Amsterdam, The Netherlands: International Food Policy Research Institute (IFPRI), Climate Focus. http://ebrary.ifpri.org/cdm/ref/collection/p15738coll2/id/130125

30

RELEVANCE – A NEGLECTED FEATURE OF SUSTAINABILITY INDICATORS

Svatava Janoušková, Tomáš Hák, and Bedřich Moldan

Introduction

Since the first notion of sustainable development in the 1980s, the world has racked its brains over how to assess overall development. There are many sustainability assessment concepts, frameworks and methods (Graymore, Sipe, & Rickson, 2008; Singh et al., 2009; Dahl, 2012) often using simple or compound indicators and indices. A wide range of indicators suitable for various aspects of the development agenda, including sustainability assessment are already in place. At present, hundreds of different indicators have been suggested and are used in many differing contexts, by different users and for diverse purposes. However, despite all the efforts of many scientists and organizations as OECD, Eurostat, UN agencies and others, it is obvious that the whole process faces weaknesses, most of which stem from an insufficiently developed conceptual framework. Many experts, even 40 years ago, called for more theoretical and methodological work rather than an increase in the amount of developmental statistics and indicators (Bunge, 1975; Rickard et al., 2007).

Ten years ago, a project called "Assessment of Sustainability Indicators" (implemented jointly by SCOPE and UNEP, together with the International Human Dimensions Programme on Global Environmental Change [IHDP] and the European Environment Agency [EEA], under the sponsorship of ICSU) reviewed progress in sustainability indicator development in three domains – conceptual challenges, methodological frontiers, and policy relevance. It revealed key factors constituting concepts, methods, and relevance of sustainability indicators (Hák, Moldan, & Dahl, 2007).

Reporting requirements to provide data and information at all levels (company, municipality, region, country, and planet) have increased to such an extent that they generate significant demands in terms of quality. A review of various approaches and criteria used for the quality evaluation of SIs used in more than twenty major organizations (e.g. European Environmental Agency, Organization for Economic Cooperation and Development, United Nations Environment Programme, World Health Organization, US National Research Council, Eurostat, US Environmental Protection Agency, World Bank, etc.) revealed that the organizations formulated similar requirements for the indicators they use. In compliance with Parris and Kates (2003), they can be characterized by three overarching attributes: relevance (also called salience), credibility, and legitimacy. A detailed look shows that the most frequent criterion/characteristic of indicator quality, in general, is relevance. However, although some these criteria are well-defined, the rules for application (i.e. their operationalization) in practical use are far from being ready to use (Ramos and Caeiro, Chapter 32). Thus we are aware of the importance of SIs being relevant but neither SI developers nor users fully understand the concept behind them and have no clue about how to recognize that the indicator really is relevant. Rosenström (2009) interviewed many SI users and found that both scientists and practitioners agreed that indicators have little chance of being accepted and used for policy and/or decision-making unless they prove certain qualities (to be relevant, scientifically sound, feasible, effective, etc.) defined and evaluated against operationalized criteria.

As a starting point, we take these commonly agreed assumptions:

- There are already over 20 years of experience and sufficient knowledge in the development of sustainable development indicators (hereinafter called sustainability indicators – SIs) to ensure the development of reliable measurement yardsticks.
- In order for SIs to measure and assess sustainability in a realistic, reliable way and convey true information they must meet certain quality criteria (Eurostat, 2012). Unless the Sis' quality characteristics are operationalized they are of little benefit in practical use.
- Relevance is an (the most) important indicator characteristic – it corresponds with the finding that users may be willing to accept methodological weaknesses in an indicator if it provides really important information (Kurtz et al., 2001).
- Relevance is a difficult concept that needs to be first theoretically elaborated with regards to SI use. Then there will be a need for operationalization of relevance in order that this important characteristic might be applicable in practice (in decision-making).

The goal of this chapter is to review the concept of relevance in SI domains (approaches, applications, etc.), distinguish and define different types of relevance and propose an easy-to-use tool for application of the relevance criteria in indicator-based decision-making. Thus, the chapter's ambition is to contribute to both better understanding and more extensive application of this important component of the overall SI quality profile.

Relevance – what is it?

In some contexts – the importance of something – the relevance concept may be intuitively understood. In other contexts and meanings – the relationship of something to the matter at hand – it is very difficult to define. Thus, when SI developers and users speak about relevance it is often totally unclear what they mean (Relevance of what? In which meaning? For whom?).

Besides the conceptual complicatedness of the relevance concept, it is also interchanged and confused with another concept underlying the development of indicators – validity. Some authors (e.g. Girardin et al., 1999; Bockstaller & Girardin, 2003) propose a process of indicator validation. It is based, inter alia, on a definition of adequacy for a specific purpose: The indicator is validated if it is scientifically designed, if the information it supplies is relevant and if it is useful and used by end users. In general, validity is a measure that explores whether a concept or measurement is well founded and if it corresponds accurately to the real world. The validity concept is commonly used in social sciences – pedagogics, sociology, psychology, etc. (validity of testing), and in medicine (e.g. validity of Body Mass Index as an indicator of health and obesity). By definition, the validity of a measurement tool is the degree to which the tool measures what it claims to measure. Since the concept of scientific validity addresses the nature of reality, it is also an epistemological and philosophical issue; however, for the purpose of this article we pursue only the measurement aspect. Validity is important because it helps to determine what types of tests to use, and determine methods that truly measure the idea or construct in question. Thus, it is very close to indicator relevance, as we demonstrate below. It is peculiar that SI developers – at least in the social domain – have not routinely applied the validity criterion to their indicators.

Another confusing concept is reliability, since it also has to do with the quality of measurement. Simply put, reliability is the consistency or repeatability of measurements and/or measures. Without getting into details on types of measurement error (errors play a key role in degrading reliability) and types of reliability,[1] it is good to realize that there are relationships between reliability and validity in measurement. Reliability – similar to validity – is also related to relevance. For example, da Costa Pereira, Dragoni and Pasi, (2012) proposed a new model for aggregating multiple criteria for relevance assessment of documents where relevance is modelled as a multidimensional property consisting of aboutness, coverage, appropriateness, and reliability.

Relevance – while sometimes intuitive and easy to understand (people wish for information that is important, useful, and to the point even without knowing the weird term "relevance") – it is mostly a very difficult concept despite the fact that it is often applied as e.g. a selective criterion). Therefore, it has already become a major area of study of information science (Cosijn & Ingwersen, 2000). Besides information, what sort of things may be relevant? Relevance is a potential property of observable or perceptible facts – physical (e.g. a weather event like a tornado) or abstract (e.g. utterances), but also a property of thoughts, memories, and conclusions of inferences. Relevance, and the maximization of relevance, is thus the key to human cognition (Sperber et al., 1986). People pay attention to some phenomena rather than to others; they represent these phenomena to themselves in one way rather than another; they process these representations in one context rather than another. These facts raise a question: What is it that determines these choices? Sperber and Wilson (1986) suggest that humans tend to pay attention to the most relevant phenomena available; that they tend to construct the most relevant possible representations of these phenomena, and to process them in a context that maximizes their relevance. An input (a sight, a sound, an utterance, a memory) is relevant to an individual when it connects with background information he has available to yield conclusions that matter to him: say, by answering a question he had in mind, improving his knowledge on a certain topic, settling a doubt, confirming a suspicion, or correcting a mistaken impression. In relevance-theoretic terms, an input is relevant to an individual when the processing thereof in a context of available assumptions yields a positive cognitive effect. This has an important consequence for the theory of communication. A communicator, by the very act of claiming an audience's attention, suggests that the information he is offering is relevant enough to be worthy of the audience's attention (the communicated information creates an expectation of relevance). The authors conclude that information is relevant to people if it interacts in a certain way with their existing assumptions about the world.

Relevance of SIs in the above sense is not always evident and easily visible. Therefore, information on SI relevance must be mediated for users – in particular politicians and the public – in appropriate ways (see below).

Types of relevance (in an indicator context)

Let's think a bit about a well-known indicator – e.g. CO_2 emissions. Can we decide if it is a relevant indicator? How do we find out? Relevant to what? To whom? What does it mean for indicator developers and/or users? Despite the fact that we cannot cover all these very legitimate questions in one chapter, we will further seek to explore at least the key issues. To follow the above example, we know (based on current scientific knowledge) that CO_2 emissions are related to climate change. Since climate change is placed very high on both political and scientific agendas, as well as the agendas of many ordinary people, and communities and cities already affected by unstable climate, the indicator shows high thematic significance. We may put an equal sign between the theme and indicator in this case – relevance of the theme directly determines the relevance of the indicator. Another interesting aspect of the use of this particular indicator is how well this indicator informs us about the particular theme of climate change. It is obvious that this will be much more difficult to disclose. Even non-experts may know that there are many indicators somewhat related to climate change – besides CO_2 these may include emissions of other greenhouse gases, atmospheric concentrations of greenhouse gases, various temperatures (land, sea), precipitation, river flooding, drought, sea level, ocean acidity, etc. So a very practical question of the potential user of the CO_2 emissions indicator is: Are they all equal/equivalent or do some indicators report better on climate change than the others? In our terminology: Are all these indicators equally relevant? And additional questions follow: What are all the factors to be considered? For whom are they important (who are the stakeholders)? (Bell and Morse, Chapter 12). Does the world view of stakeholders play a role? (Spangenberg, Chapter 9).

From the above we may deduce what SI relevance is: A relevant indicator provides information that responds to people's concerns, and captures appropriate, pertinent, and correct information about various facts. To make this definition operational and usable for practical purposes, we distinguish two types of relevance (Hák, Kovanda, & Weinzettel, 2012):

- The thematic relevance denotes the importance of sustainability or policy themes represented by particular indicators (the themes may include resource efficiency, social inclusion, circular economy, etc.). The policy themes are sustainability challenges finding their way onto political agenda.
- The indicator relevance is conceived as representativeness of a given indicator for the sustainability theme (how well it answers the question – i.e. precisely, comprehensively, closely, etc. – the particular indicator captures the nature of the theme).

SIs are mostly quantitative expressions of narratives (Garnåsjordet et al., 2012). The thematic relevance of SIs may be straightforward and easy to evaluate – it seems to be intuitively understandable "why some things matter more than others" – especially when a policy theme is well narrated. Also, there is a vast amount of literature researching this issue from many perspectives – philosophical and psychological (e.g. Ruti, 2016), and political (Garnåsjordet et al., 2012), etc. Boushey (2010) states that the more tolerable and acceptable a concept or policy is for people, the less complex it is and the more meaningful (emotionally important) the information becomes. Even though it is obvious that different people – SIs users – will perceive thematic relevance differently. Further to that, it is necessary to keep in mind that there are many factors influencing thematic relevance (conditions and contexts of surrounding reality).

Indicator relevance comprises the content and suitability of the indicator to appropriately measure the facts considered (objects, object properties, phenomena, and processes) (Bunge, 1975). It corresponds with the "indicator quality profiles" approach used by the European Statistical Office (Eurostat, 2012) and such a view of indicator relevance is also elaborated by Rametsteiner et al. (2011). He emphasizes the need to find the right approach to representing a given issue through an indicator. Despite its critical importance, this phase in indicator development is inchoate and thus difficult to accomplish. For theoretical determination, we follow the concept of indicator relevance that Bunge (1975) developed for quality of life indicators. He sees an indicator as a symptom of some condition: e.g. high unemployment may indicate a sick economy. More precisely, an indicator is an observable variable assumed to point to, or estimate, some other (usually unobservable) variable. Based on this definition, some indicators are fairly relevant because they can be checked through further indicators or, in some cases, because there are well-confirmed theories containing formulas relating indicators to what they indicate (a theme). In most cases, however, it is a hypothesis that is beyond indicator relevance. And because this "indicator-indicated fact" relation is a hypothesis, it must pass certain empirical tests to become valid (e.g. a battery of indicators).

As in the case of thematic relevance, a user's perspective influences perception of indicator relevance. Further, interpretation of the sustainability theme can influence how different societal perspectives on sustainability express their priorities for selection of indicators and choice of policy. And just using narratives in science–policy communication (framing the sustainability issue within a policy theme) is a tool for describing and organizing information of high complexity (Allen & Giampietro, 2006). Each such narrative and primary means for organizing, processing, and conveying information (for sustainability/policy themes as e.g. "resilient settlements" or "water ecosystems") provides a particular context or framing for data, indicators, and policies.

To summarize: The theme relevance assesses whether a theme, to which the indicator relates, is of concern (and if need be, to what extent), while the indicator relevance for the theme tells us how closely the indicator is related to the theme.

Thematic relevance and indicator relevance – the user's perspectives

The relevance concept has different implications with regards to particular groups of users. *Ex definitione*, SIs should be useful to decision-making, i.e. provide unambiguous and definite information leading to legislative, regulatory, financial, etc. actions. Politicians and political actors and processes should ensure that the given sustainability theme (presented as a political/policy theme) – e.g. resource efficiency, access to education, prosperity or sustainable economic growth – is meaningful to a broad audience. Their main interest and task – with the help of media and many civil society structures – is to get the public interest and support for political action within the particular theme. Therefore, they must care about the thematic relevance of the indicators developed/selected for the theme. Also, in terms of indicator relevance, politicians need to know that they work with highly relevant indicators in order not be blamed for using improper or even false information (indicators). Since it is a difficult task, they assign it to experts. The expert community (both scientists and practitioners often including civil servants with experience and expertise in a particular sustainability theme such as transport, agriculture, education, etc.)[2] has an exclusive role in the application of the relevance concept. It should ensure that crucial sustainability issues are not missed or underestimated in decision- and policymaking (i.e. the thematic relevance of indicators) and it should seek verification that the selected indicators are closely related to the theme (i.e. indicator relevance). Since politics and policymaking have social effects, we may assume citizens wish to express their opinions and that the particular sustainability themes are publicly debated. Raising publicly appealing themes and communicating them by means of relevant indicators may lead to positive emotions of identification with the sustainability goals and principles, and give rise to public sentiment. As Abraham Lincoln noted: "Public sentiment is everything" (Holzer, 2004). It is only through increased participation that society moves towards a sustainable development path (Warburton, 2013). Based on the literature, we assume many factors must be considered by users when applying SIs in decision-making (e.g. Hezri & Dovers, 2006; Hák, Moldan, & Dahl, 2007; UNEP, 2009; Bauler, 2012). They are, in particular, the following: (1) The stage of the policymaking cycle; (2) (causal) relations between assessed/reported facts (DPSIR framework); and (3) an indicator's functions (instrumental, conceptual, and political/symbolical). There is a vast amount of literature on all of them, and therefore the elements regarding SI relevance will be discussed further.

Despite the many various concepts of a policy cycle, it always includes policy aspects and conceptual aspects (also called frameworks). The policy cycle is then a simple model of the policy process highlighting the significance of the policy domain or subsystem (see e.g. Barkenbus, 1998; Jann & Wegrich, 2007). In terms of SI use, politicians start thinking of thematically relevant indicators during the policy legitimation phase when they request scientific knowledge and evidence from scientists that is to attract support for envisaged political measures. Development of highly relevant indicators – closely linked to policy themes – and applying them during the policy evaluation phase is then the ultimate task of experts (testing, data collecting, interpreting, etc.). They thus contribute substantially to assessing the extent to which the policy was successful or the policy decision was correct; and if implementation had the desired effect. Since policy evaluation takes place as a regular and embedded part of the political process and debate, scientific evaluation has been distinguished from administrative evaluations conducted or initiated by public administration and political evaluation carried out by diverse actors in the political arena, including the wider public and the media.

The "cause and effect" thinking is well established theoretically (the DPSIR Framework) and in people's minds. Most decision-makers would like to know the causes of current situations in order to foresee potential impacts. Despite the fact that DPSIR is not analytical (Bell & Morse, 2001), the notion of causality is important for SI use: Some indicators will provide information on the pressure on climate systems (e.g. GHG emissions) while others will provide information on the impact of the changing climate system (e.g. number of floods). Thus, it is a challenge for policymakers, civil servants, etc. to apply this conceptual framework to describe environmental problems and their relationships with the socio-economic domain, in a meaningful policy way. It is designed to present the indicators with reference to political objectives related to the problem addressed; and to focus on causal relationships by analyzing them (Smeets & Weterings, 1999; Matthies, Giupponi, & Ostendorf, 2007).

Relevant indicators, in general, should inform us about things that matter (see also Jesinghaus, Chapter 26); thus SIs should provide comprehensive information on facts important for understanding socio-economic and environmental trends and for guiding policies accordingly. However, there are many possible uses of SIs ensuing from their multiple functions. For understanding the role of SIs in policy (and politics), it is common to distinguish between instrumental, conceptual, and political (symbolic) uses. The instrumental role is the most visible – indicators are seen as objective information tools to improve policymaking. Typically, the discourse used at this level is about solving problems and providing information for planning, target setting, interventions, and assessment of policy effectiveness, etc. In this case an indicator has an influence when it is "used" directly by a policymaker and this consciously influences their decisions (see e.g. Weiss, Murphy-Graham, & Birkeland, 2005; Hezri & Dovers, 2006). The conceptual role of indicators helps the politician establish a broad information base for decisions by shaping conceptual frameworks, mostly through dialogue, public debate, and argumentation. In this way, indicators might affect the problem definition of decision-makers and provide new perspectives and insights, rather than targeted information for a specific point in decision-making. Since users' personal value orientation projects itself onto the conceptual role – and conversely indicators may influence and form users' personal values – the indicators also employ an educational function (Rinne, Lyytimäki & Kautto, 2013). The symbolic role means that the indicator is used as support for policy decisions – it conveys a message and thus becomes a communication tool among stakeholders. This support may be of a strategic or tactical nature, but it always serves to legitimize the decisions made. The excerpted literature suggests that direct instrumental use of indicators shows limited potential, whereas conceptual use is the key for enhanced indicator influence in the long term.

While considering the above factors that influence indicator relevance, it is important to always also consider the users for whom the indicator is intended. SIs serve a multitude of purposes, with users representing different societal, professional, and political interests and demands for statistical information (for more on SI users see e.g. Rosenström & Kyllönen, 2007; Bell & Morse, 2011). As such, we categorize relevance of SIs first and foremost by the user to which they refer: i.e. from policy, science, and public perspectives (see Table 30.1).

So how may the SI user take advantage of the knowledge on different relevance types and different perspectives of SIs when using them during decision-making? Since we assume a positive loop between the information on SI relevance and the SIs used in decision-making, we have developed an "indicator user factsheet" model. This informational aid summarizes and emphasizes the (meta)information about an indicator's use and impact.

Indicator user factsheets

Bell and Morse (2014) believe that the most "used" indicators are those that are relevant and hence match a need. If an indicator is in demand by a stakeholder (e.g. a politician or policy-maker) then that indicator is more likely to continue to exist and develop. At the same time, only few indicators are so powerful as to be able to "find their way" without a degree of marketing. If we consider SIs a market product to be "sold" to users (mostly politicians, educational organizations, civic organizations, and increasingly also to businesses), then the product must evince a proper quality. The SI providers and promoters are becoming increasingly aware of this – e.g. they develop attractive web platforms with visualizations often allowing the involvement of users, etc. to "get the right messages across" (Eurostat, 2014).

Table 30.1 Policy, science, and public perspectives of sustainability indicators with regard to thematic and indicator relevance

	Thematic relevance	*Indicator relevance*
Public perspective (relevance regarded by public)	Requiring and participating in a public debate on relevant themes based on comprehensible information (i.e. also indicators) ideally leading to "public sentiment"	
Science perspective (relevance regarded by scientists)	Exploring and elaborating sustainability themes challenging the current or future policy	Testing, verifying, and validating indicators (to ensure that selected indicators have a close relationship to the policy themes)
Policy perspective (relevance regarded by politicians)	Promoting, giving publicity to the selected indicators (via attractive narratives interpreting the policy themes)	Interacting with science and ensuring that indicator relevance for SIs used is an issue

Soon after their origin, SIs became equipped with "methodological factsheets" – the UN Commission on Sustainable Development published them in a so-called "Blue book", and the European Environmental Agency followed suit with very detailed factsheets comprising about 25 items, etc. (UN, 2004; EEA, 2006). While these factsheets look like technical manuals of a product (the indicators), the ultimate indicator users need more a concise list of arguments for the use of the product. While the former is useful for indicator professionals and increases harmonization and standardization of indicators and thus also their credibility, the latter helps to strengthen the indicators relevance and therefore their uptake by decision-makers. There is a strong assumption that the niche for such a communication aid may be filled by the "indicator policy fact sheets" (Hák et al., 2015). Its purpose is to provide the most important information about indicator producers'/promoters' intentions and the indicators' use and their known or potential impacts. Therefore, indicator user factsheets are not designed for performing a thorough scientific review of the indicator, but rather to highlight its relevance important for main user groups: politicians, scientists/experts, and public. The indicator user factsheets thus complement methodological sheets and highlight less known and/or unreported information. And if the hypothesis that matching a user's need has a greater influence on an indicator's use than its scientific quality is true, then the indicator user factsheets should be a necessary part of the "meta-information package" of all SIs.

Indicator user factsheets open with some basic indicator characteristics (Name of the indicator, Author/Developer, Periodicity, Country coverage, Brief description, Way of presentation, Data sources, Source of information on the indicator). The potential user will find there a concise description of the indicator excerpted from a methodological sheet or other recommended sources. More importantly, the user factsheets provide information on important factors related to indicator use from various users' perspectives. The main purpose is to quickly inform users (mostly politicians and policymakers) on an indicator's potential for decision-making and communication with target groups (mostly media, civic society organizations, and the lay public). To reflect that – and to clearly distinguish user factsheets from indicator methodological sheets – we further call them "indicator policy factsheets". They may, although simple and modest, become effective aids for understanding and applying the concept of SI relevance.

Indicator policy factsheets – GDP and ANS examples

This section presents the benefits of the policy factsheets on examples of two indicators – gross domestic product (GDP) and adjusted net savings (ANS). Let's imagine a very common situation of a SI user wishing to employ some suitable indicator concerning economic sustainability. A search for suitable indicators will likely result in several candidates equipped with more or less useful meta-information depending on its source (media, policy reports, scientific papers, public discussions, etc.). Thus, the user will likely learn – because of the overwhelming imperative of exactness and accuracy at least in the Western world – about the construction of the indicators, the data needed and current results, and much less on the potential use and influence of the selected indicator.

The example indicators – GDP and ANS – are often referred to as "bad, inappropriate, abused", etc., or as "good, appropriate and underused" when there has been a call for better indicators of economic sustainability (more in Costanza et al., Chapter 7; Bartelmus, Chapter 15). For more on economic sustainability see e.g. Spangenberg, 2005; Stiglitz et al., 2009; Bartelmus, 2010; or see websites of "Beyond GDP"[3] by the European Commission and "Measuring Well-being and Progress"[4] by OECD.

Indicator policy factsheets offer information on important factors related to indicator use from various users' perspectives. It comes from relevant sources (SI developers and promoters, as well as final users) mostly through a desk-based analysis and it provides the information that SI users have missed or could not easily access to date. The user factsheets do not duplicate methodological sheets – rather, they are to clearly demonstrate if the indicator may be related to policy targets, the methodology is settled and accepted by the scientific community, and how widely the indicator is used, etc.

Public perspectives (the "Indicator Factors from a Public Perspective" category)

In general, an indicator with high public relevance provides information that responds to people's concerns. This category therefore informs the main user-politician on an indicator's attractiveness for the public (topicality, comprehensibility, accessibility, linkage to other important issues, etc.). Public interest strengthens the chance of symbolic use of the indicator.

The example policy factsheets (Table 30.2 and Table 30.3) show that despite the fact that an appropriate indicator to measure/assess economic sustainability – ANS – is in in place (regardless some conceptual shortcomings), it is almost unknown to the public at large. The problem is likely the low public appeal of the theme "economic sustainability" in contrast to the quite high appeal of the theme "wealth".

Scientific perspectives (the "Indicator Factors from a Scientific Perspective" category)

Politicians need reliable SIs that can be employed for both instrumental use (accountable decision-making) and for communication with other stakeholders (symbolic use) (Waas et al., 2014). Therefore, it is important to establish the correctness and trustworthiness of the indicator – the main task of the scientific and expert community.

The example policy factsheets show that despite the lesser interest of scientists in ANS (conceived as an "alternative" to GDP despite the fact each measures something else), both indicators have similar strengths for policymaking from a scientific perspective: standardized and internationally agreed methodologies, and large analytical potentials.

Policy perspective (the "Indicator Factors from a Policy Perspective" category)

Politicians enforce programmes and policies that they deem have public utility or support. At the same time, politicians must defend such programmes from competition both inside and outside their political party. This and other factors dictate a choice of themes for policymaking. In this category we therefore include additional information on possible uses of the indicator (more effective communication, comparison with other subjects – benchmarking, policy and/or sustainability target setting, context for the policy, etc.). Also, we include information on media interest here,[5] taking it to be a proxy for interest in the topic or indicator for both the public and experts, with higher incidence denoting higher interest. Media analysis of selected SIs has also been undertaken by Morse (2013).

The example policy factsheets reveal differences between both indicators from a policy perspective: Simply speaking, the indicators are suitable for measuring different facts (Fleurbaey & Blanchet, 2013). GDP was developed to measure income and growth (in terms of expansion of output of goods and services) (see Figures 30.1 and 30.2), while ANS is capable of measuring how sustainable investment policies are (see Figures 30.3 and 30.4). So far, GDP has been

Table 30.2 Indicator policy factsheet for "gross domestic product" indicator

Name of indicator/index	Gross Domestic Product (GDP)
Organization/author	Simon Kuznets (author)/UN statistics/national statistical offices
Year created/periodicity/ last publication	1934 (first use)/annually used since 1954
Brief (policy relevant) description	GDP mainly measures market production – expressed in monetary units. It captures all final goods in an economy, whether they are consumed by households, firms, or government. Valuing them with their prices is a way of capturing, in a single number, how well off society is at a particular moment.
Country coverage	More than 200 countries
Way of presentation	

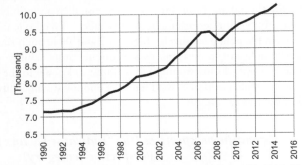

Figure 30.1 GDP per capita (constant 2010 US$); world, 1990–2015

Figure 30.2 GDP per capita (constant 2010 US$); world, 2015

Data sources	World Bank national accounts data, and OECD National Accounts data files (http://data.worldbank.org/indicator/NY.GDP.PCAP.KD)
Source of information on the indicator	UNDESA: Indicators of Sustainable Development: Guidelines and Methodologies – Third edition. Methodology sheets (www.un.org/esa/sustdev/natlinfo/indicators/methodology_sheets/econ_development/gdp_percapita.pdf)

Name of indicator/index	Gross Domestic Product (GDP)
Public perspective	Although the methodology behind the index is quite complicated, its meaning is intuitively understandable to lay people (the higher the GDP growth, the larger the potential spending and material wealth). GDP is a powerful communication tool between politicians and the public – even if incorrectly used as a measure of a country's overall performance or welfare/well-being.
Scientific perspective	The GDP data are mostly collected by national statistical offices, which assure their robustness and overall quality. The GDP methodology is based on well-proven and regularly refined methodology developed by official economic experts. GDP is a challenging topic for experts in terms of methodological development and applications in numerous analyses.
User perspective (mostly policy)	GDP is usually used for comparing the wealth of one country to another or over time. It enables one to rank the countries according to their economy health and performance, and compare national economic prosperity over the long term (from the remote past until the present). GDP enables effective economic planning (target setting) and is a unique tool for communication among the politicians worldwide (nearly each country uses this indicator). • Total number of results 1,309 mil. • Newspapers 596 thousand • Journals 206 thousand • Reports 294 thousand • Wire feeds 153 thousand The media analysis shows that GDP was largely used in the past 30 years. The number of total results illustrates the public's immense interest in the GDP index. Hundreds information about/with the index can be found in different types of media worldwide on a daily basis. However, GDP has often been mistakenly used as a broader measure of a country's overall performance or welfare.

published in all kinds of media significantly more (by two orders of magnitude) often than ANS. When politicians realize the need to measure sustainability and not current economic performance and wealth, they will have to promote ANS (or other appropriate indicator) to overcome incorrect but traditional GDP use (a force of habit). Users will likely get used to it quickly because of its easy interpretation – a positive ANS indicates that a country is adding to its overall wealth and that its economic growth is on a sustainable path.

Discussion and conclusion

We have witnessed an indicator boom recently, which is, however, often weakly supported by scientific background information. The current UN's Sustainable Development Goals (SDGs) is an example of a policy indicator-based initiative with somewhat underdeveloped relevance issues (Hák, Janoušková, & Moldan, 2016; see also Reijnders, Chapter 20). The idea of global goals accompanied by concrete indicators was officially introduced at the Rio+20 Conference in 2012. SDGs in their recent form are a large set of goals, targets (169), and indicators (243) that UN member states will use to frame their agendas and policies over the next 15 years

Table 30.3 Indicator policy factsheet for "adjusted net savings" indicator

Name of indicator/index	Adjusted net savings (including particulate emission damage) (also called informally genuine savings)
Organization/author	World Bank
Year created/periodicity/ last publication	1997, 2006, 2011
Brief (policy relevant) description	ANS seeks to provide national-level decision-makers with a clear, relatively simple indicator of how sustainable their country's investment policies are. It measures the true rate of saving in an economy after taking into account investments in human capital, depletion of natural resources and damages caused by pollution. Thus it gives an account of the net creation or destruction of national wealth on a yearly basis.
Country coverage	Over 190 countries
Way of presentation	

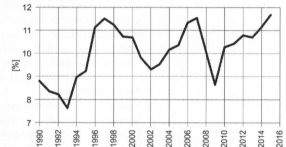

Figure 30.3   Adjusted net savings (including particulate emission damage) (% of GNI); world, 1990–2014

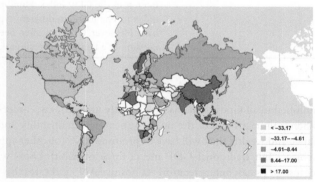

Figure 30.4   Adjusted net savings (including particulate emission damage) (% of GNI); world, 2014

Data sources	Internet source: World Bank: Adjusted net savings http://data.worldbank.org/indicator/NY.ADJ.SVNG.GN.ZS Publications: World Bank: The Little Green Data Book; The World Development Indicators

Name of indicator/index	Adjusted net savings (including particulate emission damage) (also called informally genuine savings)
Source of information on the indicator	UNDESA: Indicators of Sustainable Development: Guidelines and Methodologies – Third edition. Methodology sheets www.un.org/esa/sustdev/natlinfo/indicators/methodology_sheets.pdf (Also see: Bolt, Matete & Clemens, 2002; Thiry & Cassiers, 2010).
Public perspective	ANS is an appropriate indicator to measure/assess economic sustainability. However, it is almost unknown to the public at large. It is not because of its conceptual or methodological difficulty (in fact, it is a macroeconomic indicator of the same caliber as GDP) but because of its infrequent and discreet use. The notion of economic sustainability appeared more intensively as late as the economic crises of 2008–2012 (Geels, 2013).
Scientific perspective	For some years now, the World Bank has produced estimates of ANS for most of the world's economies.
	The combination of capital theory and the incorporation of the maximin criterion in the neoclassical theory of value in the 1970s formed the basis of the empirical work at the end of the 1980s which first defended the utility of ANS as a sustainability indicator. The indicator then gradually entered widespread use in the first decade of the 21st century. However, ANS is not without criticism; e.g. it is a national measure of weak sustainability that overlooks key international externalities, underlying a model based on consumption growth which is more suited to proving the sustainability of developed countries, etc. There is still a lot of work to improve the measure.
User perspective (mostly policy perspective)	ANS is often cited as a suitable indicator of economic sustainability. Unlike GDP, the net savings framework takes the broader view that natural and human capital is an asset upon which the productivity and therefore the well-being of a nation rest. Since depletion of a non-renewable resource (or overexploitation of a renewable one) decreases the value of that resource stock as an asset, such activity represents a dis-investment in future productivity and well-being. In the same way, the creation of an educated populace and a skilled workforce – a nation's human capital – increases the value of that resource and might better be seen as an investment. NS follows the "weak sustainability" rule (assuming that any type of capital is perfectly substitutable for natural capital as an input to production). The indicator can be easily used for international comparison.
	The media analysis shows the overall disinterest in the ANS indicator over past 30 years. On average, only three articles containing information on ANS have appeared in newspapers worldwide every month. Incidence of this topic in the specialized media (journals, wire feeds) was quite marginal.
	• Total number of results 1681
	• Newspapers 1137
	• Journals 129
	• Wire feeds 126

(2015–2030). A frequent term around SDGs is relevance: SDGs are supposed to be relevant to sustainable development to frame the entire Agenda 2030, to be relevant to policy formulation, to be relevant to all countries, etc. However, without clear conceptualization and interpretation of the goals and targets and operationalization of indicators (including their key characteristics – relevance) it will remain more policy newspeak than a real effort to assess global sustainability (e.g. ICSU & ISSC, 2015).

SDGs are already firmly embedded within a policy framework: during the course of their development they went through a political process and the "Zero Draft" evolved from broad political negotiations (UNSD, 2015). It required the goals and targets to be accompanied by relevant indicators. We argue that it can only be done by the conceptualization and operationalization of targets. Only that will transform them from being vague and mostly theoretical to tools, which are clearly understandable in terms of empirical observations that can be measured or described by appropriate indicators. No matter how measurable or applicable, the development or selection of indicators does not necessarily contribute to designing the right concepts beyond the targets. Operationalization of the targets through indicators would be methodologically incorrect and might lead to distortions in the development of the policy agenda (such an approach might cause the false interpretation whereby only that which can be measured is important to our lives). In other words: The concept of the target cannot be simply defined by a pack of statistics and indicators, regardless of how relevant they are. The concept, based on best scientific knowledge, must precede and then be operationalized as far as possible by the available data (This step will be important particularly for the targets which have a broad, multi-theme definition). Operationalization means the elaboration of clear-cut and detailed formulations of working hypotheses on the measurement of particular facts (phenomena, objects, processes). It may be that some components of the concept thus remain without currently available indicators, yet they remain integral elements of the concept and thus inspire further research and define future data requirements.

For assessing SDGs there are many more or less suitable indicators already at our disposal. In terms of their relevance, this means that there will be indicators backed by hypotheses verified to a different extent: from not verified at all (and then our assumption that an indicator measures the given fact equates to mere speculation) to an "indicator-indicated fact" relation verified by a proven theory or by an empirical test. The experience so far shows that measurement of most of the facts – regardless of the theme but especially in the social domain – will require the employment of a battery of indicators where an indicator is just one component of a vector pointing to a condition of a fact.

Despite the fact that the process of assessing SDGs and their indicators has just started, the framework for indicator selection and formulation does not seem to be based on the necessary conceptual considerations but primarily given by the definitions of individual SDGs. Therefore, there is a risk of matching various ready-to-use indicators/sets of indicators to individual targets on the basis of terminological or content affinity without verifying, or even considering, the "indicator-indicated fact" relation. Naturally, the vague definition of the targets will allow – and will tempt to allow – such a solution. That is why we do not criticize various existing indicators and indices – in fact, we do exactly the opposite. A huge amount of work in the field of indicators has been undertaken and this work must be fully utilized. We merely argue for the rigorous application of conceptual and methodological approaches for the targets' conceptualization and operationalization resulting in the selection or development of highly relevant indicators.

Generally, for selecting and/or developing SIs, we emphasize the following:

• Many sustainable development aspects may be accessed and handled by indicators (both quantitative and qualitative). Special attention must be paid to neglected or insufficiently explored SD aspects: immeasurables and intangibles (e.g. Bell & Morse, 1999; Attaran, 2005; Burford et al., 2013) since methodologies for their application and analysis are infrequently developed or applied

- SIs should be thematically relevant
- SIs should be inherently relevant, i.e. closely linked to indicated facts.

Indicator policy factsheets are a modest attempt to respond to the findings of recent studies on the use of indicators by decision-makers. The proposed indicator policy factsheets are designed to help SI users (most often decision- and policymakers) choose and use the most appropriate indicators for assessing particular sustainability issues. Decision-makers themselves have not stipulated their need – neither content-wise, nor in terms of required impacts, target audiences, etc. They have rather intensified their call for better, alternative, "Beyond GDP" indicators. But their availability is not sufficient to guarantee their use. The availability of such indicators nowadays is already good and, moreover, competition and innovation is ongoing – more and better indicators will inevitably emerge.

Indicator policy factsheets are open, dynamic tools. They are adaptable depending on the results of further research or policymaker needs. The frequency of these updates will follow methodological and other advancements in the field of indicators. The question remains as to who should develop the indicator policy factsheets further and put them into practice. The simple answer is – knowledge brokers. An expert who acts as a link between researchers and decision-makers (Findlay, 2004) and/or intermediary organizations which have an increasing role in promoting sustainable development (Cash et al., 2003). In general, while the key interest in bringing indicators closer to policymakers or other end users is held by the developers of indicators, for the sake of objectivity as well as in terms of available expertise and experience, this phase of indicator development should be undertaken by a third party – knowledge brokers – and reviewed by experts.

Notes

1 www.socialresearchmethods.net/kb/reltypes.php
2 This notion is congruent with the basic democratic understanding of elected politicians making decisions which are then carried out by a neutral public service.
3 EC 2016: Beyond GDP (http://ec.europa.eu/environment/beyond_gdp/index_en.html)
4 OECD 2016: Measuring Well-being and Progress: Well-being Research (www.oecd.org/statistics/measuring-well-being-and-progress.htm)
5 We have done a simple media analysis using the ProQuest databases that cover hundreds of US, Canadian, and international newspapers, and thousands of journals, dissertations, reports, and other expert publications (written in English). (For more details visit www.proquest.com)

References

Allen, T.F.H. & Giampietro, M. (2006). Narratives and transdisciplines for a post-industrial world. *Systems Research and Behavioral Science, 23*(5), 595–615.

Attaran, A. (2005). An immeasurable crisis? A criticism of the millennium development goals and why they cannot be measured. *PLoS Med, 2*(10), e318.

Barkenbus, J. (1998). *Expertise and the Policy Cycle.* University of Tennessee. Available at www.gdrc.org/decision/policy-cycle.pdf

Bartelmus, P. (2010). Use and usefulness of sustainability economics. *Ecological Economics, 69*(11), 2053–2055.

Bauler, T. (2012). An analytical framework to discuss the usability of (environmental) indicators for policy. *Ecological Indicators, 17,* 38–45.

Bell, S. & Morse, S. (1999). *Measuring the Immeasurable: The Theory and Use of Sustainability Indicators in Development.* London: Earthscan, 192.

Bell, S. & Morse, S. (2001). Breaking through the glass ceiling: Who really cares about sustainability indicators? *Local Environment*, 6(3), 291–309.

Bell, S. & Morse, S. (2011). An analysis of the factors influencing the use of indicators in the European Union. *Local Environment*, 16, 281–302.

Bell, S. & Morse, S. (2014). Groups and Indicators in Post-Industrial Society. *Sustainable Development*, 22(3), 145–157.

Bockstaller, C. & Girardin, P. (2003). How to validate environmental indicators. *Agricultural Systems*, 76, 639–653.

Bolt, K., Matete, M., & Clemens, M. (2002). *Manual for Calculating Adjusted Net Savings*. World Bank. Available at http://siteresources.worldbank.org/INTEEI/1105643-1115814965717/20486606/Savingsmanual2002.pdf

Boushey, G. (2010). *Policy Diffusion Dynamics in America*. New York, NY: Cambridge University Press.

Bunge, M. (1975). What is a quality of life indicator? *Social Indicators Research*, 2(1), 65–79.

Burford, G., Hoover, E., Velasco, I., Janoušková, S., Jimenez, A., Piggot, G., Podger, D., & Harder, M.K. (2013). Bringing the "missing pillar" into sustainable development goals: Towards intersubjective values-based indicators. *Sustainability*, 5(7), 3035–3059.

Cash, D.W., Clark, W.C., Alcock, F., Dickson, N.M., Eckley, N., Guston, D.H., & Mitchell, R.B. (2003). Knowledge systems for sustainable development. *Proceedings of National Academy of Science U.S.A.*, 100(14), 8086–8091.

Cosijn, E. & Ingwersen, P. (2000). Dimensions of relevance. *Information, Processing and Management*, 36(4), 533–550.

da Costa Pereira, C., Dragoni, M., & Pasi, G. (2012). Multidimensional relevance: Prioritized aggregation in a personalized information retrieval setting. *Information processing & management*, 48(2), 340–357.

Dahl, A.L. (2012). Achievements and gaps in indicators for sustainability. *Ecological Indicators*, 17, 14–19.

EEA. (2006). *The Indicator Fact Sheet Model*. Available at www.isprambiente.gov.it/contentfiles/00000900/926-water-eeaindicator-fact-sheet-model.pdf/view

Eurostat. (2012). *Quality Assurance Framework of the European Statistical System*. Version 1.1. Available at http://epp.eurostat.ec.europa.eu/

Eurostat. (2014). *Getting Messages across Using Indicators*. Luxembourg: Eurostat.

Findlay, S.S. (2004). *Knowledge brokers: Linking Researchers and Policy Makers*. Workshop held on June 28, 2003 at Canmore, Alberta, Canada. 2004. Available at www.ihe.ca/documents/HTA-FR14.pdf

Fleurbaey, M. & Blanchet, D. (2013). *Beyond GDP: Measuring Welfare and Assessing Sustainability*. Oxford: Oxford University Press.

Garnåsjordet, P.A., Aslaksen, I., Giampietro, M., Funtowicz, S., & Ericson, T. (2012). Sustainable development indicators: From statistics to policy. *Environmental Policy and Governance*, 22(5), 322–336.

Geels, F.W. (2013). The impact of the financial-economic crisis on sustainability transitions: Financial investment, governance and public discourse. *Environmental Innovation and Societal Transitions*, 6, 67–95.

Girardin, P., Bockstaller, C., & van der Werf, H.M.G. (1999). Indicators: Tools to evaluate the environmental impacts of farming systems. *Journal of Sustainable Agriculture*, 13, 5–21.

Graymore, M.L., Sipe, N.G., & Rickson, R.E. (2008). Regional sustainability: How useful are current tools of sustainability assessment at the regional scale? *Ecological Economics*, 67(3), 362–372.

Hák, T., Janoušková, S., & Moldan, B. (2016). Sustainable development goals: A need for relevant indicators. *Ecological Indicators*, 60, 565–573.

Hák, T., Janoušková, S., Whitby, A., Abdallah, S., & Kovanda, J. (2015). Indicator policy factsheets: A knowledge brokerage tool. *Sustainability*, 7(3), 3414–3429.

Hák, T., Kovanda, J., & Weinzettel, J. (2012). A method to assess the relevance of sustainability indicators: Application to the indicator set of the Czech Republic's Sustainable Development Strategy. *Ecological Indicators*, (17), 46–57.

Hák, T., Moldan, B., & Dahl, A. (Eds.) (2007). *Sustainability Indicators: A Scientific Assessment*. SCOPE, vol. 67. Washington, Covelo, London: Island Press.

Hezri, A.A. & Dovers, S.R. (2006). Sustainability indicators, policy and governance: Issues for ecological economics. *Ecological Economics*, 60(1), 86–99.

Holzer, H. (Ed.) (2004). The Lincoln-Douglas debates. *The First Complete*. Unexpurgated Text. Fordham University Press.

ICSU & ISSC. (2015). *Review of the Sustainable Development Goals: The Science Perspective*. Paris: International Council for Science.

Jann, W. & Wegrich, K. (2007). In: Fischer, F., Miller, G.J., Sidney, M.S. (Eds.), Theories of the policy cycle. *Handbook of Public Policy Analysis: Theory, Politics and Methods*, 43–62. Boca Raton, London, New York: CRC Press.

Kurtz, J.C., Jackson, L.E., & Fisher, W.S. (2001). Strategies for evaluating indicators based on guidelines from the Environmental Protection Agency's Office of Research and Development. *Ecological Indicators*, (1), 49–60.

Matthies, M., Giupponi, C., & Ostendorf, B. (2007). Environmental decision support systems: Current issues, methods and tools. *Environmental Modelling & Software*, 22(2), 123–127.

Morse, S. (2013). Out of sight, out of mind: Reporting of three indices in the UK national press between 1990 and 2009. *Sustainable Development*, 21, 242–259.

Parris, T.M. & Kates, R.W. (2003). Characterizing and measuring sustainable development. *Annual Review of Environment and Resources*, 28, 13.1–13.28.

Rametsteiner, E., Pülzl, H., Alkan-Olsson, J., & Frederiksen, P. (2011). Sustainability indicator development – Science or political negotiation? *Ecological Indicators*, 11(1), 61–70.

Rickard, L., Jesinghaus, J., Amann, Ch., Glaser, G., Hall, S., Cheatle, M., Le Kama, A.A., Lippert, E., McGlade, J., Ruffing, K., & Zaccai, E. (2007). Ensuring Policy Relevance. In: Hák, T., Moldan, B., and Dahl, A. (Eds.), *Sustainability Indicators: A Scientific Assessment*. A SCOPE, Vol. 67. Washington: Island Press, pp. 65–82.

Rinne, J., Lyytimäki, J., & Kautto, P. (2013). From sustainability to well-being: Lessons learned from the use of sustainable development indicators at national and EU level. *Ecological Indicators*, 35, 35–42.

Rosenström, U. (2009). Sustainable development indicators: Much wanted, less used? *Monographs of the Boreal Environment Research*, No. 33.

Rosenström, U. & Kyllönen, S. (2007). Impacts of a participatory approach to developing national level sustainable development indicators in Finland. *Journal of Environmental Management*, 84(3), 282–298.

Ruti, M. (2016). Why some things matter more than others: A Lacanian explanation. *Constellations*, 23(2), 201–211.

Singh, R.K., Murty, H.R., Gupta, S.K., & Dikshit, A.K. (2009). An overview of sustainability assessment methodologies. *Ecological indicators*, 9(2), 189–212.

Smeets, E. & Weterings, R. (1999). *Environmental Indicators: Typology and Overview*. Copenhagen: European Environment Agency, 19.

Spangenberg, J.H. (2005). Economic sustainability of the economy: Concepts and indicators. *International Journal of Sustainable Development*, 8(1–2), 47–64.

Sperber, D. & Wilson, D. (1986). *Relevance: Communication and Cognition* (Vol. 142). Cambridge, MA: Harvard University Press.

Stiglitz, J., Sen, A., & Fitoussi, J.P. (2009). *The Measurement of Economic Performance and Social Progress Revisited: Reflections and Overview*. Paris: Commission on the Measurement of Economic Performance and Social Progress.

Thiry, G. & Cassiers, I. (2010). Alternative Indicators to GDP: Values behind Numbers. Adjusted Net Savings in Question, Institut de Recherches Economiques et Sociales (IRES). Discussion Paper 2010–18.

UN. (2004). *Indicators of Sustainable Development: Guidelines and Methodologies*. New York: United Nations Publications.

UNEP. (2009) *Integrated Policy-making for Sustainable Development. A Reference Manual*. Nairobi: UN Environment Programme.

UNSD. (2015). *Discussion Paper on Principles of Using Quantification to Operationalize the SDGs and Criteria for Indicator Selection*. ESA/STAT/441/2/58A/14. New York: UN Statistical Division.

Waas, T., Hugé, J., Block, T., Wright, T., Benitez-Capistros, F., & Verbruggen, A. (2014). Sustainability assessment and indicators: Tools in a decision-making strategy for sustainable development. *Sustainability*, 6, 5512–5534.

Warburton, D. (2013). *Community and Sustainable Development: Participation in the Future*. London, Sterling: Earthscan.

Weiss, C., Murphy-Graham, E., & Birkeland, S. (2005). An alternate route to policy influence: How evaluations affect D.A.R.E. *American Journal of Evaluation*, 26, 12–30.

31

MEASUREMENT MATTERS
Toward data-driven environmental policy-making

Daniel C. Esty*

Environmental decision-making has long been plagued by uncertainties and incomplete information. Historically, governments, companies, communities, and individuals have lacked the data necessary for thoughtful and systematic action to minimize pollution harms and to optimize the use of natural resources. As a result, choices were made on the basis of generalized observations, average exposures, and best guesses – or worse yet, rhetoric and emotion. But breakthroughs in information technologies now permit a much more careful, quantitative, granular, empirically grounded, and systematic approach to pollution control and natural resource management. This chapter explores why and how better and cheaper data and greater emphasis on statistical analysis promise to strengthen environmental policy-making.

A shift toward performance measurement and data-driven analysis is helping to make environmental decision-making much more rigorous, as discussed in the Bell and Morse introduction to this volume. It has long been understood that better analytic underpinnings generate better environmental outcomes. Information has a cost, however, so there are always limits to how much investment in environmental data and knowledge makes sense in any particular decision context. In an ideal world, environmental choices would be made on the basis of many factors, including levels of emissions from every relevant pollution source, who and what is being affected, how much ecological or epidemiological harm each "receptor" is suffering, how much value to place on these injuries, what options exist for mitigating the harms, and the costs and benefits of the alternative harm-reducing interventions. In the data-constrained 20th century, gathering and analyzing all this information came at a very high price (Esty, 2004). Indeed, our existing environmental law and policy framework reflects an acute sensitivity to the lack of available information on actual ambient circumstances and the high cost of acquiring and analyzing data. This reality translated into stark trade-offs – notably the reliance on a "command and control" regulatory model centered on national-government-mandated uniform rules, rather than regulations tailored to specific conditions and individual requirements (Esty, 2017). While many of these limitations persist today, the expansion and evolution of data and information collecting efforts offer policy-makers new and more effective tools with which to confront many of the planet's critical environmental challenges, as detailed in the Almassy and Pintér chapter in this volume.

New challenges, new possibilities

Today's environmental challenges differ significantly from those that motivated the birth of modern American environmentalism in the 1970s. Severe environmental crises, such as the air pollution that felled dozens in Pittsburgh or the Los Angeles smog that left drivers unable to see six traffic lights ahead on many days, led to the adoption of sweeping environmental statutes in the United States and around the world. These laws led to substantial progress in reducing air and water pollution, cleaning up toxic waste sites, and expanding parks (Lehner, 2008). As a result, today's environmental problems – while no less urgent or critical – are harder to see, more difficult to address, and often present less clear cost-benefit ratios. In many respects, environmental policy-makers have already picked the proverbial low-hanging fruit (Herman et al., 2008). Addressing 21st-century environmental problems, such as climate change, will therefore demand a more sophisticated strategy of careful risk analysis and refined policy targeting (Chertow & Esty, 1997).

Fortunately, even as the environmental challenges have grown in complexity, advances in information technologies have shifted out the policy possibility frontier, promising to produce better outcomes at lower costs (Esty, 2017). The Digital Age has changed in fundamental ways how we live and communicate, how companies make and sell goods and services, and even how baseball teams pick players (McAfee & Brynjolfsson, 2012; Lewis, 2003). The data scarcity that plagued policy decision-making in the 1970s is no more. Instead, we are entering the era of "Big Data" – or, as some have described it, the 4th Industrial Revolution (Schwab, 2016). The Internet, improvements in sensors and data communications, and recent information technology breakthroughs give the science community access to a vastly wider knowledge base and much more fine-grained data – at ever-lower expense. At the same time, computer-powered statistical tools have enabled faster, more sophisticated, and less costly analyses of policy options. And while these technological advancements continue to push the boundaries of human and scientific knowledge, innovations in smart systems, "the internet of things", and other devices powered by artificial intelligence have augmented the ways in which this new information can be channeled into action and on-the-ground results. Thus, we now live in an era of data abundance rather than scarcity. This reality offers the prospect of transformed approaches to environmental protection and energy strategy – and ultimately a sustainable future. Jonathon Porritt's Foreword to this volume spells out the scope of the challenge.

In sum, the need for measurement and data-driven analysis in environmental policy-making has grown significantly over the past four decades (Esty, 2004). But so too have the set of information tools available to individuals, businesses, and government officials. As the pages that follow explain and the chapters in this volume demonstrate, a shift towards data-oriented decision-making promises to usher in a new and more efficient environmental policy paradigm, one that is equipped to address the most pressing environmental problems of the 21st century. The Pintér *et al.* and Dahl chapters in this volume both highlight the theoretical opportunities that a broader base of sustainability metrics offers and review the evolving practice of environmental policy-making as decision-makers become more data driven and empirical.

Reducing uncertainty

Pollution impacts and natural resource management issues are often hard to see and, therefore, easily overlooked or underestimated (Lazarus, 2009). In some cases, such as automobile exhaust, the harm arises from numerous sources of emissions that are individually infinitesimally small but cumulatively very significant. Likewise, the impact of a single fisherman or fishing boat on fish stocks seems minute, but collectively, fishing fleets can deplete entire fisheries. Good data provide the perspective needed to see such aggregate effects and to spot "tragedies of the commons" in the making.

In other cases, emissions mix in ways that are difficult to sort out and make sense of. Air pollution in any major metropolitan area is a complex "soup" derived not only from millions of cars and trucks emitting particulates, oxides of nitrogen (NOx), carbon monoxide, volatile organic chemicals (VOCs), and other by-products of combustion in their exhaust, but also released from hundreds of thousands of households and tens of thousands of factories and other facilities that discharge a range of pollutants and other harmful substances. Sorting out responsibility for environmental damage across these many types and sources of harm can seem daunting. But sophisticated monitors, sensors, and data tracking systems can help to identify the separate "ingredients" and pollution sources (Snyder et al., 2013).

In other circumstances, emissions spread spatially in ways that make analysis difficult. The effects of sulfur dioxide and other acid rain precursors spewed from coal-burning power plants, for instance, would be quite noticeable if concentrated. But tall smokestacks spread the emissions widely, making the harm hard to monitor and control. Data on downwind impacts (cases of respiratory distress, acidification of lakes, etc.) can help to sharpen the focus on such diffuse emissions. Perhaps the most difficult categories of pollutants are those that are dispersed not only across space but also over time (Lazarus, 2004). Greenhouse gas emissions, for example, can persist in the atmosphere for several centuries. The nearly impossible-to-observe buildup of these gases creates the risk of climate change. But numbers permit patterns to be spotted and trends to be traced. And with sophisticated computer modeling and improved processing speed, correlations can be established, causal linkages identified, and future effects forecasted.

Simply put, better metrics and data analysis can make the invisible visible, the intangible tangible, and the complex manageable. The "realization" effect of numbers can be transformative. For example, while none of us can see the ozone layer, credible measurements of the thinning of this shield against the sun's ultraviolet rays convinced the public and politicians of the need for action (Benedick, 1991). Computer-supported data collection and analysis allows us to "see" many more environmental problems and to begin to disentangle the full range of risk factors implicated. Moreover, Information Age gains in other fields (such as statistics, epidemiology, and genomics) promise to further strengthen our capacity to track ecological and public health threats and to identify how best to reduce these harms.

Perfect information for environmental decision-making will never, of course, be achieved (Farber, 2015). Significant environmental uncertainties will persist long into the future. Some questions are inherently difficult to answer and require political judgment, making a purely quantitative decision process not just impossible but unwise (Sagoff, 1982; Wagner, 1995). How much, for example, is a pretty view worth? Or what intergenerational discount rate should be used to determine the social cost of carbon? (Revesz & Shahabian, 2011; Kysar, 2007). But the inappropriateness of rigid numerical decision-making algorithms does nothing to diminish the value of undergirding environmental choices with strengthened and expanded data and analysis.

Scientific progress and evolving technologies will also constantly reshape the decision-making context and demand for new data and information. Ten years ago, no one was asking whether nanotechnologies or genomic interventions pose safety risks. But today, these questions are real – and require a recast approach to data and analysis. Unintended consequences and countervailing risks, moreover, regularly emerge – and require risk calculations to be rethought

(Graham & Wiener, 1997). For example, MBTE seemed like a useful gasoline additive in the 1990s, but a decade later, we understood that too often it leaked from gas tanks and contaminated water supplies. Identifying all of the relevant variables and elements of a comprehensive analytic framework thus represents an enormous undertaking. But tracking many moving parts is exactly what today's information and communications technologies (ICT) breakthroughs permit.

One must also remember that the "environment" is not a narrow category or a single issue but rather a multidimensional concept demanding attention to a panoply of issues. Policy-makers must simultaneously analyze an array of pollution control and natural resource management concerns – and optimize across many vectors. Good decision-making thus requires a "systems" approach, guided by metrics and data across a range of variables (Rose, 2005). The factors to be considered must include not just environmental impacts but also economic costs and benefits as well as the consequences in other policy domains (Stewart, 1995).

Complexity will remain a hallmark of the environmental realm, but it can be managed. With better metrics and ever-improving data analytic tools, sloganeering and guesswork can be supplanted by a hard-nosed focus on key problems and the search for effective and efficient solutions. The 21st century thus promises to solidify the foundations of environmental decision-making, which have too often been shaky, leading to the entire environmental field being dismissed as "soft" (Esty & Porter, 2000).

Enhancing comparative analysis

Environmental decisions almost always turn on comparisons and trade-offs. Decision-makers must identify the pluses and minuses of a particular policy choice – weighing, for example, the costs and benefits of further investments in pollution abatement (Breyer, 1993; Revesz, 2015). In deciding whether the risk reduction to be obtained justifies the expenditure entailed, good data and refined analysis are critical (Revesz & Livermore, 2008). Are the public health gains from reducing arsenic in water worth the filtration and other control costs? Would a tighter standard for particulate emissions be justified by lower incidence of respiratory disease? Does it make sense to invest in a new smokestack scrubber or to switch from coal to natural gas to reduce SO_2 emissions? Carefully constructed environmental metrics facilitate such analyses and offer the promise of systematically better outcomes over time.

Comparative analysis also makes it possible to target environmental spending and ensure the best returns for investments made in pollution control and natural resource management (Arrow et al., 1996). In a world of chronic governmental budget shortfalls and tight limits on corporate spending, every dollar, euro, yen, or yuan spent on environmental protection needs to deliver maximum returns. With data on risks, their relative significance, and alternative ways of dealing with the most pressing issues, decision-makers can set priorities and evaluate competing policy options.

Comparisons, furthermore, spur competition (Esty & Rushing, 2006). And competition, in turn, unleashes innovation (Porter, 1990). Everyone loves rankings, and no one likes to be revealed as a lagging performer (Stephan, 2002). Just as knowledge that a competitor in the marketplace has higher profits or faster-growing sales drives executives to redouble their efforts, evidence that others are outperforming one's country, community, or company on environmental criteria can sharpen the focus on opportunities for improved pollution control and resource-use management. This ability to highlight leaders, spur on laggards, and identify best practices was one of the core motivations for the launch of the Environmental Performance Index (EPI), as discussed in detail in the Esty and Emerson chapter in this volume.

Finding points of leverage

Beyond providing a snapshot of current circumstances and a basis for systematic environmental decision-making, data can be used to identify the "drivers" of environmental outcomes. With data that are relevant, valid, and reliable, statistical analysis can reveal the correlates of good performance. Empirical evidence should be used much more widely by both governments and businesses as a foundation for their environmental decisions. As time series data become readily available, causal relationships will increasingly emerge, making it easier to identify the determinants of top-tier environmental performance at the policy and corporate levels (Esty & Cort, 2017).

Data-driven decision-making is firmly established in other fields. Corporations spend a great deal of time and money on accounting to get a vantage point on their various activities and to understand better the strengths and weaknesses of their business strategies (Kaplan & Norton, 1992). With the right numbers, executives can methodically analyze options – for capital expenditures, choices of product lines, marketing and advertising, etc. – and systematically track progress. Data also allow goals to be set based on both internal targets (for example, derived from observed results within the company at other facilities or in other product lines) and with reference to external benchmarks, such as industry-wide financial returns. Investments that pay off are continued or augmented; those that do not are discontinued.

Empirically based decision-making is critical for another reason: intuition is often wrong. Robyn Dawes (2001) and others have demonstrated in a number of fields – from the diagnoses of emergency room doctors to the ability of parole officers to identify likely recidivists – that good statistical analysis beats "expert" judgment nearly every time. Cass Sunstein (2001) has similarly analyzed why people are prone to significant errors in making risk assessments, building on the work of Paul Slovic (2000) in understanding the limits of human cognition. It is becoming increasingly clear that intuition can "top up" data analytics, but cannot replace it. The advantages of quantification and statistical analysis have long been recognized in other disciplines, but only recently has the same logic begun to transform the environmental realm.

Improved performance measurement

Greater emphasis on data can also help to shift the focus of environmental decision-making to outcomes rather than inputs. Too often in the past, environmental performance has been assessed based on how much money has been spent or how many inspections have been completed or, worse yet, how big someone's environmental staff is or how many rules have been adopted. These input measures are not necessarily indicative of progress (Metzenbaum, 2002; Mintz, 2014). Actual environmental success should be judged "on the ground" as a matter of reduced public health or ecological impacts. Results – improved air and water quality, reduced waste, and more sustainably managed natural resources – are what matter.

In a world where good intentions are not enough and implementation is key, quantitative policy evaluation is essential. In business, not every new product sells. In government, not every program works. Finding the failing efforts is thus an important element of good environmental management (Graham, 1997). Historically, the environmental community has not been supportive of rigorous evaluation and the weeding out of unsuccessful policies, strategies, and approaches, perhaps fearful that negative reviews would result in lower overall environmental spending. But tough-minded 21st-century environmentalists are now insisting on having all programs monitored continuously against empirically defined benchmarks – and on redeploying the resources of initiatives that do not measure up to those standards.

Comparative data and a focus on output measurement can improve corporate environmental performance as well (Esty & Simmons, 2011). Facility-by-facility results allow executives to track pollution control and resource management practices within their own companies. Such data can be used to identify top-tier performance, establish targets, and build programs to move all of a corporation's operations toward leading-edge standards (Esty & Winston, 2009). Industry-wide performance data provide another basis for goal setting, while results identified by international bodies or the scientific community can generate guidelines for feasible environmental action.

Similar opportunities are available at the household level. Electric bills in most places, for example, show how much energy was consumed in the prior month. They may even provide a comparison with the same month last year. But they often don't tell the ratepayer what he or she really needs to know: how much an average household of comparable size in the same geographic locale consumes – or better yet, what the most energy-efficient families are able to achieve under similar circumstances. Such targets – now provided by some utilities with the help of data analytics firms such as Opower – are easily understood and can spur consumer action (Allcot & Rogers, 2016). These electricity consumption programs are just beginning to roll out nationwide, but the potential for improved energy efficiency and reduced pollution is substantial.

Benchmarking and best practices

To the extent that many environmental efforts fall short in implementation (Giles, 2013), a more data-intensive approach to policy-making offers special opportunities. Measurement facilitates policy evaluation, performance comparisons, and identification of superior regulatory approaches. In fact, enormous environmental gains can be obtained simply by moving lagging jurisdictions toward the "best practices" of those with top-ranked results. Quantitative measures also provide a basis for judging which specific regulatory tools, technologies, or strategies are succeeding and which require rethinking (Eccles et al., 2001).

The potential to use benchmarking to drive progress applies at many scales and across a diverse set of environmental issues and actors. Comparing results across environmental challenges (air versus water versus waste) and jurisdictions (California versus Texas versus Connecticut, or the United States versus France versus Germany) can spotlight conspicuous achievements or difficulties, thereby facilitating movement toward better results over time. Moreover, in the Information Age, the benchmarking and dissemination of information on best practices, strategies, and technologies promise to become ever cheaper as computer and telecommunications technologies advance.

As Yale's EPI has demonstrated, comparisons to a relevant *peer* group are particularly helpful (Emerson et al., 2010). Indeed, every country ranked in the EPI study lags its peers on some issues. Spotting these opportunities for improvement, and having access to the information on what leading jurisdictions are doing, sharply clarifies the policy challenge. The EPI experience over nearly two decades further reveals the importance of highlighting a range of peer comparisons – by level of development, geography, demography, etc. – and allowing decision-makers to judge their performance against those that they see as the most relevant peers. Haiti was never going to be motivated by the knowledge that its performance fell short of that of Finland or Switzerland, but the fact that it lags the Dominican Republic on so many critical sustainability indicators is seen as meaningful in the policy-making context. As Angel Hsu's chapter in this volume explains, China and other countries have taken up the EPI model to drive environmental progress based on domestic benchmarking across states or provinces, thereby demonstrating the further potential for comparative analysis and the identification of best practices across peer groups at sub-national scales.

A similar logic applies to the corporate sector. The availability of information on firm pollution performance and resource management puts pressure on companies to improve their own sustainability practices. Indeed, there has been a groundswell of interest in socially responsible investing in recent years, with trillions of dollars of assets now managed in sustainable investment vehicles (GSIA, 2014). As mainstream investors have begun to recognize the profit upsides to sustainability leadership, companies are under increasing pressure to report on their environmental and social risks and impacts. While some critical information is kept confidential because of its strategic value or because it creates exposure vis-à-vis regulatory authorities, a great deal of data is now available. And the Internet puts the answers to many pollution control or natural resource management questions just a few clicks away. A key challenge for this space will be organizing these data into a set of comprehensible corporate sustainability metrics that are correlated with financial performance and allow for meaningful comparisons across investments in a portfolio (Esty & Cort, 2017).

Performance data and identification of best practices thus promote an action orientation and stronger environmental performance in several ways (Esty & Rushing, 2006). First, clear numerical measures highlight what is possible, as a matter of fact, in improved environmental results. In many cases, governments, corporations, and households do not have a clear picture of what might be obtainable in pollution control or resource management gains. Data on the performance of others can help decision-makers construct appropriate sustainability targets or goals. Second, benchmarking can be used to reveal best practices and to provide a roadmap towards improved strategies, technologies, or policies that laggards can follow. With the Internet making the dissemination of information on best practices much easier and cheaper, the excuses for continuing sub-par performance become ever more limited. Third, as noted earlier, comparative data often stimulate competitive pressures and thus drive innovation that can lead to improved results (Porter, 1990).

Absent data and appropriate benchmarks from comparable jurisdictions, it is hard to spot lagging performance. Complacency and inertia are hard to overcome, but when citizens (or environmental groups or the media) find out that other cities, states, or countries are delivering much better environmental results than their own government, they have a basis for complaint. Indeed, Belgium's poor showing in Yale's 2002 Environmental Sustainability Index (a forerunner to the 2018 EPI) – ranking 125th, far behind its neighbors France, Germany, and the Netherlands – caused a huge uproar in Brussels and led to a significant focus on the country's pollution problems. While the environmental facts before and after the publication of Yale's rankings remained unchanged, the comparative analysis gave the Belgians (and especially the Belgian media) a context for understanding their pollution numbers and a benchmark for judging their government's relative performance.

Businesses also benefit from comparative information on government activities and policy results. It gives companies operating in jurisdictions with inefficient regulatory systems an independent (and not purely self-interested) basis on which to press for better government performance. The prospect of focused oversight by citizens, NGOs, the media, and the regulated community also tends to induce better government performance. In particular, the presence of data and benchmarks from other jurisdictions can trigger a process of "regulatory competition" among governments that yields more effective and cost-conscious environmental controls (Esty & Geradin, 2001). It can also improve cooperation between and highlight coordination gaps across different levels of government – leading to more efficient forms of "co-opetition" (Esty & Geradin, 2000).

Greater efficiency

Many environmental problems arise from market and regulatory failures, but other issues can be traced to inefficiency and waste, reflecting ignorance or mistakes on the part of polluters and natural resource users. In fact, a significant percentage of pollution arises not from emissions intentionally sent up the smokestack or out the effluent pipe to avoid control costs (uninternalized externalities) but from materials or energy that are unwittingly underutilized in fabrication or elsewhere in a product's life cycle. Such "inadvertent" pollution can be traced to poorly designed goods, outdated technologies, unnecessarily wasteful packaging, and general inattention to the dictates of environmental management (Esty & Winston, 2009). Data on the losses attributable to such mistakes, as well as easy access to information about alternative production or consumption practices, promise to improve resource productivity, enhance consumer welfare, and improve corporate competitiveness (Porter & van der Linde, 1995; Esty & Porter, 1998). The U.S. Environmental Protection Agency's Toxic Release Inventory highlights the potential in this regard. Simply requiring companies to tabulate the amount of chemicals flowing out of a facility into the land, air, and water pushed many firms to adopt waste minimization programs (Karkannian, 2001).

Where excess emissions can be attributed to inefficiency, policy-makers can generally induce polluters to shift to less harmful production or consumption practices by informing them of better alternatives. No government mandate is needed. The opportunity for individual gain or competitive advantage provides all the incentive needed. Without any regulatory mandate, for instance, the U.S. EPA's "Green Lights" initiative convinced thousands of enterprises to substitute high-efficiency fluorescent lighting for traditional incandescent bulbs – reducing electricity use (and thus the emissions from power generation) and lowering company costs. Likewise, the U.S. DOE's Energy Star program – a consumer-oriented scheme that identifies and labels energy efficient appliances – has led to sizeable reductions in energy use (Gillingham et al., 2004).

Further waste reductions will likely be achieved through data mining by corporations eager to understand their markets and data-enabled mass customization by businesses trying to meet the precise needs of their customers. Catalog companies, for example, used to send out mass mailings based on generalized assumptions about the buying habits of people living in certain zip codes. Today, they can select and solicit customers on a much more refined basis, saving literally tons of paper. In a similar vein, Dell uses state-of-the-art information systems to customize their computers to each customer's needs, a strategy that translates into reduced material inputs, less waste, and lower pollution (Sharma et al., 2010).

Data links may also facilitate efficiency gains up and down the value chain and even beyond. Online connections between suppliers and customers have helped a number of companies, from General Electric to 7-Eleven, shrink inventories, limit spoilage, and cut waste. While the full potential of e-commerce has not yet been realized, and there may be downsides as well as upsides, the potential for Internet-driven efficiency gains is already visible (Esty, 2001). Companies increasingly are looking upstream and downstream to find ways to reduce costs and increase value. Walmart, for example, now requires its more than 50,000 suppliers to report on a wide array of sustainability metrics, covering everything from greenhouse gas emissions to food waste (Gunther, 2013). Meanwhile, customer-supplier data exchanges and networks are deepening commercial relationships, and interconnected companies often find it easier to identify the "least cost avoider" from a pollution perspective (Esty & Porter, 1998).

Policy efficiency and regulatory reform

As noted above, more refined environmental metrics can improve regulatory procedures and outcomes. In a more information-rich world, governments can shift away from government-mandated technology standards toward more sophisticated approaches to controlling pollution and managing shared natural resources. In particular, refined data make possible the deployment of "market mechanisms", which put a price on emissions or resource consumption, thereby "monetizing" environmental harms and allowing for more flexible and cost-effective compliance strategies.

In other instances, metrics tracked in real time allow for a "property rights" approach to management of pollution or scarce natural resources (Demsetz, 1967; Ackerman & Stewart, 1985). New Zealand's fisheries, for example, have been revived over the past 20 years under a "catch shares" system with tradable fish quotas – all enabled by technologies that track and measure all fish landings (Pearse & Walters, 1992). In the United States, acid rain emissions have been cut in half since 1990 under an SO_2 control regime based on tradable pollution allowances (Stavins & Whitehead, 1997). The acid rain reduction program depends heavily on smokestack monitors that transmit data on power plant emissions on a real-time 24-hour-a-day basis (Goulder, 2013).

Fundamentally, market-based approaches to environmental protection are most effective if the transaction costs involved in exchanging (and enforcing) environmental property rights are low (Coase, 1960; Williamson, 1989). High transaction costs may lead to market failures. Better data, however, can help to bring down these costs by making property boundaries easier to delineate, lowering the cost of vindicating environmental rights, and allowing environmental property rights markets to operate more smoothly (Esty, 1996; Esty, 2004). Just as barbed wire diminished the risk of overexploitation of rangeland by making it possible to fence off individual ranches in the American West (Rose, 1998), data can serve as virtual barbed wire, enabling property rights in various shared resources to be demarcated and protected.

Even where market-based regulation is not feasible, better data can improve the effectiveness of "command and control" mandates (Cole & Grossman, 1999). More precise pollution information allows regulators to address problems at the scale of the harm, avoid overly broad uniform rules, and tailor control strategies to individual circumstances. In effect, low-cost and easily accessible data make it easier to refine regulations and, thus, to accommodate diversity across the regulated community (Esty, 1999). As noted earlier, data and analysis enable more regular and careful policy evaluations leading to continuous improvement in regulatory design. When substandard results are observed more readily, special interest lobbying and other manipulations of the regulatory process become more difficult. Thus, a data-driven policy process may be less susceptible to "public choice" failures.

Better and cheaper data also tend to increase transparency (Candeub, 2013). As discussed earlier, governments face greater scrutiny than in the past due to the increase in information that is available to opposition leaders, the media, business critics, and NGOs. Similarly, government regulators, environmental groups, community activists, and the media all have extraordinary access – via the Internet, YouTube, etc. – to facts and figures about corporate environmental activities. Bad acts and poor results are now almost impossible to hide. Although some companies and governments may feel uncomfortable under this more intense public spotlight, a world of instantaneous connections, open access, and transparency promises to draw attention to key pollution problems and natural resource management, speed up feedback loops, and increase the pace of environmental progress.

Bumps in the road

More data does not necessarily translate into more knowledge in either the policy or corporate domains. Some metrics may be deceptively framed. Others may suffer from inconsistent reporting or validation. In the context of comparative analyses, misinformation and disinformation can pose very serious risks to environmental progress. Likewise, too much data can overwhelm decision-making processes and create space for special interest influences. The fact, for instance, that there is no required set of environment/social/governance (ESG) metrics that all companies must report on following a standardized methodology undermines efforts by investors to understand who the sustainability leaders are in the corporate world (Esty & Cort, 2017). In this regard, a recent survey of corporate sustainability reports from 94 Canadian companies identified nearly 600 different indicators of sustainability performance, with little in the way of issue overlap (Roca & Searcy, 2012). Mechanisms will therefore be needed to ensure quality control and methodological consistency across metrics.

Data in the wrong hands, moreover, can also be deployed for malicious purposes. Recently, the U.S. Federal Trade Commission highlighted the potential for big data analytics to be used to discriminate or exclude low-income communities from credit and employment opportunities (Federal Trade Commission, 2016). In some instances, an information-rich world may actually constrict, rather than expand, consumer choice and civil liberties (Bollier, 2010). At the same time, big data raises important privacy concerns. Major data breaches at Target, Yahoo, JPMorgan Chase, and others have underscored the vulnerability of virtual information to hackers. Thus, a commitment to data security will be critical to building public confidence in data-driven policy-making. Likewise, there is a growing need to guard against the fabrication of false information. The rise of "fake news" during the Brexit vote and the 2016 U.S. presidential election has focused attention on the influential power of social media platforms and raised important questions about whether and how to regulate incorrect or misleading information (Allcot & Gentzkow, 2017). Ultimately, how society processes false data may be just as important to governance as how it uses real data.

While data can enrich environmental debates and facilitate "triangulation" on answers in the face of uncertainties, more information can also diminish the quality of policy dialogues, translate into a battle of numbers, fuel chaos, and lead to breakdown in the decision-making process. What will be determinative are the relevance, validity, and reliability of the new data flows – and the emergence of institutions to promote quality assurance of both the raw information and the analysis that flows from it.

Numbers, moreover, are not value neutral. What is measured and how things are measured builds on presumptions about what is important, which in turn reflects the values of those engaged in the data exercise (Wagner, 1995; Kahan, Jenkins-Smith, & Braman, 2010). As the Spangenberg chapter in this volume explains, indicator choices and frameworks reflect the data team's choices and assumptions about what matters rather than an "objective reality". But the politicization of statistics, and of science more generally, can be overplayed. Even if precise quantitative results cannot be developed or cardinal rankings are susceptible to challenge, comparative data often will provide an indicative picture of the scale and importance of environment challenges or generate an ordinal ranking of policy options.

More fundamentally, concerns about the framing of metrics argue not for less reliance on data and analysis but rather for more transparency and openness with regard to data sources and methodologies. Open disclosure of data sources and systematic use of sensitivity analyses to test whether underlying assumptions are robust can help to put metrics and comparative analyses in perspective. Concerns about data subjectivity can, however, be taken too far. Indeed, as the environmental science of data analytics advances and various indicators are framed and debated, some consensus will emerge on what matters – and thus what metrics should be tracked and how these metrics should be constructed.

The path forward

Today's environmental policy-makers operate in a dramatically different world than their 20th-century counterparts. Data and information are no longer scarce, and the threats posed by climate change and other environmental hazards are clear. If policy-makers are to address and manage these critical issues, they must work to make their environmental decision-making more systemic, data driven, and analytically rigorous. As this volume demonstrates, data-driven policy-making has shown the potential to help deliver a more sustainable future.

Note

* Chapter 31 derives from a prior work (Esty, D. C. & Cornelius, P. K. 2002. *Environmental Performance Measurement: The Global Report 2001–2002*. New York: Oxford University Press.)

References

Ackerman, B. A. & Stewart, R. B. 1985. Reforming Environmental Law. *Stanford Law Review*, 37(5), 1333–1365.
Allcot, H. & Gentzkow, M. 2017. *Social Media and Fake News in the 2016 Election*. NBER Working Paper No. 23089.
Allcot, H. & Rogers, T. 2016. *Opower: Evaluating the Impact of Home Energy Reports on Energy Conservation in the United States*. Cambridge: Abdul Latif Jameel Poverty Action Lab.
Arrow, K. J., Cropper, M. L., Eads, G. C., Hahn, R. W., Lave, L. B., Noll, R. G. 1996. Is There a Role for Benefit-Cost Analysis in Environmental, Health, and Safety Regulation? *Science*, 272(5259), 221–222.
Benedick, R. 1991. *Ozone Diplomacy: New Directions in Safeguarding the Planet*. Cambridge, MA: Harvard University Press.
Bollier, D. 2010. *The Promise and Peril of Big Data*. Washington, DC: Aspen Institute.
Breyer, S. 1993. *Breaking the Vicious Circle: Toward Effective Risk Regulation*. Cambridge: Harvard University Press.
Candeub, A. 2013. Transparency in the Administrative State. *Houston Law Review*, 51(2), 385–416.
Chertow, M. & Esty, D. C. (eds.). 1997. *Thinking Ecologically: The Next Generation of Environmental Policy*. New Haven: Yale University Press.
Coase, R. H. 1960. The Problem of Social Cost. *Journal of Law and Economics*, 3, 1–44.
Cole, D. H. & Grossman, P. Z. 1999. When is Command-and-Control Efficient? Institutions, Technology, and the Comparative Efficiency of Alternative Regulatory Regimes for Environmental Protection. *Wisconsin Law Review*, 590, 887–938.
Dawes, R. M. 2001. *Everyday Irrationality: How Pseudo-Scientists, Lunatics, and the Rest of Us Systematically Fail to Think Rationally*. Boulder, CO: Westview Press.
Demsetz, H. 1967. Toward a Theory of Property Rights. *American Economic Review*, 57(2), 347–359.
Eccles, R., Herz, R. H., Keegan, M. E., & Phillips, D. 2001. *The Value Reporting Revolution: Moving Beyond the Earnings Game*. New York: John Wiley and Sons.
Emerson, J., Esty, D. C., Levy, M. A., Kim, C. H., Mara, V., de Sherbinin, A., & Srebotnjak, T. 2010. *2010 Environmental Performance Index*. New Haven: Yale Center for Environmental Law and Policy.
Esty, D. C. 1996. Revitalizing Environmental Federalism. *Michigan Law Review*, 95(3), 570–653.
Esty, D. C. 1999. Toward Optimal Environmental Governance. *New York University Law Review*, 74(6), 1495–1574.
Esty, D. C. 2001. Digital Earth: Saving the Environment. *OECD Observer*. Summer 2001, 68–70.
Esty, D. C. 2004. Environmental Protection in the Information Age. *New York University Law Review*, 79(1), 115–211.

Esty, D. C. 2017. Red Lights to Green Lights: From 20th Century Environmental Protection to 21st Century Sustainability. *Environmental Law*, 47(1), 101–175.

Esty, D. C. & Cort, T. 2017. Corporate Sustainability Metrics: What Investors Need and Don't Get. *Journal of Environmental Investing* (Fall). 8(1), 1–43

Esty, D. C. & Geradin, D. 2000. Regulatory Co-Opetition. *Journal of International Economic Law*, 3(2), 235–255.

Esty, D. C. & Geradin, D. 2001. Regulatory Co-opetition. In Daniel C. Esty and Damien Geradin (eds.), *Regulatory Competition and Economic Integration: Comparative Perspectives*. New York: Oxford University Press.

Esty, D. C. & Porter, M. E. 1998. Industrial Ecology and Competitiveness. *Journal of Industrial Ecology*, 2(1), 35–43.

Esty, D. C. & Porter, M. E. 2000. Measuring National Environmental Performance and Its Determinants. In Michael E. Porter, Jeffrey Sachs, et al. (eds.), *The Global Competitiveness Report 2000*. New York: Oxford University Press.

Esty, D. C. & Rushing, R. 2006. *Governing by the Numbers: The Promise of Data-Driven Policymaking in the Information Age*. Washington, DC: Center for American Progress.

Esty, D. C. & Simmons, P. J. 2011. *The Green to Gold Business Playbook: How to Implement Sustainability Practices for Bottom-Line Results in Every Business Function*. Hoboken: Wiley.

Esty, D. C. & Winston, A. 2009. *Green to Gold: How Smart Companies Use Environmental Strategy to Innovate, Create Value, and Build Competitive Advantage*. Hoboken: Wiley.

Farber, D. A. 2015. Coping with Uncertainty: Cost-Benefit Analysis, The Precautionary Principle, and Climate Change. *Washington Law Review*, 90(4), 1659–1726.

Federal Trade Commission. 2016. *Big Data: A Tool for Inclusion or Exclusion? Understanding the Issues*. Washington, DC.

Giles, C. 2013. Next Generation Compliance. *The Environmental Forum*, 23. 22–26.

Gillingham, K., Newell, R., & Palmer, K. 2004. *The Effectiveness and Cost of Energy Efficiency Programs*. Washington, DC: Resources for the Future.

Global Sustainable Investment Alliance. 2014. *2014 Global Sustainable Investment Review*. Available at: www.ussif.org/Files/Publications/GSIA_Review.pdf

Goulder, L. H. 2013. Markets for Pollution Allowances: What Are the (New) Lessons? *Journal of Economic Perspectives*, 27(1), 87–102.

Graham, J. D. 1997. Legislative Approaches to Achieving More Protection against Risk at Less Cost. *University of Chicago Legal Forum*, 1997(1), 13–58.

Graham, J. D. & Wiener, J. B. 1997. Confronting Risk Tradeoffs. In John D. Graham and Jonathan B. Wiener (eds.), *Risk vs. Risk: Tradeoffs in Protecting Health and the Environment*. Cambridge, MA: Harvard University Press.

Gunther, M. 2013. Game on: Why Walmart Is Ranking Suppliers on Sustainability. *GreenBiz*. Available at: www.greenbiz.com/blog/2013/04/15/game-why-walmart-ranking-suppliers-sustainability.

Herman, C., Schoenbrod, D., Stewart, R. B., & Wyman, K. M. 2008. Breaking the Logjam: Environmental Reform for the New Congress and Administration. *New York University Environmental Law Journal*, 17(1), 1–18.

Kahan, D., Jenkins-Smith, H., & Braman, D. 2010. Cultural Cognition of Scientific Consensus. *Journal of Risk Research*, 14(2), 147–174.

Kaplan, R. S. & Norton, D. P. 1992. The Balanced Scorecard – Measures that Drive Performance. *Harvard Business Review*.

Karkannian, B. 2001. Information as Environmental Regulation: TRI and Performance Benchmarking, Precursor to a New Paradigm? *Georgetown Law Journal*, 89(2), 257–370.

Kysar, D. A. 2007. Discounting on Stilts. *University of Chicago Law Review*, 74(1), 199–144.

Lazarus, R. J. 2004. *The Making of Environmental Law*. Chicago: University of Chicago Press.

Lazarus, R. J. 2009. Super Wicked Problems and Climate Change: Restraining the Present to Liberate the Future. *Cornell Law Review*, 94(5), 1153–1234.

Lehner, P. 2008. The Logjam: Are Our Environmental Laws Failing Us or Are We Failing Them? *New York University Environmental Law Journal*, 17(1), 194–209.

Lewis, M. 2003. *Moneyball: The Art of Winning an Unfair Game*. New York: Norton.

McAfee, A. & Brynjolfsson, E. 2012. Big Data: The Management Revolution. *Harvard Business Review*. Available at: https://hbr.org/2012/10/big-data-the-management-revolution

Metzenbaum, S. 2002. Measurement that Matters: Cleaning up the Charles River. In Donald F. Kettl (ed.), *Environmental Governance: A Report on the Next Generation of Environmental Policy.* Washington: Brookings.

Mintz, J. A. 2014. Measuring Environmental Enforcement Success: The Elusive Search for Objectivity. *Environmental Law Reporter*, 44(9), 10751–10756.

Pearse, P. H., & Walters, C. J. 1992. Harvesting Regulation under Quota Management Systems for Ocean Fisheries: Decision Making in the Face of Natural Variability, Weak Information, Risks and Conflicting Incentives. *Marine Policy*, 16(3), 167–182.

Porter, M. E. 1990. *Competitive Advantage of Nations*. New York: Free Press.

Porter, M. E. & van der Linde, C. 1995. Toward a New Conception of Environment-Competitiveness Relationship. *Journal of Economic Perspectives*, 9(4), 97–118.

Revesz, R. L. 2015. Toward a More Rational Environmental Policy. *Harvard Environmental Law Review*, 39(1), 93–106.

Revesz, R. L. & Livermore, M. A. 2008. *Retaking Rationality: How Cost-Benefit Analysis Can Better Protect the Environment and Our Health*. New York: Oxford University Press.

Revesz, R. L. & Shahabian, M. R. 2011. Climate Change and Future Generations. *Southern California Law Review*, 84(5), 1097–1162.

Roca, L. C. & Searcy, C. 2012. An Analysis of Indicators Disclosed in Corporate Sustainability Reports. *Journal of Cleaner Production*, 20(1), 103–118.

Rose, C. M. 1998. The Several Futures of Property: Of Cyberspace and Folktales, Emissions Trades and Ecosystem. *Minnesota Law Review*, 83(1), 129–182.

Rose, C. M. 2005. Environmental Law Grows up (More or Less), and What Science Can Do to Help. *Lewis & Clark Law Review*, 9(2), 273–294.

Sagoff, M. 1982. We Have Met the Enemy and He Is Us or Conflict and Contradiction in Environmental Law. *Environmental Law*, 12(2), 283–316.

Schwab, K. 2016. *The Fourth Industrial Revolution*. Cologny: World Economic Forum.

Sharma, A., Iyer, G., Mehrotra, A., & Krishnan, R. 2010. Sustainability and Business-to-Business Marketing: A Framework and Implications. *Industrial Marketing Management*, 39(2), 330–341.

Slovic, P. 2000. *The Perception of Risk*. Sterling, VA: Earthscan Publications.

Snyder, E. G., Watkins, T. H, Solomon, P. H., Thoma, E. D., William, R. W., Hagler, G. S. W., . . . Preuss, P. W. 2013. The Changing Paradigm of Air Pollution Monitoring. *Environmental Science & Technology*, 47(20), 11369–11377.

Stavins, R. & Whitehead, B. 1997. *Market-Based Environmental Policies*. In Marian R. Chertow and Daniel C. Esty (eds.), *Thinking Ecologically: The Next Generation of Environmental Policy*. New Haven: Yale University Press.

Stephan, M. 2002. Environmental Information Disclosure Programs: They Work, but Why? *Social Science Quarterly*, 83(1), 190–205.

Stewart, R. B. 1995. United States Environmental Regulation: A Failing Paradigm. *Journal of Law and Commerce*, 15(585).

Sunstein, C. R. 2001. Cognition and Cost-Benefit Analysis. In Mathew Adler and Eric Posner (eds.), *Cost-Benefit Analysis: Legal, Economic, and Philosophical Perspectives*. Chicago: University of Chicago Press.

Wagner, W. 1995. The Science Charade in Toxic Risk Regulation. *Columbia Law Review*, 95(7), 1613–1723.

Williamson, O. E. 1989. Transaction Cost Economics. In Richard Schmalensee and Robert D. Willig (eds.), *Handbook of Industrial Organization*. New York: Elsevier Science Publishers.

32

META-EVALUATION OF SUSTAINABILITY INDICATORS

From organizational to national level[1]

Tomás B. Ramos and Sandra Caeiro

Introduction

Although there are well-known indicator selection criteria and it has been significantly explored over the last two and half decades since Agenda 21 first called for sustainability indicators, sustainable development indicators (SDIs) have not yet fully matured and little effort has been put into their validation (Bockstaller and Girardin, 2003; Ramos et al., 2004; Meul et al., 2009; Ramos, Alves, Subtil and Melo, 2007), in particular into evaluating how, jointly, as a framework, they respond to sustainability questions, from the standpoint of a meta-evaluation and/or sensitivity analysis. It is important, therefore, to question the effectiveness of SDIs in an effort to continue advancing and facilitating sustainability (Wilson et al., 2007) and to illustrate to what degree the outcomes achieved correspond to the goals intended (Lyytimäki and Rosenström, 2007). In this way validation verifies whether the indicator possesses a degree of "accuracy" consistent with its intended application and a degree of "credibility" conducive to the potential users' confidence in it and the information derived from it, and hence their willingness to use it (Meul et al., 2009). In fact, validation means the achievement of overall objectives or the production of the intended effects, but as pointed out by Bockstaller and Girardin (2003), the use of any evaluation tools should be formalized in a real test and not simply limited to a descriptive work. The validation process for an indicator can be separated into two stages: (1) conceptual validation, which is based on data, information and a description of the indicator and (2) empirical validation, which is based upon the analysis of the behaviour of the indicator outputs (Mantese and Amaral, 2017), outcomes and impacts, for which different evaluation approaches could be used. A key component of effective evaluation is how information is presented, which will depend on the purpose of the evaluation, the target audience and their familiarity with the information. Simplification of the results is a key factor (Becker, 2004).

Meta-evaluation is not a new concept and in fact it was initiated by Scriven (1969). Meta-evaluation is an evaluation of an evaluation. It is a critical assessment of the strengths and weaknesses of an evaluation, and draws conclusions about its overall utility, accuracy, validity, feasibility and propriety. Meta-evaluation can serve a valuable function as a self-assessment quality-control tool during the implementation of an evaluation. It could use methods such as a checklist to help the evaluator to be sure that nothing important has been missed out (Patel, 2002).

Some work has been carried out to evaluate the performance of developed environmental and sustainability indicators and indices. For example, Jackson et al. (2000); Kurtz et al. (2001); Bockstaller and Girardin (2003) and Meul et al. (2009); Caeiro et al. (2012); Ramos et al. (2014); Mascarenhas et al. (2014) have discussed or explored methodologies to evaluate ecological/environmental indicators, where end-users play an important role in determining indicator applicability or effectiveness. Ramos et al. (2004; Ramos, Alves, Subtil and Melo, 2007) specifically focused this discussion with novel approaches and concepts on meta-level monitoring and meta-performance indicators, respectively. Cloquell-Ballester et al. (2006) have developed methodologies for the validation of indicators within the environmental impact assessment of project studies, where the core of the validation is to access the correct performance of new indicators in terms of concept, coherence, operationality and utility. Other studies have compared several national sustainable development index metrics, evaluating their consistency and meaningfulness (Böhringer and Jochem, 2007; Wilson et al., 2007). Others also discuss the constraints and need to standardize indicators that assess sustainability at the local level (Moreno Pires et al., 2014) or evaluate the use of indicators in the context of local governance (Moreno Pires and Fidélis, 2012, 2015).

Despite the proliferation of sustainability indicator approaches, frameworks cases and tools, mainly implemented at the country level, few of these initiatives include meta-evaluation procedures and, to even lesser extent, indicators to operate this kind of analysis. Even though national experience of SDI frameworks, e.g. that of Spain (Gallego, 2006), Germany (Walz, 2000), Finland (Rosenström and Kyllönen, 2007), considers the requirements of indicator selection, including public participation approaches to support SDI development, few of them include a meta-evaluation of the SDI systems themselves or their components, procedures and indicator outcomes and impacts, such as the Portuguese case (Ramos, Alves, Gervásio and Liberal, 2007) and APA, (2008). Lyytimäki and Rosenström (2007) analyze the effectiveness of different national conceptual frameworks for communicating SDIs in Finland and concluded that it is important to pay more attention to the indicators as a set than on an individual basis and that specifically tailored frameworks should be employed for specific uses. According to these authors, it is easy to list the characteristics of an ideal framework, but not so easy to find frameworks that actually contain these ideal characteristics. The same situation applies to stipulating and implementing the criteria for individual indicators. When a comprehensive list of ideal characteristics has been compiled, it is left for someone else to come up with actual work that meets all these criteria. In addition, a long list of indicators or extensive frameworks may be introduced that fail to meet the criteria. Monitoring and evaluating how indicators are used and learning from the information acquired are at least as important as the development work aimed at improving the ability of a framework to depict the reality objectively. This may be considered the key challenge for future research on SD frameworks and indicators (Lyytimäki and Rosenström, 2007), where still doubts exist.

The main aim of this chapter is to present a conceptual approach to design and assess the effectiveness of the sustainability indicators, which do not usually include an evaluation of themselves. A set of key-factor and meta-performance indicators is proposed that allow the implementation of the described tool. Additionally, some examples of its application worldwide are presented and briefly discussed.

The conceptual meta-performance evaluation framework

This framework assumes a definition of sustainability meta-performance evaluation that is supported by the concept presented in Ramos, Alves, Subtil and Melo (2007), as applied to public sector environmental performance evaluation. The developed tool aims to assess the effectiveness of the sustainability assessment instruments themselves, where indicators are one of the most widely used and well-known tools. Meta-performance is understood here as part of performance management and assessment procedures. Sustainability meta-performance evaluation indicators could be the practical instruments for verifying the assessment, in showing how appropriate the SDIs are and allowing an evaluation of the overall performance of the assessment processes and results (see Figure 32.1). The sustainability indicator system itself, the entire structure of the indicators and the methodological features of the latter will be the target of the meta-performance evaluation process.

Based on Ramos and Caeiro (2010), an updated framework to conduct meta-performance evaluation of sustainability indicators was developed with the aim of identifying how to put the sustainability meta-evaluation challenges into practice (Figure 32.2). This framework was designed to be potentially applied to national, regional, local and organizational SDI initiatives, supporting indicator validation and allowing continuous assessment of these tools. Meta-evaluation may be seen as one process or component within an entire SDI system, but looking from above, mainly aimed at indicator revision and updating and system improvement. The development of sustainability indicators, when analyzed as a system where different processes occur, includes a series of actions and decisions with various data and information flows. Approaches to sustainability indicators should define various principal components, to assure a coherent development process. They may be divided into the following main categories: (1) planning and conceptualization (including all the design components and processes); (2) implementation: the whole process of data collection, processing and analysis; (3) operation and action: outcomes are presented through reporting and communication tools, leading to different kinds of reaction (e.g. policy measures; stakeholder participation); establishment of flow links with other SDIs, at the local, regional, national and international levels, and with strategic tools/instruments (policies, plans or programmes); (4) follow-up: updating and reviewing, mainly based on a meta-performance evaluation process.

This framework seeks to incorporate a systems analysis approach that integrates the main relationships among different components of the meta-performance evaluation of sustainability

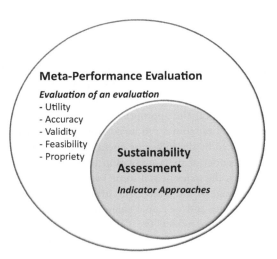

Figure 32.1   General meta-performance evaluation features of sustainability assessments

Figure 32.2   Conceptual framework for meta-performance evaluation of sustainability indicators

indicators. As with any planning or management process, SDI systems should be flexible and dynamic, and should have a follow-up procedure for reviewing and monitoring, and improving the robustness and overall quality of the sustainability assessment results produced by the indicators. The procedure for the meta-performance evaluation of sustainability indicators starts with a definition of the main objectives and the scope of this process, which will depend on various fundamentals that characterize the SDI system and its indicators. On the basis of current and well-established principles and guidelines for environmental and sustainability indicator development, key good-practice factors should be selected in order to develop a tool that can be operationalized through the construction of a checklist and the corresponding meta-performance evaluation indicators. These factors will cover two main levels of evaluation: Level 1 – Performance of the SDI system, including the main processes, and the respective actors and methodological approaches; Level 2 – performance of individual and aggregate indicators, including their inputs, outputs and outcomes/impacts. Meta-performance evaluation indicators will allow the following: (1) an evaluation of overall assessment activities, to measure how well the indicator initiative is going; (2) the appropriacy of the sustainability indicators, including the methodological aspects and outcomes produced and (3) an evaluation of the sustainability measures and actions originated by the indicator operation and analysis.

The key good-practice factors of meta-evaluation include various aspects, e.g. the type of SDI management framework, the existence of some sort of collaborative/participative process, the target audience, the coverage of the subject, the structure of the indicator organization (e.g. sustainability dimensions/themes and/or causal chain frameworks, such as the STRESS model [Rapport and Friend, 1979] from which the OECD [1993] pressure-state-response [PSR] framework was developed), the number of indicators, the relationship with sustainability indicators developed at different levels (national, regional, local and organizational), the regularity of the reporting, the sustainability indices, and the indicator report format/platform (the medium used to communicate the report information). In this way, for the assessment of the progress towards sustainability, participatory sustainability assessment frameworks should be used. Most of the works listed earlier, also used participation processes to validate indicators (Jackson et al., 2000; Walz, 2000; Kurtz et al., 2001; Bockstaller and Girardin, 2003; Gallego, 2006; Cloquell-Ballester et al., 2006; Rosenström and Kyllönen, 2007; Meul et al., 2009; Mascarenhas et al., 2014, Ramos et al., 2014).

Exploring Ramos et al. (2014) approach, the meta-evaluation performance can be *formal* and *informal*, designed on the assumption that we should integrate two dimensions of meta-evaluation, that are complementary and synergistic. *Formal*, which is mainly led by the experts/technical staff and reflect mandatory or official procedures, and the *informal*, mainly represented by voluntary, ad hoc, non-regular or private initiatives (facts and figures, views, ideas, desires, needs and/or perceptions), conducted by different types of stakeholders. Informal stakeholders participation can include lays, general citizens, public and private organizations, non-governmental organizations, universities, media and research institutions. The stakeholder's contributions for the meta-evaluation evaluation process can be integrated using different techniques and tools, namely (Ramos et al., 2014): (1) computer systems for collaborative data uploads – raw treated and analyzed data – and mailing lists for data exchange; (2) participative workshops, focus groups brainstorming meetings; (3) social networks, wikis; (4) Participatory Rural Appraisal (PRA) tools for lay and traditional knowledge data input and gathering; (5) interviews and questionnaires surveys or self-assessment checklists. The informal contributions to the meta-evaluation process could be put into practice through the implementation of a sort of collaborative Sustainability Assessment Forum, as explored in Ramos and Caeiro (2010). The results of the comparison between formal and informal evaluation will be used for cross-validation of the sustainability meta-evaluation outcomes.

This framework was designed to improve the quality of indicators, by facilitating their development and evaluation, and produce better sustainability assessments. As stressed by Kurtz et al. (2001), this kind of approach can be used to target gaps in knowledge and formulate future research directions. When the meta-performance is conducted a more effective reviewing process is implemented, with readjustments and improvements to the SDIs through an adaptive scheme.

The proposed meta-performance evaluation framework will not directly measure the full real outcome or value of a certain SDI system in assessing sustainability, given the complexity and uncertainty of sustainability issues. Nevertheless, it will help the user to ascertain if the indicator initiative is well developed, implemented and managed, and will give important signals about the credibility and accuracy of the SDI set.

Key good-practice factors and indicators for meta-performance evaluation

To put the proposed framework into practice, the core meta-evaluation components – the key good-practice factors and meta-performance evaluation indicators – were developed (see Table 32.1). A great amount of work already published presents the ideal criteria to select and develop environmental and sustainability indicators, in particular the Bellagio Principles (Hardi and Zand, 1997), and various other pieces of work (e.g. Mascarenhas et al., 2015; Morenos Pires et al., 2014; Mascarenhas et al., 2012; Bell and Morse, 2008; Niemeijer and Groot, 2008; Ramos, Alves, Subtil and Melo, 2007; Cloquell-Ballester et al., 2006; Spangenberg, 2002; HMSO, 1996; Ott, 1978). In the development of the proposed framework it was assumed that various guidelines and criteria for the selection and development of sustainability indicators could be adapted

Table 32.1 Key good–practice factors and meta–performance evaluation indicators for sustainability assessment. Summary of rationale and recommendations for each factor available at Ramos and Caeiro (2010)

Key good-practice factors	Meta-performance evaluation indicators (checklist examples): name and measurement units/scale (in brackets)
Level 1 – Performance of the SDI System: planning and conceptualization processes, actors and methodological approaches	
Objective, scope and scale effects (scale integration and spatial extent)	• Main dimensions covered by the SDI system: environmental economic, social and institutional (yes, no, not clear, for each SD dimension) • Themes related to particular territorial features – national, regional, local or organizational, depending on the main SDI scale (%; no.) • Indicators for comparison/integration among different spatial scales (type and no.)
Target audience and type of language	• Identification of the central indicator audience (yes, no, not clear)
Management model and institutional cooperation	• Identification of the management model (yes, no, not clear) • Institutions involvement and cooperation (type and number of institutions and their roles)
Technical and educational skills of the staff	• Staff profile: type and diversity of staff (total number of personnel; no. per type of background or expertise; number of personnel by function and time spent) • Training personnel for particular indicator tasks (number of persons allocated to SDI development who follow training initiatives)
Indicator organization and structuring	• Use of a conceptual framework – by sustainable development dimension or theme, DPSIR, PSR or others – for SDI organization and structuring (yes, no, not clear) • SDI size (total no. and no. by type) • Indicator subsets (type of indicator subsets for particular purposes, e.g. headline indicators; common sectoral, regional or local indicators)
Regularity issues, revision and updating procedures	• Revision of the entire SDI system processes, including a review of the general methodological approach and related procedures as well as a reselection of the indicators (yes, no, not clear; no. of revisions planned versus accomplished) • Regular SDI updating and reporting (yes, no, not clear; no. reports and updates planned versus accomplished)
Governance and public participation process	• Participative/collaborative processes undertaken in each stage of the SDI development, from the design to the operation and revision stages (yes, no, not clear; total no. and type of stakeholders involved in each participative phase) • Stakeholders' feedback to SDI development (no. year^{-1} of messages received by email/letter or through personal contacts) • Institutional cooperation with other public institutions for SDI development and implementation (yes, no, not clear; no. of formal and informal protocols)
Relationships with SD policies, strategies or plans	• SDS goals and objectives covered by the sustainability indicators (yes, no, not clear; no.; %)

Key good-practice factors	Meta-performance evaluation indicators (checklist examples): name and measurement units/scale (in brackets)
Intra-territorial (or sectoral or organizational) asymmetries	• Use of particular methodological procedures to measure territorial, organizational or sectoral asymmetries (yes, no, not clear)
Communication and promotion/ dissemination	• Reporting and communication to stakeholders (no. reports, workshops, internet sites, email list)
Cost-benefit analysis	• Implementation of public sector projects as outcome of SDI results (no.; $year^{-1}$)
	• SDI planning/conceptualization and maintenance investments and expenses (10^3 € $indicator^{-1}$ $year^{-1}$)
Decision-makers' and stakeholders' responses	• Linkage between sustainability indicators and output and outcome indicators for policies, plans and programmes (yes, no, not clear)
	• Decisions, actions/recommendations and measures to reverse or prevent negative trends and to maintain or increase positive trends (no.; % by type of sector)
	• Identification of unexpected sustainability effects through the SDI measurements (no.; %)
	• Willingness of potential end-users to effectively use the SDI systems (% of positive answers from potential end-users submitted to an interview survey)

Level 2: Performance of individual and aggregate indicators at the implementation and operation/action stage

Conceptual coherence and relevance to sustainability assessment	• Indicators that are not supported in published scientific or technical work (no.; %)
Relevance to the conceptual category, theme and/or sub-theme	• Stakeholders that use the indicator in their sectoral activity assessment (no.; %)
	• Direct relationships between the indicator title and its category (yes, no, not clear; no.; %)
Sensitivity and sustainability targets/thresholds	• Indicator targets reached (no.)
Methodological approaches for data collection and analysis	• Indicators without clear methods of data analysis and/or collection (no; %)
	• Periodicity of new data collection for indicators (no.; %);
	• Chemical use in indicator data-collection activities (loads of monitoring reagents reaching environment: $indicator^{-1}$ $year^{-1}$)
	• Use of environmentally preferable products and equipment in indicator measurement (no. of environmentally preferable products: $indicator^{-1}$ $year^{-1}$)
Quality control	• Identification of quality control objectives for each indicator (yes, no, not clear)
	• Identification of the means and methods to audit indicator quality (yes, no, not clear)
	• Analytical measurements and related detection levels (no. of indicator measurements under analytical detection level $year^{-1}$)
Spatial and temporal scales	• Indicators within socio-economic and/or homogeneous spatial/biogeographical units (no.; %)

(Continued)

Table 32.1 (Continued)

Key good-practice factors	Meta-performance evaluation indicators (checklist examples): name and measurement units/scale (in brackets)
Logistical requirements and information management	• Identification of logistics requirements for each indicator (yes, no, not clear) • Identification of information management procedures for each indicator (yes, no, not clear)
Costs	• Average cost of sustainability indicators (10^3 € indicator^{-1} year^{-1})
Understanding and social utility	• Indicators easily understandable by the end-users (no.; % of positive answers from potential end-users submitted to a survey)

to suit meta-evaluation needs. This framework takes into account certain evaluation guidelines that were developed with similar purposes but different scopes or targets in mind, in particular the work of Jackson et al. (2000) and Kurtz et al. (2001) on evaluation guidelines for ecological indicators. The research work of Meul et al. (2009); Niemeijer and Groot (2008); Ramos et al. (2008); Ramos, Alves, Subtil and Melo (2007); Ramos (2009); Cloquell-Ballester et al. (2006); and Bockstaller and Girardin (2003) was also considered for the key good-practice factors developed.

These key good-practice factors could be viewed as the basis for a checklist, providing aspects that an SDI initiative should be able to cover, though they must be adapted to each particular indicator system. A universal and standardized list of criteria for meta-evaluation is not desirable, since it is not realistic to expect a wide consensus on this subject, and also because each specific case requires a customized meta-evaluation tool. Additionally, it will be very difficult to include all the factors desired, so an SDI system could define a prioritizing scheme for key-factor accomplishment, on the basis of the defined objectives and scope of the meta-evaluation. This would result in various stages of performance that could be achieved in different periods of time. It should also be stressed that to conduct or supervise the meta-evaluation process a different institution than the one in charge of the SDI system should be involved, thus assuring independent external verification. This can be considered a fundamental step towards guaranteeing the reporting quality, robustness and credibility of the meta-evaluation.

Despite the efforts to obtain a manageable but balanced core set of factors and indicators, the total number is still high. Though a problem, this is mitigated by the fact that different factors and related indicators can be implemented in gradual stages, with a view to accomplishing partial meta-evaluation goals. A user's guide can be produced to explain the methodology in greater detail.

To avoid a too complex and resource-demanding process, the list of factors could be scored according to a qualitative assessment, based on expert knowledge, of how well the SDI system or indicator meets the requirements. An ordinal scale based on five categories can be defined to classify each meta-performance evaluation factor, in a range from 1 to 3: poor – 1; medium – 2, good – 3. The aggregated and final result value can be computed using an arithmetic or heuristic algorithm. As an alternative or complement to the scoring method, a summary analysis taking in each specific key factor could be also conducted to produce a qualitative integration of the main meta-evaluation outcomes.

Overview of application examples

The presented approach for meta-evaluation of SI has already been used or adapted in different thematic contexts and scales, demonstrating its relevance and practical utility. The framework application was found by searching in the Google Scholar research papers that cited the "meta-performance evaluation of sustainability indicators" conceptual framework (published in Ramos and Caeiro, 2010). Some of these international cases and related key factors/indicators used are analyzed below (see also Table 32.2).

Table 32.2 Meta-evaluation indicators or good-practices factors used by the application examples, based on meta-performance evaluation indicators suggested by Ramos and Caeiro, 2010

Meta-evaluation good-practices factors	Scale	Author
• Degree of reporting of environmental performance indicators in the EIS • Improved registration of master data and data transactions in the EIS • Revisions of environmental performance indicators • Implementation of new environmentally friendly practices/routines based on assessments of environmental performance • Evaluation of environmental performance: investments and expenses	Organization	Myhre et al. (2013)
• Conceptual coherence and relevance to sustainability assessment • Relevance to the conceptual category, theme and/or sub-theme • Sensitivity and sustainability targets/thresholds • Methodological approaches for data collection and analysis • Quality control • Spatial and temporal scales • Logistical requirements, information management, and costs	Municipality	Teixeira et al. (2016)
• Careful, transparent construction • Few key indicators • Appropriate type of indicators • Analysis of cross-linkages • Comparative indicators • Rising benchmarks over time • Broad coverage of indicator system • Practical tools • Transparent data collection • Data quality control • Easy to communicate and to understand • Learning process • Commissioning of indicators by government • Consideration of governmental structures • Participation of citizens • Budget	Municipality	Krank and Wallbaum (2011)

(*Continued*)

Table 32.2 (Continued)

Meta-evaluation good-practices factors	Scale	Author
• Agreement on indicators • Political support • Policy-oriented tools • Legal framework • Long-term implementation • Consideration of social, cultural environment • Appropriate promotion of indicator system • Compulsory participation • Awarding process • Accompanying measures		
• Target audience and type of language • Objective, scope and scale effects • Relationships with regional strategies • Decision-makers' and stakeholders' responses • Communication and promotion/dissemination • Technical and educational skills of the staff • Cost-benefit analysis • Governance and public participation process • Regularity issues, revision, updating procedures • Indicator organization and structuring • Management model and institutional cooperation	Organization	Gibson, 2017
• Indicator organization and structuring • Number of indicators • Dimensions covered by the SDI System • Methodological approaches used for indicator measurements • Common set of indicators • Governance and public participation process	Municipality	Torrico et al., 2011

At the local level, the model presented here was used to evaluate the energy efficiency indicators of sanitation services in the municipality of Loulé, Portugal (Teixeira et al., 2016). Seven key good-practices factors at the implementation stage of the performance indicators were checked by experts showing optimal performance for most of the indicators, confirming the added value of the performance indicator matrix for sustainability assessment of water-energy management at the municipality level.

Also at the municipal level, Krank and Wallbaum (2011) conducted a meta-performance evaluation of seven sustainability indicator programmes in developing countries of Asia (Indonesia, Thailand, China and India). The evaluation was conducted through a qualitative assessment by expert interviews and the meta-performance evaluation was carried out at the two levels (SDI system and individual indicators – see Table 32.2). This meta-evaluation allowed identifying crucial strengths and weaknesses of the sustainability indicator programmes, linking the success factors to their contexts. The results include innovative approaches to indicator types, data collection and data quality control, and a correlation between the anchoring of programmes in approved development plans and long-term implementation. According to the authors the results of this research can provide valuable guidance to users of existing sustainability indicator programmes and planners of new indicator programmes.

Another application at local level was conducted by Torrico et al. (2011). These authors developed a meta-performance evaluation of sustainability indicators in Spanish municipalities that have an Agenda 21 process. Six good-practices meta-performance factors were applied identifying the weaknesses, threats, strengths and opportunities and potential of the SDI, to allow comparison between similar municipalities and their progress towards a more sustainable development.

At the organizational level, Myhre et al. (2013), developed a conceptual framework of environmental performance indicators (EPI) for the Norwegian Defence sector, supported by an environmental information system (EIS). This framework was applied to the Norwegian Defence sector and included five meta-performance evaluation indicators (see Table 32.2). Meta-performance indicators intended to show how appropriate the EPI are, which leads to a review and improvement of these components. Furthermore, these meta-performance indicators showed an evaluation of overall monitoring activities and results, including the environmental impact of the data collecting process itself, and an evaluation of the sector's environmental performance measurement system and impact mitigation action.

At the organizational level, Gibson (2017), applied 11 good-practice factors of meta-performance evaluation of the Higg Index 2.0 in the textile and apparel industry in the USA. Industrials experts through online surveys conducted the evaluation. The meta-performance evaluation allowed improvements in the Higg Index 2.0 and other sustainability assessment tools, namely the need of: (1) training to use this index, (2) adding a scalable model for smaller industries, (3) marketing, (4) a more simple interface, (5) sustainability enforcement, (6) certification/verification process. As Searcy (2012) highlights, these meta-performance applications can help to evaluate the effectiveness of indicator systems use for successful implementation of Corporate Sustainability Performance Measurement Systems. Evaluation at corporate level is still scarce compared to local, regional or country-level SDI systems.

Also at the organizational level, Hsieh and Jeon (2010), developed sustainable development indicators to evaluate hotel environmental awareness and commitment, following the categories defined by Ramos and Caeiro (2010): planning and conceptualization, implementation, operation and act, follow-up. The results allowed assessing the pro-environmental policies that are being implemented in the hotel industry.

Other studies didn't adopt yet the framework but advise and propose guidelines for its use, namely in the context of a geographical area, like a natural park (Marques et al., 2013), or at regional level (Mascarenhas et al., 2014) or national level (Ramos and Caeiro, 2010), with emphasis on informal and self-assessment processes.

Most of the examples presented earlier give emphasis or have the collaboration of technical staff and stakeholders in the meta-performance assessment process. The selection of a diverse group of experts is critical to ensure the credibility, transparency and robustness of the sustainability assessment processes (Jasinski et al., 2016). As Ramos et al. (2014) stress and as highlighted in this chapter, stakeholders' involvement (non-experts and experts) can effectively contribute to the design, data gathering and evaluation of sustainability indicators and respective meta-evaluation process.

As some authors emphasize, examples of meta-evaluations are beginning to emerge but still underdeveloped and are rare (Krank and Walbaum et al., 2011; Wallis et al., 2011; Morse, 2015; Morse, 2016). Nevertheless, they are possible and should be pursued, as presented and explored in this research. Adaptations to the needs and constraints of each particular case are necessary and meta-performance evaluation factors and indicators (see Table 32.1) can be selected or tailored to each specific situation.

Final remarks

Although the advantages of SDI systems as tools to assess and report sustainability and the extent to which sustainability indicator frameworks have proliferated, mainly at the country and local levels, most of these frameworks do not include meta-evaluation and/or sensitivity analysis procedures or – even less – indicators to operate this kind of analysis. Some work has been carried out to meta-evaluate sustainability indicators and indices, but none of it has tried to meta-evaluate an SDI system as a whole. It is mainly focused on analysis of the sensitivity of mathematical algorithms that support indices or on more particular thematic tools or domains, such as EIA, or ecological indicators.

In this chapter, a framework was presented to design and assess the effectiveness of sustainability indicators. This approach is based on a list of key meta-evaluation factors of good practice and indicators that will allow a more objective and transparent evaluation of overall performance monitoring activities and results. The proposed framework should be implemented through gradual and prioritized steps to mitigate practical difficulties, due to the complexity of institutional reporting processes.

The presented meta-evaluation approach assumes the collaborative contribution of stakeholders in the whole process. Stakeholders' roles in this method move beyond the simple checking and passive consultation of sustainability indicators, to act as committed co-meta-evaluators.

As argued by Ramos and Wallis (2017), sustainability indicators and related approaches have long been used to assess sustainability, therefore now is a good time to rethink their roles and applicability. Researchers in this area are faced with several challenging issues, and many of them are directly and indirectly related with the need of meta-evaluation of sustainability indicators, such as: How useful are indicators for the society and for effective stakeholders' use? How effective have indicators been at progressing sustainability/sustainable development? How do we assess the impact of sustainability indicator assessments? How should indicators be tailored to produce real impact on decision-making and policy processes? What are the strengths/benefits, drawbacks, opportunities and threats/barriers of using indicators? How resilient is the indicator concept and what innovations can be expected? The sustainable development goal posts keep changing; are we as indicator researchers keeping abreast of change? And if so, how?

Finally, are indicators flexible enough to include emerging issues and deal with overlooked aspects of sustainability? Particularly those involving global changes and threats, goal and target/limit uncertainty, sustainability ethics, cultural, aesthetics and general non-material values, blurred distinction between peacetime and wartime, collaborative learning, voluntary monitoring and crowd sourcing, and "new" versus "old" limits of the natural human system (Ramos, 2009).

Note

1 This chapter is an adapted and updated version of the work conducted by Ramos and Caeiro (2010).

References

APA (Agência Portuguesa do Ambiente). 2008. *Sistema de indicadores de desenvolvimento sustentável – SIDS Portugal*. Lisboa: Agência Portuguesa do Ambiente, 351 p.

Becker, J. 2004. "Making sustainable development evaluations work". *Sustainable Development* 12: 200–211.

Bell, S. and Morse, S. 2008. *Sustainability Indicators: Measuring the Immeasurable?* Second Edition. London and Sterling, VA: Earthscan.

Bockstaller, C. and Girardin, P. 2003. "How to validate environmental indicators". *Agriculture Systems* 76: 639–653.

Böhringer, C. and Jochem, P.E.P. 2007. "Measuring the immeasurable – a survey of sustainability indices". *Ecological Economic* 63: 1–8.

Caeiro, S., Ramos, T.B., and Huisingh, D. 2012. "Procedures and criteria to develop and evaluate household sustainable consumption indicators". *Journal of Cleaner Production* 27: 72–91.

Cloquell-Ballester, V.A., Cloquell-Ballester, V.A., Monterde-Díaz, R., and Santamarina-Siurana, M.C. 2006. "Indicators validation for the improvement of environmental and social impact quantitative assessment". *Environmental Impact Assessment* 26: 79–105.

Gallego, I. 2006. "The use of economic, social and environmental indicators as a measure of sustainable development in Spain". *Corporate Social Responsibility and Environmental Management* 13: 78–97.

Gibson, C.E. 2017. *Evaluation of the Higg Index 2.0 and Other Sustainability Assessment Tools.* Master of Science Thesis. Graduate Faculty of North Carolina State University. Raleigh, North Carolina.

Hardi, P. and Zand, T. 1997. *Assessing Sustainable Development: Principles in Practice.* Winnipeg, Canada: International Institute of Sustainable Development, 175 p.

Her Majesty's Stationery Office (HMSO). 1996. *Indicators of Sustainable Development for the United Kingdom.* London: HMSO Publications Centre, Indicators Working Group, Environmental Protection and Statistics and Information Management Division, Department of the Environment, 96 p.

Hsieh, Y.J. and Jeon, S.M. 2010. *Hotel Companies' Environmental Awareness & Commitment: A Review of Their Web Pages.* International CHRIE Conference-Refereed Track. 13 p. Available at http://scholarworks.umass.edu/refereed/CHRIE_2010/Saturday/13. [Accessed 15 March 2017].

Jackson, L.E., Kurtz, J.C., and Fisher, W.S. (Eds.). 2000. *Evaluation Guidelines for Ecological Indicators.* U.S. Environmental Protection Agency, Office of Research and Development, Research Triangle Park, NC (EPA/620/R-99/005).

Jasinski, D., Meredith, J., and Kirwan, K. 2016. "A comprehensive framework for automotive sustainability assessment". *Journal of Cleaner Production* 135: 1034–1044.

Krank, S. and Wallbaum, H. 2011. "Lessons from seven sustainability indicator programs in developing countries of Asia". *Ecological Indicators* 11: 1385–1395.

Kurtz, J., Jackson, L.E., and Fisher, S. 2001. "Strategies for evaluating indicators based on guidelines from the Environmental Protection Agency's Office of Research and Development". *Ecological Indicators* 1: 49–60.

Lyytimäki, J. and Rosenström, U. 2007. "Skeletons out of the closet: Effectiveness of conceptual framework for communicating sustainable development indicators". *Sustainable Development* 16 (5): 301–313.

Mantese, G.C. and Amaral, D.C. 2017. "Comparison of industrial symbiosis indicators through agent-based modelling". *Journal of Cleaner Production* 140: 1652–1671.

Marques, A.S., Ramos, T.B., Caeiro, S., and Costa, M.H. 2013. "Adaptive-participative sustainability indicators in marine protected areas: Design and communication". *Ocean and Coastal Management* 72: 36–45.

Mascarenhas, A., Nunes, L., and Ramos, T.B. 2014. "Exploring the self-assessment of sustainability indicators by different stakeholders". *Ecological Indicator* 39: 75–83.

Mascarenhas, A., Nunes, L., and Ramos, T.B. 2015. "Selection of sustainability indicators for planning: Combining stakeholders' participation and data reduction techniques". *Journal of Cleaner Production* 92: 295–307.

Mascarenhas, A., Ramos, T.B., and Nunes, L. 2012. "Developing an integrated approach for the strategic monitoring of regional spatial plans". *Land Use Policy* 29: 641–651.

Meul, M., Nevens, F., and Reheul, D. 2009. "Validating sustainability indicators: Focus on ecological aspects of Flemish dairy farms". *Ecological Indicator* 9 (2): 284–295.

Moreno Pires, S. and Fidelis, T. 2012. "A proposal to explore the role of sustainability indicators in local governance contexts: The case of Palmela, Portugal". *Ecological Indicators* 23: 608–615.

Moreno Pires, S. and Fidelis, T. 2015. "Local sustainability indicators in Portugal: Assessing implementation and use in governance contexts". *Journal of Cleaner Production* 86: 289–300.

Moreno Pires, S., Fidelis, T., and Ramos, T.B. 2014. "Measuring and comparing local sustainable development through common indicators: Constraints and achievements in practice". *Cities* 39: 1–9.

Morse, S. 2015. "Developing sustainability indicators and indices". *Sustainable Development* 23 (2): 84–95.

Morse, S. 2016. "The success of sustainable development indices in terms of reporting by the global press". *Social Indicators Research* 125: 359–375.

Myhre, O., Fjellheima, K., Ringnesa, H., Reistada, T., Longvaa, K.S., and Ramos, T.B. 2013. "Development of environmental performance indicators supported by an environmental information system: Application to the Norwegian defence sector". *Ecological Indicators* 29: 293–306.

Niemeijer, D. and Groot, R. 2008. "A conceptual framework for selecting environmental indicator sets". *Ecological Indicators* 8: 14–25.

OECD (Organisation for Economic Co-operation and Development). 1993. *OECD Core Set of Indicators for Environmental Performance Reviews.* Environment Monographs No. 83, OCDE/GD(93)179. Paris: Organization for Economic Co-Operation and Development.

Ott, W.R. 1978. *Environmental Indices – Theory and Practice.* Michigan: Ann Arbor Science, 357 p.

Patel, M. 2002. "A meta-evaluation, or quality assessment, of the evaluations in this issue, based on the African Evaluation Guidelines". *Evaluation Program Planning* 25: 329–332.

Ramos, T.B. 2009. "Development of regional sustainability indicators and the role of academia in this process: The Portuguese practice". *Journal of Cleaner Production* 17 (12): 1101–1115.

Ramos, T.B., Alves, I., Gervásio, I., and Liberal, P. 2007. *Revisão do Sistema de Indicadores de Desenvolvimento Sustentável e Apoio na Elaboração, Revisão de Conteúdos e Divulgação do Relatório do Estado do Ambiente.* Relatório Final do Projecto desenvolvido no âmbito do Protocolo de Cooperação Técnico científica n.8 22/2005, estabelecido entre o Instituto do Ambiente e a Universidade do Algarve, Faro.

Ramos, T.B., Alves, I., Subtil, R., and Melo, J.J. 2007. "Environmental performance policy indicators for the public sector: The case of the defence sector". *Journal of Environmental Management* 82: 410–432.

Ramos, T.B. and Caeiro, S. 2010. "Meta-performance evaluation of sustainability indicators". *Ecological Indicators* 10: 157–166.

Ramos, T.B., Caeiro, S., Douglas, C., and Ochieng, C. 2008. "Environmental and sustainability impact assessment in small islands: The case of Azores and Madeira". *International Journal of Environmental Technology and Management* 10 (2): 223–240.

Ramos, T.B., Caeiro, S., and Melo, J.J. 2004. "Environmental indicator frameworks to design and assess environmental monitoring programs". *Impact Assessment and Project Appraisal* 20 (1): 47–62.

Ramos, T.B., Martins, I.P., Martinho, A.P., Douglas, C.H., Painho, M., and Caeiro, S. 2014. "An open participatory conceptual framework to support State of the Environment and Sustainability Reports". *Journal of Cleaner Production* 64: 158–172.

Ramos, T.B. and Wallis, A. 2017. *Call for Abstracts of – Track 1b: Sustainability Assessment and Indicators.* 23rd Annual International Sustainable Development Research Society Conference, June 14–16, 2017, Bogotá, Colombia. Available at: www.isdrsconference.org/site/view/154/track-1b/ [Accessed in Mach 2017].

Rapport, D. and Friend, A. 1979. "Towards a comprehensive framework for environmental statistics: a stress-response approach". *Statistics Canada,* Catalogue 11–510, Ottawa.

Rosenström, U. and Kyllönen, S. 2007. "Impact of a participatory approach to developing national level sustainable development indicators in Finland". *Journal of Environmental Management* 84: 282–298.

Scriven, M. 1969. "An introduction to meta-evaluation". *Educational Product Report* 2 (5): 36–38.

Searcy, C. 2012. "Corporate sustainability performance measurement systems: A review and research agenda". *Journal of Business Ethics* 107: 239–253.

Spangenberg, J. 2002. "Institutional sustainability indicators: An analysis of the institutions in Agenda 21 and a draft set of indicators for monitoring their effectivity". *Sustainable Development* 10, 103–115.

Teixeira, M.R., Mendes, P., Murta, E., and Nunes, L. 2016. "Performance indicators matrix as a methodology for energy management in municipal water services". *Journal of Cleaner Production* 125: 108–120.

Torrico, E.E.U., Sánchez, G.F., Lopez, F.R., and Ordonez, M.I. 2011. "Agenda 21 En Los Municipios Españoles. Análisis De Los Sistemas De Indicadores Urbanos". XV Congreso Internacional de Ingeniería de Proyectos Huesca, 6–8 de julio de 2011, 565–576.

Wallis, A.M., Graymore, M.L.M., and Richards, A.J. 2011. "Significance of environment in the assessment of sustainable development: The case for south west Victoria". *Ecological Economics* 70: 595–605.

Walz, R. 2000. "Development of environmental systems: Experiences from Germany". *Environmental Management* 25 (6): 613–623.

Wilson, J., Tyedmers, P., and Pelot, R. 2007. "Contrasting and comparing sustainable development indicator metrics". *Ecological Indicators* 7: 299–314.

33

ECOLOGICAL FOOTPRINT ACCOUNTS

Criticisms and applications[1]

*Mathis Wackernagel, Alessandro Galli, Laurel Hanscom, David Lin,
Laetitia Mailhes and Tony Drummond*

Introduction

With the emergence of the sustainable development debate and the increasing attention to global warming, food security and environmental degradation, the question of the scale or size of the human economy compared to its host planet has become more prominent. While theorized about in economic debates such as Herman Daly's "Steady State Economics" (1973, 1977) or modelled in early computer simulations on systems dynamics such as World3 which underpinned *Limits to Growth* (Meadows et al., 1972), discussions on how to limit or even reduce the metabolism of current economies has become widespread. The latest five-year plan of China is advocating Ecological Civilization (The People's Republic of China, 2015). One hundred and ninety countries have signed the Paris Climate Agreement asking for reducing carbon emissions to an extent that climate would not warm beyond 1.5° or 2° C. The UN Sustainable Development Goals urge the world to operate within the ecological possibilities of our ecosystems (UN, 2015).

The Ecological Footprint is an accounting system that sheds light on the size of economies' material metabolism by answering one particular question: *How much of the biosphere's (or any region's) regenerative capacity does any human activity demand?* This is a relevant question because sustainable development or long-term economic success depends on keeping humanity's material demands within the amount the planet can renew (Wackernagel et al., Chapter 16). In this chapter we first highlight some applications and then address criticism that Ecological Footprint accounting has received.

Scales of Ecological Footprint assessments and their policy relevance

Ecological Footprint and biocapacity assessments can be applied at any scale.[2] Biocapacity can be calculated for a particular plot of land, a region or the entire biosphere. Footprints can be assessed for any activity at any scale, be it for a single activity, the lifestyle of a person, a city, a nation or even humanity as a whole. Note though that organizations do not have a Footprint per se, since they are mental constructs, not physical entities. However, organizations' activities have Footprints. Hence when analyzing resource demands of organizations, the inquiry has to start by defining which organizational activities are being analyzed.

Ecological Footprint accounts, like any accounting system, are documenting the past and are limited by global data availability, mainly UN data sets. In 2018, the Ecological Footprint accounts have the ability to provide data for over 200 nations for 54 years (data sets correspond to 1961–2014, Global Footprint Network, 2018). All results are available on the open data platform at data.footprintnetwork.org. The historical time series help inform discussions about likely future trends. Additionally, any scenario outputs can be translated into Footprint and biocapacity outcomes (Moore et al., 2012).

The Ecological Footprint is a diagnostic tool that can be used to inform decision-makers of their current position in comparison to other nations of the world. While this tool cannot tell policy-makers what exactly to implement, it can identify key problem areas and potential options for increasing an economy's resource security. Similar to financial bookkeeping, Footprint accounts provide the context for decision-making, not prescribed solutions. This principle applies at all levels of analysis, including the personal level. For instance, a variety of Footprint Calculators have been developed, including one by Global Footprint Network (www.footprint-calculator.org) geared towards individuals, which offer diagnostics to inform decision-makers about potential actions to take. These 'yardsticks' for resource use can help people make better choices.

One particular value that the national data sets provide, as available through the data.footprintnetwork.org data platform, is the ability to compare the economic and political history of countries to their biocapacity and Footprint trends. Common patterns can be analyzed to distinguish which socio-economic developments may have been shaped by its resource contexts or to what extent economic and political changes shifted the resource availabilities for societies (Niccolucci et al., 2012).

The power of the Ecological Footprint is often recognized for its ability to communicate to wide audiences (Costanza, 2000; Deutsch et al., 2000; Stiglitz et al., 2009). However, this often also leads to the criticism that it promises too much. If the user understands the research question behind the concept, the meaning of the results should be fairly clear. While the wider public may not know the exact research question driving Ecological Footprint accounting, essentially 'how much nature people use compared to how much there is', the interpretation of 'how many planet Earths would it take if all of humanity lived your lifestyle' is a clear and accurate reflection of what Ecological Footprint accounts compute.

The link between Ecological Footprints and sustainable development

Many users misunderstand the Ecological Footprint as a measure of sustainability. As pointed out by the Footprint standards (www.footprintstandards.org), the Footprint is more accurately described as a metric of 'unsustainability'. For instance, if humanity's Footprint is larger than the world's biocapacity, humanity is in an unsustainable state. The Footprint and biocapacity metrics describe a necessary condition for sustainability, not a sufficient one. In this section, we further describe the link between Ecological Footprints and sustainable development.

Sustainable development implies a commitment to giving all people the opportunity to lead fulfilling lives within the means of planet Earth. This kind of development continues to be identified as the primary overarching policy goal, as exemplified most recently by the UN's Sustainable Development Goals, as well as the OECD's Green Growth strategy, and in the 'Green

Economy' debate stemming from Rio+20 (2012). Yet when it comes to actual environmental strategies and policies, are decision-makers asking the right questions to lead us towards this goal? Over the last decades, the global sustainable development debate has been unfocused. Definitions abound, and long agendas are drawn up in international forums that lack specificity and consistency with the reality of planetary limits. This lack of clarity is surprising, since the much earlier 1972 United Nations Conference on the Human Environment in Stockholm ran under the theme 'Only one Earth'.

The current lack of specificity and consistency could be overcome with science-based benchmarks and quantitative tracking. Sustainable development, after all, builds on the UN's original focus: economic and social development (as expressed in UNDP, 2011, the *Millennium Development Goals*, 2000, or the UN's 1948 Universal Declaration of Human Rights), and it is complemented by the adjective 'sustainable', recognizing that this development has to fit within our one planet. Sustainable development therefore becomes the marriage of these two dimensions: 'sustainable' and 'development'. The interplay between these two dimensions – the human development goal and the environmental boundary condition – is also at the heart of the Brundtland Commission's sustainable development definition. Their approach postulates to meet current needs without compromising the ability of future generations to meet their own needs (WCED, 1987).

By emphasizing the two dimensions of sustainable development, it becomes possible to track the concept through a science-based measurement framework (Boutaud, 2002a, 2002b; Moran et al., 2008). By 'science-based', we mean that the two objectives, 'sustainable – or does it fit within the confines of one planet?' and 'development – are human lives becoming measurably better?' can be tracked through evidence-based outcome metrics. The first dimension, 'sustainable', or to what extent such development can be supported within the means of planet Earth, is measured by the ratio between Footprint and biocapacity. The second dimension, 'development', depends on how progress is interpreted, and what the key outcomes are that determine such progress. One of the most prominent outcome measures of development, particularly for comparing nations, is UNDP's Human Development Index (HDI). They are described in detail below.

Sustainable development occurs at the intersection of these two dimensions. A first necessary condition for living within the means of nature occurs if the Footprint is within the available biocapacity. Currently, there are 1.7 global hectares of biocapacity available on the planet per person, but some of that biocapacity is also needed to support wildlife. The Ecological Footprint therefore compares a population's demand on the Earth's resource against the Earth's or a region's biocapacity (that is, its ability to regenerate resources and ecosystem services). Second, UNDP considers an HDI of more than 0.7 to be 'high human development'. Now being used by organizations such as WWF, the World Business Council for Sustainable Development (WBCSD, 2011), the UNEP's Green Economy initiative, this two-dimensional framework, breaks down sustainable development into its core components: a commitment to human well-being, and development within the means of planet Earth.

The resulting global graph provides a high-level snapshot view of countries' or populations' current development position.[3] It can also be used to show progress over time, to compare the situation of one community with another one, or to illustrate patterns.[4] Figure 33.1 depicts countries and exemplifies the challenge of creating a globally reproducible resource demand which also secures a high level of human well-being. In other words, they produce thriving lives at a Footprint level that all people could replicate without overshooting the planet's ecological resource base.

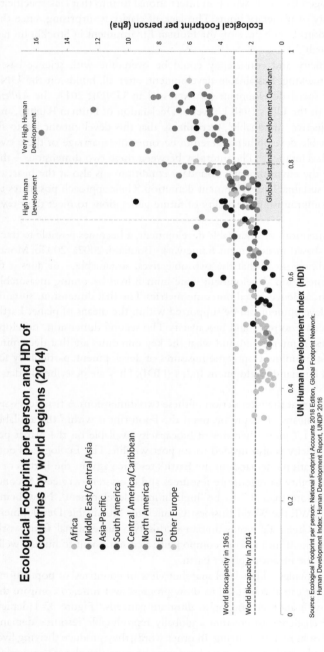

Figure 33.1 Mapping sustainable development outcome: HDI and the Footprint of nations, in 2013. Global sustainable development is assessed using UNDP's Human Development Index (HDI) as an indicator of human development, and the Ecological Footprint as a measure of human demand on the biosphere (based on the 2017 edition). The presented results reflect the situation in 2013 (UNDP, 2016). An Ecological Footprint significantly less than 1.7 global hectares per person makes those resource demands globally replicable (it would need to be significantly less, as the deficit would also need to provide for wildlife). Despite growing adoption of sustainable development as an explicit policy goal, most countries do not meet both minimum requirements. Since every country has different amounts of biocapacity within its national boundaries, this analysis can also be adapted to each country. Also: note that the world as a whole is outside the global Sustainable Development quadrant.

This framework can also be used to analyze the recently launched Sustainable Development Goals (SDGs). When SDG achievement is measured by the Bertelsmann SDG index (Sachs et al., 2016) and compared against these sustainable development outcomes, it becomes evident that high performance on SDGs correlates with higher HDI, but also with higher Footprints. In other words, SDGs may not be formulated with sufficient focus on resource security to keep powering the development (Wackernagel et al., 2017). If this indeed proves to be the case, SDGs as formulated today could therefore put the long-term opportunities for sustainable human development at risk.

Making sustainable development measurable will not only accelerate the global debate, but it will also provide decision-makers with a robust metric to support them in exploring potential trade-offs and options. The simple, empirical framework proposed here could empower nations as it identifies risks to their own performance. Therefore, it represents neither conditionality nor an approach that requires international agreements. It simply recognizes that human development depends on access to ecological assets and the resources and services they provide. Ecological Footprint accounts provide insight, enhance foresight and stimulate needed innovation.

Common questions and misconceptions

Ecological Footprints are subject to several misconceptions, which we cover in this section. Some people misunderstand the measure, or believe that it covers aspects that are not actually calculated in these accounts (for example, some might believe that the Footprint is a pollution measure). There is also confusion between the idea of the Footprint and its actual execution, which is limited by available data. We also address a number of common issues raised in the academic and policy literature. These issues are taken from the Stiglitz Report (Stiglitz et al., 2009); Eurostat (Schaefer et al., 2006); Best et al. (2008); Kitzes et al. (2009); van den Bergh and Grazi (2010); Grazi and van den Bergh (2012); Giampietro and Saltelli (2014); Goldfinger et al. (2014); Galli, Giampietro et al. (2016); and Blomqvist et al. (2013).

Is the term 'Ecological Footprint' misleading?

Ecology is the study of nature's household. One significant lens of the science of ecology is tracking the metabolism and energy flows of nature. That's what 'ecological' refers to in 'Ecological Footprint'. Further, most of nature is heavily disturbed (or shaped) by human activity. However, since the field of ecology is so vast, there is the potential that the name 'Ecological Footprint' could be misunderstood. This is why Global Footprint Network emphasizes that 'Ecological Footprint' is a name for a particular research question: how much biocapacity is demanded by a given human activity? It is the research question that counts when analyzing the concept, not the name. Yet it is now a widely used phrase that is intuitive and that many people can readily understand. The name 'Footprint' reflects 'area demand' as in 'footprint of a satellite' or 'footprint of a building'.

The originators of the Footprint (Bill Rees and Mathis Wackernagel) as well as Global Footprint Network have deliberately not trademarked the term, making it available for public use. To protect its integrity, Global Footprint Network has developed standards and has created a partner network that is committed to using the term 'Ecological Footprint' consistently. The more that large institutions such as WWF, WBCSD, UNDP, UNEP or EEA use the term consistently, the less confusion is generated.[5]

Why focus on biocapacity?

The Ecological Footprint tool is built upon the premise that the quantity of human and non-human life on this planet is limited by the biosphere's regenerative capacity. This limitation also includes access to non-renewable resources from the lithosphere. For instance, the use of today's primary lithosphere resource, fossil fuel, is most restricted by the planet's biocapacity – not by underground availability. The biosphere has a limited capacity to absorb waste from fossil fuel use (more specifically, the CO_2 emissions released when fossil fuels are burnt). In other words, if humanity burned all the fossil fuels already discovered, the carbon concentration in the atmosphere might grow beyond 1700 ppm (UK Institution of Mechanical Engineers, 2009).[6]

Conversely, if CO_2 emissions were restricted to the 450 ppm CO_2 concentration threshold in the atmosphere (which many climate scientists consider to be too high for securing ecosystems stability (Hansen et al., 2008; Lovejoy, 2008), then humanity has already found five times more fossil fuels in the ground than can be burned (Leaton, 2012). The divergence between the carbon that humanity has found in the lithosphere and the carbon that can be 'safely' released into the atmosphere makes it clear that waste absorption is the limiting factor for sustainable fossil fuel use, not supply.

Ores are another resource from the lithosphere, largely used to provide society with metals. Unlike fossil fuels, metals are used, not used *up*. Society may need more metals, or metal in use erodes and gets dispersed. Therefore, the use of metals depends on humanity's ability to concentrate the elements. Given existing technology, this ability is largely limited by energy inputs. However, since the majority of industrial energy is sourced from fossil fuels, the limiting factor ultimately becomes biocapacity for ores as well.[7]

In a time of increasing ecological constraints, the research question behind Ecological Footprint accounts could be the most critical one for the twenty-first century. More importantly, it is one that humanity cannot afford to ignore. Failing to live within nature's budget will eventually lead to ecological bankruptcy and societal collapse. Thus there may be no research endeavour more important than building an accurate understanding of humanity's demand on the biosphere. Answering such a research question therefore requires an open, transparent and replicable process, based on empirical evidence. In other words, solid answers depend on rigorous scientific inquiry.

Why measure biocapacity in 'global hectares', and not in TW or tonnes of carbon?

The sun powers planet Earth with about 175 000 terawatts (TW) of solar energy. This translates into as little as about 100 TW of biomass production in the biosphere, terrestrially and in the ocean (100 TW according to Nealson and Conrad, 1999; 75 TW according to Haberl et al., 2007). Possibly close to half of the biocapacity of the planet might be used for food production (Global Footprint Network 2017 National Footprint Accounts), meaning that this biomass production, plus significant fossil fuel input (approximately 2–3 TW of fossil fuel for the food portion of human consumption), turn into less than one TW of food (10 000 kilo joules/day per person times 7+ billion people).

This example illustrates a long energy cascade, along which less and less energy is available, and the remainder is dissipated as energy waste. In other words, no energy is lost, but the quality of the energy (or its exergetic value) is; as a result, along the cascade, less and less energy becomes available. For this reason, expressing flows of biocapacity in terms of energy, or more precisely energy flows (such as TW), while scientifically valid, is difficult for both communication as well as scientific work, since one TW means something very different along the energy cascade – by orders of magnitude. Every TW would need to be described by 'what kind of TW?' Direct comparisons of results would become challenging and potentially confusing.

An alternative is to express biocapacity in terms of biomass production. In ecological sciences, this is called Net Primary Productivity (NPP). Much of the Ecological Footprint work is inspired by such assessments as, for instance, the one by Vitousek et al. (1986) and the many highly interesting and more detailed studies by the Social Ecology group in Vienna guided by Fischer-Kowalski and Haberl (Fischer-Kowalski and Haberl, 1993, 1997, 2007; Haberl and Schandl 1999, Haberl 1997; Haberl et al., 2002). A number of papers have described the link and differences between Ecological Footprint accounting and approaches such as HANPP (human appropriation of net primary productivity) – see for instance Haberl et al. (2004) and Moffatt (1999).

Focusing on one segment of the energy cascade (i.e., where sunlight is transformed into biomass) makes NPP or Footprint studies sharper, and less prone to confusion between different types of joules along the energy cascade (or more precisely, joules of different entropic value) than general studies of energy flows. Yet NPP studies faces two other challenges compared to Footprint accounting:

1   How can we meaningfully compare one ecosystem to another? For instance, crop areas are not managed for producing maximum NPP, but rather to produce maximum amount of the desired crop. The same area of cropland left as a forest might produce significantly higher NPP than the wheat field it currently hosts. Potential NPP helps to compare various biologically productive surfaces more meaningfully – even though it is difficult to measure since it depends on assumptions and extrapolations – but these can be tested against empirical evidence. Therefore, potential NPP results, if robust global data sets were available, would be an important improvement to Ecological Footprint accounts, as they would lead to more robust estimates of equivalence factors (as discussed in more detail below).

2   An even more significant challenge is the difficulty for NPP assessments to compare supply and demand. For instance, in a forest, which parts need to be included in the assessment of availability: tree trunks, obviously, but what about branches? Leaves? Soil? Undergrowth such as ferns, bushes and mushrooms? Roots? How then is demand assessed? Does it include the branches of a tree, even though they are left back in the forest after harvest? What about the leaves, the disturbed undergrowth, the roots of the cut tree? How can the 'harvestable limit' be defined?

The Ecological Footprint's agricultural perspective, while more limited and mechanical than an assessment of an ecosystem's entire NPP, makes the demand and supply comparison more direct. For instance, foresters can estimate the timber increment a forest generates, and inversely, the number of cubic metres of timber that are removed from a forest can also be measured.

For these reasons, expressing demand on the biosphere, and availability of regenerative production of the biosphere in agricultural terms, in terms of biologically productive surfaces, allows researchers to assess, with some degree of accuracy, human demand against nature's regeneration. And luckily, the measurement units of such an analysis are also easy to understand by a wide public, thanks to the visual power of surface.

Are the equivalence factors adequate?

Equivalence factors attempt to compare hectares across various land uses. They are needed for consistent aggregation of biocapacity. Equivalence factors translate the area of a specific land-use type available or demanded into units of world average biologically productive area (expressed in global hectares). Thus, they vary by land-use type and year. Ideally, the equivalence factors should reflect the ratio of the maximum potential ecological productivity of world average land of a specific land-use type (like cropland) and the average productivity of all biologically productive lands on Earth.

In the absence of such data, currently Global Footprint Network's National Footprint Accounts define equivalence factors as the ratio of the maximum agricultural potential of land of a specific land-use type (like cropland) and the average productivity of all biologically productive lands on Earth. To this effect, the accounts use the suitability indexes from FAO's Global Agro-Ecological Zones (GAEZ) assessment combined with information about actual areas of cropland, forest and grazing area from FAOSTAT, a UN database provided by FAO (FAOSTAT; FAO and IIASA, 2000). The GAEZ model divides all land globally into five categories, each of which is assigned a suitability score:

Very Suitable – 0.9
Suitable – 0.7
Moderately Suitable – 0.5
Marginally Suitable – 0.3
Not Suitable – 0.1

The current equivalence factor calculation assumes that the most productive land is put to its economically most productive use. The calculations assume that the most suitable land available will be planted to cropland, the next most suitable land will be under forest, and the least suitable land will be grazing area. The equivalence factor is calculated as the ratio of the average suitability index for a given land type divided by the average suitability index for all land types. This means that current (and future) equivalence factors are based on global-average agricultural suitability of various biomes.

Still, Global Footprint Network also agrees with Eurostat's perspective (Schaefer et al., 2006) that the equivalence factors need to be strengthened, since they are at the core of Ecological Footprint accounting. Ideally, equivalence factors would be based on spatially explicit measures of potential net primary productivity. Globally consistent and reliable data sets on potential net primary productivity do not yet exist. However, approximations are needed to improve on the current even more basic estimates of equivalence factors.

Better equivalence factors could help bridge the current gap between theory and practice of measuring global hectares. In ideal theory, a global hectare is independent of the chosen land use. However, in practical application this is not fully realized. Still, if a piece of forest is converted into cropland, it is incorrect to assume that biocapacity automatically goes up. While the equivalence factor goes up (cropland hectares represent typically higher biocapacity than forest hectares), the yield factor may drop. The latter factor drops because relatively high-yielding forest may be converted into relatively low-yielding cropland. But there is still a research and method development gap in that changes in land use in current accounts would most likely shift the resulting biocapacity estimate.

To isolate the portion of yield change that is human-induced, and to present it as a separate factor, National Footprint Accounts also employ an 'intertemporal yield factor' (Borucke et al., 2013). It captures the change of productivity over time. This factor enables us to more meaningfully depict time series. With the help of this factor, the measurement unit of global hectares can be mapped against 'constant global hectares'. This constant-global-hectares logic is similar to dollar measurements being expressed in constant (in this case 'inflation adjusted') dollars. These constant global hectares represent a set portfolio amount of products and services that an average hectare was able to provide in a given year. In this way, a given level of consumption (and production) can more meaningfully be compared across years. When expressing National Footprint Account results, Global Footprint Network calls the units 'global hectares' rather than 'constant global hectares' to keep communication simple.

Do Ecological Footprints provide a pollution measure?

The Ecological Footprint attempts to measure demand on biocapacity. It does not include aspects outside of that scope. For instance, pollution affecting human health, but not biocapacity (such as noise, or urban air pollution, radioactivity), is not captured by the Footprint (Kitzes et al., 2009). However, pollution that affects biological productivity (or bioproductivity) should be included. The limitation is that the demand of those kinds of pollution on biocapacity is not systematically tracked, therefore there are no globally comparable data sets to include those impacts in Ecological Footprint accounts. Examples of such pollution are acidification or eutrophication (some local Footprint studies have, however, included such pollution impacts) (Wackernagel et al., 1999).

Note, however, that as these pollution effects change biocapacity, this change will be recorded by future biocapacity accounts. But ideally, in more perfect accounts, this change in biocapacity should be debited against the present Footprint. This omission indicates the general bias of Footprint accounts: the high likelihood that they exaggerate biocapacity and underestimate Footprints.

Is the Ecological Footprint biased against international trade?

Some critics have argued that Ecological Footprints are biased against international trade (van den Bergh and Verbruggen, 1999; Grazi et al., 2007; Stiglitz et al., 2009). The Ecological Footprint does not bias against trade, but instead simply reports the world as it currently stands. It documents that many countries are running biocapacity deficits and may therefore depend upon biocapacity from external sources or on local overuse. Some of this dependence may be covered in the form of net-imports. Just as money can be used to describe trade flows, so can Footprint accounting describe these flows in terms of embodied biocapacity. The Ecological Footprint approach is parallel to that of the many studies dealing with carbon (for example, Davis et al., 2011; Hertwich and Peters, 2009; Peters and Hertwich, 2006; Peters et al., 2011) or water (Hoekstra and Chapagain, 2007) embedded in international trade. The Ecological Footprint simply expands the analysis to assess a broader range of ecological resources and services embedded in internationally traded products. While it is true that some users of Ecological Footprint results have made anti-trade claims (Willey and Ferguson, 1999), the Footprint method as such offers no prescriptions about trade regimes.[8] Rather it helps to show that resources within the world are limited and to recognize that if all nations run at a biocapacity deficit then this will inevitably lead to a global depletion of the planet's ecological assets.

Is the carbon portion of the Footprint exaggerated?

Some critics have questioned the rationale behind the carbon portion of the Footprint (Ayres, 2000; IMV, 2002; Neumayer, 2013). The Ecological Footprint builds on the premise of capital maintenance. Its accounts answer the question of how much biocapacity is needed to provide all the services demanded by people. If people demand more services than are being regenerated ('overshoot') then the accounts calculate how much more biocapacity is needed to cover this demand. In the case of the carbon Footprint, the accounts calculate how much biocapacity is needed in order to not increase the carbon concentration in the atmosphere in that year (that is, not leaving a debt for future years). If carbon is absorbed through human means or techno-logical intervention, then it is not counted. The accounts only include the carbon that human-ity leaves for the biosphere to take care of. Given humanity's significant dependence on fossil fuels, it is not surprising that the carbon Footprint component currently makes up such a large proportion of the Ecological Footprint (60% globally in 2016). But a century ago, and for most lower-income countries, the carbon Ecological Footprint is quite small (see Galli, Kitzes et al., 2012). Moreover, if humanity complies with the Paris goal, humanity's carbon Footprint should be (close to) zero by 2050.

Hence, the dominance of carbon within the overall Ecological Footprint is by no means exaggerated, but simply represents the real amount of carbon dioxide that is emitted most pro-lifically through the burning of fossil fuels. To strengthen the case, Global Footprint Network recalculated the average sequestration capacity of forests using the newest available data sets. And as mentioned above, the conclusion was a 25% smaller sequestration rate per global hectare than previously calculated (Mancini et al., 2016).

Over the last few years there has been a tendency to focus on carbon emissions, but this is not the only problem. The Ecological Footprint captures many more issues than the emission of carbon dioxide. For instance, it makes the connection between emissions and land-use aspects, a link also acknowledged in the Paris Climate Agreement of 2015. Further, since the Foot-print accounts track availability of and demand on natural resources from different land types, this information is useful for understanding the availability of space for biodiversity. Again, the accounts do not prescribe how much of the biocapacity should be left for wild species. Obvi-ously the amount of biocapacity left for biodiversity shapes biodiversity outcomes, together with other factors such as invasive species, toxicity, fragmentation and management. Also, the Foot-print accounts for the forestry land that is cut down and converted to cropland and therefore implies a loss of biodiversity and ecosystem services.

If indeed humanity should decide to move aggressively out of fossil fuels, Footprint account-ing helps to identify to what extent this move leads to a burden shift to other land types (for example, cropland for biofuels or fuel wood), or truly reduces humanity's demand on biocapac-ity. Lack of biocapacity also indicates risk, should it become necessary to move out of fossil fuels and require more biomass as energy source. Also, less availability of cheap fossil fuels may have a significant impact on agricultural productivity, potentially increasing the land demand for agri-culture. All these effects are captured by Footprint accounting.

What about nuclear energy?

While in earlier Footprint accounts (up to 2007) nuclear energy was included, assuming that the Footprint of nuclear electricity would be at par with that of coal-powered electricity (in order to avoid the debate whether coal or nuclear is better), accounts since the 2008 National Foot-print Accounts Edition no longer include nuclear apart from the CO_2 emitted through con-struction and use of the plants. But it is also emphasized that Ecological Footprint methodology is not the most relevant framework for assessing the risks and benefits of nuclear energy. More significant are questions of costs, operational risks, long-term waste storage and the potential for nuclear proliferation.

Still, Footprint assessments can reveal certain impacts. For instance, a more recent study, published by WWF Japan, showed the biocapacity impacts from the Fukushima nuclear accident in 2011. The exclusion zone, or 'warning zone' as it is officially called, with a 20 km radius, represents 2.7% of Japan's biocapacity. The report does not provide information on how long the exclusion zone may be unsafe for human use. But if this zone is not inhabitable or usable by people for 1000 years, it would imply that this one accident occupied 27-fold Japan's biocapacity of that year. Also, the report documents that the area currently contaminated to a level that is higher than pre-accident legal limits is about 10% of Japan's biocapacity (WWF Japan and Global Footprint Network, 2012).

How do Ecological Footprint accounts relate to planetary boundaries?

Planetary boundaries (Rockström et al., 2009; Steffen et al., 2015) identify key physical quantitative conditions that are needed to maintain the integrity of the biosphere. Nine areas have been identified, in which transgressions could lead to shifts in the integrity, potentially irreversibly moving the biosphere out of the stable conditions which characterized the Holocene.

Therefore, one could interpret the planetary boundaries as well as the inverse of the ingredients for healthy, productive ecosystems that can maintain their integrity. In other words, staying within the safe operating zone with each of the nine ingredients enables the productivity of the biosphere, which Ecological Footprint accounting calls the biosphere's 'biocapacity'. These boundaries translate into the specific ingredients that could be called 'the production factors' to enable biocapacity:

- Stable climate
- Healthy biodiversity
- Sufficient nutrients
- Protective ozone layer
- Absence of pollutants
- Clean and sufficient fresh water
- Absence of acidification in both water and soils

The Ecological Footprint does not quantify, in contrast to the planetary boundaries, trigger points that lead to irreversible change. Rather, it tracks human demand against biological regeneration. If demand exceeds regeneration, the resulting natural capital loss or degradation will eventually become a trigger point since one cannot indefinitely take more from ecosystems than they can renew. It summarizes the overall outcome of transgressing planetary boundaries and quantifies this transgression in one 'biocapacity' number representing the regenerative capacity of the biosphere.

There is strong complementarity between planetary boundaries and Ecological Footprint. Ecological Footprint is less complex, and not a broad field of academic inquiry, but rather a biophysical accounting approach focused on a key output of the biosphere: biocapacity. Ecological Footprint is basic, using the fundamental thermodynamic laws and biological principles (such as competition for space to feed organisms, differences in NPP of various ecosystem configurations) enabling this biocapacity accounting by adding up all the mutually exclusive spaces people use to provide for people's demands (their Footprint), which then can be compared with the productive spaces available (biocapacity). The planetary boundaries concept is more granular on the biocapacity side, documenting the key parameters that enable stable, productive biocapacity around the globe.

Research arguments that strengthen Ecological Footprint accounting and its development

As originators of the method and stewards of the most widely used Ecological Footprints accounts in use today, Global Footprint Network (www.footprintnetwork.org) is the first to acknowledge that the Footprint accounts can and must be improved. Global Footprint Network considers the current National Footprint Accounts as evidence that biocapacity accounting is possible, with far more potential for accuracy and detail. As a scientific organization aiming to implement policy-relevant tools and analyses, Global Footprint Network asks others to test and review the results, and depends on input and suggestions from others regarding calculation methods and potential improvements.

Global Footprint Network scientific testing goes a long distance beyond academic peer reviews. It proactively seeks the review of the ultimate users of Footprint accounts – national governments. The main reason is that nations are the ultimate risk bearer of biocapacity deficits, and their governments need to have access to results they have confidence in.

To build this confidence, Global Footprint Network's comprehensive review efforts start with transparency: the method is published on the Network's website and in academic journals. Of course, it also engages in academic peer reviews – but peer review is just one element, because such reviews do not go deep enough, and the academic community does not depend on the reliability of results in the same way that national governments do. In addition, therefore, Global Footprint Network directly invites national governments (and their respective agencies) to verify the assessments – including suggesting improvements. About 12 such assessments have been completed and some of them are listed on Global Footprint Network's website at www. footprintnetwork.org/reviews. Completed assessments include that from the European Parliament (ECOTEC, 2001), Switzerland (von Stokar et al., 2006; Frischknecht et al., 2016), Luxembourg (Hild et al., 2010), United Arab Emirates (Abdullatif and Alam, 2011; Galli, Martindill et al., 2016), European Commission (Best et al., 2008), Japan (see for details WWF Japan and Global Footprint Network, 2012, p. 49), or the UK (RPA, 2007). An interesting example of a government review is that of the French SOeS institute (SOeS, 2010), which independently reproduced the French Footprint time series within 1 to 3% of Global Footprint Network's results, using their own data and the method described on Global Footprint Network's website.

In the academic and the public policy literature, there are numerous valid criticisms that challenge the Ecological Footprint method or its results, many of which form the basis for an active research agenda, a good summary of which is provided by Kitzes et al. (2009).

In general, there are two types of criticisms: *fundamental* (is this a valid approach?) versus *incremental* (how can the approach be improved?). Fundamental criticism is essential and to be valid of any research, it needs to follow a logical sequence, with each step building on the one before (see Box 33.1). The sequence starts with testing whether the research is based on an empirically testable research question. If it is, then critics should probe the relevance of the research question to make sure it provides information that is relevant to public policy. Step 3 involves assessing whether a better method exists elsewhere to answer the research question (and if not, then reviewers can suggest possible ways to make the examined method stronger). Finally, if an examined study passes these three steps, critics can still reject it if they can show that society would be better off without the study's results. This may be the case if the proposed answers are deemed to be more misleading than informing.

Box 33.1   Logical sequence for reviewing and criticizing research

1   Does it build on a clearly defined, testable research question?
2   If yes, is the research question relevant to the intended audiences?
3   If yes, are there more accurate methods available elsewhere for answering this particular research question?
4   If not, is society better off without the results this method generates?

Much criticism against the Ecological Footprint criticism arises from the reviewers' apparent confusion about what the research question behind Footprint accounting actually is. Because Footprint accounting takes a systems view, people often assume it covers issues that it is not designed to measure. Examples of such Footprint criticism are found in arguments made by van den Bergh and Verbruggen (1999), Grazi et al. (2007), van Kooten and Bulte (2000), Fiala (2008), Grazi and van den Bergh (2012), Giampietro and Saltelli (2014) or Blomqvist et al. (2013). None of these studies include step 1 and 2 of this logical sequence in their argumentation. As a result, many of these studies are irrelevant to the Footprint's research question. Following steps 1 and 2 would avoid such fallacies. The actual premises and scope for the Footprint accounting are outlined in the research questions addressed in the previous section.

Others question the validity of the Footprint for conclusions they make themselves, rather than addressing the four steps outlined in Box 33.1. As a consequence, they present immaterial conclusions. Examples are given in Box 33.2 and also include the Stiglitz Report (Stiglitz et al., 2009) or van den Bergh and Verbruggen (1999), which refute Footprint accounts for being anti-trade when in reality the Footprint accounts are not.

Box 33.2   'The Footprint is not perfect; therefore, we should not use it'

Some government agencies have used scientific reviews in order to legitimize their unwillingness to adopt Footprint accounting in their own practice. The argument boils down to the statement: 'Footprint results are not perfect; therefore, they should not be used'. An example of such an approach is RPA (2006) and RPA (2007), two consecutive studies commissioned by DEFRA, the UK's ministry of environment. Mathematically speaking, such a statement is true for any research, because by definition, scientific inquiry is never perfect, but a continuous process of learning and improving. While rhetorically, such an argument generates the perception that diligent scientific analysis showed that the Footprint is unfit for use by the agency, the scientifically relevant and honest question to answer should have been: why would the agency be better off not having the analysis? (step 4). Therefore, we include the plea in this chapter to make sure criticism is driven by an honest scientific inquiry (as outlined in Box 33.3) rather than by rhetorical convenience. Obviously, this is true for any research, particularly research critical for public welfare.

In the same vein, few studies on fundamental Footprint criticisms explicitly discuss whether the Footprint question is relevant or not (a notable exception is Schaefer et al., 2006). Discussing the relevance of the research (step 2 of Box 33.1) should be a prerequisite for any fundamental criticism. Global

---

Footprint Network's position is that the Footprint research question is central to sustainability. It holds that sustainability cannot be meaningful unless the availability or regenerative capacities of the ecological constraints of nature, within whose boundaries sustainable development must act, are known. Just as it is important for farmers to know the size of their farm, whether their farmland extends over 5000, 500 or 5 hectares, as having this knowledge about the capacity of the land makes a significant difference to the opportunities that are available to the farmer, one could contend that the same logic applies to a region or even the whole world. By understanding the restrictions of the planet's capacity and where the limitations lie, humanity can move towards sustainability in an informed manner.

Incremental criticism addresses the question: *How can the method be improved?* Most published criticism is of this incremental nature – and this is the area on which Global Footprint Network's current development of the methodology is also focused. For example, Global Footprint Network is working on making the trade assessments of the National Footprint Accounts compatible with the newest insights and analysis from Multi-Regional Input-Output (MRIO) models. But there is still significant work to be done to harmonize the approaches (Ewing et al., 2012; Galli, Weinzettel et al., 2012). Global Footprint Network is currently focusing on an MRIO-assessment based on the newest Global Trade Analysis Project (GTAP) database from Purdue University, GTAP9 (Aguiar et al., 2016). This provides a parallel methodology for analyzing resource flows, in addition to the classical National Footprint Accounts trade analysis based on product flows documented by the United Nations' COMTRADE database that tracks trade flows based on customs statistics of imports and exports. Other MRIO assessments are also emerging, such as the EXIOPOL model (Tukker et al., 2009) and the EORA model (Lenzen et al., 2012, 2013; Moran et al., 2017).

One challenge is that MRIO models do not offer the same level of detail of temporal, categorical or spatial coverage as the National Footprint Accounts. (GTAP9, upon which the Footprint based MRIO builds, covers the years 2004, 2007 and 2011, and divides the world into 140 nations, territories and regions, using only 57 categories; in contrast, current National Footprint Accounts include data for 1961–2014 for approximately 240 countries, of which around 150 are published).

One key application of MRIOs is that they allow the overall consumption Footprints to be broken up into activity fields. We call this breakdown the "Consumption Land-Use Matrix" or CLUM for short. The robustness of these assessments can be compared by comparing various years of results against each other, and comparing the distribution of consumption among countries with similar consumption profile. These CLUMs have a number of applications, including opening the possibility to downscale Ecological Footprint results to subnational applications using relative consumption statistics describing the difference between the national demand and that of the analyzed subnational population, whether it is a city, a region or a socio-economic group (Wackernagel, 1998).

Given the significant noise in the trade data sets, MRIO analysis compared over various years, and contrasting them over various years of NFA-based trade assessments, provides insight into ways how to separate data noise from data signal, an aspect current MRIO analysis is still weak on.

Harmonizing National Footprint Accounts with the emerging MRIO models, together with the aforementioned search for understanding the 'fragility of biocapacity', represent the most significant research frontiers in the Footprint accounting science, opening significant analytical possibilities such as the possibility of tracking trade flows more consistently as well as to the country of origin. Further, it allows researchers to break overall demand into final demand categories.

Conclusions

Ecological Footprint accounting is an answer to just one basic question emerging from the need to make our societies and economies operate within the means of our planet. It attempts to quantify the 'scale question' that is at the core of the Ecological Economics discipline (Daly, 1977; Daly and Farley, 2004). While there is still much room for improvement, a number of independent reviews by government agencies – as mentioned above – have confirmed the validity of the assessment.

Criticism is needed for improving the accounts so they can better answer the underlying research question. Much criticism is valid and is being addressed in the research agenda of the Footprint community. But there is also much criticism based on misconceptions about what Footprint accounting really is. Hopefully this contribution helps to clarify the distinction between these two types of criticism.

Notes

1 This chapter builds on Mathis Wackernagel, Gemma Cranston, Juan Carlos Morales, Alessandro Galli, (2014). "Chapter 24: Ecological Footprint Accounts: From Research Question to Application", in Giles Atkinson, Simon Dietz, Eric Neumayer and Matthew Agarwala (eds), 2014, *Handbook of Sustainable Development*: second revised edition. Edward Elgar Publishing, Cheltenham, UK ISBN-13: 978–1782544692

2 A comprehensive review of Ecological Footprint applications is provided by Collins and Flynn, 2015.

3 This approach was originally developed as part of Aurélien Boutaud's PhD dissertation (2002a). His approach was developed further in a collaboration between Boutaud and Global Footprint Network (Moran et al., 2008; Global Footprint Network, 2009).

4 Note that the comparison with global average biocapacity mainly provides a global overview. This then can be taken a step further, comparing with local biocapacity. For many countries, local availability of biocapacity (and financial means to access biocapacity from elsewhere) are a more significant determinant of resource access than the global average.

5 The promotion and slight distortion of the carbon Footprint by BP was, in the eyes of Global Footprint Network, a lucky occurrence. Global Footprint Network had been concerned about the possibility that a large organization like BP could significantly distort and confuse the concept. But in this case, it has, in spite of the slight distortion from the original concept, helped to promote rather than thwart the understanding that there are global limits, and that consumption is an ultimate driver of resource demand (Fill and Hughes, 2008, p. 156; Safire, 2008).

6 In their 2009 Climate Change Adaptation Report, they state:

> The report's point of departure is that we are unlikely to be far more successful at curbing our CO_2 emissions in the near future than we have been over the past decade or so. And even with vigorous mitigation effort, we will continue to use fossil fuel reserves until they are exhausted. However, by then, atmospheric CO_2 levels may have risen to about 1700ppmv compared to an average of 383ppmv today. (www.imeche.org/Libraries/Key_Themes/ClimateChangeAdaptationReportIMechE.sflb.ashx)

7 In addition to energy for concentrating metals, mining itself can also affect biocapacity, not only through the loss of potentially productive areas but also through mining refuse and other waste products.

8 Humanity has maintained use of resources outside the realms of settlements since the beginning of civilization. Indeed, most current communities are far from self-sustaining, and exist by drawing upon the resources beyond their borders. Even hunter-gatherer tribes depended on far larger areas than the settlements themselves. Thus the space required to sustain populations has historically been far larger than the main living space of communities. A footprint application in this context, commissioned for a Canadian court case, is explained on Global Footprint Network's website at https://www.footprintnetwork.org/2014/07/18/canada-ecological-footprint-instrumental-supreme-courts-ruling/ (accessed March 22, 2018).

References

Abdullatif, L. and Alam, T. (2011), 'The UAE ecological footprint initiative', available at: http://d2ou-vy59p0dg6k.cloudfront.net/downloads/en_final_report_ecological_footprint.pdf (accessed 28 December 2016).

Aguiar, A., Narayanan, B., & McDougall, R. (2016), 'An overview of the GTAP 9 data base', *Journal of Global Economic Analysis*, **1**(1), (June 3), 181–208.

Ayres, R.U. (2000), 'Commentary on the utility of the Ecological Footprint concept', *Ecological Economics*, **32**(3), 347–349.

Best, A., Giljum, S., Simmons, C., Blobel, D., Lewis, K., Hammer, M., Cavalieri, S., Lutter, S., and Maguire, C. (2008), 'Potential of the Ecological Footprint for monitoring environmental impacts from natural resource use: Analysis of the potential of the Ecological Footprint and related assessment tools for use in the EU's Thematic Strategy on the Sustainable Use of Natural Resources', Report to the European Commission, DG Environment, available at: http://ec.europa.eu/environment/natres/pdf/footprint.pdf (accessed 28 December 2016).

Blomqvist, L., Brook, B.W., Ellis, E.C., Kareiva, P.M., and Nordhaus, T. (2013), 'The ecological footprint remains a misleading metric of global sustainability', *PLoS Biol*, **11**(11), e1001702. doi:10.1371/journal.pbio.1001702

Borucke, M., Moore, D., Cranston, G., Gracey, K., Iha, K., Larson, J., Lazarus, E., Morales, J.C., Wackernagel, M., and Galli, A. (2013), 'Accounting for demand and supply of the Biosphere's regenerative capacity: The National Footprint Accounts' underlying methodology and framework', *Ecological Indicators*, **24**, 518–533.

Boutaud, A. (2002a), 'Elaboration de critères et indicateurs de développement durable', Doctorate Thesis, Ecole des Mines de Saint-Etienne, Centre SITE, available at: http://wwwv1.agora21.org/publications/ademe-boutaud.pdf (accessed 28 December 2016).

Boutaud, A. (2002b), 'Développement durable: Quelques vérités embarrassantes', *Economie & Humanisme*, **363**, 4–6, available at: www.revue-economie-et-humanisme.eu/bdf/docs/r363.pdf

Collins, A. and Flynn, A. (2015), *The Ecological Footprint: New Developments in Policy and Practice*, Edward Elgar Publishing Ltd; UK, 223 pages.

Costanza, R. (2000), 'The dynamics of the ecological footprint concept', *Ecological Economics*, **32**, 341–345.

Daly, H. (1973, May), *Toward a Steady-state Economy*, W.H. Freeman & Co Ltd, San Francisco.

Daly, H. (1977), *The Steady-State Economics*, Earthscan Publications, London.

Daly, H.E. and Farley, J. (2004), *Ecological Economics: Principles and Applications*, Island Press, Washington, DC.

Davis, S.J., Peters, G.P., and Caldeira, K. (2011), 'The supply chain of CO_2 emissions', *Proceedings of the National Academy of Sciences*, **108**(45), 18554–18559.

Deutsch, L., Jansson, Å., Troell, M., Rönnbäck, P., Folke, C., and Kautsky, N. (2000), 'The ecological footprint: Communicating human dependence on nature's work', *Ecological Economics*, **32**, 351–355.

ECOTEC Research & Consulting Limited. (2001), *Ecological Footprinting*, Technical Report commissioned by European Parliament, Directorate General for Research, Directorate A, The STOA Programme to the STOA Panel, Workplan Ref.: EP/IV/A/STOA/2000/09/03, available at: www.europarl.europa.eu/RegData/etudes/etudes/join/2001/297571/DG-4-JOIN_ET%282001%29297571_EN.pdf (accessed 28 December 2016).

Ewing, B.R., Hawkins, T.R., Wiedmann, T.O., Galli, A., Ercin, A.E., Weinzettel, J., and Steen-Olsen, K. (2012), 'Integrating ecological and water footprint accounting in a multi-regional input – output framework', *Ecological Indicators*, **23**, 1–8.

FAOSTAT (Food and Agriculture Organization of the United Nations Statistics). Available at: www.fao.org/faostat/en/#home

FAO and IIASA (Food and Agriculture Organization and International Institute for Applied Systems Analysis). (2000), *Global Agro-Ecological Zones*. Available at: http://webarchive.iiasa.ac.at/Research/LUC/GAEZ/index.htm (accessed July 2017).

Fiala, N. (2008), 'Measuring sustainability: Why the ecological footprint is bad economics and bad environmental science', *Ecological Economics*, **67**(4), 519–525.

Fill, C. and Hughes, G. (2008), *The Official CIM Coursebook: Marketing Communications: CIM Coursebook 08/09*, Taylor & Francis, Oxford.

Fischer-Kowalski, M. and Haberl, H. (1993), 'Metabolism and colonization, modes of production and the physical exchange between societies and nature', *Innovation in Social Sciences Research*, **6**(4), 415–442.

Fischer-Kowalski, M. and Haberl, H. (1997), 'Tons, joules, and money: Modes of production and their sustainability problems', *Society and Natural Resources*, **10**(1), 61–85.

Fischer-Kowalski, M. and Haberl, H. (2007), *Socio-ecological Transitions and Global Change: Trajectories of Social Metabolism and Land Use*, Edward Elgar, Cheltenham, UK and Northampton, MA, USA.

Frischknecht, R. with Eaton, D. and Wackernagel, M. (2016), *Comparison and expert statement on the ecological footprint 2011 of Switzerland*, Memo to the Swiss Ministry of Environment (BAFU), treeze. File Memo_comparison_CH-EF-2011_GFN_treeze_v1.0

Galli, A., Giampietro, M., Goldfinger, S., Lazarus, E., Lin, D., Saltelli, S., Wackernagel, M., and Müller, F. (2016), 'Questioning the Ecological Footprint', *Ecological Indicators*, **69**, 224–232, Available at: http://dx.doi.org/10.1016/j.ecolind.2016.04.014 (accessed 28 December 2016).

Galli, A., Kitzes, J., Niccolucci, V., Wackernagel, M., Wada, Y., and Marchettini, N. (2012), 'Assessing the global environmental consequences of economic growth through the ecological footprint: A focus on China and India', *Ecological Indicators*, **17**, 99–107.

Galli, A., Martindill, J., Lin, D., and Iyengar, L. (2016), 'UAE National Footprint Accounts 2016', *Data Verification Report*. Global Footprint Network for UAE EF Committee. August 31, 2016.

Galli, A., Weinzettel, J., Cranston, G., and Ercin, A.E. (2012), 'A footprint family extended MRIO model to support Europe's transition to a one planet economy', *Science of the Total Environment*, available at: http://dx.doi.org/10.1016/j.scitotenv.2012.11.071

Giampietro, M. and Saltelli, A. (2014), 'Footprint facts and fallacies: A response to Giampietro and Saltelli (2014) footprints to nowhere', *Ecological Indicators*, **46**, 260–263.

Global Footprint Network. (2009), *Africa Factbook*, Global Footprint Network, Oakland, CA, available at: www.footprintnetwork.org/resources/publications (accessed 14 July 2017).

Global Footprint Network. (2017), *National Footprint Accounts 2017*, available at: http://data.footprintnetwork.org (accessed 28 June 2017).

Goldfinger, S., Wackernagel, M., Galli, A., Lazarus, E., and Lin, D. (2014), 'Footprint fact sand fallacies: a response to Giampietro and Saltelli (2014) footprints to nowhere', *Ecological Indicators*, **46**, 622–632.

Grazi, F. and van den Bergh, J.C.J.M. (2012), 'L'empreinte écologique et l'utilisation des sols comme indicateur environnemental: Quel intérêt pour les politiques publiques?', *Agence Française de Développement*, working paper no. 127, available at: www.afd.fr/webdav/site/afd/shared/PUBLICATIONS/RECHERCHE/Scientifiques/Documents-de-travail/127-document-travail.pdf (accessed 28 December 2016).

Grazi, F., van den Bergh, J.C.J.M., and Rietveld, P. (2007), 'Spatial welfare economics versus ecological footprint: Modeling agglomeration, externalities, and trade', *Environmental and Resource Economics*, **38**(1), 135–153.

Haberl, H. (1997), 'Human appropriation of net primary production as an environmental indicator: Implications for sustainable development', *Ambio*, **6**(3), 143–146.

Haberl, H., Erb, K.H., Krausmann, F., Gaube, V., Bondeau, A., Plutzar, C., Gingrich, S., Lucht, W., and Fischer-Kowalski, M. (2007), 'Quantifying and mapping the human appropriation of net primary production in Earth's terrestrial ecosystems', *Proceedings of the National Academy of Sciences*, **104**, 12942–12947.

Haberl, H., Krausmann, F., Erb, K.H., and Schulz, N.B. (2002), 'Human appropriation of net primary production', *Science*, **296**, 1968–1969.

Haberl, H. and Schandl, H. (1999), 'Indicators of sustainable land use: Concepts for the analysis of society – nature interrelations and implications for sustainable development', *Environmental Management and Health*, **11**(3), 177–190.

Haberl, H., Wackernagel, M., Krausmann, F., Erb, K.H., and Monfreda, C. (2004), 'Ecological footprints and human appropriation of net primary production: A comparison', *Land Use Policy*, **21**, 279–288.

Hansen, J., Sato, M., Kharecha, P., Beerling, D., Berner, R., Masson-Delmotte, V., Pagani, M., Raymo, M., Royer, D.L., and Zachos, J.C. (2008), 'Target atmospheric CO_2: Where should humanity aim?', *Open Atmospheric Science Journal*, **2**, 217–231.

Hertwich, E.G. and Peters, G.P. (2009), 'Carbon Footprint of nations: A global, trade-linked analysis', *Environmental Science & Technology*, **43**(16), 6414–6420.

Hild, P., Schmitt, B., Decoville, A., Mey, M., and Welfring, J. (2010), *The Ecological Footprint of Luxembourg – Technical Report*, version 4.2, extended Scoping Study Report, CRP Henri Tudor/CRTE, Luxembourg.

Hoekstra, A.Y. and Chapagain, A.K. (2007), 'Water Footprints of nations: Water use by people as a function of their consumption pattern', *Water Resources Management*, **21**(1), 35–48.

IMV. (2002), *Assessing the Ecological Footprint*, Danish Environmental Institute, Copenhagen.

Kitzes, J., Galli, A., Bagliani, M., Barrett, J., Dige, G., Ede, S., Erb, K., Giljum, S., Haberl, H., Hails, C., Jolia-Ferrier, L., Jungwirth, S., Lenzen, M., Lewis, K., Loh, J., Marchettini, N., Messinger, H., Milne, K., Moles, R., Monfreda, C., Moran, D., Nakano, K., Pyhälä, A., Rees, W., Simmons, C., Wackernagel, M., Wada, Y.,

Walsh, C., and Wiedmann, T. (2009), 'A research agenda for improving national Ecological Footprint accounts', *Ecological Economics*, **68**(7), 1991–2007.

Leaton, J. (2012), 'Unburnable carbon: Are the world's financial markets carrying a carbon bubble?', *Carbon Tracker Initiative*, available at: www.carbontracker.org/wp-content/uploads/downloads/2012/08/Unburnable-Carbon-Full1.pdf (accessed 12 January 2013).

Lenzen, M., Kanemoto, K., Moran, D., and Geschke, A. (2012), 'Mapping the structure of the world economy', *Environmental Science & Technology*, **46**(15), 8374–8381.

Lenzen, M., Moran, D., Kanemoto, K., and Geschke, A. (2013), 'Building Eora: A Multi-region Input–Output Database at High Country and Sector Resolution', *Economic Systems Research,* **25**, 20–49, doi:10.1080/09535314.2013.769938

Lovejoy, T. (2008), 'AAAS-Hitachi Lecture', *AAAS Conference 2008*, available at: www.aaas.org/news/releases/2008/1118hitachi.shtml (accessed 12 January 2013).

Mancini, M.S., Galli, A., Niccolucci, V., Lin, D., Bastianoni, S., Wackernagel, M., and Marchettini, N. (2016), 'Ecological Footprint: Refining the carbon Footprint calculation', *Ecological Indicators*, **61**, 390–403.

Meadows, D., Meadows, D., Randers, J., and Behrens, W. (1972), *Limits to Growth: A Report for the club of Rome's Project on the Predicament of Mankind*, Universe Books, USA. available at: www.donellameadows.org/wp-content/userfiles/Limits-to-Growth-digital-scan-version.pdf

Moffatt, I. (1999), 'Is Scotland sustainable? A time series of indicators of sustainable development', *International Journal of Sustainable Development & World Ecology*, **6**(4), 242–250.

Moore, D., Galli, A., Cranston, G.R., and Reed, A. (2012), 'Projecting future human demand on the Earth's regenerative capacity', *Ecological Indicators*, **16**, 3–10.

Moran, D. and Kanemoto, K. (2017), 'Identifying species threat hotspots from global supply chains', *Nature Ecology & Evolution*, **1**, Article number: 0023, doi:10.1038/s41559-016-0023

Moran, D., Wackernagel, M., Kitzes, J., Goldfinger, S., and Boutaud, A. (2008), 'Measuring sustainable development: Nation by nation', *Ecological Economics*, **64**(3), 470–474.

Nealson, K.H. and Conrad, P.G. (1999), 'Life: past, present, future', *Philosophical Transactions of the Royal Society B*, **354**, 1923–1939.

Neumayer, E. (2013), *Weak versus Strong Sustainability: Exploring the Limits of Two Opposing Paradigms*, 4th edn, Edward Elgar, Cheltenham, UK and Northampton, MA, USA.

Niccolucci, V., Tiezzi, E., Pulselli, F.M., and Capineri, C. (2012), 'Biocapacity vs Ecological Footprint of world regions: A geopolitical interpretation', *Ecological Indicators*, **16**, 23–30.

The People's Republic of China. (2015), *The 13th Five-Year Plan for Economic and Social Development of the People's Republic of China (2016–2020)*, Central Compilation and Translation Press, Beijing. Available at: http://en.ndrc.gov.cn/newsrelease/201612/P020161207645765233498.pdf

Peters, G.P. and Hertwich, E.G. (2006), 'Structural analysis of international trade: Environmental impacts of Norway', *Economic Systems Research*, **18**(2), 155–181.

Peters, G.P., Minx, J.C., Weber, C.L., and Edenhofer, O. (2011), 'Growth in emission transfers via international trade from 1990 to 2008', *Proceedings of the National Academy of Sciences*, **108**(21), 8903–8908.

Rockström, J., Steffen, W., Noone, K., Persson, A., Chappin, F.S.I., Lambin, E., Lenton, T.M., Scheffer, M., Folke, C., Schellnhuber, H.J., Nykvist, B., De Wit, C.A., Hughes, T., Van Der Leeuw, S., Rodhe, H., Sornlin, S., Snyder, P., Constanza, R., Svedin, U., Falkenmark, M., Karberg, L., Corell, R.W., Fabry, V.J., Hansen, J., Walker, B., Liverman, D., Richardson, K., Crutzen, P., and Foley, J. (2009), 'A safe operating space for humanity', *Nature*, **461**, 472–475.

RPA – Risk & Policy Analysts Ltd. (2006), 'Sustainable consumption and production: Development of an evidence base', *Study of Ecological Footprinting*, Defra, London, available at: http://randd.defra.gov.uk/Default.aspx?Menu=Menu&Module=More&Location=None&Completed=1&ProjectID=13146 (accessed 28 December 2016).

RPA – Risk & Policy Analysts Ltd. (2007), 'A review of recent developments in, and the practical use of, ecological footprinting methodologies: A report to the Department for Environment, Food and Rural Affairs', Defra, London, available at: www.footprintnetwork.org/download.php?id=402 (accessed 28 December 2016).

Sachs, J., Schmidt-Traub, G., Kroll, C., Durand-Delacre, D., and Teksoz, K. (2016), SDG Index and Dashboards – Global Report. New York: Bertelsmann Stiftung and Sustainable Development Solutions Network (SDSN). Available at: http://www.sdgindex.org/

Safire, W. (2008), 'On language: Footprint', *New York Times*, 17 February, available at: www.nytimes.com/2008/02/17/magazine/17wwln-safire-t.html. (accessed 28 December 2016).

Schaefer, F., Luksch, U., Steinbach, N., Cabeça, J., and Hanauer, J. (2006), *Ecological Footprint and Biocapacity: The World's Ability to Regenerate Resources and Absorb Waste in a Limited Time Period*, Office for Official

Publications of the European Communities, Luxembourg, available at: http://ec.europa.eu/eurostat/documents/3888793/5835641/KS-AU-06-001-EN.PDF (accessed 28 December 2016).

SOeS, French Ministry of Sustainable Development. (2010), 'Une expertise de l'empreinte écologique', *Etudes & Documents*, No. 16, January, available at: www.developpement-durable.gouv.fr/IMG/pdf/ED16_cle584d56_1_.pdf (accessed 28 Dec 2016).

Steffen, W., Richardson, K., Rockstrom, J., Cornell, S.E., Fetzer, I., Bennett, E.M., Biggs, R., Carpenter, S.R., de Vries, W., de Wit, C.A., Folke, C., Gerten, D., Heinke, J., Mace, G.M., Persson, L.M., Ramanathan, V., Reyers, B., and Sorlin, S. (2015), 'Planetary boundaries: Guiding human development on a changing planet', *Science*, **347**(6223). doi:10.1126/science.1259855

Stiglitz, J.E., Sen, A., and Fitoussi, J.P. (2009), 'Report by the Commission on the Measurement of Economic Performance and Social Progress', *Commission on the Measurement of Economic Performance and Social Progress*, available at http://library.bsl.org.au/jspui/bitstream/1/1267/1/Measurement_of_economic_performance_and_social_progress.pdf (accessed 28 December 2016).

Tukker, A., Poliakov, E., Heijungs, R., Hawkins, T., Neuwahl, F., and Rueda-Cantuche, J.M. (2009), 'Towards a global multi-regional environmentally extended input-output database', *Ecological Economics*, **68**(7), 1928–1937.

UK Institution of Mechanical Engineers. (2009), 'Climate change: Adapting to the inevitable?', available at: www.imeche.org/docs/default-source/key-themes/ClimateChangeAdaptationReportIMechE.pdf?sfvrsn=0 (accessed 28 December 2016).

United Nations (UN). (1948), 'Universal Declaration of Human Rights', available at: www.un.org/en/universal-declaration-human-rights/index.html (accessed 28 December 2016).

United Nations. (2000), *Millennium Development Goals* (established in 2000), available at: www.un.org/millenniumgoals/bkgd.shtml (accessed 14 July 2017).

United Nations Development Programme. (2011), *Human Development Report 2011. Sustainability and Equity: A Better Future for All*, United Nations Development Programme, New York.

United Nations Development Programme. (2016), *Human Development Report 2016: Human Development for everyone*, United Nations Development Programme, New York.

United Nations (UN), Sustainable Development Goals (SDG). (25 September 2015), 'Part of a New Sustainable Development Agenda', available at: www.un.org/sustainabledevelopment/sustainable-development-goals/www.un.org/ga/search/view_doc.asp?symbol=A/RES/70/1&Lang=E (accessed 14 July 2017).

van den Bergh, J.C.J.M. and Grazi, F. (2010), 'On the policy relevance of ecological footprints', *Environmental Science & Technology*, **44**, 4843–4844.

van den Bergh, J.C.J.M. and Verbruggen, H. (1999), 'Spatial sustainability, trade and indicators: An evaluation of the "Ecological Footprint"', *Ecological Economics*, **29**(1), 61–72.

van Kooten, G.C. and Bulte, E.H. (2000), 'The ecological footprint: Useful science or politics?', *Ecological Economics*, **32**, 385–389.

Vitousek, P.M., Ehrlich, P.R., Ehrlich, A.H., and Matson, P.A. (1986), 'Human appropriation of the products of photosynthesis', *BioScience*, **36**, 363–373.

von Stokar, T., Steinemann, M., and Rüegge, B. (2006), 'Ecological Footprint of Switzerland', Technical Report, INFRAS, Neuchâtel, available at: www.bfs.admin.ch/bfs/de/home/statistiken/nachhaltige-entwicklung/oekologischer-fussabdruck.assetdetail.500264.html (accessed 28 December 2016).

Wackernagel, M. (1998), 'The ecological footprint of Santiago de Chile', *Local Environment*, **3**(1) (February), 7–25.

Wackernagel, M., Hanscom, L., and Lin, D. (2017), 'Making the sustainable development goals consistent with sustainability', *Frontiers in Energy Research*, **5**, 18. doi:10.3389/fenrg.2017.00018

Wackernagel, M., Lewan, L., and Hansson, B. C. (1999), 'Evaluating the use of natural capital with the ecological footprint: Applications in Sweden and subregions', *Ambio*, **28**(7), 604–612.

Willey, D. and Ferguson, A. (1999), *Carrying Capacity Ethics*, Optimum Population Trust, London.

World Business Council for Sustainable Development (WBCSD). (2011), *Vision 2050*, Geneva, available at: www.wbcsd.org/Overview/About-us/Vision2050 (accessed 14 July 2017).

World Commission on Environment and Development (WCED). (1987), *Our Common Future* ('Brundtland Report'), transmitted to the UN General Assembly as an annex to document A/42/427 – 'Development and International Co-operation: Environment, Report of the World Commission on Environment and Development' (WCED), available at: www.un-documents.net/wced-ocf.htm

WWF Japan and Global Footprint Network. (2012), *Japan Ecological Footprint Report 2012*, WWF, Japan, Tokyo, available at: www.footprintnetwork.org (accessed 28 December 2016).

In conclusion

34

WHAT NEXT?

Simon Bell and Stephen Morse

A bird's-eye view

We began this book with the following quote from Elizabeth Cady Stanton:

> *The moment we begin to fear the opinions of others and hesitate to tell the truth that is in us, and from motives of policy are silent when we should speak, the divine floods of light and life no longer flow into our souls.*
>
> — *Elizabeth Cady Stanton*

A truly existential issue faces us it would seem and, in this crisis of truth, indicators hold a key part to play.

In this book, a distinguished group of authors have contributed to map out the past experience of indicators and indices marking the experience of sustainability accountability over time. As we noted in the introduction, our style as editors was purposefully very 'hands off'. Other than asking contributors to cross-refer to other chapters in the book where appropriate our approach was to leave them to it. Our emphasis was far more at the strategic level; to make sure the rich and diverse landscape of sustainability indicators was covered as much as possible. This is a challenge given the nature of the field, and we acknowledge, based upon previous experience, that some readers will no doubt be upset at what they see as important omissions. We obviously cannot expect our contributors to cover every indicator and index in detail, and there are some topics that are arguably under-explored. For example, the development and use of indicators in the private sector could perhaps have received far more attention as indeed could the emerging field of 'Planetary Boundaries' (Steffen et al., 2015). No doubt other readers will be upset that their own favourite indicator or index has been omitted. Clearly there is a limit to what a book such as this can cover as publishers do, after all, want to be able to market something that can be carried in the hands. But we do hope that the book, despite omissions, has provided the reader with much food for thought.

To provide a summary of the topics covered in the book is never really an adequate exposition of the richness of the original, but in order to base our forward thinking on a sound basis here are the main themes you will have encountered in the book.

In our first section on History and Theory László Pintér, Peter Hardi, André Martinuzzi and Jon Hall review the manner in which in 1997 a global group of leading measurement and assessment experts developed the Bellagio Principles –– which has become the reference point for measuring sustainable development now updated in the Bellagio Sustainability Assessment and Measurement Principles (BellagioSTAMP). Arthur Dahl complements the BellagioSTAMP focus looking at and subsequently the Environmental Vulnerability Index and Environmental Performance Index. He notes that the indicators for targets under the Sustainable Development Goals raise new challenges for more integrated indicator design and for the practicality of data collection and implementation. Walter J.V. Vermeulen argues that despite the endless condemnations of the vagueness of the concept and definition of sustainable development (SD), in practice we can see a rough consensus on what it includes. A core structure exists and is being widely worked with. Daniel C. Esty and John W. Emerson describe how the Environmental Performance Index (EPI) emerged from an interdisciplinary team of researchers who believed that a data-driven approach to environmental policymaking would make it easier to spot problems, track trends, benchmark performance, highlight leaders and laggards, spotlight policy successes and failures, and identify best practices. They demonstrate that the policy impact of the EPI has been far-reaching. In Chapter 6 Sarah Rotz and Evan Fraser compare and contrast resilience and sustainability indicators (SIs) and consider how each conceptual tool may build and enhance one another and conclude by considering the utility of SIs and resilience for our study and illustrate various conceptual and programmatic tensions, as well as possible ways forward. Robert Costanza, Maureen Hart, Ida Kubiszewski, Steve Posner and John Talberth look at lessons in the history of GDP, arguing that it was never designed as a measure of national progress, prosperity or well-being, and yet it has become the most widely accepted and influential goal for national economic policy. They argue that now we need new visions of a sustainable and desirable world and new ways to measure progress that have as broad a consensus and are therefore as influential as GDP has been in the past. Finally, in the first section of the book Paul-Marie Boulanger argues that the recent burgeoning of sustainability indicators, sustainability impact assessments methods and practices, etc., can be sociologically interpreted as the progressive emergence of a new functional system structured around the sustainable/unsustainable binary code.

The Theory and History section tells a story of a struggle to achieve consensus on the definition and understanding and measurement of what we mean by sustainable development. Progress has been made but the field remains agitated and unsure of itself (despite the assurances of specific subject specialists).

In Part 2 we looked at Methods and Joachim H. Spangenberg reviews the confusing blend of objectivity and subjectivity in indicator method development. His chapter explains different approaches and how they influence the indicator selection. Catalina Turcu focusses on the role that SIs play in measuring sustainability in the built environment and concludes by discussing some of the problems associated with the use of sustainability indicators and certification schemes in the built environment. Jonathan Chenoweth moves the debate into that of water scarcity, which stems from the spatial and temporal mismatch between the supply and demand for freshwater. Water and the range of indicators have been developed to assess water scarcity and the adequacy of access to water of appropriate quality faced by different human societies. He argues that indicators attempting to measure the sustainability of global human water consumption compared to the environment's ability to cope with that consumption have been proposed but require further development. In Chapter 12 Steve and I return to the issue of subjectivity, definition and participation in SI development. We argue that 'stakeholder participation' has two contestable elements; just what is a stakeholder and what is participation? Dóra Almássy and

László Pintér provide an overview of some of the most widely known environmental indices. The methodological soundness is presented based on the ten-step OECD-EC JRC composite indicator development methodology. Roefie Hueting and Bart de Boer argue that information can be given with the aid of indicators that are measurable in cardinal units and that are arguably influencing welfare; however, environmentally sustainability national income (eSNI) is the production level that does not threaten future generations. In Chapter 15 Peter Bartelmus reviews green accounting and suggests that the greening of the national accounts, as suggested by the System of Environmental-Economic Accounting, corrects the accounting indicators for hitherto ignored environmental costs. He suggests that in internalizing these costs into the budgets of households and enterprises and into environmental-economic policies would ground the integration of environmental and economic policies on facts rather than rhetoric. Mathis Wackernagel, Alessandro Galli, Laurel Hanscom, David Lin, Laetitia Mailhes and Tony Drummond overview the progress made with the Ecological Footprint and the focus on how much of the biosphere's (or any region's) regenerative capacity any human activity demands.

Part 2 provides a vast range of methods and processes and an engagement with subjective and objective forms of assessment in a range of methods and practices. There is surely no silver bullet to answer all issues.

In Part 3 we took the methods espoused in Part 2 and looked directly at Agency Experience. Angel Hsu examines and compares the sub-national EPIs in China, Malaysia and Viet Nam and notes that these countries face common challenges including issues of poor data availability and quality, institutional fragmentation and organizational constraints. Giangiacomo Bravo assesses the Human Sustainable Development Index (HSDI) which has been proposed as a way to amend the United Nations' Human Development Index (HDI) by adding an environmental dimension. Giangiacomo critically reviews the HSDI, with a description of the procedure leading to its calculation and a critical assessment of its relation with some established environmental indicators. Elisabeth Conrad and Louis F. Cassar look at the Maltese experience of the Environmental Performance Index (EPI) which ranked the Mediterranean island state of Malta 9th out of 180 countries. Despite issues in the use and calculation of the EPI the authors argue that the EPI's utility could potentially be enhanced via modifications tailoring the index to reflect regional and/or local priorities. Lucas Reijnders notes that indicator sets for sustainability or sustainable development constructed for governments vary very much. The indicator set proposed in 2016 for the 2030 Sustainable Development Goals is to be based on objective statistics yet justice between the generations and the conservation of natural capital appear not to be central to the development of the sustainability-related indicator sets constructed for governments surveyed. Lucas suggests that there is a case for refocussing on inter-generational justice and on the conservation of natural capital as a prerequisite to sustainable development in the construction of indicator sets. Looking at the Finish experience of SDIs, Ulla Rosenström notes that Finland has been among the forerunners in developing SDIs since the late 1990s and has made special efforts to enhance their use. Gilberto C. Gallopin attempts to clarify the concepts of sustainable development, sustainability and indicators using a systemic approach which has been officially employed by Argentina and the Catalonian Region of Spain. Arthur Lyon Dahl identified that after 15 years, 66 countries were using indicators in national environmental reporting. Simon Joss and Yvonne Rydin describe how real-world innovation is enabled and constrained by divergent systems of motivations; it does not flow in a linear fashion from abstract principles of urban sustainability, however these may be defined. Ana Rita Domingues, Rodrigo Lozano and Tomás B. Ramos argue the case that stakeholders can, and should, become part of the environmental and sustainability indicator initiatives, especially when they feel that their opinions are part of decision-making processes that have impacts in their daily lives or are important for their community. Jochen Jesinghaus suggests that after decades of watching the news, the brainwashed voter will believe that a good government is one that cares for GDP growth and the Dow Jones. This absurd situation has triggered numerous initiatives to either 'green' GDP, or to replace it with an index composed of the most relevant indicators, e.g. in areas like health, equity, environment, justice, etc. The chapter by Dwi Amalia Sari, Chris Margules, Agni Klintuni Boedhihartono and Jeffrey Sayer propose that outcome metrics will differ for all situations and that generalizable indicators will rarely be available. However process indicators will be valuable in confirming best practice and the deployment of appropriate process indicators should ensure that measurable outcome indicators will be identified. Wytze Marinus, Esther Ronner, Gerrie W. J. van de Vena, Fred Kanampiu, Samuel Adjei-Nsiah and Ken E. Giller illustrate that many of the decisions made in developing an indicator framework are subjective and that they include important but easily overlooked details.

The Methods section provides more evidence for the massive energy exerted in the field of indicator collection across many variable and varied fields of activity. Again, as with earlier sections, issues of objectivity and subjectivity, interpretation and renewal are lively topics of engagement.

The final section of the four deals with critiques. In Chapter 29 Philip Grabowski, Mark Musumba, Cheryl Palm and Sieglinde Snapp review progress with sustainable agricultural intensification (SAI) and the authors summarize several important challenges that make it difficult to implement a system of indicators for sustainable agricultural intensification. Relevance is the core of the chapter by Svatava Janoušková, Tomáš Hák and Bedřich Moldan. Looking at thematic relevance and indicator relevance the authors categorize relevance first and foremost by the user to which they refer: i.e. from policy, science and public perspectives. Daniel C. Esty assesses the manner in which environmental decision-making has been plagued by uncertainties and incomplete information. This is a matter of profound interest to this book and Daniel explores why and how better and cheaper data and greater emphasis on statistical analysis promise to strengthen environmental policymaking. Tomás B. Ramos and Sandra Caeiro seek to present a conceptual framework to design and assess the effectiveness of the sustainability indicators themselves. In this work stakeholder involvement is an essential component of the proposed framework. Our final chapter by Mathis Wackernagel, Alessandro Galli, Laurel Hanscom, David Lin, Laetitia Mailhes and Tony Drummond describe the range of applications of the Ecological Footprint and the criticisms of it.

The 33 chapters of this book have a number of things in common:

1   The authors recognize the complexity of the indicator/indices fields – no one (well, no one informed) is suggesting that metrics in this area is straightforward, uncontested or trivial.
2   There is no attempt to gloss over the shortcomings of any statistical means to address complex truths – all authors grapple with the continuing, chronic issues of accuracy and inclusiveness.
3   The field is seen as evolving – and the rate of this evolution is not steady or stable – and
4   Issues of objectivity and subjectivity continue to exercise the formulation of indicator selection, assessment and resulting decision-making.

In short, we know that to pursue our objective of measurable and manageable sustainability we are in a fight. The nature of this fight and its implications are key to strategies for further development.

Fake indicators?

As we have noted, one of the other aspects that stands out across all the chapters is the contested nature of the indicator, including SIs, field. While our chapter authors, and indeed ourselves, have used the terms 'indicator' and SI almost interchangeably they are of course different. Not all indicators may be SIs of course, but given the breadth of concerns within sustainable development a case could certainly be made for very many of them. By and large all of the contributors to the book have relied on the largesse of the reader to accommodate such inclusion. Similarly, there is 'no one SI to rule them all' (although some agencies have exhibited a Mordor-esqe attitude to SIs on occasion) but a wide diversity of approaches and indicators, each emerging in their own time and space and designed to meet a defined set of objectives. Thus, we have seen indices such as the HDI (and HSDI), Ecological Footprint (EF) and EPI becoming popular and at the time of writing we have the emergence of the targets and indicators linked to the Sustainable Development Goals (SDGs) covered by a number of chapters in the book. Indices such as the HDI and EPI have evolved over time in response to feedback from researchers and practitioners, and the ever-increasing availability of data (albeit of varying qualities and arguably still not enough) also acts as a spur to change. But at their heart we all know that indicators and indices are simplifying tools designed to capture complexity and help convey information to non-specialists. This is, of course, well known and in many of the chapters we have seen how this process of simplification results in trade-offs; decisions to exclude and include and to manipulate data. These are human decisions and while they are rationalized by their 'owners' they are nonetheless subjective. It has to be acknowledged that not all will agree with those decisions and the reader need look no further than the numerous debates that have resonated over the years regarding the HDI (Morse, 2004). Indicators and indices are not 'laws of nature' but human constructs that reflect the biases, intentions and worldview of their creators. In that sense all indicators and indices can be labelled as 'fake' by at least someone and they can provide 'evidence' (based on different biases, intentions and worldviews) to back it up; uncomfortable reading indeed for those of us in the indicator business.

Of course, given that indicators and indices occupy that nexus between developers and users, it seems almost inevitable that there could be an element of selection-bias by the latter. No matter what the motives of the indicator developers, some people may indeed want to make selective use of indicators to convey a message. For an example of that the reader need look no further than the 2016 'Brexit' referendum and heated debate in the UK which we have already alluded to in the introduction. One of the most oft-quoted phrases by those on the 'leave' campaign (those in favour of Brexit) was that the UK was the '5th largest economy' in the world and thus well-able to do well outside of the EU. The phrase was repeated and is still a key element of the Brexiteers (those who support Brexit) lexicon.

The phrase is based on a metric and statistics but is it true?

Well, of course, much depends on the indicators one uses. Economies can be measured in various ways and the World Bank has been collating that information for many years. The data are readily available at https://data.worldbank.org/. Several indicators could be employed but here we have focussed on just four. In each case, the indicator is founded upon the Gross Domestic Product (GDP; Coyle, 2014) where, using the World Bank's definition:

> GDP is the sum of gross value added by all resident producers in the economy plus any product taxes and minus any subsidies not included in the value of the products. It is calculated without making deductions for depreciation of fabricated assets or for depletion and degradation of natural resources.

In effect, GDP calculated on the basis of expenditures is given by:

$$GDP(expenditure) = C + G + I + (EX - IM)$$

where:

C = consumers' expenditure on goods and services
G = government expenditure on goods and services
I = investment
EX = exports
IM = imports

The components in this equation are discussed in more detail in Morse (2004). In essence, the higher the level of GDP then the greater the 'size' of the economy, with an implied assumption that this is 'good'. Jochen Jesinghaus in his chapter (26) certainly makes a good case for treating GDP with care when it comes to sustainable development and care does need to be taken in assuming that GDP growth is always a good thing, at least for most of a population. As Peter Bartelmus has noted in his chapter, the GDP has often been "accused of being a misleading measure of well-being". Clearly it is not such a measure and was never intended to be, but it has become the key barometer of national economic performance and in the minds of many this is very much associated with well-being. In itself, GDP is not a 'bad' indicator, and as Bartelmus has noted, we do need to be careful not to discard the GDP:

> There is indeed no other place where standardized measures of economic activities can be found and presented to policy makers in a meaningful "nutshell". Individuals, corporations, and trade unions can compare information on their economic situation and prospects with those of their own country and other nations.

One can indeed use GDP for international comparisons by converting local currencies to the US$ using exchange rates (GDP current US$). To allow for fluctuations in currency value over time, caused by inflation for example, GDP could be based on a single reference point and the World Bank could provide an estimate of GDP using exchange rates for 2010. A further refinement is to adjust the GDP to allow for changes in the 'purchasing power' of currencies. The latter accommodates the issue that one US$ will buy different quantities of goods and services across the globe. As the World Bank defines it:

> PPP GDP is gross domestic product converted to international dollars using purchasing power parity rates. An international dollar has the same purchasing power over GDP as the U.S. dollar has in the United States.

PPP-adjusted GDP could also be based on current exchange rates and an exchange rate fixed to one particular year (as above). Table 34.1 provides a summary of the four indicators.

Using these four indicators of 'size' the ranking of the UK amongst the countries of the globe is shown in Figure 34.1. Also shown are the numbers of newspaper articles published each year that mention the phrases "5th largest economy" and "fifth largest economy" in relation to the UK. These data have come from the Nexis database of global media publications (www. lexisnexis.com/en-us/products/nexis.page) but specifically searching newspapers where these phrases appear in English referring to the UK. The Nexis database has been applied in a number of published studies designed to explore reporting of indicators in the media (Morse, 2013,

Table 34.1 Summary of four indicators of economic 'size'

Indicator name	Notes (as provided by the World Bank for each indicator)
GDP (constant 2010 US$)	Data are in constant 2010 U.S. dollars. Dollar figures for GDP are converted from domestic currencies using 2010 official exchange rates. For a few countries where the official exchange rate does not reflect the rate effectively applied to actual foreign exchange transactions, an alternative conversion factor is used.
GDP (current US$)	Data are in current U.S. dollars. Dollar figures for GDP are converted from domestic currencies using single year official exchange rates. For a few countries where the official exchange rate does not reflect the rate effectively applied to actual foreign exchange transactions, an alternative conversion factor is used.
GDP, PPP (constant 2011 international $)	Data are in constant 2011 international dollars.
GDP, PPP (current international $)	Data are in current international dollars. For most economies PPP figures are extrapolated from the 2011 International Comparison Program (ICP) benchmark estimates or imputed using a statistical model based on the 2011 ICP. For 47 high- and upper middle-income economies conversion factors are provided by Eurostat and the Organisation for Economic Co-operation and Development (OECD).

2014, 2016, in press). Unsurprisingly, the number of 'mentions' of the phrase surges in 2016, and is also higher than the 2010–2014 norm in 2015 when speculation over the referendum was rife and in 2017 as the UK attempts to negotiate the terms of its exit from the EU. Prior to the 2015–2017 period the terms do appear in the press, but the incidence was less than 100 articles per annum.

But does the use of the term match the reality? Well, with GDP (current US$) and GDP (constant 2010 US$) the answer seems to be 'no'. The UK tends to fluctuate between rank 6 and 7 between 2010 and 2016, although it did hit a peak of 5th in 2015 for the GDP (current US$) indicator. Nonetheless the '5th largest economy' claim that was so loudly proclaimed in 2016 is hardly convincing. But let us provide some benefit of the doubt here as such calculations are complex and say that the GDP (current US$) and GDP (constant 2010 US$) are at least in the right ballpark and the ranking based on GDP (current US$) is close to being true. The same cannot be said of the two GDP indicators adjusted for purchasing power; a commonly applied technique for adjusting GDP over many years (Officer, 1976). With these PPP-adjusted measures, the UK typically ranks between 9 and 10; some considerable distance away from the '5th largest economy' claim. It should be noted that PPP has attracted criticism from some economists (Hyrina and Serletis, 2010), but there is a logic in the sense that PPP adjustments are designed to allow for differing purchasing power across economies, and hence reduce any distortions that might arise. Yet there is little, if any, evidence to suggest that the PPP-adjustment GDPs were employed by those advocating for Brexit. Similarly, while Figure 34.1 does not include the figures if the GDP and GDP PPP are calculated on a per capita basis, then the UK drops even further in the rankings. Per capita adjustments allow for the fact that GDP may be linked to population size; the larger the population then the greater the flow of money in the

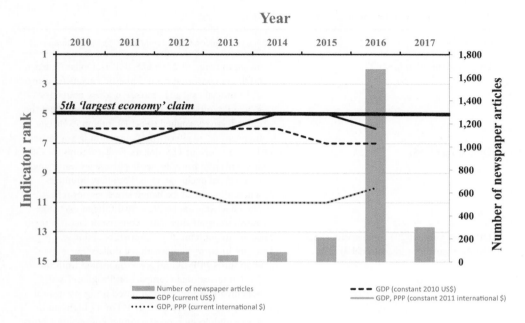

Figure 34.1 Four indicators of measuring the size of the UK economy and the rank of the UK in the global 'league table' using those measures

system. This is not always the case, of course, and can distort the rankings as countries with small populations and low corporate tax regimes can rank very high purely because companies introduce processes to ensure that a lot of money flows through them, but it is a widely used adjustment of GDP nonetheless. The HDI, for example, uses the GDP PPP adjusted on a per capita basis and the United Nations Development Programme (UNDP) has long argued in favour of that as an indicator of income, even though the HDI engineers have sought to cap high values of GDP PPP/capita in various ways to prevent a distorting effect on the index (Morse, 2014). Yet all of these adjustments were ignored by the Brexit supporters and instead the focus was on the most 'favourable' measure for their case – the GDP based on current US$. It is the case that all of the adjustments to GDP can be criticized, but then so can the GDP itself.

We as indicator developers and practitioners should not be surprised by any of this, and indeed it does have to be stressed that while we have used the Brexit 'hot house' period of intense debate to illustrate the selective used of indicators this is by no means an issue solely linked to that time and place. It goes with the 'indicator territory' and we must accept, whether we like it or not, that the indicators we develop or promote may be 'used' in ways that we did not intend or that users may be highly selective in their choices. Indicators do not have any special privileges in the 'messy' real world of decision-making where those who take the decisions are being influenced by a myriad of concerns and pressures. In a sense, we are part of that mess and are playing the same game as everyone else; maybe we just don't know it. As Rotz and Fraser have noted in Chapter (6)

> we must remain focused on understanding the conditions within which sustainability and resilience get manipulated in the interests of political-economic and social

empowerment and capital accumulation. How are these concepts deployed by different groups, and for what possible ends?

If we wish to produce an indicator that will somehow be above all of this then maybe we are chasing the end of a rainbow. If we are in the business of producing indicators to help make a difference by influencing those with power then we must expect that power to also have an impact on the uses it puts to those indicators. We cannot have it both ways. But does this mean that we have to stop trying and accept that we will always be producing and promoting 'fake' indicators; at least in the eyes of some? Well no – not at all. We live in a world where many people get their news from Twitter and Facebook. Complex events are reduced to 'tweets' of just a few hundred characters, yet these can influence the thinking of many people. At the time of writing Twitter has over 300 million 'active' users across most countries of the globe, and even Presidents of the USA are using it to get their points over directly to the public. In short, there is an appetite for communication tools that seek to present complexity in ways that busy people can interact with. Indicators and indices are trying to do the same thing and there is also an appetite for them, but as with Twitter there are dangers to such simplification. This brings us neatly into what we think the messages in the book tell us about the future of SIs?

The future of sustainability indicators

Some of the authors in this collection have made various and wide-ranging suggestions with regard to future work on SIs. The following are but a few examples we have selected to illustrate this breadth of opinion. The examples have been selected by us as they resonate with thoughts we have also had over the years.

1   More case studies on the development/use of SIs

Pintér et al. (Chapter 2) call for a "richer selection of case studies" to help create "practical and more useful guidance" regarding Sustainability Assessment and Measurement Principles (STAMP). The book has a number of 'case study' chapters which discuss the development and application of SIs; see for example Elisabeth Conrad and Louis F. Cassar's chapter (19) on experiences with the EPI in Malta and Ulla Rosenström's chapter (21) on SIs in Finland. There is certainly a need for more research of this type to allow for the identification of patterns as to what works best, or not. Case-study-based research certainly has its critics, as those of us who have tried to publish case-study-based research findings have repeatedly found to our cost, but in the case of SIs it allows us to know much about that critical interface with indicator users albeit in what can be quite context-specific spaces. The dilemma, and one that is so often espoused by paper reviewers, is that case study findings are not readily generalizable. While the latter may be true to some extent, we nonetheless agree with Pintér et al. that a case-study-based body of knowledge can allow for some patterns to emerge. What we perhaps need is a meta-analysis of SI experiences, but in order to do this we need the case studies in the public domain. This is very challenging work but also valuable.

2   Alternatives to GDP

Dahl in his chapter (3) on the 'Contributions to the Evolving Theory and Practice of Indicators of Sustainability' reiterates the need for alternative indicators to GDP and suggests material flow analysis as an integrating approach in sustainability assessment. There are echoes here with the chapter written by Costanza et al. (7) and their intriguing call for a "New Bretton Woods" to help achieve a broad consensus regarding alternative indicators to allow us to move beyond GDP and achieve "measures of what we really want and to achieve these goals". Our Brexit example above is just one illustration of the power of the GDP and not just amongst politicians. The media also had a major role to play and, of course, there is an ongoing interaction between the public, the media and the politicians with each influencing the other. While we are sympathetic to moves to raise the profile of other indicators, and the "New Bretton Woods" idea is tantalizing, these calls to explore alternatives to GDP have been with us for some years with little obvious success to date.

3   Data provision

Esty and Emerson (Chapter 5) and Esty (Chapter 31) and Hsu (Chapter 17) note the potential of indicators to help support environmental decision-making but both point to continuing problems of data limitation, even if there has been much improvement and data are no longer as scarce as they once were. We very much agree, as without an adequate availability of good quality indicators there is a likelihood that indicators may be deeply flawed and hence readily dismissed. Ulla Rosenström in her chapter makes the interesting observation about how digitalization has done little to improve the timeliness of data provision or "created new opportunities to measure sustainable development. Too much of the data is still presented on an annual basis when more real-time databases could be created". The question, of course, is what it would it take to achieve this?

4   A systems perspective

Vermeulen in Chapter 4 suggests that "we need to build indicators and index systems based on a clear guiding vision and key elements". In related vein, Rotz and Fraser (Chapter 6) call for a greater acknowledgement that "conceptual and instrumental challenges" of sustainability and resilience are deeply linked and that "indicators need to be nested in a broader analysis that helps to make sense of context-specific dynamics". Gilberto Gallopin also calls for a more integrated approach that considers linkages, synergies and antagonisms between goals and targets (and their associated SIs of course) rather than simple listings as we see with the Sustainable Development Goals (SDGs). It is hard to disagree with that or indeed his sombre conclusion that "given that linear thinking is still dominant in most institutions (including governments), the outlook is rather pessimistic, at least in the short and medium term". Herein rests a significant challenge. It is relatively easy for us to 'talk the talk' of such systems approaches to sustainability and SIs but linear thinking and desires for strict accountability over relatively short time periods can work against 'walking the talk'.

5   Top-down vs. bottom-up

A further point linked to the systems perspective is the role of SIs in helping to facilitate the development of an appreciation of what sustainability and resilience are in any particular context. Hence it is not solely a case of SIs following on from an understanding of sustainability and resilience as an operational output but SIs as a catalytic precursor to such an understanding. SIs can help ground such discussions and provide tangible representations of what is seen as relevant and important. We have often advocated such a dialectic and others in the book have also made the point. For example, Dwi Amalia Sari and colleagues in their chapter on SIs in complex, multi-functional forest landscapes suggest that "the role of criteria and indicator processes in these complex and contested situations is perhaps more to allow a structuring of the debate than to provide a set of boxes to be ticked".

However, one of the dilemmas here is what to do with the SIs that emerge out of such a dialectic? Once the SIs have allowed an 'arrival' at an understanding and have no doubt passed through a process of discussion, sieving and modification then it is possible that they may not necessarily match the SIs that have been set in a more 'top-down and one-way' process by government or others. This is certainly not to say that 'top-down and one-way' SIs are bad or irrelevant; they may well have an strong antecedence of their own and offer advantages such as cross-country and timeline comparison. Simon Joss and Yvonne Rydin in Chapter 24 address this 'bottom-up and dialectic' – 'top-down and one-way' space in the context of urban sustainability and come to understandable conclusion that:

> What constitutes an appropriate balance between the standard aspects of urban sustainability frameworks and the local variation of particular applications remains an open discussion in need of ongoing conceptual and practical exploration.

6   Aggregation of indicators

One of the fascinating aspects that emerges from the chapters is the varied views on aggregation of indicators into indices. Many of the chapters include examples where this has been done, for example with the EPI (e.g. Esty and Emerson, Chapter 5) and a derivative of the HDI called the HSDI (Bravo; Chapter 18) but there are also some stark warnings as well. As Jochen Jesinghaus passionately puts it in Chapter 26, "Aggregation is evil when it gives mediatic power to numbers that do not deserve it". We do not detect a clear consensus amongst the authors that more integration is required, and Dahl in Chapter 23 while summarizing the outcomes of a UN Commission on Sustainable Development (CSD)-led process to identify SIs reflects this by noting that "despite repeated requests from governments, reviews of progress, and the best efforts of the scientific community, no consensus emerged on highly aggregated indices". This raises an interesting dilemma. On the one hand, one of the 'givens' in the indicator world is that aggregated indices are useful tools as they help us present complexity in simple ways and this book is replete with examples. But on the other hand we all seem to know the risks involved as aggregation can 'hide' key decisions over what to aggregate and how that can in turn significantly influence the result. Indeed, the creators of the HDI say that they have resisted major changes to the index for that very reason and go to great lengths to present 'standardized' (in methodological terms) versions of the HDI to allow for time-series comparisons. But it seems that the experts have yet to arrive at a clear consensus.

What we do we think about the future of SIs as editors? Well as we have already said we know that we are in a fight, and we recognize the reality that interests will always make selective and distorted use of indicators. That is the price we pay for being in the indicator business. So, what we would like to see is a greater emphasis in research on the uses to which SIs are put and how that information can feed back into the development and presentation of SIs. As Giangiacomo Bravo succinctly puts it in Chapter 18:

> Any index inevitably is the product of a number of more or less arbitrary choices (not only scientific ones, since politics often plays a major role).

There is no magic bullet or one-size-fits-all here; no SI can ever be made immune to distortion and we need to be aware of our own biases; a point echoed by Joachim H. Spangenberg in his chapter:

> Indicator users should be aware of the limitations each indicator, index or indicator system has, partly from the method of calculation, but also from the often-hidden assumptions inherent to the world views from which they have been derived. Practitioners should choose and combine the indicators they use carefully, being fully aware of these biases and their impacts on both the measurement and the messages derived from it, implicitly or explicitly.

But that should not dissuade us for further development of SIs and seeking new ways for presenting them to a defined group (or groups) of consumer(s). We just need to be smarter about this and have a better sense who our consumers are, what they are looking for and how we can best help. To date, SI development has been almost entirely 'creator-led' with little input from consumers of those SIs. That balance needs to shift so that we as creators move towards a model of co-creation with the voices of SI consumers being part of the process. This is not a new call, of course, and we amongst many others have been saying it for years, including Almássy and Pintér in their chapter (13) in this book, but we still feel that more progress is required. As Ulla Rosenström has noted in her chapter (21):

> good indicators are of little influence and importance if they are not used in any way. Although use does not guarantee the desired influence, aiming at use is well argued for. Hence efforts to create opportunities for use and disseminating information remain crucial.

The 'Indicator Policy Factsheets' proposed by Svatava Janoušková and colleagues in Chapter 30 are one tangible suggestion to "help SI users (most often decision- and policymakers) choose and use the most appropriate indicators for assessing particular sustainability issues". But maybe there is a deeper issue at core. Maybe the indicator community (along with many other areas of rationalism) were labouring under a misapprehension that we are – as Steven Pinker suggested in his opus –*The Better Angels of our Nature* (Pinker, 2011) – living in a more rational world. A world where instinctive and knee-jerk reactions are beginning to fade out in the on-rush of rational and objective decision-making. Of course, this has been a dream for time out of mind. Since Plato's 'Philosopher Kings' through to Saint Simon and Auguste Comte's concepts of a new social doctrine based on science and today's algorithmic governance by global data corps like Facebook, humankind has sought what we may consider to be an illusion of a rational world. A world governed by clear data, uncontestable facts and wise administration. To some extent the whole SI debate might be seen as a subset of this project – a project to save human beings from their instinctive and irrational selves.

Sadly, this does not seem to be working terribly well. Plato's *Republic* remains a paper dream only, Saint Simon and Comte's technocracy could not dispel the terror of the French Revolution and the power of global algorithms raise as much *1984* and *Brave New World* angst as they do hopes for a better world. Indeed, the total transparency which Facebook might argue is provoking, is mimicked and played to horrific levels in David Eggers book: The Circle and appears only as a nightmare of algorithm-led social engineering. Knee-jerk reactions, the denial of evidence-based 'facts' with disdain, the assumption of subjective 'truth' and the trust in instinct seems to be prevalent and has been argued to lead to more terror, fear and even an amplification of fear based on compounding cycles of unreasonable social fear (for a fuller analyis of this see Bell, 2017).

The experiences of the authors of this book with the complexity of the indicator/indices fields, the shortcomings of any statistical means to address complex truths, the uneven and evolving nature of the field and the issues of objectivity and subjectivity remain as ongoing tactical issues, logistic complexities set against a much more troubling background – the human proclivity to the irrational and the dupes of the sellers of snake oil.

Kahneman suggested that our instincts lead us astray and make us fear the wrong thing. The sellers of snake oil and the charlatans of politics continue to make mass movements out of bias and prejudice. Young men and women continue to be swept up in the suicidal dreams of death cults – reason often seems to be more of an aspiration than a working reality.

It is into this malaise that this book tries to make its modest contribution.

Our book bears witness to the long, hard and arduous task of understanding. Understanding how human beings interact with social, technical and environmental issues, how the psychology of the human attempts to measure the immeasurable and make sense of the world so that in future there will be a world to make sense of.

The pages of this book are a testimony to the noble attempt at the measurement of the immeasurable. They are a step towards sustainability, resilience and what we have called "saving the human project" in the sub-title of another book (Bell and Morse, 2012). This book is a retrospective, reviewing progress made so far in this noble cause. Great progress has been made. Hosts of indicators and indices have been constructed to try and influence people with power (including the public) to do the 'right thing', important second order work in terms of reflection on the formulation of indicators by experts and communities has been completed, the strategic, tactical and operational value of indicators has been begun and early forms of assessment have been mulled over. We are not at the end of the sustainable indicator process but we may be at the end of the beginning.

References

Bell, S. (2017). *Formations of Terror*. London: Cambridge Scholars Publishing.

Bell, S. and Morse, S. (2012). *Resilient Participation: Saving the Human Project?* London: Earthscan.

Coyle, D. (2014). *GDP: A Brief but Affectionate History*. Princeton and Oxford: Princeton University Press.

Hyrina, Y. and Serletis, A. (2010). Purchasing power parity over a century. *Journal of Economic Studies*, 37(1), 117–144.

Morse, S. (2004). *Indices and Indicators in Development: An Unhealthy Obsession with Numbers*. London: Earthscan.

Morse, S. (2013). Out of sight, out of mind: Reporting of three indices in the UK national press between 1990 and 2009. *Sustainable Development*, 21(4), 242–259.

Morse, S. (2014). Stirring the pot: Influence of changes in methodology of the Human Development Index on reporting by the press. *Ecological Indicators*, 45, 245–254.

Morse, S. (2016). Measuring the success of sustainable development indices in terms of reporting by the global press. *Social Indicators Research*, 125, 359–375.

Morse, S. (2017). Focussing on the extremes of good and bad: Media reporting of countries ranked via index-based league tables. *Social Indicators Research*, 21 August, 1–22.

Officer, L. (1976). The purchasing power parity theory of exchange rates: A review article. *International Monetary Fund Staff Papers*, 23, 1–60.

Pinker, S. (2011). *The Better Angels of Our Nature: A History of Violence and Humanity*. London: Penguin.

Steffen, W., Richardson, K., Rockström, J., Cornell, S. E., Fetzer, I., Bennett, E. M., Biggs, R., Carpenter, S. R., de Vries, W., de Wit, C. A., Folke, C., Gerten, D., Heinke, J., Mace, G. M., Persson, L. M., Ramanathan, V., Reyers, B., and Sorlin, S. (2015). Planetary boundaries: Guiding human development on a changing planet. *Science*, 347(6223).

INDEX

Page numbers in *italics* indicate figures and in **bold** indicate tables on the corresponding pages.

academic disciplines 60
accountability **68**
accounting *see* green accounting
active leadership 32
adequate scope, STAMP 29
Adger, Neil 106
adjusted net savings (ANS) 149, 484–487, **486–489**
Adriaanse, Albert 43, 349, 354, 392
Africa Capacity Indicators **208**, 213, **214**, 217, 218
African smallholder farming: aggregation of results in 437–444, *438–443*; concluding remarks on 444–446, *445–446*; developing an indicator framework for 429–437, **432–433**, *436*; introduction to 427–428; *see also* sustainable agricultural intensification (SAI)
AfricaRISING project 430, 454, 467–471, *469–470*
Agenda 21, 125, 151; indicators agenda 348; inter-agency coordination 349–350; introduction to 347–348; principal stakeholders 348–349; System of integrated Environmental and Economic Accounting (SEEA) 237
aggregation: dashboard of sustainability 392–405; of sustainability indicators, future 553–555; and weighting of environmental indices 217
agriculture: African smallholder farming 427–437; data on women in 436; in Malta 296; in Ontario, unsustainable systems of 107–111, **109–110**
air quality in Malta **301**, 302
Albo, Y. 218
Allan, T. 178, 181
Almassy, D. 494
Alves, I. 508–509, 511, 517

Anderies, J. M. 106
Anders, Gunther 133
Anthropocene 36
Araral, E. 215
Arnstein, Sherry 192, **193**
Arts, J. 383
ASEM Eco-Innovation Index 206, **209**
Asia Water Governance Index **207**, **214**, 215–218, 220
AtKisson, Alan 359
Australian Treasury 27
Available Water Remaining (AWARE) index 180
avoidance costs 394–395, *395*

Bakkes, Jan 43, 349
Balaton Group 333
Balint, P. J. 422
Barbados Conference of Small Island Developing States 47
Barnett, G. B. 384
Barroso, José Manuel, 205
Bartelmus, Peter, 43, 45, 349, 354
Bartram, J. 180
"basket of baskets" approach 95
Bauman, Zygmunt 126
Beeson, M. 268
Bell, Simon 1, 134, 195, 380, 386, 432, 483, 494
Bellagio Principles 6, 22, 25, 26; *see also* sustainable development (SD)
Bellagio Sustainability Assessment and Measurement Principles (BellagioSTAMP) 6, 21–37, 218, 359, 544, 551
benchmarking and best practices using performance measurement 499–500

Berry, David 359

Bertelsmann Sustainable Governance Indicators **209**

Better Angels of our Nature, The 554

Big Data 495

binary coding 128–131, **129**

biocapacity 246, 248–249, 286, 526–527, 531

biodiversity: and habitats in Malta 299–300; indicator systems 151

Biosphere Eco-City Programme 369

Birdlife International 409

bird's-eye view of indicators 543–546

Blesh, J. 111

"blue book" 45

Blueprint for Survival 124

Bockstaller, C. 507

Bonanno, G. 300

Börhringer, C. 304

Bosch, P. R. 231–232

Bossel framework 333–334

Boulay, A. M. 180

boundary work in urban sustainability 371

Bourdeau, Philippe 354

Brave New World 554

BREEAM Communities 9, 156, 167, 170, 371

Bretton Woods Conference 118, 121

Brexit 547–551, *550*

broad participation, STAMP 32

Brooks, D. 180

Brown, Katrina 106

Brundtland Report 124, 146, 156, 176

Buhler, U. 199

Building Research Establishment (BRE) 167

built environments: certification schemes for sustainable buildings and 167–171, **168–169**; conclusions on 171–174, *172–173*; sustainability indicators for the 158–167, *159–160*, *161*, **162–163**, *165–166*

Bunge, M. 480

Caeiro, S. 509, 511, 517

"Cake Share Model" 396–397, *397*

Canadian Index of Wellbeing 27

Canadian Sustainability Indicators Network (CSIN) 26

Canadian Water Sustainability Index **207**

cannibals with forks 73

Capacity Building Index 43

capital approaches 69–70

Caribbean, the *341*, 341–344, **342–343**

Carson, Rachel 133

CASBEE-UD certification 171

Center for International Earth Science Information Network (CIESIN) 48, 94

certification schemes: conclusions on 171–174, *172–173*; introduction to 157; measuring sustainability and 157–158; sustainability

indicators for the built environment 158–167, *159–160*, *161*, **162–163**, *165–166*; for sustainable buildings and built environment 167–171, **168–169**; for urban sustainability 368–369

CGSDI *see* Consultative Group on Sustainable Development Indicators (CGSDI)

Chambers, Robert 193

Checkland, Peter 199–200

Chenoweth, J. 178, 180, 183

Chidiak, Martina 329

China: Ecological Civilization plan 521; Environmental Performance Index (EPI) in 269–272, *272*, 279–281; environmental performance legitimacy in 268; local and regional government indicator sets 310–311; Ministry of Environmental Protection (MEP) 268, 270

Chinese Academy for Environmental Planning (CAEP) 271

Christianson, K. 335

Circle, The 554

City Biodiversity Index **207**, 366, 367

City Performance Tool 368

civic science 25

civil society 59; initiatives 26

climate and energy in Malta 300

Climate Change Adaptation Report 535n6

climate change and Ecological Footprint 252–253

Climate Change Performance Index 206, **207**

Climate Competitiveness Index (Climate Accountability Subindex) **208**

Climate Laws, Institutions and Measures Index (CLIMI) **208**, 213, 214, **214**, 216, 217, 220

Climate Positive Development Program 366, 369, 375

Cloquell-Ballester, V. A. 508

Closing Circle, The 124

CO_2 emissions 495–496; Ecological Footprint and 252

Commission on Sustainable Development (CSD) 44, 48, 62, 309, 311–317, **313**; complementary processes 358–359; indicators programme 354–358; indicators work programme preparation 350–354, **351–353**; inter-agency coordination 349–350; introduction to 347–348; on systemic frameworks 333; wider outreach 359–360

Commission on the Measurement of Economic Performance and Social Progress 21

Community Capital Tool 365, 369

community engagement in urban sustainability 371–372

Community Indicators Consortium (CIC) 26

comparative analysis enhanced by performance measurement 497

composite indicators (indices) 10

composite indices 435, 441–444

conceptual framework 30
Conference of European Statisticians Recommendations on Measuring Sustainable Development 317
Congress for New Urbanism (CNU) 170
Conrad, C. C. 384
Conrad, C. T. 384
Conservation International 409
Consultative Expert Group Meeting on Environmental and Sustainable Development Indicators 43
Consultative Group on Sustainable Development Indicators (CGSDI) 13, 43, 49–50, 398–401, *399–400*
content analysis of UN SDGS *91–92*
continuity and capacity STAMP 33
Cook, J. 385
Cooke, B. 195
cost benefit analysis (CBA) **159**
Costanza, R. 119
cost-benefit analysis 35
costs: avoidance 394–395, *395*; damage *395*, 395–398
Coutinho, V. 384
crucial choices 61
cultural politics 3
Cyrus the Younger 193

da Costa Pereira, C. 479
Dahl, Arthur Lyon 42, 43, 354, 402
Daly, Herman 119, 121, 143, 521
damage costs *395*, 395–398
Danielsen, F. 384
Danish Cooperation for Environment and Development (DANCED) 273
Daoust, T. 384
Dasgupta, P. S. 225
dashboard of sustainability 158, 392–394, *393*; aggregation as evil and 404–405; avoidance costs in 394–395, *395*; Consultative Group on Sustainable Development Indicators (CGSDI) and, 398–401, *399–400*; damage costs in *395*, 395–398; notes on the methodology in, *401*, 401–404, *403–404*
data collection 3; and indicator systems 33
data interpretation 3
data manipulation **67**
data specification **67**
data-based decision making 23; *see also* measurement, performance
data-driven policymaking 93
Davies, William 2, 3–4
Davis, K. E. 267
Dawes, Robyn 498
DDT 436
de Boer, B. 231–232
de Groot, R. S. 430–431
de Jouvenel, Bertrad 133

de Kruijf, H. A. M. 315
De Olde, E. M. 435
Dellink, R. 232
Delors, Jacques 392
demarcation between causes and impacts 61
democracy 24
Depardieu, Gérard 250–251
design and planning frameworks for urban sustainability 369–370
Deurer, M. 183
development gap 63
Diazabakana, A. 455
Digital Age 495
discovery metadata 25
divergence, three processes of 60
Division for Sustainable Development (DSD) 44
Döll, P. 179
Dong Zhanfeng 272
Dopazo, Hernan 329
Dow Jones Sustainable Development Index 247–248
DPSIR Framework 481–483
Dragoni, M. 479
driver-pressure-state-impact-response model 69
driving force-pressure-state-impact-response (DPSIR) 333
driving-force/state-response (DSR) framework 6, 44–45
Dunning, C. 314
Durkheim, Emile 126

Earthwatch 13; CSD indicators programme and 354–358; indicators agenda 348; inter-agency coordination 349–350; introduction to 347–348; principal stakeholders 348–349
EC JRC Framework 77
ECLAC *see* Economic Commission for Latin America and the Caribbean (ECLAC)
Eco Principle: Ecology and Economics in Symbiosis, The 359
Eco^2 Cities 366, 369–370
Ecological Communication 136
Ecological Footprint (EF) 11, 22, 135–136, 151, 158, **159**, 286; accounting 1; accounting principles in 246–247; addressing all demands on nature, from carbon emissions to food and fibres 244–246; biased against international trade 529; carbon portion exaggeration 529–530; climate change and 252–253; common questions and misconceptions 525–532; comparison of approaches to **258–260**; conclusions on 253–254, 535; data for National Footprint Accounts 251–252; equivalence factors 527–529; focus on biocapacity 526; function and measurement of 246–251, *249*; fundamental sources and description for data used within National

Footprint Accounts **261–263**; of Gérard
Depardieu 250–251; introduction to 521;
link between sustainable development and
522–525, *524*; measuring biocapacity in global
hectares 526–527; nuclear energy and 530–531;
Planetary Boundaries and 253, 543; providing
a pollution measure 529; research arguments
that strengthen accounting and development
of 532–535; scales and policy relevance of
521–522; terminology 525
Ecological Indicators 360
Economic Commission for Latin America and the
Caribbean (ECLAC) 329, 357; *see also* socio-
ecological system (SES)
economic growth 10
economic stability 75
economics, subject of 224
ecosystem condition 28
Ecosystem Services (ES) 158, **159**
ecosystem vitality in Malta 296–300, **297**
effective communications STAMP 31–32
efficiency and performance measurement 501
Eggers, David 554
Ellul, Jacques 133
Emerson, John W. 93
employment 10
end-outcome 64
Energy Trilemma Index **208**
enset production 467–471, *469–470*
Environment Impact Assessments (EIAs) 167
environment/social/governance (ESG) metrics
503
Environmental Capital Index 43
Environmental decision-making 16
Environmental Democracy Index **209**, 214, **215**,
220
environmental functions 10, 225–226
environmental governance indicators and indices
204; analysis of 212–220; brief overview of *205*,
205–206; coherence and soundness of 216–218;
conclusions on 220–221; index structure
and indicator selection 213–216, **214–215**;
presentation and application 218–220, *219*;
review of 206–212, **207–209**, *210–211*;
sensitivity and correlation analysis 217–218;
theoretical frameworks 213; weighting and
aggregation 217
environmental health in Malta 300–302, **301**
Environmental Impact Assessment (EIA) 34
environmental indicators 5
environmental management (EM) 4
Environmental Performance Index (EPI) 6, 7, 11,
22, 48–49, 93–95, *98*, 205–206, 517, 544; 2002
reconceptualization 96–99; in China 269–272,
272, 279–281; compared to the HDSI 286,
288, 290–291; creating the index 95–96;
creation of 269; discussion 279–281; emerging

policy conclusions 96; framework 2016, *270*;
introduction to 267–269, 294–295, *295*; in
Malaysia 273–275, 279–281; in Malta 295–305;
member countries 269; as proximity-to-target
indicator 294–295, *295*; results 99–100; in Viet
Nam 275–281, *278*
Environmental Policy Stringency Index **209**, 214,
215, 216, 218, 220
Environmental Sustainability Index (ESI) 7, 48, 94,
207, 210, 212, 247
Environmental Sustainability National Income
indicator (eSNI): concept of environmental
functions and 225–226; defined 231; intent of
232–233; subject of economics and 224; theory
of and necessary statistics for 232; valuation in
226–231, *228*, *230*
environmental sustainability-related policy
initiatives 10
environmental vulnerability index (EVI) 6,
47–48, 49
environmental-economic accounting 10
environmentally adjusted net domestic product
(EDP) 237–239, *239*
environmentally sustainability national income
(eSNI) 10
environment-related policy mechanisms 10
EPI *see* Environmental Performance
Index (EPI); environmental performance
index (EPI)
epistemology 143
Equity index in water and sanitation **208**
equity 63
equivalence factors, Ecological Footprint (EF)
527–529
ESI *see* environmental sustainability index (ESI)
Espeland, W. E. 131
essential considerations, STAMP 27–29
Estrella, M. 381
Esty, Daniel C. 93
Ethiopia, ex ante SAI assessment with enset in
467–471, *469–470*
European Common Indicators (ECIs) **160**,
160–161, 162
European Environment Agency (EEA) 47, 393,
477
European Statistical Office 480
Eurostat 316, 392
EVI *see* environmental vulnerability index (EVI)
evidence-based decision-making 33
evidence-based policy-making 23
evidence-informed practice 24
expert-biased processes 9
extractive practices of human societies 62

fake indicators 547–551, **549**, *550*
Falkenmark water scarcity index 177, 184
Falkenmark, M. 177

Federal Land Development Authority (FELDA) Malaysia 273
Federal Trade Commission, U. S. 503
Findicator service 13
Finland, sustainable development indicators in: conclusions on **326**, 326–328; four phases of development of 322–326; introduction to 321–322
Fischer-Kowalski, M. 150–151, 527
fisheries in Malta 298–299
Florin, M. J. 430–432
Food and Agriculture Organization (FAO) 177
forest landscapes management: forest area data and 288; in Indonesia 407–423; in Malta 298
Forest, Land and REDD+ Governance Index **208**, 214, 215, **215**, 218, 220
Forest Stewardship Council (FSC) 408
formal meta-evaluation 511
four pillar model 44
Framework for Indicators of Sustainable Development (FISD) 43
Framework for the Development of Environment Statistics (FDES) 43
Framework for the Development of Environmental Statistics (FDES) 332
Frewer, L. 199
Fukushima nuclear accident, Japan 531
future of sustainability indicators 551–555

Gallopin, Gilberto 43, 329, 335, 359
Gaventa, J. 381
Gaviglio, A. 455
Genuine Progress Index (GPI) 22
Genuine Progress Indicator (GPI) 236
Genuine Savings 149
GEOCities initiatives 26
Geographic Information Systems (GIS) 46
Gho, Carlos 329
Gibson, C. E. 517
Gibson, R. B. 381
Giddens, Anthony 126
Girardin, P. 507
Global Agro-Ecological Zones (GAEZ) 528
Global Environment Facility (GEF) benefits index for biodiversity 288
Global Environment Outlook (GEO) 35
Global Environmental Monitoring System (GEMS) 348
Global Environmental Vulnerability Indicators 48
Global Footprint Network 253, 286, 522, 525, 528–529, 532, 535n5; research arguments 532–535
global hectares 248, 250, 526–527
global initiatives for societal impact characterization *80*
Global Innovation Index 216

Global Oceans Commission 52
Global Reporting Initiative (GRI) 7, 26
Global Reporting Initiatives (GRI) 382
Global Resource Information Database (GRID) 348
global stakeholder representation organizations 61
Global Trade Analysis Project (GTAP) 534
global water resources 9
goal-oriented concept 61
goal-oriented indicators 45
Godfray, H. C. J. 455
Goodland, R. 225
Gouveia, C. 383–384, 385
Gove, Michael 2
Great Depression 117
green accounting 235, *236*; further work on 241; GDP bashing and 236–237; as practical step toward redesigning the economy 237–240, *238–240*; System of integrated Environmental and Economic Accounting (SEEA) 237, *238*, 239
Green City Index **161**, *161*, 206, **208**, 210
Green City Index 367–368
Green Communities 369
Green Star South Africa (GSSA) framework 369
Greenpeace 393
gross domestic product (GDP) 10, 23
Gross Domestic Product (GDP) 235; aggregation and 404–405; alternatives to 551–552; dashboard of sustainability and 392–405; defined 547–548; fake indicators and 547–550; green accounting and bashing of 236–237; in history of effort to create better indicators 117–122; indicator relevance and 484–487, **486–489**; indicators as reduction of complexity and 133–134; modificationists and 148, 150; way forward with measures using 120–122
Gross National Happiness Index 316–317
Gross National Product (GNP) 122n1, 125
Guide for Sustainable Intensification Indicator Assessment Framework 456
guiding vision, STAMP 27

Haberl, H. 527
Habermas, Jürgen 126
Hai, L. T. 310
Half-Earth 245
Hall, Jon 21
Halvorsen, K. E. 198
Hammond, Allen 43, 349, 354, 359
Hardi, Peter 21, 44, 359
Hardin, Garrett 396
Hawkins, N. 274
Heal, G. M. 225
health impacts in Malta 300–301, **301**
Hennipman, P. 224
Herath, I. 182–183

Hickey, S. 195
hierarchical approach of principles, criteria, and indicators 430–432, **432–433**
Higg Index 517
Hilchey, K. G. 384
Hoekstra, A. Y. 181–182, 183
Hoekstra, R. 311, 314
Holden, M. 164
Honduras *341*, 341–344, **342–343**
Hotkes, M. W. 232
Howard, G. 180
HQE²R certification scheme 170
Hsieh, Y. J. 517
Hsu, A. 277, 499
Huang, C. 308–309, 310, 318
Hueting, R. 230, 231–232
Huisingh, D. 382
Human Development Index (HDI) 11, 22, 284, 523, 553; water scarcity and 178
Human Development Report HDSI 285–286
human mind 4
Human Sustainable Development Index (HSDI) 11, 151, 206, 553; comparison with other indicators 286–291, *287–290*; conclusion on 291–292; definition of 284–285; *Human Development Report* 2015, 285–286; introduction to 284; relation with the environmental footprint 289–290, *290*; relation with the EPI 286, 290–291
Human Welfare Index 43
human wellbeing 28
Hung, P. Q. 181–182
Hunsberger, C. A. 381

Illich, Ivan 133
impact assessment procedure 34
impact assessments or appraisals 34
impact categories approach 79
ImPACT 69–70
inclusive political institutions 75
income distribution 10
indicator business 1–2; development 3
indicator community 3, 4
indicator construction and application *68*
indicator user factsheet 16
indicator-based sustainability assessments in agriculture 23
indicators of sustainability 42; CSD work programme 44–45; integration 47; CGSDI 49–50; EPI 48–49; ESI 48; EVI 47–48; new directions 50–51; research dimension 45–47; starting 42–44; UN 2030 Agenda 51–53
Indicators of Sustainability: Reliable Tools for Decision Making 360
Indicators of Sustainable Development: Guidelines and Methodologies 358

Indonesia, forest management in: audit criteria in 415–416; Audit Design Matrix (ISSAI) 412–413, *413*; audit objectives in 413–415, *414*; case of integrated forest management units in 408–409; conclusions on 423; methods and evidence in conducting landscape audits 416–422, **417–421**; potential ways forward in 409–412, *412*
Industrial Efficiency Index 43
Industrial Revolution, 4th 495
informal meta-evaluation 511
information and communications technology (ICT) 25
Integrated Environmental Assessments (IEAs) 35
Inter-Agency Committee on Sustainable Development (IACSD) 349–350
Interagency working group, U. S. 315
Intergenerational Equity Index 43
intermediate outcomes 64
internalities 74
International Bank for Reconstruction and Development (IBRD) 118
International Council for Science (ICSU) 52
International Council of Scientific Unions (ICSU) 45
International Development Research Centre (IDRC) 43
International Human Dimensions Programme on Global Environmental Change (IHDP) 47, 477
International Institute for Information Design (IIID) 32
International Institute for Sustainable Development (IISD) 22, 46, 79, 359, 398
International Monetary Fund (IMF) 118, 213
International Panel on Climate Change (IPCC) 252
International Social Science Council (ISSC) 52
International Sustainability Indicator Network (ISIN) 26
International Union for Conservation of Nature (IUCN) 44
International Union for the Conservation of Nature (IUCN) 309
IPAT 69–70
Iribarnegaray, M. A. 216

Japan 531; CASBEE-UD certification 171
Jeon, S. M. 517
Jesinghaus, Jochen 44, 359, 360
Jochem, P. E. P. 304
Joint Research Centre of the European Commission 48, 99, 212, 216

Kahneman, Daniel 4, 555
Kalow, J. 314
Key Performance Indicators (KPIs) 268
knowledge utilization literature 31

Kobus, H. 198
Kolb, D. 193, 464
Kolb's learning cycle 464
Kothari, U. 195
Krank, S. 516
Kurtz, J. 511
Kuznets, Simon 119, 404

labour conditions 10
ladder of participation 192
Latin America *341*, 341–344, **342–343**
leadership: active 32; strong 32; weak 32
Lee, Y. 308–309, 310, 318
LEED environments 9, 156; LEED NC 369;
   LEED ND 170, 369
leisure time 10
Leverington, F. 299
liberalism 4
Life Cycle Assessment (LCA) 7, 76, **159**, 183–184
life cycle costing 74
Life Cycle Sustainability Assessment (LCSA) 7
Limits to Growth, The 50, 124, 521
"linked socioecological" systems 24
Living Planet Index (LPI) 47, 206
Living Planet Reports 253
logic model concepts **71–72**
logic models 65
long-term impact **68**
Low-carbon competitiveness Index **207**
Lozano, R. 382
Luhmann, Niklas 125–133, **129**, 135; Ecological
   Footprint and 135–136
L'vovich, M. I. 177
Lyytimäki, J. 508

Malaysia: Environmental Performance Index
   (EPI) in 273–275, 279–281; environmental
   performance legitimacy in 268
Malta 295–296; discussion and conclusions on
   303–305; ecosystem vitality in 296–300, **297**;
   environmental health in 300–302, **301**; EPI
   results in 296–302, **297, 301**; public assessment
   of environmental performance in 302–303, **303**
Manuel-Navarrete, David 329
Marinus, W. 432, 435
market arena 60
market-based transactions 25
marketplaces 25
Marques, A. S. 382
Martinuzzi, André, 21
Marx, Karl 126
Mascarenhas, A. 381
Material Flow Analysis (MFA) 150
Material intensity per unit of service (MIPS) **159**
McCulla, S. H. 118
Meadows, Donella 44, 354, 359
Measham, T. G. 384

measurement, performance 494; benchmarking
   and best practices using, 499–500; bumps in
   the road in 503; enhancing comparative analysis
   497; finding points of leverage 498; greater
   efficiency using 501; improved 498–499;
   meta-evaluation 518; new challenges, new
   possibilities in 495; path forward in 504; in
   policy efficiency and regulatory reform 502;
   reducing uncertainty 495–497
Measuring Sustainable Development 317
Melo, J. J. 508–509, 511, 517
Mercator Research Institute on Global Commons
   and Climate Change 245
Mercer Quality of Life Ranking 248
MESMIS approach 430, 460, 471
meta-evaluation of sustainability indicators 16;
   application examples overview in **515–516**,
   515–517; conceptual meta-performance
   evaluation framework 508–511, *509–510*;
   final remarks on 518; introduction to 507–508;
   key good-practice factors and indicators for
   511–514, **512–514**
metrics 94
Millennium Development Goals (MDGs) 181,
   235, 523
modern society as unsustainable 126–128
modificationists: indices and indicators systems of
   148–150; transformationists versus, 143–147,
   145
Modinger, J. 198
Modvar, Cecilie 329
Moeller, Hans-Georg 126
Moffatt, I. 527
Mohan, G. 195
Mol, A. P. J. 279
Moldan, Bedrich 44, 349, 354, 358–359, 360
Molden, D. 178
Monet stock-flow model 334–335
monitoring phase in stakeholder-driven initiatives
   383–385
monitoring systems 35
Moreno Pires, S. 310
Moriguchi, Yuchi 359
Morse, Stephen 1, 134, 380, 386, 432, 483, 494
Multi Criteria Analyses (MCA) 150
multi-criteria analysis 35
"multi-method" approaches 23
Multi-Regional Input-Output (MRIO) 253, 534
multi-scale integrated assessment 35
Mumford, Lewis 133
Murayama, A. 167
Myhre O. 517

N2Africa project 428–429; *see also* African
   smallholder farming
Najam, Adil 359
National Environmental Policy Act (NEPA) 34

National Footprint Accounts 247, 251–252; fundamental sources and description for data used within **261–263**
national governments, indicators sets for 314–317
national income 10
Natural Carbon Accounting (NCA) 158
Natural Resources Defence Council (NRDC) 170
Nature Conservancy 409
neoliberal doctrines of economy 111
Net International Product 43
Net Primary Productivity (NPP) 527
Net Resource Product 43
New Urban Agenda 364–365
Newig, J. 198
Niemeijer, D. 430–431
non-governmental organizations (NGOs) 93
non-human-made physical surroundings 10
Nooteboom S. 383
nuclear energy 530–531
Nunes, L. M. 382

O'Connor, John 44, 349, 359
One Planet Living Framework 365, 369, 375
Ontario agri-food context 107–111, **109–110**
Organisation for Economic Co-operation and Development (OECD) 204, 323, 392, 509, 522–523; environmental indices and 210, 212, 216; green growth strategy of 240
Ortiz, Laura 329
Our Common Future 309, 315–316
outreach **68**
Owens, S. 158

Pareto, Vilfredo 126
Paris Climate Agreement 244, 521, 530
Parkin, S. 157
Parsons, Talcott 126
participation, origins of 193–196, *195*
participatory action research processes (PAR) 464–467, *465*
participatory approaches for development and evaluation of sustainability indictors: conclusions and call to arms for 201–202; examples of 196–198; getting to the stakeholder in 190–192, *191*, **193**; how's of participation in 198–199; introduction to 188–189; origins of participation and 193–196, *195*; stakeholders and 189–190; visualisation in 199–200, *200*
Participatory Learning and Action (PLA) 193–196; how's of participation in 198–199; visualisation in 199–200, *200*
Participatory Rural Appraisal (PRA) 193–196; how's of participation in 198–199; visualisation in 199–200, *200*
partnership facilitation in urban sustainability 372–373
Pasi, G. 479

Pastor, A.V. 179
Pathways Model of Nutrition Sensitive Agriculture 461, *462*
Pedzisa, T. 198
people, planet, profit (PPP) 73
performance assessment framework for urban sustainability 367–368, **368**
performance evaluation, meta- *see* meta-evaluation
performance legitimacy 268
performance measurement *see* measurement, performance
Perrini, E. 383
Pfister, S. 182
pilot environmental sustainability index 95
Pinker, Steven 554
Pintér, L. 310, 494
Pintér, László, 21, 44
Pittelkow, C. M. 454–455
Planetary Boundaries, Ecological Footprint (EF) and 253, 543
'planet'-related impacts 76
Plato 554
pluralist 75
policy efficiency and performance measurement 502
policy goals 62, 64
policy-oriented indices 43
policy outputs 64
political arena 60
political institutions 75
Population Bomb, The 124
Porritt, Jonathon 495
post-normal science 24
post-statistical society 4
post truth: definition 1–2; phenomenon 4; politics 2; Weltanschauung 2
poverty 63
pressure/state/response (PSR) approach 43
Pressure-State-Response (PSR) framework 333
pressure-state-response model 69
problem of vagueness 60
process indicators 15
Programme for the Harmonisation of Forest Certification (PEFC) 408
PROIntensAfrica 432
Project ESALC (Evaluation of the Sustainability of Latin America and the Caribbean) 329–330
"proximity-to-target" methodology 7
public participation 32

Quality Criteria of Transdisciplinary Research guide 34

Rametsteiner, E. 480
Ramos, T. B. 382, 508–509, 511, 517, 518
Rapid Rural Appraisal (RRA) 193–196; how's of participation in 198–199; visualisation in 199–200, *200*

Raskin, P. 178, 179
Raw Material Consumption (RMC) 150
Rawls, J. 309, 315, 317, 318
ReCiPe2016 approach 77
reduction of complexity, indicators as 133–136
Reference Framework for Sustainable Cities (RFSC) 161, 162, **162**
regulatory reform and performance measurement 502
Reijnders, L. 231
relevance: defining 478–479; discussion and conclusion on 487–491; GDP and ANS and 484–487, **486–487**, **488–489**; indicator user factsheets and 483–487, **486–487**; introduction to 477–478; thematic and indicator 481–483, **483**; types of 479–481
Report by the Commission on the Measurement of Economic Performance and Social Progress 317
Republic 554
resilience 7; aligning SIs and 106–107; conclusions on 112–113; introduction to 103–104; limits of 112; scholarship on 105–106; sustainability indicators and 104–107; in unsustainable systems in Ontario 107–111, **109–110**
resilience-sustainability analysis 8
Resilient Participation: Saving the Human Project? 188
Resource Governance Index **208**, **215**, 217, *219*, 220
Revenga, C. 179
Revi, Aromar 354
Review of World Water Resources by Country 177
Ridoutt, B. G. 182
Rijksinstituut voor Volksgezondheid en Milieu (RIVM) 43, 349, 392
Rio Earth Summit 9, 42
Robleto, María Luisa 329
robustness of assessment and endorsement in urban sustainability 373
Rockefeller Foundation's Bellagio Center 22
Rogge, N. 294
Ronner, E. 432, 435
Roosevelt, Franklin D. 117
Rosenström, U. 478, 508
rough consensus in global scholarly practices *83*
rough consensus, substantiating 59–61; confusions 73–76; environmental issues 76–78; goal definition and indicator development 65–69; linking problems with practices 69–73; SDGs 81–84; social issues and societal issues 78–81; sustainable development 62–64
Rowe, J. 199
rules for categorization 61

SAI *see* sustainable agricultural intensification (SAI)
Saisana, M. 217
Saltelli, A. 217

Sandker, M. 415
Sanz, F. S. 382
Sarkar, S. 415
Sauder, M. 131
Sayer, J. 409, 415, 423
Schoenaker, N. 318
Schon, Donald 193
Schumacher, Fritz 133
Schuschny, Andrés 329
Schut, M. 431
Scientific Committee on Problems of the Environment (SCOPE) 45, 358–359, 359–360; projects 13, 46, 47
Scientific Workshop on Indicators of Sustainable Development 46
SCOPE/UNEP/IHDP/EEA Assessment of Sustainability Indicators (ASI) 47
Scriven, M. 507
Searcy, C. 517
Seckler, D. 177
SEEA *see* System of integrated Environmental and Economic Accounting (SEEA)
Seghezzo, L. 216
sensitivity analyses 99
Serageldin, Ismail 44, 359
Shah, Reena 45
Sharifi, A. 167
Shen, L. 311
Sierra Leone 50
SIs *see* sustainability indicators (SI)
Slovic, Paul 498
Smakhtin, V. 179
Small Island Developing States (SIDS) 47
Smith, S. 118
Smits, J. P. 311, 314
Social Equity Index 43
social multi-criteria evaluation 35
social, environmental (or ecological) and economic elements (SEE) 73, 74
societies initiative, progress 26
socio-ecological system (SES) 13, 329; basic dimensions of sustainable development and 330; concluding remarks 344; framework for indicators in 331–333; as integrative analytical framework 335–337, *336*; results for Honduras and for Latin America and the Caribbean *341*, 341–344, **342–343**; sustainability and sustainable development and 330–331; sustainable development indicators of 338, **339–340**; systemic frameworks in 333–335
socio-economic indicators 46
Soil, Food and Healthy Community (SFHC) 466
solar energy **159**
solidarity 63
South Pacific Applied Geoscience Commission (SOPAC) 48
SPeAR certification 171

Spencer-Brown, George 133
Spengler, Oswald 133
Sperber, D. 479
stakeholder-driven initiatives 14; conclusions on 386–387; enhancing the interactive process 381–386; introduction to 379–381; monitoring phase in 383–385; selecting, developing, and evaluating indicators for 382–383; sustainable agricultural intensification (SAI) 466; technology-based 385–386
stakeholders: categorization of 78; defining 189–190; identifying 189–190; participation by 10; participation in process by 190–192, *191*, **193**
stand-alone water footprints 181–183
standardisation frameworks for urban sustainability 370
Standardized City Data to Meet UN SDG Targets 370
Stanton, Elizabeth Cady 1, 543
statistics 4
"Steady State Economics" 521
Steffen, W. 180
Steves, F. 216
Stiglitz Report 533
Stiglitz-Sen-Fitoussi Commission on the Measurement of Economic Performance and Social Progress 27, 150
STIRPAT 70
Strategic Environmental Assessment 34
STRESS model 509
strong leadership 32
structural couplings 128–131, **129**; with nature or technologies 131–133
Struik, P. C. 431
Subtil, R. 508–509, 511, 517
Sunstein, Cass 498
Sustainability Assessment and Measurement Principles (STAMP) 6, 21–27; accuracy standards 36; application of 33–36; impact assessments 34; principle 1: guiding vision 27; principle 2: essential considerations 27–29; principle 3: adequate scope 29; principle 4: framework and indicators 29–30; principle 5: transparency 30; principle 6: effective communications 31–32; principle 7: broad participation 32; principle 8: continuity and capacity 33; promoting 34; propriety standards 36; utility standards 35–36; *see also* Bellagio Sustainability Assessment and Measurement Principles (BellagioSTAMP)
sustainability dashboard *see* dashboard of sustainability
Sustainability Index for Taipei 308
sustainability index 96
sustainability indicators (SI) 1–4, 3, 5, 7, 9, 14, 16, 42, 94; African smallholder farming

429–437, **432–433**, *436*; to audit performance of complex, multi-functional forest landscapes 407–423; bird's-eye view of 543–546; and certification schemes for the built environment 156–174; CGSDI integration 49–50; CSD work programme integration 44–45; Environmental Performance Index (EPI) 267–281, 294–305; EPI integration 48–49; ESI integration 48; EVI integration 47–48; fake 547–551, **549**, *550*; future of 551–555; Human Sustainable Development Index (HSDI) 284–292; identification 9; and indexes 5, 59, 65; integration 47; meta-evaluation of 507–518; new directions 50–51; participatory approaches for development and evaluation of 188–202; as reduction of complexity 133–136; relevance in 477–491; research dimension 45–47; resilience and 103–113; socio-ecological system (SES) approach to 329–344; stakeholder-driven initiatives using 379–387; starting 42–44; sustainability-related 308–318; sustainable development, in Finland 321–328; systems-theoretical perspective on 124–137; UN 2030 Agenda 51–53; world views and 147–151
sustainability science 33
sustainability 28
Sustainability-adjusted Global Competitiveness Index **209**
sustainability-focused policy-making 22
sustainability-related indicators 12; concluding remarks 318; indicators sets for national governments 314–317; introduction to 308–310; local and regional government indicators sets 310–311; UN indicator sets 311–314, **313**
sustainability-related initiatives 14
sustainable agricultural intensification (SAI) 15; challenges (and responses) in developing indicators of 456–471, **459**, **461**, *462*, *465*, *469–470*; complex tradeoffs, synergies and unintended consequences in assessment of 460–464, *462*; conclusion on 472; diverse values and priorities in 464–467, *465*; establishing relevant spatial and temporal boundaries for assessment in 457–460, **459**, **461**; ex ante assessment with enset in Ethiopia 467–471, *469–470*; indicator assessment next steps 471–472; introduction to 453–454; sustainability indicators and the intensification of agri-food systems and 454–456, *456*
Sustainable Cities and Communities 370
sustainable development (SD) 6, 42; assessment of progress 27; basic dimensions of 330; business interpretation 26; concept *60*; definition 4, 23, 27; framework for indicators in 331–333; principles 24; scientific articles published *62*, *63*; SES system indicators for 338, **339–340**;

sustainability and 330–331; temporal scale 29; urban (*see* urban sustainability)

Sustainable Development Goals (SDGs) 6, 7, 12, 59, 100, 235; African smallholder farming and 427–428; Ecological Footprint (EF) 525; Ecological Footprint (EF) and 522–523; indicator relevance and 490; Indonesian forest management and 415–416; proposed indicators or targets for **163**; steps in the logic model *82*; sustainable agricultural intensification (SAI) and 453–454; on water scarcity and consumption 176; world views and 148

sustainable development indicators (SDIs) 12, **66–68**

Sustainable Development Solutions Network (SDSN) 383

sustainable development solutions network (SDSN) 52, 70

sustainable intensification of agriculture 15

Sustainable Seattle (S2) indicators 164, *165*

Sustainable Water Governance Index **208**, 213, **215**, 216

Switzerland, Monet model in 334–335

System of integrated Environmental and Economic Accounting (SEEA) 22, 43, 149, 158, 237, 241

systemic frameworks 333–335

systems analysis 432–434

systems perspective on sustainability indicators 552

systems-theoretical perspective: binary coding, structural couplings and indicators 128–131, **129**; conclusion on 136–137; Ecological Footprint and 135–136; indicators as reduction of complexity and 133–136; introduction to 124–126; structural couplings with nature or technology and 131–133; on why (or how) modern society is unsustainable 126–128

Talberth, D. J. 120

Tanguay, G. A. 311

technology-based stakeholder initiatives 385–386

Tencati, A. 383

terawatts (TW) 526–527

Terborgh, J. 410

terrestrial and marine protected area data 288

Teytelboym, A. 216

Thayer, C. A. 268

thematic relevance of SI indicators 481–483, **483**

Theory of Justice, A 309

theory of political transitions 75, 79

Thinking Fast and Slow (Book) 4

Tittonell, P. 437

Tomorrow's City Today 365

Tönnies, Ferdinand 126

top-down vs. bottom-up sustainability indicators 105, 552–553

Töpfer, Klaus 354

Torrico, E. E. U. 517

total life cycle costs 74

Total Material Consumption (TMC) 150

Total Material Requirement (TMR) 150

Touraine, Alain 126

Towards a Framework for Indicators of Sustainable Development 349

transformationists: indicators and indicator systems of 150–151; modificationists versus 143–147, **145**

Transforming Our World. The 2030 Agenda for Sustainable Development 311–312, 311–314, **313**

transparency, STAMP 30

triangulation 503

triple bottom line (TBL) 25–26, 84

Trump, Donald 200

Tschirley, Jeff 349

Turcu, Catalina 164, 165

Turner, B. L. 112

2030 Agenda for Sustainable Development 312–314, **313**

UN 2030 Agenda 51–53

UN Conference on Environment and Development (UNCED) 42

UN Development Programme (UNDP): creation of environmental indices 210; Ecological Footprint (EF) and 523–525, *524*; Viet Nam and 276–277

UN Environment Programme (UNEP) 33, 35, 42, 43; assembling the principal stakeholders 348–349; CSD indicators programme and 354–358; green-economy report 240; indicators agenda 348; inter-agency coordination 349–350; introduction to 347–348

UN Statistical Division (UNSTAT) 349, 353

UN Statistical Office (UNSTAT) 43, 44

uncertainty reduction 495–497

UNICEF 181

United Kingdom and Brexit 547–551, *550*

United Nations Global Compact 26

United States Agency for International Development 409, 454

University of Teknologi – Malaysia (UTM) 274, 277

unsustainable development 6

urban sustainability: certification frameworks for 368–369; conclusions on 375–376; design and planning frameworks for 369–370; global trends 367–370; governance challenges in 370–373; introduction to 364–365; key dimensions of frameworks for 365–366; partnership facilitation in 372–373; performance assessment frameworks 367–368, **368**; policy and practice lessons in 373–375; robustness of assessment and endorsement in 373; standardisation frameworks for 370

Urban water and sanitation governance index **209**
US Green Building Council (USGBC) 170
Usefulness of Indicators for Sustainability 360

Valentinov, Vladimir 126, 128, 131
valuation 226–231, *228, 230*
value theory 145–146
van de Ven, G. W.J. 432, 435
van den Bergh, J. C. J. M. 533
Van Vuuren, D. P. 315
Variable Monthly Flow (VMF) method 179–180
Verbruggen, H. 232, 533
Vermeulen, Walter J.V. 59
Viet Nam: Environmental Performance Index
 (EPI) in 275–281, *278*; environmental
 performance legitimacy in 268
Vilches, Rodolfo 329
visualisation in participatory processes 199–200,
 200
Vitousek, P. M. 527
von Carlovitz, Hans Carl 156
vulnerability index 47

Walker, David 28–29
Wallace Global Fund 49
Wallace, Robert B. 43, 359
Wallbaum, H. 516
Waller-Hunter, Joke 351
Wallis, A. 518
Wang, J. 268
Warriors, The 193
Water and Wetland Index **207**, 212
water footprint indicators, 181–184; as part of
 Life Cycle Assessment 183–184; stand-alone
 181–183
Water Footprint Network (WFN) 182–184
water scarcity stems 9
water scarcity: conclusions on 184; indicators of
 water stress and 177–180; intensity of water use
 index and 178–180; introduction to 176–177;
 water access indicators and 180–181; and water
 and sanitation resources in Malta 296, **297, 301,**
 301–302; water footprint indicators and 181–184
Watershed Sustainability Index 206, **207**
weak leadership 32
Web 2.0, 25
web-based databases 25
Weibo, H. 312

Weitz, N. 312
welfare 10; and welfare-related indicators 49
White, G. F. 177
*Why Nations Fail – The Origins of Power, Prosperity
 and Poverty* 75
Wiel, Stephen 396
Williams, C. 375–376
Wilson, D. 479
Wilson, E. O. 245
Winograd, Manuel 44, 349, 354
Wismer, S. K. 381
Wittman, H. 111
women in agriculture 436
*Working Guidebook to the National Footprint Accounts
 2016*, 253
Workshop on Environmental Indicators 43
World Bank 118–119, 149, 349, 369, 409, 547;
 Worldwide Governance Indicators 218
World Conservation Strategy 309
World Economic Forum (WEF) 48, 94, 286
World Health Organization (WHO) 44, 181
World Resources Institute (WRI) 43, 44, 94,
 348–349
world views: conclusion on 152–153; introduction
 to 143; modificationists' indices and indicator
 systems and 148–150; modificationist versus
 transformationist 143–147, **145**; sustainable
 development indicators and 147–151;
 transformationists' indicators and indicator
 systems and 150–151; unhappy coexistence in
 mixed systems and 151–152
World War II 117–118
World Wildlife Fund (WWF) 206, 253, 409;
 creation of environmental indices 210, 212
Worldwide Fund for Nature (WWF): Living
 Planet Index 47, 206
Worldwide Governance Indicators 218
WTO-ITC 79

Xenophon 193
Xi Jinping 271

Yu, D. 215
Yuan, W. 310
Yurick, Sol 193

Zomer, A. 277
Zoological Society of London 253

For Product Safety Concerns and Information please contact our
EU representative GPSR@taylorandfrancis.com Taylor & Francis
Verlag GmbH, Kaufingerstraße 24, 80331 München, Germany